International Taxation of Energy Production and Distribution

Series on International Taxation

VOLUME 65

Series Editors

Prof. Ruth Mason, University of Virginia School of Law
Prof. Dr Ekkehart Reimer, University of Heidelberg

Introduction & Contents

The Series on International Taxation deals with a wide variety of topics in the global tax arena. The authors include many of the field's leading experts as well as talented newcomers. Their expert views and incisive commentary have proven highly useful to practitioners and academics alike.

Objective

The volumes published in this series are aimed at offering high-quality analytical information and practical solutions to international tax practitioners.

Readership

Practitioners, academics and policy makers in international tax law.

Frequency of Publication

2-3 new volumes published each year.

The titles published in this series are listed at the end of this volume.

International Taxation of Energy Production and Distribution

John Abrahamson

Wolters Kluwer

Published by:
Kluwer Law International B.V.
PO Box 316
2400 AH Alphen aan den Rijn
The Netherlands
E-maill: international-sales@wolterskluwer.com
Website: lrus.wolterskluwer.com

Sold and distributed in North, Central and South America by:
Wolters Kluwer Legal & Regulatory U.S.
7201 McKinney Circle
Frederick, MD 21704
United States of America
Email: customer.service@wolterskluwer.com

Sold and distributed in all other countries by:
Air Business Subscriptions
Rockwood House
Haywards Heath
West Sussex
RH16 3DH
United Kingdom
Email: international-customerservice@wolterskluwer.com

Printed on acid-free paper.

ISBN 978-90-411-9101-4

e-Book: ISBN 978-90-411-9120-5
web-PDF: ISBN 978-90-411-9121-2

Printed in the United Kingdom.

Table of Contents

Preface

This book introduces and discusses international tax issues relating to energy production and distribution. The book is intended to benefit accountants, lawyers, economists, financial managers, and government officials by explaining practical energy production and distribution international tax issues. These issues include examples of country tax regimes, energy issues including upstream oil and gas and mining tax regimes, export and investment tax incentives, permanent establishment issues relating to service structures, VAT and customs duties, and international tax issues relating to interest and dividend flows, capital gains, and foreign tax credits. The book reviews related topics, including management of intangible property, mergers and acquisitions, group treasury operations, and transfer pricing issues. The book includes updates on the most recent international tax developments affecting manufacturing and distribution, including the OECD Action Plan on Base Erosion and Profit Shifting (BEPS), and the 2017 OECD Transfer Pricing Guidelines.

The book is based on courses on international taxation that I have presented in London, Aberdeen, Durham, Jersey, Paris, Nice, Amsterdam, Rotterdam, Zurich, Lugano, Copenhagen, Warsaw, Limassol, Hong Kong, Singapore, Kuala Lumpur, Seoul, Sydney, Melbourne, Brisbane, Canberra, Perth, Sao Paulo, Rio de Janeiro, Mexico City, and Houston.

I would like to express my thanks to Simon Bellamy and the team at Kluwer Law who made this book possible, and especially to Brian and Valerie Abrahamson. I am deeply indebted to Professor Donald R Rothwell, Professor Harry Reicher, and Professor Malcolm D H Smith, for their encouragement and inspiration in international law.

Questions and comments on this publication are very welcome. Contact details: j.abrahamson@sheltonsgroup.com (www.sheltonsgroup.com)

John Abrahamson
Sydney, January 2018

CHAPTER 1

Introduction

ENERGY PRODUCTION AND DISTRIBUTION

The book is designed to give the reader a strong understanding of the most significant issues in the international taxation of energy production and distribution. The book has a broad scope, including related issues such as upstream oil and gas taxation, renewable energy, customs tariffs, VAT, group treasury, withholding taxes, mergers and acquisitions, asset finance and leasing, derivatives, and related transfer pricing issues. This book does not deal with all aspects of energy taxation, but rather is intended to provide the best introduction to the most significant international tax issues:

- The first part of the book, Chapters 1 to 4, reviews the major systems of energy production and distribution taxation. This is followed by a review of selected countries tax systems, including taxation of interest and dividend flows, capital gains, foreign tax credits, and tax losses.
- The second part of the book, Chapters 5 to 13, examines specific issues relating to energy production and distribution, including upstream oil and gas taxation, tankers and pipelines, oil refineries, coal mining, power stations and electricity networks, renewable energy incentives, and carbon taxes and trading.
- The third part of the book, Chapters 14 to 28, examines international tax structuring issues, including intangible property, group treasury companies, mergers and acquisitions, leasing, derivatives, thin capitalisation and controlled foreign corporations.
- The fourth part of the book, Chapters 29 to 36, examines transfer pricing issues relating to energy, including arm's length pricing, transfer pricing methodologies, specific energy transfer pricing issues, OECD BEPS measures, and design of energy fiscal systems, followed by some general conclusions.

The related case studies that follow these chapters are an opportunity to apply international tax analysis to specific examples, and particularly to gain practice in identifying and discussing relevant international taxation issues.

International tax issues includes the essential characteristics of the tax regime of each country, any special provisions for upstream oil and gas activities including additional petroleum taxes, production sharing contract (PSC) and service contract regimes, incentives for renewable energy, carbon taxes and carbon trading regimes, tax issues relating to investment into other countries, the treatment of dividends, interest, royalties and payments for services when these payments are made to other countries, and transfer pricing provisions which require 'arm's length' pricing, essentially market prices, for goods and services provided between related companies in different countries in a multinational group.

Regional purchasing, marketing, service, and intangible property (IP) management structures may be used to perform services for the multinational group. These activities may potentially be located in a lower taxing country.

Global treasury structures may be used by multinational groups to borrow funds from international financial markets, provide group funding to subsidiaries worldwide, and provide related services such as foreign currency transactions, risk hedging, and centralising the cash management for the multinational group.

VAT and customs tariffs are significant issues for international energy production and distribution, where free trade agreements and customs unions can reduce or eliminate VAT and tariffs on related transfers of oil, gas, coal, refined products and related equipment. Related tax planning may include the location of the principle trading entity, VAT group relief, the timing of invoices, maximising foreign VAT refunds and partial exemptions, and exemptions under free trade zones.

Largest Oil and Gas Producing Countries and Regions

The following summaries of the largest countries and regions with oil and gas reserves, and the largest oil and gas companies, demonstrate the international nature of upstream oil and gas activities.

	Largest Oil Producing Countries	*Barrels per day (bbl/day[1])*
1	Russia	10,250,000
2	Saudi Arabia	10,050,000
3	United States	9,415,000
4	China	4,278,000
5	Iraq	4,054,000
6	Canada	3,677,000
7	Iran	3,300,000
8	United Arab Emirates	2,820,000
9	Kuwait	2,562,000
10	Venezuela	2,500,000

	Largest Oil Producing Countries	*Barrels per day (bbl/day[1])*
11	Brazil	2,437,000
12	Nigeria	2,317,000
13	Mexico	2,302,000
14	Angola	1,842,000
15	Kazakhstan	1,653,000
16	Norway	1,610,000
17	Qatar	1,532,000
18	European Union	1,411,000
19	Algeria	1,370,000
20	Colombia	1,006,000
21	Oman	982,000
22	United Kingdom	893,300
23	Azerbaijan	848,500
24	Indonesia	785,900
25	India	761,000

1. CIA World Fact Book – 2017.

Largest Gas Producing Countries

	Largest Gas Producing Countries	*Cubic meters (cu m)[1]*
1	United States	766,200,000,000
2	Russia	603,900,000,000
3	Iran	174,500,000,000
4	Qatar	160,000,000,000
5	Canada	151,500,000,000
6	European Union	132,300,000,000
7	China	123,500,000,000
8	Norway	108,800,000,000
9	Saudi Arabia	102,400,000,000
10	Algeria	83,290,000,000
11	Turkmenistan	76,000,000,000
12	Indonesia	73,450,000,000
13	Netherlands	70,280,000,000
14	Malaysia	65,420,000,000
15	Australia	62,640,000,000
16	Uzbekistan	61,740,000,000

	Largest Gas Producing Countries	*Cubic meters (cu m)*[1]
17	United Arab Emirates	54,240,000,000
18	Egypt	48,800,000,000
19	Mexico	44,370,000,000
20	Nigeria	43,840,000,000
21	Thailand	42,150,000,000
22	Trinidad and Tobago	41,590,000,000
23	Pakistan	39,070,000,000
24	United Kingdom	38,580,000,000
25	Argentina	35,400,000,000

1. CIA World Fact Book – 2017.

These tables show the wide variety of locations for upstream oil and gas and the consideration needed for the different country fiscal systems. This includes whether oil and gas exploration and production is conducted by state owned oil and gas companies, and the terms of relationships with foreign oil and gas companies, such as partnership or joint venture arrangements. There is also a specific issue whether particular oil and gas fields are conducted as joint ventures or partnerships, where one oil and gas company is generally the operator responsible for oil and gas operations, and the other partners or joint venture parties have a more passive investment role.

These countries may apply tax and concession regimes, where the oil and gas company owns the oil and gas and pays tax and royalties, PSC regimes, where the company obtains a share of oil and gas production as profit oil, or service contract regimes, where the company receives payment for exploration and development services. A distinctive feature of upstream oil and gas is the wide range of countries with large oil and gas companies.

Largest Public Oil and Gas Companies

	Company	*Million Barrels of Oil Per Day (MMBOPD)*[1]
1	Gazprom – Russia	8.38
2	Rosneft – Russia	5.07
3	ExxonMobil– US	4.10
4	PetroChina – China	4.07
5	BP – UK	3.24
6	Royal Dutch Shell – Netherlands	2.95
7	Chevron – US	2.62
8	Petrobras– Brazil	2.55

	Company	*Million Barrels of Oil Per Day (MMBOPD)*[1]
9	Lukoil– Russia	2.40
10	Total – France	2.35
11	Statoil – Norway	1.81
12	Eni – Italy	1.69
13	ConocoPhillips – US	1.59
14	Surgutneftegas – Russia	1.49
15	CNOOC – China	1.36
16	China Petroleum & Chemical (Sinopec) – China	1.32
17	Oil and Natural Gas Corp. – India	1.07
18	Anadarko Petroleum – US	0.84
19	Canadian Natural Resources – Canada	0.79
20	Devon Energy – US	0.68
21	Ecopetrol – Colombia	0.67
22	Occidental Petroleum – US	0.65
23	Suncor Energy – Canada	0.58
24	EOG Resources – US	0.57
25	Repsol – Spain	0.56

1. Forbes 2016, reported in Oil & Gas 360, https://www.oilandgas360.com/2016-worlds-largest-public-oil-gas-companies/ at 8 May 2017.

The largest public oil and gas companies in this list include national production-based oil companies, which may not be involved in significant investment outside their respective countries. International tax issues will arise for companies providing related services, particularly seismic surveys, geological and geophysical (G&G) analysis, exploratory and production drilling, terminal services, and international pipelines and shipping.

The list also contains the large multinational oil companies which have subsidiaries in many other countries. There are several related international tax issues, including the different oil and gas taxation regimes in production countries, interest and royalties, taxation issues relating to mergers and acquisitions and the sale of assets, the financing of operations within the group, management of intellectual property, withholding taxes on payments such as dividends, and transfer pricing for the sales of oil and gas and provision of goods and services between companies in the group.

Selected Electric Utility Companies

	Company	Parent	Approximate Market Capitalisation (USD billion/equivalent)
1.	NextEra Energy	US	73
2.	Duke Energy	US	57
3.	Enel	Italy	56
4.	Dominion Resources	US	53
5.	Southern Company	US	50.5
6.	National Grid	UK	48
7.	Engie	France	42.6
8.	China Yangtze Power	China	42.3
9.	Iberdrola	Spain	42
10.	Exelon	US	39.6
11.	EDF	France	32.2
12.	Korea Electric Power Corporation	Korea	19.1
13.	SSE	UK	17.2
14.	E.On	Germany	16.9
15.	Tokyo Electric Power Company	Japan	6.1

1. Sources include Justin Walton, Investopedia, The World's Top 10 Utility Companies, 2017, https://www.investopedia.com/articles/investing/022516/worlds-top-10-utility-companies.asp on 23 February 2018. The table includes several estimations to provide a general listing of the selected companies.

The largest electric utility companies may have activities which are mainly based in one country, such as several of the large US electric utilities, or may be multinational groups with energy generating assets in many countries.

Selected Renewable Energy Companies

	Company	Parent Country	Revenue (USD/equivalent billion)
1.	Siemens Wind	Germany	13.5
2.	Vestas	Denmark	12.3
3.	Tesla	US	7.0

	Company	Parent Country	Revenue (USD/equivalent billion)
4.	Xinjiang Goldwind	China	4.1
5.	GCL-Poly Energy	China	3.2
6.	Trina Solar	China	3.0
7.	First Solar	USA	2.9
8.	Canadian Solar	Canada	2.8
9.	Acciona	Spain	2.3
10.	Ming Yang Wind Power	China	1.0

1. Sources include 'As You Sow', Clean200 list, https://www.asyousow.org/clean200 on 23 February 2018. The table includes several estimations to provide a general listing of the selected companies.

Renewable energy activities are also increasingly being carried out within multinational groups with other activities, for example Shell has established division to focus on renewable energy and technologies to lower carbon emissions,[1] and Lockheed Martin has established a compact fusion research unit.[2]

There is a very broad range of multinational energy groups. These groups are based in a wide range of countries, and generally have a large number of subsidiaries and branches in other countries. The international tax issues include local country taxation of oil and gas exploration and production, mining, power stations and electricity distribution, and renewable energy incentives.

1. Reuters, Shell sees rising investment in renewables, 10 July 2017, https://www.reuters.com/article/us-shell-renewables/shell-sees-rising-investment-in-renewables-idUSKBN19V0L9 on 21 September 2017.
2. Lockheed Martin, Compact Fusion, https://lockheedmartin.com/us/products/compact-fusion.html on 23 February 2018.

CHAPTER 2

Overview of International Taxation and OECD BEPS Measures

INTRODUCTION

This book introduces and analyses the significant international tax issues relating to energy production and distribution activities, extending from the tax regime in the country where the oil, gas and coal exploration and production activities are located, through to transportation using pipelines, tankers, and bulk carriers, to the taxation of power stations and electricity transmission and distribution networks.

The analysis includes the domestic tax laws relating to energy production and distribution company profits. There are international tax issues relating to income flows, including the payment of interest on related or third-party loans, and the payment of dividends to the related holding company. These income flows can also include management or service fees for functions performed by the parent company and other companies in the group, such as information technology support, human resources, legal support, and finance and accounting functions, and royalties for the use of intangible property (IP). There are also taxation issues where the energy production and distribution activities are conducted by a branch, rather than a company, including the repatriation of branch profits, and the allocation of head office and related company expenses.

The analysis of international tax includes the potential application of transfer pricing provisions, which many countries use to require arm's length pricing for goods and services which are provided between related companies. The analysis also includes the examination of the related terms of international tax treaties, which are agreements between countries with the principal purpose of eliminating double taxation of income and the exchange of tax related information.

There are several international tax planning structures reviewed in the following chapters, however, it is not proposed that tax planning structures should be adopted unless:

- There is a dominant commercial purpose, rather than a dominant tax purpose, for adopting the related arrangements.
- The entities concerned all have real commercial substance located in the respective countries, including directors, staff and business risks appropriate to the activities performed.
- The transfers of all goods and services under these arrangements are made at arm's length prices, which are essentially the prices for the same goods and services which would be charged between independent parties.

There are also specific tax issues as to whether business activities are performed by a taxable entity such as a company, or by an entity which is a transparent, pass-through, or disregarded entity for tax purposes. This may include the limited partnership, where at least one member is a general partner which makes business decisions and is liable for business debts, and at least one member is a limited partner which invests money but has minimal control over business decisions and is generally not personally liable for business debts.

The use of entities which may be transparent for tax purposes has been increasing. In the United States (US), for example, the limited liability company (LLC), master limited partnership (MLP) and business development company (BDC) structures may be transparent for tax purposes, so that US tax applies to the members or investors in the entity rather than the entity itself.

There are also taxation issues relating to the tax status of investors in energy production and distribution businesses, for example a sovereign wealth fund (SWF) is a state-owned fund which is generally tax exempt in its own country.[1]

Other forms of investment structures include the variable interest entity (VIE) which may have control over an operating company located in another country under contract or service arrangements.[2]

MERGERS AND ACQUISITIONS

There are several international tax issues relating to mergers and acquisitions. One primary issue is whether to acquire a target business by acquiring the company's shares, which is most common for large-scale international and domestic acquisitions, or alternatively, to acquire the business and assets of that company. The related tax analysis includes the use of structures to obtain interest deductions in the country of the acquisition, which is generally known as debt push down.

There may be tax planning opportunities relating to depreciation deductions for the assets involved in an acquisition, such as allocating a greater part of an agreed

1. The Economist, *Briefing: The New American Capitalism – Rise of the Distorporation* 25 (The Economist, 26 October 2013). Commercial issues relating to these structures include that protections under corporation laws may not apply, and that the opportunity for the public to invest is limited because these interests are generally not listed on stock exchanges.
2. The structure may potentially allow overseas investment while complying with foreign direct investment (FDI) restrictions.

purchase price for the acquisition to the depreciable assets to increase future depreciation deductions, which is generally known as asset step up. Retaining and utilising any tax losses in a target company may also be a significant issue. There are also tax issues for the seller, which may prefer to sell shares if this is potentially exempt from tax, for example under participation exemption provisions in most European countries. In relation to commercial considerations, a share sale may require greater due diligence by the purchaser to determine the tax position than an asset transaction, as the purchaser will acquire the company together with all its liabilities, however most large-scale acquisitions are structured as share acquisitions.

There are also taxation issues relating to the terms of the related sale and purchase agreements, and whether there are effective warranties and indemnities in these agreements relating to tax. These terms may determine whether the buyer or seller will pay the potential tax on the transaction, whether the seller is responsible for the stated value of any carry-forward tax losses, and which party will be responsible for tax in the period after the contract is signed until the final closing date.

DIVIDEND, INTEREST, AND ROYALTY FLOWS

The primary taxation issue with international income flows generally concerns the payment of dividends out of the profits of the local country company to the parent company in another country, and whether the local country imposes withholding tax on these dividend payments. There may also be tax imposed when the local country branch of a foreign company remits profits to its head office company, which is known as a branch remittance tax.

Dividends are generally not deductible expenses for the local country company which pays the dividends, however the dividends may be free of tax to the parent company shareholder. This exemption can arise, for example, under the participation exemption rules in many European countries, including exemptions under the European Union Parent Subsidiary Directive.[3] Dividends may also be effectively free of tax for the parent company where the dividend is taxed, but the related country then allows a foreign tax credit for the tax paid by the subsidiary, and not just a credit for any withholding tax. This is generally known as an underlying foreign tax credit.

The remittance of branch profits will not be deductible, however the income received by the head office company may be exempt if that country does not tax profits of foreign branches, or allows a related underlying foreign tax credit.

There are several tax issues relating to interest payments on loans or corporate bonds. A common tax planning objective is to maximise the local country interest deductions on loans from the parent company or the group treasury company to reduce taxable profits. The availability of tax deductions for interest on related party debt is subject to restrictions in many countries. The most common restriction are thin capitalisation rules, which can potentially deny interest deductions on portion of

3. *Council Directive 90/435/EEC of 23 July 1990 on the Common System of Taxation Applicable in the Case of Parent Companies and Subsidiaries of Different Member States*, Article 5(1) (L 225, 20/08/1990) (Parent Subsidiary Directive) (European Union).

related party debt which is considered to be excessive. On this basis the company is considered to be thinly capitalised, generally because the company has too little share capital compared to the amount of the related party debt. This approach has been broadly extended in several countries into a limit on excessive interest deductions including all the company's debt, such as the interest barrier rules in Germany, the United Kingdom (UK), Italy, and Denmark.

There are also issues relating to withholding tax, which is commonly imposed on dividend, interest, and royalty payments made to other countries. Withholding tax rules require the paying company to deduct tax from the dividend, interest, or royalty payment as the tax liability of the recipient of that income, and then forward the tax collected to the local country tax office. Several countries also impose withholding tax on other types of income, such as the use of technical service fees to service providers which are located in other countries. Withholding taxes are often reduced under the related terms of tax treaties as discussed below. There may also be domestic tax exemptions from tax, such as interest paid on certain unrelated party borrowings, in the US, or on interest on borrowings made on financial markets in the UK and Australia.

There are several multinational group structures which are intended to reduce taxes by using companies located in lower taxing countries to derive income from within the group. The structures have been used for holding companies to derive dividends, group treasury centres to derive interest income, and IP holding companies to derive royalties. There are generally tax issues with these structures where such companies are located in tax havens, as withholding tax is likely to be imposed on payments to these companies at higher rates. Accordingly these companies are more likely to be located in countries with tax treaty networks.

These structures generally require sufficient commercial substance, such as locally based management, skilled employees, and business capital, so that the arrangements are less likely to be disregarded for tax purposes under anti-tax avoidance provisions. The management of these companies should be based on a majority of local directors and related board meetings in that country, to reduce the risk of being treated as tax resident in another country.

There is also an issue of the timing of income flows. Tax deductions for interest, royalties and technical services may not be utilised unless there are sufficient profits. This may mean that the related deductions cannot be utilised for several years, while the related income may be fully taxable when interest or royalties are paid. There may be scope to use equity funding initially, and then increase debt once the related interest deductions can be effectively used to reduce tax.

CORPORATE INCOME TAX

A primary tax consideration is the corporate tax regime under the domestic tax laws of each country where a multinational energy group has subsidiaries and business operations. Taxes on exploration, production, power generation, transmission, and distribution activities may include corporate tax, royalties imposed on payments for the use of intellectual property, and indirect taxes such as Value Added Tax (VAT) and customs tariffs on the importation of goods. The tax regimes are reviewed with several country examples in Chapter 4.

A country's tax laws may have provisions which define when a foreign company is treated as having a local permanent establishment (PE) which is subject to tax. Where individuals are transferred to another country, for example, there is a risk that their presence and related activities may constitute a taxable PE. In general terms these employees should be sent under secondment to be employees of a local company to minimise the PE risk. Where there is a taxable PE, such as a branch, then a significant issue will commonly be to determine the proportion of head office and related company expenses should be allowed as deductible for the PE.

There are also differences in country tax laws as to whether capital gains are taxable, for example on the sale of shares in a company or the sale of a business. A related issue is whether such gains are also taxed when a foreign company or ultimate holding company sells foreign subsidiaries with interests in local country companies or assets, generally known as 'tracing up' to tax gains at a higher level in the multinational group.

Country tax rules also differ as to whether they provide tax consolidation or group relief, in which losses in one company can offset profits in a related company. This is an important consideration with mergers and acquisitions transactions, where a local purchasing company may borrow to acquire a local target company, and the objective is to use the interest deductions in the purchasing company to reduce tax on profits of the target company.

The tax laws of a country will also provide whether withholding tax is imposed on dividends, interest, royalties and technical service fees, and the repatriation of profits from branches. A related issue is that some countries, such as India, Canada, and Australia, provide that the purchaser of certain assets is responsible for the seller's taxes, and is required to withhold tax from payments to the seller.

Taxation may potentially apply to the sale of shares of a foreign holding company. In the *Vodafone* case in 2007,[4] there was a USD 2.5 billion tax dispute with the Indian Income Tax Department over the purchase shares in Hutchison Essar Telecom services. The shares in a Cayman Island holding company which held the business in India were sold in the transaction. The Supreme Court held in 2012 that Vodafone was not taxable because a non-resident had sold shares in a foreign company to another non-resident.[5] The Indian government revised the related laws to apply to these cases.

4. *Vodafone International B.V. v. Union of India & Anr.* Supreme Court of India, Civil Appeal No. 733 of 2012 (India).
5. PricewaterhouseCoopers, *BEPS Action Plan: Action 6 – Treaty Abuse,* (PricewaterhouseCoopers, 2015) <http://www.pwc.com/gx/en/tax/tax-policy-administration/beps/treaty-abuse.jhtml>.

TAXATION ISSUES FOR DERIVATIVES AND HEDGING

The term hedging generally refers to strategies used to reduce risk of price changes using derivatives such as call options, put options, short-selling, or futures contracts. Hedging may also be used to offset a potential loss on one investment with an investment that is expected to perform in the opposite way. Energy groups have made significant use of hedging, particularly with respect to commodity prices of oil, gas, coal, and uranium used in energy production, electricity prices for power generators and distributors, and movements in foreign currency exchange rates. The more common hedging arrangements include the following examples:

- A refinery business may expect that the price of commodity such as crude oil will rise over the next month, and so the company buys crude oil to avoid the expected price increase.
- A US battery distributor may intend to buy products in the UK to hold for a period of six months until expected resale when prices are higher, and therefore converts US dollars (USD) into UK pounds (GBP) to make the purchase. Once the products are purchased, the US company is exposed to the risk that the exchange rate will move by the time the asset is sold. This will decrease the return, for example, if the USD strengthens, as they will receive less USD for their GBP sale proceeds. The exposure can be partially reduced using hedging, for example by the forward purchase of USD at the expected value of the sales in six months.
- A multinational group treasury company may use an interest rate swap to hedge against movements in interest rates. For example, a company may have borrowed by issuing five-year floating interest rate notes based on the one-month LIBOR floating interest rate. The company is concerned, however, that the LIBOR rate will increase over the term of the loan. The company may use a fixed to floating rate swap, where the company pays interest at a fixed rate under the swap, and receives floating rate interest under the swap to meet its floating interest rate obligations on the notes.

The tax treatment of such hedging transactions includes whether countries treat certain transactions as made on capital account rather than relating to normal business operations. These countries may, for example, treat a hedging loss which relates to the capital structure of the business as made on capital account, and therefore not deductible. Countries may also have different tax treatments for unrealised gains and losses at the end of the financial year, and whether such unrealised gains and losses are taxable or deductible. There is also a trend to introduce tax regimes for financial arrangements and derivatives. Examples include the Taxation of Financial Arrangements (TOFA) regime in Australia, and the loan relationship provisions in the UK. There are also taxation issues relating to foreign exchange gains and losses, and whether there are specific county tax provisions relating to this issue such as Subpart

J in the US.[6] The tax treatment may be based on accounting standards, and this may include International Financial Reporting Standard IFRS 9, Classification and Measurement of Financial Assets.[7]

MULTINATIONAL GROUPS AND TRANSFER PRICING

Transfer pricing provisions are based on the requirement in many countries for companies to use 'arm's length' pricing for goods and services provided between related companies, which generally means the prices which would be paid between independent parties. The purpose of these rules is to prevent profit shifting to reduce tax by manipulating pricing between related companies. A company in a high taxing country, for example, may try to reduce its own tax liability by paying excessive prices for goods and services purchased from related companies in lower taxing countries.

The OECD has issued suggested methods for transfer pricing to determine an arm's length price for these related party transactions. These methods include the comparable uncontrolled price (CUP), resale price method (RPM), cost plus method (CPM), transactional net margin method (TNMM), and the profit split methods (PSM).

Transfer pricing is currently a very significant area for tax audits, and some of the largest tax adjustments have related to transfer pricing issues. Companies are required to establish transfer pricing documentation files which analyse their business and functions, select the most accurate transfer pricing methodology, and document that the companies in the group have adopted arm's length pricing. There have also been developments in transfer pricing with the increased use of Advance Pricing Agreements (APAs), which are agreements on transfer pricing with the tax authorities.

Transfer pricing is a significant issue for the exploration, production, power generation, transmission, distribution, intellectual property, treasury, and in-house banking structures within a multinational energy group. The potential advantages of several tax planning structures may not be realised if there is the related use of non-arm's length pricing which results in significant tax adjustments and penalties.

GROUP TAX PLANNING AND ANTI-AVOIDANCE PROVISIONS

Multinational group tax planning structures and the related transactions may potentially be subject to anti-avoidance provisions, which can eliminate benefits such as increased interest deductions, deriving income in low-taxing countries, maximising depreciation and other capital allowances, reductions in withholding tax on payments to non-residents, and the receipt of tax-free dividends or foreign branch income.

Specific anti-avoidance measures include thin capitalisation which limit interest deductions on related party debt, or interest barrier rules can interest deductions based on earnings before net interest, tax, depreciation and amortisation (EBITDA).

6. *Tax Reform Act of 1986*, Public Law 99-514, 100 Stat. 2085 (22 October 1986), 1986-3 C.B. Vol. 1, 1, *see* §601.601(d)(2) (United States).
7. International Financial Reporting Standard IFRS 9, Classification and Measurement of Financial Assets, www.ifrs.org/IFRSs/Pages/IFRS.aspx on 13 March 2014.

Controlled Foreign Corporation (CFC) rules can potentially tax the parent company on the income of foreign subsidiaries in tax havens.

Legal systems which are based on a civil code, such as France and the Netherlands, have legal doctrines which can prevent tax avoidance. In France, for example, the abuse of law doctrine, *abus de droit*, may permit a transaction to be disregarded where a transaction has no other purpose than to avoid tax and leads to a tax advantage contrary to the purpose of the tax regulations, Article L 64 of the French Code of Tax Procedure.[8]

Countries with legal systems based on common law also have legal doctrines which can address anti-avoidance issues. In the US, for example, the courts have applied the substance over form doctrine, which allows disregarding the legal form of the transaction for the economic substance of the transaction. The principal related case was *Gregory v. Helvering.*[9]

In relation to changes in tax laws, common law countries are also increasingly introducing general anti-avoidance rules (GAAR) provisions. An example of a GAAR is Part IVA in Australia, which applies to arrangements with a sole or dominant purpose of obtaining a tax benefit.[10]A significant development was the adoption of a GAAR in the UK in 2013.[11]

BASE EROSION AND PROFIT SHIFTING: THE OECD BEPS ACTION PLAN

One current issue is the focus relating to international measures to address tax avoidance contained in the OECD Action Plan on Base Erosion and Profit Shifting (BEPS), which was released in 2013, and the related Final Reports issued in 2015.[12] The treaty-related BEPS measures have been incorporated in the BEPS Multilateral Instrument (MLI) which was signed by representatives of seventy-one countries on 7 June 2017.[13]

The BEPS measures that are most likely to impact energy companies and related service providers include the following:[14]

8. *Livre de Procédure Fiscale*, (Code of Tax Procedure), Article L 64 (France).
9. *Gregory v. Helvering*, 293 US 465 (1935) (United States).
10. *Income Tax Assessment Act 1936*, Part IVA, sections 177A and 177D (Australia).
11. *Finance Act 2013*, c. 29, Part 5 and Schedule 43 (United Kingdom).
12. OECD, *Action Plan on Base Erosion and Profit Shifting* (OECD Publishing, 2013), http://dx.doi.org/10.1787/9789264202719-en.
13. Multilateral Convention to Implement Tax Treaty Related Measures to Prevent Base Erosion and Profit Shifting, opened for signature 7 June 2017), http://www.oecd.org/tax/treaties/multilateral-convention-to-implement-tax-treaty-related-measures-to-prevent-beps.htm on 21 September 2017.
14. EY, OECD releases final reports on BEPS Action Plan, Global Tax Alert, (EY, 6 October 2015) http://www.ey.com/Publication/vwLUAssets/OECD_releases_final_reports_on_BEPS_Action_Plan/$FILE/2015G_CM5818_OECD%20releases%20final%20reports%20on%20BEPS%20Action%20Plan.pdf on 21 September 2017.

Action 2: Neutralise the Effects of Hybrid Mismatch Arrangements

Action 2 includes developing model treaty terms and recommendations for the design of domestic tax rules to neutralise the effects of hybrid mismatches, including double non-taxation, double deduction, and long-term tax deferral outcomes.[15] The recommendations may include both primary and secondary measures, where primary measures relate to the action expected to be taken first by one country, and the secondary measures by the other country where the primary measure was not taken. This approach can enable the use of anti-hybrid measures where one country is not applying anti-hybrid rules.

The scope of the anti-hybrid recommendations varies, with some recommendations only applying to transactions within the same control group, or implemented under structured arrangements where the hybrid mismatch is priced into the terms of the arrangement, or the facts and circumstances indicate that it is designed to produce a hybrid mismatch.

In relation to hybrid entities, these measures include:

- Recommendation 3: Payments by Hybrid Payer – This applies to deductions claimed in one country where there was non-inclusion/tax exemption in another country (D/NI). The primary rule is that countries deny the taxpayer's deduction for the payment to the extent it exceeds dual inclusion income, which is the amount not included in taxable income. The defensive rule is to include this amount in the payee's taxable income.
- Recommendation 4: Reverse Hybrid Entities – This applies to deductions claimed in one country with non-inclusion/tax exemption in another country (D/NI) and which used reverse hybrids, which are entities that are transparent for tax purposes in the local country. There is only a primary rule which requires that the payer jurisdiction should deny the payer's tax deduction. The rule requires the transaction to be in the same control group or made under a structured arrangement.
- Recommendation 6: Double Deductions – This applies to hybrids providing deductions in two or more countries for the same expense for double deduction/double dips (DD). The primary rule is to deny parent entity deduction. The defensive rule is to deny the payer deduction. The defensive rule requires the transaction to be in the same control group or under a structured arrangement.

In relation to hybrid instruments the measures include:

- Recommendation 1: Hybrid Financial Instrument – This applies to deductions in one country with non-inclusion/tax exemption in another country (D/NI). The primary rule is that countries deny taxpayer's deduction to the extent of the D/NI outcome. The defensive rule is to include in payee ordinary income

15. OECD, Neutralising the Effects of Hybrid Mismatch Arrangements, Action 2: 2015 Final Report.

to the extent of the D/NI outcome. This rule requires the transaction to be in the same control group or under a structured arrangement.

- Recommendation 2: Specific Hybrid Financial Instrument – This applies to deductions in one country with non-inclusion/tax exemption in another country (D/NI) – where the instrument has been designated by countries. The primary rule is to deny a dividend exemption for deductible payments.

The imported mismatch rules include:

- Recommendation 8: Imported Mismatch Rule – This applies to hybrid entities and instruments between other countries and a related deduction in the local country. This includes a local deduction, a chain of related income flows, and hybrids used higher up in the income flow structure. There is a primary rule only to deny the payer deduction. This rule requires the transaction to be in the same control group or under a structured arrangement.

Action 3: Designing Effective Controlled Foreign Company Rules

The Action 3 measures are intended to respond to the risk that taxpayers with a controlling interest in a foreign subsidiary can reduce the tax base of their country of residence or of other countries by shifting income into a CFC.[16] The measures provide guidance on related issues, including:

- Definition of a CFC – The CFC rules generally apply to foreign companies that are controlled by shareholders in the parent jurisdiction. The report sets out recommendations on how to determine when shareholders have sufficient influence over a foreign company for that company to be a CFC.
- CFC exemptions and threshold requirements – The CFC rules should only apply to controlled foreign companies that are subject to effective tax rates that are meaningfully lower than those applied in the parent jurisdiction.
- Definition of income – The CFC rules should include a definition of CFC income, and the report sets out a non-exhaustive list of approaches or combination of approaches that CFC rules could use for such a definition.
- Computation of income – The CFC rules should use the rules of the parent jurisdiction to compute the CFC income to be attributed to the shareholders.
- Attribution of income – The attribution threshold should be tied to the control threshold, and the amount of income to be attributed should be calculated by reference to the proportionate ownership or influence over the CFC.
- Prevention and elimination of double taxation – The report emphasises the importance of both preventing and eliminating double taxation, and

16. Designing Effective Controlled Foreign Company Rules, Action 3: 2015 Final Report.

recommends that jurisdictions with CFC rules allow a credit for foreign taxes actually paid.

Action 4: Limiting Base Erosion via Interest Deductions and Other Financial Payments

The Action 4 measures recommend that countries implement a fixed ratio rule to limit net interest deductions claimed by an entity, or a group of entities operating in the same country, to a fixed percentage of EBITDA.[17] This ratio should be between 10% and 30% of the applicable EBITDA. The measure is designed to provide meaningful limits on net interest expense, while still allowing most multinationals to deduct all of their third-party interest expenses.

Action 4 also recommends a group ratio rule, where an entity with net interest expense above a country's fixed ratio could deduct the interest expense up to the level of the net third-party interest/ EBITDA ratio of the worldwide group.

Action 6: Inappropriate Treaty Benefits

The Action 6 measures are intended to prevent inappropriate access to treaty benefits, and include the following measures to be included in the OECD Model Tax Convention:[18]

- A clear statement included in tax treaties is proposed that the states that enter into a tax treaty intend to avoid creating opportunities for non-taxation or reduced taxation through tax evasion or avoidance, including through treaty shopping arrangements.
- A specific anti-abuse rule is proposed for treaties, which may include the limitation on benefits (LOB) rule that limits the availability of treaty benefits to entities that meet certain conditions. The conditions are based on the legal nature, ownership in, and general activities of the entity, and seek to ensure that there is a sufficient link between the entity and its state of residence.
- A more general anti-abuse rule may be used in treaties, based on the principal purposes of transactions or arrangements in the principal purposes test (PPT). If one of the principal purposes of transactions or arrangements is to obtain treaty benefits, the benefits are denied unless it is established that granting these benefits would be in accordance with the object and purpose of the treaty.

17. OECD, Limiting Base Erosion Involving Interest Deductions and Other Financial Payments, Action 4 – 2016 Update.
18. OECD, Preventing the Granting of Treaty Benefits in Inappropriate Circumstances, Action 6: 2015 Final Report.

Action 7: Prevent Artificial Avoidance of PE Status

The Action 7 measures concern structures used to avoid having a taxable PE in a particular country.[19] These measures include:

- Commissionaire arrangements and similar strategies – These measures apply to commissionaire arrangements, where an agent sells the products on behalf of the principal. The measures also concern arrangements where a dependant agent does not habitually conclude contracts but substantially negotiates those contracts. The BEPS Multilateral Instrument (MLI) provides the option that the PE extends to where the agent does not conclude contracts but habitually plays the role leading to the contracts in Article 12.
- Fragmented Contracts using specific activity exceptions – This issue concerns contracts which are artificially divided or split up with the intention of allocating the resulting split contracts to a different related party in order to avoid the existence of a PE. The resulting several small operations under the separate contracts are then argued to be merely engaged in preparatory or auxiliary activities which do not constitute a PE. The MLI contains the related optional anti-fragmentation rule in Article 13.
- Other strategies for avoidance of PE status and the splitting up of contracts – These issues include the time exception for construction sites and the related practice of splitting-up contracts between closely related enterprises, so that each contract is below the time threshold to be treated as a PE. The MLI provides an option which can aggregate these contracts in Article 14.

Action 8–10: Aligning Transfer Pricing Outcomes with Value Creation

The BEPS Actions 8–10 measures relate to transfer pricing issues.[20] Action 8 concerned transfer pricing issues relating to intangibles. Action 9 concerned the contractual allocation of risks and the resulting allocation of profits which may not correspond with the activities actually carried out. Action 10 included the scope for addressing profit allocations resulting from transactions which are not commercially rational for the individual enterprises concerned.

The related measures included:

- General Revisions to the OECD Transfer Pricing Guidelines – The revisions include guidance on identifying actual transactions undertaken, what is meant by control of a risk, and the circumstances in which the actual transaction undertaken may be disregarded for transfer pricing purposes.

19. OECD, Preventing the Artificial Avoidance of Permanent Establishment Status, Action 7: 2015 Final Report.
20. OECD, Aligning Transfer Pricing Outcomes with Value Creation, Actions 8–10: 2015 Final Reports.

- Cost contribution arrangements (CCA) – The pre-requisite for participating in a CCA is the expectation of mutual benefit. Participants are also required to have the functional capacity to control the related risks under the CCA. The value of the contributions made by the participants is required to be in proportion to their reasonably anticipated benefits.
- Transfer Pricing Aspects of Intangibles – The use of a cost-plus markup approach was considered unlikely to reflect the arm's length price for the contribution of an R&D service provider where that R&D service provider has unique skills and experience relevant to the research, bears risk related to commercialisation, uses its own intangibles, or is managed or controlled by a party other than the legal owner of the intangibles.
- Global Supply Chain – This approach identifies the full range of activities undertaken to bring a product or a service from its conception to its end use by final consumers. This approach assists each country's tax authorities to understand their relative contribution within global value chain, to determine whether their return is commensurate with their respective functions, assets, and risk (FAR) contributions.

The Action 8–10 measures were incorporated in the 2017 OECD Transfer Pricing Guidelines for Multinational Enterprises and Tax Administrations.[21]

Action 13: Country-by-Country (CbC) Reporting

The BEPS Action 13 for CbC reporting is one of the most significant BEPS measures, and requires multinationals with annual consolidated group revenue equal to or exceeding EUR 750 million to file information on activities in countries where they have activities.[22] These measures will provide tax authorities with information about global and local operations and the related global value chain. The measures also include development of formats for the electronic exchange of CbC information. The required reports comprise:

- The master file that provides tax administrations with high-level information regarding a multinational enterprise's (MNE's) global business operations and transfer pricing policies.
- The local country file that provides a local tax administration with information regarding material related party transactions, the amounts involved, and the company's analysis of related transfer pricing determinations. The local county file may also be adapted to obtain additional information.

21. This includes related revisions to guidance on the Arm's Length principle in Chapter 1, p. 33, Special Considerations for Intangibles, Chapter 6, p. 247, and Cost Contribution Arrangements, Chapter 8, p. 345.
22. OECD, Transfer Pricing Documentation and Country-by-Country Reporting, Action 13: 2015 Final Report.

- The CbC report that provides the amount of revenue (related and unrelated party), profits, income tax paid and taxes accrued, employees, stated capital and retained earnings, and tangible assets annually for each tax jurisdiction.

The CbC Reporting measures were incorporated in the 2017 OECD Transfer Pricing Guidelines for Multinational Enterprises and Tax Administrations.[23]

Action 14: Dispute Resolution

The Action 14 Dispute Resolution measures relate to cases where taxpayers have double taxation, for example under transfer pricing disputes where once country has made tax adjustments, such as increased prices for tax purposes applying to sale to foreign related parties, where these adjustments have not subsequently been accepted by the other country. The BEPS measures include the following minimum standards:[24]

- Ensuring that treaty obligations related to the mutual agreement procedure (MAP) are fully implemented in good faith and that MAP cases are resolved in a timely manner.
- Ensuring the implementation of administrative processes that promote the prevention and timely resolution of treaty-related disputes.
- Ensuring that taxpayers can access the MAP process where they are eligible.

Action 14 also includes peer review measures for monitoring implementation of the MAP minimum standards, and the option for countries to adopt compulsory binding arbitration to resolve disputes.

Action 15: Multilateral Instrument (MLI)

The MLI is intended to implement treaty-related BEPS measures by modifying existing bilateral tax treaties where the respective countries both agree that their treaty should be included as a covered agreement.[25] The MLI includes both minimum required standards and optional provisions from the BEPS Action Plans, including:

- Action 2 – Hybrid entities and securities, MLI Article 3. This includes: (1) revision of Article 1 of the Model Tax Convention to address fiscally transparent entities; and (2) application of the exemption method to relieve double taxation, such as using credits against other income, and the use of underlying tax credits.
- Action 6 – Minimum standard on treaty abuse, MLI Articles 6 and 7. This includes: (1) purpose of a covered agreement; (2) the principal purpose test or

23. Chapter 5 Documentation, p. 229.
24. OECD, Making Dispute Resolution Mechanisms More Effective, Action 14 Final Report.
25. OECD, Developing a Multilateral Instrument to Modify Bilateral Tax Treaties, Action 15: 2015 Final Report, and Multilateral Convention to Implement Tax Treaty Related Measures to Prevent Base Erosion and Profit Shifting, opened for signature 7 June 2017).

simplified limitation on benefits tests to prevent treaty abuse such as treaty shopping, savings clause that treaties do not restrict a State's right to tax its own residents; and (3) specific anti-abuse rules related to dividend transfer transactions, transactions involving immovable property holding companies, dual-resident entities, and treaty shopping using third-country PEs.
- Action 7 – Avoidance of PE Status, MLI Articles 12–14. This includes: (1) measures to address commissionaire arrangements and related tax planning; (2) modifications to specific activity exemptions under Article 5(4) and the addition of an anti-fragmentation rule to prevent using different entities and claiming each is merely engaged in preparatory or auxiliary activities; and (3) addressing splitting-up of contracts to abuse the time exception for building site, construction, or installation projects in Article 5(3).
- Action 14 – Minimum standards and best practices on dispute resolution, MLI Articles 16 and 17. This includes: (1) changes to Article 25(1)-(3) of the OECD Model regulating MAPs, and (2) inclusion of Article 9(2) implementing secondary transfer pricing adjustments.

The MLI also includes optional mandatory binding arbitration provisions which only apply if these measures are adopted by both states concerned (MLI Articles 18–26).

TAX RISK MANAGEMENT

Tax risk management relates to the identification and management of potential tax risks. One preliminary comment that should be made is the importance of tax risk within a multinational group due to the substantial amounts of tax generally involved, and the potential penalties arising from tax audits. A major role of the multinational group's tax department is therefore ensuring that tax risks are effectively identified and managed.[26]

Tax risk identification and management issues include analysing the business, its international income flows, and the tax planning arrangements in use. These functions also include the tax reporting and payment procedures with the local country tax authorities, and the tax reporting in the group's financial accounts. This process can include the analysis of large book to tax differences to highlight areas of potential tax risks, and the review of the most material tax issues and risks at the multinational parent board level.

These functions also include the management of tax disputes and related litigation, particularly for tax cases with high potential costs and penalties. This function requires a close working relationship with the group's legal department, as the related cases may combine specialised tax issues with the ability to conduct high value litigation.

26. P.J. Henehan & Aidan Walsh, *Global Tax Risk Management* (2007).

The management of transfer pricing issues requires close cooperation with many other business areas to explain the transfer pricing issue, and to engage support to establish a strong basis for transfer pricing and minimise the potential tax audit adjustments and penalties. Arm's length pricing is required to be in place during each year, and the tax department therefore needs to have management support to have an effective transfer pricing structure in place for the group's related party transactions.

The multinational group will generally not have in-house tax experts available in all the respective countries of operations, and one key to successful tax administration is having a close relationship with international accounting and legal firms to assist with technical issues. This issue is seen, for example, in large merger and acquisition proposals, where a team of the group's tax experts together with external advisers may need to be organised on short notice for a number of countries.

The use of external advice on large-scale potential transactions is particularly important, where tax department transaction approval may require a positive risk analysis by particular trusted external advisors.

Developments in best practice include the adoption of high-level tax risk assessments to review a multinational group's internal controls over tax. The Tax Cube approach used by Deloitte, for example, includes analysis of the related tax governance framework, people, processes, data and systems.[27] The results of this analysis can be used to benchmark a multinational group's tax risk management framework against other organisations, and highlight areas for potential changes and improvements.

The effectiveness of the multinational group's tax organisation is a key issue which can impact all the international tax topics discussed in this book.

27. Deloitte, The Tax Cube, https://www2.deloitte.com/ie/en/pages/tax/articles/tax-cube.html on 21 September 2017. This is based on a set of specifically designed tax questions based on Deloitte's view of good practice in the area of tax risk management. The approach categorises and scores responses into four interrelated components – governance, people, processes, and data & systems, which together form an integrated risk framework for internal controls over tax.

CHAPTER 3

Tax Treaty Provisions

INTRODUCTION

Tax treaties are primarily used to allocate taxing rights between countries, and in particular to avoid double taxation. Taxation in many cases can arise in the source country, where the income is earned or derived, and also may be taxed in the residence country, such as where an investor or lender is located. The use of source and residence taxation in many countries can potentially lead to double taxation.

Tax treaties generally prevent double taxation by allocating taxing rights between the country of residence and the country of source:

- They assign taxing rights between source of income country, and the residence of the recipient of income country, to reduce or eliminate double taxation.
- They oblige the residence country to relieve double taxation where the treaty allocates shared taxing rights.
- Double taxation is relieved by way of exemption or credit. Treaties generally do not provide taxing rights that do not already exist under domestic legislation. However, there can be exceptions such as the deemed source Articles.
- They create a framework for tax authorities to cooperate administratively and provide a mechanism for resolving tax disputes.

There are also more restrictive types of treaty including Exchange of Information Agreements and Airline Profits Agreements.

The OECD Model Tax Treaty was developed to be a framework for treaties to eliminate double taxation and for the exchange of information. There have been several updates, including the most recent update in 2017.[1] The OECD has issued related commentaries to clarify the meaning of the Model Tax Treaty in different

1. OECD, *Model Tax Convention on Income and on Capital* (2017) <http://www.oecd.org/ctp/treaties/2014-model-tax-convention-articles.pdf>.

circumstances. The Model Tax Treaty is very helpful to understand the basic structure of tax treaties, however it is essential to note that all tax treaties are different, and it is always necessary to review the exact terms of the relevant tax treaty.

The state of residence is defined in the treaty, and may be based on the place of incorporation or on the place of management and control of a company. The treaty generally provides a tie-breaker provision so that an entity is only resident in one of the states for treaty purposes, e.g., Article 4(3) of the 2017 Model.

There is an important issue in relation to tax residence concerning entities which are transparent, pass-through, or disregarded for tax purposes. These entities are generally not treated as resident in the country of registration by most tax treaties. The OECD commented that a fiscally transparent collective investment vehicle (CIV) would not be treated as a resident of the contracting state in which it is established because it is not liable to tax in that state.[2] The tax authorities would generally look to the tax residence of the related investors in these entities for tax treaty purposes.

Tax treaties generally contain some partial source definitions, for example dividends are included where they are paid by a company resident in a contracting state under Article 10(1) of the 2017 Model, and interest is deemed to arise in a Contracting State when the payer is a resident of that State under Article 11(5).

There are several important limitations on the use of tax treaties which can potentially apply in 'treaty shopping' cases, where there is insufficient commercial substance in a particular company used to claim tax treaty benefits. These cases include where treaty benefits are claimed to reduce withholding tax for a company on the basis that it is a resident of one of the treaty states, however that company has no substantial directors or employees in that state. Examples of these potential limitations include the requirement to be the 'beneficial owner' of the related income must be a resident in a treaty state, for example in relation to dividend income in Article 10(2), interest income in Article 11(2), and royalty income in Article 12(1).[3] This term has been applied in certain cases to mean that the ultimate owner of the related income must be resident in a treaty state, ignoring the use of intermediate companies which may have been established to obtain treaty benefits. The related cases and rulings include the following:

- The United Kingdom (UK) *Indofood* case in 2006,[4] concerned whether a loan from an intermediate holding company in Mauritius to the Indonesian borrower should be replaced with loan from an intermediate holding company in Netherlands. This was done by the companies concerned in response to the termination of the Indonesia/Mauritius tax treaty. The issue was whether an interposed Netherlands company would be regarded by Indonesia as the beneficial owner of the interest, in which case it would be entitled to reduced Indonesian withholding tax on the interest payments. The Court of Appeal

2. OECD, *The Granting of Treaty Benefits with Respect to the Income of Collective Investment Vehicles* (OECD, 2010) 16.
3. OECD, *Model Tax Convention on Income and on Capital* (2017).
4. *Indofood International Finance Ltd v. JP Morgan Chase Bank NA* [2006] EWCA Civ 158.

held that the Netherlands Co would not be regarded by Indonesia as the beneficial owner entitled to any treaty benefits.[5]

- The Canadian *Prévost* case[6] in 2009 concerned whether a Canadian company could use the lower treaty withholding tax rate for dividends paid to a Netherlands Co, when the shareholders of the Netherlands Co were in fact residents of the UK and Sweden. The Court held that the beneficial ownership issue should not result in disregarding the interposed company, except where such an interposed company is without discretion in how to apply the related funds.[7]
- A related development was Circular 601 issued by China's State Administration of Taxation (SAT) on 26 October 2009.[8] The Circular provides for an approach of looking through interposed companies, including agent companies and companies established for transferring profits and which conduct no business work, to determine beneficial ownership.[9]

A similar limitation relating to the use of treaties is made under the 'limitation on benefits' (LOB) clauses under United States tax treaties. The United States (US)/Luxembourg tax treaty, for example, requires at least 50% Luxembourg ultimate ownership, and at least 50% of income ultimately paid to Luxembourg persons, for a company to obtain the benefits of the treaty under Article 24.[10]

There are also domestic provisions against the abuse of tax treaties. In Germany, for example, the anti-treaty shopping provision of section 50d(3),[11] amended from 1 January 2012, provides treaty reduction of withholding tax on dividends where there are economic or other substantial reasons for the interposition of the holding company, and to the extent relevant income results from the company's own active business activities. This provision can allow treaty benefits for dividends from a corporation which is actively managed by holding company; and where the holding company has adequate business operations for its business purpose and the company participates in general commerce. The anti-treaty shopping requirements do not apply if the foreign holding company is listed on a stock exchange, or if the holding entity is a qualified investment vehicle.

5. Gareth Green (ed.), *Transfer Pricing Manual* 86 (2008).
6. *The Queen v. Prévost Car Inc*, 2009 FCA 57 (FCA) (Canada).
7. Gareth Green (ed.), *Transfer Pricing Manual* 84 (2008).
8. *Circular on How to Understand and Recognise the 'Beneficial Owner' in Double Taxation Agreements, Circular Guoshuihan [2009] No. 601* (Circular 601), State Administration of Taxation (China).
9. These rules may apply where 60% of the company's income is transferred to a third country within twelve months, there is no business except holding assets and rights, the company's activities are small in scale and do not match the company's income, there is no control of assets by the company, there are agreements with counties with lower taxes, or where the company has back-to-back loans.
10. *Convention between the Government of the United States of America and the Government of the Grand Duchy of Luxembourg for the Avoidance of Double Taxation and the Prevention of Fiscal Evasion with Respect to Taxes on Income and Capital* (3 April 1996).
11. *Income Tax Act* (EStG) section 50d(3) (Germany).

Domestic provisions against treaty abuse include Decree BRB 62 of 1962 in Switzerland, which was designed to prevent the abuse of Swiss treaties and Swiss intermediate companies, by residents of other countries, to reduce their taxes in other countries.[12] The decree can apply where a substantial portion of the benefit passes to an individual or company which are not qualified for benefits under the treaty. In these cases payments to other countries may be treated as dividends subject to 35% Swiss withholding tax. There are related commercial substance requirements for benefits relating to dividends which are based on a set of tax administration questions. The provisions are not applicable to European Union recipients provided they hold 30% equity in the Swiss company.

The mutual agreement procedure (MAP) in most tax treaties is based on Article 25 of the Model Tax Treaty, which allows a person to petition the designated government competent authority in the country where they are resident for assistance where the actions of treaty countries results in double taxation.

The United Nations has developed a Model Tax Convention which can provide increased taxing rights to developing states compared to the OECD Model. The differences between the model treaties include a broader definition of permanent establishment to include six-month construction projects, the right to tax income from sales and business activities similar to those performed by a permanent establishment, allowing the source state to impose withholding tax on royalty payments, and including payments for use of equipment in the definition of royalties.

There is a significant trend to develop exchange of information procedures outside of tax treaties. The Foreign Account Tax Compliance Act (FATCA) provisions of the US,[13] for example, requires individuals to report details of their financial accounts held overseas, and foreign financial institutions to report on the financial accounts of US clients, to the Internal Revenue Service (IRS). The US has entered into a series of treaties with other countries to support the implementation of these provisions.[14]

Another development is the Convention on Mutual Assistance,[15] by the OECD and the Council of Europe, which is open for ratification by all countries. The convention provides countries with the power to seek, and the obligation to provide, administrative assistance in the exchange of taxpayer information, the recovery of tax debts, and the service of related documents.

---

12. *Bundesratsbeschluss betreffend Massnahmen gegen die ungerechtfertigte Inanspruchnahme von Doppelbesteuerungsabkommen des Bundes*, 14 December 1962 (SR 672.202) ('BRB 62') (Switzerland).
13. *Foreign Account Tax Compliance Act* 26 USC §§ 1471–1474, and §6038D (*'FATCA'*) (United States).
14. An example is the *Agreement between the Government of the United Kingdom of Great Britain and Northern Ireland and the Government of the United States of America to Improve International Tax Compliance and to Implement FATCA*, 12 September 2012.
15. *Convention on Mutual Administrative Assistance in Tax Matters*, 25 January 1988 (entered into force 27 May 2010).

The OECD Action Plan on Base Erosion and Profit Shifting (BEPS) includes measures to prevent treaty abuse in Action Plan 6.[16] The measures include a Principal Purpose Test (PPT) applying where the main purpose of a transaction was in obtaining a treaty benefit, unless granting that benefit would be in accordance with the object and purpose of the relevant provisions of the treaty in question. The measures also include a LOB clause similar to the LOB clauses in US treaties discussed above.

These measures were adopted as minimum standards in the OECD BEPS Multilateral Instrument (MLI) to implement treaty-related BEPS measures by modifying existing bilateral tax treaties.[17] These measures have also been incorporated in the OECD Model Tax Treaty 2017 in Article 29 Entitlement to Benefits.[18]

One related comment is to note the importance of using the latest version of a tax treaty between two countries, to ensure that any changes to the treaty or the related protocols are considered. The online treaty databases generally used to include the Bloomberg BNA Tax Treaties Analysis,[19] and the International Bureau of Fiscal Documentation (IBFD) Tax Treaties Database.[20]

SELECTED OECD MODEL TREATY ARTICLES

The OECD has issued the Model Tax Agreement together with related commentaries with periodic updates.[21] There are always differences between actual tax treaties and the OECD Model, however, and it is always necessary to review the specific tax agreement in any particular case. The following are some selected articles of the current Model Tax Agreement which are likely to be most relevant to international taxation of multinational energy businesses:

Chapter I Scope of the convention

Article 1 Person covered

Article 1 establishes the scope of the application of the Convention by providing for it to apply to persons who are residents of one or both of the Contracting States.

Article 2 Taxes covered

Tax treaties generally do not cover VAT, customs duties, state taxes and duties, or estate tax and duties.

Article 3 General Definitions

The definitions include person, company, competent authority, and international traffic.

---

16. OECD, *Action Plan on Base Erosion and Profit Shifting* (OECD Publishing, 2013), http://dx.doi.org/10.1787/9789264202719-en.
17. Multilateral Convention to Implement Tax Treaty Related Measures to Prevent Base Erosion and Profit Shifting, opened for signature 7 June 2017.
18. OECD, *Model Tax Convention on Income and on Capital* (2017), Article 29.
19. Bloomberg BNA Tax Treaties Analysis, www.bna.com/Tax-Treaties-Analysis-p8638/.
20. IBFD Tax Treaties Database www.ibfd.org/IBFD-Products/Tax-Treaties-Database.
21. Model Convention with Respect to Taxes on Income and on Capital, 2014, OECD, http://www.oecd.org/ctp/treaties/model-tax-convention-on-income-and-on-capital-2015-full-version-9789264239081-en.htm on 1 September 2017.

Chapter II Definitions

Article 4 Residence

Article 4 defines who is a resident of a treaty country and so can take advantage of the tax treaty. For companies, the OECD Model includes any person who, under the laws of that State, is liable to tax therein by reason of his domicile, residence, place of management or any other criterion of a similar nature.

The definition of resident exists for:

- Defining the personal scope of the treaty (Article 1)
- The tie breaker rule (Article 4)
- Specific provisions on payments or gains to residents, including dividends (Article 10), interest (Article 11), royalties (Article 12) and capital gains (Article 13).
- Double tax relief is limited to residents (Article 23).
- Article 4(3) has the tie breaker test for companies which are potentially resident in both states. Residence for treaty purposes is usually determined by the place of effective management.

Article 5 Permanent Establishments (PEs)

The PE concept has several functions in tax treaties:

- Jurisdictional threshold test – Sufficient presence must generally exist before a country can tax business profits derived there under Article 7.
- Source rule – This attributes the source of income to the country in which the activity is undertaken.

PE is defined in Article 5(1) as being 'a fixed place of business through which the business of an enterprise is wholly or partly carried on.' Thus, under Article 5(1) for a PE to exist:

- There must be a place of business;
- The place of that business must be fixed (both in terms of physical location and in terms of time); and
- The business of the enterprise must be carried on through this fixed place of business.

Article 5(2) lists examples of typical PEs. However, these examples will only constitute a permanent establishment if the primary definition in Article 5(1) is satisfied:

- a place of management;
- a branch;
- an office;
- a factory;
- a workshop;
- a mine, an oil or gas well, a quarry or any other place of extraction of natural resources.

Article 5(3) generally provides that a building site or construction or installation project constitutes a permanent establishment only if it lasts for more than 12 months.

Article 5(4) provides that permanent establishment is deemed not to include:

- the use of facilities solely for the purpose of storage, display or delivery of goods or merchandise belonging to the enterprise;
- the maintenance of a stock of goods or merchandise belonging to the enterprise solely for the purpose of storage, display or delivery;
- the maintenance of a stock of goods or merchandise belonging to the enterprise solely for the purpose of processing by another enterprise;
- the maintenance of a fixed place of business solely for the purpose of purchasing goods or merchandise or of collecting information, for the enterprise;
- the maintenance of a fixed place of business solely for the purpose of carrying on, for the enterprise, any other activity of a preparatory or auxiliary character;
- the maintenance of a fixed place of business solely for any combination of activities mentioned in subparagraphs a) to e), provided that the overall activity of the fixed place of business resulting from this combination is of a preparatory or auxiliary character.

These measures were updated in Article 5(4) of the OECD Model Tax Treaty 2017 to require the overall activity to be of a preparatory or auxiliary nature for the PE exemptions to apply.

Article 5(5) deems an enterprise to have a PE if a person acts on its behalf in the other country where that person has and habitually exercises an authority to conclude contracts on behalf of the enterprise (a dependent agent) unless the activities are of a preparatory or auxiliary character.

Article 5(6) states that a business carried on through an independent agent will not give rise to a PE provided that the agent is acting in the ordinary course of their business.

Chapter III Taxation of Income

Article 6 Income from Immovable Property

Article 6 preserves taxing rights to the source state for income from immovable property. Article 6(1) provides that income derived by a resident of a Contracting State from immovable property, including income from agriculture or forestry, situated in the other Contracting State may be taxed in that other State. Immovable property is stated to have the same meaning as the country where the property is located.

Article 7 Business Profits

Article 7 concerns the division of business profits between a branch (PE) and its head office. Article 7(1) provides that the profits of an enterprise of a Contracting State shall be taxable only in that State unless the enterprise carries on business in the other Contracting State through a permanent establishment situated therein. If the enterprise carries on business through such a permanent establishment, then the profits of the enterprise may be taxed in the other State but only so much of them as is attributable to that permanent establishment.

Article 7(2) provides that the profits that are attributable in each Contracting State to the permanent establishment are the profits it might be expected to make, in particular in its dealings with other parts of the enterprise, if it were a separate and independent enterprise engaged in the same or similar activities under the same or similar conditions, taking into account the functions performed, assets used and risks assumed (FAR) by the enterprise through the permanent establishment and through the other parts of the enterprise. The OECD approach is to apply the arm's length principle of Article 9, as articulated in the OECD Transfer Pricing Guidelines, to the PE under Article 7(2).

Article 8 International transport

Article 8(1) allocates the profits of an enterprise from the operation of ships or aircraft in international traffic to be taxable only in the State in which the place of effective management of the enterprise is situated.

Article 9 Associated Enterprises – Transfer Pricing

Article 9 deals with associated enterprises, such as parent and subsidiary companies and companies under common control. Article 9(1) authorises transfer pricing adjustments for the reallocation of profits between related enterprises between contracting States on an arm's length basis where the commercial or financial arrangements between the enterprises differ from those that might be expected to operate between unrelated enterprises dealing wholly independently with one another. Article 9(2) requires corresponding adjustments, where the other State to make an appropriate adjustment to relieve the double taxation where the rewriting of transactions between associated enterprises may give rise to economic double taxation.

Article 10 Dividends

Article 10(1) allocates unlimited taxing rights to country of residence of a shareholder who is paid dividends by a company resident in another State. Article 10(2) allows source country to also tax the dividends, but tax charged on the gross amount of dividends paid to the non-resident beneficial owner is limited, typically, to a rate not exceeding 5%, where there is a significant ownership percentage, or 15% in all other cases. Article 10(3) provides the definition of dividends, which means income from shares, 'jouissance' shares or 'jouissance' rights, mining shares, founders' shares or other rights, not being debt-claims, participating in profits, as well as income from other corporate rights which is subjected to the same taxation treatment as income from shares in the state where the company making the distribution is a resident. Article 10(4) excludes dividends arising from a business conducted through a PE in the country of source, which is dealt with under Article 7.

Article 11 Interest

Article 11(1) assigns the taxing rights to interest to country of residence of the lender. Article 11(2) allows source country to also tax the interest. Where the beneficial owner of the interest is a resident in the other state, the tax charged on the gross amount of interest paid to the non-resident beneficial owner is limited to a rate not exceeding 10%. Article 11(4) excludes interest arising from a business conducted through a PE in the country of source, which is dealt with under Article 7. Interest is defined in Article 11(3) and includes income from debt-claims of any kind.

Article 12 Royalties

Article 12 provides that royalties are taxed in the state in which the beneficial owner resides. Article 12(3) excludes royalties which are effectively connected with a PE in the other state, where Article 7 will then apply.

Royalties are defined in Article 12(2) as 'payments of any kind received as a consideration for the use of, or the right to use, any copyright of literary, artistic or scientific work, including cinematographic films, any patent, trade mark, design or model, plan, secret formula or process, or for information concerning industrial, commercial or scientific experience.' Article 12(3) excludes royalties arising from a PE, where Article 7 will then apply.

Article 13 Capital Gains

Under Article 13 the source country has the right to tax gains on the alienation of:

- immovable property in the jurisdiction, Article 13(1);
- shares deriving 50% or more of their value directly or indirectly from immovable property in the jurisdiction, Article 13(4);
- movable property that is a business asset of a local PE, Article 13(2); and
- the alienation of such a PE, whether sold directly, or due to the sale of the head office, Article 13(2).

The country of place of effective management has exclusive right to tax ships, aircraft and related movable property, Article 13(3), while the country of residence has exclusive right to tax gains on all other assets, Article 13(5).

Article 21 Other income

Article 21 provides rules for the allocation of taxing rights between the contracting countries with respect to items of income not dealt with in the other articles. Article 21 provides that income derived by a resident, where ever arising, which is not dealt with in the previous articles shall be taxable only in the country of residence. The provision does not apply to income which is effectively connected with a PE in the other country, in which case Article 7 will apply.

Chapter V – Elimination of Double Taxation

The OECD Model Tax Treaty allows countries to adopt either of two methods to eliminate double taxation

- Article 23A Exemption method – this requires the residence country to exempt the income from the source country.
- Article 23B Credit Method – This applies so that the residence country of dividends, interest and royalties allows a credit for the source country withholding tax

A typical example is where the source country imposes withholding tax on interest, and so the resident country is required to either exempt the dividends from tax, or to provide a credit for the withholding tax to eliminate double taxation.

Chapter VI Special Provisions

Mutual Agreement Procedure (MAP)

Article 25(1) provides that a person who considers that the actions of the Contracting States result in a tax outcome inconsistent with the treaty may present a case, within 3 years of notification of the action, to the competent authority of the State of which the person is a resident or, where a non-discrimination issue, the State of which the person is a national. Article 25(5) permits arbitration to be used to assist in resolving cases where the competent authorities cannot reach agreement within 2 years from when the case was first presented.

Entitlement to Benefits

Article 29 of the 2017 Model Tax Treaty is particularly significant in adopting the BEPS anti-treaty abuse measures. This is intended to address tax planning arrangements such as treaty shopping. The adoption of the respective clauses is to be agreed by the contracting states. This includes the limitation on benefits test in Article 29(1) to (7), and the principal purpose test in Article 29(9).[22]

THE UNITED NATIONS MODEL TREATY

The United Nations has also issued a Model Tax Agreement which has a number of important differences intended to increase the allocation of taxing rights to developing countries.[23] The most significant differences compared to the OECD Model include:[24]

- Article 5(3)(a) on the definition of a PE has a six-month duration test for building sites, as compared to twelve months in the OECD Model Convention.
- Article 5(3)(b) addresses services PEs within a Contracting State for a period or periods aggregating more than six months within any twelve-month period.
- Article 5 omits 'delivery' from the Article 5(4) exemptions from a PE, so that delivery alone is an activity that can constitute a PE.
- Article 7(1) on the taxation of business profits of a PE has a limited force of attraction rule in Article 7(1) to allow taxation of certain profits not actually attributable under normal rules to the PE, but which relate to sales of similar goods or merchandise in the source country, as well as other business activities of the same or similar kind carried on by the enterprise in the source country.
- Article 8 on Shipping and Air Transport provides an alternative to allow limited source country taxation of international shipping where the shipping activities arising from such operation in the other Contracting State are more than casual.
- Article 9(3) on associated enterprises relating to transfer pricing provides that a corresponding adjustment is not required where one of the enterprises concerned is liable to penalty with respect to fraud, gross negligence, or wilful default. Double taxation can potentially arise on this basis.
- Article 12 provides for source country taxation of royalties.

22. OECD, *Model Tax Convention on Income and on Capital* (2017), Article 29.
23. United Nations Model Double Taxation Convention between Developed and Developing Countries, United Nations 2011, http://www.un.org/esa/ffd/documents/UN_Model_2011_Update.pdf on 1 September 2017.
24. Michael Lennard, The UN Model Tax Convention as Compared with the OECD Model Tax Convention – Current Points of Difference and Recent Developments, Asia-Pacific Tax, IBFD, January/February 2009.

THE OECD BEPS MULTILATERAL INSTRUMENT (MLI): CHANGES TO TAX TREATIES INCLUDING TREATY SHOPPING

As discussed, the MLI is part of the OECD BEPS measures, and is a multilateral agreement to implement treaty-related BEPS measures by modifying existing bilateral tax treaties.[25] Representatives of sixty-eight countries signed the MLI in June 2017. The BEPS Actions and related MLI articles include both BEPS minimum standards applying to all BEPS participating countries and also optional provisions, including:

- MLI Article 3 relates to BEPS Action 2, addressing hybrid entities and securities including: (1) revision of Article 1 on persons covered of the OECD Model Tax Convention to address fiscally transparent entities; and (2) issues with application of the exemption method to relieve double taxation, such as using credits against other income, and the use of underlying tax credits.
- MLI Articles 6 and 7 relate to BEPS Action 6, minimum standard on treaty abuse, including: purpose of a covered agreement, the principal purpose test or simplified LOB tests to prevent treaty abuse such as treaty shopping, savings clause that treaties do not restrict a State's right to tax its own residents, and specific anti-abuse rules related to (1) certain dividend transfer transactions; (2) transactions involving immovable property holding companies; (3) situations of dual-resident entities; and (4) treaty shopping using third-country PEs. The OECD 2017 Model Tax Treaty adopted the LOB test in Article 29(1) to (7), and the principal purpose test in Article 29(9).
- MLI Articles 12–14 relate to BEPS Action 7, addressing avoidance of PE Status, including: (1) measures to address commissionaire arrangements and similar planning; (2) modifications to the specific activity exemptions under Article 5(4) and addition of an anti-fragmentation rule to prevent using different entities and claiming each is merely engaged in preparatory or auxiliary activity; and (3) measures to address splitting-up of contracts to abuse the time exception for building site, construction, or installation projects in Article 5(3).
- MLI Articles 16 and 17 relate to BEPS Action 14, minimum standards and best practices on dispute resolution including: changes to Article 25(1)-(3) of the OECD Model regulating MAPs, and inclusion of Article 9(2) implementing secondary transfer pricing adjustments.
- MLI Articles 18–26 include mandatory binding arbitration provisions. These measures only apply if adopted by both states concerned.

25. Multilateral Convention to Implement Tax Treaty Related Measures to Prevent Base Erosion and Profit Shifting, opened for signature 7 June 2017.

CHAPTER 4

Examples of Country Fiscal Systems

INTRODUCTION

This chapter provides a series of brief summaries of selected country fiscal regimes, including specific regimes for upstream oil and gas operations. The principal purpose of the summaries is to provide an overview of how different forms of fiscal regimes are combined in different countries. In relation to upstream oil and gas, these regimes range from licence/concession regimes, which apply corporate tax on profits, to production sharing contract (PSC) regimes where the oil and gas company derives profit oil as provided under specific PSC terms. The summaries also demonstrate how these tax regimes are generally combined with other sources of government revenue, particularly royalties.

These summaries are based on information from several sources, including the country surveys in the Ernst & Young Global Oil and Gas Tax Guide 2017,[1] the World Fiscal Systems for Oil and Gas courses by Pedro van Meurs of Van Meurs Corporation,[2] and the country analysis in the online subscription Wood Mackenzie Upstream Service.[3] These sources are recommended for further reading. It is important to highlight that fiscal regimes are subject to quite frequent changes in many countries, and it is therefore advisable to review the most recent available summaries of country tax regimes. This review should be followed by advice from a tax advisor in the specific country concerned for any specific transactions.

The type of fiscal regime can impact tax in the foreign holding company and whether tax imposed in one country can be credited in the parent company's country. This issue is particularly important for multinational groups with subsidiaries in other countries, where the parent country may tax the related dividends but may allow a

1. EY, Global Oil and Gas Tax Guide 2017 (EY, 2017).
2. World Fiscal Systems for Oil and Gas courses by Pedro van Meurs of Van Meurs Corporation, www.vanmeurs.org/Training.aspx on 8 May 2017.
3. Wood Mackenzie Upstream Service, www.woodmacresearch.com on 8 May 2017.

foreign tax credit for tax paid by the foreign subsidiary company. The tax regime in the holding company country is also significant as it may provide an exemption for dividends paid from subsidiaries.

An important consideration for the countries with corporate income tax (CIT) regimes is whether there is tax consolidation, also known as group relief, which generally allows losses from one company to offset taxable profits in another related company. The issue may require business activities to be in the same company to allow losses to offset profits if no consolidation between companies is allowed in that country.

Tax consolidation is also significant for mergers and acquisitions. A common structure for international acquisitions is to establish a new local acquiring company or special purpose vehicle (SPV), which borrows from related parties or independent financial institutions to provide funding for the acquisition of the local target company. Consolidation generally allows the related interest deductions in the acquiring company SPV to offset the profits of the target company. This structure allows interest deductions in the country of the acquisition, known as debt push down. In the absence of consolidation, similar results may be achieved in a downstream merger, where the acquiring company SPV mergers with the target company, so that the interest deductions and profits are in the same target company after the merger.

Tax regimes may have special rules relating to foreign contractors. Brazil, for example, has several indirect taxes and withholding tax regimes, and related structures include the use of a local service company to reduce the impact of these taxes. Countries may also tax foreign contractors on the basis of deemed permanent establishments where their activities relate to oil and gas operations.

Taxation in several countries may be imposed at federal, state, and municipal levels. These additional levels of tax need to be considered to determine the total tax position. Examples of state or provincial taxation regimes include the states of Texas and Alaska in the United States (US), and the province of Alberta in Canada.

Countries may have different tax regimes for upstream oil and gas operations and for other commercial activities, with a higher tax rate applying to the oil and gas activities. This may result in the use of a service company structure, where functions such as administration are performed in a specific service company which is taxed at the lower general tax rate.

There are different tax rules applying to the sale of an upstream investment, and may tax indirect transfers where a foreign company with interests in local oil and gas fields is sold. Several countries have 'tracing upwards' provisions to tax the sale of shares in foreign companies which directly or indirectly hold local oil and gas licence interests.

Ring fencing provisions can prevent losses from one oil and gas field to offset profits from another field, and this restriction can result in significantly higher taxation. Ring fencing can also apply to prevent losses from any non-oil and gas businesses in a country from reducing taxable profits in the oil and gas operations in that country. Examples in the country summaries include ring fencing between fields in Kazakhstan, and ring fencing between oil and gas and other businesses, described in the Denmark and United Kingdom (UK) summaries.

The ring fencing issue arises in different ways under PSC regimes. PSCs are generally contracts between the oil and gas company and the government or the national oil company (NOC) relating to specific licence blocks or oil and gas fields. The oil and gas company may therefore be conducting operations under several PSCs in the same country. PSC terms do not generally allow expenses which are allowed as cost oil under one PSC contract to be recovered as cost oil under a different PSC. On this basis, expenses must be carried forward under each PSC until there is production from the related oil and gas field, instead of being immediately recovered as cost oil under a different PSC.

ALGERIA

Algeria applies the current fiscal regime under to contracts generally signed from 2005. Most contracts used in Algeria are PSCs.[4] The Petroleum Income Tax applies on the value of production less deductible expenses, generally at rates from 20% to 70% on the basis of the profitability of the project, which is generally paid from the national oil company Sonatrach's profit oil share. The Additional Profits Tax generally applies to oil and gas profits at 30%. Tax losses may be carried forward for up to five years. Group tax consolidation is allowed providing there is at least 90% common ownership between the respective companies.[5]

Royalties under the current PSC contracts are imposed at rates from 5.5% to 23% on the value of production.[6]

The older fiscal regime applies to contracts signed before 2005.[7] The regime applies Income Tax at 38% which is paid by Sonatrach on the Operator's behalf, together with royalties at 10% to 20%, and the Tax on Extraordinary Profits (TPE) at 5% to 50% of gross income where the oil price is over USD 30 per barrel.

The surface area tax under the recent contracts applies at DZD 4,000 (USD 54) to 16,000 (USD 216) per square km in the exploration period, DZD 16,000 (USD 216) to 32,000 (USD 432) in the exploitation period.[8]

There is a transfer tax of 1% of value on the transfer of PSC interests, and the government considers that this transfer tax also applies to the older PSCs.[9]

ANGOLA

Angola imposes tax on upstream oil and gas operations under the Law on Taxation of Petroleum Activities.[10] Most contracts used in Angola are PSCs. The Petroleum Income

4. Law No. 05-07 and Law No. 13-01.
5. EY, Global Oil and Gas Tax Guide (EY, 2017) p. 1.
6. Law No. 05-07.
7. Law No. 86-14.
8. Law No. 05-07.
9. Law No. 86-14.
10. Law on Taxation of Petroleum Activities (Law No. 13/04 (2004)).

Tax (PIT) is generally imposed at 50% on income from a specific block.[11] This tax is assessed on profit oil, which is petroleum produced in excess of:

(i) the percentage deemed as cost oil; and
(ii) that used in the operations after being shared with the state oil and gas company Sonangol.

Incentives under the tax regime include the investment allowance uplift for development expenses from 30% to 40%, production allowances, tax reductions, and exemptions from customs duty. Surface fees are imposed at USD 300 per square kilometre. The Training Tax Contribution applies at USD 0.15 per barrel for production companies, at USD 100,000 for companies owning a prospecting licence, at USD 300,000 for exploration companies, and at 0.5% for service companies. The consumption tax generally applies to the importation and supply of goods and services at a rate of 10%.

Stamp duty at 0.1% applies to the value of new share issues. Stamp duty also applies on specific transactions including certain contracts, transactions, and licence farm outs.

The LNG taxation regime uses a separate tax structure, with petroleum income tax generally 35%, and the training tax contributions at 0.15% together with a gas surcharge.

An example of Angolan tax and PSC terms is based on sales of crude oil in a year of USD 1 million. Cost oil is allowed at 55%, and so USD 550,000 is therefore allowed for the oil and gas company to recover costs. The profit oil is the remaining USD 450,000. The production share under the particular PSC for this field is 20% to the state oil company Sonangol, and 80% to the oil and gas company, allowing the oil and gas company to retain profit oil of USD 360,000. The Petroleum Income Tax due on the company's profit oil at the 50% rate is therefore USD 180,000.

In relation to mergers and acquisitions, gains made on the sale of licence interests are subject to tax in Angola.

AUSTRALIA

Australia imposes Federal income tax under the Income Tax Assessment Act 1936,[12] Income Tax Assessment Act 1997,[13] and the Income Tax Rates Act 1986,[14] with the rate on larger companies at 30%. The reduced rate for Small Business Entities is 27.5% for 2017/2018 for businesses under an annual turnover threshold of 25 million. Sale of depreciable assets such as plant and machinery is generally taxable under a depreciation balancing charge up to their original cost, and any excess is taxed as a revenue

11. EY, Global Oil and Gas Tax Guide (EY, 2017) p. 8.
12. Income Tax Assessment Act 1936 (Act No. 27 of 1936).
13. Income Tax Assessment Act 1997 (Act No. 38 of 1997).
14. Income Tax Rates Act 1986 (Act No. 107 of 1986).

gain.[15] Gains on other assets are generally subject to Capital Gains Tax (CGT).[16] Capital losses under these provisions are not deductible against other income. There is no ring fencing applied between different oil and gas fields under the income tax system. Tax consolidation is allowed on the basis of a single taxable entity for 100% commonly owned companies.[17] The thin capitalisation provisions can potentially deny interest deductions where the debt exceeds the related safe harbour amounts. These tests include the safe harbour debt amount, where related and unrelated party debt does not exceed a debt-to-equity ratio of 1.5:1 (60% debt-to-total assets ratio).[18]

Australia imposes Petroleum Resource Rent Tax (PRRT) under the PRRT Assessment Act 1987,[19] on petroleum projects, including onshore and offshore oil and gas licences, and coal seam gas, with a 40% tax rate applying on a project basis. Exploration expenditure can be transferred between projects, and a 100% deduction is allowed for exploration costs incurred under an exploration licence. Specific costs are not deductible for PRRT, including financing costs, private royalty payments, income tax, goods and services tax (GST), cash bidding payments, and indirect administrative costs. Unused deductions are compounded annually at set rates and are allowed as deductions in later years. PRRT is deductible under the income tax system.

Crude oil excise is a tax imposed on crude oil and condensate production from coastal waters, onshore areas, and the North West Shelf project area, with marginal tax rates of up to 30%. The first 30 million barrels of crude oil and condensate from a field are excise exempt.[20]

Federal royalties are imposed on the value of all petroleum including gas production from the North West Shelf offshore project area at 10% and 12.5% of the wellhead value. The royalties are shared by the federal government with the Western Australia state government.[21]

State royalties generally apply to onshore oil and gas projects or projects in state territorial waters at rates of 10% to 12.5%, based on the wellhead value, with deductions allowed for processing, storing, and transportation.

GST applies to value added on the supply of goods and services on a similar basis as a VAT at the rate of 10%, and registered businesses are allowed a credit for GST paid on purchases. Exports are generally treated as GST-free, so that GST is not included in the price of exports, while credits may still be claimed for GST on related purchases.[22]

In relation to mergers and acquisitions, Australian resident companies and Australian branches are generally subject to capital gains tax on the sale of company shares. A participation exemption is available for dividends and gains on foreign

15. These rules generally apply for assets acquired after 30 June 2001. The excess is taxed under Capital Gains Tax rules where the asset was acquired from 20 September 1985 to 30 June 2001.
16. Part 3-1 Income Tax Assessment Act 1997. CGT generally applies where the assets were acquired on or after 20 September 1985.
17. Divs 701 and 703, Income Tax Assessment Act 1997.
18. Div. 820 Income Tax Assessment Act 1997.
19. Petroleum Resource Rent Tax Assessment Act 1987 (Act No. 142 of 1987).
20. Excise Tariff Act 1921. The provisions apply for oil discovered from 18 September 1975.
21. Offshore Petroleum and Greenhouse Gas Storage Act (2006), section 75.
22. A New Tax System (Goods and Services Tax) Act 1999 (Act No. 55 of 1999).

non-portfolio company shares, where that company is an active business, and taxpayer has at least a 10% voting interest, for at least twelve months.[23]

Profits on sale of oil exploration permits, retention leases and production licences assets acquired after 30 June 2001 are taxed under the uniform capital allowance rules, as a taxable balancing charge and revenue profit.[24]

Non-residents of Australia are subject to tax on gains on sale of 'taxable Australian real property' (TARP). This includes assets of a permanent establishment in Australia, and Australian shares, where the company, directly or indirectly, primarily holds taxable Australian assets, including land, fixtures to land, and Australian oil and gas exploration permits and production licences. Purchasers are generally required to withhold tax at the rate of 12.5% of the purchase price as a non-final tax where they purchase TARP assets with value above AUD 750,000 from a non-resident of Australia.[25]

BRAZIL

Brazil imposes CIT or IRPJ under the National Tax Code,[26] together with the related Social Contribution Tax (CSLL), for a combined rate 34%. Depreciation is allowed at concessional rates for upstream operations. A deduction is allowed for certain dividends under the Interest on Net Equity (INE) rules, with dividends treated as deductible interest subject to 15% withholding tax, or 25% when paid to tax haven jurisdictions. The INE amount is limited to the highest of 50% of annual profits or 50% of accumulated earnings and profits.

There is no tax consolidation in Brazil. Accordingly, there may be advantages in using the downstream merger structure to obtain interest deductions, where a Brazilian acquiring company with debt deductions merges with the Brazilian target company. Tax losses of a target company can be retained on change of ownership providing that there is no change in business activities. There is no ring fencing for taxation of oil and gas fields.[27]

The thin capitalisation provisions were introduced from 2011, and generally impose a 2:1 debt to net equity limit on related party debt, which may be reduced to 0.3:1 where there is a tax haven lender. A Brazilian parent company is taxed on the income of foreign subsidiaries where the parent company has control, significant influence, or at least 20% ownership, although this may be limited by tax treaties. The provisions can apply to multiple levels of foreign companies where the companies are included in accounting consolidation.

The Special Participation Tax (SPT) applies to oil and gas income at rates from 10% to 40%. Royalties are imposed generally at 10% of the value of oil and gas

23. Div. 768 and section 118-12 Income Tax Assessment Act 1997.
24. Profits on such assets acquired from 20 September 1985 to 30 June 2001 are subject to capital gains tax, with capital losses not deductible against other income.
25. Div.14-D Taxation Administration Act 1953. The provisions apply from 1 July 2016, with the current rate applying to transactions from 1 July 2017.
26. National Tax Code (Law No. 5172 (1966).
27. EY, Global Oil and Gas Tax Guide 2017 (EY, 2017) p. 63.

production. Tax losses are allowed an indefinite carry-forward, however the use of the losses is limited to 30% of taxable profits in each year. Signature bonuses are imposed on the winning bidder for a block licence, with the bonuses amortised for CIT, and deductible for SPT.

The PSC regime was introduced from 2010 for new 'pre-salt' areas and areas deemed strategic by the government. The state oil company, Petrobras, may be the field operator with a minimum 30% interest.[28]

Federal, state, and municipal indirect taxes are allowed under the Federal Constitution.[29] Federal indirect taxes include the Contribution for Social Integration (PIS), Contribution for Social Security (COFINS), Excise Tax (IPI), Import Tax (II), Special Contribution (CIDE), and tax on credit, exchange, insurance and security transactions (IOF).[30] The principal state indirect tax is the Tax on Goods and Services (ICMS). The principal municipal tax is the Service Tax Importation (ISS). Complex issues arise with these taxes, such as the requirement to purchase a listed item to obtain PIS/COFINS credits. The combination of indirect taxes on transactions can be summarised as follows:

- Imported goods: II 5%–15%, IPI 5%–20%, PIS/COFINS 9.25% or 10.25%, ICMS 18%, IOF 0.38%.
- Imported services: IRRF 15%, CIDE 10%, PIS/COFINS 9.25%, ISS 5%, IOF 0.38%.
- Brazilian goods: IPI 5%–20%, PIS/COFINS 9.25%, ICMS 18%.
- Brazilian services: PIS/COFINS 9.25%, ISS 5%.

An example of the calculation for imported services, which includes an issue of tax imposed on tax, is as follows: Net WHT withheld by the recipient is 25%, which comprises 18.75% corporate tax (15% corporate tax on service, WHT and ISS), plus 6.25% ISS (5% tax on service, WHT and ISS). The service provider is responsible for 10% CIDE, and 9.25% PIS/COFINS. The total withholding tax, including indirect taxes, is approximately 50%.

Tax developments include the State of Rio de Janeiro Law in 2015 which makes extraction of crude oil in the state subject to ICMS. ICMS previously only applied to subsequent transactions in the chain of production and sale.[31]

The Repetro regime allows a suspension, or reduction to 3%, for Federal indirect taxes on imported goods which are to be exported at a later date (II, IPI, PIS, COFINS). One current issue is the suspension of this regime in the State of Rio de Janeiro.[32]

In relation to mergers and acquisitions, assets sales are treated as capital gains or losses. Share sales by non-residents are taxed at 15%, or at 25% if the seller is resident in a low-tax jurisdiction.

28. Ben H Welmaker, Jr and Steven P Otillar, Baker & McKenzie, 'Production Sharing Contracts: Implications for Pre-Salt Development in Brazil'.
29. Constitution of the Federative Republic of Brazil (1988), sections 153–156.
30. Tax on Credit, Exchange Operations, and Insurance, or on Securities, Law No. 5143 (1966).
31. State of Rio de Janeiro, Law 7,183/15.
32. Legislative Decree 2/2016.

The IOF is a tax on financial operations which applies at the rate of 0.38% on foreign currency transactions. In a merger and acquisition transaction, the tax can effectively apply twice, applying to the purchase of Brazilian reals (BRL) required for payment, and applying again on conversion by seller from BRL received to their home currency.

The Ltda limited liability partnership entity may be a preferred structure to hold assets in Brazil, rather than a company. The Ltda entity does not require 10% of its share capital to be held in a bank account. The Ltda requires a second 'partner' to hold a nominal interest, in addition to the main parent company.

CANADA

The Canadian Income Tax Act,[33] imposes corporate tax at 25%, which is reduced to 15% by abatement of 10% for taxable income allocated to a province or territory. Corporate tax is also imposed by the provinces. Canada does not provide tax consolidation. Capital gains have a reduced level of tax, with only half the gains taxed at normal rates. Capital losses can only offset capital gains.[34] Tax credits and allowances relating to upstream oil and gas include:

- A deduction of 10% is allowed each year for the costs of oil and gas rights pooled in the Canadian Oil and Gas Property Expense (COGPE).
- A deduction of 100% is allowed each year for exploration costs including seismic, geological and geophysical, and drilling costs of discovery wells pooled in Canadian Exploration Expense (CEE).
- A deduction of 30% is allowed each year for development costs accumulated in Canadian Development Expense (CDE).

An investment tax credit is available at the rate of 15% for scientific research and experimental development (SR&ED) expenses including the development of oil and gas technology. The credit is allowed in addition to tax deductions for the expenses.

GSTs applies to value added on the supply of goods and services on the same basis as a VAT at the rate of 5%, with GST free 'zero rated' treatment applying to exports.[35]

Capital transactions such as sale of shares and partnership interests have a reduced rate of tax for corporations and individuals, with 50% of the gain generally taxed at normal tax rates.

Corporate tax applies to a non-resident's sale of taxable Canadian property (TCP), or shares in private companies, where more than 50% of value is taxable Canadian property, including Canadian oil and gas assets. This tax may be reduced or eliminated by tax treaty. Non-resident vendors are required to provide the purchaser

33. Income Tax Act (RSC 1985, c 1).
34. EY, Global Oil and Gas Tax Guide 2017 (EY, 2017) p. 103.
35. Excise Tax Act, Part IX.

with a related certificate, otherwise the purchaser is required to withhold and remit to the tax authorities 50% of the asset price or 25% of the share purchase price.[36]

Asset sales may be taxable as revenue transactions, including recoupment of claimed pool deductions for plant and machinery.

Canadian Provincial Tax

The Canadian province and territories impose CIT at rates from 11% to 16%.

Royalties are imposed by province and territory governments on the production of oil and gas in relation to government-owned lands at rates from 10% to 45% on the value of production, with special regimes for Arctic, Atlantic offshore, and oil sands. Royalties may be payable at varying rates to private land owners. Royalty payments are generally deductible for corporate tax purposes.

Alberta

Alberta imposes provincial CIT at 12% in 2017,[37] with no deduction allowed for royalty payments. There is a nominal property tax, and there are no provincial capital taxes or sales taxes.

Royalties on the production of oil and gas are determined on a sliding scale, with the rate increasing with the production from each well, and also adjusted for current oil and gas prices.[38] The royalty rates under the modernised system introduced from 2017 are up to 40% for oil and natural gas. There are also several royalty incentives, including a 5% rate on production from horizontal drilling for the first year, and for an additional one to three years depending on the well depth.

Alberta imposes a property tax regime on the oil and gas industry on the market value of property in Alberta which is not owned by the Crown, generally levied at 4% of the related revenues.[39]

British Columbia

British Columbia imposes CIT rate at 11%.[40] There is a 10% tax credit allowed on scientific research and experimental development (SR&ED) expenses including the development of oil and gas technology.

British Columbia also imposes a royalty on the value of oil and gas production.[41] The royalty rate for oil varies up to 40% depending upon the volume of oil, whether the oil is produced from Crown or freehold land, classification of the oil as new oil, old oil,

36. EY, Global Oil and Gas Tax Guide 2017 (EY, 2017) p. 108.
37. Alberta Income Tax Act, RSA 2000, c A-26.
38. Petroleum Royalty Regulation, 2017, under the Mines and Minerals Act, RSA 2000 c M-17 (Alberta).
39. Freehold Mineral Rights Tax Act (RSA 2000 c F-26 (Alberta).
40. Income Tax Act, RSBC 1996, Ch. 215, Division 3.
41. Petroleum and Natural Gas Act (British Columbia).

third tier oil, or heavy oil, and the net sales price. The royalty rate for gas varies up to 27%, depending on whether the gas is produced from Crown or freehold land, whether classified as conservation gas or non-conservation gas, the reference price determined monthly, and the select price set annually.[42]

British Columbia introduced the Provincial Sales Tax (PST) on the sale of specific goods and services generally at a rate of 7%.[43] The PST replaced the prior Harmonised Sales Tax (HST).

CHINA

CIT in China is imposed under the *Enterprise Income Tax Law* (EIT) applying from 2008 at 25%.[44] The tax rate may be reduced under incentives for specific industries, for example high and new technology enterprises incorporated from 2008 in the Shanghai Pudong New Area, or the Special Economic Zones (SEZ) such as Hainan, Shantou, Shenzhen, Zhuhai, and Xiamen. Capital gains are treated as taxable income. Capital gains derived by non-residents which have a source in China are subject to a 10% withholding tax. Tax losses may be carried forward for up to five years. There is generally no tax consolidation relief.[45]

The fiscal regime that applies to upstream oil and gas is generally based on PSCs, together with special oil gain levies, VAT, resource tax, and CIT.[46] The special oil gain levy is based on a formula in circumstances where the monthly average weighted price per barrel of crude oil sold is greater than USD 65 per barrel from 1 January 2015.

Royalties are imposed at rates from 0% to 12.5%. Royalties are not applicable to PSCs concluded after 1 November 2011. Bonus payments may be required under specific PSCs based on the volume of petroleum resources and the economic value of the field. The resource tax applies at 6% of the sales price from 1 December 2014.

China has thin capitalisation provisions which can potentially disallow interest deductions where the debt-to-equity ratio of a company exceeds 2:1, or 5:1 for financial institutions.

China provides several tax incentives for qualifying R&D activities.[47] These include the Research & Development expenditure super deduction at 150% for CIT purposes, and a reduced CIT rate for High and New Technology Enterprises (HNTE) of 15%.[48]

42. Oil and Gas Royalty Handbook (2014) British Columbia Ministry of Finance, www.sbr.gov.bc.ca/business/Natural_Resources/Oil_and_gas_royalties/handbook.htm at 6 August 2013.
43. Provincial Sales Tax Act 2012, SBC 2012 Chapter 35 (British Columbia).
44. *Enterprise Income Tax Law of the People's Republic of China*, adopted at the 5th Session of the 10th National People's Congress of the People's Republic of China on 16 March 2007 (China).
45. EY, Worldwide Corporate Tax Guide 2017 (EY, 2017) p. 301.
46. EY, Global Oil and Gas Tax Guide 2017 (EY, 2017) p. 125.
47. *Enterprise Income Tax Law of the People's Republic of China*, Article 27, and *Enterprise Income Tax Law Implementing Regulations*, Article 93 (China).
48. KPMG, Securing R&D Tax Incentives in China, <www.kpmg.com/CN/en/IssuesAndInsights/ArticlesPublications/Documents/Securing-Research-Development-Tax-Incentives-in-China-201210.pdf>.

The Chinese VAT provisions generally apply to the sale of goods and services.[49] The standard VAT rate is 17%, with lower rates for specific items such as agricultural products and utility services at 13%, transportation at 11%, and information technology services at 6%.[50]

DENMARK

Denmark imposes Corporation Income Tax on hydrocarbon activities at the 'Chapter 2' corporate tax rate of 25%,[51] and taxes other income at the ordinary CIT rate of 22%. Exploration costs for taxable production are fully deductible. Ring fencing provisions apply, so that losses from non-oil and gas activities cannot be used to offset profits from hydrocarbon production. Tax losses have an indefinite carry-forward period. The thin capitalisation rules limit interest deductions where a company's debt-to-equity ratio exceeds 4 to 1. There are also additional limits on interest deductions under the interest ceiling rule, where interest expenses exceed 3.4% of assets, or an earnings before interest and tax (EBIT) rule, where interest exceeds 80% of EBIT.[52]

Denmark imposes Hydrocarbon Tax on oil and gas production activities, generally at the 'Chapter 3A' rate of 52%.[53] Transitional measures apply to the tax rate older licences previously under 'Chapter 3' provisions.

The overall combined tax rate for Chapters 2 and 3A is 64%, as the Chapter 2 taxes paid are deductible in determining Chapter 3A income.

In relation to mergers and acquisitions, the participation exemption applies to the sale of subsidiary company shares, where the parent company holds at least 10% of the subsidiary's share capital, or sale of group company shares where the company and its shareholder are under Danish domestic or Danish international tax consolidation rules.

Farm out transactions are generally treated as taxable asset disposals which are taxed at the 25% corporation tax rate, and the 52% hydrocarbon tax rate.

FRANCE

The corporate tax rate in France is 33.3%, together with a standard surtax of 3.3% of the corporate tax, resulting in total tax of 34.43%.[54] Capital gains generally also are taxed at the same rate.[55]

49. *Provisional Regulations of the People's Republic of China on Value Added Tax Detailed Rules for its Implementation* 13 December 1993 (VAT) (China).
50. KPMG, 'VAT in China: significant reforms – time to prepare', www.kpmg.com/global/en/issuesandinsights/articlespublications/frontiers-in-tax/pages/vat-china-significant-reforms.aspx on 4 December 2013.
51. State Tax Act Statute of 1922 on Income Taxation to the State (Statsskatteloven) and Corporate Income Tax Act, Law 111 of 19 February 2004 (Selskabsskatteloven).
52. EY, Global Oil and Gas Tax Guide 2017 (EY, 2017) p. 193.
53. Act on Taxation of Income in connection with Hydrocarbon Exploration and Production in Denmark (Hydrocarbon Tax Act), Consolidated Act No. 792 (1993) as amended.
54. EY Worldwide Corporate Tax Guide 2017 (EY, 2017) p. 485.
55. General Tax Code (Code Général des Impôts, CGI) (France).

France has a territorial tax system, so that foreign sourced income is generally not taxed. The participation exemption applies to qualifying dividends which are effectively only taxed at 5%.[56] CIT applies to 12% of the gross capital gains on qualifying participations from 31 December 2012 for effective tax rate of 4%. The profits of foreign branches are tax exempt unless the branch derives passive, low-taxed income. The French CFC provisions can apply to tax to foreign companies with a foreign effective tax rate which is less than 50% of the French tax rate.[57]

Tax consolidation is allowed where there is 95% common ownership between the respective companies and the parent company has elected tax consolidation for a five-year period.[58] Losses incurred after 2003 may be carried forward indefinitely, however the use of carry-forward tax losses in any year cannot exceed EUR 1 million plus 50% of the taxable profit above that amount. Tax losses may be carried back one year. Carry-forward tax losses may cease to be available in the event of a significant change in business activity, such as the addition or a termination of a business that relates to at least 50% of revenue, or the average of headcount and fixed assets.

France generally allows a deduction for interest expenses subject to: (a) an arm's length test that an independent party would lend on the same terms, and (b) the higher of: (i) a thin capitalisation limit where debt exceeds a debt-to-equity ratio of 1.5:1; (ii) the interest exceeds an earnings threshold of 25% earnings before related interest, tax, and depreciation; or (iii) the interest income threshold of the amount of interest received from related parties. These limitations may not apply however where the consolidated debt-to-equity ratio of the group is higher than the debt--to-equity ratio of the French company.[59]

France provides several incentives for R&D including the tax credit for R&D expenses (*crédit d'impôt recherche* – CIR), which is generally a credit of 30% of eligible expenses up to EUR 100 million, and 5% over this threshold.[60]

The principal indirect tax is the *Taxe sur la Valeur Ajoutée* (TVA), which is the French VAT regime on goods and services.[61] Under these provisions, VAT is imposed on any supply of goods or services, other than an exempt supply, made in France by a taxable person. The VAT rate is generally 20%, with reduced rates for items including agricultural products and foodstuffs. The export of goods and services to a person in another country is generally outside the scope of VAT, also known as zero-rated supplies, which allows a credit for the related input VAT paid.[62]

---

56. General Tax Code (CGI) Articles 145 and 216 (France).
57. General Tax Code (CGI) Article 209 B (France).
58. General Tax Code (CGI) Article 223 (France).
59. EY, Worldwide Corporate Tax Guide 2017 (EY, 2017) p. 489.
60. General Tax Code (CGI) Article 244 quater B.
61. European Commission, Trade Export Helpdesk, http://www.exporthelp.europa.eu/thdapp/display.htm?page=rt/rt_ValueAddedTax.html&docType=main&languageId=EN on 13 September 2017.
62. *General Tax Code* (CGI) Article 266 (France) and *Livre des procédures fiscales* (Manual of Tax Procedures) (France).

GERMANY

The German federal CIT rate under the *Corporate Income Tax Act* is 15%, together with a 5.5% solidarity charge, resulting in an effective tax rate of 15.825%.[63] Capital gains are generally taxed on the same basis as business income. Dividends and capital gains from participations of at least 10% in other companies are effectively only taxed on 5% of the dividend payment or capital gain under the participation exemption. Income from foreign treaty country branches is generally exempt, and losses of other branch are allowed as deductions if the branch is an active business.

Tax consolidation is available between German companies where the shareholders of one company have the majority of voting rights in the related company. There is an indefinite carry-forward of tax losses, however the use of these losses in each year is limited to EUR 1 million for each tax year plus 60% of annual taxable income exceeding EUR 1 million. Tax loss carry forwards may potentially be forfeited proportionally where, within a five-year period, more than 25% of the shares of the entity are directly or indirectly transferred to a single new shareholder or group, and entirely forfeited where more than 50% of the shares are transferred within a five-year period, under provisions introduced in 2008.

Municipalities impose Trade Tax on business income at an average rate of 14%. The tax is based on taxable income on a similar basis to Corporate Tax, however the related add-back adjustments include 25% of interest on debt, 6.25% for licence payments, 5% for lease payments on movable assets, and 12.5% for lease payments on immovable assets. The tax base is distributed between the related municipalities according to the payroll at each location.[64]

Interest deductions are subject to an interest barrier limit applying from 2008 based on 30% of earnings before net interest, tax, depreciation and amortisation (EBITDA). The rule applies to debt owed to resident and non-resident creditors, including debt owed to third parties and debt owed to related parties.[65]

Germany does not provide specific tax incentives for R&D, and there is also currently no patent box regime.[66]

The Turnover Tax, *Umsatzsteuergesetz* (UStG) is the German VAT indirect tax regime on goods and services.[67] The tax is imposed on any supply of goods or services, other than an exempt supply, made in Germany by a taxable person. The rate is generally 19%, with a reduced rate of 7% applying to certain goods and services including food, books, public transport, and hotel accommodation. Exempt supplies include supplies relating to land and buildings, financial transactions, insurance,

---

63. Corporate Income Tax Act (Körperschaftsteuergesetz) (KStG) (Germany).
64. EY, Worldwide Corporate Tax Guide 2017 (EY, 2017) p. 537.
65. *Income Tax Act*, section 4(h) (EStG), *Corporate Income Tax Law*, section 8(a) ('KStG') (Germany).
66. Christiane Malke, Ina Schlie & Christoph Spengel, *Germany* in *Tax Incentives on Research and Development (R&D), Cahiers de droit fiscal international*, vol. 100A, 319, 332.
67. Turnover Tax Law (*Umsatzsteuergesetz)* (UStG) of 2 March 2005, BGBl I 2005, 386), and Turnover Tax Implementing Ordinance (*Umsatzsteuer-Durchführungsverordnung*) (UStDV) of 2 March 2005, BGBl I 2005, 434) (Germany).

education, and medical services. Exempt with credit supplies, also known as zero-rated supplies, allow the recovery of credits for input tax paid, and include the export of goods and services to a person in another country.[68]

GREENLAND

Greenland applies income tax on company profits under the Administration of Taxes Act 2006,[69] and the Income Tax 2006.[70] CIT terms will generally apply to upstream oil and gas operations, with the state oil company Nunaoil participating in the oil and gas licence. Income Tax applies to oil and gas company profits, with the current rate generally at 30%. Greenland applies ring fencing for tax purposes, where oil and gas exploration and exploitation income or expenses cannot offset other income or expenses, however there is no field ring fencing. Greenland does not provide tax consolidation or group taxation. Depreciation allowances are available on a reducing balance basis at rates of up to 30% a year. Exploration costs are allowed as fully deductible. Dividends are fully deductible for the distributing company for Income Tax purposes. Greenland requires a locally incorporated company to be used for oil and gas production.[71]

Dividend payments are subject to WHT generally at 37% unless this is reduced by a tax treaty. This may be a significant issue for oil and gas companies as Greenland has limited tax treaties with other countries, including Denmark, Norway, Faroe Islands, Iceland, and specific items under the Denmark/Canada Tax Treaty. Greenland is not a member of the European Union (EU), and the EU Parent Subsidiary directive does not apply to reduce WHT on dividends.

The royalty regime relating to current oil and gas licences depends on the specific licence terms. In the 2002 licensing round, a three-tier surplus royalty system applied, with rates of 7.5%, 10%, and 12.5% on net cash flow. The royalty in each tier was payable if there was a positive balance after adjusting for prior year expenses at specified interest rates.

The government is reviewing the hydrocarbons tax model. The current proposals include: (1) the corporation and dividend tax in force at any time; (2) a turnover royalty of 2.5%; (3) profit-based royalties of 7.5%, 17.5%, and 30%, which will be paid when the accumulated income exceeds the accumulated costs by 35%, 45%, and 55%, respectively; and (4) participation in the home-rule company Nunaoil A/S, with a share of 6.25% in the exploration phase.[72]

Farm outs are taxable at 30%, however as exploration expenses are fully deductible, the consideration may defray the seller's exploration expenses.

---

68. European Commission, Trade Export Helpdesk, 'VAT Overview for Germany', www.exporthelp.europa.eu/thdapp/taxes/show2Files.htm?dir = /taxes/notes&reporterId2 = DE&file2 = ehit_de13_05v001/de/main/ovr_vat_de_0612.htm&reporterLabel2 = Germany&languageId = en&status = PROD > at 12 December 2013.
69. Landsting Act No. 11 on the Administration of Taxes 2006.
70. Landsting Act No. 12 on Income Tax 2006.
71. EY, Global Oil and Gas Tax Guide 2017 (EY, 2017) p. 243.
72. Government of Greenland, Greenland's Oil and Mineral Strategy 2014–2018, 55.

INDIA

The corporate tax rate in India is 30%, with an additional surcharge of 12% for domestic companies where income exceeds INR 100 million, and education cess tax at 3%,[73] resulting in an effective tax rate of up to 34.61%. The tax rate for branches of foreign companies is 40%, with a surcharge of 5% where the total income exceeds INR 100 million and education cess tax at 3%,[74] resulting in an effective tax rate of up to 43.26%. The Minimum Alternative Tax (MAT) can apply at a rate of 18.5% of book profits where this exceeds corporate tax.[75] The tax rate on capital gains is generally 20%.

There are no provisions allowing tax consolidation. Carry-forward tax losses are generally available for eight years, which is then subject to a 51% continuity of ownership test to be available for closely held corporations. There are specific rules for amalgamations relating to carry-forward losses on mergers which generally require a continued 75% shareholding relationship, that the amalgamating company has been engaged in business for three years, and that there is a continuous holding of 75% of fixed assets.[76]

There are no specific thin capitalisation provisions, however the Indian foreign exchange regulations can potentially limit related party debt using on a 4:1 debt-to-equity ratio.

There is an exemption for long-term capital gains on the sale of shares or units on a recognised stock exchange where Securities Transaction Tax (STT) has been paid, and a 15% rate applies for short-term gains with a less than twelve-month holding period.[77]

There is a tax exemption for dividend income received from a domestic company. The dividend paying company is required to pay dividend distribution tax (DDT) of 15% together with surcharges and education cess, which may be reduced by the amount of dividends received from subsidiaries on which the subsidiary has paid DDT. No branch remittance tax is imposed in India.[78]

India provides several incentives for R&D, including deductions for revenue and capital R&D expenditure.[79] There is a 100% super deduction for certain in-house R&D revenue and capital expenditures.[80] The Patent Box regime provides a 10% tax rate for royalty income for patents developed and registered in India.

73. *Finance (No. 2) Act 2004*, Act 23 of 2004, section 81 (India).
74. *Income Tax Act 1961*, Act 43 of 1961 (India).
75. *Income Tax Act 1961*, Act 43 of 1961, section 115JB (India).
76. EY, Worldwide Corporate Tax Guide 2017 (EY, 2017) p. 655.
77. If STT has not been paid, the tax rate on the sale of shares for domestic companies is 30% short-term, and 20% long-term holdings, foreign institutional investors is 30% short-term and 10% long-term gains respectively, and other non-residents is 40% short-term and 20% long-term gains, respectively.
78. EY, Worldwide Corporate Tax Guide 2017 (EY, 2017) p. 642.
79. Gautam Chopra & Isha Sekhri, *India* in *Tax Incentives on Research and Development (R&D)*, *Cahiers de droit fiscal international*, vol. 100A, 383.
80. Deloitte, *2014 Global Survey of R&D Tax Incentives*, 19.

Indirect taxes in India include the central value added tax (CENVAT) imposed by the central government on goods manufactured in India. Sales Tax is imposed on the sales of goods by the central government known as central sales tax, on interstate sales at various rates. The state governments impose indirect tax on intrastate sales at various rates which is generally referred to as Value Added Tax.[81] Service tax is imposed on specific services including banking and finance, insurance, scientific and technical consultancy, information technology, telecommunication and consulting at 12.36%.

The STT applies to the purchase and sale of securities such as shares, derivatives, and units of an equity fund, which are transacted on a recognised stock exchange. The rate on shares is generally 0.1% imposed on the buyer of the shares and 0.1% imposed on the seller of the shares.[82]

JAPAN

Japan imposes tax on business income at a rate of 23.4% under the Corporation Tax Act.[83] This rate added to local taxes provides an effective tax rate of approximately 31%. Corporations Tax also applies to capital gains at the same rate.[84] There is generally a tax exemption for dividends from other Japanese corporations net of related interest costs where the parent has a shareholding of 25% or more, with a 50% tax exemption if the parent holds less than a 25% shareholding. Foreign dividends are allowed a 95% exclusion from taxable income where the Japanese company has at least a 25% shareholding in the foreign company. The tax rules allow tax consolidation where the respective companies have 100% common ownership. Tax losses may be carried forward to be utilised against future taxable income for up to nine years.

Japan provides several tax incentives for R&D, which generally includes: (1) a permanent credit, for larger companies at 8% to 10% of R&D expenditure, limited to 25% of the CIT liability; (2) a credit for joint R&D with or contracted R&D by university or public research institution at 12% of the gross special R&D cost; and (3) a temporary incremental credit till 2017 of the higher of: (i) 5% to 30% of incremental R&D costs; or (ii) R&D costs in excess of 10% of the average sales times a tax credit ratio generally based on R&D costs compared to average annual sales.[85]

There are also thin capitalisation provisions which can potentially limit tax deductions for interest on related party debt where the debt-to-equity ratio exceeds 3:1. Japan introduced earnings-stripping rules from 1 April 2013 which can also limit the deductibility of interest. These rules can potentially apply where interest is paid by corporations to related persons in excess of 50% of the corporation's adjusted taxable income.[86]

81. EY, Worldwide Corporate Tax Guide 2017 (EY, 2017) p. 657.
82. *Finance (No. 2) Act 2004*, Act 23 of 2004, section 86 (India).
83. *Hōjin Zei Hō* (Corporation Tax Act), Act No. 34 of 1965 (Japan).
84. EY, Worldwide Corporate Tax Guide 2017 (EY, 2017) p. 777.
85. Deloitte, *2014 Global Survey of R&D Tax Incentives*, 26.
86. EY, Worldwide Corporate Tax Guide 2017 (EY, 2017) p. 784.

Stamp duty may be imposed on transfer agreements for the sale of real estate and businesses at up to JPY 600,000, share certificates at up to JPY 20,000, and merger agreements and demerger agreements at up to JPY 40,000. There is no stamp duty on the transfer of shares.[87]

Japan imposes Consumption Tax (CT), on a similar basis to a VAT, to the sale or lease of an asset in Japan and the supply of services in Japan. The Consumption Tax rate is 8%, and expected to increase to 10% from 1 October 2019.[88] Exported goods and exported listed services are zero rated, so that no tax applies to the sale, while allowing the recovery of tax paid on the related inputs. Specific financial transactions including loans, guarantees, distributions from investment trusts and insurance premiums are generally non-taxable supplies, so that no tax applies to the sale with no recovery of the tax paid on inputs.[89] Input credits are limited where taxable supplies including zero-rated supplies are less than 95% of turnover, based on a pro-rata allocation, using ratio of taxable supplies to total supplies, or based on the direct attribution of credits.[90]

KAZAKHSTAN

Kazakhstan provides PSC terms for upstream oil and gas with the related profits being subject to CIT under the Tax Codes at a 20% rate.[91] Withholding tax is imposed on dividend payments at 15%, which may be reduced by tax treaties. Branch profits tax also applies to the after tax income of permanent establishments of foreign companies at 15%, which results in total tax on branches of 32%. Kazakhstan applies ring fencing terms between PSC contracts, and between oil and gas production and other activities. Depreciation allowances are provided at double rates for oil and gas producers, prospecting and preparatory expenses depreciated once production has commenced. Thin capitalisation provisions can disallow interest deductions on related party debt, debt guaranteed by related parties, or interest paid to tax havens, where the related debt-to-equity ratio exceeds 4 to 1. Tax losses may be carried forward for up to ten years.[92]

Excess profits tax may apply at rates from nil to 60% to the extent that net after tax income exceeds 25% of deductions.

87. *Inshi Zei Ho* (Stamp Tax Act), Act No. 23 of 1967 (Japan).
88. PricewaterhouseCoopers, *Asia Pacific Tax Newsalert*, 'Japan announces consumption tax increase and investment incentive proposals', 21 October 2013. www.pwc.com/en_US/us/tax-services-multinationals/newsletters/asia-pacific-tax/assets/pwc-japan-consumption-tax-increase.pdf at 6 December 2013.
89. KPMG, *Japan, Country VAT/GST Essentials* (KPMG, 2012).
90. EY, Worldwide VAT, GST and Sales Tax Guide 2017 (EY, 2017) p. 523.
91. Code of the Republic of Kazakhstan dated 10 December 2008 No. 99 on Concerning Taxes and Other Obligatory Payments to the Budget; Law of the Republic of Kazakhstan dated 20 December 2008 No. 100 on Concerning the Implementation of the Code of the Republic of Kazakhstan on Concerning Taxes and other Obligatory Payments to the Budget, and Code of the Republic of Kazakhstan on Taxes and other Obligatory Payments to the Budget 2013.
92. EY, Global Oil and Gas Tax Guide 2017 (EY, 2017) p. 333.

The Minerals Extraction Tax (MET) applies as a royalty on the value of oil and gas condensate production at rates from 0.5% to 18%, with the tax rate reduced by 50% if the oil or gas is processed in Kazakhstan. A 10% MET rate applies to exported natural gas.

Rent tax on exports applies to the value of exported oil and gas condensate at rates of up to 32%. Customs export duty is imposed on crude oil from 2016 based on market prices at up to USD 236 per ton.

Kazakhstan applies signature bonuses on oil exploration contracts and oil production contracts, and bonuses on commercial discovery.

CIT generally applies to gains on the sale of interests in subsurface use contracts, the sale of shares in Kazakhstan companies with subsurface use contracts, and the sale of shares of foreign companies with more than 50% value from Kazakhstan subsurface use contracts. Non-residents may be taxed on the related gains on the basis of 15% WHT, unless this tax is reduced by domestic laws or tax treaties. Corporate tax may apply to gains made on farm out transactions.

MEXICO

The fiscal regime in Mexico was updated in 2014 Income Tax Law and the Hydrocarbon Revenue Law. The law provides for the use of licence contracts, profit and PSCs, and service contracts: (1) Licence contract terms include a signing bonus, exploratory phase fees, royalties, and a percentage of operating profits or the contract value of hydrocarbons, in addition to taxes under the Income Tax Law. (2) Profit sharing and PSC terms include exploratory phase fees, royalties, and a percentage of operating profits. In the profit sharing contract all production is delivered to the state marketer, whereas the PSC requires a portion of production to be delivered to the state marketer, and (3) Service contract terms which require the contractor to provide services for cash consideration.

Mexico imposes CIT under the Federal Fiscal Code 1981 and the Law on Income Tax 2002, at a rate of 30% including capital gains. Non-residents are subject to a 25% tax rate on gross income or a 35% rate on net income. The thin capitalisation rules can disallow deductions for the interest paid to foreign related parties where debt-to-equity exceeds a 3 to 1 ratio. Tax consolidation is not available to companies which are in the business exploration and extraction of hydrocarbons. Tax losses may be carried forward for up to ten years, or for up to fifteen years for losses derived from deep-water contracts.[93]

VAT applies generally at a 16% rate. An 11% VAT rate may apply in certain border zones, and the rate is 0% for activities carried out with the Mexican oil fund. Companies which have employees are required to distribute 10% of their adjusted taxable income to the employees.

Royalties are imposed on the production of oil at 7.5% for prices up to USD 44.78 per barrel, and using a formula of (0.134 x contract price) + 1.5% for higher prices.

93. EY, Global Oil and Gas Tax Guide 2017 (EY, 2017) p. 396.

Royalties are imposed on gas associated with oil at contractual price divided by 93.30. Royalties are imposed on non-associated gas for prices up to USD 4.67 per million BTUs at nil, ([contractual natural gas price – 4.67] × 60.5)/contractual price for prices up to USD 5.15 per million BTUs, and contractual price divided by 93.30 for higher prices.

In relation to mergers and acquisitions, disposals are generally taxed unless they are qualified for relief as reorganisations. There is no specific regime for farm in or farm out transactions. The sale of shares in a Mexican company is taxable at 25% on the gross proceeds, at 35% on the net gain, or at 40% of the gross proceeds if there is a tax haven seller. The sale of shares in a foreign company is taxable if more than 50% of the value of the shares relates to Mexican real property.

NIGERIA

Nigeria uses licence/concession, PSC, and Risk Service Contract regimes. Nigeria applies the Petroleum Profits Tax Act 2004,[94] to licences, generally at a rate of 85%, with a lower rate for new entrants for the first five years of 65.75%, and a tax rate of 50% on the oil and gas company's profit under PSCs. There is an Annual Allowance on qualifying capital expenditure of 20%, and a Petroleum Investment Allowance for the first year of qualifying expenditure at rates of 5% for onshore activities, and at 10% to 20% for offshore activities. There is also an Investment Tax Credit or Investment Tax Allowance of 50% for qualifying expenditure under PSCs.[95] Risk Service Contracts are subject to the standard CIT rate at 30%.

Resource Rent Tax applies on an area used basis at NGN 200 per square kilometre for oil prospecting licences at NGN 300 per square kilometre for non-producing leases, and at NGN 500 per square kilometre for producing leases. VAT is generally imposed at a 5% rate. VAT is not payable on exported goods and services including oil and gas products.

Royalties apply to the value of oil and gas produced. The rates are generally 20% for onshore production, 18.5% for territorial waters and offshore to 100m depth, and 16.67% for offshore waters over 100m depth. The rates for deep offshore and inland basis PSCs vary from 10% for inland basin, 16.67% to 200m depth, 12% to 500m depth, 8% to 800m depth, 4% to 1000m depth, and 0% over 1,000m depth.

Capital gains are taxed at 10% under the Capital Gains Tax Act, including farm in and farm out transactions. Rollover relief may be available for capital gains if the proceeds are used in acquiring a new related asset. The sale of shares is generally not taxed.

94. Petroleum Profits Tax Act 2004 (CAP P13 LFN 2004).
95. EY, Global Oil and Gas Tax Guide 2017 (EY, 2017) p. 447.

NORWAY

The Norwegian Act relating to the Taxation of Subsea Petroleum Deposits,[96] and the Income Tax Act of 1999,[97] impose a total 78% tax rate on oil and gas operations in 2017, comprising corporate tax at 24%, together with Special Tax at 54%. This combined rate also applies to onshore support activities. Norway provides incentives including depreciation uplift for expenditure on offshore production facilities, pipelines and installations, for an additional 22% deduction over four years. The tax value of exploration expenses not utilised in the current year against taxable profits are also refunded in cash at 78%. Norway applies ring fencing measures so that only 50% of onshore losses may be used to offset offshore profits.[98]

Tax loss grouping is provided where there is at least 90% common ownership between companies, however grouping does not apply to the Special Tax regime. There is an indefinite tax loss carry-forward, and a two-year tax loss carry-back. There is a specific limit to interest deductions relating to the Special Tax regime, based on interest costs, times 50%, times tax value of offshore related assets, divided by the average interest bearing debt. Norway limits related party interest deductions to 25% of taxable ordinary income, with the add-back of tax depreciation and net interest expenses (tax EBITDA). This limit does not currently apply to interest allocated to the 78% tax regime.

There are no royalties or bonus payments required.

There has been an issue whether appraisal wells are exploration eligible for refund, or are development expenses which are not immediately refunded. Oil and gas wells which are primarily drilled to ascertain whether a commercial field exists should generally be treated as exploration costs under these measures. There has also been an issue concerning the allocation of interest expense between the offshore and onshore tax regimes.

In relation to mergers and acquisitions, licence sales may be exempt under 'section 10' provisions, where the transfer is non-taxable to the seller and non-deductible for the buyer, with assets retaining the same basis for depreciation. The related sale and purchase agreement should confirm that section 10 applies, and state that the cash consideration is non-taxable and non-deductible.

If the acquisition relates to exploration assets, buyers may commonly pay 22% of the asset value. This buyer's payment, together with the seller's 78% exploration deduction, then meets 100% of the seller's exploration costs.

Gains on the sale of shares are not taxable if the gains are made by qualifying companies under the tax exemption system. This includes companies which are resident in another EEA Member State and non-EEA resident companies not in low-tax jurisdictions which have held at least 10% of capital and votes for more than two years.

One structuring issue is that there is no tax consolidation for upstream oil and gas subject to the combined offshore 78% tax rate. Accordingly, related ownership

---

96. Act of 13 June 1975 No. 35 relating to the Taxation of Subsea Petroleum Deposits. etc.
97. Income Tax Act 26 March 1999 No. 14.
98. EY, Global Oil and Gas Tax Guide 2017 (EY, 2017) p. 456.

structures may use one Norway licensed holding company to allow profits and losses to offset between different fields. There is also a planning issue that there is no 78% deduction for interest on share acquisitions, and the deduction is only allowed at the 28% tax rate.

QATAR

Qatar imposes taxes on profits arising under PSCs and the more recent development and fiscal agreements (DFA) under the Income Tax Law 2009.[99] The tax applies on taxable income which is defined under the PSC or DFA. The tax rate for fields approved from 2010 is 35%, and the tax rates for fields approved at earlier dates are from 35% to 55%. Ring fencing measures apply so that losses under PSC or other contracts cannot be used to offset profits under other PSCs or contracts, however the most recent agreements have not applies this limitation. Interest costs are generally not allowed as allowable costs under PSCs.[100]

Royalties may apply on the value of production at the rates specified under DFAs and some PSCs. Bonus payments may also be required under the specific terms of some PSCs.

Commercial activities other than exploration and production, such as oil and gas service activities, may be taxable at a 10% rate. There are exemptions for specific activities conducted in the Qatar Science and Technology Park.

The sale of licence interests are generally not taxable under PSC terms. No transfer taxes apply to farm in and farm out transactions.

RUSSIA

Corporate profits tax generally applies at rates from 15.5% to 20%, comprising 13.5% to 18% payable to regional governments, and 2% payable to the central government. Capital gains are taxed as ordinary income. There is an exemption for capital gains realised by foreign companies with no permanent establishment in Russia on the disposal of shares in Russian companies where immovable property does not exceed 50% of total assets, or shares in Russian companies traded on a securities market. Carry-forward tax losses may generally be utilised for up to for ten years, however this limit may not apply to the industrial special economic zones. Russia generally does not have tax consolidation provisions, unless a controlled group of companies' (CGC) approval has been granted.[101]

Russian taxation of upstream oil and gas includes:

- A substantial portion of Russian income from upstream oil and gas is derived from the Export Duty regime, with rates from 35% to 60% on crude oil, and natural gas at 30%. No export duty applies to LNG.

99. Income Tax Law 2009 (Law No. 21 of 2009 issuing the Income Tax Law).
100. EY, Global Oil and Gas Tax Guide 2017 (EY, 2017) p. 523.
101. EY, Worldwide Corporate Tax Guide 2017 (EY, 2017) p. 1295.

- MET applies royalties based on crude oil RUB 446 per tonne, natural gas RUB 509 per 1,000 cubic metres, condensate RUB 556 per tonne with adjustments.
- Russia applies Corporate Profits Tax at 20%.

Russian provides specific exemptions or reductions from export duty and MET in relation to production from new offshore hydrocarbon deposits (NOHDs) regions.[102]

The principal incentive for R&D is a 150% super deduction for companies conducting eligible R&D activities.[103]

The thin capitalisation provisions can apply to limit interest deductions on loans from foreign entities which directly or indirectly hold more than 20% of the Russian entity, loans from their Russian affiliates, or loan guaranteed by these entities. The provisions potentially apply where the debt-to-equity ratio exceeds 3:1, or a 12:1 ratio for banks and leasing companies. The excess interest is treated as the payment of dividends for withholding tax purposes.[104]

Indirect tax in Russia is principally based on the VAT on goods sold and services provided with the rate generally imposed at 18%. A concessional rate of 10% is available on items such as listed foodstuffs, children's goods and medical goods, and a 0% rate allowed for exports where no VAT is imposed and which allow related input tax credits.[105]

SAUDI ARABIA

Saudi Arabia requires upstream oil companies to operate under petroleum concession agreements (PCA). Tax is imposed on related profits under the Income Tax Law of 2004.[106] The tax rate is 85% on profits from oil production. There is no ring fencing relating to fields or different business activities. Natural Gas activities are subject to natural gas investment tax at rates from 30% to 85% depending on the internal rate of return (IRR) on cumulative cash flows of the project. This regime does not apply if the oil and gas company is subject to the tax on oil and other hydrocarbons. Ring fencing between fields applies for the natural gas tax regime. Exploration and drilling costs are capitalised and are deductible at 20% each year.[107] Corporate tax at 20% applies business activities other than upstream oil and gas.

Tax losses may be carried forward indefinitely, however the use of such losses is limited to 25% of taxable profits in each year. There is withholding tax on royalties or

102. EY, Global Oil and Gas Tax Guide 2017 (EY, 2017) p. 551.
103. Deloitte, *2014 Global Survey of R&D Tax Incentives*, 37.
104. EY, *Russian Tax Brief*, November 2011 (EY, 2011) www.ey.com/Publication/vwLUAssets/RTB-2011-11-EN/$FILE/RTB-2011-11-EN.pdf on 12 December 2013. There are related transfer pricing provisions which can apply where interest is more than 20% of the interest payable under comparable conditions. The taxpayer can alternatively elect to use a limit is based on the Central Bank of Russia rate increased by a factor of 1.1 for rouble loans, and a maximum rate of 15% for foreign currency loans.
105. EY, Worldwide Corporate Tax Guide 2017 (EY, 2017) p. 1296.
106. Income Tax Law, Ministerial Resolution No. 128 of 12 January 2004.
107. EY, Global Oil and Gas Tax Guide 2017 (EY, 2017) p. 564.

related party services at 15%, other services and interest at 5%, and on management fees at 20%.

Royalties apply at the specific rates provided under the respective PCAs, and are deductible for tax purposes.

Capital gains derived from the sale of assets are generally treated as taxable income.

UNITED KINGDOM

The UK applies corporation tax on profits from all upstream oil and gas activities, referred to as the 'ring fenced' trade generally at 30% as Ring Fence Corporation Tax (RFCT).[108] The corporate tax rate on other activities is 19% in 2017, reducing to 17% in 2020.[109] Tax losses may be carried forward indefinitely, and carried back for one year. The ring fencing measures provide that onshore losses may not offset offshore profits. There is a first-year capital allowance of 100% for capital expenditure relating to the ring fenced trade. This allowance does not apply to exploration costs, however the research and development (R&D) allowance at 100% may then apply. Tax consolidation, known as group relief, is provided for corporate tax and supplementary charge purposes between companies which have at least 75% common ownership.

The corporation tax rules can limit interest deductions using a transfer pricing approach which requires 'arm's length' commercial terms.[110] The UK also announced new limits on interest deductions from 2017. These measures include: (1) a fixed ratio rule, limiting corporate tax deductions for net interest expense to 30% of a group's UK EBITDA; and (2) a group ratio rule, based on the external net interest to EBITDA ratio for the worldwide group. These new measures are consistent with OECD's BEPS Action 4 in limiting base erosion due to excessive interest deductions.[111]

The Supplementary Charge (SC) regime applies to fields which received development consent from March 1993, in addition to corporation tax, reduced to a 10% rate applying from 2016.[112] The supplementary charge is not deductible for CIT purposes. There is no deduction allowed for the supplementary charge for financing costs. The effective tax rate of corporation tax and supplementary charge on oil and gas ring fenced trade is currently 40%.

The prior Petroleum Revenue Tax (PRT) regime applied to profits on fields which received development consent prior to March 1993, in addition to corporation tax. PRT was however reduced to a nil rate from 2016.[113]

The UK gave formal notice of its intention to leave the EU on 29 March 2017. This development may have a substantial effect on CIT, and indirect taxes including VAT

108. *See* section 279 Corporation Tax Act 2010 and Finance Acts including section 2 Finance Act 2010.
109. Finance Act 2016, section 46.
110. EY, Global Oil and Gas Guide 2017 (EY, 2017) p. 679.
111. Deloitte, Interest Deductibility, http://www.ukbudget.com/2016-measures/interest-deductibility.aspx on 8 May 2017.
112. Finance Act 2016 section 58, amending CTA 2010 section 330.
113. Finance Act 2016 section 140 amending Oil Taxation Act 1975 section 1.

and customs tariffs.[114] There are also potential impacts on direct taxation with EU directives including the Parent Subsidiary Directive,[115] the Interest and Royalties Directive,[116] and the Mergers Directive.[117] EU Directives and other measures may however potentially continue to apply depending on the terms of a future exit agreement.

In relation to mergers and acquisitions, income and capital gains on the sale of upstream assets are subject to corporation tax at 30%, and the additional 10% rate under the Supplementary Charge. Reinvestment relief may apply on disposal of material upstream assets if the receipts from the sale are reinvested in upstream assets. The substantial shareholding exemption may exempt profits on the sale of shares in a trading company, where the shareholding was more than 10% and the shares were held for at least twelve months.

The farm out of undeveloped areas for nil consideration other than undertaking to pay for exploration and production expenses is generally deemed to be tax free. There is an issue whether expenditure is deductible if the farm in party pays more than their share of costs.

UNITED STATES

US federal income tax applies under the Internal Revenue Code (IRC),[118] at the rate of 21% for corporations as provided in the Tax Cuts and Jobs Act (TCJA) from 2018. This was a substantial reduction from the previous 35% rate.[119] Tax deductions are allowed for state and municipal taxes. Tax losses incurred from 2018 can generally be carried forward indefinitely with the deduction limited to 80% of taxable income. Tax consolidation is allowed for affiliated groups where there is at least 80% common US parent ownership. The thin capitalisation provisions were amended by the TCJA from 2018. The new limit is on net interest expense that exceeds 30% of adjusted taxable income (ATI). For the first four years, ATI is computed without regard to depreciation, amortisation, or depletion. From 2022, ATI is decreased by these items, based on 30% of net interest expense exceeding EBIT (earnings before interest and taxes).[120]

114. UK leaving the EU: briefing paper on direct and indirect tax implications, Deloitte, June 2016.
115. Council Directive 90/435/EEC of 23 July 1990 on the common system of taxation applicable in the case of parent companies and subsidiaries of different Member States. and Directive 2003/123/EC (Parent Subsidiary Directive).
116. Council Directive 2003/49/EC of 3 June 2003 on a common system of taxation applicable to interest and royalty payments made between associated companies of different Member States, and related measures, (Interest and Royalties Directive).
117. Council Directive 90/434/EEC of 23 July 1990 on the common system of taxation applicable to mergers, divisions, transfers of assets and exchanges of shares concerning companies of different Member States, codified with amendments in Council Directive 2009/133/EC of 19 October 2009, (Mergers Directive).
118. Internal Revenue Code, 26 USC (1986).
119. The Tax Cuts and Jobs Act, Public law no. 115-97, 131 Stat. 2054, and 'The Tax Cuts and Jobs Act', EY, 5 January 2018.
120. US Tax Cuts and Jobs Act and its impact on the energy sector, EY Global Tax Alert, 29 December 2017, EY 2017.

Depreciation allowances for plant and machinery may be based on units of production determined by current year production over total remaining reserves, or under the modified accelerated cost recovery system which generally uses a declining balance system. Asset calculations are generally made on a unit of property basis, such as a lease or oil and gas well. The TCJA provides 100% bonus depreciation on qualified property both acquired and placed in service after 27 September 2017 and before 1 January 2023. Qualified property is defined as tangible personal property with a recovery period of twenty years or less, and generally excludes real estate.

Federal tax incentives for upstream oil and gas operations are under review, however as at 2017, the incentives include:

- The Intangible Drilling Cost (IDC) incentive applies to costs which are ‘incident to and necessary for the drilling of wells and the preparation of wells for the production of oil and gas’. The incentive allows an election for 100% current year deduction of the related costs. This deduction is reduced to 70% for ‘integrated oil companies’ which have over USD 5 million annual retail oil and gas sales, or refining operations in excess of 75,000 barrels/day, with the remaining 30% required to be amortised on the same basis as lease and well equipment over five years.
- Exploration costs such as geological and geophysical (G&G) expenses are amortised over two years for independent oil and gas producers, and over seven years for integrated oil companies.
- Depletion allowances relate to the reduction in oil and gas reserves. Percentage depletion is available to independent oil and gas producers and royalty owners, excluding integrated oil companies. This incentive allows tax deductions at a fixed rate of income, based on the extent of depletion of natural resources. The deduction is generally 15% of gross income for oil and natural gas. This is an alternative to cost depletion on a unit of production basis, also used by integrated oil companies, which allows deductions of costs based on annual production over the field’s projected life.
- The enhanced oil recovery credit is allowed generally at 15% of qualified costs, which include specific tangible property, intangible drilling and development costs, and qualified tertiary injectant expenses.
- There is a domestic manufacturing tax deduction at 6% on related oil and gas income. This deduction is generally limited to 50% of wages.[121]

The Alternative Minimum Tax (AMT) regime was repealed by the TCJA for corporations from 2018. The AMT previously applied at a 20% tax rate on profits, instead of corporate income tax, where the AMT was the higher tax amount.[122]

Federal royalties are generally imposed at 18.75% of the value of production for offshore waters beyond state maritime boundaries, and rates as negotiated for Federal lands or other mineral owners. The valuation of crude oil sales has resulted in several

121. Internal Revenue Code section 199.
122. Tax Reform Act of 1969, Public Law 91–172, Tax Equity and Fiscal Responsibility Act of 1982, Public Law 97–248.

cases claiming additional royalties. The *J Benjamin Johnson v. Shell Oil Co* case,[123] for example, concerned underpaid royalties on oil extracted from land owned by the US government and Indian nations. The Federal government claims were estimated at USD 5 billion, while the total settlements were approximately USD 800 million.[124]

The changes to the US CIT system under the TCJA also include the mandatory toll charge based on the deemed repatriation of currently deferred foreign profits at a rate of 15.5% for liquid assets such as cash, cash equivalents, and certain other short-term assets, and 8% for illiquid assets such as property, plant, and equipment.[125]

In relation to mergers and acquisitions, capital gains made by companies, including the sale of shares, are taxed at the corporate rates depending on taxable income. Capital losses may only be used to offset capital gains. The excess capital loss may be carried back for up to three years, and carried forward for up to five years. Asset disposals are generally taxable unless there is a like-kind exchange or involuntary conversion of the assets. Farm in and farm out transactions may potentially not be taxable providing the consideration is only cost sharing, however the cash portion of any consideration is generally taxable.

The US adopted a partial territorial tax system from 2018 including the exemption for dividends received by US corporations from foreign corporations in which the US corporation owns at least a 10% holding. In relation to prior years and non-qualifying income, the foreign tax credit system allowed a credit for foreign taxes relating to taxable income. The system used baskets of income, generally comprising: (1) the passive income basket, for income such as interest, dividends, royalties; and (2) the general income basket, relating to other income. This was intended to prevent the use of foreign taxes on active businesses, such as the income of foreign branches, being used to shield passive income such as dividends, interest, and royalties from US tax. Specific foreign tax credit rules applied to oil and gas extraction income. These rules could disallow credits paid on oil and gas extraction income in excess of the US tax due, although the credits could be carried over to future years. These measures effectively placed oil and gas extraction income in a separate foreign tax credit basket.[126]

A significant consideration relating to foreign tax credits was whether the tax paid by the foreign subsidiary qualified as creditable to reduce US tax. Significant issues arose, for example, if the foreign tax is based on gross income, multiple tax years, or is based on a share of production.

An example of this issue was considered in the case of *PPL Corporation v. Commissioner of Internal Revenue*.[127] The court denied a foreign tax credit with respect to a UK windfall profits tax that was imposed on a number of electricity utilities that

123. *United States of America ex rel J Benjamin Johnson v. Shell Oil Company* (Civil Action No. 9:96CV66) (E.D. Tex, Lufkin Division).

124. 'Taxes on Profits of Multinational Companies and Implications for Russia', International Tax and Investment Centre, Oxford Economic Forecasting, Squire Sanders & Dempsey LLP, p. 7.

125. Tax Cuts and Jobs Act of 2017, and US Tax Cuts and Jobs Act and its impact on the energy sector, EY Global Tax Alert, 29 December 2017, EY 2017.

126. Jane G Gravelle, 'Moving to a Territorial Income Tax: Options and Challenges' (United States Congressional Research Service, 2012) 7-5700 www.crs.gov R42624, 5./

127. *PPL Corpn v. Comr of Internal Revenue* (No. 12-43) (20 May 2013, unreported), US SC.

were privatised. The court held that the windfall profits tax did not qualify for the foreign tax credit because the tax was computed on the basis of a formula whose primary variable referenced profits earned over multiple years.[128]

The significant issue for upstream oil and gas companies was whether a foreign tax credit was available for foreign oil and gas taxes. Amounts paid to a government or its agency for the privilege of using or purchasing the government's property or as payment for a special privilege may not qualify as taxes.

There was generally no foreign tax credit allowed for foreign royalties, taxes based on sales, turnover, transaction, output, production, asset, property, or VAT. The Internal Revenue Service (IRS) issued the Internal Revenue Manual which generally provides that to be creditable, the foreign tax must be a compulsory payment to a foreign government, and an income tax, or a tax in lieu of an income tax. A tax on income is required to be a tax on net gains based on three criteria:

(1) Realisation test, imposed generally when income would be realised under the Internal Revenue Code.
(2) Gross receipts test, based on the fair market value of amount realised.
(3) Net income test, where gross income is reduced by allowable expenses.

The US Treasury issued related regulations in 2005 for the related provision section 901, allowing a credit for tax obligations paid by another party provided the tax is otherwise creditable.[129] These issues may be substantially removed if the US adopts an exemption for foreign sourced dividends.

State Taxes

State CIT may apply generally at rates of up to 12%. The state taxes are deductible for Federal income tax purposes. The basis of these taxes varies between states, and may be based on income or gross receipts, and is subject to state-specific calculation rules. The states may use different methods of apportionment for income, however apportionment has been harmonised to some degree in several states based on apportioning profits to the state on the basis of state property, state payroll and state sales, using the Uniform Division of Income for Tax Purposes Act model (UDITPA).[130] Significant issues can arise with these apportionments for state CIT purposes. For example, Louisiana may not fully recognise related costs, such as IDCs, in the taxable basis on the sale of a partnership interest, where this is considered to relate to offshore oil and gas licences.

128. PriceWaterhouseCoopers, *US Supreme Court confirms creditability of UK tax in PPL* (US Outbound Newsalert, 23 May 2013).
129. Treasury Regulations Under Code section 901, Taxes of Foreign Countries and of Possessions of the United States, Reg § 1.901-1 (2005).
130. Institute on Taxation and Economic Policy, Policy Brief, 'Corporate Income Tax Apportionment and the "Single Sales Factor"' August 2012.

Most states also impose severance tax on oil and gas based on production in the state. Severance tax rates vary from 2% to 15%, and these taxes are generally based on the value of production.

States also impose royalties on oil and gas production from state-owned lands. The royalty rates vary from 12.5% to 40% on the value of production for oil and gas fields which are on land or in state territorial waters. States may also receive a share of Federal royalties from oil and gas production on Federal lands.

State franchise taxes may apply on business activities generally at rates from 0.15% to 1.0%, calculated by multiplying the value of the assets, capital stock or net worth employed in the state by the franchise tax rate.

The basis of state royalties has been subject to substantial litigation:

- The *ANS Royalty Litigation*,[131] commenced in 1977 was resolved between 1992 and 1995. This series of royalty cases was estimated at USD 2 billion by the state of Alaska against Arco, Exxon, Mobil, and Sohio. Alaska asserted that the producers were undervaluing crude oil for the calculation of royalties. Alaska collected approximately USD 750 million from the related settlements.[132]
- The *City of Long Beach v. Exxon* case[133] concerned a claim by the state of California that Exxon had underpaid royalties of USD 750 million due to the under-valuation of oil from public lands. Exxon was held not liable in 1999, on the basis that the economy and price controls in effect at the time were responsible for the price used to determine the royalties. Claims of USD 1.25 billion were made against ARCO, Shell, Chevron, Mobil, Texaco, and Unocal, and were settled for USD 345 million in 1991.[134]
- The *ExxonMobil v. Alabama* case[135] concerned a claim against ExxonMobil Corpn in relation to royalties of USD 50 million, and USD 3.5 billion in punitive damages. The dispute concerned costs, such as transportation, processing, brokerage fees, and pipeline reservation fees, reduced value of production subject to the royalty. The Alabama Supreme Court rejected the punitive damages claim.[136]

The following are examples of state taxation for Texas and Alaska.

131. *Alaska v. Amerada Hess Corpn*, Civil No IJU-77-847.
132. Richard A Fineberg, 'Securing the Take: Petroleum Litigation in Alaska' in Svetlana Tsalik, Caspian Oil Windfalls: Who Will Benefit? (2003) 53.
133. *The City of Long Beach and the State of California v. Standard Oil Co of California and Exxon Corpn*, 46 F 3d 929 (US Ct of Apps (9th cir), 1995).
134. Davan Maharaj, 'Exxon Paid Fair Oil Royalties, Jury Decides', Los Angeles Times, 31 August 1999.
135. *ExxonMobil Corpn v. Alabama Dept of Conservation and Natural Resources*, 2007 WL 3224585 (Ala. 1 November 2007).
136. 'Alabama Supreme Court Sides with ExxonMobil in Royalties Dispute', Rigzone, 2 November 2007.

Texas State Taxes

There is no state CIT in Texas.

Texas state taxes include the Oil Production Tax[137] of 4.6% of the market value of oil, and the Gas Production Tax[138] of 7.5% of the market value of gas.[139] Related incentives for the upstream oil and gas industry include:

- The High-Cost Gas program provides an incentive for high-cost gas wells based on the ratio of each well's drilling and completion costs to twice median cost for high-cost Texas wells.
- The Two-Year Inactive Wells program provides a ten-year exemption incentive for oil and gas severance taxes from a well that the Texas Railroad Commission (TRC) certifies as not producing oil or gas for two years.
- The Enhanced Oil Recovery Project allows a partial ten-year tax incentive following certification by TRC as an eligible field. Producers pay half the crude oil tax rate, i.e., 2.3%.

Texas imposes severance tax on the value of oil and gas production at a 4.6% rate for oil and condensate production, and at a 7.5% rate for gas production.

Royalties are payable to the owner of the related resources. Where the resource owner is Texas, the royalty is generally 25% on gross production from state land and territorial waters up to nine miles from the coast.[140] The royalty is the amount which was agreed under contract where there is a private resource owner.

The Texas Franchise Tax,[141] also known as Margin Tax, is generally imposed from 2016 at 0.75% of taxable margin for most entities, and 0.375% of taxable margin for retail and wholesale businesses. Texas imposes property tax at 2.5% of the net present value of property including oil and gas wells.[142]

Alaska State Taxes

Alaska imposes state CIT at rates of up to 9.4%.[143] The Alaskan basis of apportionment of a company's profits for oil and gas companies to Alaska is generally based on state extraction and state property, which differs from the UDIPTA model used in many other states.[144]

137. Texas Tax Code Ann § 202.
138. Texas Tax Code Ann § 201.
139. Glenn Hegar, A Field Guide to the Taxes of Texas, April 2017.
140. Texas Natural Resources Code Ann. § 52.
141. Texas Tax Code Ann §171.
142. Texas Tax Code Ann §11.
143. Alaska Revenue and Taxation Code Alaska Stat § 43.20.072, and regulations 15 AAC 20.490 and 15 AAC 20.500.
144. Alaska Revenue and Taxation Code Alaska Stat § 43.20.

Alaska imposes severance tax known as the Oil and Gas Production Tax,[145] at a 35% rate on the net value of production from 2013. There are tax incentive credits for specific expenditure, including:

- Exploration Incentive Credit;
- Gas Exploration and Development Tax Credit;
- Cook Inlet Jack Up Rig Credit;
- Alternative Exploration Tax Credit;
- Well Lease Expenditure Credit;
- Carried Forward Annual Loss Credit and Capital Expenditure Credit.

There is to be a production tax for Alaska Liquefied Natural Gas (AKLNG) project for gas produced on and after 1 January 2022, with the rate to be 13% of the gross value of production.[146]

Alaska state royalties apply to the gross production from state land and territorial waters up to three miles from the coast, with the rate most commonly at 12.5%. The royalty rate is the amount agreed under contract where there is a private resource owner.[147]

The Oil and Gas Property Tax applies at 2% on the value of property including oil and gas wells, generally excluding property rights to explore or produce oil and gas, oil or gas leases, oil or gas in place, in use or extracted, and intangible drilling, development or exploration expenditure.[148]

145. Alaska Revenue and Taxation Code Alaska Stat § 43.55.
146. Alaska Department of Revenue – Tax Division, Oil & Gas Production Tax – Historical Overview.
147. Alaska Public Land Code Alaska Stat § 38.05.135.
148. Alaska Revenue and Taxation Code Alaska Stat § 43.56.

CHAPTER 5

Upstream Oil and Gas Taxation: Exploration and Production

INTRODUCTION

The principal tax regimes for upstream oil and gas operations are: (1) tax imposed under licence/concession regimes, which use corporate income tax on profits, (2) Production Sharing Contract (PSC) regimes where the oil and gas company derives a share of profit oil as provided under specific contractual terms, and (3) Service Contract regimes, where the oil and gas company is essentially a contractor. Tax, PSC and Service Contract regimes are generally combined with other taxes, such as royalties, production bonuses, and indirect taxes including VAT. Examples of how these systems are combined are included in the country tax examples in Chapter 4.

Many upstream tax regimes have changed over time, and older regimes may continue to apply to specific projects, for example based on the date the specific oil and gas licence was granted. Particular care is required with PSC regimes, where precise fiscal terms are generally set out in the PSC for a particular oil field or block, and those terms may have been amended by country tax laws, or by specific contractual amendments to the PSC.

Reference has been made to the EY Global Oil and Gas Tax Guide 2017,[1] James W Bush and Daniel Johnston, International Oil Company Financial Management in Nontechnical Language,[2] Carole Nakhle, Petroleum Taxation: Sharing the Oil Wealth,[3] and the World Fiscal Systems for Oil and Gas courses by Pedro van Meurs.[4] These sources are recommended for further reference.

1. EY, Global Oil and Gas Tax Guide 2017 (EY, 2017).
2. James W Bush & Daniel Johnston, *International Oil Company Financial Management in Nontechnical Language* (PennWell Books, 1998).
3. Carole Nakhle, *Petroleum Taxation: Sharing the Oil Wealth* (Routledge, 2008).
4. World Fiscal Systems for Oil and Gas 2011 courses by Pedro van Meurs, Van Meurs Corporation, http://www.vanmeurs.org/Default.aspx on 8 September 2017.

TAX AND LICENCE/CONCESSION REGIMES

Concession regimes apply where the government transfers title to oil and gas to the oil company, and imposes tax and royalties. Countries imposing tax under licence/concession regimes include the United Kingdom (UK), United States (US), Canada, Australia, Norway, and Denmark. The oil and gas companies are allowed to own the oil and gas produced, and then pay corporate tax on their related profits. There may be additional tax or higher tax rates relating to oil and gas production. For example, Norway applies the Hydrocarbon Tax at a 50% rate on related income in addition to corporate income tax.

The tax regimes of individual countries may apply 'ring fencing' to exploration and production income. This may apply where: (1) profits from one oil or gas field cannot be offset by losses on another field, or (2) where profits from upstream oil and gas activity cannot be offset by losses on other business activities.

Tax regimes may be combined with a royalty or severance tax regime, which imposes charges based on the value of the oil or gas produced. Royalties tend to generate income for the related country sooner than income from the corporate tax system. The oil and gas company can generally utilise carried forward costs from exploration and development to defer corporate taxes for several years, whereas royalties are generally payable as soon as production has commenced.

The corporate tax regime may have specific terms for exploration and drilling costs, such as whether the costs are deductible, or must be capitalised. The tax regime may allow specific incentives, such as immediate deductions for development costs. Capital expenditure rules may allow incentives such as allowing costs to be immediately deductible, or by providing 'depreciation uplift' where a higher than actual value is used to calculate depreciation to enable higher depreciation allowances. Tax regimes may also have specific provisions for abandonment expenses, when oil and gas development ends, and equipment such as onshore and offshore installations may need to be dismantled and removed.

Repatriation of profits and other payments made to residents of other countries may be subject to withholding taxes, and a country may impose withholding tax on the payment of dividends or the remittance of branch profits. This withholding tax may be reduced by tax treaties, or other measures such as the European Union Parent Subsidiary Directive.[5] Withholding taxes may also be substantially higher for payments to countries with low effective tax rates such as tax havens.

Mergers and acquisitions are often large-scale transactions affected by country tax regimes. The related issues include whether capital gains on the sale of oil and gas assets or companies holding such assets are taxed, and whether overseas investors are protected by tax treaties. The country's tax rules may also apply to tax indirect transfers of oil and gas interests, for example the sale of a foreign holding company which holds local oil and gas assets may be taxed under these provisions. There may be different tax

5. European Union, Directive on the Common System of Taxation Applicable in the Case of Parent Companies and Subsidiaries of Different Member States (90/435/EEC) (1990) 'Parent Subsidiary Directive.'

treatments of state equity, where the government may own part of the oil and gas development, or have the option to acquire such interests.

Many countries also allow tax consolidation, where profits of one company may be offset by losses in a related company if there is sufficient common ownership. This is an issue for mergers and acquisitions, where interest costs in an acquiring company may then potentially offset profits in the acquired company where the acquiring company and the target company are in the same consolidated group.

Tax regimes may use resource rent systems, which impose tax where income exceeds expenditure adjusted at a compound interest rate based on the internal rate of return (IRR). Tax under these regimes is generally determined on a project basis, with the intention of providing effective tax revenue while compensating investors for the time value of money of their development expenses.

PSCs: COST OIL AND PROFIT OIL

In PSC regimes, also known as Production Sharing Agreements (PSAs), the government retains title to the oil and gas, but provides the right to a share of production, known as profit oil, to the oil and gas company. Countries with PSC regimes applying to all or some of their oil and gas fields include Angola, Brazil, China, Kazakhstan, Libya, and Malaysia. The oil and gas company is generally allowed to recover their costs in additional share of production. A variation of PSC regimes is the revenue sharing contract, where the contractor may receive a defined share of revenue rather than a share of the production. The oil and gas company is therefore essentially contracted to perform exploration, drilling, and production activities in return for a share of oil and gas.

The calculation of the company's return commences with determining the portion of total production retained by the contractor to recover their costs as cost oil subject to limits on recovery under the specific PSC.

The remaining oil, including any surplus of cost oil over the amount needed for cost recovery, is profit oil to be divided between the government and the contractor using the formula in that PSC. The government may impose tax on the profit oil, or may deem the company's tax to be paid by government from the government's profit oil share.

Variations in PSC terms include how the split of profit oil between the government and the oil and gas company is determined. This may be based a fixed percentage, or other methods such as a sliding scale. The sliding scale may be based on different factors, including 'R Factors' based on different formulas such as daily production, cumulative production, or the internal rate of return. One example of an R factor is cumulative production over cumulative costs, with a higher government profit oil share in a given year where there is a higher R Factor in that year. R Factors may also be used to determine tax rates or royalty rates.

The government may have the option to acquire an interest in the oil and gas field, and there may be different terms for government payment to acquire the interest.

The following example of oil and gas company profit under a PSC regime is based on calculation by Bush and Johnston.[6] The specific methods of calculation will differ under the terms of different PSCs.

EXAMPLE

In this example, tax is applied to the company's profit oil. Oil production in the year is USD 100 million, the royalty rate is 10%, and the corporate tax rate is 40%. The annual development costs are USD 30 million, the profit oil split is 60% to the government /40% to the oil company, and the recovery of cost oil capped annually at 50% of gross oil income, with the excess costs carried forward to later years.

The calculations are based on USD 100 million production, less the royalty of USD 10 million, leaving USD 90 million after the royalty. The cost recovery of USD 30 million is deducted to meet expenses, and these expenses are below the 50% of income annual cap of USD 50 million. This leaves USD 60 million of profit oil after deduction. The government therefore receives 60% of profit oil for USD 36 million, and the company receives 40% of profit oil for USD 24 million. The company's profit oil share of USD 24 million is then taxed at 40% for a total of USD 9.6 million tax. The net cash flow to the company is USD 14.4 million. The total government share is based on the USD 10 million royalty, plus the USD 9.6 million of tax, plus the USD 36 million of profit oil, with the total income to the government therefore at USD 55.6 million.

The specific fiscal terms under each PSC should be considered, as there are many variations in key contract terms. These issues include how profit oil is determined, where there may be a deemed oil or gas price, any requirement for sale of oil and gas to the government at specific prices, or transfer pricing rules on related party sales of oil and gas. One example of PSC terms is the 2012 Egypt Concession Agreement for Gas and Crude Oil Exploration and Exploitation.[7]

The PSC will state the specific allowable costs for cost oil, and financing costs such as interest are generally not recoverable. The PSC may also require that competitive bid contracts are used for recoverable costs. There may be incentives in the PSC in determining cost oil, for example increased allowances for depreciation of plant and equipment such as depreciation uplift.

The amount of costs which are recoverable as cost oil in each year is generally capped, for example as a fixed percentage of annual oil and gas production, with unused costs over the cap carried forward to future years. The cost oil cap generally results in higher profit oil to be shared with the government. There are several related practical issues, including the government's record on approving costs to be allowed as cost oil.

6. James W Bush & Daniel Johnston, *International Oil Company Financial Management in Nontechnical Language* (PennWell Books, 1998) 152.
7. Egypt Concession Agreement for Gas and Crude Oil Exploration and Exploitation. *See* Article VII, Recovery of Costs and Expenses and Production Sharing, Egyptian Natural Gas Holding Company (EGAS): www.egas.com.eg/BidRound2012/MODEL_AGREEMENT_2012_new.pdf on 8 November 2017.

The PSC may also provide exemptions from further direct taxes and indirect taxes such as VAT, import and customs duties. In these cases, there may be a related issue in obtaining government VAT refunds, which can apply where the oil and gas company has paid VAT on purchases while the export of oil and gas is VAT exempt. The PSC may extend the VAT exemption to suppliers of goods and services to the oil and gas company.

The PSC may allow an exemption from dividend withholding tax or branch profit repatriation tax, interest, royalty, or service fee withholding tax, or exemptions from tax on the direct or indirect sale of the oil and gas interest.

Significant developments in PSC terms include the new Indonesia model contract announced in January 2017. These PSCs essentially provide for contractors to be allocated a higher percentage share of gross production, in exchange for the removal of any cost recovery mechanism. These PSCs potentially replace the complex administration of PSC cost recovery terms, and gross production is allocated between the state and the contractor based solely on production splits. The contractor's net income is then determined after deducting the applicable income tax. The related issues with the new PSCs include the state's title to the assets used in petroleum operations, given that the cost of these assets would not be recovered.[8]

Service Agreement or Service Contract regimes apply where the oil and gas company essentially receives a fee for exploration, drilling, and production services. In regular service contracts, the fee is paid for services performed irrespective of the outcome of the development. In risk sharing contracts, the contractor risks economic losses if the venture is unsuccessful. The regime allows a fee to the oil and gas company which may potentially increase with increased production. There is no direct entitlement to the oil and gas produced. Service agreements are currently used in countries including Saudi Arabia, Mexico, and Iraq. is The 2009 Iraqi Model Producing Oil Field Technical Service Contract[9] is a recent example of a service contract based on cost plus margin terms.

Service agreements can be used where oil and gas has been discovered and reserves confirmed, and where the oil and gas company's financial risks are therefore very low. Service contracts are potentially less appropriate to encouraging oil and gas exploration and development as there is a much lower profit incentive under these arrangements. The Mexican government is therefore adopting PSCs which allow more generous terms than the service contract regime.[10]

---

8. Indonesia abandons cost recovery mechanism for new production sharing contracts, Ashurst, Oil and Gas Update, 20 January 2017, and Minister Regulation No. 8 of 2017.
9. 2009 Iraqi Model Producing Oil Field Technical Service Contract. *See* Article 19, Supplementary fees and service fees, available at Platform online: platformlondon.org/documents/PFTSC-23-Apr-09.pdf on 8 November 2017.
10. Simon Gardner, Reuters, 'Exclusive: Mexico energy reform won't offer private oil concessions -ruling party leader' 11 August 2013, www.reuters.com/article/2013/08/11/us-mexico-reforms-idUSBRE97A0CS20130811 on 8 September 2017.

ROYALTIES

Royalties and severance payments are generally based on the amount or value of oil and gas produced. There are several variations in royalty systems, may be based on different values such as:[11]

- Royalties may use a fixed percentage, for example the US Federal royalties.
- Royalties are an amount bid to get the oil and gas licence, as applied in several states in the US, for example in Louisiana.
- Royalties vary with geological features, for example the Nigeria offshore royalties which decrease with the geological features of greater water depth.
- Sliding scale royalties which increase with higher production, for example in China and Abu Dhabi.
- Sliding scale royalties which may increase based on several factors, for example in Alberta in Canada, which are based on production and price.
- Sliding scale royalties depending on IRR, for example as currently proposed in Greenland.

In the US, royalties or severance taxes are paid to the mineral owner. This may be federal royalties applying to offshore oil fields in federal waters beyond state territorial sea jurisdiction, state royalties applying to onshore and state territorial sea fields, or private royalties paid to the private resource owner. These royalty amounts may be based on fair market prices, the wellhead price, the field terminal price, the export terminal price, or based on deemed prices.

Several states in the US impose severance taxes at 2% to 10% of the volume of oil and gas produced, or the taxes may be based on a percentage of gross receipts.

Excise taxes are also based on value of production, and the term may be used to distinguish the excise from royalties with different methods of calculation and revenue sharing arrangements. For example, in the Australia North West Shelf, Federal crude oil excise applies to production from the project area. Federal royalties also apply which are shared with the Western Australia state government.

Royalties are combined with other tax systems, such as Concession and PSC regimes, because they give rise to income to the state as soon as production commences. Government revenue from licence/concession or PSC regimes is delayed as the oil and company uses tax losses or recoverable costs carried forward from prior years.

SIGNATURE AND PRODUCTION BONUSES

Several countries impose signature and production bonuses to be paid at certain stages of exploration and production. Bonuses may be agreed as part of the bidding process for a new exploration and development licence, or may be imposed under standard terms of PSC contracts.

11. Pedro van Meurs, *World Fiscal Systems for Oil and Gas* (2011).

These bonus payments may include:[12]

- Signature bonuses, which are payable on signing the oil and gas agreement, for example on signing of the PSC or block exploration and development licence.
- Capacity building bonuses, which are payable to assist in the development of facilities such as project infrastructure, and generally payable at an early stage in the contract.
- Bonuses which are payable on discovery, commercial discovery, licence application, specific levels of production, or levels of cumulative production.

Signature bonuses generally provide compensation to the government for costs in conducting the bidding process, and also provide income for government oil and gas administration where there are dry wells. The much larger production bonuses include significantly higher amounts are paid on meeting agreed oil and gas production milestones.

Bonuses are generally not recoverable costs under PSC regimes, so that the oil and gas company does not retain cost oil to meet these payments. Bonuses may qualify for tax relief under tax regimes, for example lease bonuses are amortised for US federal tax purposes.

Bonuses are significant as amounts which generally apply at agreed levels of production, and therefore may increase where an oil and gas development becomes more successful. They are distinguished from royalties as they are not payments for oil and gas resources, and may be considered as sharing the benefits of a project which reaches specific production milestones.

RENTALS

Rentals are amounts which may be payable under licence/concession or PSC regimes, and are based on the land or sea area used. The rental amount may be a fixed fee, or may be based on the area of an exploration block or on the area of a specific oil and gas field. The basis of the rental may also increase, for example the rental regime may apply at USD 10 per square kilometre during the first exploration period, USD 20 per square kilometre during the next exploration period, and then increasing to USD 500 per square kilometre during the development and production phase.

Rentals are significant in fiscal regimes as a source of income from the use of land, rather than a tax on profits, or royalty for the use of oil and gas resources. The rental regime may provide an income stream of a type which would arise from other uses of land or sea region. Rentals may form part of municipal and state revenue or paid to local communities in respect of the land use required for the oil and gas facilities.

Rentals may significantly increase in the later stages of development to encourage relinquishment by the oil and gas company of the parts of an exploration block which will not be used. The government may then offer the remaining relinquished area to other oil and gas companies to conduct exploration activities. Area rentals can be large

12. Pedro van Meurs, *World Fiscal Systems for Oil and Gas.*

amounts as the total area in an exploration block, particularly for offshore oil and gas exploration, is typically very large.

STATE EQUITY AND CARRIED INTERESTS

The government may have an equity interest in the oil and gas field, or may have an option to acquire an equity interest. The equity may be in the form of a full working interest, where the equity is paid up on commercial terms. State equity may also be made on concessional terms, where the government acquires its equity share at a below-market price. The government may have an option to acquire the interest if the project is successful, for example after a commercial discovery has been made.

The government may have a carried interest, where the government's share of explorations and development expenses is initially paid by the oil and gas company. The government may pay for its equity share and share of expenses from the proceeds of oil or gas production if the project proceeds to the production stage, and may pay interest on the outstanding balance of carried costs. The oil and gas company then carries the risk of not being reimbursed for the expenses if the project does not result in significant production.

State equity may be acquired in return for a reduced tax liability on the oil and gas company, or for a non-cash contribution, such as government provision of project infrastructure, such as harbour facilities, roads, and pipelines.

State equity is a significant issue for the financial modelling of an oil and gas project. The structure of state equity is not a tax, sharing of profit oil, or a royalty, however, the state may effectively obtain an additional large portion of profits, for example exercising an option to acquire a 25% share of a project.

This is an issue for new investments and also for mergers and acquisitions, where the state equity, or the option for the government to acquire state equity, may significantly affect the oil and gas company's potential investment return.

EXPORT DUTY

Export duties on oil and gas are applied on the amounts of production exported from the production country. They are generally combined with other taxes. The export duty essentially applies for the rights to the country's oil and gas, rather than as a tax on production such as VAT. Export duties are substantially different from other indirect taxes such as VAT, which provide exemptions for exports. The amounts may be imposed as export duties so that domestic oil and gas prices are not directly affected, and so target large-scale oil and gas developments which aim to generate profits from international oil and gas sales.

The issue of whether oil and gas developments impact local prices applies in several countries. The most recent example is the US, where issuing of LNG export permits and terminal approvals is expected to increase US domestic prices. The use of an export duty as used in Russia may potentially address this issue, by ensuring that part of taxation does not apply to domestic oil and gas sales.

INDIRECT TAXES AND VAT

Value Added Tax (VAT) is an indirect tax imposed in many countries on the value of a company's sales, where a company registered for VAT applies VAT on its own sales, and is allowed a credit for VAT paid on their related purchases. VAT therefore applies to the value added by each stage from production to final sale. The sale to an unregistered party, such as a consumer, then carries the full VAT charge.

Exporting oil and gas is generally 'zero rated' for VAT purposes, so that VAT is not chargeable on the export sales, however the company is entitled to a refund of the VAT paid on its related purchases. The oil and gas company therefore applies for refunds on VAT paid on its purchases, and does not charge VAT on its zero-rated export sales. The use of zero rating may then result in a credit refund issue as to whether refunds are allowed, are provided promptly, or there are substantial delays. VAT refunds may also be restricted to the related joint venture, rather than being made available to the investing companies. This issue may be addressed where tax regimes and PSCs provide specific exemptions from VAT to avoid the refund issue. This may be extended to local suppliers to upstream oil and gas companies.

Alternative methods of indirect taxation include the gross turnover taxes applied in many states in the US. These taxes are essentially different to VAT because they are single stage taxes which apply to the final sale to the consumer.

Countries may also impose significant customs tariffs or duties on the importation of equipment used for exploration and production. Several countries allow specific exemption under their PSCs or tax regimes from indirect taxes where the equipment used in oil and gas activities is subsequently exported after use. These exemptions include:

- The Brazilian Repetro regime allows an exemption from federal indirect taxes on the importation on goods which are to be re-exported (II, IPI, PIS, COFINS taxes).
- Indonesia allows an import duty, VAT, and income tax exemption for related importation.

Customs tariffs are a significant issue for the importation of oil and gas. There may be exemptions or reductions under international trade agreements, such as under the North American Free Trade Agreement (NAFTA) between the US, Canada, and Mexico.[13]

Related issues include whether crude oil and natural gas qualify for tariff reductions based on their source, for example because oil and gas is sourced in a NAFTA country under the NAFTA rules of origin. This issue has arisen, for example, when oil and gas companies blend crude oil with condensates or diluents from non-NAFTA states to transport the oil by pipeline, or where these companies blend

13. North American Free Trade Agreement, 17 December 1992, 32 ILM 289, Article 302, entered into force 1 January 1994 (NAFTA).

natural gas with gas originating in non-NAFTA states.[14] The US duty rate on crude oil imports from Canada, for example, may then increase from the NAFTA rate of 'free' to 5.25 cents or 10.5 cents per barrel.

OTHER INTERNATIONAL TREATIES: THE LAW OF THE SEA AND JOINT DEVELOPMENT ZONES

Oil and gas exploration and development may also be affected by other international treaties where these activities are undertaken in ocean areas with disputes over national sovereignty. There are several international joint development agreements which have established joint development zones (JDZs) relating to areas of ocean with overlapping sovereignty claims. These JDZ agreements generally provide for the sharing of the resources of the disputed areas, and may also provide for the regulatory regimes for the joint development of offshore oil and gas.

The United Nations Law of the Sea Convention (LOSC)[15] which came into force on 16 November 1994 is the basis of the international law of the sea, and over 160 countries have now ratified the convention.[16] The use of JDZ agreements is consistent with LOSC, for example Article 83(3) requires states with opposite or adjacent coasts to make every effort to enter into provisional arrangements of a practical nature pending agreement on the final delimitation of the continental shelf between them in a manner consistent with international law.

An early example of resource sharing which has similarities to a JDZ agreement was the Svalbard Treaty in 1920.[17] This was a treaty agreed between Norway, USA, Denmark, France, Italy, Japan, the Netherlands, Great Britain and Ireland and the British Overseas Dominions, and Sweden. It gave sovereignty over the Svalbard islands to Norway, but also allowed use of resources by other countries. There are now a number of successful JDZ agreements with significant oil and gas production, such as the Malaysia/Thailand Agreement for Joint Development in 1979.[18] There are also

14. Glenn A Cranker & Harold K Andersen, Stikeman Elliott LLP, 'Exporting Canadian Oil and Gas: The Challenge of NAFTA Compliance', www.acc.com/legalresources/quickcounsel/exognafta.cfm on 31 July 2017.
15. Law of the Sea Convention (opened for signature 10 December 1982, 1833 UNTS 396) came into force on 16 November 1994 (LOSC).
16. United Nations, Division for Ocean Affairs and the law of the Sea, Chronological lists of ratifications of, accessions and successions to the Convention and the related Agreements, http://www.un.org/depts/los/reference_files/chronological_lists_of_ratifications.htm on 8 September 2017.
17. Treaty concerning the Archipelago of Spitsbergen, including Bear Island, 9 February 1920, 2 LNTS 8, (entered into force 14 August 1925) (Svalbard Treaty).
18. Memorandum of Understanding between the Kingdom of Thailand and Malaysia on the Establishment of a Joint Authority for the Exploitation of the Resources of the Seabed in a Defined Area of the Continental Shelf of the two countries in the Gulf of Thailand, 24 October 1979, (entered into force 15 July 1982), reprinted in Jonathan I Charney & Lewis M Alexander (eds), International Maritime Boundaries (1993) vol. 1, 1099.

cancelled or suspended agreements, such as the Joint Declaration between the UK and Argentina relating to the Falkland Islands region.[19]

The fiscal terms of JDZs vary in many cases. The best model may be the Malaysia/Thailand Joint Development Area,[20] where the income of upstream oil and gas companies derived from activities/services in the JDZ is subject to taxes by both countries under their respective legislation, subject to reduction by 50% of the tax chargeable by each country. Related provisions in this JDZ agreement include profit split and cost oil rules under PSCs, payment of royalties, and excise duties on exports.

THE INTERNATIONAL SEABED AUTHORITY

LOSC established or modified several maritime zones, including the territorial sea, continental shelf, exclusive economic zone (EEZ), and the Area beyond national claims. LOSC contains provisions which impose royalties from activities in respect of a state's continental shelf beyond 200 nautical miles from the coast,[21] and also requires payments in relation to activities in the deep seabed ('the Area').

LOSC requires the coastal state to make payments or contributions in kind in respect of the exploitation of the non-living resources continental shelf beyond 200 miles from the state's coast.[22] The payment regime applies on all production at a site after the first five years of production at that site. The payments are made to the International Seabed Authority (ISBA), which is required to distribute these amounts to parties to LOSC on the basis of 'equitable sharing criteria, taking into account the interests and needs of developing states, particularly the least developed and the land-locked among them'. The payment rate is currently 1% of the value or volume of production at the site commencing in the sixth year of production, increasing by 1% for each subsequent year until the twelfth year, and 7% thereafter.

The LOSC regime in Part XI relating to the 'Area' concerns 'the sea-bed and ocean floor and subsoil thereof, beyond the limits of national jurisdiction'. The significance of the Part XI provisions is large because the Area is estimated to comprise 50% of the earth's surface.[23] Part XI provides that the mineral resources beyond state jurisdiction are to be used to benefit all states, and establish a regime for oversight of the

19. Joint Declaration on Cooperation over Offshore Activities in the South West Atlantic between the United Kingdom and Argentina (27 September 1995, 35 ILM 301).
20. Malaysia Thailand Joint Authority, 'Fiscal Regime for the JDA', www.mtja.org/fiscalregime.php at 8 November 2017).
21. LOSC Article 76 provides the limit of the continental shelf. This limit is firstly based on the foot of slope feature on the seabed floor, plus the greater of: (i) the line where the sediment thickness on the seabed floor is 1% of the distance to the foot of slope; or (ii) 60 nautical miles from the foot of slope. The area is then limited to the greater of: (i) the 2,500 metre isobath (water depth line) plus 100 nautical miles; or (ii) the coast baseline plus 350 nautical miles. The continental shelf is limited to 350 nautical miles in respect of submarine ridges, however this limit does not apply to 'submarine elevations that are natural components of the continental margin, such as its plateaux, rises, caps, banks and spurs'.
22. LOSC Article 82(2).
23. Donald R Rothwell & Tim Stephens, *The International Law of the Sea* (2010) p. 123.

exploitation of resources. LOSC Annex III provides for payments by states or companies carrying out commercial production in the Area.[24]

The LOSC Area regime currently has very limited relevance for offshore oil and gas, due to the extreme depth of the related seabed areas beyond the continental shelf. The Area royalty provisions are also currently based on seabed mining activities rather than the development of oil and gas. This position may potentially change with time due to technological and safety improvements, however, in the longer time frame.

It should be noted that certain LOSC provisions may also potentially apply to states which have not ratified LOSC, such as the US, where specific provisions are considered to have been absorbed into customary international law.

FINANCIAL REPORTING: RESERVES RECOGNITION

The financial reporting issues for upstream oil and gas include the requirements for the recognition of oil and gas reserves. Net proved reserves of an upstream oil and gas company are generally the estimated quantities that geoscience and engineering data demonstrate with reasonable certainty to be economically producible in the future from known reservoirs under existing economic conditions, operating methods and government regulations, and exclude royalties and interests in oil and gas which are owned by others.

There is a significant advantage for oil and gas companies under licence/concession regimes, most production and revenue sharing contracts and some risk service contracts, where these arrangements allow for a significant portion of oil and gas discovered in the project to be reported as oil and gas reserves. The related factors which can support reserve reporting are:[25]

(1) Elements which may support reserve reporting include:
   - The right to extract the oil or gas.
   - The right to take produced oil or gas volumes in kind or share in the proceeds from their sale.
   - There is exposure to market risk and technical risk.
   - There is opportunity for reward through participation in producing activities.

(2) Elements which may not support reserves reporting include:
   - Participation which is limited only to the right to purchase volumes.
   - The use of supply or brokerage arrangements.
   - Agreements for services or funding that do not contain aspects of risk and reward or convey an interest in the oil and gas.

24. LOSC Part XI Annex III previously provided for a specific production-based charge, or production-based charge combined with a share of net proceeds. This was amended by the 1994 Agreement Relating to the Implementation of Part XI of the United Nations Convention on the Law of the Sea of 10 December 1982, 28 July 1994, Annex section 8.
25. Elliott Young, Reserves Entitlement and Reporting, presentation to Society of Petroleum Evaluation Engineers, Houston, 2 October 2013.

Reserve disclosures are affected by different accounting rules. In general, for licence and concession agreements, US Generally Accepted Accounting Principles (US GAAP) Financial Accounting Standard FAS 69 requires the disclosure of proved reserves and proved developed reserves, and the US Securities and Exchange Commission (SEC) requires foreign private issuers in the oil and gas industry which use International Financial Reporting Standards (IFRS) to also provide FAS 69 disclosures.

There is currently no standard disclosure of reserves under IFRS, or related formal definitions of proved, probable or possible reserves. The International Accounting Standard Board (IASB) is however considering the accounting for mineral resources and reserves as part of its Extractive Activities project.[26] Most companies therefore follow the disclosure rules their home country, or use the US GAAP rules for reserve definitions and disclosures. The UK Oil Industry Accounting Committee's Statement of Recommended Practice (OIAC SORP, for example, permits disclosure of either proved and probable or proved developed and undeveloped reserves.

In relation to PSCs, US GAAP FAS 69 potentially allows disclosure of related oil and gas in consolidated reserves depending on the terms of the contract. If the enterprise participates in the operation of the properties in which the oil or gas is located, or otherwise serves as the producer of the reserves, they may disclose these amounts separately.[27] The reserves are based on cost recovery plus profit hydrocarbons that are recoverable under the contract. In relation to the similar revenue sharing contracts, reserves are generally based on the economic interest held or the financial benefit received. On this basis, for both PSCs and revenue sharing contracts, the contractor's share of oil and/or gas production and reserves therefore varies over time, and is dependent on prices, costs, and specific contract terms.

There is a related issue of the accounting policy adopted. Under US GAAP accounting many integrated oil and gas companies use the successful efforts method (SE), where costs incurred in finding, acquiring and developing reserves are capitalised on a field-by-field or well-by-well basis when there has been a discovery of commercially viable or proven mineral reserves. When a commercial discovery has not been achieved, these costs are charged to expense. The alternative full cost method (FC) provides that all costs incurred in searching for, acquiring and developing the reserves in a large geographic cost centre are capitalised. Under IFRS, however, costs should generally be capitalised only when it is probable that the recognised amount will be recoverable in full.[28]

In summary, reserves recognition is likely to be higher under licence/concession regimes, with significant recognition available under PSC and revenue sharing contracts subject to the contract terms.

26. PricewaterhouseCoopers, Financial reporting in the oil and gas industry, International Financial Reporting Standards, 2nd Edition, 16, www.pwc.com/energy on 11 September 2017.
27. EY, *US GAAP v. IFRS*, The basics: Oil and gas, Ernst & Young, May 2009, 14.
28. PricewaterhouseCoopers, Crunch Time, Embedding International Financial Reporting Standards in the Oil and Gas and Utilities Industries, 7.

FINANCIAL REPORTING: DEFERRED TAX

A second significant issue for upstream oil and gas financial concerns deferred tax accounting, where adjustments to financial statements are generally required by International Accounting Standard IAS 12 Income Taxes and similar accounting rules.

This issue relates to temporary or timing differences between book income compared to taxable income, due to items of revenue or expense that are recognised in one period for taxes, but in a different period for the financial accounts. IAS 12 requires that deferred tax should be calculated in respect of all taxes that fall within the scope of income taxes, including all domestic and foreign taxes which are based on taxable profits. Income taxes also include taxes, such as withholding taxes, which are payable by a subsidiary, associate, or joint venture on distributions which are made to the reporting entity.

Oil and gas taxes which are calculated by applying a tax rate to volume, or a measure of revenue not adjusted for expenditure, are however generally outside the scope of IAS 12. These revenue-based and volume-based taxes, including royalties and excise taxes, are to be recognised when the revenue is recognised.[29] The IAS 12 rules relate to deferred tax as follows:

- Deferred tax assets are items which are expected to reduce tax in the future, such as carry-forward tax losses.[30]
- Deferred tax liabilities are items which are expected to result in more tax to be payable in the future, such as accelerated tax depreciation allowances and tax amortisation of goodwill.[31]

The deferred tax balances are to be calculated separately for each tax, based on the temporary differences between the IFRS carrying amount and the corresponding tax base.[32] The deferred tax assets and liabilities should be measured at the tax rates that are expected to apply to the period when the asset is realised or the liability is

29. IAS 8, para. 8.
30. IAS 12, para. 24 provides that deferred tax assets should be recognised for all deductible temporary differences to the extent that it is probable that taxable profit will be available against which the deductible temporary difference can be utilised, unless the deferred tax asset arises from the initial recognition of an asset or liability in a transaction that: (a) is not a business combination; and (b) at the time of the transaction, affects neither accounting profit nor taxable profit or tax loss.
31. IAS 12, para. 15 provides that deferred tax liabilities should be recognised for all taxable temporary differences, except for: (a) liabilities arising from initial recognition of goodwill for which amortisation is not deductible for tax purposes; (b) liabilities arising from the initial recognition of an asset/liability other than in a business combination which, at the time of the transaction, does not affect either the accounting or the taxable profit; and (c) liabilities arising from undistributed profits from investments where the entity is able to control the timing of the reversal of the difference and it is probable that the reversal will not occur in the foreseeable future.
32. Financial reporting in the oil and gas industry, (PricewaterhouseCoopers, 2011), pp. 85–90, www.pwc.com/gx/en/energy-utilities-mining/pdf/ifrsog.pdf.

settled, based on tax laws enacted or substantively enacted by the end of the reporting period. These amounts should therefore reflect the expectations, at balance sheet date, as to the manner in which the carrying amount of its assets and liabilities will be recovered or settled. The deferred tax assets and liabilities should not be discounted.

Consideration is also required for permanent differences between book income compared to taxable income, which are differences that never reverse because they are items of book or tax revenue or expense in one period, but which are never items of tax or book revenue or expense in later periods. These amounts include income which is exempt from tax, and expenses which will never be deductible for tax purposes. These amounts are disregarded when determining both the tax payable currently and the deferred tax asset or liability.

Issues which require accounting analysis include any additional petroleum taxes which are applied in addition to ordinary corporate income taxes. This may relate to specific areas or fields, and the amounts may be deductible for corporate income tax. The required financial reporting calculations may include barrels that are free of tax, accelerated depreciation, and additional investment tax credits. These issues generally need to be separately evaluated and accounted for under IAS 12.[33]

Deferred tax relating to overseas subsidiaries may require recognition of these issues and adjustments in the oil and gas company's consolidated accounts. This recognition may not be required where related profits will not be repatriated to the parent country, generally known as the permanent or indefinite reinvestment assertion, under US Financial Accounting Principles Board (FASB) APB 23,[34] and similar, though less stringent, provisions under International Accounting Standard IAS 12 paragraph 39, based on whether there is control over the timing of the reversal of temporary differences, and whether it is probable that the temporary differences will not reverse in the foreseeable future.[35]

There are also specific deferred tax issues relating to PSCs. The sharing of profit oil, for example, is generally not a tax under IAS 12, and so the provisions for deferred tax therefore do not generally apply to profit oil. The costs paid by the oil and gas company under a PSC are to be recorded using the full cost or successful efforts method of accounting, while the proceeds from the sale of cost oil are recorded as oil revenue. The proceeds from the sale of profit oil are also to be recorded as oil revenues. The oil and gas company should not recognise revenue for the share of production passed to the national oil company (NOC). As the oil and gas company bears much of the risk under a PSC, they generally disclose the reserves as their own even though the company never legally owns the related hydrocarbons until they are produced. In cases where the country then also imposes corporate tax on profit oil, the deferred tax rules under IAS 12 may then apply to that taxation.

---

33. Financial reporting in the oil and gas industry, (PricewaterhouseCoopers, 2011) 86.
34. APB 23 is codified as Accounting Standards Codification (ASC) ASC 740-10-25-3.
35. Barry Jay Epstein & Lawrence G Macy, 'The Differential Influence of U.S.GAAP and IFRS on Corporations' Decisions to Repatriate Earnings of Foreign Subsidiaries', International Tax Journal (CCH, 2011) pp. 29, 35 and 37.

Other specific differences between US GAAP accounting and IFRS which impact the reporting of upstream oil and gas operations. These differences include rules for reporting exploration and production activities, risk sharing arrangements, joint venture accounting, PSCs, decommissioning liabilities, regulated assets, and reserves disclosures.[36]

36. Ernst & Young, *US GAAP v. IFRS*, The basics: Oil and Gas (Ernst & Young, 2009), p. 10, www.ey.com.au/UL/en/AccountingLink/Publications-library-US-GAAP-vs–IFRS–The-Basics at 8 September 2017.

CHAPTER 6
Tankers and Bulk Carriers

INTRODUCTION

This chapter concerns the transportation crude oil, gas, refined petroleum products, coal, and uranium from the place of extraction to refinery or processing plant to downstream distributors. These activities are known as the midstream in relation to oil and gas. A significant role in this process is the use of crude oil and LNG tankers to transport oil and gas between countries or within countries between production fields and related terminals.

Vessels such as oil tankers, LNG tankers, and coal bulk carriers may be provided by third parties, or multinational groups may hold the related vessels in specialised companies, with the vessels then provided under charters to other group companies.

The principal charter types for hiring vessels are: (1) bareboat charters, using agreements for the hiring of the vessel where no crew or provisions are included under the agreement, and (2) time charters, using agreements for the hiring of the vessel for a specific period of time where the owner still manages the vessel, the charterer selects the ports and directs the vessel, and the charterer pays daily hire to the owner of the vessel and pays related expenses including fuel and port charges.

The taxation of tanker and bulk carrier activities is generally based on the tax regime applying to the ship owning or operating company, and in practice taxation is also determined by tax treaty provisions relating to international shipping, and by the concessional tonnage tax regimes used by many countries. There may also be state and municipal taxation relating to income from shipping activities.

TANKERS, BULK CARRIERS, AND TAX TREATIES

The OECD Model Tax Treaty, Shipping and Air Transport Article 8, generally provides that profits from the operation of ships in international traffic are only taxable in the contracting state where the place of effective management of the enterprise is located.[1] International traffic excludes transportation solely within one of the contracting states. Accordingly where the shipping article of the related tax treaties are based on the OECD Model, profits of tanker or bulk carrier owners, or operators transporting crude oil, LNG or coal between international ports is generally protected from tax in other states except for the country of management.

The United Nations Model Tax Treaty, by comparison, permits the source state to tax income from operation of ships in international traffic, if such income is derived through more than casual activities. This is likely to include regular or frequent visits of a shipping enterprise's ships to a contracting state.[2]

In relation to tax treaties, a time charter of the vessel is determined under the shipping article in Article 8, on the same basis as the profits from the carriage of cargo.[3] A bareboat charter of the tanker or carrier, however, where the vessel is provided without crew and supporting services, is not treated as profits form the operation of ships, and is therefore taxed under the business profits provision of Article 7 which generally requires profits to be related to a permanent establishment in the source country.[4]

Tankers and carrier vessels may be treated as the place where the business is carried on, however this would not be treated as a fixed place of business unless the vessel was operating in a restricted geographical area, such as a tanker used for oil storage in association with a particular oil or gas field, or shuttle tankers transporting oil from the field to a terminal in the same country.[5] Tankers may also be used for longer term storage purposes, for example where crude oil prices are low and oil is stored in tankers for sale at a later date when prices are higher.[6] These tankers may potentially be treated as a fixed place of business.

There may be an issue relating to the place of effective management for treaty purposes. The OECD comment, for example, that the place of effective management of a subsidiary may potentially not lie in its alleged state of residence but, rather, lies in the state of residence of the parent company so as to make it a resident of that latter state for domestic law and treaty purposes.[7]

The shipping and air transport Article 8 has potentially quite broad scope. The OECD comment that shipping and air transport enterprises invariably carry on a large variety of activities to permit, facilitate or support their international traffic operations. Article 8 includes profits from activities directly connected with such operations, as well as profits from activities which are not directly connected with the operation of the enterprise's ships or aircraft in international traffic as long as they are ancillary to such

1. OECD *Model Tax Convention on Income and on Capital* (2014), Article 8(1).
2. United Nations Model Double Taxation Convention between Developed and Developing Countries, Article 8B(2).
3. OECD *Model Tax Convention on Income and on Capital* (2014), Commentary C(8)-2-5.
4. OECD *Model Tax Convention on Income and on Capital* (2014), Commentary C(8)-2.
5. Maja Stubbe Gelineck, 'Permanent Establishments and the Offshore Oil and Gas Industry', Bulletin for International Taxation, April 2016, 208, 217.
6. Brian Wingfield, Oil Tanker Storage Hits a 2017 Record Despite OPEC's Cuts, Bloomberg, 20 June 2017.
7. OECD, *Model Tax Convention on Income and on Capital* (2014), C(1)-10.

operations. This includes activities which make a minor contribution relative to the operation of ships or aircraft in international traffic but are so closely related to such operation that they should not be regarded as a separate business or source of income.[8]

The use of treaty benefits may potentially also be affected by adoption of treaty states of the OECD BEPS Action 6 measures to prevent treaty abuse, and the related provisions in the OECD BEPS Action 15 Multilateral Instrument (MLI). The related MLI measures include the principal purpose test or simplified limitation on benefits tests, to prevent treaty abuse such as treaty shopping.[9] This issue may potentially require related commercial substance in treaty countries with low-tax regimes claiming sole taxing rights under tax treaty clauses based on the OECD Model Article 8 Shipping and Air Transport article.

There are significant variations in tax treaties. Several of India's tax treaties, for example permit India as a source state to tax to a certain extent a foreign shipping enterprise's income from operation of ships in international traffic.[10] An example of the related issues is the decision of the Indian Income Tax Appellate Tribunal (ITAT) in *A.P. Moller, Maersk Agency India (P.) Ltd.*[11] ITAT considered the taxation of slot fees, relating to payments for allocated space on a container vessel, derived by a Danish shipping company. ITAT concluded that Indian taxation was governed by the shipping article of the India/Denmark tax treaty, rather than the business profits article, and that the income was therefore taxable in India.

In the absence of tax treaties, tax on international shipping activities may be collected by countries on a withholding tax basis where treaty exemptions do not apply:

- The United States (US) excludes income from the international operation of ships or aircraft from the gross income of certain foreign corporations that grant an equivalent exemption to the US.[12] Income attributable to transportation that begins or ends in the US is treated as being 50% derived from US sources.[13] Foreign corporations are subject to a 4% tax on their US sourced gross transportation income which is not effectively connected to a US trade or business.[14] Taxation of shipping activities by states within the Unites States is restricted by the tonnage tax prohibition in the US Constitution.[15]

8. OECD *Model Tax Convention on Income and on Capital* (2014), C(8)-2.
9. Multilateral Convention to Implement Tax Treaty Related Measures to Prevent Base Erosion and Profit Shifting, opened for signature 7 June 2017, Articles 6 and 7.
10. Amar Mehta, 'Taxation of Shipping Income under Tax Treaties – Development of Case Law in India', Asia-Pacific Tax Bulletin, (2015), vol. 21(3).
11. *A.P. Moller, Maersk Agency India (P.) Ltd*, ITA No. 4372/Mum/1992, dated 27 January 2003.
12. Internal Revenue Code, section 883(a).
13. Internal Revenue Code, section 863(c).
14. Internal Revenue Code, section 887.
15. United States Constitution, Article I, §10, cl. 3, and cases including *Polar Tankers, Inc. v. City of Valdez*, Alaska, (No. 08-310) 182 P. 3d 614, decided 15 June, 2009.

- Australia provides that ship owners or charterers with their principal place of business outside Australia are taxed on 5% of gross fares or freight charges receivable for outward carriage from Australia of passengers, mail or freight.[16]

TAX TREATY PLANNING

There are significant variations in tax treaties, for example the US/Austria tax treaty provides that profits of an enterprise of a Contracting State from the operation in international traffic of ships or aircraft shall be taxable only in that State.[17]

One example of potential related tax planning may include a structure for a US based group with an Austrian subsidiary which holds a Cayman Islands subsidiary. The Cayman Islands company derives the related shipping management income. Austria may exempt the dividends from the Cayman Islands company under the participation exemption. The US parent may elect fiscal transparent treatment of the Cayman Islands company under the entity classification 'check the box' rules, so that the Austrian company is treated as deriving the related income.[18] The US/Austria tax treaty may then potentially prevent US taxation of the shipping management income.[19]

A second example relates to US investors with interests in a Canadian trust. The trust derived transportations income which is protected from tax under the US/Canada tax treaty. The trust is taxed in Canada, however a deduction is allowed for the distributions to the investors. In the US the trust is treated as a foreign corporate entity under the entity classification 'check the box' rules.[20] The structure may potentially prevent Canadian tax, and allow a deferral of US tax.[21]

The use of such tax treaty exemptions is potentially subject to any anti-treaty shopping provisions in the related treaties, and anti-treaty shopping measures are included in the OECD BEPS Action 6 minimum standards on treaty abuse,[22] and the related in the BEPS Action 15 Multilateral Instrument.[23]

16. Income Tax Assessment Act 1936, section 129-135A.
17. Convention Between the United States of America and the Republic of Austria for the Avoidance of Double Taxation and the Prevention of Fiscal Evasion with Respect to Taxes on Income, 31 May 1996, Article 8(1).
18. Treasury Regulation 26 CFR 301.7701-3.
19. Jeffrey Rubinger & Summer LePree, *Tax Planning for International Transportation Income, Taxes without Borders* (Bilzin Sumberg, 27 April 2015).
20. Treasury Regulation 26 CFR 301.7701-3.
21. Jeffrey Rubinger & Summer LePree, *Tax Planning for International Transportation Income, Taxes without Borders* (Bilzin Sumberg, 27 April 2015).
22. Preventing the Granting of Treaty Benefits in Inappropriate Circumstances, Action 6: 2015 Final Report.
23. Multilateral Convention to Implement Tax Treaty Related Measures to Prevent Base Erosion and Profit Shifting, opened for signature 7 June 2017, Articles 6 and 7.

TONNAGE TAX REGIMES

Shipping industry tax regimes and concessions are discussed in several sources including PWC, in Choosing Your Course – Corporate taxation of the shipping industry around the globe,[24] and EY, in the Shipping Industry Almanac 2016.[25] The principal tax concession is the availability of tonnage taxation regimes in several countries, where a charge is payable is calculated on the basis of the tonnage of the vessels, rather than the actual profits from the use of the vessel. These regimes generally provide that only certain shipping activities qualify for the tonnage tax regime. Tonnage tax regimes usually apply to maritime transport, as the transport of goods and persons by sea in international traffic. Certain tonnage tax regimes also include towage, cable and pipe-laying, dredging and ship management activities. These regimes provide that the shipping company must own the vessel or have the right to use the vessel under a bareboat charter. The shipping company is generally permitted to charter out vessels on time charter basis. Chartering a vessel to a third party under a bareboat charter usually does not qualify under most tonnage tax regimes. The tonnage tax regimes may require that strategic and commercial management are undertaken directly by the company owning the vessel.

Tonnage tax regimes based on the Netherlands model are based on the net tonnage of the vessels.[26] Tonnage tax regimes based on the Greek model are based on the gross tonnage of the vessels in a fixed number of tonnage size groups and the age of the vessel, and generally include vessels and all shipping activities.[27] Other requirements may include:

- Qualifying activities – The basic requirement is the operation of a vessel in international traffic at sea. This may be extended for example to dredging and towing activities. PWC comment that the vessel owner or bareboat charterer usually exercises management activities relating to the vessel.
- Qualifying persons – This may include individual entrepreneurs, foundations, legal entities, partnerships, and permanent establishments.
- Ownership tests – Tonnage tax regimes generally apply to owned vessels and vessels used under a bareboat charter arrangement. Vessels used under a time charter arrangement may also qualify where additional ownership requirements are met.

24. PWC, Choosing Your Course – Corporate taxation of the shipping industry around the globe, 2015, https://www.pwc.com/kr/ko/publications/industry/pwc-choosing-your-course.pdf at 22 February 2018.
25. EY, Shipping Industry Almanac 2016, 483, http://www.ey.com/Publication/vwLUAssets/EY-shipping-industry-almanac-2016/$FILE/EY-shipping-industry-almanac-2016.pdf on 10 August 2017.
26. PWC comment that the Netherlands tonnage tax model is used in Belgium, Bulgaria, Denmark, Finland, France, Germany, India, Ireland, Italy, Japan, South Korea, Netherlands, Norway, Poland, South Africa, Spain, Taiwan, United Kingdom, and the United States.
27. The Greek tonnage tax model is used in Greece, Cyprus, and Malta.

- Flag registration – The vessel is generally required sail under the flag of the country in which the tonnage tax state. European Union (EU) countries may allow another EU or European Economic Area (EEA) flag.
- Ship management activities – The standard tonnage tax model generally excludes ship management activities from the regime. PWC have however identified a significant number of countries which extend the tonnage tax regime to these activities.

In the United Kingdom (UK), tonnage tax is available to a qualifying company which has qualifying ships and which meets specific obligations to train seafarers:[28]

- A company is a 'qualifying company' for tonnage tax purposes if it is within the charge to corporation tax, it operates one or more qualifying ships, and those ships are strategically and commercially managed in the UK.[29]
- A qualifying ship requires that the ship is seagoing, is of 100 tons or more gross tonnage and has either a valid International Tonnage certificate or other valid certificate, is used for one or more of: carriage of passengers by sea, carriage of cargo by sea, towage, salvage, or other marine assistance carried out at sea, transport in connection with other services of a kind necessarily provided at sea, is not used for the provision of goods or services of a kind normally provided on land, and is not in the category of excluded vessels.[30]
- Companies are required to provide training for seafarers. They will have to find or fund places for an agreed number of officer trainees according to the size of its fleet and the number of officers employed. This is called the minimum training obligation (MTO), comprising the core training commitment (CTC) and the end of period adjustment (EPA).[31]

The company must own or charter in the ship. It will generally not be eligible if it charters it out the ship on bareboat charter terms. The company may, however, bareboat charter the ship out for a term of no more than three years, provided the ship is temporarily surplus to the company's requirements, or to bareboat charter the ship to another member of the same group. The company may not time charters in, on average, more than 75% of its net tonnage, except where this is on an intra-group basis.[32]

28. HMRC Internal Manual, Tonnage Tax Manual, https://www.gov.uk/hmrc-internal-manuals/tonnage-tax-manual/ttm03001 on 10 August 2017.
29. Finance Act 2000, Schedule 22, Part III.
30. Finance Act 2000, Schedule 22, Part III, section 19.
31. Finance Act 2000, Schedule 22, Part IV, and UK Department of Transport, Guidance on Application and Reporting Requirements, https://www.gov.uk/government/publications/tonnage-tax-guidance-application-and-reporting-requirements.
32. Watson, Farley & Williams, Summary of UK Tonnage Tax Legislation, http://www.wfw.com/wp-content/uploads/2009/06/WFW-UKTonnageTaxLegislation.pdf on 10 August 2017.

The tonnage tax rates are based on total net tonnage and deemed profit per day per 100 tons in GBP:[33]

Up to 1,000 0.60
1,001 to 10,000 0.45
10,001 to 25,000 0.30
Over 25,000 0.15

OTHER SHIPPING INCENTIVES

Countries may also provide other tax incentives for shipping companies, by narrowing the tax base, lowering the tax rate, or providing complete tax exemption. PWC commented on related tax incentives provided by several countries, including:[34]

- *China* – For foreign international shipping companies, shipping income derived from outbound transportation shipment departing from China ports is subject to a Corporate Income Tax (CIT) rate of 1.25% where treaty exemptions do not apply.
- *Hong Kong (China SAR)* – Freight income is exempt from Hong Kong profits tax for ships under a Hong Kong flag uploading cargo in Hong Kong and navigating to international waters. Taxpayers resident outside Hong Kong but carrying on a shipping business in Hong Kong are tax exempt where there is reciprocal tax treatment in that country for a Hong Kong resident taxpayer, including New Zealand and South Korea.[35]
- *Malaysia* – An income tax exemption of 70% of the statutory income is available to a Malaysian resident company in relation to its income from the carrying on of business of a Malaysian ship.
- *Philippines* – International shipping companies doing business in the Philippines are liable to income tax of 2.5% based on Gross Philippine billings, which may be reduced by related treaties, together with percentage tax of 3% on gross receipts.

TANKERS, BULK CARRIERS, AND TAX SHELTERS

An alternative to the use of tonnage tax and other shipping incentives is to derive the related income in a high taxing country but to derive related capital allowances and

33. EY, Shipping Industry Almanac 2016, 483, http://www.ey.com/Publication/vwLUAssets/EY-shipping-industry-almanac-2016/$FILE/EY-shipping-industry-almanac-2016.pdf on 10 August 2017.
34. PWC, Choosing Your Course – Corporate taxation of the shipping industry around the globe, 2015, 26.
35. PWC, Solutions for shipping companies: Opportunities in Hong Kong, https://www.pwchk.com/en/industries/transportation-and-logistics/solutions-for-shipping-companies-opportunities-in-hong-kong.html on 9 August 2017.

interest deductions. Based on the circumstances and the related depreciation allowances this can provide a tax shelter, based on the related net tax deduction position for the earlier years of the structure.

Several countries have tax provisions to address the tax shelters based on asset ownership and related leasing structures. The use of tax shelter arrangements in the US, for example, was substantially limited by the passive activity loss rules in section 469 of the Internal Revenue Code.[36] These rules prohibit taxpayers from using losses derived from passive activities to offset income earned on activities in which the taxpayer materially participates, so that passive losses can be used only to offset passive income. Taxpayers are therefore generally interested in maximising the number of business activities that qualify as non-passive, where the taxpayer materially participates. US based planning structures which may generate tax losses are therefore generally based on active participants rather than passive investors.[37]

TRANSFER PRICING

Specialised entities in a multinational group providing transportation services are typically paid on a basis of: (1) crewing services, remunerated through a cost-plus arrangement, and (2) internal broking and vessel operation, receiving rates established with reference to the market. The larger returns may typically be paid to the vessel owner, on the basis of assuming the risks associated with the vessel, and the risk that they may not recover their original asset investments.[38] Information on market tanker rates includes Drewry Maritime Research,[39] Shipping Intelligence Weekly,[40] and S&P, Platts Marine – Tankers.[41]

36. 26 U.S. Code § 469 – Passive activity losses and credits limited.
37. Baker Tilly, Insights, 25 April 2012, Passive activity losses: Complying with section 469 rules.
38. PWC, LNG Shipping – Transfer Pricing Considerations, https://www.pwc.co.uk/tax/assets/lng-shipping-transfer-pricing-considerationsng.pdf on 4 August 2017.
39. Drewry Maritime Research, Tanker Forecaster, https://www.drewry.co.uk/maritime-research-products/tanker-forecaster-annual-subscription on 4 August 2017.
40. Shipping Intelligence Weekly, http://www.crsl.com/acatalog/shipping-intelligence-weekly.html#enqanchor on 4 August 2017.
41. S&P, Platts Marine – Tankers, https://www.platts.com/shipping/tankers on 4 August 2017.

CHAPTER 7
Pipelines

INTRODUCTION

Oil and gas pipelines are a vital component in the global supply chain. The success of upstream oil exploration and production activities, and of related downstream activities such as refining and distribution, may be dependent on the related pipeline infrastructure. Oil and gas pipelines may be purely domestic, or may be cross-border pipelines connecting production and consumption countries and may also pass-through transit countries.

Alternatives to pipelines include crude oil tankers where there is effective port access and longer transport distances. Liquefied natural gas (LNG) processing and tanker transportation may provide an alternative to natural gas pipelines over longer distances.

The related tax issues include whether pipelines are permanent establishments in respective countries, the attribution of income and expenses to permanent establishments, and the use of treaties to allocate income between source, transit, and destination countries.

References on these issues include the detailed analysis cross-border pipelines by Knut Olsen, including discussion including permanent establishments, profit attribution, and related pipeline treaties.[1] The United Nations Development Programme (UNDP) and the World Bank have analysed case study examples of large cross-border and domestic pipeline systems.[2]

Key developments include the adoption of treaties between different countries for cross-border pipelines, which can provide greater certainty of revenue sharing and tax regimes particularly for large-scale pipeline projects.

1. Knut Olsen, Characterisation and Taxation of Cross-Border Pipelines (IBFD 2012).
2. Joint UNDP/World Bank Energy Sector Management Assistance Programme (ESMAP), Cross-Border Oil and Gas Pipelines: Problems and Prospects, June 2003.

PIPELINE EXAMPLES

There have been a large number of cross-border and domestic oil or gas pipeline projects, and a number of examples of successful and unsuccessful projects. The UNDP/World Bank report reviewed several large cross-border and domestic pipeline systems, including:[3]

- TransMed Pipeline, Algeria, Tunisia, and Italy.
- Trunk Oil Pipeline System of Russia, Russia (Transneft), Ukraine, Belarus, Latvia, and Lithuania.
- Suez–Mediterranean pipeline (SuMed), Egypt.
- Iraqi crude oil export pipelines, Iraq, and Turkey.
- Baku's Early Oil Project, Russia, and Georgia.
- Maghreb-Europe Gas Pipeline, Algeria, Morocco, and Spain.
- Caspian Pipeline Consortium, Kazakhstan, and Russia.
- Express Pipeline, Canada and United States (US).
- Bolivia–Brazil Gas pipeline.
- Baltic Pipeline System (BPS), Russia, Finland, and Latvia.
- GasAndes Pipeline (Gasaducto GasAndes), Argentina and Chile.

Based on its analysis of the respective case studies for these pipeline examples, the UNDP/World Bank concluded that conditions which create conflict or the potential for conflict include:

- Different parties, each with different interests, are involved.
- There is no overarching legal regime that can be used to police and regulate activities and contracts.
- The context created by the characteristics invites conflict because profit and rent are to be shared between the various parties and mechanisms exist to encourage one or other party to seek a greater share of that profit and rent.

The report highlighted differences between oil and gas pipelines as follows:

- There is normally much greater rent associated with oil than with gas.
- Security of supply is more important for gas than for oil, where gas outages may involve greater reconnection problems.
- Gas pipeline transportation involves different technical issues from those of oil; for example, in terms of issues such as grid balancing.
- Environmental threats from oil and gas pipelines differ significantly.
- The extent of competition from other transport methods differs.

The report considered the historical background of these projects, including successful examples together with cases with conflict and disruption to pipeline

3. *Ibid.*

operations, and commented that the four principal conditions of best practice are as follows:

- The rules are clearly defined and accepted.
- Projects are driven by commercial considerations.
- There are credible threats to deter the obsolescing bargain.
- There are mechanisms to create a balance of interest.

The analysis highlighted the need for clearly defined and accepted rules in bilateral or multilateral pipeline treaties, and in relation to international tax these treaties may contain specific provisions for revenue sharing between the respective countries.

PERMANENT ESTABLISHMENTS

Oil and gas pipelines activities which are performed by a local resident company are taxed under the related domestic tax rules. One of the primary issues relating to oil and gas pipelines, however, is whether these activities constitute a permanent establishment when performed by a foreign company in respective origination, transit, or destination countries. Tax treaties based on the OECD Model generally provide that a country may tax only a foreign company on business profits under Article 7 of the OECD Model if these profits attributable to a permanent establishment in the local country under Article 5. The absence of a permanent establishment can therefore provide treaty protection from source country taxation for the foreign company.

Significant issues with the permanent establishment provisions of the OECD Model Treaty and the classification of pipeline related activities were discussed by Knut Olsen.[4] These issues include whether pipelines are potentially considered to be immovable property, or as another source of business profits to which permanent establishment and attribution rules should apply:[5]

- The 2014 OECD Commentary on the Model Tax Treaty notes that where pipelines constitute immovable property then Article 6 can apply, which allows source country taxation of the owner or operator from their use by other enterprises.
- The OECD Commentary however also notes that where an enterprise owns and operated a pipeline solely for the purpose of transporting its own property and that transport is incidental to the business of that enterprise, then that may be an exception to permanent establishment under Article 5(4)(a) as the use of facilities solely for the purpose of storage, display, or delivery of goods or merchandise belonging to the enterprise.
- An enterprise may be a customer of the pipeline service provider. In this case the enterprise is merely obtaining transportation services provided by the

4. Knut Olsen, *Characterisation and Taxation of Cross-Border Pipelines* (IBFD 2012).
5. OECD, *Model Tax Convention on Income and on Capital* (2014), C(5)-26.

pipeline operator is not considered a permanent establishment of that enterprise.

The 1996 *German Pipeline* case concerned a Netherlands company which remotely managed and controlled an underground pipeline to deliver oil within Germany. German companies maintained the related delivery stations that supplied customers. Maintenance and repair of the pipeline was done by independent contractors. The Netherlands company's business was the transport of oil, and the Federal Fiscal Court therefore held that the pipeline is the way the Netherlands company conducted its business. The pipeline was therefore a permanent establishment of the Netherlands company in Germany.[6] The pipeline was not used solely for auxiliary purposes, rather the transportation of oil for other enterprises was the core activity of the company.[7]

Pipelines may also be defined to be permanent establishments in tax treaties, such as in the Norwegian, United Kingdom (UK), and Kazakhstan tax treaties. Canada, Denmark, Ireland, Norway, and the UK have also made reservations to the OECD Model Tax Treaty to reserve the right to insert related provisions in their tax treaties.[8]

The permanent establishment issue may also be affected by the OECD BEPS measures. BEPS Action 7 addresses the avoidance of PE Status, including modifications to the specific activity exemptions under Article 5(4).[9] There measures have also been incorporated in optional measure in the Multilateral Instrument (MLI) Article 13.[10] These measures may apply so that the permanent establishment exception only applies where the overall activity of the fixed place of business is of a preparatory or auxiliary character.

TRANSFER PRICING AND ATTRIBUTION OF INCOME

Transfer pricing is a significant issue where oil or gas transportation is provided for related upstream or downstream parties in a multinational group. A separate pipeline company in a particular country may require functional analysis of the business and related party transactions, review of potential internal and external comparables such as prices for similar transportation services, and selection of the most appropriate transfer pricing method. Where the pipeline is a permanent establishment, an arm's length attribution of income and expenses is required under tax treaties, based on Article 7 of the OECD Model Treaty.

The pipeline company may be providing services to unrelated parties which may establish comparable income, or third parties may be providing pipeline services at

6. Bundesfinanzhof (Federal Fiscal Court, BFH), Decision of 30 October 1996, II R 12/92 (1996),Betriebs-Berater 1997.
7. Knut Olsen, *Characterisation and Taxation of Cross-Border Pipelines* (IBFD 2012).
8. *Ibid.*
9. OECD, Preventing the Artificial Avoidance of Permanent Establishment Status, Action 7: 2015 Final Report, 28.
10. Multilateral Convention to Implement Tax Treaty Related Measures to Prevent Base Erosion and Profit Shifting.

known prices. In other cases a more complex analysis may be required using detailed analysis of the functions performed, assets used, and risks undertaken (FAR).

Significant related issues in determining an arm's length profit where oil and gas transportation is provided to related parties include:

- Determining the value to assign to the pipeline infrastructure as the most significant asset, and what value to assign to supporting services and intangible assets.
- Pipeline income can be vulnerable to interruptions, where any part of the pipeline is unable to operate.
- A pipeline is part of a larger supply chain, and the value of the pipeline may be partly dependant on the success of the multinational's upstream and downstream business.
- Income may be dependent on variations in oil and gas prices. There may also be value to a pipeline owner in a vertically integrated oil business to restricting access to the line by third parties to limit competition.[11]
- There are also issues in analysing significant risks such as pollution damage, and this can vary with the political and geographical circumstances, insurance terms, and the age of the pipeline.
- There are issues with the attribution of capital and level of related party debt with pipeline activities, particularly when funding large-scale investments.

PIPELINE FINANCING

Long distance oil and gas pipelines generally have significant capital and operating costs, and financing and related tax issues are a dominant consideration:

- Integrated oil and gas multinationals may have access to lower cost borrowings by issuing corporate debt by the parent company or the group treasury company on international financial markets. The related tax issues include thin capitalisation for the local pipeline subsidiary for the related party debt, and transfer pricing concerning the interest rate charged on that debt.
- Project finance may be used in other cases where investors including financial institutions provide funding on a non-recourse basis to the pipeline assets.[12] This funding is generally at a higher cost, however it may be useful to the multinational group to diversify sources of finance.

Norton Rose commented that a pipeline requires a high level of initial investment and does not generate any revenue to finance debt repayment until the pipeline is

11. Joint UNDP/World Bank Energy Sector Management Assistance Programme (ESMAP), Cross-Border Oil and Gas Pipelines: Problems and Prospects, June 2003, 18.
12. Norton Rose Fulbright, Project Financing of Cross-Border Pipelines, 1 April 2005, http://www.nortonrosefulbright.com/knowledge/publications/154213/project-financing-of-cross-border-pipelines on 22 August 2017.

completed. This non-completion risk is an important issue in project funding, and may require express commitments from the project sponsors. In addition, most cross-border pipelines involve a number of parties with diverse interests:

- Cross-border pipelines may involve both the public and the private sectors. In the public sector, the country of production usually wants the highest price for the exported hydrocarbons, the country of transit wants the highest tariff, and the country of receipt wants the lowest price and the lowest tariff.
- There is also a divergence of interests in the private sector, to the extent that different entities are involved in the supply, transportation, and purchase of the relevant hydrocarbons.

A stable regulatory and tax regime are likely to significantly lower the project risks, and enable funding for the pipeline project to be secured. The most recent developments include specific treaties for large-scale cross-border pipeline projects.

CROSS-BORDER PIPELINE MODEL AGREEMENT: ENERGY CHARTER SECRETARIAT

The Energy Charter Secretariat has issued the Model Intergovernmental Agreement (IGA) and Model Host Government Agreements (HGA) for cross-border pipelines. Article 13 of the second edition of the Model Intergovernmental Agreement contains the related tax clauses, which are summarised as follows:[13]

- No less favourable treatment – The tax treatment of project investors, interest holders, shippers, or contractors with respect to any part of project activities will be no less favourable than that applicable to its nationals in the same circumstances under its general tax legislation.
- VAT and customs duties – No non-recoverable VAT or sales taxes is imposed on imports, exports, or the supply of goods, works, or services with respect to all or any part of specific project activities. No customs duties or other levies is imposed or withheld with respect to project activities.
- Fair and transparent application of taxes – Each state shall cooperate with the other states to ensure a fair and transparent application of taxes with respect to project investors, shippers, or contractors.
- Taxation of profits, tax exemptions, or credits – Tax shall be limited to the profits of such project Investor or Contractor which is attributable to such project activities in each state. Each state will grant relief from double taxation of such profit either by exemption from taxes or credit against taxes.
- Transfer pricing and allocation keys – For the purpose of computing taxes, the aggregate amount of revenues, costs, and expenses shall be allocated between the states, and the principles of the OECD, especially concerning transfer

13. Energy Charter Secretariat, Model Intergovernmental and Host Government Agreements for Cross-Border Pipelines, Second Edition.

pricing, shall apply. For each of the revenues and costs of the Project, uniform and appropriate allocation keys to be determined jointly by the project investors and the states, as agreed in the HGA, shall be used to allocate revenues and costs between the states.

- Withholding taxes – No state shall impose withholding tax or other taxes on cash transfers to bring liquidity to the project investor, interest holder, shipper, or person who provides goods, works, technology, or services as far as they are not paid into the stated capital of a legal entity unless explicitly admitted by a relevant double tax treaty.
- No extension of benefits – States are not obliged to extend the benefits of any treatment, preference, or privilege resulting from any existing or future tax agreement or granted by one state, under a multilateral agreement, to a resident or national of another state.
- No taxes on capital or assets – No Taxes shall be levied on the asset value, equity value, or stated capital of the entity or permanent establishment located or domiciled in the host state, or on the value of the pipeline system, or petroleum or natural gas transported through the pipeline system, on the value of any project activities related assets, except as expressly provided in the HGA.
- No withholding taxes – No taxes shall be imposed or withheld with respect to payments, including taxes on payments of interest, royalties, fee for services and dividends, or other distributions or remittances of profit, or deemed payments associated with project activities, except as expressly provided in the HGA.
- No tax on related services – No taxes shall be imposed by any state on any project investor, shipper, or person who provides goods, works, technology, or services, except as expressly provided in the HGA.

The Energy Charter Model Agreements refer to the principles set out in Article 7 of the OECD Model Tax Agreement for the allocation of income, and then go a step further as the parties would agree on an uniform allocation key in advance, would should reduce the risk of disputes, double taxation, and uncertainties.[14] The Host Government Agreement also requires the parties to execute a Profit Tax Agreement concerning carrying forward of tax losses, deductible cost, deductibility of interest and foreign exchange gains and losses, capitalisation criteria, and pooling of assets for tax deprecation.[15] Agreements based on the Model Agreements include the Trans-Caspian Aktau-Baku Agreement between Kazakhstan and Azerbaijan.[16]

14. Knut Olsen, *Characterisation and Taxation of Cross-Border Pipelines* (IBFD 2012).
15. Olsen commented that parties which use the Energy Charter's Model Agreement should clarify the allocation of income and expenses in advance and avoid time-consuming and costly disputes.
16. Knut Olsen, *Characterisation and Taxation of Cross-Border Pipelines* (IBFD 2012).

CHAPTER 8

Downstream Taxation: Refineries and Processing Plants

INTRODUCTION

Oil refineries process crude oil into refined products such as gasoline, diesel fuel, aviation fuel, heating oil, kerosene, liquefied petroleum gas (LPG), and raw materials for other products such as plastics. Refineries typically include related facilities such as oil depots for storage, and transportation infrastructure for crude oil or petroleum products. There is considerable variation in the capabilities of oil refineries, such as the ability to process lower quality crude oil and to produce specialised products. Natural gas processing plants are generally used to remove impurities in raw natural gas. Gas liquefaction plants are used to convert gas into liquefied natural gas (LNG) for ease of transportation and storage.

There are a significant number of taxation issues which apply to oil refineries and gas processing or liquefaction plants, particularly for transfer pricing where crude oil or gas is purchased for related party domestic or foreign producers. References used include Transfer Pricing Associates, Transfer Pricing Handbook for the Oil & Gas Industry.[1]

REFINING AND PROCESSING IN THE GLOBAL SUPPLY CHAIN

The refinery is typically supported by research and development (R&D) and intangible property (IP), including production processes, specifications, technical equipment, instructions manuals, and safety protocols. This may be recognised using royalty payments for bundled IP, and/or the payment of time based charges for technical support from engineers and other experts.

1. Transfer Pricing Associates, Transfer Pricing Handbook for the Oil & Gas Industry, August 2012.

The refinery will have substantial property and equipment, and taxation issues arise in relation to the design, construction, and testing stages together with any later upgrade programmes. The related tax issues include whether the design and construction activities constitute a permanent establishment (PE) in the local country, and how profits are then attributed to the permanent establishment under transfer pricing rules. Recent developments include BEPS Action 7 measures to address the artificial avoidance of PE status commissionaire arrangements, strategies to negotiate contracts locally and conclude the contracts in another country, fragmenting contracts to use the specific activity exceptions, and contract splitting in large construction and engineering projects.

There may also be related party investment and funding structures, particularly where the refinery is part of a multinational business including upstream oil and gas exploration and production. The related tax planning includes debt push down and related interest deduction limitations such as thin capitalisation and transfer pricing rules. A refinery project may potentially benefit from a lower cost of funds compared to the upstream oil and gas activities of a parent oil and gas multinational, for example where the refinery is considered to have lower economic risks than a new oil and gas exploration project. The refinery may also have access to local third-party funding opportunities.

Support services are likely to be provided by the multinational head office or other support centres. The OECD 2017 Transfer Pricing Guidelines support a 5% cost plus basis for low value-adding services. The OECD discuss the related allocation keys used to allocate services to group companies, and give several examples including headcount for services related to people, total users for information technology (IT) services, share of total vehicles for fleet management services, total relevant transactions, or the share of total assets for accounting support services, and also comment that in many cases the share of total turnover may be a relevant key.[2]

Refineries and processing plants may benefit from sustained demand for petroleum related products even where crude oil and unprocessed gas prices are low, so that an energy multinational group may generate significant profits from the refinery business when upstream sectors are less profitable.[3] There are also opportunities for greater certainly of supply where upstream and refinery businesses have common ownership, so that there is a guaranteed market for crude oil and gas upstream to benefit the upstream business, and the refinery has a more stable source of supply.

There is also an issue for the downstream retail petrol and gas distribution businesses, where retail market conditions may generate profits when the refinery is less profitable. Tax consolidation provisions may provide opportunities for the losses in one business to offset profits in the other business, and ring fencing provisions which separate upstream and downstream profits and losses may potentially not apply to consolidating profits and losses which are just within the downstream business.

2. OECD Transfer Pricing Guidelines for Multinational Enterprises and Tax Administrations 2017, 341.
3. Alan Farley, The 2016 Outlook For Oil Refiners, Investopedia, 25 February, 2016, http://www.investopedia.com/articles/markets/022516/2016-outlook-oil-refiners.asp on 31 July 2017.

CHARACTERISATION OF REFINING OR PROCESSING ACTIVITIES

The refinery may have different characteristics in terms of functions performed, assets used and risks undertaken (FAR). This classification will have a significant impact of the expected level of profits under transfer pricing analysis in determining whether related party transactions such as the purchase of crude oil or unprocessed gas, and the sale of refined petroleum products and gas is made on an arm's length basis:[4]

- Refinery as a profit centre – This structure is based on a fully stand-alone organisation which includes the main decision makers and intangible assets. The comparable uncontrolled price method is often applied for transfer pricing purposes, with related issues including the use of internal comparables based on purchases or sales with third parties, compared to external comparables such as advertised prices for equivalent oil and gas products.
- Refinery as a cost centre – This structure is based on the refinery performing functions on a contracted or tolling basis, so that the refinery does not make purchase or sale decisions or have significant intangible assets. The transactional net margin method (TNMM) based on return on assets or return on equity or a markup on total costs may be used.

Related tax planning for a refinery which is located in a higher taxing country may include conversion of the facility into a contract refinery. This may involve excluding specific activities so that the refinery is only processing on instructions of the principal. The excluded activities may include purchasing of crude oil, trading, or any trading support activities, and the sale of the refined products.

INTERNATIONAL TRANSFER PRICING: RELATED PARTY PURCHASES AND SALES

Refineries which are members of a multinational oil and gas group may purchase crude oil or gas from related parties, and sell refined petroleum products or processed gas to related parties. The purchase of crude oil or gas from related parties may involve the use of procurement hubs, where an entity in the group in a low-taxing country purchases from related or unrelated parties, and then sells the crude oil or gas to the refinery or processing plant. The sale of refined petroleum products and processed gas may also raise the marketing hub issue, where an entity in the group in a low-taxing country purchases from the refinery or processing plant and then sells the product to related or unrelated parties.

4. Transfer Pricing Associates, Transfer Pricing Handbook for the Oil & Gas Industry, August 2012, 44.

Transfer pricing provisions require related party transactions to be made on arm's length basis under the laws of many countries and in accordance with the OECD 2017 Transfer Pricing Guidelines.[5]

The OECD BEPS Action 13 Country-by-Country (CbC) reporting measures may impact the use of group procurement and marketing entities.[6] The CbC reports will generally include these entities under the Main Business Activity heading in the Purchasing or Procurement category for procurement hubs, and the Sales, Marketing and Distribution category for marketing hubs. The CbC report information includes related and unrelated party revenues, profits before tax, income tax paid, and number of employees. These measures were adopted in the 2017 OECD Transfer Pricing Guidelines.[7]

DOMESTIC TRANSFER PRICING

Several countries also have domestic transfer pricing provisions which can apply to transactions relating to tax holidays, differential tax rates, or carry-forward tax losses. In relation to oil refineries and gas processing plants, the provisions can apply to the sale of crude oil or gas from an upstream exploration and production business to a downstream oil refinery or gas processing plant in the same country. Examples of countries with transfer pricing provisions which can apply to domestic transactions include:

- Australia – There are domestic transfer pricing provisions relating to upstream oil and gas in the in the Petroleum Resource Rent Tax (PRRT),[8] and in relation to domestic transactions between trusts and companies in stapled structures, where investors hold shares and trust units which must be purchased and sold together.[9]
- India – The Indian transfer pricing provisions were extended to Specified Domestic Transactions (SDT) in 2013. These transactions include payments to related parties, transfers of goods or services of tax holiday entities with other taxpayer entities, and transactions of tax holiday entities with other closely connected entities.[10]
- Malaysia – The transfer pricing rules and related guidelines are applicable to controlled transactions where at least one party is chargeable to tax in Malaysia, so that both cross-border and domestic-related party transactions are within the scope of these provisions.[11]

5. OECD Transfer Pricing Guidelines for Multinational Enterprises and Tax Administrations, 2017, Chapter V, p. 233.
6. OECD Transfer Pricing Documentation and Country-by-Country Reporting, BEPS Action 13: 2015, Final Report.
7. OECD Transfer Pricing Guidelines for Multinational Enterprises and Tax Administrations, 2017, Chapter V, p. 233.
8. Petroleum Resource Rent Tax Assessment Act 1987, sections 56–58.
9. Income Tax Assessment Act 1997 sections 275-605, and Law Companion Guide LCG 2015/15.
10. Income Tax Act 1961 section 92BA.
11. Income Tax Act 1967 section 140A, and Income Tax (Transfer Pricing) Rules 2012.

- The Netherlands – The transfer pricing rules issued in 2002 apply where there is an understatement of the taxable income reported by a Dutch group company because of non-arm's-length related party transactions. The provisions cover both transactions among domestic-related entities and among internationally related entities.[12]
- United Kingdom (UK) – The rules apply where an enterprise has lower taxable profits or greater allowable losses than if calculated on the basis of the arm's-length provision as an 'advantaged person'. This can include transactions between the ring fenced trade rate for upstream oil and gas and the general corporate tax rate.[13]

INTEGRATED PRODUCERS: UPSTREAM AND REFINING BUSINESS

Refining activities may also impact a group's tax position where combined with upstream and midstream oil and gas activities. In the United States (US), capital allowances are significantly affected for integrated businesses. The related classifications are:[14]

- An integrated producer is defined as a company, or a 5% or more related party, that has exploration and production activity, and either: (1) gross receipts in excess of USD 5 million in US retail sales of oil and gas for the taxable year, or (2) refinery runs located anywhere in the world that average in excess of 75,000 barrels of throughput per day.
- A major integrated oil company is defined as producers of crude oil that have average daily worldwide production of at least 500,000 barrels, gross receipts in excess of USD 1 billion for the last taxable year ended during the 2005 calendar year and at least a 15% ownership in a crude oil refinery.
- An independent producer or royalty owner is defined as any taxpayer that is not an integrated producer.

Taxation allowances affected by these classifications include:

- Geological and geophysical (G&G) costs may be amortised and deducted over a twenty-four-month period, or seven years for a major integrated oil company.
- Intangible Drilling Cost (IDC) incentive for costs incident to and necessary for the drilling of wells and the preparation of wells for the production of oil and gas with an election for 100% current year deduction. This is reduced to 70%

12. Corporate Income Tax Act 1969 Article 8b.
13. Taxation (International and Other Provisions) Act 2010, Part 4. An exception for United Kingdom to United Kingdom transactions was removed from the prior rules in 2004.
14. Ernst & Young, Global oil and gas tax guide 2016, 666, and Deloitte, Oil and gas taxation in the United States, Deloitte taxation and investment guides, 2, www.deloitte.com/taxguides on 25 July 2017.

for integrated oil companies, with the remaining 30% amortised over sixty months.

- Percentage depletion available to independent oil and gas producers and royalty owners generally at 15% of the gross income from the property. Integrated oil companies are required to use the cost depletion method.

VAT, CUSTOMS TARIFFS, AND DUTIES

Customs tariffs and indirect taxes such as Value Added Tax (VAT) are imposed by a substantial number of countries. The principal issue for refineries and gas processing plants is whether import VAT and customs tariffs applies to the importation of crude oil and unprocessed gas.

In relation to customs tariffs, oil and natural gas, for example, may be subject to the General Agreement on Tariffs and Trade (GATT) updated as a result of the Uruguay Round negotiations concluded in 1993 under the World Trade Organisation (WTO).[15] The updated GATT sets out tariff limits agreed by different member countries.[16]

There may be other exemptions from customs tariffs under multilateral agreements. One example is the exemption arrangement between Canada, Mexico, and the US under the North American Free Trade Agreement (NAFTA).[17] Related issues include whether crude oil and natural gas qualify as sourced in a trade treaty country under the related rules of origin. For example, when oil and gas companies blend crude oil with condensates or diluents from non-NAFTA states to transport the oil by pipeline, or blend natural gas with gas originating in non-NAFTA states.[18] In relation to customs tariffs in the European Union (EU), the Common Customs Tariff (CCT) has set a zero rate.[19]

In the UK, imports of gas by all means and in all forms including liquefied natural gas (LNG) are relieved from import VAT. When crude oil is imported into a UK refinery, the product is duty and VAT suspended. Supplies within the warehousing regime are treated as outside the scope of UK VAT. Once the crude oil is refines the resulting

15. General Agreement on Tariffs and Trade 1994, 15 April 1994, Marrakesh Agreement Establishing the World Trade Organization, Annex 1A, 1867 U.N.T.S. 187, 33 I.L.M. 1153 (1994).
16. United Nations Conference on Trade and Development (UNCTAD),Trade Agreements, Petroleum And Energy Policies, 2000, UNCTAD/ITCD/TSB/9, Crude oil (HS 2709) Table K p. 138, and Hydrocarbons (HS 2901-2907) Table M p. 144, http://unctad.org/en/docs/itcdtsb9_en.pdf at 31 July 2017.
17. North American Free Trade Agreement, Article 302, (17 December 1992, 32 ILM 289, entered into force 1 January 1994).
18. Glenn A Cranker & Harold K Andersen, Stikeman Elliott LLP, 'Exporting Canadian Oil and Gas: The Challenge of NAFTA Compliance', www.acc.com/legalresources/quickcounsel/exognafta.cfm on 31 July 2017. The United States duty rate on crude oil imports from Canada, for example, may increase from the NAFTA rate of 'free' to 5.25 cents or 10.5 cents per barrel.
19. Commission Implementing Regulation (EU) 2016/1821 of 6 October 2016 amending Annex I to Council Regulation (EEC) No. 2658/87 on the tariff and statistical nomenclature and on the Common Customs Tariff, Official Journal of the EU, L 294/210, EN 28.10.2016, CN codes 2707 and 2709, p. 210.

products are new products with UK origin which are subject to VAT.[20] Excise duties are generally levied on the refinery or gas processing plant as the producer of oil and gas products.

20. United Kingdom Oil Industry Tax Committee, Indirect Taxes Committee, The North Sea Memorandum, pp. 9, 10, and 24.

CHAPTER 9

Coal Exploration and Production

INTRODUCTION

The coal industry is a principal contributor to global energy production, and in many countries coal is the main energy source for electric power stations. The coal mining process includes exploration for coal reserves, followed by the mining production taking place on the surface or underground. Coal processing includes crushing, screening, and beneficiation to remove impurities such as ash and sulphur, with higher quality coal potentially used for export. Coal production includes coking coals used to make coke for use in blast furnaces used for metal production, and energy, steaming or thermal coal used for heating purposes such as consumption in power stations generating electricity. Coal production requires significant transportation infrastructure such as road, rail, and port services, and shipping using bulk carriers.

Large-scale coal production required significant capital expenditure (CAPEX) on mining, processing, and transportation equipment, and appropriate funding structures are therefore extremely important. Debt push down structures may be used to borrow funds in the mining country and provide related interest deductions to offset mining income. Multinational groups may also use related party funding structures where interest is paid by the local mining company to a low-taxed group treasury company.

There is also large-scale ongoing operating expenditure (OPEX) on personnel, services, and technology, which may be provided to the local mining company by service hubs within the multinational group.

TAXES AND INCENTIVES

Tax on mining activities is generally based on corporate income tax on the mining company's profits, combined with royalties applying to production. The cash flow profile of a coal mine typically involves large expenses in the initial development of a mine, with the related income only derived once the mine is in full scale operation. This profile is somewhat similar to an upstream oil and gas cash flow profile, except that the exploration risk is lower in coal mining, and long-term political risks may potentially be considered higher.

The availability of tax concessions such as accelerated depreciation or tax holidays, for example, defers taxation and therefore the amount of un-recouped investment at risk.[1] Limitations on the use of carry-forward tax losses to a set period may be a significant issue for longer term projects, where there may be some years before production becomes profitable.

In the United States (US), for example, federal tax incentives for mining include:[2]

- Expensing of Exploration and Development Costs – Taxpayers can immediately deduct coal mine exploration expenditures, with deducted amounts recaptured once the mine is producing or is sold. C corporations, which are generally taxed separately from their owners, can only expense 70% of qualifying costs, with the remaining 30% recovered over five years. Alternatively, mine exploration expenditures can be amortised over a ten-year period.
- Percentage Depletion – Capital costs can be recovered using percentage depletion. For coal, depletion deductions equal to 10% of gross income from the property are allowed. The deduction is limited to 50% of taxable income from the property.
- Coal Royalties Treated as Capital Gains Income – Dispositions of coal royalties are treated as long-term capital gains which may be taxed at reduced rates.
- Credit for Investment in Clean Coal Facilities – A 30% tax credit is available for integrated gasification combined cycle (IGCC) and advanced coal-based electricity generation technologies (ACBGT) projects.
- Exclusion of Special Benefit for Disabled Coal Miners – Certain disability payments are excluded from taxable income.

Several tax systems apply ring fencing to mining operations, so that profits on one mine cannot offset profits on another mine. Examples of countries with ring fencing provisions for mining include Ghana, Kazakhstan, and Tanzania.[3] The use of the corporate income tax system, rather than other fiscal systems such as the production sharing contracts (PSC) in the upstream oil and gas industry, generally means that there is no project ring fencing to restrict the use of mining losses within a company. The availability of a tax consolidation regime may facilitate the use of tax losses by related companies in the same country.

1. Corlie Hazell, Aligning the tax agenda with the business agenda, EY Global mining and metals tax survey, 2013, http://www.ey.com/Publication/vwLUAssets/Global_mining_and_metals_tax_survey/$FILE/Global_mining_and_metals_tax_survey.pdf on 14 August 2017.
2. Marc Humphries & Molly F Sherlock, Congressional Research Service, U.S. and World Coal Production, Federal Taxes, and Incentives, 14 March 2013, 16, https://fas.org/sgp/crs/misc/R43011.pdf on 16 August 2017.
3. PWC, Corporate income taxes, mining royalties and other mining taxes, A summary of rates and rules in selected countries, 2, https://www.pwc.com/gx/en/energy-utilities-mining/publications/pdf/pwc-gx-miining-taxes-and-royalties.pdf on 16 August 2017.

The availability of interest deductions on financing costs is a significant issue. Many countries have thin capitalisation provisions which limit tax deductions for related party interest payments. The OECD BEPS Action 4 measures recommend that countries implement a fixed ratio rule that would limit net interest deductions claimed by an entity to a fixed percentage of earnings before interest, taxes, depreciation and amortisation (EBITDA). The proposed ratio should be between 10% and 30% of applicable EBITDA. The measure would provide caps on net interest expense, while still allowing deduction for third-party interest expenses.[4]

There may be taxation imposed at federal, state and municipal levels. In the largest coal producing state of Wyoming in the US, for example, no state income tax applies, however other state taxes include property tax at an average effective rate of 0.62%, sales and use tax and municipal tax at 4%, and excise and severance tax on surface coal at 7%.[5]

TRANSFER PRICING

There are also ongoing challenges in the ability of developing countries to apply transfer pricing approaches to mineral product transactions. These issues include the basis for coal commodity prices to determine related party arm's length prices, and the related adjustments required to determine arm's length prices for particular markets. A related concern is the use of hedging arrangements against risks such as price fluctuations, and whether the coal producer would enter into hedging on the related terms and conditions.

Related party financing is also a core topic for transfer pricing, and this issue includes whether large-scale related party loans are provided to the mining country on arm's length terms and conditions. Related structures may include interest charged on advance payments by the parent or group treasury company to the local mining company, based on the period between shipping from the production country and the sale of coal to the final customer. Parent or group treasury company loans may also be used to fund equipment provided by related companies to the mining company.

Transfer pricing also relates to the prices charged for services provided by related companies in the multinational group, including realisation charges for processing, transport, insurance, and freight. There are significant differences in coal mining compared to upstream oil and gas, as joint operating agreements (JOA) and consortia are less common in mining, and so oversight and review of related party payments by third parties is less common. The OECD has highlighted the use of marketing/trading

4. OECD Base Erosion and Profit Shifting Project, Limiting Base Erosion Involving Interest Deductions and Other Financial Payments, Action 4 – 2016 Update.
5. For a summary of United States and Canadian provincial taxes, *see* Industry Standard for Mining Cost Estimating Mining Cost Service, State/Provincial Mining Taxes for U.S. and Canada, http://costs.infomine.com/costdatacenter/miningtaxes.aspx on 16 August 2017.

hubs or intermediaries as a common feature for possible base erosion and profit shifting through transfer pricing.[6]

Transfer pricing in the mining sector has been a focus for international review, including a major World Bank report in 2017.[7] The report commented that in centralised business structures in the coal industry, the exploration and mining entities stripped of their main risks and assets are being regarded as performing routine services, and are compensated with a limited markup on top of their costs. The United Nations position is that the location saving and synergies of having access to the source of coal may justify the local group companies involved in the exploration and mining activities claiming a premium on top of what otherwise would be a typical 'cost plus' price. The additional uplift to take into account potential location savings and synergies would be determined through a process of negotiation between the parties as if they were independent entrepreneurs dealing at arm's length.

The World Bank report included a discussion of tax audit case selection relating to multinational enterprises (MNE) engaged in mining activities, including tax administrations gaining an understanding of:[8]

(1) Which MNEs conduct mining operations in their country.
(2) The business structure, both legal and operational, used by each MNE to undertake mining operations in the country and how that structure fits within the MNE's global legal and operating structure.
(3) The high-level financial performance of those MNEs globally and of their mining subsidiaries and other entities in the host country.
(4) The relative performance of the various MNEs and mining companies that operate in the host country. It can be difficult to separate poor financial performance due to profit shifting through transfer pricing and poor financial performance caused by other reasons, such as inadequate administrative capacity, macroeconomic factors, and business conditions including cost and capital expenditure constraints. Insights to filter out those miners more likely to be undertaking profit shifting or transfer pricing can be obtained by comparing line item costs and profitability against:
    (a) Peers, with similar but unrelated mining operations. This may include comparing prices achieved for sale of the same or similar commodities by other miners or published market prices and general industry trends (e.g., if the industry reflects increasing demand and higher prices it would

6. Dan Devlin & Howard Mann, OECD Tax and Development Programme and Intergovernmental Forum on Mining (IGF), Tackling Revenue Leakages, Building on BEPS, December 2016, 133, https://www.oecd.org/dev/inclusivesocietiesanddevelopment/Session%206A%20and%206B%20-%20Tackling%20Revenue%20Leakages,%20Building%20on%20BEPS%20_Minerals%20Traded%20in%20Intermediate%20Forms.pdf on 14 August 2017.
7. Pietro Guj, Stephanie Martin, Bryan Maybee, Frederick Cawood, Boubacar Bocoum, Nishana Gosai & Steef Huibregtse, Transfer Pricing in Mining with a Focus on Africa A Reference Guide for Practitioners, World Bank, January 2017, http://documents.worldbank.org/curated/en/801771485941579048/Transfer-pricing-in-mining-with-a-focus-on-Africa-a-reference-guide-for-practitioners on 15 August 2017.
8. *Ibid*, 149.

be unusual for a mining company to be reflecting losses or decreasing profitability).

(b) Parts, relating to other parts of the MNE's business involved in the mining chain, especially those in other countries.

(c) Past, relating to historical results.

This information may then be used for the risk assessment, based on functional, profitability, tax, and mining chain analysis. The ranking of taxpayers on this basis, along with estimated likelihood of occurrence and value of its consequence results, would then form the pool of potential tax audit cases.

Contract Mining

Contract mining is an example of limited functions assigned to local exploration and manufacturing companies. This typically takes place where a company performs core services on behalf of the principal, such as production drilling and blasting mineral deposits, and can extend to a complete turn-key mining operation including haulage, crushing, and conveyance to facilities for processing. The contract miner may work for a range of mining companies, providing the people and plant to extract the resources from their mines. The mineral deposits therefore belong to the principal, and the contract miner typically received a cost plus return for the services provided.

These arrangements may potentially limit the taxable profits in the mining country, for example where only the contract miner is subject to local country taxation. The use of contract mining arrangements was included in a discussion of mining tax avoidance schemes by Joseph Nonde of the Zambia Revenue Authority.[9]

Safe Harbours

The World Bank report discussed the potential use of safe harbours for the mining industry.[10] The report notes in particular the advantages of using a safe harbour for pricing of routine low-risk functions. This can provide certainty for a taxpayer, potentially reducing the costs of complying with transfer pricing administration, reducing the need to perform comparable studies, and free up resources so that tax authorities and taxpayers can concentrate on more important transfer pricing matters, such as restructuring, intangible transactions, and high-risk transactions where reliable comparables are not available. The safe harbours would be accompanied by disclosure and review requirements.

9. Joseph Nonde, Zambia Revenue Authority, Mining tax Avoidance Schemes, Presentation at the International Association of Prosecutors' Africa Regional conference, Livingstone, Zambia, 2–5 March 2014, http://www.iap-association.org/getattachment/Conferences/Regional-Conferences/Conference-Documentation-Zambia/3AIORC_Zambia_P3_Joseph_Nonde.pdf.aspx on 14 August 2017.
10. Pietro Guj, Stephanie Martin, Bryan Maybee, Frederick Cawood, Boubacar Bocoum, Nishana Gosai & Steef Huibregtse, Transfer Pricing in Mining with a Focus on Africa A Reference Guide for Practitioners, World Bank, January 2017, 176.

Coal Sale at the Mine

There are also issues where contracts provide for the sale of coal at the mine. This may potentially be a much lower value that at an export terminal. One example concerns coal in the US which is mined in the state of Wyoming, and then transported by rail to an export terminal in Washington state. The coal mined in Wyoming results in a state severance tax liability, and country ad valorum tax, based on the value of the coal at the mine at USD 9–10 per tonne. While in transit to the export terminal, the coal is in interstate commerce and is therefore not subject to Washington state sales tax. Businesses engaged in transportation or export would be responsible for their respective business, payroll taxes, property, and sales taxes. The coal terminal would pay taxes on its income from loading coal on bulk carriers, the profits from a fee of USD 9–10 per tonne. The coal mined from taxpayer property would then be sold for USD 80–120 a tonne on the international market. There may potentially be no obligation to pay Federal tax in the US where an international business uses an international subsidiary to buy the coal at the mine.[11]

INDIRECT SALE OF MINING INTERESTS

The sale of mining interests is generally subject to tax in most countries as relating to immovable property. This is consistent with the OECD Model Tax Treaty, and Article 13 of the 2014 model provides that gains derived by a resident of a contracting state from the alienation of immovable property referred to in Article 6 and situated in the other contracting state may be taxed in that other state. Article 13 also includes certain indirect sales relating to immovable property, by providing that gains derived by a resident of a contracting state from the alienation of shares deriving more than 50% of their value directly or indirectly from immovable property situated in the other contracting State may be taxed in that other state.[12]

Immovable property is generally defined in Article 6 by reference to the law of the state in which the property is situated, however newer treaties such as the Germany/Australia treaty specifically include in the definition ‘a right to explore for mineral, oil or gas deposits or other natural resources, and a right to mine those deposits or resources’.[13]

A common concern with these provisions is the use of tax planning where splitting or bifurcation of assets and revaluation of other assets in the company may

11. Charles West, Chinadialogue, 4 December 2012, US Tax loopholes driving up coal exports to Asia, https://www.chinadialogue.net/article/show/single/en/5405-US-tax-loopholes-driving-up-coal-exports-to-Asia on 14 August 2017.
12. OECD, Model Convention with respect to Taxes on Income and on Capital, 2014.
13. Agreement between Australia and the Federal Republic of Germany for the Elimination of Double Taxation with Respect to Taxes on Income and on Capital and the Prevention of Fiscal Evasion and Avoidance, Article 6(2)(f).

dilute the proportion attributable to immovable property.[14] In these cases the company which is sold may have less than 50% of its value relating to immovable property after transfers of assets made before the sale.

The related issues include whether the indirect sale is actually declared. Responses from tax administrations include Indian provisions on the taxation of indirect transfers,[15] the Taxable Canadian Property (TCP) rules in Canada,[16] and the Australian provisions requiring withholding tax on the sale of taxable Australian real property (TARP) by the purchaser.[17]

MINE REHABILITATION

Mine rehabilitation can be a significant expense relating to coal mining. Different parties may have responsibility for rehabilitation, and there are variations as to whether the funding for rehabilitation is provided without security, provided with security such as assets, parent company guarantee, or a bank letter of credit, or provided on the basis of contribution to a fund owned by the government or by an independent fund.

The principal tax issue is similar to the decommissioning issue in upstream oil and gas, in that deductions for the related expenses are generally only available at the end of a project, after the majority of income has been earned. As a result the company incurring these costs may not be able to use the related deductions.

Many countries may only allow a deduction when the rehabilitation expense is incurred, generally including Australia, Denmark, Norway, Zambia, Chile, Peru, and the United Kingdom (UK). The US allows deductions when expenses are incurred or on an accruals basis by election.[18]

There have been several structures intended to provide deductions in such counties at an earlier time, for example on the basis of the payment of a fee in advance to carry out the reclamation at a future time. The availability of such deductions depends on the anti-avoidance rules and any restrictions on prepayment of future expenses.[19]

---

14. Pietro Guj, Stephanie Martin, Bryan Maybee, Frederick Cawood, Boubacar Bocoum, Nishana Gosai & Steef Huibregtse, Transfer Pricing in Mining with a Focus on Africa A Reference Guide for Practitioners, World Bank, January 2017, 85.
15. Income Tax Act, 1961–2017 section 9(1)(i), as amended in 2012 after the Vodafone case: *Vodafone International Holdings B.V v. Union of India*, Supreme Court of India Civil Appellate Jurisdiction, Civil Appeal No. 733 of 2012. Section 9(1)(i) Explanation five states: 'For the removal of doubts, it is hereby clarified that an asset or a capital asset being any share or interest in a company or entity registered or incorporated outside India shall be deemed to be and shall always be deemed to have been situated in India, if the share or interest derives, directly or indirectly, its value substantially from the assets located in India.'
16. Section 116, Income Tax Act.
17. Income Tax Assessment Act 1997 section 855-30, and Taxation Administration Act 1953 Div.14-D.
18. Internal Revenue Code §468, and Becky McLaughlin & Daniel Love, Basics of U.S. Mining Taxation, 2012 Americas School of Mines, 37, https://www.pwc.com/gx/en/mining/school-of-mines/2012/pwc-basics-of-mining-taxation-us.pdf on 15 August 2017.
19. Australian Taxation Office, Taxpayer Alert TA 2009/3.

A number of countries have reclamation provisions which allow deductions on the basis of contributions to a related fund, including Ghana, India, Mozambique, South Africa, Zambia, and Canada.[20] In Canada, the Qualifying Environmental Trust (QET) provisions allow a deduction for contributions made to a QET with the sole purpose of funding the reclamation of a site in Canada which was used for specified activities including mining. The income earned in the QET subject to tax at the trust level. The beneficiary is also required to report the income and is allowed a credit for tax paid by the QET.[21]

ENVIRONMENT ISSUES AND COAL TAXES

Countries may impose specific taxes on coal, as compared to carbon taxes which apply to several energy sources. In India, the National Clean Energy Fund (NCEF) was created in 2010 based on a clean energy cess coal tax. The tax rate in 2017 of INR 200 per tonne of coal or lignite sold applies to coal mined in India and imported coal. The use of the funds raised may include loans and direct funding to support renewable and clean environment projects:

- Carbon dioxide (CO2) emissions are a major concern with coal power stations. This issue can potentially be controlled by measures including carbon capture and storage (CCS), which captures CO2 emissions before or after the coal is burnt, and then stores the CO2 in a secure and permanent manner.[22]
- Coal-fired power stations emissions also include particulate matter, sulphur dioxide, and nitrogen oxides. The NCEF has reported that in India, coal-based thermal power plants are responsible for a disproportionate share of emissions from the industrial sector. Manufacturers including Mitsubishi, GE-Alstom, and BHEL have related pollution-control technologies which can be fitted to existing power stations.[23]

On the basis there may be a significant improvement in the environment performance of coal as a principal energy source.[24] Specific project funding, together

20. H. Choudhury, O. Fjellsa, C. Sanger & B.G. Twomey, United Nations Tax Committee's Subcommittee on Extractive Industries Taxation Issues for Developing Countries, Guidance Note on the Tax Treatment of Decommissioning for the Extractive Industries, October 2016 Draft, 14, http://www.un.org/esa/ffd/wp-content/uploads/2016/10/12STM_CRP3_AttachmentA_Decommissioning.pdf at 15 August 2017.
21. Income Tax Act, Subsection 211.6(1), and KPMG, A Guide to Canadian Mining Taxation, Third Edition, 29 February 2016. https://assets.kpmg.com/content/dam/kpmg/pdf/2016/04/KPMG-Mining-Taxation-Guide-2016.pdf on 15 August 2017.
22. Chevron, Gorgon Project Fact Sheet, Carbon Dioxide Injection Project, https://www.chevronaustralia.com/docs/default-source/default-document-library/fact-sheet-gorgon-co2-injection-project.pdf?sfvrsn = 16 on 14 August 2017.
23. Indian Government, Centre for Science and Environment, Policy Brief, Using the National Clean Energy Fund to Clean Coal Power Plants, 2017, 6, http://www.cseindia.org/userfiles/NCEF.pdf on 14 August 2017.
24. Indian Government, Centre for Science and Environment, Policy Brief, Using the National Clean Energy Fund to Clean Coal Power Plants, 2017, http://www.cseindia.org/userfiles/NCEF.pdf on 14 August 2017.

with loans and grants sourced from coal taxes, may potentially address these environmental concerns.

VAT AND IMPORT TARIFFS

Value Added Tax (VAT) or equivalent taxes may be imposed by many producing countries on the production of coal for domestic use, and by importing countries on coal importation.[25] The VAT is paid by the producer or importer, and then included in the coal sale price to purchasers, with VAT registered business purchasers then allowed a credit for the VAT paid. VAT is commonly zero-rated for coal exports, where VAT is not charged but the exporter is able to recover VAT on their related purchases. There may also be lower VAT rates which apply to coal, for example in Ireland where coal is offered for sale solely as fuel.[26]

A significant consideration for coal exporters is import tariffs, which may be imposed by the importing country based on the value of imported coal.[27] Examples of free trade agreements relating to the largest coal exporting countries include:

- The China Australia Free Trade Agreement (ChAFTA),[28] which eliminates the Chinese 3% import tariff on coking coal and the 6% import tariff on thermal coal.[29]
- Import duties from the US to the European Union (EU), which commonly transfer coal to other EU states via the Netherlands at nil under EU tariff rules.[30]
- The Agreement on Trade in Goods of the China-ASEAN Free Trade Agreement,[31] which eliminates China's import tariffs on coal imports from Indonesia.[32]

25. For example, imported coal is generally subject to the VAT standard rate on importation to the UK from a non-EU country, U Government, Commodity information for 2701121000, https://www.trade-tariff.service.gov.uk/trade-tariff/commodities/2701121000 on 16 August 2017.
26. Value Added Tax Consolidation Act 2010, section 46 and Schedule 3, section 17(1). The standard 23% rate is reduced to 13.5%.
27. The primary Harmonised System (HS) Code for coal generally used in trade agreements is 2701.
28. Free Trade Agreement between the Government of Australia and the Government of the People's Republic of China, 17 June 2015, [2015] ATS 15 (entry into force on 20 December 2015).
29. Australian Department of Foreign Affairs and Trade, Chine-Australia Free Trade Agreement, 2016, http://dfat.gov.au/trade/agreements/chafta/fact-sheets/Documents/fact-sheet-resources-energy-and-manufacturing.pdf on 16 August 2017.
30. TARIC measure Information, Goods nomenclature Code 2701, http://ec.europa.eu/taxation_customs/dds2/taric/measures.jsp?Lang=en&SimDate=20170816&Area=US&Taric=2701&LangDescr=en at 16 August 2017, also *see* European parliament, Parliamentary questions, 5 December 2006, P-4785/2006, Answer given by Mr Mandelson on behalf of the Commission, http://www.europarl.europa.eu/sides/getAllAnswers.do?reference=P-2006-4785&language=EN on 16 August 2017.
31. Agreement on Trade in Goods of the Framework Agreement on Comprehensive Economic Co-operation between China and ASEAN.
32. Products and Programme of Tariff Reduction for Early Harvest Programme, Normal Track, Normal Track 2 and Sensitive List for Trade in Goods Agreement Under the Framework Agreement on Comprehensive Economic Co-Operation Between ASEAN and the People's Republic of China, 39.

CHAPTER 10
Power Stations and Electricity Networks

INTRODUCTION

Power stations and electricity networks are generally large-scale investments, with a significant number of activities in relation to electric power generation including:[1]

- Conventional fossil fuel power generation utilising coal, gas, diesel, and waste heat fuels.
- Renewable energy including solar photovoltaic (PV), wind, solar thermal, hydroelectric, pumped hydro, tidal, geothermal, and biomass.
- Transmission and distribution networks including power lines and substations to efficiently, effectively, and reliably deliver power to meet market needs.
- Emerging energy storage technologies such as batteries, and their applications within the energy sector.
- Grid connection of both generation and large end-users, including feasibility, system modelling and negotiation of performance standards and access.
- Regulation of electricity networks, including related due diligence and advisory services.

Power stations may be categorised as: (1) Base load, which is intended to operate at almost full capacity most of the time. (2) Peaking, which is available for generation on very short notice and dispatched at times of maximum electricity need, and (3) Mid-merit, which adjusts power output as demand for electricity fluctuates throughout the day. Base load power stations may cost more to build per megawatt, but cost less to run, compared to peaking plants which may cost less to build but generate more expensive electricity.[2]

1. GHD, Power, http://www.ghd.com/global/markets/energy--resources/power/ on 23 August 2017.
2. Stephen Peppiatt, 'Introduction to Power Station Project Financing', Berkeley Journal of International Law, (1995) vol. 13(1), 50.

The power purchase agreement (PPA) is the key contract between the electricity generator and the private or government electricity distributor 'offtaker'. The PPA essentially defines the output of the generating assets and the credit of its associated income streams. These agreements may range from fifteen to thirty years, and include provisions on the related tax regime and concessions, and the effects of tax or regulatory law changes. The PPA will generally include an energy charge, to cover the electricity generated by the power station based on marginal costs incurred when the power station produces energy, and a capacity charge for the power station's ability to generate electricity to cover the costs of building and the investors' return. A 'take or pay' structure may be used in some cases to purchase irrespective of market conditions, for example based on a minimum level of electricity supply.

Long-term contracts for supply of oil, gas, coal, or uranium commodities to an electric power station operator may diminish the economic risks for the operator, and justify the investment in the operator's power station facility. These agreements may also provide the commodity seller with a reliable cash flow, and justify their own infrastructure investments to develop these natural resources. The contracts also result in a loss of flexibility, however, particularly where there are major variations in market prices in favour of the commodity seller or buyer. Responses to this issue include the use of pricing clauses with reference to spot market prices, or the use of price review clauses which require renegotiation on a regular basis such as every three or five years. Risk sharing mechanisms may also include coal, gas, oil, or uranium commodity sellers requiring a price floor, to ensure that there will always be sufficient cash flow to meet debt obligations, and the power station operator requiring price caps to ensure affordable supplies.[3]

Renewable energy power stations including hydroelectric, wind and solar power do not require these supplies for energy production. Hydroelectric power has an advantage of water storage in dams, whereas other renewable energy power plants such as wind and solar require other storage means such as batteries or the use of pumped storage, where water is pumped to higher elevations for subsequent generation of hydroelectric power. Renewable energy has historically had higher costs, which may be supported by higher feed-in tariffs and environmental tax incentives.

Electricity grid networks are primarily based on: (1) electricity transmission networks, which transfer electricity at high voltage from power stations to substations,[4] and (2) electricity distribution networks, which deliver electricity at lower voltages from substations to electricity retailers and industrial, commercial, and

3. Louis Chiam & Vishal Ahuja, Long-Term Supply Contracts – Time For Review, Australian Resources and Energy Law Journal (2006) vol. 25, 149.
4. In the United States, the North American Electric Reliability Corporation (NERC) has oversight of the network, and oversees four regional transmission organizations (RTOs) and seven independent system operators (ISOs), United States Electricity Industry Primer, U.S. Department of Energy, DOE/OE-0017. The UK has a single system operator, National Grid Electricity Transmission plc, three regional transmission operators, National Grid Electricity Transmission plc, Scottish Power Transmission Limited, and Scottish Hydro Electric Transmission plc. Ofgem, The GB electricity transmission network, https://www.ofgem.gov.uk/electricity/transmission-networks/gb-electricity-transmission-network on 24 August 2017.

domestic users.[5] These networks may be an integrated utility business including power stations, for example with a number of large United States (US) utilities.[6] The networks may also be separately owned and operated, with transmission networks able to take power from different energy producers, and distribution networks providing electricity to retailers and consumers.

The largest asset value is generally in the longer distance transmission networks, and may include step up transformer substations at power stations, and step down transformers at local substations. Network controls are required to provide for base load and peak loads and failure protection. Distribution networks may have very high commercial value however, based on their access to industrial, commercial, and retail customers.

There has also been a trend towards increasing cross-border electricity interconnections, which can be used to balance mismatches in supply and demand and peak capacity savings, integrate variable renewable energy supplies, and access remote energy resources. These interconnections have some similar tax characteristics to cross-border pipelines, such as whether the networks constitute permanent establishments, the attribution of income to permanent establishments, and the use of treaty agreements for related revenue sharing between source, transit, and destination states.[7]

The Energy Charter Secretariat has issued the Model Intergovernmental and Host Government Agreements for Cross-Border Electricity Projects.[8] The Electricity Model Agreements (EMA) comprise the Intergovernmental Agreement (IGA) and Host Government Agreement (HGA) to assist parties to negotiate a final agreement, on a similar basis to the Secretariat's Pipeline Model Agreements (PMA). Large-scale current and planned electricity interconnection arrangements include:[9]

- European Network of Transmission System Operators for Electricity (ENTSO-E) was established in 2008, between forty-two transmission system operators (TSOs) in thirty-five European Union (EU) and non-EU countries.[10]

5. *Ibid*, the UK has fourteen licensed distribution network operators.
6. US integrated power utilities include Duke Energy, NRG Energy, Southern Company, NextEra Energy, and American Electric Power, Reuters, Factbox: Largest U.S. electric companies by megawatts, customers, http://www.reuters.com/article/us-efh-bankruptcy-utilities-idUSBREA3S0P420140429 on 24 August 2017.
7. OECD and International Energy Agency, Large-Scale Electricity Interconnection Technology and Prospects for Cross-regional Networks, 2016, https://www.iea.org/publications/freepublications/publication/Interconnection.pdf on 24 August 2017.
8. Energy Charter Secretariat, Model Intergovernmental and Host Government Agreements for Cross-Border Electricity Projects, http://www.energycharter.org/fileadmin/DocumentsMedia/Legal/EMAs_en.pdf on 25 August 2017.
9. Karolis Gudas, Cross-border electricity infrastructures and efficient use of renewable energy sources.
10. Related EU measures include Directive 2009/72/EC concerning common rules for the internal market in electricity, Regulation (EC) No. 714/2009 on conditions for access to the network for cross-border exchanges in electricity, and Regulation (EC) No. 713/2009 of the European Parliament and of the Council of 13 July 2009 establishing an Agency for the Cooperation of Energy Regulators. ENTSO, European Network of Transmission System Operators for Electricity, https://www.entsoe.eu/Pages/default.aspx on 25 August 2017.

- Southern African Power Pool (SAPP) was established in 1995 with twelve member countries.[11]
- Central American Electrical Interconnection System, *Sistema de Interconexión Eléctrica de los Países de América Central* (SIEPAC) is the interconnection of power grids of six countries.[12]
- The Gobitec and Asian Supergrid (ASG) projects are intended to produce energy from renewable sources in the Gobi Desert for transmission to Russia, Mongolia, China, South Korea, and Japan.[13]

The use of treaties and model agreements should assist in project negotiations, providing transparency regarding present practices in the areas of cross-border electricity project construction, operation and investment, shortening lead-times for the mobilisation of project-specific investment, and reducing the cost of project implementation. The Energy Charter models follow the general structure of the pipeline models, with significant issues including the way in which the physical infrastructure fits into the electricity systems of the jurisdictions involved.

PROJECT FUNDING

A large proportion of power station and electricity network developments are funded on a project finance basis, where lender's primary sources of security are the assets and cash flows of the project. This enables the project sponsors not to assume balance sheet risks for large projects. There may be a significant reduction in funding costs where loans, loan guarantees or insurance has been provided by an export credit agency (ECA) which provides support to goods and services exporters from their respective countries, or multilateral development banks (MDB) such as the World Bank and the Asian Development Bank.[14]

On a similar basis to other large-scale energy infrastructure, power stations and electricity networks requires a high level of initial investment, and do not generate revenue to finance debt repayment until the station is completed. The non-completion

11. Related agreements include the Intergovernmental Memorandum of Understanding, Inter-Utility Memorandum of Understanding, Agreement Between Operating Members and the Operating Guidelines. Southern Africa Power Pool, http://www.sapp.co.zw/ on 25 August 2017.
12. The SIEPAC member counties are Panama, Costa Rica, Honduras, Nicaragua, El Salvador, and Guatemala. SEMI, SIEPAC: An innovative electric interconnection system in Central America, http://www.semi.es/news/siepac-an-innovative-electric-interconnection-system-in-central-america.html on 25 August 2017.
13. International Energy Charter, Gobitec and the Asian Supergrid for Renewable Energy Sources in Northeast Asia (2014), http://www.energycharter.org/what-we-do/investment/investment-thematic-reports/gobitec-and-the-asian-supergrid-for-renewable-energy-sources-in-northeast-asia-2014/ on 25 August 2017.
14. Multilateral Development Banks include the World Bank, International Fund for Agricultural Development (IFAD), European Investment Bank (EIB), Islamic Development Bank (IsDB), Asian Development Bank (ADB), European Bank for Reconstruction and Development (EBRD), CAF – Development Bank of Latin America (CAF), Inter-American Development Bank Group (IDB, IADB), African Development Bank (AfDB), and Asian Infrastructure Investment Bank (AIIB).

is an important issue in power station funding, and may require express commitments from the project sponsors or relate to ECA or MDB guarantees.

Funding structures for power stations or electricity networks include public-private partnerships (PPP) between the public and private sectors for the provision of power station assets or electricity. These agreements generally allocate risks between the partners, and may create efficiency incentives for the service provider by linking payments to performance criteria. The private sector is required to provide the related capital expenditure, and the public sector purchases power over a specified period of time. PPP arrangements include build–operate–transfer (BOT) and build–own–operate–transfer (BOOT) models, where private entities receives a concession from the public sector to finance, design, construct, own, and operate the facility.

The World Bank issued a report on power project finance in developing countries.[15] The report commented that changes in tax laws can increase project costs, and that in many cases the power purchase agreement specifies that cost increases resulting from these changes may be passed through to the utility under the power tariff. In some cases project sponsors can exercise options to terminate the project, triggering the obligation by the utility or host government to buy out the project. This may apply where the sponsor's investment is materially reduced by new or modified laws or regulations, or tax stability clauses for agreed periods of power revenues.

TAX ISSUES

The taxation issues for the funding structure include the use of debt and equity, and the deductions available for local country interest costs. This includes the use of thin capitalisation provisions which may deny deductions where the interest rate exceeds an arm's length amount. These measures have been based on measures such as a debt-to-equity ratio. Measures which are based on earnings before interest, taxes, depreciation and amortisation (EBITDA) have been adopted by an increasing number of countries and are proposed in the OECD BEPS Action 4.[16] The EBITDA approach may potentially result in additional interest disallowance in cases such as low electricity market prices or the use of carry-forward tax losses.

Profit repatriation and withholding tax is a significant planning issue, including whether withholding tax applies to dividends paid from the local country, and whether the tax rate can be reduced by favourable tax treaties. Treaty shopping structures which use intermediate holding companies in countries with favourable treaty networks are addressed OECD BEPS measures, including BEPS Action 6 on inappropriate treaty benefits,[17] and related minimum standards in the BEPS Action 15 Multilateral

15. Suman Babbar & John Schuster, World Bank, Power Project Finance, Experience in Developing Countries, RMC Discussion Paper Series, Number 119, 1998, 31.
16. OECD, Limiting Base Erosion Involving Interest Deductions and Other Financial Payments, Action 4 - 2016 Update, 2016.
17. OECD, Action 6, 2015 Final Report, Preventing the Granting of Treaty Benefits in Inappropriate Circumstances, p. 17.

Instrument (MLI) Article 7.[18] These measures can include the principal purpose test or limitation on benefits tests to potentially deny treaty benefits in treaty shopping cases.

Local country tax concessions may include tax holidays and reduced tax rates for the power generation industry. Vietnam, for example, provides a concessional 10% tax rate for the fifteen-year period beginning with the first year of revenue may be available for income from new investment projects that are engaged in the development of power plants.[19] Asset depreciation rates also have a significant effect on local country taxation, including the extent to which the very high value plant and machinery in power stations and electricity transmission and distribution networks can qualify for accelerated depreciation rates.

There is also an issue with tax grouping and other tax consolidation regimes. Integrated utilities which combine power generation, transmission, and distribution may benefit from tax consolidation where different parts of the business are profitable or in losses due to market forces such as cost of coal or gas used in power stations, maintenance, or repair of transmission networks, or competition in retail electricity markets.

The availability of tax loss carry forwards is a significant issue for the industry because of the costs of the initial planning and construction stages of a new power plant or electricity distribution network. Limitations on the loss carry-forward period may result in tax losses which cannot be used to offset future income.

TRANSFER PRICING

Transfer pricing issues can relate to power station and transmission projects in separate legal entities in different countries, with a foreign head office or regional head office company providing development, engineering, and management services, group treasury companies for hedging and related derivatives, and the use of group IP management companies.

Development Process – The development process for power stations and electricity distribution networks has several key components, including:[20]

- Site assessment, energy capacity evaluation, resource availability, community responses, and land use rights.
- Procurement, financing, capital costs, and construction.
- Ongoing operations can include plant operation and ongoing power sales.

The key milestones are generally the operational approval for the project, and the PPA, and the earlier stages of the development carry a higher risk. For transfer pricing

18. OECD, Action 15, 2015 Final Report, Developing a Multilateral Instrument to Modify Bilateral Tax Treaties, and the Multilateral Convention to Implement Tax Treaty Related Measures to Prevent Base Erosion and Profit Shifting, opened for signature 7 June 2017, Article 7.
19. EY, Worldwide Corporate Tax Guide 2016, 1634.
20. Shannon Blankenship, Allison Easley & Christine Piar, Deloitte, Renewables: Transfer Pricing and Selected Tax Issues for Renewable Energy, International Tax Review, 9 July 2012, http://www.internationaltaxreview.com/Article/3057712/Renewables-Transfer-pricing-and-selected-tax-issues-for-renewable-energy.html on 23 August 2017.

purposes, a higher development fee may therefore apply where the developer has borne the related risks for a longer period.[21]

Engineering and management – The engineering and management services which may be provided by related companies to a power station project include:[22]

- Conceptual design and feasibility studies;
- Power plant sitting;
- Engineering design;
- Procurement services;
- Construction and project management;
- Engineering, Procurement, Construction Management (EPCM);
- Owner's Engineer and Independent Engineer roles;
- Operations phase asset management;
- Power plant performance assessment and audit;
- Maintenance planning and remaining life assessments; and
- Due diligence of power generating assets.

The group engineering company may provide specialised services to independent clients as well as related parties, and may charge a fee to its independent clients based on a fixed hourly rate that compares with the hourly rate charged by competitors for similar services in the same market. For transfer pricing purposes, the provision of similar services to a related party power company may potentially be made on the same basis using the price charged to independent clients as an internal comparable price. Issues may arise however if the power station country also has engineering expertise and comparable rates within the country are lower for the same quality of work.[23]

Commodity Purchases – Power station may purchase oil, gas, coal, or uranium from related mining or production or procurement companies, and the transfer pricing issue will be whether these purchases are made at arm's length prices. In general commodity prices are published and provide some guide to appropriate prices which would have been paid by independent parties, however in practice there can be substantial variations in prices due to factors such as quantities and delivery terms. Related OECD BEPS developments include Country-by-Country (CbC) reporting which can show the financial returns of the related group companies.[24]

Hedging Arrangements – Power station and transmission companies may enter into hedging or foreign exchange arrangements with related parties, for example: (1) using derivatives such as forward contracts or swaps to hedge the future purchase of

21. *Ibid*, United States cost sharing regulations can take into account the related risk profile. Analysis under the income method for comparable uncontrolled transaction (CUT) and comparable profits method (CPM), include risk adjustments.
22. GHD, Power Generation, http://www.ghd.com/global/services/power-generation/ at 23 August 2017.
23. OECD Transfer Pricing Guidelines for Multinational Enterprises and Tax Administrations, 2017, para. 9.130 p. 412.
24. OECD BEPS Action 13 Transfer Pricing Documentation and Country-by-Country Reporting Action 13: 2015 Final Report, and OECD Transfer Pricing Guidelines for Multinational Enterprises and Tax Administrations 2017, (Chapter 5 Documentation) p. 229.

coal or gas required for electricity generation with group procurement or trading companies, (2) transmission or distribution companies using hedging arrangements for electricity supply prices, or (3) companies using swaps in relation to foreign currency risks relating to borrowings from group treasury companies. The related transfer pricing issues include whether independent entities would have entered into these arrangements, and what term would have been provided by independent trading companies or banks.

Distribution Networks – There are also transfer pricing issues in relation to the intangible property (IP) used in electricity distribution networks. For example, related trademarks recognised by industrial, commercial, and domestic users may be purchased by a Group IP management company as part of an acquisition, and royalties may then be paid by the distribution company for the use of the trademarks. The related OECD BEPS measures include Actions 8–10,[25] and the OECD Transfer Pricing Guidelines 2017,[26] where the returns on the use of intangibles should not be based solely on the ownership of the IP.

25. OECD, Aligning Transfer Pricing Outcomes with Value Creation, Actions 8–10: 2015 Final Reports, p. 73.
26. OECD Transfer Pricing Guidelines for Multinational Enterprises and Tax Administrations 2017, Chapter 6, para. 6.32, 257.

CHAPTER 11

Renewable Energy: Supply, Funding, and Taxation Incentives

INTRODUCTION

Incentives for renewable energy include feed-in tariffs to purchase renewable energy, grants and loan funding for new projects, tax incentives for R&D, and tax credits and capital allowances for new project spending.

SUPPLY AND FUNDING INCENTIVES

Supply and funding incentives are available in many countries for renewable energy projects. The related incentives, including comments from a World Bank report, are as follows:[1]

- Power Purchase Arrangements – Feed-in Tariffs and Renewable Portfolio Standards – Governments may agree to purchase power from specific renewable projects at set or minimum feed-in tariffs (FIT) prices to encourage non-government equity and loan funding for the investment. Renewable Portfolio Standards (RPS) places an obligation on electricity supply companies to produce a required portion of electricity from renewable energy sources.
- Equity or Project Loan Funding – This incentive may involve a government agency providing equity, loans, or guarantees to specific renewable energy projects. The level of government support may then provide the basis for non-government co-investors in the renewables project.

1. Nathalie McGregor & Sebastian James, Providing Incentives for Investments in Renewable Energy, Advice for policymakers, World Bank Group, Investment Climate in Practice, No. 19 November 2011.

- Grants – Grants are non-loan payments which can provide substantial assistance to renewables projects. This may include grant support for the construction of large solar power stations and the development of a range of renewable energy technology. Grants may also be combined with loan funding, for example by providing a combined 20% grant/80% loan support for renewable power projects.
- Research and Development (R&D) funding – This type of funding may be allocated through competitive grants. The Word Bank report commented that at least twelve countries offer R&D funding for renewable energy technology.
- Equipment rebates – These rebates usually target specific types of renewable energy technology, including rebates for photovoltaic equipment to support solar power. At least fifteen countries provide equipment rebates.

TAXATION INCENTIVES

There is a wide range of incentives which can apply to renewable energy producers. The incentives, including comments from the related World Bank report, are as follows:[2]

- Investment subsidies and tax holidays – This may include investment tax credits, investment allowances, and accelerated depreciation linked to the amount of the related investment. Investment allowances are generally one-time deductions of capital costs in addition to regular depreciation, such as the allowance in India for 100% deduction of the capital costs of renewable energy projects. Tax incentive may also include tax holidays, which exempt the profits of renewable energy producers for a fixed term. A related issue is that renewable projects are long-term investments, so that tax losses from the early years of projects generally need to be carried forward to later years when firms start to generate profits.
- Spending on research and development – Renewable energy technology is currently evolving, and many countries provide additional deductions for R&D spending which allow for 100% or higher tax deductions for related costs.
- Production-based incentives – Production-based incentives provide tax deductions, based on the amount of energy produced, to encourage generation of renewable energy.
- Indirect tax reductions – Value added tax, sales tax, and import duty exemptions may be provided which lower the cost of inputs, such as equipment and systems, required to generate renewable energy. Property tax exemptions may be allowed for land purchased or leased to generate renewable energy.

2. *Ibid.*

COUNTRY EXAMPLES

The related funding and, taxation and incentive measures for renewable energy are subject to significant changes over time. The following summaries are therefore provided as examples of related measures, and current developments should always be reviewed for the analysis of specific countries. The principal references used include Taxes and incentives for renewable energy, 2015, by KPMG International,[3] and the Deloitte 2017 Survey of Global Investment and Innovation Incentives.[4]

Australia

The principal Australian Federal Government measures to support renewable energy include development and commercialised funding together with the R&D tax incentive.

Australian Renewable Energy Agency

The Australian Renewable Energy Agency (ARENA) is an Australian Government agency created in 2012 to increase the competitiveness of renewable energy and increase its supply in Australia. Renewables project are required to have an identified pathway to commercialisation and co-investment from the project proponent and/or other financial supporters:[5]

- The Emerging Renewables Program (ERP) includes: (1) Project funding available for renewable energy and enabling technologies and products as they move through the technology innovation chain generally from AUD 2 million to AUD 30 million, and (2) Measure funding available for initiatives that involve a renewable energy industry capacity building activity, skills development activity, or a preparatory activity for an ARENA Project generally up to AUD 3 million.
- The Supporting High value Australian Renewable Energy Knowledge (SHARE) initiative includes: (1) the Research and Development Program (RDP) which is focused on supporting R&D activities that will contribute to increasing the commercial deployment of renewable energy with up to AUD 300 million in grants allocated, and (2) the Accelerated Step Change Initiative (ASCI) which supports breakthrough projects not otherwise eligible under other programmes, with contributions of AUD 5 million or more and overall project cost over AUD 20 million.

---

3. KPMG, Taxes and incentives for renewable energy, 2015, KPMG International (kpmg.com/energytax on 17 July 2017).
4. Deloitte, 2017 Survey of Global Investment and Innovation Incentives, March 2017, https://www2.deloitte.com/content/dam/Deloitte/us/Documents/Tax/us-tax-surveyof-global-investment-and-innovation-incentives.pdf on 17 July 2017.
5. Australian Renewable Energy Agency, Annual Report 2015–2016, https://arena.gov.au/assets/2017/02/AR21288-ARENA-Accessibility-file_LR.pdf on 17 July 2017.

Clean Energy Finance Corporation

The Clean Energy Finance Corporation (CEFC) was established by the Australian Government in 2012 as a commercially oriented financing entity which would make a positive return on its investments. CEFC focuses on technologies and projects that are in the later stage of development, which can produce a positive rate of return, and which provide the ability to repay capital. The aim is to accelerating delivery of projects that use renewable energy, energy efficient, or low-emissions technologies to reduce energy consumption while lowering carbon emissions. CEFC had made commitments of AUD 2.43 billion on projects with total value of AUD 5.7 billion by 2016.[6]

It was announced in 2016 that Clean Energy Innovation Fund would be established to be jointly managed by ARENA and the CEFC. The Fund will provide equity and/or debt to clean energy, low emissions, and energy efficiency projects.

Feed-in Tariffs: State Government and Retailer Measures

Feed-in tariffs are offered under mandatory or voluntary schemes in several Australian states and territories, including buyback rates for unused electricity provided by retail customers back to the electricity grid. Mandatory schemes are based on a minimum required to be paid by energy retailers to small scale providers under state regulations, whereas voluntary schemes are based on rates determined by electricity retailers.

As in 2017, the state systems and approximate tariff rates paid to small scale producers such as home solar power installations were: Tasmania, mandatory system at 7¢/kWh, Victoria, voluntary 6–10¢/kWh; Queensland, voluntary or mandatory at 6–8¢/kWh in regional areas; New South Wales, voluntary system at 6–12¢/kWh; South Australia, voluntary system at 6–12¢/kWh; Australian Capital Territory, voluntary system at 6–8¢/kWh; and the Northern Territory, variable rate set by the respective power retailers.[7]

Research and Development Tax Incentive

The R&D tax incentive encourages companies to engage in R&D benefitting Australia, by providing a tax offset for eligible R&D activities. The incentive provides:[8]

- A 43.5% refundable tax offset for eligible entities with an aggregated turnover of less than AUD 20 million per annum, provided they are not controlled by income tax exempt entities.

6. Clean Energy Finance Corp, Annual Report 2015–2016, http://annualreport2016.cleanenergy financecorp.com.au/media/1243/cefc-annual-report-2015-16.pdf on 17 July 2017.
7. Solar Choice, State Solar Feed-In Tariffs, https://www.solarchoice.net.au/solar-rebates/solar-feed-in-rewards on 17 July 2017.
8. Research and development tax incentive, Australian Taxation Office, https://www.ato.gov.au/business/research-and-development-tax-incentive/about-the-program/ on 17 July 2017.

- A 38.5% non-refundable tax offset for all other eligible entities (entities may be able to carry forward unused offset amounts to future income years).

The rate of the R&D tax offset is reduced to the company tax rate for that portion of an entity's notional R&D deductions that exceed AUD 100 million for an income year.

Generally, only R&D activities conducted in Australia qualify for the R&D tax incentive. However, R&D activities conducted overseas also qualify if approved by Innovation and Science Australia. The R&D activities must be classified as either core R&D activities or supporting R&D activities:

Core R&D activities are experimental activities:

- Whose outcome cannot be known or determined in advance on the basis of current knowledge, information, or experience, but can only be determined by applying a systematic progression of work that is based on principles of established science; and proceeds from hypothesis to experiment, observation, and evaluation, and leads to logical conclusions.
- Are conducted for the purpose of generating new knowledge, including about creating new knowledge or improved materials, products, devices, processes, or services.

Supporting activities are directly related to core R&D activities, or are undertaken for the dominant purpose of supporting core R&D activities such as activities which relate to producing goods or services.

The Australian Taxation Office (ATO) and the Department of Industry, Innovation, and Science jointly administer the R&D tax incentive. The R&D activities must be registered with the Department of Industry, Innovation, and Science before the tax offset is claimed, and the ATO then determines if the expenditure is eligible for the R&D tax offset.

China

Incentives for renewable energy in China include feed-in tariffs, government funding, and allowances, the super deduction for eligible R&D, and reduced tax rates for High-New Technology Enterprises.

Feed-In Tariffs

Feed-in tariff incentives may be provided under the Renewable Energy Law effective from 2010 on the price of on-grid electricity generated by renewable energies determined by the related price department of the State Council. The National Development and Reform Commission published 2017 rates feed-in tariffs, including rates for photovoltaic (PV) energy including solar power of between CNY 0.65/kWh and CNY

0.85/kWh, depending on the region. The new tariff structure was designed to encourage the eastern region to develop new energy sources, reduce coal consumption and greenhouse gas emissions, and promote air quality improvement.[9]

Government Funding and Allowances

Government funding is available to facilitate the development of renewable energy relating to scientific and technical research, standardisation processes and model engineering projects, renewable energy projects in rural and pastoral areas, construction of stand-alone electricity generation system in remote areas and islands, renewable energy resource surveys, evaluation and construction of information systems, and the localisation of manufacturing facilities used in the renewable energy sector. Funding may also be made to meet the higher costs charged by renewable energy plants and indirectly borne by the grid for the purchase of electricity from these plants.[10]

Reduced Tax Rates for Related Projects

A reduced Corporate Income Tax (CIT) rate of 15% is available to qualified advanced and new technology enterprises in fields including solar energy, wind energy, biomaterial energy, and geothermal energy. A three-year exemption of the CIT is followed by a 50% reduction for another three years of the standard CIT rate for income derived from specified Clean Development Mechanism (CDM) projects. This reduction is also allowed for income derived from qualified environmental protection and energy or water conservation projects.[11]

Qualified energy service companies (ESCOs) which develop, install, and arrange financing for projects that improve the energy efficiency of facilities can receive incentives including tax exemption in the first three years and a tax reduction by half (an effective rate of 12.5%) over the following three years, starting from the tax year in which the revenue from the project first arises. Where an EPC project lasts less than six years, the ESCO shall be entitled to the incentives based on the actual project period.

Super Deduction for Eligible R&D

A super deduction provides an extra 50% deduction for eligible R&D expenses. Tax losses attributable to R&D super deductions may be carried forward up to five years. The related expenses include direct and indirect labour expenses, depreciation, amortisation, design and testing, and other directly related expenses. Several industries

9. China unveils 2017 FIT rates and urges local tenders, Recharge, http://www.rechargenews.com/solar/1202461/china-unveils-2017-fit-rates-and-urges-local-tenders on 18 July 2017.
10. KPMG, Taxes and incentives for renewable energy, 2015, KPMG International, 23 (kpmg.com/energytax on 17 July 2017).
11. *Ibid*, 22.

are excluded under a negative list introduced in 2016, however energy production and power generation is included in the concession. Up to 80% of arm's length fees paid to contractors to perform research on the taxpayer's behalf also qualify for the concession.[12]

Reduced Tax Rates for High-New Technology Enterprises

A reduced 15% CIT rate is available for companies with High-New Technology Enterprise (HNTE) status. The qualifying activities include the development of new technology, new products, and new production techniques, and HNTE status is granted for a three-year term, with an annual review of the status during the three-year period. From 2016, companies qualify only where the technology plays a core supporting role in the main product/service of the company, and is included in one of the specified state-encouraged technology areas, including new energy and energy conservation, and resources and the environment.[13]

Germany

German incentives for renewable energy include loan funding from the KfW government-owned development bank, financial support under the market premium system, and R&D cash grants.[14]

KfW Programmes

The KfW Renewable Energies Programme supports projects related to the environment plants for electricity generation from renewable energy sources such as solar/photovoltaic (PV), biogas, hydro, onshore wind or geothermal energy, and heat generation in combined heat and power (CHP) systems. The funding is generally made as a long-term, interest-reduced loan of up to 100% of the investment costs up to EUR 25 million for each project.

The KfW Offshore Wind Energy Programme promotes offshore wind energy projects in the German Exclusive Economic Zone (EEZ) of the North and Baltic Seas, with the related measures including direct loans of to 70% of the total project debt and EUR 700 million for each project.

The KfW Energy Efficiency Programme provides low interest rates and repayment bonuses for commercial enterprises to invest in energy efficiency measures up to EUR 25 million per project for: (1) Production Systems/Processes; and (2) Energy-efficient construction and rehabilitation.

12. Deloitte, 2017 Survey of Global Investment and Innovation Incentives, March 2017, 38.
13. *Ibid*, 39.
14. KPMG, Taxes and incentives for renewable energy, 2015, KPMG International, 56 (kpmg.com/energytax on 17 July 2017).

KfW Energy Turnaround Financing Initiative loans up to EUR 100 million per project are available for large-scale investment projects in Germany in energy efficiency, innovative projects in energy conservation, electricity generation, storage and transmission, and use of renewable energy.

Ministry Funding

The Federal Ministry for the Environment, Nature Conservation, Building and Nuclear Safety (BMUB) funds major pilot projects in environmental sectors, including loans of up to 70% of project costs.

Financial Support

Financial support is currently available under the Renewable Energy Sources Act, *Erneuerbare-Energien-Gesetz* (EEG) 2017, with the level of financial support generally based on an auction process which replaced the previous FIT. To receive the market premium, *marktprämie,* from the grid operator, project developers bid in technology-specific auctions for certain tender volumes. The tender system generally applies to all onshore wind power plants, offshore wind power plants, solar power plants, and biomass power plants, with exceptions for small plants and prototypes. Geothermal energy will continue to use the feed-in tariff system. The renewable energy plant operator receives the market premium from the grid operator together with the agreed purchase price from the direct marketing counterparty. The average market premium in February 2017 was 6.58 ¢/kWh, with 9.17 ¢/kWh for ground-mounted solar power.[15]

R&D Cash Grants

R&D activities for the cash grants are generally required to be conducted in Germany, with exploitation of the results in Germany or the European Union (EU), and with the created IP held in Germany or the EU.[16]

General cash grants are available for qualifying activities, including: (1) industrial research, based on research with a specific practical objective aimed at developing new products, processes, or services, or at improving existing ones; (2) experimental development and demonstration actions, based on demonstration of new applications and/or research results; and (3) development of business models, based on analysis and implementation of innovative business models.

There are also targeted R&D grants, including: (1) energy efficiency research for industrial production, buildings, cities, power supply and storage, or renewable energy until 31 December 2018. Large enterprises may receive cash grants up to 50% of

15. Norton Rose Fulbright, German Renewable Energy Act 2017 (EEG 2017) – what you should know, April 2017.
16. Deloitte, 2017 Survey of Global Investment and Innovation Incentives, March 2017, 56.

eligible costs, and small and medium-sized enterprises (SME) may receive an additional 10% bonus; (2) digitisation and automation of production processes, including the Innovation for the production, services and work of tomorrow, Convergent ICT, and Human-machine interaction schemes.

India

Indian incentives for renewable energy include funding, feed-in tariffs, renewables purchase obligations, National Solar Mission, R&D super deductions, and the Patent Box regime.[17] Several related tax holiday incentives on infrastructure projects, including incentives for power generation projects, expired in 2017.

Funding

The Indian Renewable Energy Development Agency (IREDA) was established as a financing agency to promote and finance renewable energy projects.

Feed-in Tariffs

The Generation Based Incentive scheme can apply to wind power projects INR 0.50 per unit of power provided to the grid for up to ten years, subject to a ceiling of INR 10 million per MW.

Renewables Purchase Obligation

The Renewables Purchase Obligation (RPO) requires power distribution companies to purchase a percentage of total power requirements from renewable energy sources. State-level RPOs currently vary from 2% to 14% of total energy demand.

National Solar Mission

This initiative includes development of large-scale rooftop projects, solar parks, and other large-scale solar projects. These measures include auctions of solar projects by the Solar Energy Corporation of India (SECI).

R&D Super Deduction

India has several R&D incentives based on super deductions for R&D activities conducted in India:[18]

17. KPMG, Taxes and incentives for renewable energy, 2015, KPMG International, 38 (kpmg.com/energytax on 17 July 2017).
18. Deloitte, 2017 Survey of Global Investment and Innovation Incentives, March 2017, 56.

- The super deduction is available for R&D expenses of an R&D facility approved by the Department of Scientific and Industrial Research (DSIR). The deduction is at 150% until 31 March 2020 and applies to taxpayers engaged in the business of biotechnology, or manufacturing or producing products.
- The 100% super deduction is available from 2017 for specified payments made to a scientific research company, research association, university, college, or other institution for the purpose of scientific and statistical research. A higher 150% rate applies to payments to specific institutions until 2020.
- A 100% deduction is available for R&D expenses, other than land, that do not qualify for the super deductions.

Patent Box

The Indian Patent Box regime provides that from the 2016–2017 tax year, royalty income of an Indian resident that owns a patent developed and registered in India is taxed at a rate of 10% plus applicable surcharge and cess.

Japan

Incentives for renewable energy in Japan include the feed-in tariff and research and development tax incentives.[19]

Feed-In Tariff

Feed-in tariffs are available including rates in 2016 of JPY 29.16/kW for solar energy, and JPY 23.76/kW for wind power. The related requirements include government approval of the development plan, interconnection with the power company, and documentation on the related land and equipment purchases.

Research and Development Tax Incentives

The 2017 Tax Reform included an R&D tax credit generally allowed at 8% to 10%, with the rate depending on the increase or decrease ratio compared to prior years, with a temporary maximum 14% credit to 31 March 2019. The credit is limited to 25% of corporate tax before credit, with a 35% limit to 31 March 2019. There is also a 30% credit for joint R&D with a university or public research institution or where R&D is contracted to these entities.[20]

---

19. KPMG, Taxes and incentives for renewable energy, 2015, KPMG International, 44 (kpmg.com/energytax on 17 July 2017).
20. PWC, Japan, Corporate – Tax credits and incentives, http://taxsummaries.pwc.com/ID/Japan-Corporate-Tax-credits-and-incentives on 20 July 2017.

United Kingdom

The United Kingdom (UK) offers a substantial number of incentives which include FIT, renewables obligation, contract for differences, the Patent Box regime, and R&D tax incentives.[21]

Feed-In Tariff

Eligible renewable energy plants with a capacity of up to 5 MW must generally undergo an accreditation process, which may differ according to plant size and energy source. Once this process is completed and the plant has been accredited, the electricity exported to the grid by the plant is bought by the electricity supplier licensee at fixed rates.

Renewables Obligation

The Renewables Obligation is an example of a RPS, and is based on a quota obligation and certificate system. The Renewables Obligation Orders impose the obligation on electricity suppliers to prove that a certain proportion of electricity supplied was generated from renewable sources based on presentation of Renewables Obligation Certificates (ROC). The quota system applies to power plants above 5 MW, while plants between 50 kW and 5 MW can choose between the feed-in tariff system and the Renewables Obligation. The scheme was closed to new generating capacity on 31 March 2017.

Contract for Differences

The Contract for Difference (CfD) is based on contracts between a power generator and the Low Carbon Contracts Company (LCCC) owned by the UK Government. The CfD is based on the difference between the market price and an agreed strike price. Where the strike price is higher than market price, LCCC pays the difference to the power generator. Where the market price is higher than strike price, the power generator pays the difference to LCCC.

Patent Box Regime: Tax Incentive

The UK Patent Box regime taxes income relating to patents and certain other intellectual property at a rate of 10% by means of an additional deduction. The regime includes patents granted by UK and European patent offices and certain other patent offices in the European Economic Area. The concession applies to income arising from

21. Georgios Maroulis, Promotion in the United Kingdom, Legal Resources on Renewable Energy, http://www.res-legal.eu/search-by-country/united-kingdom/tools-list/c/united-kingdom/s/res-e/t/promotion/sum/204/lpid/203/ on 17 July 2017.

the patents, including royalties and income from the sale of patents, together with profits from the sale of products, services, and processes with embedded patents. Changes to the regime effective after 30 June 2016 apply to new IP or new claimants, and restricts the concession where the claimant company has outsourced development to a significant extent to related parties or has acquired the related IP.[22]

R&D Relief: Tax Incentive

The UK introduced R&D Relief provisions including the Large Company scheme for tax relief to be available for large companies by way of a deduction of 130% of qualifying R&D expenditure.[23] The R&D project must 'seek to achieve an advance in overall knowledge or capability in a field of science or technology through the resolution of scientific or technological uncertainty'. The R&D must be related to the company's trade, either as an existing trade, or a trade intended to be started up based on the R&D results. The provisions do not require ownership of the R&D, under changes from 9 December 2009. In relation to upstream oil and gas, the concession applies generally for R&D not directly relating to exploration and appraisal. Exploration and appraisal expenditure qualifies, however, for 100% deduction for corporation tax and supplementary charge. The related scheme for small- or medium-sized enterprises allows deductions of 230%.[24]

United States

The majority of state government in the United States (US) offer incentives including RPS. The US federal government offers incentives which include the Investment Tax Credit and Research Tax Credit.

Renewable Portfolio Standards

As in 2017, twenty-nine states have RPS.[25] The standard may be measured by percentages of kilowatt hours of retail electric sales, specific amounts of renewable energy capacity, or as a percentage of peak demand. The system in California, for example, provides a renewable portfolio standard as an obligation on electricity supply

22. Ernst & Young, 2016 Worldwide Corporate Tax Guide, 1535; Part 8A, Chapters 1–7 Corporation Tax Act 2010; and HM Revenue and Customs, Policy paper, Corporation Tax: Patent Box – compliance with new international rules, 9 December 2015.
23. Corporation Tax Act 2009, Part 13, Chapter 5, and HM Revenue and Customs, Guidance, Corporation tax: Research and Development Tax Relief for large companies.
24. HM Revenue and Customs, Guidance, Corporation Tax: Research and Development tax relief for small- or medium-sized enterprises, 19 October 2016.
25. Jocelyn Durkay, State Renewable Portfolio Standards and Goals, National Conference of State Legislatures, http://www.ncsl.org/research/energy/renewable-portfolio-standards.aspx on 24 July 2017.

companies to produce 50% of electricity from renewable energy sources by 2030.[26] The respective state requirements can differ in only applying to investor-owned utilities (IOUs), or also including municipalities and electricity cooperatives.

Investment Tax Credit (ITC)

The US provides the investment tax credit (ITC) for certain energy-related investments. The incentive was enacted in 1978 and has been substantially modified over time.[27] The ITC for non-solar technologies has generally been limited:[28]

- There is a permanent 10% ITC for solar and geothermal technologies. Temporarily, the credit rate for solar is 30% through 2019, 26% in 2020, and 22% in 2021, before reverting to 10% after 2021.
- Other property placed in service by the end of 2016 was also eligible for the ITC. Investments in small wind property of 100 kilowatts or less) may qualify for a 30% ITC, as can investments in fuel cell power plants. The credit for fuel cells is limited to USD 1,500 per 0.5 kilowatts in capacity. Investments in micro-turbines, combined heat and power (CHP) systems, and geothermal heat pumps qualify for a 10% ITC.
- The ITC for investments in geothermal energy property is permanent under current law with a 10% credit rate.

Research Tax Credit

The US provides a non-refundable research tax credit that can be applied to reduce income taxes under Internal Revenue Code (IRC) section 41 as an increment of qualified research spending exceeding a base amount. Qualifying R&D expenses are deductible, however taxpayers must reduce the current deduction by the amount of the tax credit. Taxpayers can elect to report one of the following research tax credits:[29]

- Traditional research tax credit – This credit is 20% of the amount of the qualified research expenses (QREs) exceeding a base amount. The base amount is determined by: (i) first determining the ratio of QREs to gross receipts for the period of 1984–1988. The fixed base percentage then is multiplied by the average annual gross receipts of the taxpayer for the four years preceding the credit year. There is a minimum base amount of 50% of the current year QREs.

26. Cal. Public Utilities Code §399.11, Cal. Public Resources Code §25740, CA A 327 (2013), and CA S 350 (2015).
27. Internal Revenue Code (IRC) section 48.
28. The Energy Credit: An Investment Tax Credit for Renewable Energy, Congressional Research Service, 7 October 2016.
29. Deloitte, 2017 Survey of Global Investment and Innovation Incentives, March 2017, 183.

- Alternative Simplified Credit – The alternative simplified credit (ASC) is 14% of the excess of the QREs over 50% of the average of the previous three years' QREs. The ASC base amount is easier to determine than under the traditional method, and most taxpayers therefore elect to use this method.

Qualifying R&D can include product development, product enhancement, process development, process improvement, and software development. Qualifying costs include wages for in-house labour, 65% of contract research, and supplies which are used in the research process, but exclude overheads and capital expenditure.

Other targeted R&D credits include a 20% basic research credit for funding research undertaken by universities and research organisations that have no commercial objective, and a 20% credit for payments to energy research consortiums.

RPS: Quota Obligation

This standard places an obligation on electric supply companies to produce a specified portion of their electricity from renewable energy sources, and includes mechanisms to achieve compliance such as renewable energy credits (RECs).[30] Currently no federal RPS legislation has been enacted. A total of twenty-nine states and the District of Columbia have an RPS.[31]

Conclusions

There have been substantial changes in the nature and extent of government support for renewable energy. Countries may impose renewable energy on electricity systems that may not need new capacity where demand is in decline. This approach may potentially push down electricity prices which may discourage new investment. The Economist commented that electricity markets deregulated in the late twentieth century typically use a 'merit order' system for supply. In these systems demand is met by taking electricity first from the cheapest supplier, then the next-cheapest, until all the required power is secured. The price paid to power generators is set by the most expensive source in use at that time.

Renewables generators do not need to buy fuel, and their marginal costs are therefore generally low. Renewables plants are intermittent suppliers, however, with output based on solar and wind conditions. This issue may result in capacity shortages in the absence of traditional power generators. This issue has required capacity payments, which are subsidies for plants that would otherwise be uneconomic. This may require markets that have sold power as a commodity may need to be transformed

30. KPMG, Taxes and incentives for renewable energy, 2015, KPMG International, 74 (kpmg.com/energytax on 17 July 2017).
31. The states currently include Arizona, California, Colorado, Connecticut, Delaware, Hawaii, Illinois, Indiana, Kansas, Maine, Maryland, Massachusetts, Michigan, Minnesota, Missouri, Montana, Nevada, New Hampshire, New Jersey, New Mexico, New York, North Carolina, Ohio, Oregon, Pennsylvania, Rhode Island, Texas, and Washington.

so that consumers pay for guaranteed services.[32] The availability of power supply may be addressed by the use of cash grants or targeted FIT to meet key needs such as the storage of renewable energy, such as the provision of battery backup systems for solar and wind power projects.[33]

32. Renewable energy, A world turned upside down, Economist, 25 February 2017.
33. One example to provide stability services for renewable energy is the 100mw battery for the Hornsdale Wind Farm project in South Australia, Jay Weatherill, Premier of South Australia, Tesla to pair world's largest lithium ion battery with Neoen wind farm in SA, https://www.premier.sa.gov.au/index.php/jay-weatherill-news-releases/7736-tesla-to-pair-world-s-largest-lithium-ion-battery-with-neoen-wind-farm-in-sa on 24 July 2017.

CHAPTER 12

Carbon Taxes and Emissions Trading Schemes

INTRODUCTION

One of the most significant fiscal and regulatory changes relating to energy production and distribution is the development of carbon taxes and emission trading schemes (ETS). These measures have been adopted to address climate change known as global warming, caused by emissions of greenhouse gases which cause rises in global temperatures. The most recent summary was made in the Fifth Assessment Report (AR5) of the Intergovernmental Panel on Climate Change (IPCC).[1] The principal framework for addressing climate change is the United Nations Framework Convention on Climate Change (UNFCCC).

Significant milestones in the process of addressing climate change include the Paris Agreement in 2015,[2] and the Kyoto Protocol to the United Nations Framework Convention on Climate Change.[3] It should be noted that the United States (US) withdrew from the Paris Agreement in 2017.

The Paris Agreement and the Kyoto Protocol include agreements to limit emissions of greenhouse gases. Carbon taxes and ETS are essentially national and regional measures designed to reduce greenhouse gas emissions to meet the targets set under these agreements.

Carbon taxes and Emissions Trading Schemes prices are generally expressed in

1. Climate Change 2014- Synthesis Report (Intergovernmental Panel on Climate Change, 2014) http://www.ipcc.ch/report/ar5/syr/ on 22 February 2018.
2. Paris Agreement, 12 December 2015, UNTS Registration Number 54113 (entered into force 4 November 2016) https://treaties.un.org/Pages/showDetails.aspx?objid=0800000280458f37 on 26 June 2017.
3. Kyoto Protocol to the United Nations Framework Convention on Climate Change, 11 December 1997 (entry into force 16 February 2005) 2303 UNTS 162.

currency amount per 1 tonne of carbon dioxide (CO_2) equivalent (tCO2e), for example the European Union (EU) carbon price was EUR 4.87 tCO2e in June 2017.[4]

CARBON TAXES

A carbon tax is a tax on energy sources which emit greenhouse gases including carbon dioxide. These taxes aim to address activities which impose pollution costs on others, including the potential impacts of global warming caused by greenhouse gas emissions. The carbon tax places a cost on these activities to reduce emissions of greenhouse gases using a tax on the burning of coal, petroleum products, and natural gas, in proportion to their carbon content.

Carbon taxes have several potential advantages:[5]

- They may place a limit on the costs of emissions reduction where they are transparent, simple, and have a wide coverage. Carbon taxes may also be implemented quickly by amending tax provisions.
- The related costs of a carbon tax may be predictable, which can provide relatively stable price signals to assist business and consumers plan energy spending. This potentially provides greater certainty for investments in energy efficiency with large initial costs.
- Carbon taxes act as a permanent incentive to reduce emissions because the price of emissions does not change, compared with price volatility in the operation of a market-based carbon trading system.
- The taxes are not susceptible to distortions in markets for trading emissions under an ETS, for example, where companies purchase a large number of permits and resell them for a profit.
- The taxes are a revenue source, which may allow other taxes to be reduced, or provide compensation to those most affected, so that introduction of a carbon tax remains revenue neutral.

The potential disadvantages of carbon taxes include:

- Carbon dioxide emissions may not decline if the consumption of the goods and services that produce carbon emissions remains unresponsive to price increases. This may apply, for example, to carbon taxes which result in increased consumer electricity prices.
- The rate of tax to produce the best outcomes is difficult to predict, and may require several changes before becoming effective.

---

4. EU European Emission Allowance quotations include the European Energy Exchange, https://www.eex.com/en/market-data/environmental-markets/spot-market/european-emission-allowances#!/2017/06/29 on 30 June 2017.
5. Carbon Taxes, Parliament of Australia, Parliamentary Library, http://www.aph.gov.au/About_Parliament/Parliamentary_Departments/Parliamentary_Library/Browse_by_Topic/ClimateChangeold/responses/economic/carbontax on 15 June 2017.

- Lobby groups may be successful in securing exemptions for highly affected industries, and this may substantially reduce the effectiveness of carbon taxes.
- Activities may relocate to a country that does not have carbon taxes, particularly where the tax is set at a high level.
- The tax is potentially regressive as it is likely to have the highest proportionate effect on the lowest income households. The imposition of an additional tax is therefore likely to be politically unpopular.

EMISSIONS TRADING SCHEMES

ETS are based on establishing tradable property rights to provide incentives to reduce emissions of greenhouse gases. The four main variations on carbon trading systems are as follows:[6]

Cap-and-trade – This is a system of tradeable permits which allows a set amount of emissions for related enterprises. The fixed number of permits limits the amount of emissions in any period, and the permits can be traded subject to related rules. An enterprise firm with activities with carbon emissions which may exceed the level of permits must generally invest in pollution control equipment, or purchase more permits. Enterprises which emit less than their allowance may sell their surplus permits to other enterprises. This allows enterprises with the lowest abatement costs an incentive to control more emissions, and those with high abatement costs have an incentive to buy permits. The market therefore determines the most efficient way to control pollution within this regulatory framework. The EU's Emission Trading System is one example of this system.

Baseline-and-credit – This system allows enterprises a certain baseline amount of allowable emissions. Enterprises are required to surrender enough emissions credits to account for their emissions above the baseline. Third parties create these credits through various renewable energy projects and sell these credits to enterprises and other market participants. Enterprises are therefore not under a strict emissions cap, but are required to purchase offsetting emission credits. Enterprises baseline emissions may be lowered so that the overall amount of emissions is potentially reduced.

Project based schemes – These schemes are based on a feature of the Kyoto Protocol providing flexible mechanisms intended to lower the overall cost of reducing, or offsetting, unwanted greenhouse gas emissions.[7] The Clean Development Mechanism allows industrialised countries with a greenhouse gas reduction commitment to invest in projects that reduce emissions in developing countries, as an alternative to more expensive emission reductions in their own countries. The Joint Implementation

---

6. Emissions trading, Parliament of Australia, Parliamentary Library, http://www.aph.gov.au/About_Parliament/Parliamentary_Departments/Parliamentary_Library/Browse_by_Topic/ClimateChangeold/responses/economic/emissions/emissionstrade on 15 June 2017.
7. Kyoto Protocol to the United Nations Framework Convention on Climate Change, Kyoto, 11 December 1997 (2303 UNTS 162).

Project relates to investments in another country which also has emission reduction obligations under the Kyoto Protocol.

Hybrid Schemes – These schemes combine features of the above approaches, such as a cap on emissions to regulate the quantity of pollution, combined with an adjustment mechanism, such as a carbon price floor or ceiling, to keep the price of a permit within acceptable limits.

Emissions trading schemes have several potential advantages:[8]

- Emissions trading can achieve the environmental objective of reduced emissions at the lowest cost. Cap and trade is designed to deliver an environmental outcome, so that the cap must be met, or there are sanctions such as fines. Allowing trading within that cap is an effective way of minimising the cost.
- Emissions trading may be better able to respond to economic fluctuations than other policy tools, by allowing the open market to set the price of carbon allows for better flexibility and avoids price shocks or undue burdens. In Europe, for example, prices will fall during a recession as industrial output and related emissions fall.
- Emissions trading incentivises innovation and identifies the lowest-cost solutions to make businesses more sustainable. The combination of an absolute cap on the level of emissions permitted and the carbon price signal from trading helps firms to identify low-cost methods of reducing emissions, such as investing in energy efficiency.
- Cap and trade has proven to be an effective policy choice. In the US the acid rain programme reduced pollution levels at a lower than expected cost. The EU Emissions Trading System has shown that cap and trade can be extended to carbon, and create a price on carbon that drives emissions reductions.
- Emissions trading can provide a global response to a global challenge. Cap and trade provides a way of establishing rigour around emissions monitoring, reporting, and verification. The use of offsets can help involve other jurisdictions in the reduction of greenhouse gas emissions, and may even inspire them to establish their own emissions trading system.
- As emissions trading spreads around the world, there are a number of opportunities to link systems, which may enhance their effectiveness and potentially reduce costs. Connecting emissions trading systems, such as with California and Québec, potentially widens the pool of participants to reduce costs.

There are significant issues with ETS which need to be addressed. These issues include:

- Determination of the related carbon pricing including the effective control of allowances. The EU ETC carbon price, for example, has declined from an average of EUR 13 /tonneCO2e in January 2010 to EUR 3.90 /tonneCO2e by

8. IETA, Benefits Of Emissions Trading, March 2015, http://www.ieta.org/resources/Resources/101s/ieta-emissions-trading-101-library-april2015.pdf on 26 June 2017.

April 2013.[9] This fall was primarily due to the oversupply of emissions allowances, particularly in the original Phase I of the ETS, where the verified emissions reported by EU countries were less than the allowances allocated to installations. The price of an ETS allowance was EUR 4.87 /tonneCO2e in June 2017. Related measures to address these issues in Phase III from 2013 to 2020 include the setting of an overall EU cap, with allowances then allocated to EU members, tighter limits on the use of offsets, limiting banking of allowances between Phases II and III, and a trend from credit allowances to credit auctioning.

- An ETS generally needs to deliver a more stable carbon price which necessary for long-term, low-carbon investment decisions. An example of measures to address this issue is the carbon price floor introduced by the United Kingdom (UK) at GBP 18/tonneCO2e (EUR 20/tonneCO2e). France has not implemented the proposed carbon price floor of EUR 20–30 /tonneCO2e proposed in the French 2017 Finance Bill.[10]
- There is an issue concerning the effectiveness of carbon offsets. The related issues include demonstrating that the benefits of such projects were additional to any savings which might have happened in any event, and the independent audit of carbon offset benefits.

Effective emissions trading scheme are likely to include a supported carbon floor combined with an efficient basis for the auctioning of emission allowances.

UPSTREAM OR DOWNSTREAM SCHEMES

There is an issue of whether carbon taxes or ETS should be made on an upstream or downstream basis. An upstream carbon tax or ETS is imposed at the point of their extraction, import, processing, or distribution in the fossil fuel supply chain on the carbon content of fossil fuels. On this basis, almost all of the carbon entering the economy would be accounted for, while this approach potentially keeps administration of the system as simple as possible.[11]

An upstream carbon tax or ETS may not apply effectively where fossil fuel supplies do not lead to significant carbon emissions downstream, such as power plants or factories with effective carbon capture and storage, or where crude oil is used to make petrochemicals. A downstream carbon tax or ETS can apply effectively to sectors like power generation and heavy industry with a relatively small number of carbon

9. Anita Talberg and Kai Swoboda, Emissions trading schemes around the world, Parliament of Australia, http://www.aph.gov.au/About_Parliament/Parliamentary_Departments/Parliamentary_Library/pubs/BN/2012-2013/EmissionsTradingSchemes on 30 June 2017.
10. France suspends carbon floor price planned on 1 January 2017, Enerdata, 24 October 2016, https://www.enerdata.net/publications/daily-energy-news/france-suspends-carbon-floor-price-planned-1-january-2017.html on 26 June 2017.
11. *Carbon Taxes v. Carbon Trading, Pros, cons and the case for a hybrid approach*, PricewaterhouseCoopers, March 2009, 22.

emitters. The EU ETS is an example of a system which applies on such a downstream basis.

There may be scope to combine an efficient downstream ETS on a small number of emitters in power generation and heavy industry, together with upstream measures such as a carbon tax on other sectors of the economy such as road transport.[12]

COUNTRY ADOPTION OF CARBON TAXES OR EMISSIONS TRADING SCHEMES

There has been substantial adoption of carbon taxes or ETS by many countries. There are also substantial differences in the measures adopted. The tax systems and rates are subject to substantial changes, and the following should therefore only be used as a general guide to illustrate the different country approaches:[13]

- Canada – Canada does not have a federal carbon tax. The Canadian provinces of Quebec and British Columbia have carbon taxes.[14] Ontario has also introduced a cap-and-trade scheme. Alberta implemented emissions trading in 2006 and Quebec in 2013.
- Chile – Chile enacted a carbon tax in 2014 to be implemented from 2017 at USD 5 per tonne of CO2 equivalent applying to boilers and turbines with the summation of sources to have a thermal plant capacity equal to or greater than 50 MW.[15]
- China – The emissions trading scheme is being introduced from 2017. The cap-and-trade scheme will be combined with a reduction on reliance on coal in the power sector and increased use of renewable energy. Pilot carbon markets were introduced in Beijing, Chongqing, Guangdong, Hubei, Shanghai, Shenzhen and Tianjin.
- Denmark – Denmark has had a carbon tax since 2002, with a rate in 2017 of 170 DKK /tCO2e. The carbon tax applies to all energy users, however industrial companies are taxed differently depending on the process the energy is used for, and whether the company has entered into a voluntary agreement to apply energy efficiency measures.[16]
- EU – The EU ETS began in 2005. The ETS currently covers approximately 11,000 power stations and manufacturing plants in the Member States plus Iceland, Liechtenstein, and Norway, as well as aviation activities in these countries. The ETS is a cap-and-trade system, with the cap set on the total amount of certain greenhouse gases that can be emitted. The cap is reduced

12. *Carbon Taxes v. Carbon Trading, Pros, cons and the case for a hybrid approach*, PricewaterhouseCoopers, March 2009, 23.
13. Carbon taxes and emission trading schemes around the world, SBS News, 8 December 2016.
14. British Columbia, Carbon Tax (2008).
15. Carbon Tax, Law No. 20780 (2014), and Carbon Tax Guide, A Handbook for Policy Makers, Appendix: Carbon Tax Case Studies, World Bank Group 2017, 22.
16. Carbon Tax (1992), Green Energy Package (1996), and Carbon Tax Guide, A Handbook for Policy Makers, Appendix: Carbon Tax Case Studies, World Bank Group 2017, 28.

over time so that total emissions fall. Within the cap, companies receive or buy emission allowances which they can also trade. Companies can also buy limited amounts of international credits from emission-saving projects around the world. The ETS is the world's largest emissions trading market, accounting for over three quarters of international carbon trading. A carbon tax was proposed by the European Commission in 2010, but a carbon tax has not been agreed upon by the Member States.[17]

- Iceland – Iceland introduced a carbon tax in 2010. The tax covers oil, gas, and other gaseous hydrocarbons. Coal is exempt from the carbon tax, but most industries in Iceland that use coal are covered by the EU ETS. The tax rate was set at IKR 1120/tCO2e in 2014.[18]
- India – India introduced a nationwide carbon tax in 2010. The rate from 2016 is INR 400 per tonne of coal produced or imported in India.[19]
- Ireland – Ireland introduced a carbon tax in 2010 applying to fossil fuels based on each fuel's CO2 emissions, the rate from 2014 has been EUR 20/tCO2e. The carbon tax applies primarily to residential heating, transport, commercial buildings, and small industry.[20]
- Finland – Finland introduced the world's first carbon tax in 1990, initially with exemptions for specific sectors. Later changes included the implementation of a border tax on imported electricity. Natural gas has a reduced tax rate. The tax from 2013 for heating fuels is EUR 35/tCO2 and the rate for liquid traffic fuels is EUR 60/tCO2.[21]
- France – France imposes a carbon price on the use of fossil fuels not covered by the EU ETS. In 2017 the tax is EUR 30.50/tCO2e, and is then expected to increase to EUR 56/tCO2e in 2020 and EUR 100/tCO2e in 2030.[22]
- Japan – Japan legislated for a carbon tax in 2012, and the rate from 2016 is JPY 289/tCO2. Tax revenues are to be used to promote low-carbon technologies, energy efficiency improvements, and renewable energy. Japan also introduced emissions trading schemes in the Tokyo and Saitama regions.[23]

17. Directive 2003/87/EC of the European Parliament and of the Council of 13 October 2003 establishing a scheme for greenhouse gas emission allowance trading within the Community and amending Council Directive 96/61/EC, and EU related measures, and The EU Emissions Trading System (EU ETS), https://ec.europa.eu/clima/policies/ets_en on 26 June 2017.
18. Kolefnisgjald Á Fljótandi Jarðefnaeldsneyti – Carbon Tax on Carbon of Fossil Origin (2010), and Carbon Tax Guide, A Handbook for Policy Makers, Appendix: Carbon Tax Case Studies, World Bank Group 2017, 45.
19. Clean Environment Cess, Chapter VII, section 83, Finance Act (2010), and Carbon Tax Guide, A Handbook for Policy Makers, Appendix: Carbon Tax Case Studies, World Bank Group 2017, 50.
20. Carbon Tax – Finance Act (2010) and Carbon Tax Guide, A Handbook for Policy Makers, Appendix: Carbon Tax Case Studies, World Bank Group 2017, 55.
21. Hiilidioksidivero CO2 Tax (1990), and Carbon Tax Guide, A Handbook for Policy Makers, Appendix: Carbon Tax Case Studies, World Bank Group 2017, 34.
22. Carbon Tax – Domestic Consumption Tax on Energy Products (2013), Law on the Energy Transition to Green Growth (2015), and Carbon Tax Guide, A Handbook for Policy Makers, Appendix: Carbon Tax Case Studies, World Bank Group 2017, 40.
23. Tax For Climate Change Mitigation (2010), and Carbon Tax Guide, A Handbook for Policy Makers, Appendix: Carbon Tax Case Studies, World Bank Group 2017, 61.

- Mexico – Mexico introduced the carbon tax in 2014. The tax is applied upstream, to producers and importers, and natural gas is not taxed. The tax rate varies by fuel since the tax rate is based on the difference between the emissions that would have occurred if natural gas had been used. The tax rate in 2016 was set at a maximum of MXN 18.77/tCO2e.[24]
- The Netherlands – The Netherlands introduced a carbon tax in 1990. The current taxes include the Energy Tax, with the rates for electricity applying from EUR 0.1013 kWh up to 10,000 kWh, with reducing rated down to EUR 0.00053 kWh over 10m kWh for businesses in 2017, and a levy on the supply of energy to develop sustainable energy.[25]
- New Zealand – The New Zealand Government set up an emissions trading scheme in 2008. The scheme covered forestry initially, and was then expanded in 2010 to cover stationary energy, transport, liquid fossil fuels, and industrial processes.[26]
- Norway – Norway introduced a tax on carbon in 1991. The tax rate was NOK 29–446/tCO2e from 2016. The carbon tax applies upstream to oil and gas companies operating on the continental shelf. The carbon tax applies midstream to fuels, as sales taxes have to be paid to the Norwegian Tax Administration by midstream suppliers after collection from downstream users. Norway also implemented the first phase of an Emissions Trading Scheme in 2005 and joined the EU ETS in 2008.[27]
- South Africa – South Africa has proposed implementation of a carbon tax from 2017 or 2018. The tax would include measures to help businesses adapt to the tax, which would see a price of the effective tax rate will be between ZAR 6–48/tCO2e. South Africa introduced a carbon tax on new vehicle sales in September 2010.
- South Korea – South Korea passed legislation in May 2012 for an emissions trading scheme to start from 1 January 2015. The emissions trading scheme covers facilities producing more than 25,000 tonnes of greenhouse gas emissions for about 450 of the country's largest carbon emitters.
- Sweden – Sweden enacted a tax on the use of coal, oil, natural gas, petrol and aviation fuel used in domestic travel in 1991. The tax rate is SEK 1,120/tCO2e, with reduced rates for certain users.[28]

24. Carbon Tax – Ley del Impuesto Especial sobre Producción y Servicios (2014), and Carbon Tax Guide, A Handbook for Policy Makers, Appendix: Carbon Tax Case Studies, World Bank Group 2017, 65.
25. Energy Tax (Energiebelasting) – Tables tariffs environmental taxes, http://www.answersforbusiness.nl/regulation/energy-tax on 19 June 2017.
26. Climate Change Response Act 2002 and related provisions, and New Zealand Ministry for the Environment, New Zealand Emissions Trading Scheme http://www.mfe.govt.nz/climate-change/reducing-greenhouse-gas-emissions/new-zealand-emissions-trading-scheme on 26 June 2017.
27. Carbon Tax – Act Concerning Sales Tax, Act Relating to Tax on Discharge of Co2 in the Petroleum Activities on the Continental Shelf (1990), and Carbon Tax Guide, A Handbook for Policy Makers, Appendix: Carbon Tax Case Studies, World Bank Group 2017, 72.
28. Co2 Tax (Koldioxidskatt) (1991), and Carbon Tax Guide, A Handbook for Policy Makers, Appendix: Carbon Tax Case Studies, World Bank Group 2017, 87.

- Switzerland – A carbon incentive tax was introduced in Switzerland in 2008. The rate in 2017 is CHF 84/tCO2e. The tax includes all fossil fuels unless they are used for energy. Swiss companies can be exempt from the tax if they participate in the country's emissions trading system.[29]
- UK – The UK imposes the Climate Change Levy (CCL) on energy supplied to an end user, including rates for electricity at GBP 0.00568/KWh with a potential 90% discount available for holders of a climate change agreement (CCA) with the Environmental Agency in 2017. The Carbon Price Support (CPS) rates are paid on supply of fossil fuels for electricity generation at GBP 0.00331/kWh for gas, GBP 0.05280/kg for LPG, and GBP 1.54790/GJ for coal.[30] The prior CCL exemption on the renewable energy sector has been removed, with a transitional period from 2015 to 2018. An annual duty is imposed on licences for motor vehicles linked to CO2 emissions for cars and weight for commercial vehicles. The UK imposes a carbon price floor in relation to the EU ETS at GBP 18/tonne CO2e.[31]
- US – There is no nationwide carbon tax levelled in the USA. There are several regional carbon tax regimes, including California, Connecticut, Delaware, Maine, Maryland, Massachusetts, New Hampshire, New York, Rhode Island, and Vermont.[32]

A significant development is that corporations may set an internal price on carbon to assess the risk value of future projects when making economic investment decisions. This can be relevant to oil and gas companies, for example, which have assets that may be affected by energy policies in the future. The anticipation of carbon taxes or carbon trading may therefore have an impact on related investment decisions.

SUMMARY

The use of ETS currently appears to be more successful than carbon taxes providing there are mechanisms such as an effective floor to stabilise the related carbon price. A related issue is the effective pricing of carbon offsets, where domestic or foreign projects to reduce greenhouse emissions such as forest development can provide related emission credits, providing there is an accepted and effective audit process.

29. CO2 Levy – Federal Act on the Reduction of Co2 Emissions (2008), and Carbon Tax Guide, A Handbook for Policy Makers, Appendix: Carbon Tax Case Studies, World Bank Group 2017, 28.
30. Guidance – Climate Change Levy rates, HMRC 2016, https://www.gov.uk/government/publications/rates-and-allowances-climate-change-levy/climate-change-levy-rates on 19 June 2017.
31. Elena Ares and Jeanne Delebarre, The Carbon Price Floor, UK House of Commons, Briefing Paper Number CBP05927, 23 November 2016, http://researchbriefings.files.parliament.uk/documents/SN05927/SN05927.pdf on 5 July 2017.
32. Cutting Power Sector Carbon Pollution: State Policies and Programs, U.S. Environmental Protection Agency, August 2016, 10.

There has also been an effective use of carbon taxes for areas which are not covered by an emission trading scheme. The potential to connect emissions trading schemes is also a significant potential advantage, and this may develop in a complimentary way to the use of internal prices on carbon used by multinational groups.

CHAPTER 13

Contractor Services and Permanent Establishments (PEs)

INTRODUCTION

The production of energy requires extensive contractor services including oil and gas field construction, coal and uranium mining services, windfarm and solar installation, power station construction, electricity transmission and distribution network construction, and the provision of related maintenance and upgrade services. A common issue is whether the provision of these services constitutes a permanent establishment (PE) of the service provider in the respective country, which generally enables local country taxation on the related business profits under most tax treaties.

A PE UNDER THE OECD MODEL TAX TREATY

The principal definition of a PE in the OECD Model Tax Treaty is a fixed place of business through which the business of an enterprise is carried on. This definition includes a place of management, branch, office, factory, workshop, and mine, oil and gas well, quarry, or any other place of extraction of natural resources. A building site or construction or installation project also constitutes a PE where this lasts for a period of more than twelve months.[1]

An enterprise may also be treated as having a PE due to the activities of a dependant agent which habitually exercises authority to conclude contracts on its

1. OECD, *Model Tax Convention on Income and on Capital* (2017) Article 5(3), (OECD Model Tax Treaty) http://www.oecd-ilibrary.org/taxation/model-tax-convention-on-income-and-on-capital-condensed-version-2017_mtc_cond-2017-en on 13 October 2017.

behalf.[2] This provision does not apply to an independent agent, for example a broker, general commission agent, or any other agent of an independent status, generally providing services to several parties and acting in the ordinary course of their business.[3]

PE EXCLUSIONS UNDER THE OECD MODEL TAX TREATY

There are several exclusions from the definition of PE. These exclusions include a place of business solely for activities of a preparatory or auxiliary character, also known as a representative office.[4]

In general, a representative office which does not have the authority to negotiate or conclude contracts on behalf of its head office company may not be treated as a taxable PE. The representative office staff should, however, not undertake activities which are more directly related to sales. One measure to protect the status as a representative office, for example, is to provide terms in all related contracts that they are not binding unless signed by specific head office staff.

An example of representative office relating to upstream oil and gas may, for example, be an office of a drilling services company which advertises the company's drilling services to oil and gas companies, explains the available services, and then arranges for contacts for negotiation and conclusion of contracts with head office staff. The head office then negotiates and concludes contracts with the oil and gas companies.

A related structure is to use a separate local company to provide the local country services, so that the drilling company itself does not have employees or a PE in the country. Local country taxation may therefore be limited, or quarantined, to the local country service company, with a substantially reduced risk of taxation on the parent company. The drilling company parent may then transfer or second employees to the local company under local country employment contracts when they are required for specific projects. The local company should be taxed for the work performed relating to that country, however the parent drilling company should not be taxed as there is no PE in that country.

The use of tax treaty provisions to prevent taxation of the parent company where there is no local PE will depend on the existence of a related tax treaty between the respective countries. A multinational group may therefore have several service companies which can provide services located in different countries, and use the company located in country with a treaty with the local country to provide the required services.

2. Article 5(5).
3. Article 5(6).
4. Article 5(4)(e).

OECD BEPS ACTION 7

The OECD BEPS Action 7 measures addressed several strategies used for the artificial avoidance of PE status:

- Commissionaire arrangements and similar strategies: These arrangements may be a significant issue for the energy industry, where a dependant agent does not habitually conclude contracts but substantially negotiates those contracts. This issue is also addressed in the optional measures which may be adopted by counties under the OECD Multilateral Instrument (MLI).[5]
- Artificial avoidance of PE status using specific activity exceptions: Contracts for construction or maintenance services for energy projects may be divided between different related parties. This may potentially avoid the existence of a PE as each contract is claimed not to constitute a PE, for example because the segmented activity is then solely for storage, processing by another enterprise, or for purchasing, each of which then qualifies as an exception from a PE.[6] The MLI contains an optional anti-fragmentation rule against these structures including restricting the specific activity exemption to activities that are solely considered preparatory or auxiliary to the business as a whole.[7]
- Other strategies for the avoidance of PE status and splitting-up of contracts: Large construction and engineering projects may split up the major customer contracts into separate parts in different closely-related enterprises, so that each contract is below the time-threshold to be treated as a PE. The MLI provides an option to aggregate such contracts and so be treated as a PE.[8]

Of these changes, potentially the most important for service companies is the specific activity exemption. Examples of the related changes include:[9]

- An oilfield service company may, for example, stockpile the materials required for a project in the country of manufacture. The stockpile would previously have qualified for the specific activity exemption and therefore not been a PE in the manufacturing country, however under the new rules the stockpiling activity may not be preparatory or auxiliary to the activities of the service company as a whole.
- A related issue arises for geological and geophysical (G&G) survey activities in exploration for oil and gas, or subsurface analysis for offshore wind farms, which may have used the exemption for a PE where this relates to collecting information for an enterprise. These activities may now constitute a PE as they may not be preparatory or auxiliary to the activities of the service company as a whole.

5. Multilateral Convention to Implement Tax Treaty Related Measures to Prevent Base Erosion and Profit Shifting, opened for signature 7 June 2017 (MLI) Article 12.
6. OECD Model Tax Treaty, 2017, Article 5(4).
7. MLI Article 13.
8. MLI Article 14.
9. Deloitte, Base erosion and profit shifting, Implications for the mining sector, 10 January 2016.

THE 2017 OECD MODEL TAX TREATY

The 2017 OECD Model Tax Treaty included several measures to apply the BEPS Action 7 PE measures:

- Article 5(4) requires the overall activity of the establishment to be of a preparatory or auxiliary nature for the specific PE exemptions to apply.
- Article 5(5) includes an agent as a PE where the agent habitually plays the principal role leading to the conclusion of contracts that are routinely concluded without material modification by the enterprise.
- Article 5(6) denies the PE exception to an independent agent where that person acts exclusively or almost exclusively on behalf of one or more enterprises to which it is closely related.

PE RISK

There are several significant tax risks in the event that a PE is deemed to be present in the local country where the services are provided. In Angola, for example, obligations arising from a local PE include tax registration, reporting obligations, corporate income tax at 35% on profits attributable to the PE, and 1% stamp duty on the gross value of all receipts, and foreign exchange rules. An entity is deemed to have a PE in Angola where:[10]

(a) it has any type of fixed business installation or premises of any kind in Angolan territory through which commercial activity is carried on;
(b) it would either have personnel staying in Angola for more than ninety days (not necessarily consecutive, within any given twelve-month period), or otherwise it acts through a dependant agent that would have habitually exercised powers of attorney.

There is an issue as to whether a country's tax laws may treat a foreign company to be taxable on services performed outside the local country, and not just the services performed by the PE in the local country. This issue was considered in *Asst DIT v. M/s Clifford Chance*.[11] The case effectively overruled the previous Indian decision in *Linklaters LLP v. ITO (International Taxation)*.[12] The case held that Indian taxation would only apply to the work done by the PE.[13]

10. General Tax Code, Article 17A.
11. *Asst DIT v. M/s Clifford Chance* (ITA Nos 5034/Mum/2004, 5035/Mum/2004, 7095/Mum/2004, 3021/Mum/2005 AND 2060-61/Mum/2008) (13 May 2013, unreported), Mumbai Special Bench.
12. *Linklaters LLP v. ITO (International Taxation)* [2010] 40 SOT 51 (Mum).
13. *See* further Sudhir Kapadia and Hitesh Sharma, 'India's Special Bench rules on profit attribution to a permanent establishment under the India-UK Tax Treaty,' Ernst & Young, Global Tax Alert, 17 May 2013.

Certain tax treaties may contain force of attraction provisions. These measures may allow local country taxation on income with a source in the country but which are not derived by the PE in the country. This local country taxation can apply where that income is of the same nature as income derived by the PE. An example of this approach is provided in the United Nations Model Tax Treaty.[14]

ATTRIBUTION OF PROFITS TO THE PE

A key issue is to determine the allocation of profits to the PE. The related OECD analysis includes the 2010 Report and the most recent commentary on Article 7 of the Model Tax Treaty. The OECD approach to profit attribution is generally based on Functionally Separate Entity (FSE) analysis. The profits to be attributed to a PE are the profits that the PE would have earned at arm's length if it were a separate and independent enterprise engaged in the same or similar activities under the same or similar conditions.[15] The related analysis takes into account functions performed, assets used and risks assumed (FAR) through the PE and other parts of the enterprise.[16]

The OECD Guidance – Report on Attribution of Profits to PEs in 2010 is relevant to several key issues.[17] This Guidance rejects the force of attraction principle, which potentially treats all profits from the country as relating to the PE and therefore taxable. This basis is incorporated in the OECD Commentary of the Model Tax Treaty.[18]

The Guidance provides that the allocation of profits to the PE is generally based on significant people functions:[19]

- People functions determine allocating the risks within an entity, based on decision-making related to assuming and managing the risks.
- The allocation of tangible assets is presumptively based on use, and of intangible assets including marketing intangibles based on significant people functions on decision making for the assumption and management of related risks.

The capital allocation issue relates to the PE being treated as having an appropriate amount of 'free' (equity) capital needed to support risks and assets, which can potentially limit the amount of interest deductions claimed to relate to the PE.[20]

14. United Nations Model Double Taxation Convention between Developed and Developing Countries (UN Doc ST/ESA/PAD/SER.E/21) Article 7(1).
15. OECD, *Model Tax Convention on Income and on Capital* (2014), C(7)-39 para. 14.
16. For financial institutions, the functional analysis is based on key entrepreneurial risk-taking functions (KERT).
17. OECD Guidance – Report on Attribution of Profits to Permanent Establishments in 2010, http://www.oecd.org/ctp/transfer-pricing/45689524.pdf at 16 October 2017.
18. OECD, *Model Tax Convention on Income and on Capital* (2014), C(7)-37 para. 10.
19. OECD, *Model Tax Convention on Income and on Capital* (2014), C(7)-8 para. 20.
20. OECD, *Model Tax Convention on Income and on Capital* (2014), C(7)-47 para. 45.

CHAPTER 14
Value Added Tax

INTRODUCTION

Value Added Tax (VAT) is imposed in many countries on the value of a company's sales, with the company allowed credit for VAT paid on their purchases. VAT therefore applies to the value added by each stage added by different companies in the provision of products and services. VAT on imported purchases of goods is generally collected on the owner of the goods or their agent on entry to the country. VAT may be collected on imported services using a reverse charge method, where the local country user of the services is required to withhold and pay the related VAT on behalf of the non-resident supplier. The export of goods and services to a person in another country is generally outside the scope of VAT, also known as zero-rated supplies, however the company is allowed a credit for the VAT paid on the related purchases.

Financial services are generally exempt from VAT, known as exempt supplies. The result is that VAT is not chargeable on related income, such as interest income, or income from foreign exchange transactions. The company is, however, not entitled to a refund of the VAT paid, known as input tax, on its related purchases. This issue results in a form of hidden charge on financial services, where states have collected VAT revenue on the inputs relating to the related product or service which are not then refunded. On this basis, zero-rated supplies are better for the supplier company than exempt supplies, because the zero-rated supplies allow the company to receive input tax credits.

The issue of securities such as shares, bonds, loan notes, and debentures to raise capital, transactions in securities that are already in existence sold in the course of a business activity, and income from specific derivatives, including futures, options, and interest rate swaps, are generally also exempt supplies.[1]

1. HMRC, *VAT – Finance*, Notice 701/49 (January 2013).

Related services provided by a financial services or group treasury company may not be exempt supplies, for example equipment leasing, and investment, finance and taxation advice. If input tax relates to both taxable and exempt supplies, the company can generally deduct only the amount of input tax that relates to the taxable supplies.[2] This issue generally requires an apportionment of input tax to determine the related input tax credit, for example based on input tax, multiplied by taxable supplies, over total supplies. In the United Kingdom (UK), a general apportionment method may be based on taxable supplies divided by total supplies. This may result in reduced credits where the treasury operations are only a small part of the larger group business. Group treasury companies may therefore potentially apply for a special apportionment, based on factors such as employees or floor-space.

The rules for VAT for countries in the European Union (EU) are generally harmonised to establish a common system.[3] For example, in the UK, VAT provisions do not apply to the supply to a recipient in another EU Member State which receives the supply for business purposes, or to a recipient in a country outside the EU. The exporting company is generally able to recover the input tax relating to the zero-rated supplies in their country.

VAT PLANNING

The following review of potential VAT planning measures is based on discussions by Deloitte, Marcus Ward, and PWC.[4] These potential arrangements are intended as an introduction to VAT planning, however their use will depend on the circumstances in each case.

Maximising VAT Recovery

VAT grouping generally allows entities that are closely linked financially, economically, and organisationally to be regarded as a single VAT person. In the UK, two or more companies or limited liability partnerships can register as a single taxable person or VAT group if each body has its principal or registered office in the UK, and they are under common control, for example one or more company is a subsidiary of a parent company. If the turnover of the VAT group is over GBP 10 million per year and the group is partly owned or managed by a third party, the entities can only register as a group for VAT if no more than 50% of the benefits generated by the business go to third parties, the group uses consolidated accounting, and no third party consolidates the group into its accounts.[5] No VAT is payable on supplies between grouped companies

2. *Value Added Tax Act 1994* c. 23 (United Kingdom).
3. European Union, *Council Directive 2006/112/EC of 28 November 2006 on the Common System of Value Added Tax*, OJ L-347 11.12.2006 (European Union).
4. Piet Vandendriessche et al, *Managing in Volatile Times: Achieving Cash Savings through Tax Strategies* (Deloitte, 2009).
5. UK Government *Business Tax – Guidance, VAT Registration for Groups, Divisions and Joint Ventures*, <https://www.gov.uk/vat-registration-for-groups-divisions-and-joint-ventures>.

and only one VAT return is required. There are also opportunities to include a holding company in the VAT group, which can potentially increase VAT recovery on the holding company's overheads relating to the supply of management services to the holding company's subsidiaries. The use of VAT grouping therefore maximises tax recovery by avoiding the pre-financing of intercompany VAT or irrecoverable VAT.

There may be opportunities to increase the frequency of foreign VAT refund claims. Businesses operating in countries in which they are not established or VAT registered (i.e., non-resident businesses) can incur significant amounts of VAT on expenses paid in those countries.[6] Non-resident businesses should be able to recover some or all of the VAT incurred. There are significant potential advantages in putting processes in place to obtain the VAT refunds.

There are also opportunities to maximise VAT refunds relating to employee expenses. In the UK, for example, it is generally possible to reclaim VAT on employee expenses if they relate to business travel and subsistence such as meals, canteen facilities or accommodation, unless the employees are paid a flat rate for subsistence when no VAT is recoverable. The UK tax authorities, Her Majesty's Revenue and Customs (HMRC), generally requires the business to have invoices or receipts in the name of the company. When employees are travelling on business, however, it is possible to reclaim VAT on purchases up to GBP 250, as long as there is a receipt or invoice showing the key details, such as the supplier's name and address, nature of the goods supplied, VAT amount and the seller's VAT number. It is necessary to ensure that all employees are keeping records of their receipts.[7]

There are provisions for VAT bad debt relief. This allows claims to recover VAT paid to authorities if the company's customers are being impacted by a downturn in economic conditions, for example, and are not able to pay their invoices. In the UK, the related conditions are that the entity must already have accounted for the VAT on the supplies and paid it to HMRC, the entity must have written off the debt in their day to day VAT accounts and transferred it to a separate bad debt account, the value of the supply must not be more than the customary selling price; the debt must not have been paid, sold, or factored under a valid legal assignment, and the debt must have remained unpaid for a period of six months after the later of the time payment was due and payable and the date of the supply.[8]

It is also beneficial to review the use of the partial exemption method for VAT. When an entity incurs input tax on purchases that relate to both taxable and exempt supplies, known as 'mixed costs', it can only recover the input tax to the extent that the purchases are used to make taxable supplies. Direct attribution of input tax is the identification of VAT incurred on purchases that are used, or intend to use exclusively in making taxable supplies or other supplies that carry the right to deduct; or exclusively in making exempt supplies. The entity can also recover the amount of residual input tax that relates to taxable supplies and other supplies that carry the right

6. Olivier Hody & Jorge Franco, *European VAT Refund Guide 2013*, Deloitte Global Tax Center (Europe) (Deloitte, 2013).
7. 'When to Reclaim VAT on Your Employees' Expenses' (Raffingers Stuart, 2014).
8. HMRC, VAT Notice 700/18: relief from VAT on bad debts, 7 February 2013.

to deduct. In the UK, this amount is determined by a partial exemption calculation. This may be based on a standard attribution method, or a special method with HMRC approval.[9] The standard attribution method may be value-based, use-based, or use of previous year's recovery percentage. Special method attribution may be based on a variety of criteria, such as: the number of transactions such as the number of taxable transactions in a quarter over total number of transactions in the quarter; floor area, such as the floor area used to make taxable supplies and the floor area used to make exempt supplies; or staff numbers, such as the total staff employed in the taxable business compared to the staff numbers used in the exempt business. These methods may be quite complex as every business is different and have their own specific characteristics.[10]

Invoicing and Tax Points

The use of 'call-off' stock arrangements may potentially be used to defer the payment of VAT until the actual supply occurs. Call-off stock is the description given to the transfer of goods by a VAT registered business from one EU Member State to another to create a stock of goods from which their customer can call-off, meaning use and pay for the goods as and when they require them. This structure is generally used to integrate the supply of stock which is to be used in the manufacturing process. If the customer is aware of the details of deliveries into storage, the intra-EU movement can be treated as call-off stock.[11] VAT is then delayed until the call-off stock is received in the UK from a VAT registered business in another EU Member State. The UK business declares the call-off at the time the goods arrive in storage.[12]

There may be opportunities for the application of simplified triangulation relating to supplies within the EU. This can apply, for example, where Company A makes an intra-Community supply to company B. Company A is allowed to issue a zero-rated VAT invoice, providing the VAT identification numbers of both A and B are stated on the invoice. Company A must declare the supply in its local VAT return. Company B is also allowed to issue a zero-rated invoice, providing that it states on the invoice that the simplified triangulation procedure applies to the goods supplied to C and it lists the VAT identification numbers of both B and C. As a result, no registration in either EU Member State A or C is required for company B.[13]

The tax point for VAT is generally the time a supply is 'crystallised' and the VAT becomes due to the tax authorities and dictates the VAT return period in which VAT

9. HMRC, VAT Notice 706: partial exemption, 16 June 2011.
10. Tolley Tax Training, *Value Added Tax*, (Reed Elsevier UK Ltd, 2014).
11. In the United Kingdom, for example, call-off goods delivered to storage facilities operated by the supplier, rather than the customer, should be treated as consignment stocks, unless the customer is aware of the details of deliveries into storage. If stocks of goods are dispatched by an EU supplier direct to the UK for call-off by more than one customer, this does not qualify for treatment as call-off stock.
12. HMRC, Intrastat Information Sheets, 'Call-off and Consignment Stock' March 2012, <www.uktradeinfo.com>.
13. Bert Laman, Mazars Paardekooper Hoffman NV, *European VAT – Business and Taxation Guide* 12 (Praxity, 2013).

must be accounted for. In very general terms this is the earliest of the invoice date, receipt of payment, goods transferred, or services completed. On this basis, it may be possible to generate output tax as early as possible in a VAT period, and incur input tax as late as possible. This will give a business use of VAT money for up to four months before it needs to be paid. The timing of VAT paid on purchases can potentially be deferred by increasing the payment terms with a company's suppliers. This effectively reduces VAT pre-financing by the purchasing company.[14]

There may also be potential opportunities to determine the timing of a tax point to benefit both parties to a transaction. Businesses may have different VAT quarter dates, and so the appropriate timing of invoices may mean that the recipient business is able to recover input tax before the supplier needs to account for output tax. This issue may be particularly significant for large or one-off transactions such as property sales.[15]

Specific documentation may be used to avoid creating tax points for certain supplies. If a business supplies ongoing services, where there is no identifiable completion of those services, and the issue of a tax invoice is avoided, then VAT may potentially only be due when payment is received.[16]

There are potential advantages relating to the timing of outgoing invoices. In general, issuing invoices at the beginning of the month may increase the probability that customers have paid the full invoice amount before the VAT is due to the authorities.

Other VAT Planning Approaches

As discussed in the following chapter, import duties and tariffs may be linked to import VAT. Accordingly structures which may reduce import duties and tariffs can also potentially reduce import VAT.

There are also planning opportunities relating to imports include special provisions for Customs/VAT warehousing. These provisions generally defer payment or avoid payment where goods are kept in customs warehouses or other exemption zones, and then re-exported or shipped onward.

European VAT: Central Billing Agencies

The structures which may potentially be used by multinational groups with companies in several EU countries were reviewed by Anne Murrath and Laurent Grencon of PWC.[17] The basis of the structure is that the multinational group has a central billing agency (CBE). Groups with companies in different EU Member States which receive taxable services from suppliers established in the same EU Member State may

14. Marcus Ward Consultancy, *VAT – Top 10 Tax Point Planning Tips*, 24 February 2015.
15. Marcus Ward Consultancy, *VAT – Top 10 Tax Point Planning Tips*, 24 February 2015.
16. Marcus Ward Consultancy, *VAT – Top 10 Tax Point Planning Tips*, 24 February 2015.
17. Anne Murrath, Laurent Grencon et al, *VAT News for Multinational Companies* (PricewaterhouseCoopers SarL, 2011).

potentially use the CBE structure. The CBE entity would receive all invoices from EU service providers. The result is intra-EU services where the reverse charge mechanism applies, rather than same country supplies, where VAT must be paid by the provider. The recipient of the services therefore declares and recovers the VAT in the same return. On this basis, transactions where VAT would otherwise be pre-financed, meaning that cashflow is required to pay VAT which then may be obtained at a later date by a related entity, is replaced with a reverse charge transaction with VAT declaration and VAT recovery in the same return.

EUROPEAN COMMISSION: ANTI-AVOIDANCE MEASURES

The European Commission has reported a 'VAT gap' between expected revenue and revenue actually collected by national authorities is estimated at around EUR 170 billion, which equates to 15.2% of revenue loss. The Commission adopted the Action Plan on VAT in 2016.[18] The related measures include enhancing administrative cooperation, collectively improving the performance of European tax administrations, and improving voluntary compliance.

The European Commission concern with the present VAT system is that it splits every cross-border transaction into an exempted cross-border supply and a taxable cross-border acquisition. This is considered to be like a customs system, but lacks equivalent controls and is therefore the root of cross-border fraud. The Commission considered that VAT fraud generally occurs when a supplier pretends to have transported the goods to another Member State, but the goods are in fact consumed VAT-free locally, or where a client of a cross-border transaction purchases goods or services VAT-free and charges VAT without remitting it to tax authorities while their customer can deduct it.

The related anti-avoidance measures are proposed to include:[19]

- Improving cooperation within the EU and with non-EU countries – This will move from the existing cooperation models based on Member States exchanging information to new models of sharing and jointly analysing information and acting together. Member States should benefit from a risk management capacity at EU level, enabling them to rapidly and more effectively identify and dismantle fraudulent networks. Officials working in the Eurofisc information network would have direct access to relevant information held in different Member States, enabling them to exchange, share, and analyse key information and launch joint audits.[20]

18. Communication from the Commission to the European Parliament, the Council and the European Economic and Social Committee on an action plan on VAT Towards a single EU VAT area – Time to decide, Brussels, 7.4.2016, COM(2016) 148 final, https://ec.europa.eu/taxation_customs/sites/taxation/files/com_2016_148_en.pdf at 16 October 2017.
19. European Commission, Action Plan on VAT, https://ec.europa.eu/taxation_customs/business/vat/action-plan-vat_ at 16 October 2017.
20. Regulation on administrative cooperation and combating VAT fraud (Council Regulation 904/2010 (OJ L268 of 12/10/2010)).

- Towards more efficient tax administrations – This will develop a common agenda for tax administrations in order to build trust and to strengthen tax administrations' capacity to tackle fraud and adapt to economic developments while working together. This includes providing for a strategic discussion between the heads of the EU tax administrations, and with customs, in order to build such an agenda, facilitating agreements on minimum quality standards for core tax administration functions and evaluation, and providing platforms for knowledge and experience sharing and technical assistance to support reforms.
- Improving voluntary compliance – This will include running or sponsoring concrete projects such as effective dispute prevention and resolution mechanisms under the EU VAT Forum and will facilitate agreements between tax administrations and business sectors.
- Tax collection – New approaches to tax collection may include new reporting tools, new auditing tools, defining new roles for certain market intermediaries.
- Temporary derogation for Member States to tackle national and structural fraud – Some Member States more heavily affected by VAT fraud have asked to be allowed to implement a temporary generalised reverse charge system which would derogate from the general principles of the VAT Directive.

CHAPTER 15
Customs Duties and Tariffs

INTRODUCTION

Most countries impose significant customs tariffs on the importation of goods. Several countries also allow specific exemptions. Customs tariffs are a significant issue for the importation of goods, and a related issue is whether there are exemptions from customs duty under international agreements, for example exemptions provided under the European Union,[1] the North American Free Trade Agreement (NAFTA) between Canada, Mexico, and the United States (US).[2] There are also general agreements to reduce tariffs relating to the World Trade Organisation (WTO). In general the average rate of tariff has been significantly declining. The World Bank has commented, for example, that the average tariff rate in Latin American countries fell from 13.1% in 1996 to 4.8% in 2012.[3]

Customs tariffs are particularly important to the energy industry, with the importation of large scale machinery for upstream oil and gas exploration and production, coal and uranium mining, and plant and machinery for hydroelectric, wind, solar, and geothermal renewables projects. There are also very material customs tariff issues on the importation of oil, gas, coal, and uranium used in the generation of energy.

---

1. The Union Customs Code (UCC) was adopted on 9 October 2013 as Regulation (EU) No. 952/2013 of the European Parliament and of the Council. The substantive provisions will apply from 1 May 2016, once the related Delegated and Implementing Acts are adopted and in force. <http://eur-lex.europa.eu/legal-content/EN/TXT/?uri=CELEX:32013R0952>.
2. *North American Free Trade Agreement*, 17 December 1992, 32 ILM 289, Article 302 (entered into force 1 January 1994) ('*NAFT*'). <https://www.nafta-sec-alena.org/Home/Legal-Texts/North-American-Free-Trade-Agreement>.
3. 'Game of Zones' *The Economist*, 21 March 2015, p. 61.

CUSTOMS DUTY PROVISIONS

Customs duties on goods, generally known as tariffs, are based on reporting and payment procedures on importation. In the United Kingdom (UK), for example, Her Majesty's Revenue and Customs (HMRC) has summarised UK customs duty procedures.[4] Imports from overseas are treated differently depending on whether the goods come from countries within the European Union or from elsewhere. Within the European Union, most goods can be imported with minimal customs control and, mostly, with no import duty or VAT due to be paid. Goods in free circulation in the European Union can be moved from country to country with minimal customs control. Unless the goods are subject to excise duty, such as alcohol, or licence requirements such as agricultural goods, they generally cross European Union internal borders without any special taxes and minimal import paperwork.

Imports from outside the European Union are treated differently, and require an import declaration to customs. The importer generally must pay import duty and import VAT (plus VAT on import duty), although use of some customs procedures may suspend or relieve these taxes.[5] Imports from outside the European Union into the UK must be declared to HMRC. This is usually done using the Single Administrative Document (SAD) which are submitted electronically using the Customs Handling of Import and Export Freight (CHIEF) system, or are reported manually.

There are several methods available for the calculation of customs value. These values are also used as the basis to determine import VAT. In the UK, for example, there are six methods to calculate import valuations. Method 1 is the transaction value method, which applies to over 90% of import consignments. Method 1 cannot be used if the goods are imported on consignment, i.e., there has been no sale, or they have been supplied free of charge or on loan. The customs value is based on the price paid or payable by a buyer to a seller for the imported goods when sold for export to the European Union. The following costs must be added to the seller's price under Method 1 if they are not already included:[6]

- delivery to the European Union border;
- most commissions except buying commission;
- royalties and licence fees paid by the importer on the imported goods as a condition of sale;
- containers and packing;
- any proceeds of resale the seller will receive; and
- goods and services that the importer has provided to the seller for free or at a reduced cost – e.g., components incorporated in the imported goods, or

4. HMRC, 'Imports from outside the EU' 13 June 2013, <https://www.gov.uk/importing-goods-from-outside-the-eu>.
5. Businesses that are already involved in international trade and have an Economic Operator Registration and Identification Number (EORI), may wish to consider registering with HMRC as an Authorised Economic Operator (AEO). While the scheme is not compulsory, companies that meet the requirements will be registered as AEOs and can take advantage of simplified customs procedures that relate to the security and safety of their imported goods in transit.
6. HMRC, *How to Value Your Imports for Customs Duty and Trade Statistics* 13 June 2013.

development and design work carried out outside the European Union and necessary for the production of the imports.

The following amounts are excluded in determining the dutiable value where certain conditions are met:

- delivery costs within the European Union;
- European Union duties or taxes;
- taxes paid in the country of origin or export;
- quantity and trade discounts and those relating to cash and early settlement, that are valid at the time the goods are valued;
- dividend payments to the seller;
- marketing activities related to the imports;
- buying commission;
- export quota and licence costs;
- interest charges;
- rights of reproduction;
- post-importation work, e.g., construction or assembly; and
- management fees.

The use of other methods was summarised by the HMRC in Table 15.1.

Table 15.1 Calculation of Customs Value

	Calculate on the Basis of...	*Try the Next Method If...*
Method 1	the transaction value – the price payable to the seller	there has been no sale of goods
Method 2	the customs value of identical goods, produced in the same country as the imports	there are no identical goods
Method 3	the customs value of similar goods, which must be: produced in the same country, able to carry out the same tasks, and commercially interchangeable	there are no similar goods
Method 4	the selling price of the goods (or identical or similar goods) in the European Union	there are no European Union sales of the goods
Method 5	the production cost of the goods, including the cost of any materials, manufacturing and any other processing used in production	this production cost information is unavailable
Method 6	reasonably adapting one of the previous methods to fit unusual circumstances	N/A

Import duty and taxes are due when importing goods into the UK from outside of the European Union whether by a private individual or a commercial entity. The import duty and taxes payable are calculated on the cost, insurance and freight (CIF) value, which is the sum of the value of the imported goods and the cost of shipping and insurance. The duty rates applied to imports into the UK typically range between 0% for books to 17% for footwear. Some products such as laptops, mobile phones, digital cameras, and video game consoles are duty free. However, certain goods have been subject to additional duties depending on the country of manufacture, for example bicycles made in China carried an additional anti-dumping duty of 48.5%.[7]

BILATERAL TRADE AGREEMENTS, FREE TRADE AREAS, AND CUSTOMS UNIONS

Introduction

Preferential tariffs are lower tariff rates which can arise under international treaties. These treaties may be bilateral treaties between two specific countries, multilateral treaties within a specific group of countries generally within a geographical region such as the European Union, or multilateral treaties open to many countries such as the treaties relating to the WTO.

Bilateral trade agreements give preference to certain countries in commercial relationships, facilitating trade and investment between the home country and the foreign country by reducing or eliminating tariffs, import quotas, export restraints and other trade barriers. The US, for example, has bilateral trade agreements with twenty counties.[8]

A free trade area is a group of states which have eliminated most or all tariffs and quotas on their trade. The related agreement usually covers manufactured goods and commodities, and may also apply to services or the free movement of labour. Examples of free trade areas are the NAFTA,[9] the Association of Southeast Asian Nations (ASEAN),[10] and the Commonwealth of Independent States Free Trade Area (CIS-FTA).[11]

A customs union provides for internal free trade similarly to a free trade area, however a customs union also provides a common external tariff on imports from non-members. The members may potentially restrict their right to sign other trade agreements, and trade agreements are generally made by the union as a whole.

7. DutyCalculator, <http://www.dutycalculator.com/country-guides/>.
8. The United States has free trade agreements in force with twenty countries. These agreements are with Australia, Bahrain, Canada, Chile, Colombia, Costa Rica, Dominican Republic, El Salvador, Guatemala, Honduras, Israel, Jordan, Korea, Mexico, Morocco, Nicaragua, Oman, Panama, Peru and Singapore. The United States is also in negotiations of a regional, Asia-Pacific trade agreement, known as the Trans-Pacific Partnership (TPP) Agreement and the Transatlantic Trade and Investment Partnership (TTIP) with the European Union.
9. The members of NAFTA are Canada, the United States, and Mexico.
10. ASEAN members are Brunei, Cambodia, Indonesia, Laos, Malaysia, Myanmar, the Philippines, Singapore, Thailand, and Vietnam.
11. The members of CISFTA are Russia, Ukraine, Belarus, Uzbekistan, Moldova, Armenia, Kyrgyzstan, and Kazakhstan. All CISFTA participants except Ukraine, Uzbekistan, and Moldova are members of the Eurasian Economic Union.

Examples of customs unions are the European Union,[12] Mercosur,[13] and the Andean Community.[14]

Related issues include whether goods qualify as sourced in a treaty country, such as sourced from a NAFTA country under the NAFTA rules of origin. For example, this issue can arise where oil and gas companies blend crude oil with condensates or diluents from non-NAFTA states to transport the oil by pipeline, or blend natural gas with gas originating in non-NAFTA states.[15]

The WTO provides a forum for negotiating trade agreements. The purpose is to reduce obstacles to international trade, and therefore contribute to economic growth and development. The WTO also provides a legal and institutional framework for trade agreements, and a mechanism to resolve related trade disputes. The WTO was the outcome of the Uruguay Round of negotiations which included a major revision of the original General Agreement on Tariffs and Trade (GATT). The related classification of goods is based on cooperation between the World Customs Organisation (WCO) and the WTO. The classification of goods is based on Harmonised System (HS) originally based on GATT provisions. The WCO Technical Committee on Rules of Origin (TCRO) is responsible for harmonising rules of origin.

The Uruguay Round created new rules for dealing with trade in services, relevant aspects of intellectual property, dispute settlement, and trade policy reviews. This development included about thirty agreements and separate commitments made by individual members in specific areas such as lower customs duty rates and services market-opening. One result of the Uruguay Round was the commitment to cut tariffs and to bind customs duty rates to levels which are then difficult to increase.[16]

The World Bank reviewed the three types of tariff, being the most favoured nation (MFN), bound tariff (BND), and effectively applied tariffs (AHS).[17] They commented that virtually all countries in the world have joined at least one preferential trade agreement, under which they promise to give another country's products lower tariffs than their MFN rate.

12. The European Union members are Austria, Belgium, Bulgaria, Croatia, Republic of Cyprus, Czech Republic, Denmark, Estonia, Finland, France, Germany, Greece, Hungary, Ireland, Italy, Latvia, Lithuania, Luxembourg, Malta, Netherlands, Poland, Portugal, Romania, Slovakia, Slovenia, Spain, Sweden, and the United Kingdom. The members of the related The European Economic Area (EEA) includes the European Union countries and also Iceland, Liechtenstein, and Norway. Switzerland is not an EU or EEA member but is part of the single market.
13. The Mercosur members are Argentina, Brazil, Paraguay, Uruguay, and Venezuela. Its associate countries are Chile, Bolivia, Colombia, Ecuador, and Peru.
14. The Andean Community members are Bolivia, Colombia, Ecuador, and Peru.
15. Glenn A Cranker & Harold K Andersen, Stikeman Elliott LLP, 'Exporting Canadian Oil and Gas: The Challenge of NAFTA Compliance', <http://www.acc.com/legalresources/quickcounsel/exognafta.cfm> on 20 November 2013. The United States duty rate on crude oil imports from Canada, for example, may increase from the NAFTA rate of 'free' to 5.25 cents or 10.5 cents per barrel.
16. World Trade Organisation, 'The WTO Agreements', <https://www.wto.org/english/thewto_E/whatis_e/inbrief_e/inbr03_e.htm>.
17. World Bank, World Integrated Trade Solution, <http://wits.worldbank.org/wits/wits/witshelp/Welcome.htm>.

MFN Tariffs

The MFN tariffs are the tariffs that countries agree to impose on imports from other members of the WTO, unless the country is part of a preferential trade agreement, such as a free trade area or customs union. This means that, in practice, that MFN rates are the highest that WTO members charge one another.

In a customs union, such as the European Community or the Southern Africa Customs Union, or a free trade area such as NAFTA, the preferential tariff rate is zero on essentially all products. These agreements are reciprocal, so that all parties agree to give each other the benefits of lower tariffs. Some agreements specify that members will receive a percentage reduction from the MFN tariff, but not necessarily zero tariffs.

Some countries impose higher tariffs on countries that are not part of the WTO, or have also invoked the non-application clause of WTO/GATT agreements and chosen not to extend MFN treatment to certain other countries. Many countries, particularly the more developed ones, give developing countries unilateral preferential treatment, rather than through a reciprocal agreement. The largest of these programmes is the generalised system of preferences (GSP), which was initiated in the 1960s. The European Union, Japan and the US offer multiple unilateral preference programmes. The European Union's everything but arms (EBA) programme is one example. Exporting countries may have access to several different preference programmes from a given importing partner and for a given product.

Bound Tariffs

Bound tariffs are specific tariff commitments made by individual WTO member governments. The bound tariff is the maximum MFN tariff level for a given commodity line. When countries join the WTO or when WTO members negotiate tariff levels with each other during trade rounds, they make agreements about bound tariff rates, rather than actually applied rates. WTO members still have the flexibility increase or decrease their tariffs on a non-discriminatory basis so long as they did not raise tariffs above their bound levels. If one WTO member raises applied tariffs above their bound level, other WTO members can take the country to dispute settlement.[18]

The World Bank commented that the binding coverage share of tariff lines with WTO-bound rates also varies across countries. Until the Uruguay Round of the GATT, which ended in 1994, countries agreed to bind tariffs only on manufactured goods. During the Uruguay Round, countries committed to bind tariffs on all agricultural products. New members of the WTO have been asked to bind all manufactured tariff lines as well.

The importing country will apply the MFN tariff if the product fails to meet the country's rules that determine the product's country of origin. The World Bank

18. The World Bank commented that the gap between the bound and applied MFN rates is called the binding overhang. Trade economists argue that a large binding overhang makes a country's trade policies less predictable. This gap tends to be small on average in industrial countries and often fairly large in developing countries as illustrated below.

commentary gave the example that some former European colonies find it easier to satisfy the rules of origin under the Cotonou Agreement between the European Union and the African, Caribbean and Pacific Group of States, rather than the European Union Everything but Arms (EBA) programme even where the preferential tariffs are lower under the EBA. Accordingly satisfying the practical requirements of particular tariff schemes may be an important issue.

Effectively Applied Tariffs

States may in practice apply lower rates of tariff than the bound tariff rates. This is generally known as the effectively applied tariff and is the lowest available tariff. If a preferential tariff exists, it will be used as the effectively applied tariff.

CUSTOMS DUTIES AND ROYALTIES

There is a related issue concerning the payment of royalties. In general, royalty payments made by an importer must be included in the dutiable value where the payments are in connection with the imported goods, or the payment of the royalties is a condition for the sale and export of the goods to the importing country. Royalties are defined to include money paid for the use of patents, copyrights, and trademarks. Expenses paid for the right to domestically reproduce an imported good are not included in dutiable value. Royalties paid in connection with a patent on an imported good's production methods or the goods themselves usually need to be included in dutiable value. Royalties paid for the trademark on imported goods may, however, potentially not be included in the customs value where the actual use of the trademark is inside the importing country.

In the US, the transaction value subject to customs duties generally includes payments which are required as a condition of sale.[19] The US Customs and Border Protection (CBP) position is that, if the holder of the trademark, as the party receiving the royalties, is not the seller of the goods or its related party, and there is no other evidence that the trademark holder can control the transaction between buyer and seller, then it can accept that the payment of royalties is not a condition for the sale. Many customs authorities in Asia, including those in China, Taiwan, and Thailand, have considered that even where there is no connection between the holder of the rights and the seller of the goods, there may be assumed to be some influence on the part of the patent or trademark holder, so that the royalty payments are viewed as a condition of sale, and therefore included in the value subject to import tariffs.[20]

19. Tariff Act, 19 USC 1401a.
20. Yishian Lin, *Royalties: A Common Source of Problems in Customs Valuation* (PWC, 2015).

CUSTOMS DUTY PLANNING

Customs duty planning structures were reviewed by companies including International Trade Solutions,[21] and the former Custom Duty Compliance + Planning.[22] The most essential point is to correctly classify goods, as lower rates may be available for specific categories. There may be a further opportunity to reduce costs by stripping down the imports into individual constituent parts to achieve a lower duty rate, or alternatively, to present components at the same time in an unassembled kit form where the finished kit attracts a lower rate of duty than the individual components.[23]

There are several allowable deductions when declaring a customs value to the authorities. There are also certain additions such as freight, insurance costs and certain royalty payments. Deductions from the customs value include buying commissions and certain finance charges. These items should be specifically identified in supplier agreements so that the related deductions are clearly available.[24]

Split invoice arrangements may potentially reduce the value for duty payable by the company using a franchise fee concept. The charge for goods may be based on a split invoicing system, for example 90% relating to goods and a 10% service fee. Duty may potentially be payable on the 90% portion only.[25]

Prior sale planning is based on potentially reducing the declared value for duty by using the value of a sale that takes place before the sale to the importer. In many cases the importer may be buying from intermediaries rather than a manufacturer, and so there is a chain of sales before import. In these circumstances the importer may be able to elect an earlier sale in the chain as the basis for customs duty and remove any subsequent markups from a charge for duty. Related conditions include needing access to the earlier sales price, proving the earlier sale took place with intention to export the goods the European Union, and tracing transactions through the supply chain.[26]

There may be tariff relief where goods are imported to be used in the manufacture of goods for export. In relation to the European Union, for example, Inward Processing Relief (IPR) allows an importer to claim duty relief on raw materials, components, and goods imported for processing which are subsequently sold outside the European Union. Processing in this context could include inspecting and repacking the goods

21. '10 Ways Customs Planning Can Drive Down Your Business Costs', International Trade Solutions Ltd,. <http://www.internationaltradesolutions.co.uk/skyblucms/resources/10-ways-to-cut-customs-costs-white-paper-270611-6.pdf>.
22. Customs Duty Compliance + Planning, <http://www.cdcpireland.com/compliance-planning/> in June 2015.
23. '10 Ways Customs Planning Can Drive Down Your Business Costs', International Trade Solutions Ltd,. <http://www.internationaltradesolutions.co.uk/skyblucms/resources/10-ways-to-cut-customs-costs-white-paper-270611-6.pdf>.
24. '10 Ways Customs Planning Can Drive Down Your Business Costs', International Trade Solutions Ltd,. <http://www.internationaltradesolutions.co.uk/skyblucms/resources/10-ways-to-cut-customs-costs-white-paper-270611-6.pdf>.
25. Customs Duty Compliance + Planning, <http://www.cdcpireland.com/compliance-planning/> in June 2015.
26. '10 Ways Customs Planning Can Drive Down Your Business Costs', International Trade Solutions Ltd,. <http://www.internationaltradesolutions.co.uk/skyblucms/resources/10-ways-to-cut-customs-costs-white-paper-270611-6.pdf>.

through to more complex manufacturing. The availability of IPR is subject to specific authorisation and compliance with the related administration requirements. There may also be relief from customs duty relating to goods which are exported for processing. In the European Union, Outward Processing Relief (OPR) allows an importer to claim total or partial relief on goods sent outside of the European Union for process or repair.[27]

There are also customs duty reliefs relating to changes in classification relating to the manufacturing process. In the European Union, Processing under Customs Control (PCC) allows for relief on imported components where they are processed into finished or semi-finished products that attract nil or lower rates of duty than the components. The relief is based on the importer declaring the parts and materials under the same commodity code as the finished product.[28]

PROPOSED TRADE AGREEMENTS

There are several large scale potential trade agreements, which include the Transatlantic Trade and Investment Partnership (TTIP) between the US and the European Union, and the Trans-Pacific Partnership Agreement (TPP) between several Pacific Ocean states. The effective negotiation and completion of these proposed agreements is subject to approval of the respective governments, and the following summaries therefore relate to potential developments. There is a broad scope for both of the proposed agreements, where the reduction in tariffs is only one of several negotiating objectives, including regulatory issues such as rules governing capital flows and competition policy.[29]

Transatlantic Trade and Investment Partnership (TTIP)

The TTIP, a proposed comprehensive free trade agreement being negotiated between the US and the European Union. The objectives of the potential agreement for the US was summarised by the US Trade Representative as including:[30]

- The elimination of all tariffs and other duties and charges on trade in agricultural, industrial and consumer products between the US and the European Union, with substantial duty elimination on entry into force of the

27. '10 Ways Customs Planning Can Drive Down Your Business Costs', International Trade Solutions Ltd,. <http://www.internationaltradesolutions.co.uk/skyblucms/resources/10-ways-to-cut-customs-costs-white-paper-270611-6.pdf>.
28. '10 Ways Customs Planning Can Drive Down Your Business Costs', International Trade Solutions Ltd,. <http://www.internationaltradesolutions.co.uk/skyblucms/resources/10-ways-to-cut-customs-costs-white-paper-270611-6.pdf>.
29. 'Game of Zones' *The Economist*, 21 March 2015, 61.
30. Office of the United States Trade Representative, Transatlantic Trade and Investment Partnership, <https://ustr.gov/trade-agreements/free-trade-agreements/transatlantic-trade-and-investment-partnership-t-tip/t-tip>.

agreement, transition periods where necessary for sensitive products, and appropriate safeguard mechanisms to be applied if and where necessary.

- The elimination or reduction non-tariff barriers that decrease opportunities for exports, provide a competitive advantage to products, or otherwise distort trade.
- Providing greater compatibility regulations and related standards development processes, with the objective of reducing costs associated with unnecessary regulatory differences and facilitating trade.
- Establishing rules of origin that ensure that duty rates apply only to goods eligible to receive such treatment and define procedures to apply and enforce such rules.
- Obtaining improved market access on a comprehensive basis, and address the operation of any designated monopolies and state-owned enterprises, as appropriate; and reinforcing transparency, impartiality, and due process with regard to authorisations to supply services, obtain additional disciplines in certain services sectors, and improve regulatory cooperation where appropriate.
- Developing appropriate provisions to facilitate the use of electronic commerce to support goods and services trade, including through commitments not to impose customs duties on digital products or unjustifiably discriminate among products delivered electronically; and including provisions that facilitate the movement of cross-border data flows.
- Securing for investors important rights comparable to those that would be available under domestic legal principles and practice.
- Establishing disciplines to ensure transparent, efficient, and predictable conduct of customs operations and ensure that customs measures are not applied in a manner that creates unwarranted procedural obstacles to trade; and enhance customs cooperation.
- Expanding market access opportunities for goods, services, and suppliers of goods and services to government procurement markets; ensuring fair, transparent, and predictable conduct of government procurement and that suppliers of goods and services receive treatment as favourable as that accorded to domestic and other foreign goods, services, and suppliers.
- Obtaining appropriate commitments to internationally recognised labour rights and effective enforcement of labour laws concerning those rights, and establish procedures for consultations and cooperation to promote respect for internationally recognised labour rights.
- Obtaining appropriate commitments to protect the environment, including conserving natural resources, and to effectively enforce environmental laws, and seek opportunities to address environmental issues of mutual interest.
- Obtaining appropriate commitments that reflect the shared objective of high-level intellectual property rights (IPR) protection and enforcement, and to sustain and enhance joint leadership on related issues.

- Establishing appropriate, globally relevant disciplines on state trading enterprises, state-owned enterprises, and designated monopolies, such as disciplines that promote transparency and reduce trade distortions.
- Strengthening cooperation to enhance the participation of small and medium enterprises (SMEs) in trade between the US and the European Union.
- Obtaining improved transparency in the administration of trade and investment regimes, and rules that ensure trade and investment related measures are adopted and applied in an open and transparent manner.
- Establishing fair, transparent, timely, and effective procedures to settle disputes on matters arising under a trade and investment agreement with the European Union, including through early identification and settlement of disputes through consultation.

TPP Agreement

The TPP Agreement is under negotiation between Australia, Brunei, Canada, Chile, Japan, Malaysia, Mexico, New Zealand, Peru, Singapore, and Vietnam. The current US administration advised of its withdrawal from the TPP however on 23 January 2017.[31] The key features were described by the US Trade Representative as follows:[32]

(1) Comprehensive market access: to eliminate tariffs and other barriers to goods and services trade and investment, so as to create new opportunities for our workers and businesses and immediate benefits for our consumers.

(2) Fully regional agreement: to facilitate the development of production and supply chains among TPP members, supporting our goal of creating jobs, raising living standards, improving welfare and promoting sustainable growth in our countries.

(3) Cross-cutting trade issues: to build on work being done in APEC and other fora by incorporating in TPP four new, cross-cutting issues. These are:
    - Regulatory coherence. Commitments will promote trade between the countries by making trade among them more seamless and efficient.
    - Competitiveness and Business Facilitation. Commitments will enhance the domestic and regional competitiveness of each TPP country's economy and promote economic integration and jobs in the region, including through the development of regional production and supply chains.

31. The White House, Presidential Memorandum Regarding Withdrawal of the United States from the Trans-Pacific Partnership Negotiations and Agreement, Office of the Press Secretary, 23 January, 2017.
32. Office of the United States Trade Representative, 'Enhancing Trade and Investment, Supporting Jobs, Economic Growth and Development: Outlines of the Trans-Pacific Partnership Agreement', <https://ustr.gov/tpp/outlines-of-TPP>.

   - Small- and Medium-Sized Enterprises. Commitments will address concerns small- and medium-sized enterprises have raised about the difficulty in understanding and using trade agreements, encouraging small- and medium-sized enterprises to trade internationally.
   - Development. Comprehensive and robust market liberalisation, improvements in trade and investment enhancing disciplines, and other commitments, including a mechanism to help all TPP countries to effectively implement the Agreement and fully realise its benefits, will serve to strengthen institutions important for economic development and governance and thereby contribute significantly to advancing TPP countries' respective economic development priorities.

(4) New trade challenges: to promote trade and investment in innovative products and services, including related to the digital economy and green technologies, and to ensure a competitive business environment across the TPP region.

(5) Living agreement: to enable the updating of the agreement as appropriate to address trade issues that emerge in the future as well as new issues that arise with the expansion of the agreement to include new countries.

The broad scope of proposed agreements such as the TPP has extended well beyond the reduction in tariffs and customs duties on goods and services. Donald Robertson commented on the TPPs potential impact on the energy sector as follows:[33]

> The TPP is unprecedented in its scope and complexity. Not only does it cover a wide range of market access issues for both goods and services, it also contains provisions in relation to issues that go well beyond traditional free trade agreements. Among the TPP's sector-specific rules are regulations addressing 'modern economy' industries and issues, such as financial services, telecommunications, intellectual property and e-commerce. The TPP deals with the integrity of market processes (anti-corruption, competition, government procurement and preferential status of state-owned enterprises); the economic regulation of markets (best practice regulation and regulatory coherence); and environmental, labour and other human rights issues. It also, controversially, provides protection for investors in the form of Investor-State Dispute Settlement (ISDS) provisions.

He also commented that the chapter of the TPP on environmental regulation was of great relevance to the energy sector, as the TPP countries are required to promote cooperative efforts to address energy efficiency and the development of cost-effective, low-emissions technologies and alternative, clean and renewable energy sources.

33. Donald Robertson, Impact of Trans-Pacific Partnership on the Energy Sector, Herbert Smith Freehills, 2 November 2015, https://www.herbertsmithfreehills.com/latest-thinking/impact-of-trans-pacific-partnership-on-the-energy-sector at 21 December 2017.

CHAPTER 16

Holding Companies, Dividends, and Profit Distributions

INTRODUCTION

This chapter considers the international taxation issues relating to how profits are distributed from a subsidiary in one country to its holding or parent company in another country. Accordingly the chapter concerns where funding has been made available to the subsidiary company in the form of shares or other forms of equity, rather than made in the form of loans. There are potential advantages for equity funding, which can include exemptions from withholding tax for the payments of dividends from a country compared to the payment of interest, and exemptions on the taxation of dividends for the parent company under domestic tax rules and tax treaties. This includes measures to reduce or eliminate withholding tax under the majority of tax treaties, and the participation exemption measures under domestic tax laws and the European Union (EU) Parent Subsidiary Directive.

One preliminary comment is that the repatriation of profits depends on the tax laws of the countries concerned, including the rate of tax on the related activities, the withholding tax on dividends and other payments, whether withholding taxes are reduced by tax treaties between the paying and receiving countries, and how the related income is taxed in the parent country. The practical approach is to prepare a schedule showing income from business activities, and then showing each level of taxation, until the net amounts after tax are derived in the parent country.

In general, the repatriation of profits using dividends or from branches is not deductible in the paying countries. There may, however, be scope to reduce taxes in the local country by other means, such as maximising amounts that may be deductible including management fees or the payment of interest on loans.

There are also potential uses of branches for tax planning purposes. Branches should generally be allowed an allocation of head office and related company expenses as deductible in the branch country consistent with Article 7 of the OECD Model Tax

Treaty.[1] Related tax issues for the branch include the deductibility of the head office interest costs, and the related issue of how much capital is allocated to the branch to reduce the allocation of these head office costs.

SUBSIDIARIES: DIVIDENDS

Figure 16.1 Subsidiaries: Dividends

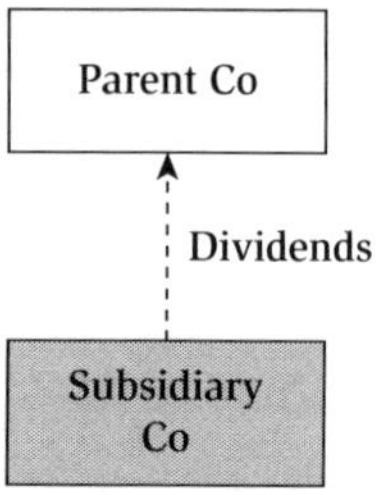

Dividends may be tax free under participation exemption

Dividends are generally not deductible

Overview

This issue concerns the taxation treatment on the repatriation of profits from subsidiaries to the parent company using dividends. The payment of dividends is generally not deductible for the subsidiary company, and may also incur dividend withholding tax.

Tax Analysis

There is generally no deduction for dividends in most countries, with very limited exceptions such as under the interest on net share equity provisions in Brazil.[2] Dividends are, however, commonly tax exempt to the parent company under participation exemption provisions, such as in the United Kingdom (UK), the Netherlands, and many other European countries. The dividends may alternatively be taxable, but with a foreign tax credit which may potentially eliminate parent country taxation when the credit is a sufficient amount.

Considerations

The principal consideration on the use of dividends to repatriate profits is the availability of tax exemptions such as the participation exemption in the parent county.

1. OECD, *Model Tax Convention on Income and on Capital*, Article 7 (OECD, 2017) (OECD Model Tax Treaty 2017).
2. *Law 9,249/1995*, Article 9 (Brazil).

Limitations on the participation exemption which can make the dividend taxable for the parent company can include where dividends are paid from tax havens. This should not be an issue where the Hold Co is the immediate holding company of a subsidiary with real business operations, as in the structure above. The issue may apply, however, if there is an intermediate tax haven holding company holding the shares of the Subsidiary Co, and where the tax haven company was then a subsidiary of the Parent Co. This type of a structure may risk the loss of the participation exemption on dividends for the Parent Co under the related participation exemption rules.

There is also an important issue of potential withholding tax on dividend payments from the Subsidiary Co. This issue generally depends on any domestic withholding tax exemptions for dividend payments in the subsidiary country, together with any reductions or exemptions in withholding tax under the relevant tax treaties. The Parent Co country in particular needs to have a good tax treaty network to generally reduce or eliminate withholding tax from the subsidiaries in other countries. There may also be a requirement for commercial substance in the Parent Co, to benefit from reduced withholding tax rates on dividends under many tax treaties. These limitations may include the requirement that the beneficial owner of the dividends must be resident in the treaty state, as in the OECD Model Tax Treaty in Article 10(2).[3] A similar limitation is made under the 'limitation on benefits' clauses under most United States (US) tax treaties, which may require ultimate ownership and use of income by in the other treaty country to obtain benefits of the Treaty, for example under Article 24 of the US/Luxembourg tax treaty.[4]

Potential Benefits

The potential benefits of the use of dividends are that the dividends are generally tax-free to the parent company, however the drawback is that the dividends are generally not deductible for the subsidiary company.

DIVIDENDS: WITHHOLDING TAX EXEMPTIONS

Tax Treaties

The principal way in which dividend withholding tax may be reduced or eliminated is under tax treaties. The OECD Model Tax Treaty limits the source country withholding tax on dividend payments to 15%, reduced to 5% if the beneficial owner is a company which holds directly at least 25% of the share capital of the company paying the

3. OECD, *Model Tax Treaty 2017*.
4. *Convention between the Government of the United States of America and the Government of the Grand Duchy of Luxembourg for the Avoidance of Double Taxation and the Prevention of Fiscal Evasion with Respect to Taxes on Income and Capital* (3 April 1996) ('United States/Luxembourg tax treaty').

dividends.[5] Dividends are generally defined as 'income from shares jouissance shares or jouissance rights, mining shares, founders' shares or other rights, not being debt-claims, participating in profits, as well as income from other corporate rights which is subjected to the same taxation treatment as income from shares by the laws of the State of which the company making the distribution is a resident'.[6] This definition is particularly significant in relation to hybrid securities, which have elements of equity and debt, and may have different tax treatments in different countries. The tax treaty treatment under this definition, including whether withholding tax reductions or exemptions are available, will generally classify the distributions as dividends if that is the classification in the dividend paying country.

European Union

The EU introduced a requirement for nil withholding tax on dividend payments made between taxable companies in EU countries where there was a sufficient shareholding under the Parent Subsidiary Directive.[7] The EU also introduced the requirement for the parent country to provide either a tax exemption or a foreign tax credit for dividends under the Directive. The Directive was amended to reduce the shareholding threshold to 10% applying from 2009.[8] EU Member States have implemented the Directive in domestic tax provisions and may provide better terms than the minimum requirements of the Directive.

Collective Investment Schemes

There are several tax issues concerning the repatriation of profits relating to entities which are not companies. There are, for example, current tax issues which apply to collective investment schemes (CIS) and collective investment vehicles (CIV), which include common EU rules for establishment, operation and regulation of these funds, called Undertakings for Collective Investment in Transferable Securities (UCITS).[9] A significant issue being considered by the OECD is whether these types of entities should qualify for tax treaty benefits to reduce withholding tax on distributions.[10]

The related developments include France introducing withholding tax exemptions for EU and European Economic Area (EEA) based schemes in 2012.[11] These

5. *OECD Model Tax Treaty 2017*, Article 10(2).
6. *OECD Model Tax Treaty 2017*, Article 10(3).
7. *Council Directive 90/435/EEC of 23 July 1990 on the Common System of Taxation Applicable in the Case of Parent Companies and Subsidiaries of Different Member States*, Article 5(1) (L 225, 20 August 1990) (Parent Subsidiary Directive) (European Union).
8. *Council Directive 2003/123/EC of 22 December 2003 Amending Directive 90/435/EEC on the Common System of Taxation Applicable in the Case of Parent Companies and Subsidiaries of Different Member States*, Article 3 (L 007, 13 January 2004) (European Union).
9. European Union, The Undertakings for Collective Investment in Transferable Securities Directives 85/611/EEC, as amended by 2001/107/EC and 2001/108/EC ('UCITS').
10. OECD, *The Granting of Treaty Benefits with Respect to the Income of Collective Investment Vehicles*, (OECD, 2010).
11. *Finance Act 2012* (France).

measures exempt distributions to UCITS from dividend withholding tax. The measures were adopted to comply the decision of the European Court of Justice (ECJ) in the *Santander* case, where the ECJ held that applying French withholding tax on dividends paid by French companies to non-French UCITS, where no withholding tax would be payable on payments to French resident UCITS, was contrary to the EU principle of the free movement of capital.[12]

DIVIDENDS: PARTICIPATION EXEMPTIONS AND FOREIGN TAX CREDITS

Introduction

A significant issue for holding company structures is whether the dividends received by the holding company from its foreign subsidiaries are effectively free of tax in the holding company country, such as under the participation exemption. There are generally related conditions, for example the exemption may not be allowed where the dividends are received from a subsidiary located in a tax haven country. The dividend is then generally taxed where the conditions for the exemption are not met, however a foreign tax credit is allowed which may reduce the effective tax on the dividend. Other countries may tax dividend income received from foreign subsidiary companies, but allow a foreign tax credit for tax paid by the subsidiary. A related issue is whether the interest expenses of the holding company on any funds borrowed which were used to invest in share capital of foreign subsidiaries are deductible. This issue applies, for example, where the financing is done at parent company level, and the parent company then provides the borrowed funds in the form of share capital to the foreign subsidiary. The tax issue arises because the related dividend income is effectively free of tax, and so the tax provisions in several countries may deny the interest deductions on the related borrowings.

Australia

Australia provides an exemption for foreign 'non-portfolio dividends'. These measures apply where the shareholding company has at least 10% voting interest in the subsidiary company.[13] Dividends derived by Australian companies from other Australian companies are generally tax exempt to the extent that the dividends have been 'franked' under the dividend imputation system. This system applies where a company payment of tax is allocated to the dividends paid by that company. The related dividends are then effectively tax exempt to the recipient to the extent that the paying company has paid tax, by including the dividend in taxable income and then allowing

12. *Santander Asset Management SGIIC and Others*, ECJ, 10 May 2012, C-338/11 to C-347/11 (European Court of Justice).
13. *Income Tax Assessment Act 1997*, section 768-A, generally replacing from 2014 the previous section 23AJ of the *Income Tax Assessment Act 1936*, and as amended by the *New International Tax Arrangements (Participation Exemption and Other Measures) Act 2004* (Australia).

a credit for the related tax paid by the dividend paying company.[14] The dividends are also exempt from withholding tax when paid to non-resident shareholders to the extent the dividends are franked.[15]

France

The French rules provide that dividends are effectively 95% exempt from tax under the participation exemption where the parent company is an SA or SARL entity, or the dividends are derived by a French branch with head office in the EU or treaty country with a non-discrimination clause in relation to permanent establishments. The parent company is required to hold at least 5% of the subsidiary company's capital.[16]

Germany

Dividends are generally exempt in Germany where the German company or branch holds at least 10% of the shares in the German or foreign company under the amended rules applying from 2013. The participation exemption requires that 5% of the dividends is added back to the taxable income of the German shareholding company as non-deductible business expenses.[17] Beginning from the 2014 tax year, the tax exemption for dividends is only allowed where the dividend payment is not tax-deductible for the distributing company, under amendments applying from 2014.[18]

Italy

The Italian participation exemption rules provide that dividends derived by resident companies from non-residents may be effectively 95% exempt from corporate income tax (IRES).[19] The exemption does not apply where the dividends are deductible to the paying company. Dividends from non-residents only qualify for the exemption where distributing company is not resident in 'black list' privileged tax regime unless tax ruling allows the exemption. Dividends which are received from an intermediate holding company resident in a jurisdiction not on the blacklist are fully taxable on the dividends to the extent they are derived from indirect subsidiaries which are resident in the black list jurisdictions.[20]

14. *Income Tax Assessment Act 1997*, Act No. 38 of 1997, Division 207 (Australia).
15. *Income Tax Assessment Act 1936*, Act No. 27 of 1936, section 128B(3)(ga)(i) (Australia).
16. *General Tax Code* (CGI) Arts 145 and 216 (France).
17. *Körperschaftsteuergesetz* (KstG) (Corporate Income Tax Act) section 8b (Germany).
18. Ernst & Young, *Worldwide Corporate Tax Guide 2014* 477 (Ernst & Young, 2014).
19. *Testo Unico Imposte sui Redditi* (TUIR) (Italian Tax Code) (Presidential Decree 917 of 22 December 1986) Article 89(2) (Italy).
20. Ernst & Young, *Worldwide Corporate Tax Guide 2014* 658 (Ernst & Young, 2014).

Netherlands

The Netherlands participation exemption rules as amended from 2007 provide that there is no tax on dividends and capital gains if the seller held a participation of at least 5% in the subsidiary company, and the participation is not held as a portfolio investment, generally meaning that the shares in the subsidiary are not merely held for the return that can be expected from normal asset management. The intention of the parent company is based on the particular facts and circumstances. The participation may still qualify if it meets the reasonable tax test, where the effective foreign tax rate is not less than 10% calculated under Netherlands tax rules.[21] The participation may also qualify if it meets an asset test, where less than half of the assets of the direct subsidiary usually consist of, directly or indirectly, low-taxed 'free' portfolio investments, including interest yielding assets, and non-participation shareholdings.[22]

United Kingdom

The UK introduced the foreign dividend participation exemption provisions for 10% or greater shareholdings in subsidiaries with effect from 2009.[23] The provisions generally allow the exemption where:

- Medium and large companies receive distributions within an exempt class, including dividends paid by a company that is controlled by the UK recipient company, dividends paid in respect of ordinary share capital that is non-redeemable, most portfolio dividends, and dividends derived from transactions which are not designed to reduce tax. The exemption also applies to small companies, with fewer than fifty employees and annual turnover or balance is less than GBP 10 million, receive dividends where the payer is resident in the UK or a qualifying territory.
- The distribution is not of a specified kind, such as capital distributions or interest treated as distributions under thin capitalisation adjustments, distributions which are tax-deductible in the paying jurisdiction, dividends subject to targeted anti-avoidance measures, and dividends paid out under a controlled foreign company acceptable distribution policy.
- No deduction is allowed to a resident of any territory outside the UK under the law of that territory with respect to the distribution.[24]

The UK may allow a foreign tax credit for foreign direct tax where the exemption is not available. The credit is limited to the UK Corporations Tax that would apply on the same profits. A credit is also allowed for underlying tax, being the tax paid by the foreign subsidiary on its own income, from 1 July 2009 irrespective of the UK

21. *Corporate Income Tax Act 1969*, Act of 8 October 1969, Article 13 (Netherlands).
22. Ernst & Young, *Worldwide Corporate Tax Guide 2014* 952 (Ernst & Young, 2014).
23. *Corporation Tax Act 2009* c. 4, section 931D, introduced by *Finance Act 2009*, c. 10, section 34 and Schedule 14 (United Kingdom).
24. Ernst & Young, *Worldwide Corporate Tax Guide 2014* 1435 (Ernst & Young, 2014).

company's voting power in the foreign subsidiary. From 2010, surplus foreign tax credits may be carried forward indefinitely to be utilised against future tax, and the credits may be carried back for two years. There are several anti-avoidance measures concerning foreign tax credits including related measures in the 2005 Budget. These provisions can potentially apply where a taxpayer claims relief for foreign tax as part of a scheme with tax avoidance as its main purpose or one of its main purposes. The available foreign tax credits will then be limited to cancel the effect of the scheme.

United States

The US has introduced an exemption system for certain foreign dividends from 2018 under the Tax Cuts and Jobs Act (TCJA).[25] The exemption applies to dividends received by US corporations from foreign corporations in which the US corporation owns at least a 10% holding.

THE OECD BEPS ACTION 2 AND HYBRID ARRANGEMENTS

Multinational groups may use hybrid entities or hybrid securities in dividend structures. One example would be where a hybrid security where the related payment by the subsidiary was treated as interest in the subsidiary country, but was treated as a tax-free dividend under the participation exemption or taxed with a foreign tax credit in the parent country.[26] As discussed, the OECD BEPS Action 2 addresses the use of hybrid mismatch arrangements as follows:[27]

- Recommendation 1: Hybrid Financial Instrument – This applies to deductions in one country with non-inclusion/tax exemption in another country (D/NI). The primary rule is that countries deny taxpayer's deduction to the extent of the D/NI outcome. The defensive rule is to include in payee ordinary income to the extent of the D/NI outcome. This rule requires the transaction to be in the same control group or under a structured arrangement.
- Recommendation 2: Specific Hybrid Financial Instrument – This applies to deductions in one country with non-inclusion/tax exemption in another country (D/NI), where the instrument has been designated by countries. The primary rule is to deny a dividend exemption for deductible payments.
- Recommendation 8: Imported Mismatch Rule – This applies to hybrid entities and instruments between other countries and a related deduction in the local country. There is a primary rule only, to deny the payer deduction. This rule requires the transaction to be in the same control group or under a structured arrangement.

25. *The Tax Cuts and Jobs Act*, Public law no. 115-97, 131 Stat. 2054 (United States).
26. Jakob Bundgaard, *Hybrid Financial Instruments in International Tax Law* (Kluwer Law International, 2016) and John Abrahamson, *Tolley's International Taxation of Corporate Finance* (LexisNexis, 2014).
27. OECD, Neutralising the Effects of Hybrid Mismatch Arrangements, Action 2: 2015 Final Report.

ALTERNATIVES TO DIVIDENDS: RETURN OF CAPITAL OR DEBT REPAYMENT

Figure 16.2 Alternatives to Dividends – Return of Capital or Debt Repayment

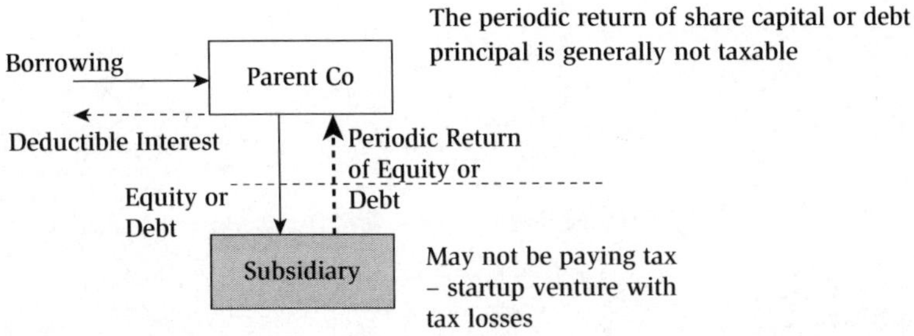

One structure which may provide an alternative to repatriating profits using dividends is based on the early return of the capital invested in a foreign subsidiary. In this structure, it may be effective to plan the early return of part of the investment as the return of share capital or as the repayment of debt. The return of capital is generally not taxed, either by withholding tax in the Subsidiary country, or by direct tax in the Parent Co country, whereas paying a dividend or interest may be taxable to the Parent Co.

The capital can be returned to the Parent Co by redeeming issued shares or a part return of share capital. In relation to the alternative of debt funding, a debt instrument can be used for the investment, such as loan note, which allows earlier repayment of part of the principal of the loan. The equity repayment or repayment of part of the loan principal is generally not subject to withholding tax as these amounts are not dividends or interest. The early return of investment capital or loan principal is also generally not income or profit, and is therefore not taxed in the Parent Co country unless there is a related capital gain.

The loan note structure may provide for the return of principal of the loan at certain dates, as well as the payment of interest at set periods. For example, EUR 100 million may be loaned for ten years. The terms of the loan note provide for 20% repayment of the loan principal in years three, five, and seven, when subsidiary expects sufficient available cash, and for the repayment of the remaining 40% of loan principal in year ten. This structure may reduce the Parent Co's tax where the investment anticipates initial losses, and where the Subsidiary Co borrower has limited use for interest deductions in the early years of operations.

BRANCHES AND PROFIT REPATRIATION

Figure 16.3 Branches and Profit Repatriation

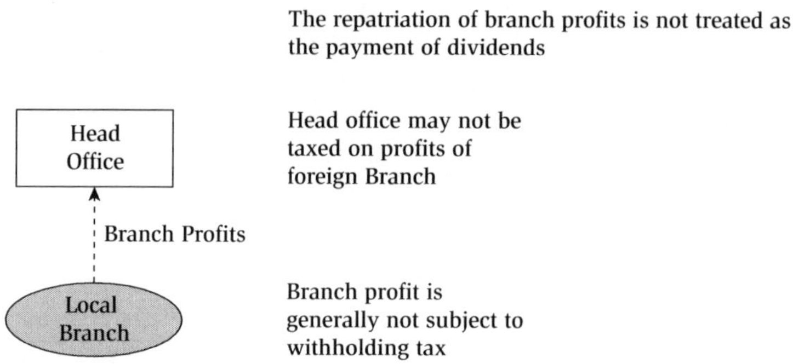

This structure concerns one potential tax advantage where a local branch of a foreign head office company may be more tax effective than using a local country subsidiary.

The repatriation of branch profits is not treated as a dividend, and in many countries the repatriation of profits may not be subject to local country withholding taxes unless that country has a branch profits repatriation tax.

The related considerations include how the Head Office company is taxed. The head office may potentially be taxed on the profits of the foreign branch, and so it may be more effective to use a local country subsidiary to ensure the foreign parent company is not subject to local country tax. The use of a local subsidiary may also have a commercial advantage in potentially limiting the legal liabilities to the subsidiary company itself rather than a separate parent company. There may also be a legal requirement to have a local subsidiary, such as a licence condition for upstream oil and gas activities. Accordingly the use of a branch may have potential tax advantages relating to withholding tax, however it is important to consider the related commercial and tax issues.

On this basis, there is likely to be no withholding tax in many countries on the remittance of branch profits to the Head Office company.

OECD BEPS MEASURES AND TREATY SHOPPING

The extension of anti-treaty shopping measures in tax treaties will have the greatest impact on holding company structures used by multinationals to reduce withholding tax and direct taxation on dividend flows. As discussed, the OECD BEPS Multilateral Instrument (MLI) Article 7 relates to BEPS Action 6, minimum standard on treaty abuse, and requires that countries adopt both limitation on benefit (LOB) and principal purpose test (PPT) measures, adopt PPT measures alone, or adopt LOB measures together with a restricted PPT rule applicable to conduit financing arrangements or domestic anti-abuse rules or judicial doctrines that would achieve a similar result.[28] These measures are incorporated in the OECD Model Tax Treaty 2017 in Article 29 Entitlement to Benefits.[29]

Accordingly a structure based on an intermediate holding company located in a country with a favourable tax treaty network which does not have a principal commercial purpose or sufficient commercial substance in may not qualify for treaty benefits, with the result that withholding taxes on dividends paid form subsidiary companies to the intermediate holding company are not reduced by tax treaties.

CBC REPORTING

The BEPS Action 13 Country-by-Country (CbC) reporting measures may impact the use of group holding companies:

- CbC reports can include holding company under the Main Business Activity heading Holding Shares or Other Equity Instruments, with related information including related and unrelated party revenues, profits before tax, income tax paid, and number of employees.
- The CbC report may assist in identifying group holding companies with high related party earnings compared to the number of related employees.
- The related analysis by tax authorities may include whether profits allocated to such holding companies are appropriate to functions performed, assets used, and risks undertaken by these entities, or suggest that the use of these companies is potentially to reduce taxable profits in the group.

The CbC measures were adopted in the 2017 OECD Transfer Pricing Guidelines for Multinational Enterprises and Tax Administrations.

EU ANTI-ABUSE CLAUSE FOR THE PARENT SUBSIDIARY DIRECTIVE

The EU Parent Subsidiary Directive (2011/96/EU) (PSD), adopted in November 2011,[30] was intended to ensure that profits made by cross-border groups are not taxed twice. The Directive requires Member States to exempt from taxation profits received by parent companies from their subsidiaries in other Member States. On 27 January 2015, the European Council adopted a binding general anti-abuse rule (GAAR) to be included

28. Multilateral Convention to Implement Tax Treaty Related Measures to Prevent Base Erosion and Profit Shifting, opened for signature 7 June 2017.
29. OECD, *Model Tax Treaty 2017*, Article 29.
30. Directive 2011/96/EU, adopted in November 2011 (Parent Subsidiary Directive).

in the Directive.[31] Member States had until 31 December 2015 to implement the GAAR into their own national law.[32] The Directive provides that:

> Member States shall not grant the benefits of the PSD to an arrangement or a series of arrangements which, having been put into place for the main purpose or one of the main purposes of obtaining a tax advantage that defeats the object or purpose of the PSD, are not genuine having regard to all relevant facts and circumstances. An arrangement may comprise more than one step or part.

For the purposes of the GAAR, the Directive provides that 'an arrangement or a series of arrangements shall be regarded as not genuine to the extent that they are not put into place for valid commercial reasons which reflect economic reality'.

These measures, in a similar manner to the OECD MLI and the 2017 Model Tax Treaty anti-treaty abuse rules, will impact the use of EU intermediate holding companies to eliminate withholding tax on payments to other EU companies.

31. Council Directive (EU) 2015/121 of 27 January 2015 amending Directive 2011/96/EU on the common system of taxation applicable in the case of parent companies and subsidiaries of different Member States.
32. EY, GAAR rising, Strengthening the European Union Parent Subsidiary Directive with a new general anti-abuse rule, 2015, http://www.ey.com/Publication/vwLUAssets/ey-a-new-gaar-for-europe-parent-subsidiary-directive/$FILE/ey-a-new-gaar-for-europe-parent-subsidiary-directive.pdf on 16 October 2017.

Chapter 17
Interest Deductions in Subsidiaries and Thin Capitalisation

INTRODUCTION

Figure 17.1 Thin Capitalisation

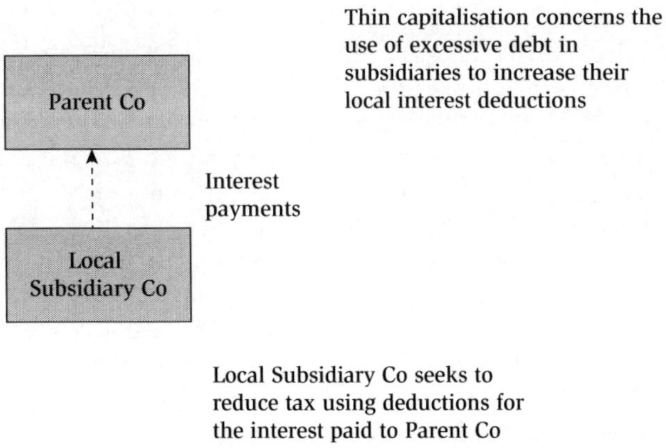

Thin capitalisation relates to the anti-tax avoidance provisions of many countries which generally limit tax deductions for interest paid on related party debt, for example for interest on loans from a parent company or a group treasury centre.[1] These provisions can potentially also limit interest deductions on debt to third parties, or where debt is considered to be excessive. In the diagram above, the Parent Co has loaned money to the Local Subsidiary Co in another country. The interest on the loan

1. Stuart Webber, *Thin Capitalization and Interest Deduction Rules: A Worldwide Survey*, (2010) 60(9) Tax Notes International, 683.

paid by the Local Subsidiary Co to the Parent Co may not be deductible if the loan exceeds that country's thin capitalisation limits.

Several countries use a debt-to-equity ratio for thin capitalisation, where interest on the amount of debt exceeding the maximum ratio of debt-to-equity is not deductible. For example, a country may have a 3:1 debt-to-equity ratio for thin capitalisation, and the debt-to-equity ratio of the local company is actually 5:1, based on USD 500 million of debt to USD 100 million of equity. The interest on the USD 200 million excess debt may be treated as non-deductible.

In some countries, thin capitalisation rules may apply to third-party loans where a parent company provides a guarantee for a third-party bank loan to a subsidiary in the group. Other countries have been introducing additional limitations on interest deductions, such as the earnings-stripping rules in the United States (US), the interest barrier rules in the United Kingdom (UK), Germany, and Denmark, the interest limits applying to the participation exemption limitation in the Netherlands, and the worldwide debt cap rules in the UK. Instead of international structures with debt exceeding the local country thin capitalisation limits, there may be opportunities to charge other expenses to the local subsidiaries which still allow local tax deductions.

COUNTRY EXAMPLES

Australia: Thin Capitalisation

The Australian thin capitalisation provisions apply to the total debt of Australian operations of multinational groups, including foreign and domestic related party and third-party debt. Interest on the excessive debt is not deductible. The rules do not apply where total debt deductions are AUD 2 million or less, or the Australian assets account for 90% or more of total assets of outward investing entities. The maximum debt amount is generally the greatest of: (1) the safe harbour debt amount using a debt-to-equity ratio of 1.5:1 (60% debt-to-total assets ratio), 15:1 debt-to-equity for non-bank financial entities, and 6% of risk-weighted assets of Australian operations for banks; (2) the arm's-length debt test which allows groups to have gearing levels that exceed safe harbour limit having regard to debt levels the entity might reasonably be expected to have, and debt levels that commercial lending institutions might reasonably be expected to have advanced on an arm's-length basis; or (3) the debt is under 100% of group's worldwide gearing ratio.[2]

Denmark: Interest Barrier Rules

The Danish interest barrier rules were introduced in 2007, and may impose limits on interest deductions. The interest ceiling rule applies where interest expenses exceed 3.5% of assets, and the earnings before interest and tax (EBIT) rule applies where

2. Div 820, Income Tax Assessment Act 1997.

interest exceeds 80% of EBIT. The provisions may apply to debt owed to resident and non-resident creditors, and debt to third parties and related parties.[3]

France: Thin Capitalisation

Interest expenses can be disallowed from 1 January 2007 under the arm's length test or under the thin capitalisation test. The arm's length test can disallow the interest deductions where the interest rate exceeds the higher of the average interest rate on loans of more than two years granted by banks to French companies in similar circumstances, or the interest rate at which the company could have borrowed from unrelated financial institutions.

The thin capitalisation test can disallow deductions where loans from related shareholders, based on a relationship of more than 50% of voting or financial rights, exceed 50% of share capital, 25% of profits, with interest, depreciation and tax added back, or the interest exceeds the interest amount received from related companies.

Germany: Interest Barrier Rules

In Germany the interest barrier rules introduced in 2008 can generally disallow interest deductions where the company's net interest expenditure exceeds 30% of the company's earnings before interest, taxes, depreciation and amortisation (EBITDA). The interest barrier rule can apply to debt to resident and non-resident creditors, and debt to third parties and related parties.[4]

Italy: Interest Limits

Italy introduced limitations on the deductibility of interest from 1 January 2008. The limits can apply to related and unrelated party debt. The rules provide that interest expenses, net of interest income, exceeding 30% of EBITDA (earnings before interest, tax, depreciation, and amortisation) are not deductible. The rules include lease payments which are treated as interest. Banks, insurance companies, and financial companies, except for holding companies, are generally excluded from the limits. Interest which is disallowed under these provisions can be carried forward without a time limit, and can be used to offset taxable income within the 30% limit in succeeding tax years.

3. *Corporate Income Tax Act*, Law 111 of 19 February 2004, ('*Selskabsskatteloven*') section 11B and 11C, and *Income Tax Act*, Statute of 1922 on Income Taxation to the State, ('*Statsskatteloven*') (Denmark).
4. *Income Tax Act*, section 4(h) (EStG), *Corporate Income Tax Law*, section 8(a) ('KStG') (Germany).

Netherlands: Participation Debt Limitation

The Netherlands has measures to limit the interest deductions relating to foreign participations in the participation debt limitation rules which apply from 2013.[5] The measures apply to interest relating to share investments where the related dividends would be tax-free under the participation exemption rules. The amount of the non-deductible interest is based on the ratio of participation debt to the company's total debt. The term participation debt is the amount by which the purchase price of the participations exceeds the parent company's equity. The Netherlands abolished the thin capitalisation ratio provisions in 2013.[6]

US: Thin Capitalisation

The US thin capitalisation provisions were amended by the Tax Cuts and Jobs Act from 2018. The US has adopted a limit based on net interest expense that exceeds 30% of adjusted taxable income (ATI). For the first four years, ATI is computed without regard to depreciation, amortisation, or depletion. From 2022, the ATI is decreased by these items, based on 30% of net interest expense exceeding EBIT (earnings before interest and taxes).[7]

UK: Thin Capitalisation

The UK announced new interest deductibility rules to apply from 1 April 2017 to limit deductions for interest by reference to a ratio of their net interest expense to EBITDA. The new provisions will include: (1) a fixed ratio rule limiting UK tax deductions for net interest to a maximum of 30% of a group's tax-adjusted UK EBITDA; (2) an optional group ratio rule that allows tax relief for interest to instead be calculated by reference to the group's net interest to EBITDA ratio; and (3) a GBP 2 million threshold for these rules based on the net UK interest expenses. The measures will allow the carry-forward of spare borrowing capacity for up to three years, and the indefinite carry-forward of restricted interest. The measures also include a modified worldwide debt cap rule to ensure that groups with low levels of external debt cannot leverage their UK operations to the new limit, together with related anti-avoidance rules.[8]

5. *Corporate Income Tax Act* (CITA) section 13L (Netherlands).
6. Ernst & Young, *Worldwide Corporate Tax Guide 2013* 915 (Ernst & Young, 2013).
7. US Tax Cuts and Jobs Act and its impact on the energy sector, EY Global Tax Alert, 29 December 2017, EY 2017.
8. Finance (No. 2) Bill 2017, section 31 and Sch 10, to add Pt 10, Taxation (International and Other Provisions) Act 2010 (TIOPA 2010).

UK: Worldwide Debt Cap

The UK has also introduced worldwide debt cap rules.[9] These provisions may apply from 1 January 2010 to the net UK debt costs of a UK group. The gateway test for disallowance applies where UK net debt, less loan receivables and debt in finance leases, exceeds 75% of the group's worldwide gross external debt.[10] The test then compares total net finance costs of UK members of a group, as the tested amount, to the gross external finance costs of whole group, as the available amount. The interest on the excess of the tested amount over the available amount is then disallowed. There is an exemption which may apply to financing income.

UK: Anti-arbitrage Interest Limits

The UK provisions counteracting hybrid and other mismatches came into force on 1 January 2017.[11] These measures apply to financial transactions and also apply to other areas, such as payments relating to intellectual property.[12] The UK is the first country to introduce anti-hybrid rules based on of OECD BEPS Action 2, The provisions define hybrid mismatches as cases where an amount is deductible in one jurisdiction but are not taxed in any other, or where an amount is deductible more than once.

THE OECD BEPS ACTION PLAN 4 AND INTEREST DEDUCTIONS

The OECD BEPS Action 4 measures include the review of base erosion arrangements using excessive interest deductions and other financial payments.

The BEPS Action 4 measures recommended that countries implement a fixed ratio rule to limit net interest deductions claimed by an entity, or a group of entities operating in the same country, to a fixed percentage of EBITDA.[13] This ratio should be between 10% and 30% of the applicable EBITDA. The measure is designed to provide meaningful limits on net interest expense, while still allowing most multinationals to deduct all of their third-party interest expenses. The Action 4 measures also recommended a group ratio rule, where an entity with net interest expense above a country's fixed ratio could deduct the interest expense up to the level of the net third-party interest/ EBITDA ratio of the worldwide group.

9. *Taxation (International and Other Provisions) Act 2010*, c. 8, and *Finance Act 2009* c. 10 (United Kingdom).
10. Nicholas Gardner & John Watson, *The Debt Cap Explained*, Ashurst LLP.
11. Part 6A TIOPA 2010.
12. EY, Global Tax Alert, 8 June 2016.
13. OECD, Limiting Base Erosion Involving Interest Deductions and Other Financial Payments, Action 4 – 2016 Update.

EUROPEAN UNION ANTI-AVOIDANCE DIRECTIVES

The Council of the European Union (EU) adopted the Anti-Tax Avoidance Directive (ATAD1) providing rules against tax avoidance practices that directly affect the functioning of the internal market on 20 June 2016.[14] The Directive required Member States to adopt minimum levels of protection against specific tax avoidance measures. In relation to interest deductions, Article 4 on the Interest Limitation rule requires that states limit the deduction of interest costs on net borrowings to essentially 30% of the EBITDA or a higher threshold of EUR 3 million, generally on a 'per country' basis.[15] The rules do not distinguish between third party and related party interest. Members may choose to exclude stand-alone entities from the interest deduction limits. There is also an exclusion where a corporate taxpayer can prove that its solvability on the basis of commercial accounts is equal or better than that of the related consolidated group allowing a 2% margin, or based on the group EBITDA. Member countries may choose to allow a carry forward of their unused interest capacity.

THIN CAPITALISATION PLANNING

There are several potential thin capitalisation tax planning structures. Any tax planning arrangements may, however, potentially be subject to the specific thin capitalisation tax rules and the anti-tax avoidance rules of the countries concerned, and consideration of OECD BEPS and EU measures is also required:

- Operating leases over plant and machinery may be provided by the parent or group treasury company to the local country subsidiary. The operating lease obligations may potentially not be treated as debt for the thin capitalisation provisions. The operating leases may also be provided in the form of a sale and leaseback transaction, which would provide the local country subsidiary with funding from the sale of some of the company's assets to the parent or group treasury company, and where the local country subsidiary would then lease back those assets.
- Debt factoring is also a potential planning approach. The local country subsidiary may sell its trade receivables, being amounts owed by its customers and expected to be paid at future dates, to the parent company at a discount to the face value of the receivables, for example they may be sold for 85% of their face value. This discount received by the parent company under the debt factoring arrangement effectively represents the time value of money for the later collection of the receivables, and this discount is therefore effectively interest received by the parent company for providing funding.

---

14. EU, Council Directive (EU) 2016/1164 of 12 July 2016 laying down rules against tax avoidance practices that directly affect the functioning of the internal market (ATAD1).
15. Loyens & Loeff, Q&A – What is the impact of the EU anti-tax avoidance Directive on investment funds?, https://www.loyensloeff.com/en-us/news-events/news/qa-what-is-the-impact-of-the-eu-anti-tax-avoidance-directive-on-investment-funds#kopje5 on 18 October 2017.

- The parent company may borrow funds and obtain interest deductions in its own country, and then provide equity to the subsidiary company to reduce the subsidiary company's related party debt. This arrangement effectively moves part of the interest deduction to the parent company. This approach may be used at several levels, where each company borrows to its thin capitalisation limit, and then provides equity funding to its subsidiary. This structure is generally known as 'debt cascading'.
- The local country subsidiary may borrow from a local bank branch, while the parent company deposits funds with the same bank's head office in its own country. The local subsidiary therefore obtains interest deductions on the local bank loan, and the local third-party bank debt may not be included in thin capitalisation limits. This structure is generally known as the use of back-to-back loans. There are several anti-tax avoidance provisions which may apply, particularly where the local subsidiary loans and the parent company deposits have similar amounts and conditions.
- The parent company may provide a guarantee of the third-party debts of the local country subsidiary in return for a guarantee fee paid by the local country subsidiary. This structure may potentially provide a deduction for the guarantee fee paid by the subsidiary, and also reduce that subsidiary's related party debt.
- An alternative to loan arrangements relates to the use of fees for treasury services. The local country subsidiary may pay the parent company or group treasury company for financial services. These services may include, for example, foreign currency spot transactions such as purchasing the subsidiary's USD derived from overseas sales, and selling local currency to meet local production expenses. These services may also include swap transactions. A foreign currency swap, for example, may exchange a series of USD payments over time with a series of payments of local currency. A fixed to floating interest rate swap can exchange a series of interest payments which are at a set or fixed rate, with a series of payments at a floating rate which can change with market conditions, such as the London interbank offered rate (LIBOR). The parent or group treasury company would derive the related fee income, and these fees may potentially be deductible for the local country subsidiary.
- The parent company or group treasury company may provide a smaller loan to the subsidiary which is within the local thin capitalisation limits. The loan is, however, charged at a higher interest rate as the loan carries higher risk. This may be applied, for example, with subordinated loans. The repayments on a subordinated loan on a winding up of a company are only made after payments are made to other creditors. The subordinated loan therefore carries a higher risk of default than other loans, and therefore potentially entitles the lender to a higher interest rate.
- An arrangement may also be used which is based on an asset transfer. The parent company or another group company transfers assets to the local country subsidiary, in exchange for share capital issued by the subsidiary company. This structure essentially increases the subsidiary's share capital

and therefore its equity for thin capitalisation purposes. This arrangement potentially allows additional related party borrowing within thin capitalisation limits based on the new higher level of the subsidiary's capital.

CHAPTER 18

Interest Flows and Hybrid Arrangements

ISSUES AND PLANNING

This chapter reviews the taxation issues arising from interest flows relating to loan financing. This review includes the issues relating to external financing from sources such as financial markets, as well as consideration of group finance structures, such as the use of a group treasury company or an in-house bank.

The principal issue is the most effective use of interest deductions to ensure that profitable subsidiaries maximise their interest deductions to reduce tax. A multinational group particularly needs to consider which subsidiaries may benefit most from the use of interest deductions. For example, there may be no way to utilise interest deductions for a particular subsidiary if it is in the early stages of new business activities, and so will not have taxable profits for several years.

Consideration should also be given to the issue of withholding tax on interest payments to foreign lenders, and whether there may be domestic tax exemptions or tax treaties which may reduce or eliminate the withholding tax. There may also be a choice of companies for lenders within a multinational group structure, and a simple reduction in withholding tax on interest may potentially be achieved by borrowing from a lender in the group which is located in a country with a more effective tax treaty network.

There is also a significant potential issue concerning controlled foreign corporation provisions (CFC), which are imposed by many countries against deriving passive income such as interest in a group subsidiary which is located in a low-taxing country such as a tax haven. These provisions may generally tax the parent company on the tax haven subsidiary company's passive income including the related interest.

INTEREST WITHHOLDING TAX REDUCTIONS AND EXEMPTIONS

Cross-border lending transactions will generally result in interest payments to non-residents, which may be subject to interest withholding tax in the country of the borrower. The withholding tax mechanism means that the borrower, as the payer of the interest, is responsible for the collection of tax from the payments on behalf of the non-resident lender, and is then responsible for forwarding these amounts to the tax authorities.

Withholding tax is imposed under a country's domestic tax provisions, however this tax can potentially be reduced or eliminated under domestic tax exemptions or under the terms of related tax treaties. Domestic withholding tax exemptions may include interest on borrowings which were offered on financial markets, for example where the funds were raised by issuing financial instruments or securities on international bond markets, or the financial instruments or securities were issued to institutional investors.

Tax Treaties

Tax treaties may reduce withholding tax on interest payments where the country of the borrower making the interest payment, as the source country, has a tax treaty with the country where the lender receiving the interest payment is a resident for tax treaty purposes. The OECD Model Tax Treaty 2017, for example, limits withholding tax to 10%.[1] Interest is generally defined as 'income from debt-claims of every kind, whether or not secured by mortgage and whether or not carrying a right to participate in the debtor's profits, and in particular, income from government securities and income from bonds or debentures, including premiums and prizes attaching to such securities, bonds or debentures'.[2]

There are significant issues concerning the requirement that the beneficial owner of the related interest income must be a resident of one of the treaty states. This condition is included, for example, in the Model Tax Treaty in relation to interest income.[3] This term may potentially be applied to mean the ultimate owner of the income, ignoring the use of intermediate companies which were set up with the intention of obtaining the benefits of specific tax treaties.

The European Union

The European Union (EU) Interest and Royalties Directive,[4] requires there to be nil interest withholding tax where there is at least 25% common direct ownership of

1. OECD, *Model Tax Convention on Income and on Capital* (2017), Article 11(2), (OECD Model Tax Treaty 2017).
2. OECD Model Tax Treaty 2017, Article 11(3).
3. OECD, Model Tax Treaty 2017, Article 11(2).
4. *Council Directive 2003/49/EC of 3 June 2003 on a Common System of Taxation Applicable to Interest and Royalty Payments Made between Associated Companies of Different Member States*, (L 157, 26 June 2003) (Interest and Royalty Directive) (EU).

capital by one company in the other company, or where a third company has a direct minimum holding of 25% in the capital of both companies; and the companies are incorporated and resident in EU Member States or are branches in the EU. There is currently a significant issue that the Directive does not apply to reduce withholding tax on interest and royalty payments where there is only an indirect ownership relationship, for example where the companies may have common ultimate ownership, but one company does not directly hold the required shareholding in the other company. The EU is currently reviewing proposals to reduce the required shareholding to 10% and to apply the Directive to indirect shareholdings.[5]

Australia

The Australian tax provisions generally apply a withholding rate on interest of 10% unless the rate is reduced by a related tax treaty or exemption. No withholding applies, however, to interest on securities which were issued under the public offer test.[6] This test allows five alternatives for exemption on interest on debenture securities. The exemptions include debentures offered to at least ten persons carrying on the business of providing finance or investing or dealing in securities in a financial market, such as banks, or which were offered for issue to 100 or more investors in securities.

United Kingdom

The United Kingdom (UK) provisions generally provide that tax at 20% must be withheld from the payment of interest to non-residents, unless reduced this rate is reduced or eliminated by a tax treaty or other tax exemptions. The domestic exemptions provide that there is no withholding tax on interest on deposits with UK banks, on interest payments to non-residents on quoted Eurobonds,[7] on the payment of short interest where the interest is paid in respect of a borrowing of less than one year, and on the payment of non-UK sourced interest.

United States

The United States (US) tax provisions impose a 30% withholding tax rate on interest, unless this is reduced by a tax treaty or under a specific exemption. The most relevant exemption is that no withholding of tax is required for portfolio interest, under the portfolio interest exemption.[8] Portfolio interest under these provisions includes:

- Discounted securities such as original issue discount securities (OID).
- Interest on obligations not in registered form.

5. KPMG, *Proposals to Address Double Taxation in the EU – Amending the Interest and Royalties Directive* EU Tax Centre, 172, 16 November 2011 (KPMG, 2011).
6. *Income Tax Assessment Act 1936*, Act No. 27 of 1936, section 128F (Australia).
7. *Income Tax Act 2007*, c. 3, section 882 (United Kingdom).
8. *Internal Revenue Code*, 26 USC (1986) section 881(c) (United States).

- Interest on obligations in registered form, where the US payer receives a statement, known as the W-8BEN, confirming that the beneficial owner is not a US person.

Portfolio interest does not include:

- Interest received by any person who has a 10% or greater ownership interest in the payer of the interest.
- Interest paid to a bank attributable to the extension of credit entered into in the course of the bank's trade or business.
- Interest paid by the borrower to a CFC by a related person.
- Contingent interest, for example where the interest payment is contingent on the amount of a company's profit.

BRANCHES AND HEAD OFFICE FUNDING COSTS

Figure 18.1 Branches and Head Office Funding Costs

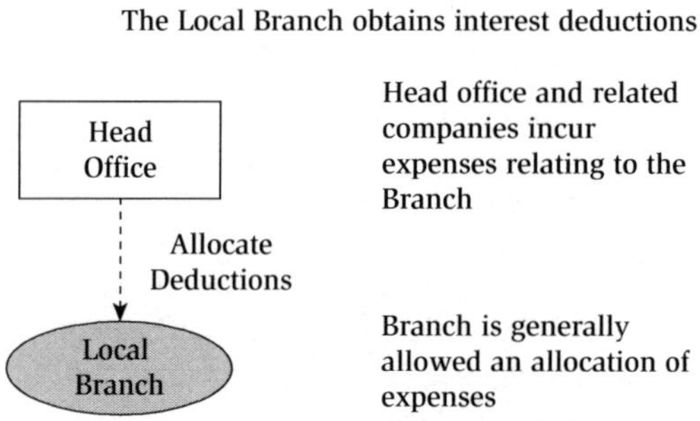

This structure relates to potential advantages of branches in relation to withholding tax. The issue concerns using a local branch for the allocation of head office and related company interest expenses.

The head office company and other group companies generally incur expenses relating to the local branch, such as administration, accounting, human resources (HR), legal, and information technology (IT) expenses. One very significant expense may be interest costs on loans by group companies which have been used in part to fund the branch. Most tax treaties allow the allocation of expenses relating to the branch as deductible in determining the local country taxation.

It is necessary to determine an arm's length basis of allocation of these expenses, as there is a common transfer pricing issue whether basis of allocation results in arm's length profits in the branch. This can be a very significant issue in local country tax audits of the branch. There may also be specific treaty limitations on expense allocations. In Article 7(4) of the UK/Mexico tax treaty, for example, there is a standard clause allowing deduction of general administrative expenses incurred on behalf of the branch, however specific limitations on deductions in the treaty include interest on loans to the permanent establishment, as follows:[9]

> In determining the profits of a permanent establishment, there shall be allowed as deductions expenses which are incurred for the purposes of the permanent establishment, including executive and general administrative expenses incurred for the purposes of the enterprise as a whole, whether in the Contracting State in which the permanent establishment is situated or elsewhere. However, no such deduction shall be allowed in respect of amounts, if any, paid (otherwise than by way of reimbursement of actual expenses) by the permanent establishment to the head office of the enterprise or any of its other offices, by way of royalties, fees or other similar payments in return for the use of patents or other rights, or by way of a commission, for specific services performed or for management, or, except in the case of a bank, by way of interest on money lent to the permanent establishment.

The deduction therefore relates to the allocation of head office and related company expenses, and not to interest charged to the branch. In general, several countries consider that the interest charged by the head office to the branch may potentially not be deductible as the head office and the branch are the same legal entity.

The potential benefit of the branch structure is that there may be additional deductions for interest expenses relating to the branch. These deductions are also not limited to the expenses incurred by the head office company in relation to the branch under Article 7 OECD Model Tax Treaty, and may also include certain interest expenses of related companies in the multinational group.

HYBRID ENTITIES AND FINANCIAL INSTRUMENTS

The term hybrid when used in tax discussions refers to hybrid entities or financial instruments which have different tax characteristics in different countries. This issue generally arises because there is a mixture of characteristics which result in different classifications under the tax rules in different counties. Hybrid entities have characteristics of companies, as well as tax-transparent entities such as partnerships. Hybrid financial instruments have characteristics of equity share capital, as well as characteristics of debt. The hybrids may be treated differently for tax purposes in different countries. The potential advantage arising from different tax treatments is generally known as tax arbitrage.

Hybrids may be used when restructuring equity and debt, for example in merger and acquisition transactions. Hybrids may provide deductions for payments in one country, while the related income is not taxed in the other country. The availability of a hybrid transaction depends on the tax rules of both countries concerned.

There are several limitations on the use of hybrid entities. The most significant limitation is that anti-tax avoidance provisions may apply. For example, US tax laws

9. Convention between the Government of the United Kingdom of Great Britain and Northern Ireland and the Government of the United Mexican States for the Avoidance of Double Taxation and the Prevention of Fiscal Evasion with respect to Taxes on Income and Capital Gains, 2 June 1994, (entered into force 15 December 1994) ('United Kingdom/Mexico tax treaty').

provide that there may be no reduction in withholding tax rates under tax treaties for payments made to hybrid entities.[10] The provisions may limit tax treaty benefits in relation to payments involving hybrid entities.

THE OECD BEPS ACTION 2 MEASURES AND HYBRID ARRANGEMENTS

Multinational groups may use hybrid instruments structures, where a hybrid financial instrument where the related payment by the subsidiary was treated as interest in the subsidiary country, but was treated as a tax-free dividend under the participation exemption or taxed with a foreign tax credit in the parent country. Hybrid entities and instruments are analysed in detail in *Hybrid Financial Instruments in International Tax Law*,[11] and *Tolley's International Taxation of Corporate Finance*.[12] The OECD BEPS Action 2 measures include the review of hybrid arrangements as follows:

> ACTION 2
>
> Develop model treaty provisions and recommendations regarding the design of domestic rules to neutralise the effect (e.g. double non-taxation, double deduction, long-term deferral) of hybrid instruments and entities. This may include: (i) changes to the OECD Model Tax Convention to ensure that hybrid instruments and entities (as well as dual resident entities) are not used to obtain the benefits of treaties unduly; (ii) domestic law provisions that prevent exemption or non-recognition for payments that are deductible by the payor; (iii) domestic law provisions that deny a deduction for a payment that is not includible in income by the recipient (and is not subject to taxation under controlled foreign company (CFC) or similar rules); (iv) domestic law provisions that deny a deduction for a payment that is also deductible in another jurisdiction; and (v) where necessary, guidance on co-ordination or tie-breaker rules if more than one country seeks to apply such rules to a transaction or structure … .

The BEPS Action 2 measures include developing model treaty terms and recommendations for the design of domestic tax rules to neutralise the effects of hybrid mismatches, including double non-taxation, double deduction, and long-term tax deferral outcomes.[13] The recommendations may include both primary and secondary measures, where primary measures relate to the action expected to be taken first by one country, and the secondary measures by the other country where the primary measure was not taken. This approach can enable the use of anti-hybrid measures where one country is not applying anti-hybrid rules.

The scope of the anti-hybrid recommendations varies, with some recommendations only applying to transactions within the same control group, or implemented under structured arrangements where the hybrid mismatch is priced into the terms of the arrangement, or the facts and circumstances indicate that it is designed to produce a hybrid mismatch.

10. Internal Revenue Code § 894(c) and Treasury Regulations § 1.894-1(d).
11. Jakob Bundgaard, *Hybrid Financial Instruments in International Tax Law* (Kluwer Law International, 2016).
12. John Abrahamson, *Tolley's International Taxation of Corporate Finance* (LexisNexis, 2014).
13. OECD, Neutralising the Effects of Hybrid Mismatch Arrangements, Action 2, 2015 Final Report.

The OECD BEPS Multilateral Instrument (MLI) can implement treaty-related BEPS measures by modifying existing bilateral tax treaties where the respective countries both agree.[14] The MLI includes optional provisions for hybrid entities and instruments:

- Action 2 – Hybrid entities and instruments (MLI Article 3). This includes: (1) revision of Article 1 of the Model Tax Convention to address fiscally transparent entities; and (2) application of the exemption method to relieve double taxation, such as using credits against other income, and the use of underlying tax credits.

It will be important to review how these recommendations are incorporated in domestic tax laws and international tax treaties. The measures are likely to come into broader effect if they are incorporated in the proposed new multilateral treaty under the BEPS proposals, which would then potentially apply the new rules to a country's existing treaties without amending each one.

EU ANTI-AVOIDANCE DIRECTIVES

The Council of the EU adopted the Anti-Tax Avoidance Directive (ATAD1) providing rules against tax avoidance practices that directly affect the functioning of the internal market on 20 June 2016.[15] The Directive required Member States to adopt minimum levels of protection against specific tax avoidance measures. In relation to hybrids, Article 9 on Hybrid Mismatches requires that:

(1) To the extent that a hybrid mismatch results in a double deduction, the deduction shall be given only in the Member State where such payment has its source.
(2) To the extent that a hybrid mismatch results in a deduction without inclusion, the Member State of the payer shall deny the deduction of such payment.

On this basis, Member States are required to introduce legislation effective from 1 January 2019 to prevent the use of hybrid entities or instruments between Member States to derive a double deduction or derive a deduction without related taxation.

The EU finance ministers reached political agreement on 21 February 2017 on the second Anti-Tax Avoidance Directive (ATAD2).[16] This would be a significant extension of the anti-hybrid rules to include arrangements with non-EU states. Member States would need to apply the provisions from 1 January 2020.

14. Multilateral Convention to Implement Tax Treaty Related Measures to Prevent Base Erosion and Profit Shifting, opened for signature 7 June 2017).
15. Council Directive (EU) 2016/1164 of 12 July 2016 laying down rules against tax avoidance practices that directly affect the functioning of the internal market (ATAD1).
16. Council Directive amending Directive (EU) 2016/1164 regarding hybrid mismatches with third countries, (ATAD2).

UK ANTI-HYBRID RULES

The UK introduced provisions counteracting hybrid and other mismatches which came into force on 1 January 2017.[17] These measures apply to financial transactions and also apply to other areas, such as payments relating to intellectual property.[18] The UK is the first country to introduce anti-hybrid rules based on OECD BEPS Action 2.

The provisions define hybrid mismatches as cases where an amount is deductible in one jurisdiction but are not taxed in any other, or where an amount is deductible more than once:

- The primary measure is to disallow a deduction where the UK is the payer jurisdiction in respect of a deduction/non-inclusion mismatch. Where the UK is the payee jurisdiction, and the primary response has not been applied in another jurisdiction, the UK will tax the related receipt.
- In the case of a double deduction, the UK will deny the deduction where it is the parent jurisdiction. Where the UK is the payer jurisdiction and the deduction is not denied in the parent jurisdiction, the UK will deny the deduction to the payer.

The scope of the provisions is also expanded to eliminate the tax advantage arising from the use of mismatches involving permanent establishments (PEs), and include counteracting excessive deductions in the permanent establishment on payments to the head office, and counteracting deductions claimed in both the permanent establishment jurisdiction and the head office country.

17. Part 6A TIOPA 2010.
18. EY, Global Tax Alert, 8 June 2016.

CHAPTER 19

Capital Gains, Group Restructures, and Private Equity

INTRODUCTION

This chapter concerns the taxation issues relating to multinational group restructures, and in particular the taxation of capital gains on the sale of subsidiary companies in a group. These transactions can result in some of the largest potential taxation of a group, where profitable subsidiaries are sold to other multinational groups, and the entire increase in the value of the subsidiary may be fully taxable. These issues include the potential use of holding companies in specific countries to hold shares in foreign subsidiary companies, so that the potential sale of shares in the foreign subsidiary is free of tax, or is taxed at a concessional rate. These issues are also relevant to private equity investors in the energy industry, including large institutional investors, pension funds, hedge funds, sovereign wealth funds, and wealthy individuals, which may invest primarily to derive a capital gain on sale after a short holding period.

A threshold issue is that the participation exemption provisions of many countries exempt a parent company on the sale of a subsidiary, in addition to allowing the dividends from the subsidiary to be free of tax. For tax planning purposes, there is a potential advantage for the parent or holding company to be located in a country with a participation exemption.

There may be other planning structures where a country has no participation exemption provisions, or the shareholding does not qualify for the exemption as the interest is too small or has not been held for a sufficient period of time. The foreign holding company may, for example, be located in a tax haven country, and the tax haven may not tax the profits on the share sale. The parent country may however potentially tax the gain on the sale of the tax haven company. A variation on the structure is to use two tax haven companies, and then to sell the lower level company. The use of such tax haven companies may, however, result in the application of anti-tax avoidance provisions in many countries. There may also be a general group policy, for reasons of reputation for example, not to use tax haven companies without a dominant commercial purpose.

The holding company should therefore generally not be located a tax haven, but preferably, be located in a country which has higher rates of tax, such as the Netherlands, which also provides specific exemptions on sales of qualifying shareholdings under the participation exemption provisions.

OFFSHORE HOLDING COMPANY EXAMPLE

Figure 19.1 Offshore Holding Company

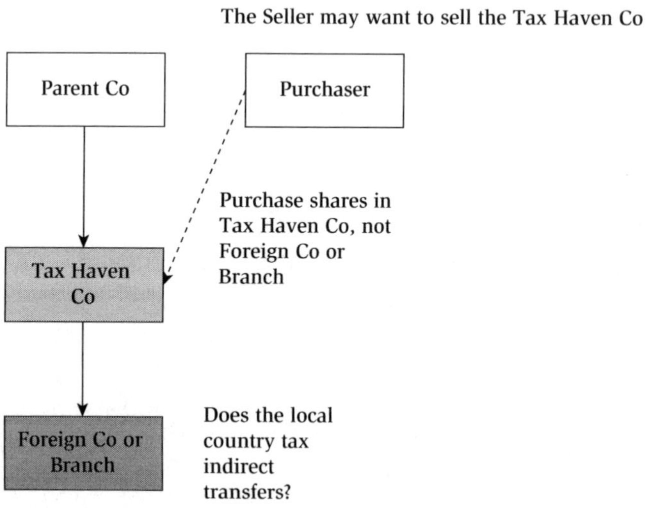

Overview

In this example the Parent Co holds assets in the Tax Haven Co offshore holding company. The Parent Co sells the shares in the Tax Haven Co rather than the Foreign Co or the Branch directly. There may be no tax on sale of shares in the tax haven. There may potentially also be no direct sale in the country of the Foreign Co or the Branch. The structure may then potentially eliminate local country tax due to the indirect transfer of Foreign Co or Branch.

The use of the structure largely depends on local Foreign Co or Branch country rules, especially whether they 'trace upwards' to tax indirect changes of ownership such as the sale of the Tax Haven Co holding company. The use of tax haven companies may be subject to local country anti-tax avoidance provisions. The structure also depends on the Parent Co's own country tax rules, which may tax gains on selling the Tax Haven Co company, such as CFC provisions which may tax profits relating to tax havens.

The IMF, OECD, UN, and World Bank Group issued a Discussion Draft on the Taxation of Offshore Indirect Transfers – A Toolkit in 2017,[1] concerning the tax treatment of 'offshore indirect transfers' (OITs) for the sale of an entity owning an asset located in one country by a resident of another. The draft suggested the need for a more uniform approach to taxation, and considered there was a strong case for taxation on a wide class of assets beyond a narrow notion of immovable assets, to include more widely those generating location specific rents, such as telecom licences and other rights issued by government.

TREATY PROTECTION EXAMPLE

Figure 19.2 Treaty Protection

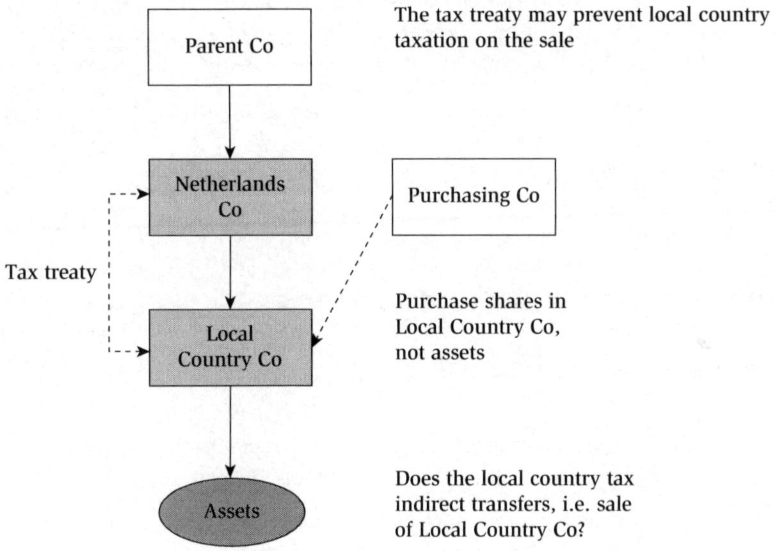

In this example, the Parent Co holds local the business assets indirectly. The Local Country Co holds the assets, and it is in turn held by the Netherlands Co intermediate holding company. The structure is based on the Netherlands Co selling the shares in the Local Country Co.

There may be no tax on sale by the Netherlands Co if the participation exemption conditions are met.[2] There may also be protection from local country taxation if there is a related tax treaty between the local country and the Netherlands which only allows

1. The Platform for Collaboration on Tax, Discussion Draft on the Taxation of Offshore Indirect Transfers–A Toolkit, (IMF, OECD, UN and WBG, 2017), http://www.oecd.org/tax/discussion-draft-toolkit-taxation-of-offshore-indirect-transfers.pdf on 19 September 2017.
2. Baker & McKenzie, *Doing Business in the Netherlands 2012*.

the residence country of the seller, in this case the Netherlands, to tax capital gains. There is no direct sale of the assets in the local country in this structure.

Considerations

The structure depends on tax treaties and local country rules, and particularly whether the local country tax rules 'trace upwards' to tax indirect transfers of ownership of assets. The use of tax treaties to eliminate tax on capital gains as shown in this example is potentially subject to the OECD BEPS measures against treaty shopping and related tax planning. These measures are included in Action 6 – Inappropriate Treaty Benefits, and include the limitation on benefits (LOB) and the principal purposes test (PPT) rules. These measures are also included in the BEPS Action 15 Multilateral Instrument (MLI), under Article 7. There should therefore be dominant commercial purposes for the related holding structures, together with significant economic substance in the related treaty holding companies. The structure may potentially eliminate local country taxation on transfer of Local Country Co shares due to the terms of the related tax treaty.

Netherlands/Denmark

The use of a structure relating to treaty protection from taxation of capital gains depends on the specific wording of the related tax treaty. This generally requires a clause that provides that only the residence country can tax capital gains, rather than the country where the local subsidiary or assets are located. The related terms are contained in Article 13(4) of the Netherlands/Denmark Tax Treaty, for example, which states:[3]

> Gains from the alienation of any property other than that referred to in paragraphs 1, 2 and 3, shall be taxable only in the State of which the alienator is a resident.

The structure also requires parent country exemption from tax. In this example the Netherlands may potentially exempt the Parent Co from Netherlands tax on the capital gains on sale of foreign company shares under the participation exemption rules. The Netherlands exemption generally requires meeting both ownership and motive tests:[4]

- The ownership test includes a participation of at least 5% in the nominal paid-up share capital of an active subsidiary company.
- The motive test requires participation held for business reasons, and not mere portfolio investment.

---

3. *Convention between the Kingdom of the Netherlands and the Kingdom of Denmark for the Avoidance of Double Taxation and the Prevention of Fiscal Evasion with respect to Taxes on Income and on Capital*, 1 July 1996 (entered into force 6 March 1998).
4. Baker & McKenzie, *Doing Business in the Netherlands 2012*.

If the motive test is not met, the exemption in the Netherlands still applies if either the subject to tax test or the asset test are met. The subject to tax test is based on whether the subsidiary in its country of residence is taxed at a rate of at least 10%. The asset test applies where the subsidiary does not hold more than 50% free portfolio investments, which are generally investments which do not have any business function.

Australia

The Australian taxation provisions generally tax capital gains on indirect transfers of assets, and these terms are contained in several of Australia's tax treaties in relation to the sale of shares in a property owning company. The provisions can apply to tax the sale of shares in a company where that company has more than 50% of its value in Australian real property. This was extended by the *International Tax Agreements Act*,[5] to tax gains from the alienation of real property through multiple levels of entities, for example to tax the sale of a foreign holding company. This scope was later extended in 2006 to tax the sale of entities holding at least 10% interests in these companies.[6] Related taxation issues in these provisions include not taking into account the sold company's liabilities in determining its value, for example loans from banks, in relation to these tests.

THE OECD MODEL TAX TREATY

Countries which have tax treaties based on the OECD Model Tax Treaty may allow an exemption from tax when a resident of the other treaty country sells shares in a company in that source country. The Model Tax Treaty was however updated in 2003 to allow the source country to tax gain on shares in real estate companies.[7]

It is important to note that several countries do not use the real estate exception, and simply exempt the seller of the shares from tax. There are also countries that do not tax these gains under their domestic tax rules. The Parent Co seller of the Subsidiary Co shares may potentially also obtain tax concessions under the participation exemption provisions where treaty protection does not apply.

THE OECD BEPS MULTILATERAL INSTRUMENT (MLI): CHANGES TO TAX TREATIES INCLUDING TREATY SHOPPING

The MLI is part of the OECD BEPS measures to implement treaty-related changes by modifying existing bilateral tax treaties.[8] The MLI Articles 6 and 7 relate to BEPS Action

5. *International Tax Agreements Act 1953*, Act No. 82 of 1953, section 3A (Australia).
6. *Income Tax Assessment Act 1997*, Act No. 38 of 1997, Div. 855 (Australia).
7. *OECD Model Tax Treaty*, Article 13(4).
8. Multilateral Convention to Implement Tax Treaty Related Measures to Prevent Base Erosion and Profit Shifting, opened for signature 7 June 2017.

6, minimum standard on treaty abuse, including treaty shopping structures which use tax treaties to prevent taxation of capital gains. The treaty shopping measures use principal purpose test (PPT) or limitation on benefits test (LOB) measures for minimum standards against treaty abuse. The MLI requires that countries adopt both LOB and PPT measures, adopt PPT measures alone, or adopt LOB measures together with a restricted PPT rule applicable to conduit financing arrangements or domestic anti-abuse rules or judicial doctrines that would achieve a similar result.

These measures have been incorporated in the OECD Model Tax Treaty 2017 in Article 29 Entitlement to Benefits, and are to be adopted as agreed by the contracting states. This includes the limitation on benefits test in Article 29(1) to (7), and the PPT in Article 29(9).[9]

This may apply, for example, to private equity investors which invest primarily to derive a capital gain on sale after a shorter holding period, rather than a flow of dividends over a longer holding period. The issues will include the extent of related commercial substance in the treaty holding country.

EUROPEAN UNION ANTI-AVOIDANCE MEASURES: GENERAL ANTI-AVOIDANCE RULE (GAAR)

The European Union Directive (EU) 2016/1164 (ATAD1) provides rules against tax avoidance practices that directly affect the functioning of the internal market on 20 June 2016.[10] The Directive required Member States to adopt minimum levels of protection against specific tax avoidance measures. Article 6 on the General Anti-Abuse Rule provides that:

> 1. For the purposes of calculating the corporate tax liability, a Member State shall ignore an arrangement or a series of arrangements which, having been put into place for the main purpose or one of the main purposes of obtaining a tax advantage that defeats the object or purpose of the applicable tax law, are not genuine having regard to all relevant facts and circumstances. An arrangement may comprise more than one step or part.
>
> 2. For the purposes of paragraph 1, an arrangement or a series thereof shall be regarded as non-genuine to the extent that they are not put into place for valid commercial reasons which reflect economic reality.
>
> 3. Where arrangements or a series thereof are ignored in accordance with paragraph 1, the tax liability shall be calculated in accordance with national law.

On this basis there may be scope to disregard the participation exemptions within the European Union on gains on the sale of companies where a tax benefit was one of the main purposes of the arrangement.

9. OECD, *Model Tax Convention on Income and on Capital* (2017), Article 29.
10. Council Directive (EU) 2016/1164 of 12 July 2016 laying down rules against tax avoidance practices that directly affect the functioning of the internal market.

CHAPTER 20

Group Procurement Companies

INTRODUCTION

The group procurement function within a multinational group relates to purchasing materials, goods and services by a procurement company, which will then be on-sold to other companies in the multinational group. These activities generally include liaising with group companies to determine their procurement needs, the analysis and selection of goods and services, the negotiation of the related purchase contracts, arranging any required funding and insurance, quality control and inspection, and making required payments to suppliers.

There are strong commercial reasons for centralising procurement functions in a group procurement company, including the more effective use of centralised procurement staff, and obtaining substantial discounts for purchasing goods and services in much greater quantities than required by individual group companies. For practical reasons, such as communications with suppliers and related time zones, there may be two or more regional procurement companies worldwide. The procurement company may also be a component of supply chain management (SCM), which is a process which seeks to rationalise the movement and storage of raw materials, work-in-process inventory, and finished goods from the point of origin to the point of consumption.

There are potential advantages in being able to negotiate better terms on a much larger contract, for example the selection of a small panel of preferred global suppliers for legal services may result in their agreement to a higher liability cap in relation to potential actions for negligence than would otherwise be agreed by the legal firms on a much smaller contract.

There may be scope to negotiate more favourable terms in relation to tax matters such as withholding tax, for example where the supplier may agree that payments are not to be grossed up for paying country withholding tax, and will instead seek to recover a tax credit in their supplying country. The procurement company therefore pays only the actual contract price without increasing the price for withholding tax.

Group procurement functions may potentially be performed by a company located in a lower taxing jurisdiction. This may include, for example, a general low tax rate such as 16.5% in Hong Kong, with potential exemption if the related income is treated as derived from sources outside Hong Kong,[1] or a low tax rate under specific tax concessions, for example the International Procurement Centre (IPC) concession in Malaysia provides a tax exemption for ten years.[2]

The procurement structure may potentially not be treated as a taxable controlled foreign corporation (CFC) under anti-tax haven rules because the procurement company conducts an active business. This tax planning advantage does not apply in all cases. The United States (US) CFC provisions under Subpart F, for example, may apply to the profits of a group procurement company when this income is treated as 'foreign base income', which include sales, service, and shipping income from transactions with related parties.[3] US taxation can therefore apply to the US parent company on the income of a procurement company located in a tax haven in relation to the sales to other companies in the same multinational group.

There is also an advantage with procurement companies for tax planning purposes because payments made to the procurement company for the purchase of materials, goods and services by other group companies would generally not be subject to withholding tax, as the payments are for the purchase of the materials, goods and services, rather than being payments of interest, dividends, royalties, or technical service fees, which may be subject to withholding tax in many countries.

There may be withholding tax in some countries where the procurement company is charged for services. It may be useful in these circumstances to have the third-party suppliers enter into contracts with group companies directly, under the terms of a global contract, also known as an 'umbrella contract' which was previously negotiated by the group procurement company and the supplier. The procurement company may be paid an administration fee by the group companies.

One significant issue with the group procurement structure is that the procurement company must use arm's length pricing for the sales to related companies in the multinational group, as additional tax and penalties may otherwise be imposed under transfer pricing provisions.[4]

1. *Inland Revenue Ordinance*, E.R. 1 of 2012, section 14(1) (Hong Kong), and *Departmental Interpretation and Practice Notes No. 21 (Revised) Locality of Profits*, DIPN 21, Inland Revenue Department, Hong Kong.
2. *Income Tax Act 1967*, Act 53, section 127 (Malaysia).
3. *Internal Revenue Code*, 26 USC (1986) Part III, Subpart F, §§ 951–965 (United States).
4. Refer to the transfer pricing discussion in Chapter 29.

GROUP PROCUREMENT STRUCTURE EXAMPLE

Figure 20.1 Group Procurement Structure

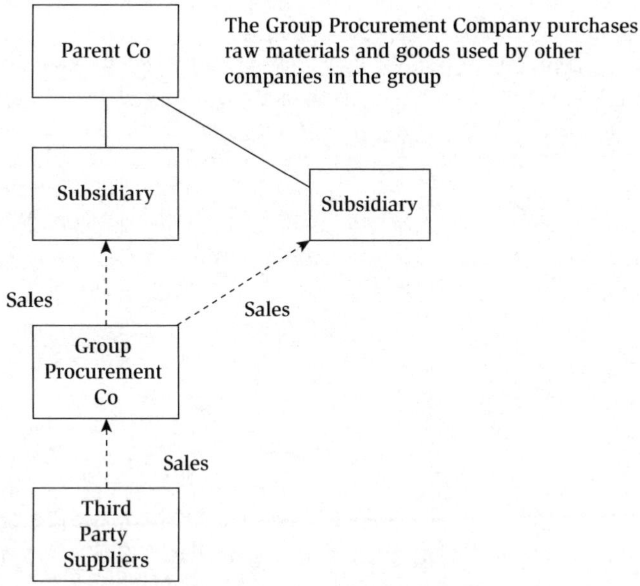

The procurement structure relates to product selection, contract negotiation, purchasing, funding and insurance, and quality control functions for materials, goods, and services required by a multinational group. These functions can be performed by a group procurement company located in a lower taxing country.

The procurement company derives a profit margin between the price paid for the purchases from suppliers, and the price received on sales to related companies in the multinational group. The related profits may be taxed at low rates depending on the location of the procurement company.

The structure requires significant management and related personnel needed for the procurement function, and the related capital needed for this business, to actually be located in procurement country, to potentially reduce the risk that anti-tax avoidance provisions of several countries may apply. Transfer pricing is also a very significant issue, and the related prices should be at arm's length amounts.

The principal potential tax advantage is that the procurement margin is potentially derived in a low-taxing country.

COUNTRY EXAMPLES

Swiss Branch of a Netherlands Co

This structure is based on having the procurement functions performed by a Swiss branch of a Netherlands company.

The related profits may potentially not be taxed in the Netherlands as foreign branch income.[5] The tax in Switzerland should apply at reduced rates under cantonal tax rulings. The procurement income should not be treated as passive income under many countries' tax regimes, and so taxation of the parent company under CFC rules may not apply.

The potential tax results are that the procurement margin is not taxed in Netherlands, and reduced Swiss tax rates should apply.

Hong Kong

This structure is based on a procurement company located in Hong Kong.

The related procurement profits are generally subject to Hong Kong Profits Tax at a rate of 16.5%. The tax rate is, however, potentially reduced to nil where the source of profits is treated as derived from outside Hong Kong under Hong Kong's territorial tax system. This tax treatment may potentially apply where the related purchase and sale contracts are negotiated and concluded outside Hong Kong.[6] A significant issue with the structure, however, is that Hong Kong is potentially more likely to be on a tax haven list under several countries' CFC taxation systems, in which case the parent company may be taxed on the related profits of the Hong Kong procurement company.

Singapore

This structure is based on a procurement company located in Singapore, and receiving concessional tax treatment under specific tax regimes available in Singapore.

The related profits of the procurement company may potentially be taxed at rates down to 0%, under the International Headquarters (IHQ) concession or the Regional Headquarters (RHQ) concession available in Singapore.[7] Singapore also has a territorial tax system under which there has generally been an exemption for income not received in Singapore. The related rules were, however, updated in 1995.[8] In relation to trading profits, the updated rules provide that income derived from outside Singapore which is applied in or towards satisfaction of any debt incurred in respect of a trade or business carried on in Singapore is taxable, as the income is treated as

5. Baker & McKenzie, Doing Business in the Netherlands 2012.
6. *Inland Revenue Ordinance*, E.R. 1 of 2012, section 14(1), and *Departmental Interpretation and Practice Notes No. 21 (Revised) Locality of Profits*, DIPN 21, Inland Revenue Department (Hong Kong).
7. *Income Tax Act* (Chapter 134), section 43E, (Singapore).
8. *Income Tax Act* (Chapter 134), section 10(19) (Singapore).

received in Singapore. On this basis the better tax result is generally to be achieved using the IHQ and RHQ concessions.

OECD BEPS ACTION 13: CBC REPORTING

The BEPS Action 13 Country-by-Country (CbC) reporting measures may apply to the use of group procurement entities:[9]

- CbC reports will generally include procurement entities under the Main Business Activity heading in the Purchasing or Procurement category, together with related information including related and unrelated party revenues, profits before tax, income tax paid, and number of employees.
- These reports may identify group procurement centres with high related party earnings compared to the number of related employees.
- The follow-up analysis by country tax authorities may include whether profits allocated to such procurement entities are commensurate with the functions performed, assets used, and risks undertaken (FAR) by these entities, or suggest that the use of the procurement entity is potentially to reduce taxable profits in the group companies making purchases from the procurement entity.

The CbC measures were adopted in the 2017 OECD Transfer Pricing Guidelines for Multinational Enterprises and Tax Administrations.[10]

9. OECD Transfer Pricing Documentation and Country-by-Country Reporting, ACTION 13: 2015 Final Report.
10. Chapter 5 Documentation, p. 229.

CHAPTER 21

Group Marketing Companies

INTRODUCTION

This chapter analyses the significant international tax issues relating to group marketing companies, such as companies marketing oil, gas, coal, and uranium produced by group subsidiaries for sale to worldwide customers. These issues include the level of taxation in the head office country where the principal is located compared to the level of taxation in the local sales country, and transfer pricing issues on the sales to the local distributing company.

Marketing companies may derive a profit margin in a lower taxing country for performing the sales, and for related services such as arranging related funding, goods inspection, delivery, foreign exchange management, and insurance. Commissionaire structures may be used where the principal retains title to the commodities and carries the most significant business risks, and the local distribution company derives a smaller profit margin. The limited risk buy/sell structure is based on a local marketing and distribution company which carries lower risks and derives a lower profit margin.

REGIONAL MARKETING COMPANIES

Figure 21.1 Regional Sales Companies

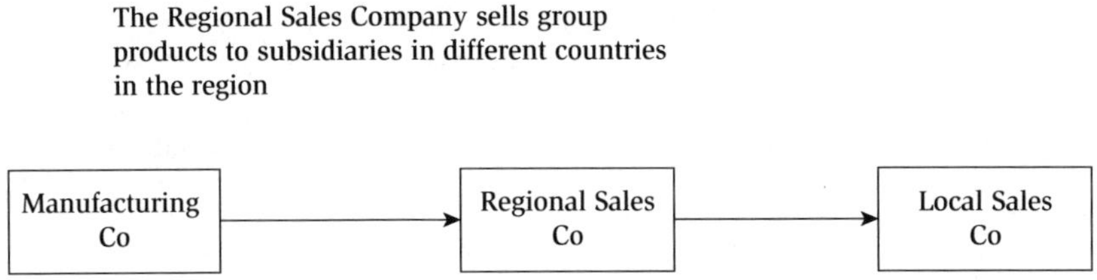

The use of regional sales companies enables common functions relating to sales, such as marketing, invoicing, insurance, shipping, quality control, and legal support, to be performed in one location to support sales in several countries in a region. This centralisation may potentially reduce costs due to economies of scale. The regional sales company may be located in a lower taxing country, so that the margin between purchase costs and sales is taxed at a lower rate.

The principle issue is the transfer pricing requirement that related party sales are made at arm's length prices. There is also the potential application of anti-avoidance provisions, which may apply for example where the regional sales company does not have commercial substance, such as employees and business capital, and does not carry real business risks.

COMMISSIONAIRE STRUCTURES

Figure 21.2 Commissionaire Structures

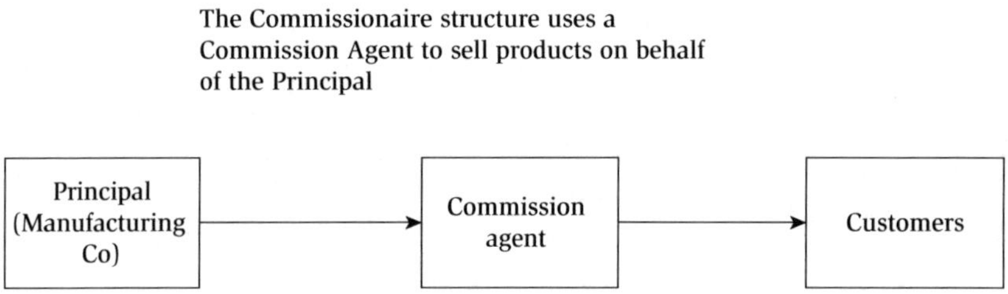

The commissionaire structure is based on local sales companies which act on a commission basis, where they sell commodities in their own name but on behalf and at the risk of the principal company. The commissionaires reduce their activities to the core business of sales.[1]

The commercial advantage of the structure is based on centralising business risks, such as inventory, bad debts and currency risks, centralising the purchase and production of commodities, reducing back office costs, and centralising the distribution of commodities.

The structure may potentially have tax benefits where these home country profits are subject to a low rate of tax. Commissionaire structures are more common in Europe. The related tax issues include the potential existence of a permanent establishment (PE) of the principal in the sales country, VAT arrangements, and the level of the commission for transfer pricing purposes.

The adoption of a commissionaire arrangement has particular tax issues, where companies which previously fully benefitted from customer relationships reduce their activities to the functions of a commissionaire. This may result in a profit decrease, and

1. PricewaterhouseCoopers *Switzerland: Commissionaire Structures – Switzerland As A Location For The Principal Supplier*, <http://www.mondaq.com/x/5424/Audit/Commissionaire+Structures+Switzerland+As+A+Location+For+The+Principal+Supplier>.

the local tax authorities may consider that there has been a taxable disposal of goodwill to a related party.

The tax authorities may also consider that the commissionaires are PEs of the principal, because the commissionaire is not legally and economically independent from the principal, and that it has, and habitually exercises, the ability to conclude contracts on behalf of the principal. The multinational group should therefore ensure that the related transactions are at arm's length, and that the commissionaire cannot bind the principal in contract.

The use of commissionaire structures to potentially avoid the presence of a taxable PE is being addressed under the OECD BEPS Action 7 measures.[2] These measures apply to commissionaire arrangements where the agent does not own the products sold on behalf of the principal. The measures also concern arrangements where a dependant agent does not habitually conclude contracts but substantially negotiates those contracts. These measures were incorporated in the BEPS Multilateral Instrument (MLI), which also provides the option that the PE extends to where the agent does not conclude contracts but habitually plays the role leading to the contracts.[3]

LIMITED RISK BUY/SELL STRUCTURES

Figure 21.3 Limited Risk Buy/Sell Structures

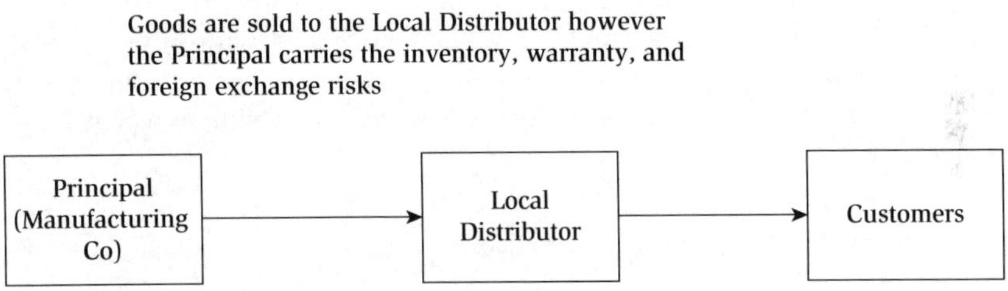

The limited risk buy/sell structure applies where the principal sells commodities to the local country distributor. The legal title to the goods therefore passes to the Distributor. The related distribution agreement may provide that the principal bears significant commercial risks such as inventory, warranty, foreign exchange, and the principal therefore has a higher markup on sale. The distributor in the structure generally bears less risk than under a standard full-risk distributorship, and derives a lower profit margin.

The structure was analysed by Cabrera, Leiman, and Skaletsky, who commented that the activities of the distributor should not result in a local PE for principal,

2. OECD, Preventing the Artificial Avoidance of Permanent Establishment Status Action 7: 2015 Final Report.
3. OECD, Multilateral Convention to Implement Tax Treaty Related Measures to Prevent Base Erosion and Profit Shifting, opened for signature 7 June 2017, Articles 12–14.

provided the parties respect the distributor's function and risks as a bona fide buy-sell distributor. Both the distribution agreement and the parties' transfer pricing analysis should include a detailed description of the risks the principal and distributor bear. The parties should act in accordance with the distribution agreement and the principal should not take any action that may result in it having a tax presence or PE in the country of the final sale.[4]

COMPARABLE COMPANY PROFITS OR COMMISSION RATES

The transfer pricing analysis of group marketing companies for energy-related commodities is based on the functions performed, assets used and risks undertaken (FAR) by the group marketing company, and the related profit margins where the commodities are purchased and sold by the marketing companies, or commission rates where the marketing company sells the commodities on behalf of the producer to derive commission income.

The analysis may typically use a transactional net margin (TNMM) based method, which examines profits of unrelated trading companies in the same business with a similar FAR profile, or a comparable uncontrolled price (CUP) method, which examines the commissions derived by unrelated trading companies in the same business with a similar FAR profile.

The selection of companies for the TNMM or CUP analysis should consider several factors, including: (1) the geographical location and the related political risks in the production countries, with lower margins likely for marketing production from lower risk locations, (2) the volumes of commodities sold with lower margins or commissions likely for larger volumes, and (3) the nature of the related markets, with lower profits or commissions likely for mature markets with a well-established customer base.

OECD BEPS ACTION 13: CbC REPORTING

The BEPS Action 13 Country-by-Country (CbC) reporting measures may impact the use of group marketing entities:[5]

- CbC reports will generally include these entities under the Main Business Activity heading as Sales, Marketing, and Distribution category, with related information including related and unrelated party revenues, profits before tax, income tax paid, and number of employees.

4. Victor Cabrera, Jose Leiman & Marc Skaletsky, *Hub-and-Spoke Arrangements May Result in a Rough Ride– Tax Issues Facing Supply Arrangements in Latin America* (KPMG LLP) 11(6) Practical Latin American Tax Strategies (2008). They also commented that there should be no unrecoverable import VAT issues for the principal as the distributor bears import duties as well as input VAT upon the acquisition of the goods, and should be able to recover input VAT upon the sale of the goods to its customer.
5. OECD Transfer Pricing Documentation and Country-by-Country Reporting, ACTION 13: 2015 Final Report.

- This may identify, for example, group trading centres with high related party earnings compared to the number of related employees.
- Once these entities are identified, the follow-up analysis may include whether profits allocated to such trading entities are commensurate with the functions performed, assets used, and risks undertaken (FAR) by these entities.

The CbC measures were adopted in the 2017 OECD Transfer Pricing Guidelines for Multinational Enterprises and Tax Administrations.[6]

6. Chapter 5 Documentation, p. 229.

CHAPTER 22

Group R&D and Intangible Property Companies

R&D AND INTANGIBLE PROPERTY IN THE ENERGY INDUSTRY

The performance of research and development (R&D) functions in an energy group and the provision of the related intangible property (IP) is often an essential part of multinational business operations. These functions include the provision of technology and related high value services, such as assistance with manufacturing methods, information technology (IT) support, and health and safety procedures. Payments for the use of intangible property may be made as royalties or management fees which are generally deductible under many countries tax regimes, or as cost contribution arrangements (CCA) where group companies share the costs and benefits of intangible property.

There may potentially be scope for a tax planning structure where royalties are paid for the use of intangible property to a company which is located in a low-taxing country that manages intangible property and owns the related patents and trademarks. The company may also provide technical assistance in return for technical service or management fees. These structures are subject to transfer pricing provisions that the royalty payments and other charges are made at arm's length prices:

- The payment of royalties may be based on estimated market value of the intangible property. In practice there are substantial databases on royalty charges, and so royalty rates may be accepted if the IP is clearly documented, and the rates are within the market range.
- The payment of technical service or management fees may be based on the related costs of the scientific or technical staff which provide the technical support. These amounts may be based on the related cost plus an acceptable margin, or on the prices charged where similar services are provided to or from third parties.

Intangible property is often a significant consideration in the larger mergers and acquisitions transactions. There may be scope, for example, to transfer the intangible property acquired from the target company or group to the acquirer's own intangible property company, and then provide for the payment of royalties from group companies for the use of that intangible property. There is generally an issue that capital gains taxes or exit taxes may be imposed where valuable intellectual property is transferred to another country. Tax may be imposed in the United States (US), for example, where intangible property is transferred from the US.

Cost Sharing Agreements (CSA) and CCA are arrangements which allow companies to share the costs incurred for a mutually beneficial purpose. CSAs are used for R&D where several companies may benefit from the development of a new patent and therefore share the related costs. The CSA structures are also used to share other costs which benefit several companies in a group, such as accounting, management, and marketing costs.

The participation in the CSA is generally made by parties that reasonably expect to gain a benefit by directly or indirectly using the results, under the OECD Transfer Pricing Guidelines,[1] and the US Treasury Regulations.[2] Participants may use the results for their own business activities, for the activities of a subsidiary company, or for transfer or licence of intangible property to other parties.

The essential principle of cost sharing is that the allocation of costs should be made on the basis of the expected benefits from the expenditure. Research expenses, for example, can be allocated on the basis of the anticipated benefits on a successful outcome such as a new product, manufacturing process or patent. The CSAs should provide for the potential adjustments in the required cost contributions to reflect any potential changes in business circumstances.

There is a potential advantage to CSAs because the related payments may not be subject to withholding taxes in many countries. The payments are not royalties for the use of intellectual property, for example, or payments for the use of equipment. There can be issues, however, as to whether the cost contribution payments are deductible in the respective countries. The company claiming the deduction for cost contribution payments needs to have a clear right to use the intellectual property when the project is completed, and there may be a tax issue if the related projects are not successful. Some countries' tax laws potentially also require that the payments must be capitalised for tax purposes as they relate to the creation of new assets.

One arrangement that may potentially be used is the contract R&D structure, which has the intangible property management company contracting for R&D work to be performed by the other subsidiaries in the multinational group and also by third parties. The payments made under these arrangements may be made on a cost plus basis to the companies performing the R&D which may lower tax in those countries. The group subsidiaries using the related intangible property would then pay royalties which should be deductible when paid at arm's length rates. The contract R&D

1. OECD *Transfer Pricing Guidelines for Multinational Enterprises and Tax Administrations (2010) Chapter VII.*
2. *Treasury Regulations*, Subchapter A, section 1.482-7 (United States).

structure may potentially be more effective than CSAs, as the structure may provide the opportunity to retain a margin in an intangible property management company located in lower taxing countries such as Switzerland, the Netherlands, and Singapore.

RESEARCH AND DEVELOPMENT TAX CONCESSIONS

There are several tax concessions for R&D included in the examples of country tax regimes in Chapter 4. Some of these tax concessions allow a tax deduction for expenses which would otherwise have been required to be capitalised, such as the original US R&D provisions.[3] Other tax concessions allow additional tax credits under the related US tax incentives,[4] or allow increased rates for the tax deduction, such as the deduction for up to 400% of the expenses under Singapore's Productivity and Innovation Credit (PIC) scheme.[5] These types of incentives are generally referred to as input tax incentives, as they relate to tax deductions, tax credits, and accelerated depreciation on the inputs in R&D activity.

The most significant recent trend in relation to tax concessions for research and development is the introduction by several countries of patent box regimes. These measures are generally classified as output tax incentives, as they relate to the income derived from the R&D activity, for example by providing a lower taxation regime for royalty income derived from the licensing of technology developed by R&D activities.

Robert Danon analysed these regimes in a general report for the International Fiscal Association (IFA) in 2015.[6] He commented that patent box regimes have been introduced within the European Union (EU) in Belgium, Cyprus, France, Hungary, Luxembourg, Malta, the Netherlands, Portugal, Spain, and the United Kingdom (UK). He considered the principles R&D incentives included: (i) internal neutrality, where the incentive was extended to all taxpayers irrespective of legal form, whether or not a permanent establishment was used, and whether or not the results were patented; and (ii) proportionality, where the incentives were directly linked to the related R&D activity, were based on a suitable definition of R&D expenditure including novelty in the country concerned, and where qualifying expenditure included staff costs, other current and capital expenditure directly linked to the R&D activity.

One essential issue is whether R&D related income which benefits from a concessional tax regime such as a patent box may be subsequently taxed if it has a parent company in a country with controlled foreign corporation (CFC) provisions. The CFC provisions may tax the parent company on the income of the patent box company on the basis that it was low-taxed income.

Related references include the EY Worldwide R&D Incentives Reference Guide 2017.[7] The following are examples of these innovation and patent box regimes.

3. *Internal Revenue Code*, 26 USC (1986) §174, and *Treasury Regulations* 1.174.
4. *Internal Revenue Code*, 26 USC (1986) §41, and *Treasury Regulations* 1.41.
5. *Income Tax Act*, sections 14A, 14D, 14R, 14S, 14T/19A, and 19B.
6. Robert J Danon, *General Report* in *Tax Incentives on Research and Development (R&D)*, *Cahiers de droit fiscal international*, vol. 100A, 17.
7. EY, *Worldwide R&D Incentives Reference Guide 2017* (EY, 2017).

The Netherlands: Innovation Box Regime

The Netherlands introduced the current Innovation Box rules from 1 January 2010.[8] The intangible property must relate to patent rights, or have a related government issued R&D declaration. The tax base of the related income is reduced by 80%, and so the effective tax rate on related income is reduced to 5%. In addition intangible property related losses can be deducted against the company's standard tax rate profits. The innovation box regime was not considered to be state aid by the European Commission, and so was not disqualified under the related rules. The Netherlands regime can apply to self-developed and patented intangible property, and also to contract R&D. The provisions primarily require sufficient commercial substance in the Netherlands entity to allow the tax concession, so that the Netherlands entity must therefore:[9]

- Bear the risks and costs relating to the R&D.
- Have sufficiently skilled personnel who manage and control the research and development process and manage and control the related risks.

Changes were made to the Innovation Box regime from 2017 which apply to intangible assets developed after 30 June 2016, in response to OECD BEPS Action Plan 5 on Countering Harmful Tax Practices. The most significant change is the nexus approach, where only a portion of the benefits attributable to innovation are eligible for the reduced tax rate. This is based on qualifying expenditure, comprising in-house development activities which are not subcontracted within the group, and expenditure on development activities subcontracted to third parties. Qualifying benefits are based on a formula where qualifying expenditure is uplifted by 30%, divided by the total expenditure, multiplied by the total IP income.[10]

Luxembourg

A second example of an intangible property regime is provided in Luxembourg. The related provisions apply from 2007 to software, copyrights, patents, trademarks, designs, or models,[11] and the concessionary treatment is available for acquired and self-developed intangible property. The regime provides a 5.93% effective tax rate, based on an 80% profits exemption with the 29.63% corporate tax rate. The related tax calculation is based on gross revenue and royalties, less expenses and amortisation of the costs of the intangible property. Related losses are fully tax deductible at the corporate tax rate, and the losses are only recouped if the related rights are sold at a later date. The concessional tax regime also provides exemption from withholding taxes on the payment of royalties to non-residents. There is also a deduction for 80% of the deemed amount that a third party would have paid as a royalty for self-developed

8. *Corporate Income Tax Act 1969* (Netherlands).
9. Baker & McKenzie, *Doing Business in the Netherlands 2012*, 164.
10. Renewed innovation box legislation as of 1 January 2017, PWC, September 2016.
11. *Luxembourg Law of 21 December 2007*, section 50 (Luxembourg).

patents which are used in-house, in addition to the deduction for the related R&D expenses.[12]

UK: Patent Box Regime

The UK introduced the Patent Box regime from 1 April 2013 for companies which own or exclusively license in patents which are granted by the UK Intellectual Property Office, the European Patent Office, and by specific countries in the European Economic Area. The patent box company or another related company must have undertaken qualifying development for the patent, which requires a significant contribution to the creation or development of the patented invention, or to a product which incorporates the patented invention. The concessional regime generally taxes the qualifying income from patents and related innovations at an effective tax rate of 10%.[13] Changes to the regime effective after 30 June 2016 apply to new IP or new claimants, and restricts the concession where the claimant company has, to a significant extent, outsourced development to related parties or has acquired the related IP.[14]

SWISS INTELLECTUAL PROPERTY BRANCH

Figure 22.1 Swiss Intellectual Property Branch

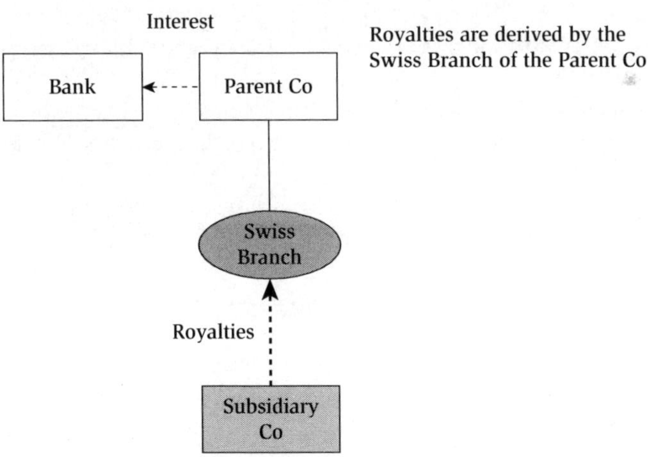

The Swiss intangible property branch structure is an arrangement where the Swiss branch of the Parent Co, a foreign head office company, derives royalty income from

12. Ernst & Young, *Luxembourg Intellectual Property Tax Regime*, April 2010.
13. *Finance Act 2012* c. 14, Schedule 2, and *Corporation Tax Act 2010* c. 4, Part 8A (United Kingdom).
14. 2016 Worldwide Corporate Tax Guide, Ernst & Young, 1535, Part 8A, Chapters 1-7 Corporation Tax Act 2010, and HM Revenue and Customs, Policy paper, Corporation Tax: Patent Box – compliance with new international rules, 9 December 2015.

licensing intellectual property to other companies within a multinational energy group.[15]

Switzerland provides several incentives at the federal, cantonal, and municipal tax levels. The incentives typically require the related royalty income to be under 25% of the branch's total income. The total effective Swiss tax rate depends on cantonal and municipal tax regimes and the availability of related rulings from the respective tax authorities. In general, Swiss cantonal and municipal tax may allow a deduction for the allocation of head office company's interest expense.

The Swiss branch structure generally requires a tax exemption for foreign branch or permanent establishment profits for the head office company, or a related tax treaty exemption from tax. The head office company in this example may potentially be located in the Netherlands or Luxembourg. There are several related tax issues with the structure, particularly the issue of exit taxes or capital gains taxes if existing intangible property within the multinational group is transferred into the structure. It is generally a much simpler approach to use the structure for new intangible property within the group. There is a need for sufficient management to be located in Switzerland to establish that there is commercial substance to the arrangement. There is also an issue whether the income derived by the branch in Switzerland is subject to CFC taxation in the ultimate parent country, for example if that parent company is located in the US.

The tax rate can potentially apply because Switzerland has domiciliary, mixed, and auxiliary company regimes. These companies are required to predominantly perform business activities with commercial effects outside Switzerland, and to host the related administrative functions in Switzerland. These activities can include the exploitation of intangibles such as intellectual property and related assets, invoicing, and group financing. On this basis the companies are generally required to have at least 80% of their income and expenses from sources outside Switzerland. In relation to these provisions, royalty income generated by intangible property which is licensed for use in foreign markets will qualify as foreign sourced income. The Swiss tax rules also generally allow tax amortisation of the related costs of intellectual property over a five-year period, and allow debt financing of the intellectual property up to 70% of the fair market value.

The Swiss federal corporate income tax rate is 8.5%, however because other taxes are deductible the effective federal tax rate is approximately 7.8%. A mixed company tax ruling generally allows only 5% to 30% of the foreign sourced income to be subject to cantonal and commune tax at the related tax rate of 1% to 4%. In addition, a significant part of a finance branch's capital may be treated as loan financing, which allows a related interest deduction. Certain Swiss cantons also allow finance branches to combine with intangible property holding and management activities, provided that their respective licensing income is less than 25% of the branch's total income.

The EU has considered whether the Swiss holding, mixed, and domiciliary company regimes may constitute state aid by encouraging businesses to be established

15. Pascal Hinny & Jean-Blaise Eckert, 'Corporate Tax: Is Swiss Corporate Tax System still Attractive Despite EU Pressure?' International Tax Review, 12 March 2013.

in Switzerland due to the related tax concessions, which may be contrary to the 1972 Agreement between the EU and Switzerland.[16] This issue may result in changes to the Swiss tax regime in the future.

OECD BEPS ACTION 13: CBC REPORTING

The BEPS Action 13 Country-by-Country (CbC) reporting measures may impact the use of group IP entities:[17]

- CbC reports can include IP related entities under the Main Business Activity heading in the Research and Development or Holding or Managing Intellectual Property categories.
- The CbC report may assist in identifying group IP centres with high related party earnings compared to the number of related employees.
- The related analysis by tax authorities may include whether profits allocated to such IP entities are appropriate to functions performed, assets used, and risks undertaken by these entities.

The CbC measures were adopted in the 2017 OECD Transfer Pricing Guidelines for Multinational Enterprises and Tax Administrations.[18]

INTANGIBLE PROPERTY PLANNING

Tax planning relating to intangible property and research and development will depend on the related concessions available in specific countries, however the following are some general planning issues, Any planning arrangements will be subject to related anti-tax avoidance rules of the countries concerned, and consideration of OECD BEPS measures which may potentially apply:

- The primary issue is identifying R&D projects and activities, to ensure that related expenditure is included in tax concession claims. There are quite broad possibilities under some concessions, for example where the development of a patent is not required for concessionary treatment.
- It is also generally effective to identify all the related expenditure which may qualify for the concession, for example related administrative and overhead expenses are allowed under several tax concession regimes.
- There may be opportunities to recharge head office and related company expenses which relate to the R&D activity, such as human resources, information technology, accounting, treasury and legal services, where these expenses potentially also qualify for the concessional tax regime.

16. Agreement between the European Economic Community and the Swiss Confederation of 22 July 1972, Article 23(1), OJ L 300, 31.12.1972.
17. OECD Transfer Pricing Documentation and Country-by-Country Reporting, ACTION 13: 2015 Final Report.
18. Chapter 5 Documentation, p. 229.

- Where a structure such as a patent box is used it is generally effective to allow al the related returns from the use of the R&D, such as royalties paid by related companies and third parties, to be taxed at the concessional rate under the patent box provisions.
- There may be opportunities to subcontract part of the R&D to related companies, and ensure that they are paid an arm's length return for the work carried out, where these subcontractor payments also qualify for the tax concession.
- The commercial substance of the R&D entity is generally enhanced if the entity subcontracts not only to related parties performing contracted R&D but also to third parties, and also provides the results of the R&D to related companies and also to third parties in exchange for royalty income.
- There is a crucial transfer pricing issue for R&D entities that the subcontractor fees paid, and the royalties received, are at arm's length amounts. In general there may be third-party comparable payments to help determine an appropriate arm's length royalty rate, however the arm's length contractor fee for R&D performed for the entity may be more difficult to determine. The related transfer pricing issues are discussed in Chapter 31.
- There may also be potential advantages in performing activities which do not qualify for the patent box regimes, for example relating to intellectual property such as business practices and safety standards, in a tax effective contract R&D entity. This entity would develop and own the intellectual property, and would license the intellectual property in return for royalty income.
- The potential for substantial tax incentives make R&D an essential issue which requires close liaison between the tax department and the related R&D entities and personnel.

CHAPTER 23

Group Treasury and In-House Banking Companies

INTRODUCTION

The primary commercial reason to use a group treasury company or in-house banking company is to centralise the treasury and finance functions within a multinational group. This approach enables borrowing by the treasury company under larger scale programmes on financial markets, which can achieve much lower interest rates than would apply to smaller loans by group subsidiaries under local bank borrowings. There may also be advantages in longer term borrowing used by the treasury company resulting in lower interest rates, compared to shorter borrowing terms for the subsidiary company loans. The result is generally a significant reduction in the multinational group's funding costs.

The group treasury company typically also undertakes related activities such as foreign exchange management, based on the currencies of business income, the needs of the subsidiaries to meet expenses, and the currencies of the group's borrowings. The treasury company may also conduct centralised foreign exchange hedging of the group's net foreign currency exposures. There may also be opportunities for the company to conduct other related financing activities, for example group leasing and insurance activities.

There is also a potential benefit from the 'netting off' function. A subsidiary may owe certain amounts to the group treasury company on funding for its local activities, for example, and may also be owed amounts by the treasury company. The two balances may be netted off, with interest only payable on the net balance. This structure generally reduces withholding taxes payable on interest by the subsidiary companies.

This use of a group treasury company usually results in a margin of profit based on the margin between the interest charged to subseries on smaller loans, and the lower interest expense on the treasury company's larger scale borrowings. There may therefore be a significant reduction in the multinational's group effective tax rate, particularly where the interest margin is derived in a lower taxing country, such as the Netherlands, Switzerland, Luxembourg, or Singapore.

TAX ISSUES

The principal tax issue is that group treasury company should be located in a country with a good tax treaty network to reduce withholding tax on payments from the borrowing subsidiaries, and withholding tax on the group treasury company's own borrowings from the financial markets.

The group treasury company generally enables interest income from group companies to be derived in a low-taxing country. Examples of concessional tax regimes which may be used potentially include:

- The Netherlands Financial Services Company (FSC) regime provides that the company is taxed based on economic substance performed in the Netherlands, rather than the company's full interest or royalty income. The Advance Pricing Agreement (APA) system, however, requires operational and economic substance for the FSC from 2014, and also requires arm's length pricing for those services. The Netherlands company is required to have professionally skilled Netherlands resident directors which will form at least half the board and have real decision-making power, major decisions must be taken in the Netherlands, and all administrative activities must be performed in the Netherlands. The company should also run real business risks and have sufficient equity capital at stake for these risks. The measures generally require a safe haven equity at risk requirement is at least 1% of outstanding receivables, with a maximum of EUR 2 million.
- Ireland has a standard tax rate from 2003 of 12.5%, which provides a beneficial tax rate under the standard tax system of a European Union (EU) country. The use of a standard tax rate, rather than a special tax regime, is also less likely to attract anti-tax avoidance provisions. Withholding tax does not apply to interest paid form Ireland to non-residents if the loans are for a period of less than one year, or interest is paid in the course of a trade or business to a company resident in a EU or treaty country.
- Switzerland provides tax concessions which can apply to group finance companies. The Swiss tax rules for finance branches, for example, requires at least 75% of assets and income to be derived from financing activities, and loans and advances to Swiss residents must not exceed 10%. Withholding tax on interest payments to the branch may be reduced by the branch's head office country tax treaties, because tax treaties generally depend on the residence of the company that receives the interest, and not the country where a branch is located. The EU has considered that the Swiss regime may potentially constitute state aid, however, by encouraging businesses to establish themselves in

Switzerland through tax concessions, which may be contrary to the EU Switzerland agreement in 1972.[1]

- The Singapore Finance and Treasury Centre (FTC) incentive has significant potential benefits for a group treasury company, including a 10% tax rate for financial income including interest.[2] The related tax concessions are provided for a period of five to ten years, and the concessions may be renewed on the basis of substantial commitments to expanding the operations in Singapore. The Singapore concessions may also include exemptions from withholding tax on interest payments to banks and related companies.

Group Treasury Centres: Reduction of the Group Tax Rate

Figure 23.1 Group Treasury Centres

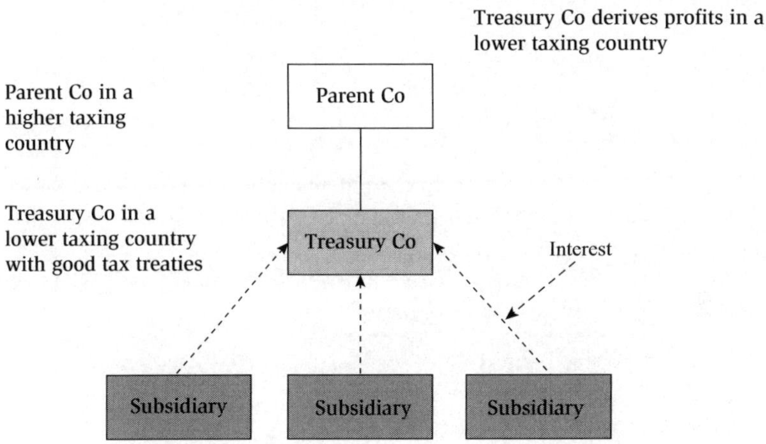

The group treasury company structure relates to the interest income of the Treasury Co derived from group subsidiaries in different countries.

The structure may provide interest deductions for group subsidiaries located in higher taxing countries, and also allow the Treasury Co derive that interest income in a country with lower tax rates.

The Treasury Co needs to be located in a country with a good tax treaty network to reduce withholding tax imposed on the interest payments in each subsidiary country. Accordingly the Treasury Co should generally not be located in a tax haven. Countries which may be considered for the Treasury Co include Switzerland, Netherlands, Luxembourg, and Singapore. It is necessary to consider rules on interest

1. *Agreement between the European Economic Community and the Swiss Confederation of 22 July 1972*, Article 23(1), OJ L 300, 31.12.1972.
2. *Income Tax Act*, Chapter 134, section 43G (Singapore).

deductions in subsidiary countries, for example thin capitalisation rules may deny deductions for related party interest where there is considered to be excessive related party debt.

MULTINATIONAL LENDING STRUCTURES

Introduction

In a common structure, the group treasury company generally lends funds to related subsidiary companies in high taxing countries. Interest is paid from those high taxing countries, allowing a deduction to reduce tax on the subsidiaries, to the group treasury company which is only taxed at concessional rates. The treasury company needs to be located in a country which has a good treaty network, so that other countries do not impose withholding tax on interest payments to the treasury company. The treasury company should also have nil withholding tax on interest it pays on its own borrowings.

The traditional type of treasury company has a flow through of interest payments. The treasury company borrows from the market or a related company. This structure may potentially be used in countries such as the Netherlands, Luxembourg, and Sweden.

There have been several related developments in tax rules which may potentially benefit group treasury companies. For example, Belgium introduced a notional interest deduction (NID) based on the Belgian company's equity from 1 January 2006, which allows a deemed interest deduction based on the company's equity less than company's equity participations and overseas permanent establishments.

Treasury Companies: Equity Example

Figure 23.2 Treasury Companies: Equity Example

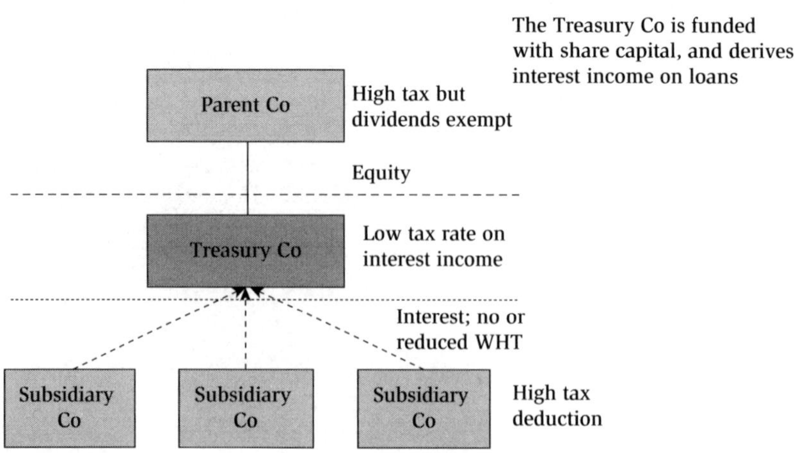

The intra-group lending structure is based on share equity provided by the Parent Co to the Treasury Co located in a country with a low effective tax rate. The Treasury Co then lends the funds to the Subsidiary Co companies in the same multinational group.

The structure may potentially result in a reduction of the group tax rate as the interest income is taxed at a low rate, while the Subsidiary Co companies potentially receive deductions at higher tax rates. This benefit may be substantial, as the Treasury Co may have limited expenses as it has been funded by equity rather than debt and therefore has high potential profits. There may, however, be controlled foreign corporation (CFC) provisions in the country where the Parent Co is located, which would then potentially tax that the Parent Co on the passive income, such as interest, derived by the Treasury Co.

The Parent Co is typically located in a country with a higher tax rate, however the dividend income from the Treasury Co may be exempt from tax, for example if the dividends qualify for the participation exemption. One issue is whether there are limitations on the participation exemption in relation to dividends from related companies such as the Treasury Co when those companies are located in low taxing countries. There is also a significant issue whether the Parent Co is allowed an interest deduction for borrowings used to provide equity to the Treasury Co. The Treasury Co is typically located in a country with a low effective tax rate on the interest income received from the Subsidiary Co companies.

The Subsidiary Co companies should potentially receive a tax deduction for the interest paid to the Treasury Co. There may however be higher withholding tax where the Treasury Co is regarded as located in a tax haven, or does not have an effective tax treaty network with the countries where the Subsidiary Co companies are located. The amount of the tax deduction in the Subsidiary Co countries is also potentially limited by the thin capitalisation provisions, which may reduce interest deductions on related party debt which is considered to be excessive.

Treasury Companies: Debt Example

Figure 23.3 Treasury Companies: Debt Example

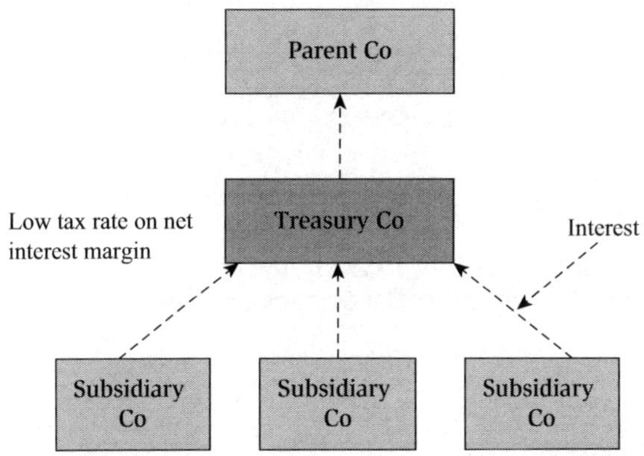

This example of an intra-group lending structure is based on loan funding from the Parent Co to the Treasury Company, rather than using share equity as in the previous example. As in the previous example, the Treasury Co company is located in a country with a low effective tax rate.

The structure may potentially result in a reduction of the group tax rate as the interest margin is derived by the Treasury Co in the lower taxing country. This profit would be less substantial than the previous structure, as the Treasury Co has been funded by debt and has a related interest expense, and therefore only derives an interest margin. There may also be CFC provisions in the country where the Parent Co is located, which potentially taxes the Parent Co on the passive income, such as interest, derived by the Treasury Co which is located in a tax haven.

The Parent Co is typically located in a country with a high tax rate. The dividend income from the Treasury Co may potentially be tax exempt under the participation exemption, subject to any conditions which may deny the exemption relating to income from companies considered to be located in low tax countries. The Treasury Co is typically located in a country with a low effective tax rate on the interest income received from the Subsidiary Co companies.

As in the prior example, the Subsidiary Co companies should receive a tax deduction for the interest paid to the Treasury Co. There may however be high withholding tax where the Treasury Co is regarded as located in a tax haven or does not have effective tax treaties with the countries where the Subsidiary Co companies are located. The amount of the tax deduction is also commonly limited by thin capitalisation provisions in the respective countries where the amount of the related party debt is treated as excessive.

IN-HOUSE BANKING

Multinational groups may use a group treasury company or in-house banking company to effectively perform banking functions, such as cash management, foreign currency management, and group funding, in a centralised treasury location. For example, an in-house banking facility may be used for management of the following issues:

- Liquidity – Surplus funds in a group subsidiary in one country can be used to fund temporary cash needs of another group subsidiary in different country.
- Foreign Exchange – A group subsidiary in one country may, for example, have surplus United States (US) dollars, which can be used to meet a need for US dollars by a subsidiary in another country.
- Funding – The treasury or in-house banking company may obtain funds from the financial markets at much lower interest rates, though larger borrowings and parent company credit support, and part of these savings can be used to lower the interest paid by subsidiary companies.

A significant benefit of group treasury and in-house banking companies is to reduce the net assets and liabilities in the group, meaning that less cash need be held in different countries as the multinational group can 'net off' the surplus cash in one country against the funding needs in other countries.

In-house banking may also be used reduce bank transaction costs. The in-house bank makes net payments to external banks on the net loan balance to external parties, rather than having each group subsidiary making payments on borrowings under their local banking arrangements. The multinational group's subsidiaries would maintain accounts with the in-house bank, which would borrow and lend funds to subsidiaries, and would also have its own accounts with funding sources such as external banks and issuing corporate bonds.

The in-house bank would generally be in a country with a good tax treaty network, principally to minimise the potential withholding tax on interest payments from the group's subsidiaries in other countries. The in-house bank may also benefit from low tax rates on in-house banking activities, such as interest margins, foreign exchange gains, and fee income that may potentially be available under related tax concessions.

THE OECD BEPS ACTION PLAN AND GROUP TREASURY COMPANIES

Several measures in the BEPS action plans may potentially impact tax planning and the use of group finance and treasury centres. The measures may particularly apply where these entities lack significant economic substance, and include:

- Action 3 Designing Effective Controlled Foreign Company Rules – The general extension of CFC rules to more countries is likely to apply parent country tax to profits derived by group treasury centres with little economic substance, such as a cash box with limited or no economic activities.[3]
- Action 4 Limiting Base Erosion Involving Interest Deductions and Other Financial Payments – The interest deductibility rules may limit the amount of deductions obtained in the related companies paying interest to the group treasury centre. This includes the recommended approach to limit an entity's net interest deductions to a percentage of its earnings before interest, taxes, depreciation and amortisation (EBITDA).[4]
- Action 6 Preventing the Granting of Treaty Benefits in Inappropriate Circumstances – These measures may apply to structuring payments to the group treasury company in a way that avoids withholding taxes, such as treaty shopping, due to the guidance provided on preventing treaty abuse, and related implementation of these measures under the Action 15 Multilateral Instrument (MLI). This includes the principal purpose test and the limitation

3. OECD, Designing Effective Controlled Foreign Company Rules Action: 2015 Final Report.
4. Limiting Base Erosion Involving Interest Deductions and Other Financial Payments Action 4 – 2016 Update.

on benefits test, which can potentially deny treaty benefits in treaty shopping cases.[5]

- Action 13 Country-by-Country (CbC) reporting – These measures may impact the use of group treasury entities.[6] The CbC reports will generally include these entities under the Main Business Activity heading as Internal Group Finance category. This will include related information including related and unrelated party revenues, profits before tax, income tax paid, and number of employees. The CbC measures were adopted in the 2017 OECD Transfer Pricing Guidelines.[7]

5. Preventing the Granting of Treaty Benefits in Inappropriate Circumstances Action 6: 2015 Final Report.
6. OECD Transfer Pricing Documentation and Country-by-Country Reporting, Action 13: 2015 Final Report.
7. OECD Transfer Pricing Guidelines for Multinational Enterprises and Tax Administrations 2017, Chapter 5 Documentation, p. 229.

CHAPTER 24

Group Service Companies

INTRODUCTION

Service company structures are based on the use of a company within a multinational group which provides services to other companies in the group. The service company is contracted to provide supporting services to related companies, and where the related services income is derived by the service company in lower taxing country. A deduction for the service payments is generally obtained by group subsidiaries in higher taxing countries.

The services provided to related companies may include:

- management and control;
- government, shareholder, and public relations;
- project evaluation and approval;
- accounting and finance;
- performance evaluation;
- technical and IT services;
- management of know-how, administration of patents, and licences;
- procurement;
- leasing;
- distribution;
- engineering;
- HR services, recruitment, and training;
- financial services, group treasury, foreign exchange;
- fund raising with bond and capital issues;
- legal and tax services including compliance and advice;
- advertising;
- research and development;

- contract manufacturing;
- contract research; and
- acquisitions and sales.

The related arrangements can include direct charges of expenses relating to particular countries and subsidiaries, or indirect charges of expenses such as overheads. Cost contribution arrangements (CCA) or cost sharing arrangements (CSA) may be used to determine charges to group companies.

POTENTIAL WITHHOLDING TAX

The related tax considerations include the potential withholding tax on the service payments from the subsidiaries to the group service company. One tax planning objective is to have the service company located in a country with lower tax rate but which still has a good tax treaty network, and so is not treated as a tax haven by the countries where the subsidiaries are located. Accordingly, the structure may generally not use tax havens for the service company. Countries which may potentially be used for the group service company include the Netherlands and Singapore.

The OECD Model Tax Treaty allows source country withholding tax to apply to income such as dividends and interest.[1] Many treaties are similar to the UN Model Tax Treaty, however, in allowing source country withholding tax on royalties.[2] A common issue is whether service fees may be subject to withholding tax where treated as royalties, to the extent that they include payments relating to the use of intangibles such as technical knowledge. Several countries such as Malaysia impose withholding tax on service fees.[3]

The service company may therefore be located in a country with related tax treaties which do not provide for withholding tax except on dividends and interest, or, while allowing withholding tax on royalties, adopt a narrow definition or royalties which would not apply to the service fees.

An example of this issue arose in the *Tech Mahindra* case in Australia, where the related payments for information technology (IT) services from the Australian customer to Indian suppliers included items, such as the correction of software code, which were considered to be royalties subject to royalty withholding tax.[4]

1. Model Convention with Respect to Taxes on Income and on Capital, 2014, OECD, Articles 11 and 12.
2. United Nations Model Double Taxation Convention between Developed and Developing Countries, Article 12.
3. Income Tax Act, 1967, section 4A, and KPMG, Malaysia: Withholding tax, royalty and service fee payments to non-residents, 21 December 2016, https://home.kpmg.com/xx/en/home/insights/2016/12/tnf-malaysia-withholding-tax-royalty-and-service-fee-payments-to-non-residents.html on 19 October 2017.
4. *Tech Mahindra Limited v. Commissioner of Taxation* [2015] FCA 1082. The case concerned the 'development and transfer' part of the royalties Article 12(3)(g) of the Australia/India tax treaty, which included technical services which related to the development and transfer of a technical plan or design, such as software design and the customisation of existing software applications.

ADVANTAGES OF TIME BASED CHARGES

The group service company is significant in multinational group structures as the company is generally charging for services rather than for the use of intangible property such as the use of proprietary technology. The charges are in many cases related to personnel costs and third-party charges which are allocated to countries and subsidiaries using allocation keys.

In relation to upstream oil and gas, Joint Operating Agreements (JOA) are frequently used to allow different oil and gas companies to cooperate in an investment in an oil and gas field, with one of the investors designated as the operator with overall responsibility for the project. JOAs will generally allow time based charges for services subject to review by the other investors, whereas other charges such as royalties are generally not allowed.

In other cases upstream oil and gas projects are undertaken under Production Sharing Contracts (PSCs), where the oil and gas company is remunerated on the basis of profit oil and recovery of costs under cost oil. Time based charges from group service companies may potentially be recoverable as costs oil, compared to royalties which are usually not allowed as recoverable costs.

Deductions for time based charges or recovery as recoverable costs under PSCs may be more likely to be accepted by country tax authorities where evidence is that the allocation has been made on a reasonable basis, and in particular, has been made under the same uniform system applied by the multinational group to all subsidiary companies.

POTENTIAL CFC TAXATION

The related issue is whether the parent company of the service company may be subject to CFC taxation, on the basis that the service fee income is defined to be passive income derived by a related company in a tax haven. The structure may potentially not be subject to CFC provisions where the activity is treated as an active business. The United States (US) CFC provisions, however, apply to foreign base company (FBC) services income, which consists of income derived by a CFC in connection with the performance outside the CFC's country of incorporation of technical, managerial, engineering, architectural, scientific, skilled, industrial, commercial, or like services for or on behalf of any related person.[5]

SERVICE COMPANY STRUCTURES AND SUBCONTRACTING

The group service company may subcontract services to companies in the same group or to third-party service providers. There may be justification for a margin to be retained in the service company based on quantity discount available for a large service

5. Internal Revenue Code § 954(e).

contract, compared to the smaller contracts which may be made by individual group subsidiaries.

There is a potential issue with tax provisions based on a Diverted Profits Tax (DPT), where tax authorities may raise additional assessments where profits are considered to have been diverted to a group service company which may not have sufficient commercial substance. This can particularly apply to subcontracting services, where the level of commercial substance in the group service company may not be substantial compared to the related profit margins. The DPT tests may include whether the group service company has the appropriate levels of staff and expertise to manage the related activities. Examples of these provisions include DPT measures in the United Kingdom (UK) and Australia.

THE OECD BEPS ACTION PLANS AND SERVICE COMPANIES

The BEPS Action 13 Country-by-Country (CbC) reporting measures may impact the use of group service companies:[6]

- CbC reports will generally include these entities under the Main Business Activity heading in the Administrative, Management, or Support Services category. The report includes information on related and unrelated party revenues, profits before tax, income tax paid, and number of employees.
- This may, for example, identify group service centres with high related party earnings compared to the number of related employees.
- Country tax authorities may perform follow-up analysis as to whether the profits allocated to the service entities are commensurate with the functions performed, assets used, and risks undertaken (FAR) by the service entities.

The CbC measures were adopted in the 2017 OECD Transfer Pricing Guidelines for Multinational Enterprises and Tax Administrations.[7]

The OECD BEPS Action Plan 8 included analysis of low-value adding intra-group services.[8]

The BEPS review also included analysis of CCA.[9] The transfer pricing issues relating to service companies, including the OECD BEPS measures, are discussed in Chapter 32.

6. OECD Transfer Pricing Documentation and Country-by-Country Reporting, Action 13: 2015 Final Report.
7. Chapter 5 Documentation, p. 229.
8. OECD, Aligning Transfer Pricing Outcomes with Value Creation, Actions 8-10: 2015 Final Reports, p. 141.
9. *Ibid*, p. 161.

CHAPTER 25
Group Insurance Companies

CAPTIVE INSURANCE ARRANGEMENTS

Captive insurance arrangements are based on the use of an insurance entity within a multinational group which insures the business risks of the parent and subsidiary companies in the group.

Figure 25.1 Captive Insurance Structure

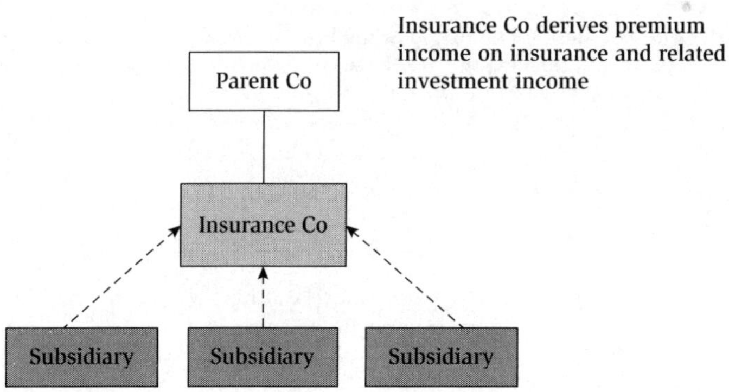

In the structure, the Insurance Co provides insurance cover to related companies in the same multinational group. The intention of the structure is that the related insurance premium together with income from investment of the premiums is then derived by the Insurance Co in lower taxing country. A deduction for the insurance premiums is generally obtained by the Subsidiaries in higher taxing countries.

The most significant tax consideration is the potential withholding tax on the insurance premium payments from the Subsidiaries to the Insurance Co. The principal objective is to have the Insurance Co located in a country with lower tax rate but which still has a good tax treaty network, and so is not treated as a tax haven by the countries where the subsidiaries are located. Accordingly, the structure should generally not use a tax haven for the location of the Insurance Co. Countries which may potentially be used for the Insurance Co include Switzerland, the Netherlands, Luxembourg, and Singapore.

The related issue is whether the parent company of the Insurance Co may be subject to CFC taxation, on the basis that the insurance premium and investment income is passive income derived by a related company in a tax haven. The structure may potentially not be subject to CFC provisions where the insurance activity is treated as an active business. The United States (US) CFC provisions, however, apply to 'foreign base income' which includes income relating to insurance risks outside the CFC's country of incorporation.

The captive insurance company may in turn offset business risks with third-party reinsurance companies. There may be justification for a profit margin in the captive insurance company based on quantity discount available for a large reinsurance contract, compared to the smaller risk contracts made with the related group subsidiaries.

THE OECD BEPS ACTION PLAN AND CAPTIVE INSURANCE

The OECD BEPS Action plan included a review of captive insurance arrangements as part of Action 4:

> ACTION 4
>
> Limit base erosion via interest deductions and other financial payments
>
> Develop recommendations regarding best practices in the design of rules to prevent base erosion through the use of interest expense, for example through the use of related-party and third-party debt to achieve excessive interest deductions or to finance the production of exempt or deferred income, and other financial payments that are economically equivalent to interest payments. The work will evaluate the effectiveness of different types of limitations. In connection with and in support of the foregoing work, transfer pricing guidance will also be developed regarding the pricing of related party financial transactions, including financial and performance guarantees, derivatives (including internal derivatives used in intra-bank dealings), and captive and other insurance arrangements. The work will be co-ordinated with the work on hybrids and CFC rules.

It remains to be seen what measures may be adopted by countries in relation to this part of the BEPS proposals. Any use of captive insurance arrangements should, however, be based on real levels of local management, appropriate levels of capital, and real business risk in the captive insurance entity.

The OECD BEPS Action plan includes review of transfer pricing relating to captive insurance arrangements as part of Action 9:

> Action 9 – Assure that transfer pricing outcomes are in line with value creation/risks and capital. This issue relates to transferring risks or excessive capital to group members, including preventing inappropriate returns solely for the provision of capital or assumption of risks.

The related OECD Public Discussion Draft proposes attention to all risk transfers including the use of captive insurance companies:[1]

> In analysing the transfer of risk, it is relevant to consider whether the arrangement provides the opportunity for both parties to the arrangement to enhance or protect their commercial or financial position on a risk-adjusted basis (the return adjusted for the level of risk associated with it). This means that risk transfer is likely to happen only if the transferee is well placed or better placed to manage risk than the transferor. Circumstances meriting particular scrutiny include those where the transferee has no risk management capability, and those where risk management is performed by the transferor.

OECD BEPS ACTION 13: CbC REPORTING

The BEPS Action 13 Country-by-Country (CbC) reporting measures may impact the use of group insurance entities:[2]

- CbC reports will generally include these entities under the Main Business Activity heading in the Insurance category, with related information including related and unrelated party revenues, profits before tax, income tax paid, and number of employees.
- This may identify group insurance centres with high related party earnings compared to the number of related employees.
- The follow-up analysis may include whether profits allocated to such insurance entities are commensurate with the functions performed, assets used, and risks undertaken (FAR) by these entities.

The CbC measures were adopted in the 2017 OECD Transfer Pricing Guidelines.[3]

1. OECD, *Public Discussion Draft, BEPS Actions 8, 9 and 10: Discussion Draft on Revisions to Chapter I of the Transfer Pricing Guidelines* (Including Risk, Recharacterisation, and Special Measures) <http://www.oecd.org/ctp/transfer-pricing/discussion-draft-actions-8-9-10-chapter-1-TP-Guidelines-risk-recharacterisation-special-measures.pdf> 23.
2. OECD Transfer Pricing Documentation and Country-by-Country Reporting, ACTION 13: 2015 Final Report.
3. 2017 OECD Transfer Pricing Guidelines for Multinational Enterprises and Tax Administrations, Chapter 5 Documentation, p. 229.

CHAPTER 26

Mergers and Acquisitions

INTRODUCTION

This chapter analyses some significant mergers and acquisitions taxation issues when energy groups acquire new companies or businesses, including the related funding requirements. The tax issues include whether the purchaser will acquire the business assets, or will acquire the issued shares of a target company. The tax issues also include the treatment of interest deductions on any loans which were made to finance the purchase, and whether it is possible to use the tax deductions for interest in the local country, which is generally known as 'debt push down'.

The acquisition may also provide potential tax advantages by the opportunity to increase the buyer's depreciation or amortisation deductions on plant, machinery, or intangible property (IP) after the acquisition. This may potentially be done allocating more of the purchase price to the assets up to their market value, which is generally known as 'asset step up'. The taxation issues also include the availability of tax losses under different country tax regimes, and particularly whether the tax losses or recoverable cost balances of a target company are retained after the acquisition.

One important consideration is that the buyer and seller may have conflicting tax objectives. For example, the seller may prefer an asset sale to utilise tax losses so that the seller is not taxed, whereas the buyer may prefer to purchase the target company to retain the target company's tax losses.

An acquisition may also involve some amount of deferred consideration, which may only be determined at a later date on the basis of the post-acquisition performance. The right to receive an unknown future amount may be regarded as an asset that must be valued for tax purposes, for example under United Kingdom (UK) tax rules.[1]

1. KPMG, *Taxation of Cross-Border Mergers and Acquisitions – United Kingdom* (KPMG International Cooperative, 2012) 9.

WHETHER TO ACQUIRE TARGET ASSETS OR TARGET COMPANY SHARES

There are several commercial and legal issues which may affect the decision to purchase business assets, or to purchase the shares of the target company which holds those assets. The most significant of these non-tax issues is that purchasing only the related business assets allows the purchaser to exclude hidden liabilities of a target company, for example there may be hidden debts or obligations in the company that held the assets.

The process of purchasing the shares of a company may generally be much simpler, for example the transfer of ownership of a company generally does not require the separate transfer of registered assets of the company. The purchase price can also potentially be adjusted for company liabilities such as external debt. The share purchase also retains the target company's structure, which may include the ownership of any subsidiary companies. The share purchase also generally provides better continuity to the target company's customers as they continue to deal with the same company. In relation to large scale acquisitions in particular, a share purchase may be done on the stock market for shares in a listed target company.

There have been several tax developments relating to the use of tax losses. European Union (EU) provisions may allow cross-border tax relief, where tax losses can be transferred between companies in different EU countries, following the European Court of Justice (ECJ) decision in the *Marks & Spencer* case in 2005.[2] Marks & Spencer had claimed group relief in the UK for losses incurred by its Belgian, German, and French subsidiaries, to utilise those losses to reduce UK tax, on the basis that refusal to allow the losses was contrary to the freedom of establishment under the Treaty on EU.[3] The ECJ held that the losses may be utilised in the UK, provided there was no local loss relief whatsoever in the EU subsidiary countries, irrespective of whether that loss relief was made under carry-back, current relief, or carry-forward tax loss provisions.

One dominant tax planning consideration is the availability of carry-forward tax losses which may potentially be retained by purchasing the target company. New business operations, for example in upstream oil and gas or mining, can result in very large balances of carry-forward tax losses in a target company, and retaining these tax losses can be an essential tax structuring issue for the acquisition.

DEBT PUSH DOWN STRUCTURES AND INTEREST DEDUCTIONS

Interest deductions are generally allowed to a company for the purchase of assets under many tax regimes, as the assets will be used to generate taxable profits. It may be more difficult to obtain interest deductions on funds borrowed to purchase shares in a target company where, for example, the related dividends may be tax exempt under participation exemption provisions.

2. *Marks & Spencer*, Case C-446/03, [2005] ECR I-10837.
3. *Treaty on EU* [1992] OJ C191/1, opened for signature 7 February 1992 (entered into force 1 November 1993) ('*Maastricht Treaty*').

There is also an issue that many countries have thin capitalisation provisions which restrict interest deductions on related party debt, or which may apply to debt which is guaranteed by related parties. The debt push down issue frequently relates to the placing of third-party debt within the multinational group, such as borrowing from unrelated banks, and in many countries interest on third-party debt is not subject to thin capitalisation provisions. There is a trend, however, towards other interest deduction limits, such as those based on interest barrier rules, for example interest compared to earnings before interest, tax, depreciation and amortisation (EBITDA).

Figure 26.1 The Debt Push Down Issue and Debt in the Wrong Place

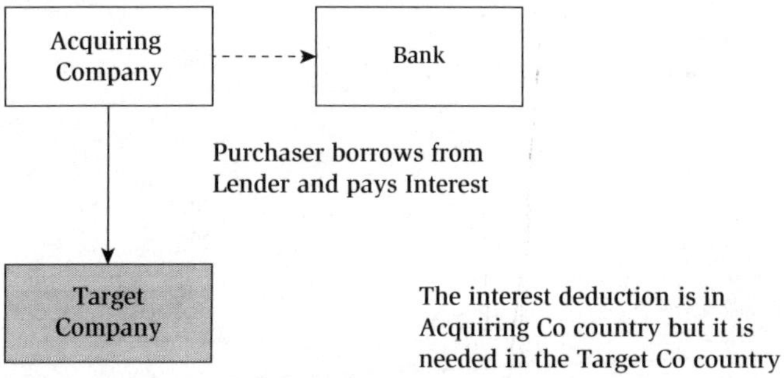

The debt push down issue concerns whether interest deductions on funds borrowed to acquire the Target Company in a cross-border acquisition can be 'pushed down' to the country of the Target Company. The objective of the structure is to utilise the interest deductions on the funds used for the acquisition to reduce tax on the Target Company.

The Acquiring Company may obtain a tax deduction in its own country, however it may not be able to effectively use those deductions if it does not have significant taxable income. The ability of a company to effectively use tax deductions is generally known as that company's 'tax capacity'.

The following pages review structures for addressing the issue of effectively utilising interest deductions. The most common approach is based on the use of structures with a new company in the target country, usually called a special purpose vehicle (SPV) or special purpose entity (SPE). The SPV borrows the required funds in the same country, and then purchases the Target Company or the Target Company's business assets.

If the structure used is one in which the Target Company is acquired, then some form of tax grouping or tax consolidation is generally needed to transfer tax losses arising from interest deductions in the SPV to reduce tax in the Target Company on the Target Company's profits. It is therefore necessary that the Target country has some form of tax consolidation or tax grouping.

A related issue is that some care is needed with the timing of adding debt in a structure with related interest deductions. The target company may be in early business stages and so have large carry-forward losses. There may be an advantage in increasing the debt at a later stage when the target company is profitable, and therefore when the interest deductions can be utilised to reduce tax.

Figure 26.2 Debt Push Down: Local SPV and Consolidation

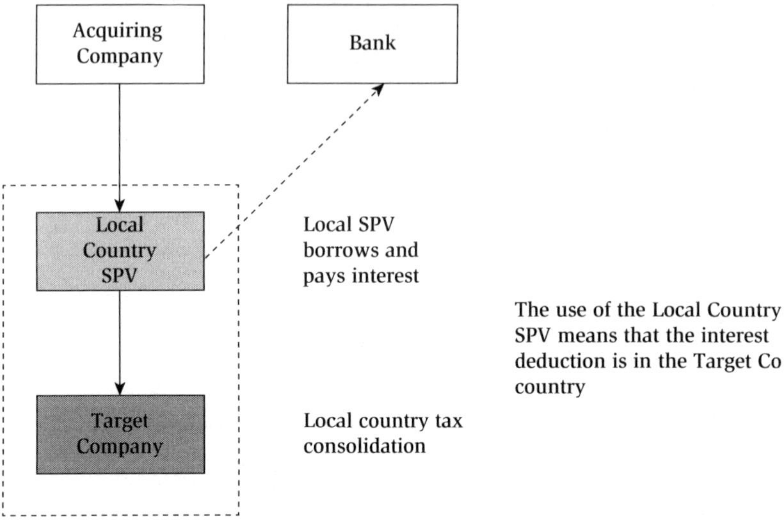

Overview

This is an illustration of the principal debt push down structure. A new company, shown above as the Local Country SPV, is established in the same country as the Target Company. Interest deductions on the debt needed for the acquisition are incurred by the SPV which borrowed the funds needed for the acquisition, and so the interest deductions are 'pushed down' to the country of the acquisition, and are used to reduce tax on the Target Company using tax consolidation. The debt is not itself transferred, however the tax effect of the structure is to notionally push down the debt for tax purposes so that the interest is effectively deducted in the Target Company.

The structure depends on the availability of tax consolidation or tax grouping under local country tax rules. The local country may have other provisions limiting deductions for interest, such as thin capitalisation or interest barrier rules. Tax consolidation is primarily used to allow the transfer of tax losses within groups of companies, such as between the SPV and the Target Company in the above examples. There may be other tax benefits, such as the transfer of assets between group companies without capital gains tax under Australian tax rules, or the payment of dividends between affiliated companies which may be made free of tax under the dividend received deduction (DRD) rules in the United States (US).

Tax consolidation can be provided under different tax rules which provide broadly similar tax outcomes. For example, fiscal unity provisions treats the related companies as one taxpayer entity, affiliated group provisions allow reporting of aggregate group income and deductions in the US, and group relief provisions allow one company to contribute its tax losses to another company within the same tax group.

The tax consolidation requirements of many countries commonly require a minimum common ownership relationship to allow the benefit of the tax concession, such as a 75% requirement in the UK, an 80% requirement in the US, and a 100% requirement in Australia. The provisions may also require that the group relationship be maintained during the full tax year, or that the companies have the same tax reporting year. Tax consolidation may also be optional or obligatory in different countries.

Countries which currently have tax consolidation or group relief provisions include Austria, Australia, Denmark, the Netherlands, Germany, Italy, Luxembourg, Singapore, Spain, Sweden, the UK, and the US. Countries without tax consolidation or group relief currently include Belgium, Switzerland, and Brazil.

Figure 26.3 Hybrid Entities and Consolidation for Debt Push Down

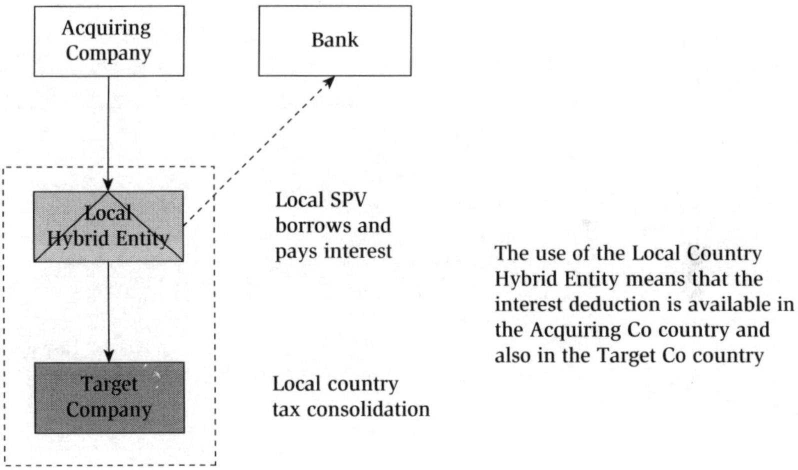

This tax planning structure is based on the use of hybrid entities, which potentially have different tax treatments in different countries. The hybrid entity structure is based on the previous tax consolidation structure except that in this structure the SPV is a hybrid entity. An SPV is established in same country as Target Company, and interest deductions in the SPV are transferred to the Target Company using tax consolidation. The structure differs however because by using a hybrid entity for the SPV there may potentially also be interest deductions allowed for the Acquiring Company.

The hybrid entity is treated as a corporate for tax purposes in the Target Company country, and is treated as a tax-transparent entity in the Parent country. On this basis, interest deductions which arise in the SPV can offset profits in the Target Company using tax consolidation.

As the SPV is treated as a tax-transparent entity, also known as a look through, pass-through or disregarded entity, in the Purchaser's country, however, there is also potentially an interest deduction for the Acquiring Company. This deduction arises because the Local Hybrid Entity is disregarded for tax purposes in the Acquiring Company country, and so its borrowing and related interest expenses are treated as if they were incurred by the Acquiring Company.

The structure requires that there is a suitable hybrid entity between the two countries concerned, and there may also be specific anti-avoidance provisions which could deny the interest deductions.

The potential benefits of the structure are that that the Local Hybrid Entity has interest deductions which can be used to offset the Target Company profits, and interest deductions can also be available in the Acquiring Company in their country. This structure is an example of an interest double dip structure, as deductions may potentially be obtained in two countries for the same interest expense.

Figure 26.4 Asset Acquisitions for Debt Push Down

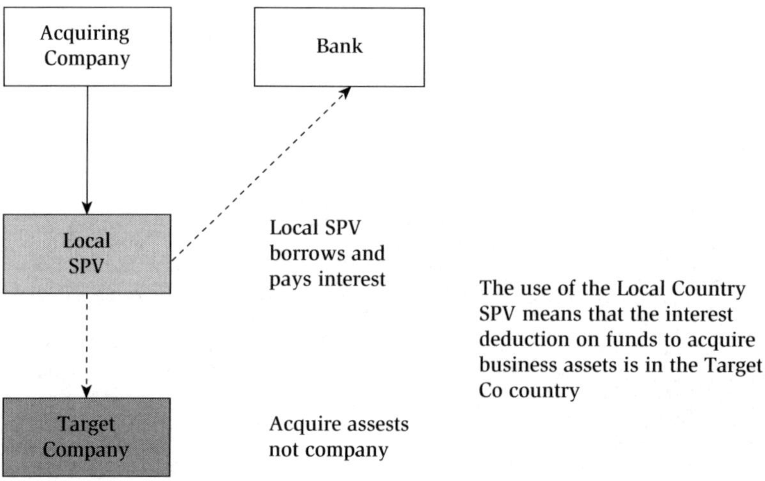

In general the acquisition of assets rather than a company is more likely to enable interest deductions on an acquisition. The structure in this example uses an SPV which is established in same country as the Target Company. The SPV will acquire the Target Company's business assets.

The local country SPV acquires the Target Company's assets, rather than acquiring the Target Company itself. Most countries allow interest deductions on loans which were made to acquire business assets which will be used to generate taxable profits.

The potential benefit of the structure is that it generally provides local country interest deductions, which can offset taxation on the future profits from the business assets. The principal drawback of this structure is that an asset acquisition generally does not allow the acquisition of any tax losses which may be in the Target Company.

DEPRECIATION ALLOWANCES AND ASSET STEP UP

Introduction

The previous structure for the acquisition of assets may also allow an 'asset step up', which refers to allocation of purchase price to depreciable assets up to their market value, rather than written down values after the prior years' tax depreciation. This allows the SPV to obtain increased depreciation allowances in future years based on the higher market value of the assets. The asset selling company is likely, however, to be taxable on the difference between the higher sale value and the tax written down value of the assets. The structure may be effective where, for example, the Seller's company has carry-forward tax losses, and so the tax losses can offset the tax on the asset sale.

For example, mining machinery may cost USD 200 million, the written down tax value after depreciation over several years is USD 20 million, and the currently market value is USD 100 million. The SPV purchasing the asset can allocate USD 100 million of the total purchase price of the business to the mining machinery, and depreciate from that stepped up value of USD 100 million over future years. The Seller, however, is likely to be taxed on the USD 80 million difference between tax written down value and the sale price of the machinery.

The use of asset step up structures may be particularly important where countries have tax regimes with accelerated depreciation, and so the written down tax values of the assets may be low compared to the current market value of those assets.

Upstream Mergers and Asset Step Up

Figure 26.5 Upstream Mergers and Asset Step Up

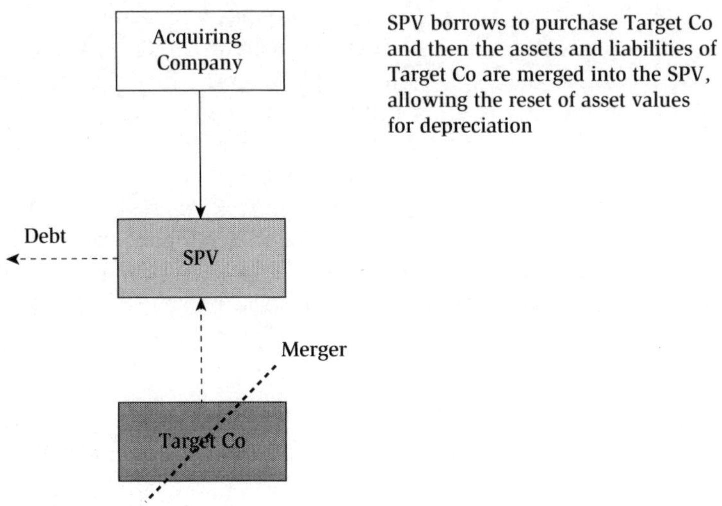

The planning objective of an upstream merger structure is to achieve an 'asset step up'. This arrangement increases the tax basis of the Target Co assets up to their market values on their transfer to the SPV, which will then increase future depreciation deductions for the SPV. In the structure, the SPV may be a new company established for the transaction, which then borrows the funds required to acquire the Target Co. The SPV then merges with the Target Co, so that the Target Co is liquidated, and the SPV is the surviving company.

The SPV as the surviving entity may be treated as having acquired the assets at their market value. There may be tax on transfers where the value of the assets exceeds their tax written down value, and there may need to be tax losses in the Target Co to offset the taxable gains. However, several countries may potentially not tax the transfers of assets between related companies on liquidation.

The new values of the assets on transfer should not exceed their market value. There is an opportunity to utilise any tax losses in the Target Co where the gains on the asset step up are taxable.

A similar result may be derived for US tax purposes, for example with a deemed liquidation where a check-the-box entity classification election is made to treat foreign companies as disregarded for tax purposes. A deemed liquidation which is not made within an affiliated group, which requires at least 80% common ownership, may be treated as a taxable event. The assets in the subsidiary including goodwill may then potentially be reset to their market values.[4]

Tax Relief for Share or Asset Sales

One important consideration is whether there may be tax relief relating to asset sale transactions such as those shown in the above structures so that the seller is not immediately taxed on any gains on the sale of assets over the tax written down value of those assets. Tax relief may be available, for example, if the asset sale is connected with the purchase of a replacement asset under tax deferral or rollover relief provisions. In the UK, business asset rollover relief may apply to defer capital gains tax due on the disposal of assets where there is an acquisition of other assets costing the same or more than the amount received for the old assets. The tax relief postpones tax on the sale of the assets until there is a disposal of the new assets.[5]

In the US, similar relief is provided for like-kind exchanges. The relief can apply where the income from the sale of assets is used to acquire similar assets, and for involuntary conversions where transfers were required by legislation.[6] The relief applies so that tax is deferred until there is a future sale of the replacement asset. The US provisions can separate real assets, such as a production licence, and tangible assets, such as plant and machinery. Tax may not fully be deferred under these provisions where the like-kind exchange or involuntary conversion does not relate to the same category of asset.

4. Internal Revenue Code, 26 USC § 334 and §7701.
5. *Taxation of Chargeable Gains Act 1992* (1992) c 12, sections 152–162 (United Kingdom).
6. *Internal Revenue Code*, 26 USC § 1031 and § 1033 (United States).

THE USE OF CARRY-FORWARD TAX LOSSES

Introduction

Figure 26.6 Carry-Forward Tax Losses

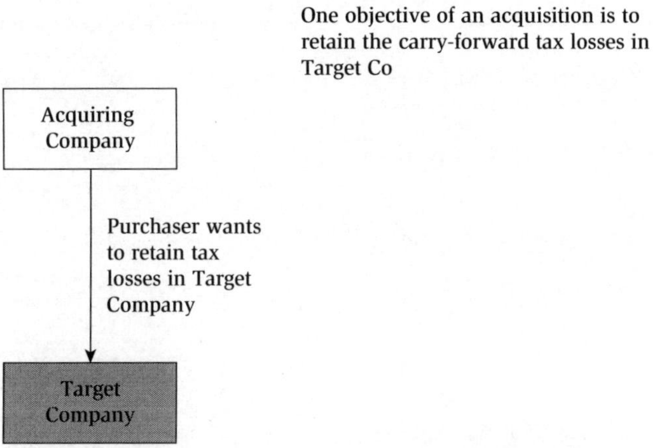

This issue relates to the acquisition of the Target Company to enable the use of that company's carry-forward tax losses. These losses can be a very valuable asset of the Target Company where the losses can be used in future years to reduce the Target Company's taxes on its future profits.

There is generally a need for the structure to acquire the Target Company, rather than its assets, in order to retain the Target Company's tax losses. Many countries tax laws may, however, potentially deny carry-forward tax losses where there is a change of ownership of the tax loss company or there is a change in the tax loss company's business. It is therefore always important to review the conditions for retention of tax losses in the Target Company country.

Carry-Forward Tax Losses: Downstream Merger

Figure 26.7 Downstream Merger

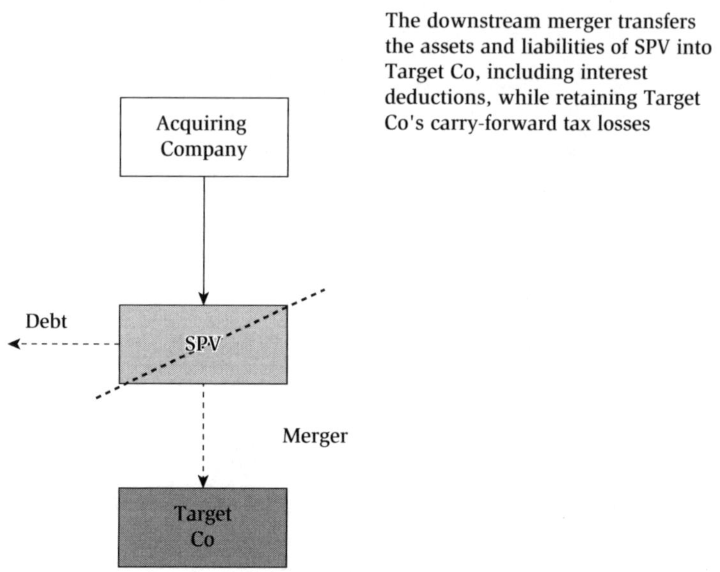

This structure is intended to retain the carried forward tax losses in the Target Co, and also to utilise interest deductions of the SPV on borrowings to fund the acquisition of the Target Co. In the downstream merger, the SPV borrows to acquire Target Co, and then SPV merges with the Target Co and is later liquidated, leaving the related debt and interest deductions in the Target Co.

The structure is particularly significant where a country does not have tax consolidation provisions, such as in Brazil. Structures which use tax consolidation to use tax deductions of the SPV to offset profits in the target are therefore not available. The downstream merger achieves a similar result by transferring the assets and liabilities of the SPV down to the Target Co. The surviving Target Co entity then has the related interest deductions, and the Target Co is also the company with the retained carry-forward tax losses.

It is necessary to ensure that the Target Co which had the carry-forward tax losses survives the merger. Countries may also have anti-avoidance provisions that potentially disallow carry-forward tax losses on a change of ownership or business activities.

The potential benefits of the downstream merger structure are to retain the carry-forward tax losses in the Target Co, and to allow interest deductions related to the acquisition are pushed down to be deductible for the Target Co.

TAX RELIEFS FOR MERGERS AND ACQUISITIONS

Example Structure: Share Exchange

Figure 26.8 Share Exchange

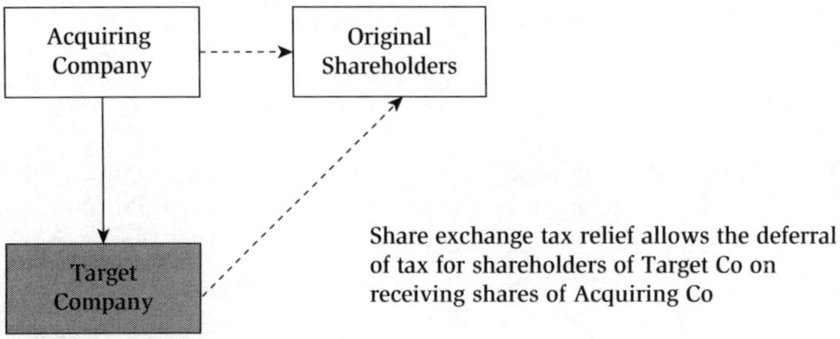

An acquisition may result in substantial taxation on the seller, for example shareholders may sell their shares in the Target Company to the Acquiring Company, and these shareholders may be taxed on the gain on the sale of their shares. There may, however, be various forms of merger relief in different countries which may defer the seller's tax on the sale transaction. The above structure is an example of this type of relief for the shareholders of the Target Company. In this example, the existing shareholders of the Target Company are not immediately taxed on a share exchange, where they receive shares in the Acquiring Company in exchange for their shares in the Target Company. Other tax relief structures may include issue of shares or business assets in exchange for the transfer of the target's business assets, or where there is a transfer of assets or shares from the target to a new company, and the issue of shares in that new company.

The relief is a tax deferral so that the original shareholders are taxed on any gain when they sell the new shares in the Acquiring Company at some future date. The tax basis of their new shares in the Acquiring Company, used to determine their gain on any future sale, is the same as the tax basis of their original shares in the Target Company.

The shareholders may potentially have other opportunities to benefit from tax relief. For example, European company shareholders may potentially benefit from the participation exemption for substantial shareholdings, which can exempt them from tax on the sale of the related shares.

European Union

The EU Merger Directive,[7] provides a system of taxation for mergers, divisions, transfer of assets, and the exchanges of shares. The Directive provides for the deferral of the taxes that could otherwise be charged on the difference between the real value of the

7. *Merger Directive* (90/434/EEC 1990) (European Union).

assets and liabilities and their value for tax purposes on transfers to other companies. The tax deferral is generally granted provided that the receiving company continues with the assets at their original tax values prior to the transfer. For example, merger relief may apply to the issuing of shares in the acquiring company to shareholders of a target company. Tax would be deferred so that the target company's original shareholders are taxed when they sell the shares in the acquiring company. The EU requires its Member States to pass legislation to implement the Directive.

United Kingdom

The UK provisions allow tax relief for reorganisations including mergers between third parties. For example, capital gains tax relief is generally available for the exchange of shares to defer tax on gains until the new shares are sold. The provisions require a holding more than 25 % shares in the acquired company.[8] The UK provisions also apply to cross-border mergers from 2007, where the relevant assets and liabilities are transferred automatically by operation of law, and where the transferor company is automatically dissolved upon the merger.

United States

The US tax provisions may allow relief for certain corporate acquisitions, divisions and other restructurings which qualify as tax-free reorganisations. The parties generally defer current tax on gains on the related share and asset transfers, and receive the tax basis of the shares or assets received on a carryover basis. The unrecognised gain is therefore deferred for later taxation on a future sale. The concessions for tax-free share reorganisations include:[9]

- *A Reorganisation* – This relates to statutory mergers and consolidations. The target shareholders receive shares in the acquirer. The tax-free treatment requires 40 % continuity of ownership of shares.
- *B Reorganisation* – This relates to stock-for-stock swaps. Both corporations concerned can issue shares to the other company's shareholders. The related tax-free treatment requires that at least 80 % of target is acquired, and the only consideration is the share issue.
- *C Reorganisation* – This relates to where the acquiring company's voting shares are exchanged for substantially all of the target company's assets.
- *Acquisitive D Reorganisation* – This applies to the transfer of substantially all of target company's assets to an acquiring corporation, and where the target company has at least 80 % control of the acquiring company after the transfer.
- *Triangular Reorganisations* – This applies to the above A, B, or C type reorganisations where these transactions involving the target selling company,

8. *Taxation of Chargeable Gains Act 1992* c. 12 section 135 (United Kingdom).
9. *Internal Revenue Code*, 26 USC (1986) § 368(a)(1) (United States).

the buyer company, and the buyer's subsidiary company. The buyer subsidiary makes the acquisition in these cases. This may be done to reduce the buyer's exposure to target liabilities.

For tax planning purposes, it is therefore important to review the availability of merger and reorganisation relief, as this may provide a tax exemption of deferral for the seller where other tax exemptions are not available. US mergers have also been deliberately made taxable, for example stock has been issued for only 60% of the total consideration so that the relief does not apply. This has been done so that the acquirer has the consideration actually paid as the cost basis in the target company, and not just the carryover basis if the relief applied. Target shareholders are taxed in this case, however the shareholders may be concessionally taxed with treatment of the transaction as a long-term capital gain.

Tax-free mergers may potentially also be available where the acquiring company is not resident of the US, providing that US shareholders receive no more than 50% of shares in the foreign acquirer, the foreign acquirer must be engaged in active trade or business outside the US for at least three years after the transfer, and the fair market value of foreign acquirer's equity must at least equal the target company's equity.[10]

10. *Internal Revenue Code*, 26 USC (1986) § 367 (United States).

CHAPTER 27

Asset Leasing

INTRODUCTION

Lease Classification

This chapter reviews the use of leasing in the energy industry. Leasing is primarily a source of financing assets at an effective rate. The company which uses the asset is the lessee, and the company which owns the asset is the lessor.[1] Leases where the lessor is in one country, and the lessee is in another country, are called cross-border leases. Leases are broadly categorised as follows:

- The lease may be treated as a finance lease where the lessee will eventually obtain ownership of the asset, and the lease is therefore essentially a form of financing the acquisition of the asset.
- The lease may be treated as an operating lease, or a true lease, where the lessee is merely renting the asset, and so the lessee is not likely to obtain ownership of the asset at a future date.

Finance lease transactions will generally result in additional debt on the balance sheet of the lessee because the transaction is essentially treated as a loan to acquire the asset. By comparison, operating leasing has generally provided an accounting advantage for lessee companies because the transaction did not result in additional debt on the lessee company's balance sheet.

The International Accounting Standards Board (IASB) published IFRS 16 Leases in January 2016 with an effective date of 1 January 2019. The new standard requires

1. For a general reference on leasing *see* Peter K Nevitt & Frank J Fabozzi, *Equipment Leasing*, 4th Edn. (Wiley, 2000).

lessees to recognise nearly all leases on the balance sheet to reflect their right to use an asset for a period of time together with the associated liability for payments.[2]

There may be a significant issue as to whether credit rating agencies, such as Standard & Poor's, Moody's Investor Service, and Fitch Ratings, decide to treat operating lease obligations as equivalent to debt.

Commercial Benefits of Leasing

The use of leasing may have significant commercial advantages compared to borrowing the required funds and purchasing an asset. The advantages can potentially include the following:[3]

- There can be gains from specialisation in the management of assets, for example there may be more efficient maintenance by the lessor.
- Leasing can address the issue of a company with large existing debt and which cannot easily borrow funds for a new project.
- The issue of the uncertainty of the resale value of the asset, known as the residual value, is transferred to the lessor. The lessor is generally more able to manage this risk by maintaining a portfolio of assets to diversify the risks.
- There may be incentives associated with leasing, for example where the lessor is also the manufacturer of the asset, and so provides better lease terms to increase their sales.

There may also be significant limitations with leasing. Conditions under existing loans, for example, may require access to all the borrower's assets in the event of default, and this may prevent the use of leasing where the lessor has access to specific assets in the event of a company's default.

Related Tax Issues

Operating leasing can have significant benefits for the lessee for tax purposes because the related payments are generally fully deductible as the lessee is treated as merely renting the asset. This compares to the tax position of finance leases, where generally only the interest component of the total lease payments will be allowed as deductible. The lessee under an operating lease is, however, not treated as the asset owner, and accordingly the lessee will not obtain depreciation deductions for the asset. Operating leases may therefore provide potential tax advantages compared to finance leases where the increased deduction of the full operating lease payment is greater than the interest component deduction and the depreciation deduction which would be allowed under a finance lease. The related tax benefit analysis usually depends on interest rates, the detailed terms of the lease, and the extent of depreciation allowances in a

2. PWC, IFRS 16: The leases standard is changing, Are you Ready? https://www.pwc.com.au/assurance/ifrs/assets/ifrs16lease-brochure.pdf on 20 October 2017.
3. Jonathan Berk & Peter DeMarzo, *Corporate Finance* 878 (Pearson, 2013).

particular country.[4] The operating lease can be expected to be more tax effective than purchase, for example, where the transaction shifts depreciation tax deductions which have a higher value to the lessor.[5]

The availability of tax treatment as an operating lease generally depends on establishing that there is no economic sale of the asset to the lessee. This issue includes reviewing the lease term compared to the economic life of the asset, and the absence of terms for the lessee to acquire the assets at less than market value. The related Netherlands tax rules, for example, generally allow operating lease treatment where the lease term does not exceed 85% of the estimated economic life of the asset, and where the lessee has a purchase option at the end of a fixed term lease of up to five years, the option price should not be below 7.5% of the asset value.[6]

VAT and Transfer Taxes

Leasing and hire purchase contracts are generally transactions which are subject to indirect taxes such as VAT. The detailed VAT provisions may vary between different countries, however in general terms, operating leases are generally treated as the supply of services with VAT payable on the respective payments. Where the lease is likely to result in transfer of ownership, such as a hire purchase, conditional sale or credit sale, then the lease may generally be treated as a supply of goods. In this case VAT may be imposed on the full selling price at the commencement of the lease. Where however the finance element of the rental payments is separately identified and disclosed to the lessee, then this part of the payments may be treated as a separate supply of finance, and such a supply may be exempt from VAT.

There are potential exemptions from VAT in the lessor state for cross-border leases. For example, the related exemptions for a lessor in a European Union (EU) state generally include:

- Exemption for the export of goods to a lessee in another EU state or to a country outside the EU.
- Exemption for the supply of services to a lessee in another EU state, where the lessee will be subject to VAT in their own EU state, or for the supply of services to a lessee outside the EU.

VAT is generally payable by the lessee under a cross-border lease. For example, VAT in relation to a lessee in a EU Member State generally relates to:

- The importation of goods from a country outside the EU.
- The importation of services from another EU state or from a country outside the EU, and where the lessee is generally responsible for VAT under the 'reverse charge' provisions.

---

4. Philip Marwood & David Maxwell, *Leasing*, KPMG Leasing Taxation (2002).
5. Jonathan Berk & Peter DeMarzo, *Corporate Finance* 877 (Pearson, 2013).
6. *Netherlands Corporate Income Tax Leasing Resolution BNB 2000/66* (Netherlands).

A VAT registered business will generally receive a VAT credit for the VAT paid on inputs, including goods and services under leasing contracts, and will have the right to a VAT refund where their VAT paid exceeds the VAT chargeable on their own sales. The EU Council Directive 2008/9/EC provides that businesses within the EU can request a refund of VAT incurred in other EU Member States.[7]

There may also be transactions taxes applying to leases, such as asset transfer taxes or stamp duty. For example, Stamp Duty Land Tax (SDLT) in the United Kingdom (UK) may apply where the leased assets are fixtures attached to land.[8]

Specific Leasing Structures

One use of a cross-border lease, is where there is a difference in the related tax treatment. There are countries which assign tax ownership, together with the related depreciation allowances, to the entity that has legal title to an asset, compared to countries such as the United States (US) which assign tax ownership and the related depreciation allowances to the entity that has the most factors indicating economic ownership. The cross-border leasing structure can potentially allow depreciation deductions in both countries.

Cross-border leases have also been used where the owner of an asset is not subject to tax and so cannot utilise depreciation allowances. The related sale and leaseback transaction typically involves the asset owner selling the asset to a lessor who can claim depreciation, and then leasing back the asset under a long-term operating lease. Cross-border leases have been used, for example, by US investors leasing assets which are used outside the US. Other countries which have acted as the lessors in similar transactions have included the UK, Germany, and Japan.

Some related arrangements include the lease in/lease out (LILO) structure, where a financial institution leases the asset from the owner, and then subleases the asset to the ultimate user. The initial lease may potentially not be treated as a sale and this treatment may therefore give rise to depreciation allowances for the financial institution in its own country. This structure was used by German state asset owners and US financial institutions.[9] The use of LILO transactions relating to the US was generally restricted under specific anti-avoidance provisions from 2004.[10] The similar sale in/lease out (SILO) structures are essentially sale and leaseback transactions, where the original asset owner sells the asset to the financial institution, which then leases the asset back to the asset seller. This structure was also based on the use of the related depreciation allowances by the financial institution.

One of the issues for cross-border leasing is whether the lease payments are subject to withholding tax. The country's domestic tax rules may define the payments to be royalties which are subject to withholding tax, or they may impose withholding

7. EU, Council Directive 2008/9/EC of 12 February 2008.
8. *Finance Act 2003*, c. 14, Part IV, Stamp duty land tax.
9. Petri Mäntysaari, *The Law of Corporate Finance: General Principles and EU Law*, (Springer, 2010) vol. III, 38.
10. *American Jobs Creation Act* 2004 (Pub.L. 108–357) (United States).

tax on the interest component of payments under a finance lease. The related withholding tax may include a combination of federal, state, and municipal taxes. A tax treaty may apply between the lessee and lessor countries to reduce or eliminate withholding tax, however this generally will not extend to the reduction of state and municipal taxes. It may be essential that the lessor is not located in a tax haven when the lessee country, for example under the tax rules in Mexico withholding tax is imposed at very high rates when payments are made to tax havens.

There are several other specialised structures relating to leasing, including the synthetic lease. In these structures a special purpose vehicle (SPV) or trust may be the legal owner of the related assets. In general certain investors may hold for example at least 3% of the equity or share capital of the SPV, and the structure would use loan funding for the remaining 97% of the required asset value. The structure potentially results in off-balance sheet accounting treatment of the SPV and the related assets.[11] In relation to tax, however, the structure may be treated as an in-substance loan, so that for tax purposes the asset may be treated as owned by the asset using company. The asset using company may potentially obtain depreciation allowances and deduction for interest component of the in-substance loan as the asset owner for tax purposes.[12]

PERMANENT ESTABLISHMENT ISSUES FOR OPERATING LEASING

The tax issues for leasing include whether high value assets may be treated as a permanent establishment of the lessor, so that the lessor is fully taxed on their leasing income in the local country. For example, in relation to leasing from Singapore to Norway, the Norway/Singapore tax treaty defines a permanent establishment in Article 5(2) as including:[13]

> The term 'permanent establishment' includes especially:
>
> (a) a place of management
> (b) a branch
> (c) an office
> (d) a factory
> (e) a workshop, and
> (f) a mine, an oil or gas well, a quarry or any other place of extraction of natural resources.

The US/Mexico tax treaty goes further to define specific assets to be a permanent establishment in Article 5(3):[14]

11. FASB Statement 13, para. L10.103, and International Accounting Standard IAS 17.
12. Chris Boobyer (ed.), *Leasing and Asset Finance: The Comprehensive Guide for Practitioners* 94 (Euromoney Institutional Investor PLC; 2003).
13. *Agreement between the Republic of Singapore and the Kingdom of Norway for the Avoidance of Double Taxation and the Prevention of Fiscal Evasion with respect to Taxes on Income,* 19 December 1997 (entered into force 17 April 1998).
14. *Convention between the Government of the United States of America and the Government of the United Mexican States for the Avoidance of Double Taxation and the Prevention of Fiscal Evasion with respect to Taxes on Income,* 18 September 1992 (entered into force 28 December 1993).

> The term 'permanent establishment' shall also include a building site or construction or installation project, or an installation or drilling rig or ship used for the exploration or exploitation of natural resources, or supervisory activity in connection therewith, but only if such building site, construction or activity lasts more than six months.

The lessor would then incur full local country taxation on the related income, rather than protection from tax relating to business profits in the absence of a permanent establishment, or from potential withholding tax on lease payments under tax treaties. This issue can partly be addressed by the split contract structure, using one company to provide just the leased equipment under a bare lease, and another company to provide any related services which may be required. The provision of equipment alone would not constitute a permanent establishment under many tax treaties. The income from the bare equipment leasing may be protected from local country taxes as business profits which are not derived from a permanent establishment.

The provision of services by a separate company, involving employees in the local country, may constitute a permanent establishment. That risk may in turn also potentially be reduced by seconding the staff required to work in the local country to a separate employment company in the local country. The local employment company is fully taxed in the local country on the fees paid for the work performed by the employees. The majority of the income, relating to the bare asset leasing, and the income from the work done outside the country, may then potentially be protected from local country tax.

SALE AND LEASEBACK ARRANGEMENTS

Figure 27.1 Sale and Leaseback Arrangements

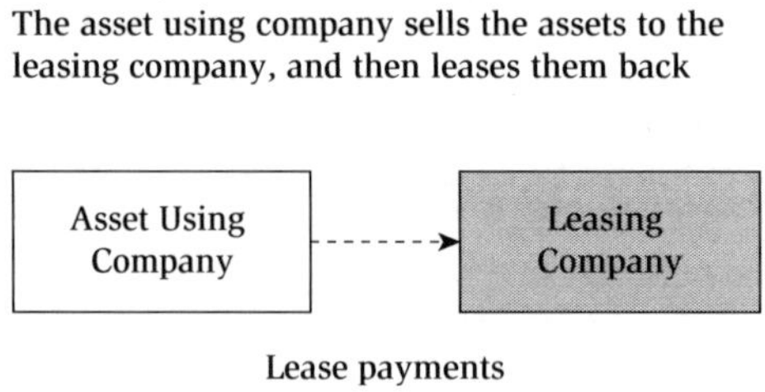

In this example of the sale and leaseback structure, the Asset Using Company sells the related assets to the Leasing Company, and obtains funding from the sale proceeds. The Asset Using Company then leases back the same assets from the Leasing Company over a ten-year period.

The asset using company would obtain operating lease deductions for the full amount of the lease payments, compared to funding itself under a loan where only the interest component of repayments would be deductible. The Leasing Company is taxed on the operating lease income, however the company may be located in a low-taxing country, utilise its own carry-forward tax losses to reduce tax, or may be based in a country with high depreciation allowances which reduce tax. The Asset Using Company may be taxed on the original sale to the leasing company under capital gains tax or depreciation recapture provisions. The asset using company may however utilise its own carry-forward tax losses or use asset rollover relief to reduce the potential tax on the sale.

The sale and leaseback structure requires assets which are suitable for leasing, such as moveable plant and equipment. The Asset Using Company would not obtain depreciation allowances after the sale, and so the structure is generally more effective where depreciation rates in the Asset Using Company's own country are low compared to the depreciation rates in the Leasing Company's country. There is generally a need to be a related tax treaty to reduce or eliminate withholding tax if this is imposed on the lease payments.

The structure potentially allows an operating lease deduction to the Asset Using company. The lease payments may also be potentially lower than payments under other forms of financing such as interest on a loan, for example where the Leasing Company shares the benefit of its depreciation allowance deductions or the use of its carry-forward tax losses.

Sale and Leaseback Transactions Within a Group

There is a potential tax planning structure where existing high value assets in a multinational group can be sold to a related company in a lower taxing country, for example in Singapore, with the subsequent lease back of the assets from that company. There are several issues including the potential application of anti-tax avoidance provisions, and there generally needs to be sufficient commercial substance in the leasing company. This issue generally requires that the leasing company would conduct a full leasing business, for example by having sufficient local directors, staff and capital for these activities, and for the company to select assets, arrange delivery, maintenance, and insurance of the related assets.

One of the tax issues for transferring existing group assets to the company concerns the potential capital gains taxes or depreciation balancing charges. This issue may require the related asset transfers to be made at the tax written down values of the assets to ensure that no additional taxation arises, however transfer pricing rules may allow the selling country to substitute the market value for such assets, and potentially impose tax on the related notional gain on their sale.

INVESTORS AND CROSS-BORDER LEASING STRUCTURES

Figure 27.2 Investors and Cross-Border Leasing Structures

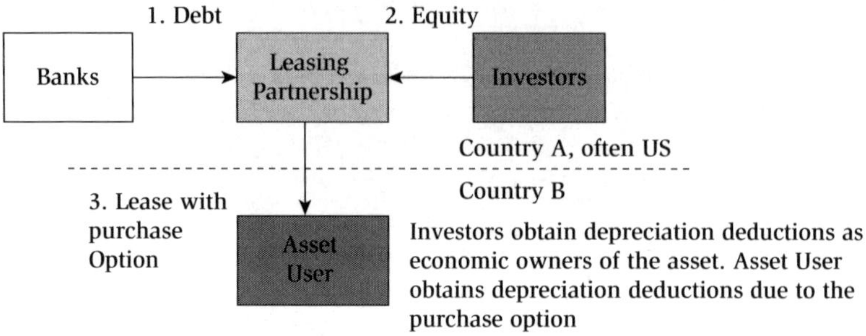

There are opportunities for investors in cross-border leasing structures. One example of these arrangements is based on a Leasing Partnership asset owner located in one country, and the Asset User Company located in another country. In this structure, the Leasing Partnership leases the asset to the Asset User Company. The Leasing Partnership may be funded, for example, with 10% equity from Investors, and 90% debt from lenders such as banks. The bank lenders would derive interest income from the structure, whereas the equity investors would potentially derive profits and would claim related expenses such as depreciation allowances and interest costs. The equity investor may have other taxable income, and then utilise the depreciation and interest deductions arising from the leasing structure to reduce their tax on other income.

These investment structures may also seek to provide a 'depreciation double dip' result. The asset may be treated as owned by the Leasing Partnership, for example based on legal ownership of the asset, and the asset may also treated as owned by the Asset User Company, for example based on the economic characteristics of the lease such as a purchase option. The result is that depreciation allowances may potentially be claimed by both the Leasing Partnership and the Asset User Company in their respective countries.

CHAPTER 28

Tax Havens and Controlled Foreign Corporations Rules

INTRODUCTION

Controlled foreign corporation (CFC) provisions are principally concerned with addressing tax avoidance structures which use tax havens. The provisions generally address the tax haven issue by taxing the local parent company on the income earned by that company's foreign subsidiaries located in tax havens or other low tax rate regimes. The CFC provisions generally apply tax on the 'passive income' of a tax haven company which is not related to an active business, such as interest, dividends and royalty income, as that income is earned in the tax haven company, rather than only taxing the income when the tax haven subsidiary pays a taxable dividend to the parent company. Accordingly CFC provisions are also known as accruals taxation regimes.

The CFC provisions may not apply to active business income, such as income from production, manufacturing, or trading activities which are actually performed in the tax haven country. The provisions may also test what proportion of the tax haven subsidiary's total income is passive income to determine whether CFC taxation should apply.

Some CFC rules use a specific list of tax havens,[1] or the rules may determine that the provisions should apply where the foreign company has a comparatively low effective tax rate. An effective tax rate generally means the tax rate calculated as if the income was derived in the parent country under the parent company tax rules, and this amount is then compared to the actual tax paid by the foreign subsidiary.

The provisions may use two related tests: (1) a shareholder test to determine whether a foreign company is a CFC because their residents have a sufficient

1. Jason Sharman & Gregory Rawlings, 'Deconstructing National Tax Blacklists – Removing Obstacles to Cross-Border Trade in Financial Services' (Paper presented at the Beyond the Level Playing Field? Symposium, London, 19 September 2005).

ownership or control of the foreign company; and then (2) test whether particular taxpayers in their country are subject to CFC taxation because they have a sufficient ownership or control in the CFC. For example, the United Kingdom (UK) provisions generally require 50% control by one or more UK residents for a foreign company to be a CFC, and then apply the CFC provisions to UK residents which hold at least 25% shareholding in that CFC.

These provisions have been adopted by many countries. Countries with similar regimes include:

- Argentina – 1999 – Law 25,239;
- Australia – 1991 – Part X ITAA 1936;
- Brazil – 1996 – A.25 Law 9.249/95 A.21 Provisional Measure 2.158-34;
- Canada – 1976 – S.91-95 Income Tax Act;
- China – 2008 – Corporate Income Tax Law, Circular 82/2009;
- Denmark – 1995 – A.8 Income Tax Law;
- France – 1980 – A.209B French Tax Code;
- Germany 1972 – S.7-14 Foreign Tax Law;
- Italy – 2002 – S.167 Income Tax Code;
- Japan – 1978 – Special Taxation Measures S.40 S.66;
- Mexico – 1997 – Chapter 4 Law for the Coordination of International Tax Affairs;
- Spain – 1994 – Law 42/1994 and 43/1995;
- Sweden – 1990 – Chapter 6 Income Tax Act;
- UK – 1984 – Part 9A Taxation (International and Other Provisions Act) 2010;
- USA – 1962 – Subpart F Internal Revenue Code.

A more recent development is the Diverted Profits Tax (DPT) regimes in the UK and Australia, which can apply taxation where profits are considered to have been artificially diverted to other countries. These regimes are generally based on whether profits are claimed to arise in a lower taxing country which does not have the related commercial substance to support those profits.

EXAMPLES OF COUNTRY CFC AND DPT PROVISIONS

United States Provisions: Subpart F

The United States (US) provisions generally apply to tax the 'Subpart F income' of foreign subsidiaries which are controlled by US taxpayers.[2] A CFC is defined as any foreign corporation where more than 50% of voting shares in that company are owned by US shareholders.[3] The provisions then tax US shareholders which own 10% or more of the foreign company. The provisions apply to several types of income, including Foreign Personal Holding Company Income (FPHCI) such as dividends, interest, rents,

2. *Internal Revenue Code*, 26 USC (1986) Part III, Subpart F, §§ 951–965 (United States).
3. U.S. Master Tax Guide (2014) CCH.

royalties, and gains from alienation of property that produces such income. The provisions may also apply to 'foreign base income' which is essentially sales, service, and shipping income from transactions with related parties, income relating to oil activities, and income from insuring risks outside the CFC's country of incorporation. The provisions generally do not apply if the income was subject to foreign income tax in excess of 90% of the related US tax rate. A foreign tax credit is allowed to reduce US taxation by allowing a credit for the related share of the foreign income taxes paid by the CFC.

UK CFC and DPT Provisions

The UK CFC provisions were substantially updated in 2013,[4] and currently apply to a non-resident company which is controlled by UK residents, and which is subject to a lower rate of tax than the UK.[5] The taxation provisions can then apply to UK shareholders with at least 25% interests in the CFC. Under these rules, CFC taxation applies to 'gateway income', which is considered to have been artificially diverted from the UK, including profits attributable to significant UK personnel functions, trading, and non-trading finance profits, and 'captive insurance' income derived from insuring related companies. The provisions do not apply to countries on an excluded territory list, which applies where the headline tax rate is not less than 75% of the UK tax rate, not more than 10% of the CFC income is concessionally taxed, and the income does not relate to intellectual property transferred from the UK. The taxation of CFC income is then generally based on UK tax rules.

The UK DPT provisions apply from 1 April 2015 to impose a charge of 25% of diverted profits where: (1) a person, whether UK resident or not, carries on activity in the UK in connection with the supply of services, goods, or any property by a foreign trading company, and it is reasonable to assume that the activities are designed to ensure that no permanent establishment (PE) is established in the UK, or where (2) a UK resident company (or a UK PE of a foreign company) is party to arrangements with an affiliated company that produce an 'effective tax mismatch' and the 'insufficient economic substance' condition is met.[6] The economic substance test in practice can include: (1) comparing the non-tax benefits of transactions and activities of the company's staff with the financial benefit of the tax reduction, and (2) on comparing income generated by activities of the parent company's staff with other income from the transactions.[7]

4. *Taxation (International and Other Provisions) Act 2010*, c. 8, Part 9A, and *Finance Act 2012* (United Kingdom).
5. KPMG, Controlled Foreign Companies – A Summary of the New Rules September 2012.
6. Pt.3 Finance Act 2015 and HMRC Diverted Profits Guidance, https://www.gov.uk/government /publications/diverted-profits-tax-guidance> on 12 May 2017.
7. Lydia Challen, Mark Middleditch & Ka Sen Wong, *Diverted Profits Tax – the UK Experience* (Allen & Overy, 2016).

Australian CFC and DPT Provisions

The Australian CFC provisions tax Australian shareholders on their share of a CFC's tainted income as it is earned, unless that income is comparably taxed offshore or the CFC derives its income almost exclusively from active business activities. A company is a CFC where: (1) five or fewer Australian residents have at least a 50% control interest, (2) a single Australian entity has at least a 40% control interest, and (3) five or fewer Australian entities have actual control of the company. CFC taxation does not apply where the CFC passes the 'active income test', where it has less than 5% of gross turnover as stated in its recognised accounts in the form of tainted income. Tainted income is generally income from investments or arrangements that are likely to be significantly affected by taxation considerations, including interest, dividends, royalties, or amounts arising from related party transactions. The rules attribute income to Australian resident controllers of the CFC: (1) tainted income derived by CFCs resident in unlisted countries; and (2) eligible designated concession income derived by CFCs resident in one of seven listed countries, Canada, France, Germany, Japan, New Zealand, UK, and US, such as where capital gains are not taxed.[8]

The Australian DPT provisions apply from 1 July 2017 to significant global entities which applies where a multinational group has global income of AUD 1 billion or more. The DPT provisions aim to ensure that the tax paid by significant global entities properly reflects the economic substance of their activities in Australia, and to prevent the diversion of profits offshore through contrived arrangements by imposing tax at 40%. The DPT can apply where a taxpayer has obtained a tax benefit in connection with the scheme in an income year, and the principal purpose, or one of the principal purposes of the scheme, is to obtain an Australian tax benefit or to obtain both an Australian and foreign tax benefit. The provisions do not apply where the Australian income does not exceed AUD 25 million, (2) the increase in foreign tax as a result of the diversion of income offshore is 80% or more of the reduced Australian tax liability, or (3) the foreign entity has sufficient economic substance.[9]

EU Issues: The Cadbury Schweppes Case

There is a EU issue whether the CFC provisions of EU Member States can apply in respect of companies established in the European Economic Area (EEA). In this respect, the European Court of Justice (ECJ) reviewed the previous UK CFC provisions in the *Cadbury Schweppes* case.[10] Cadbury Schweppes had established two indirect subsidiaries under the former International Financial Services Centre (IFSC) tax incentive provisions in Ireland. These subsidiaries provided group treasury services which were taxed in Ireland at 10%. The UK tax authorities applied the CFC provisions to tax the UK parent company on the income of the two subsidiaries. The ECJ noted

8. Income Tax Assessment Act 1936 Part X.
9. Income Tax Assessment Act 1936, section 177J.
10. *Cadbury Schweppes Plc and Cadbury Schweppes Overseas Ltd v. Commissioners of Inland Revenue*, Case C-196/04[2006] ECR I-7995.

that the Treaty on EU ('Maastricht Treaty') prohibited Member States from hindering establishment of a national in another Member State,[11] and that taxation of the parent company would not occur in relation to the income of UK subsidiaries. On this basis the CFC legislation restricted establishment or acquisition of a subsidiary in a lower taxing Member State. The ECJ held that UK CFC provisions therefore breached EU freedom of establishment rules, by imposing additional tax because the subsidiaries were located in Ireland, except where the provisions were concerned with wholly artificial arrangements.[12]

The UK tax authorities initially responded to the case stating that it would exclude that part of chargeable profits that represents the net economic value to the group arising from the work carried out by the company's staff in the business establishment in the other EU Member State.[13]

In the *Vodafone 2* case,[14] however, the UK Court of Appeal held that CFC provisions should be interpreted to conform with the ECJ decision, and accordingly that the CFC provisions should not apply to companies established in a Member State of the EEA, and carry out genuine economic activities in that state.[15] The UK therefore issued the revised CFC rules described above. France and Germany also revised their CFC provisions following the *Cadbury Schweppes* decision.[16] France amended its rules in 2005 providing an exemption where the ownership of the foreign company in a EU Member State did not constitute a wholly artificial arrangement designed to escape tax that would otherwise be payable. Germany amended its rules in 2008 to provide an exemption for companies in the EEA for income derived from genuine economic activity carried out in its country of residence.

The EU has also issued a Council Resolution on coordination of CFC and thin capitalisation rules within the EU.[17] The Resolution provides a broad and non-exclusive list of cases where Member States may potentially apply CFC provisions, including:

- where there are insufficient valid economic or commercial reasons for the profit attribution, which therefore does not reflect the economic reality;
- where there is an incorporation that does not essentially correspond with an actual establishment intended to carry on genuine economic activities;
- where there is an inadequate correlation between the company's activities and its premises, staff, and equipment; or

11. *Treaty on EU* [1992] OJ C191/1, opened for signature 7 February 1992 (entered into force 1 November 1993) ('*Maastricht Treaty*'). The treaty was substantially updated by the *Treaty of Lisbon amending the Treaty on EU and the Treaty establishing the European Community* [2007] OJ C306/01.
12. Mathieu Isenbaert, *EC Law and the Sovereignty of the Member States in Direct Taxation* 544 (2010).
13. This was set out in the prior version of the HMRC International Tax Manual INTM 210530 (superseded).
14. *Vodafone 2 v. Her Majesty's Revenue and Customs* [2009] EWCA Civ 446.
15. 'Vodafone 2 -v- HMRC: CFC rules' Ashurst Tax Newsletter, June 2009.
16. Sara Luder, *CFCs Around Europe*, Tax J., 9 May 2012.
17. *Council Resolution of 8 June 2010 on Coordination of the Controlled Foreign Corporation (CFC) and Thin Capitalisation Rules within the EU* (2010/C 156/01).

- where the taxpayer has entered into arrangements that are devoid of economic reality.

TAX HAVENS AND THE PARTICIPATION EXEMPTION

There are also anti-tax haven measures in the conditions relating to the participation exemption. Many European countries have a participation exemption which can treat dividends from other countries as tax-free or concessionally taxed in certain circumstances, including the Netherlands, Germany, Belgium, and the UK. This generally applies where the dividends are from a company in which the shareholder has a significant shareholding, known as a participation. These countries generally deny the benefit of the participation exemption where the dividend relates to passive activities performed by the subsidiary in a low-taxing country. Accordingly, while CFC taxation taxes the parent company as the income is earned by the CFC, the participation exemption restrictions generally apply tax at a later stage, when dividends are received from the low-taxed subsidiary by the parent company.

The Netherlands has participation exemption rules, for example, which can treat dividend income from foreign subsidiaries, and capital gains on the sale of the participation shares, as tax-free income.[18] The exemption, updated in 2007, generally applies if the Netherlands company has a participation of at least 5% in the foreign company, and this holding was not a 'low-taxed portfolio participation'. This exclusion applies where the effective tax rate in the foreign country is less than 10% under Netherlands tax rules, and more than 50% of the foreign company's assets are portfolio investments which are not used in the course of business.

18. *Corporate Income Tax Act 1969*, Act of 8 October 1969, Article 13 (Netherlands).

ISSUES FOR THE GROUP HOLDING COMPANY

Figure 28.1 Group Holding Company

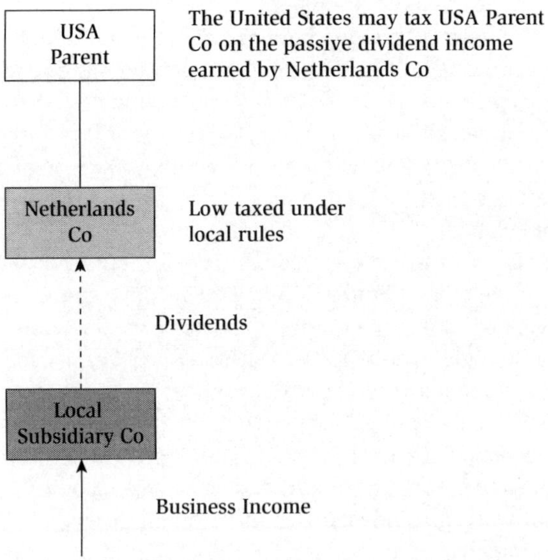

This issue concerns the ownership of local production companies through intermediate holding companies, for example in the Netherlands. In this example, the US may seek to impose CFC taxation under Subpart F on the USA Parent in relation to the dividend income that the Netherlands Co receives from the Local Subsidiary.

The Netherlands may be treated as a low effective tax rate country for US purposes due to the participation exemption, which may exempt the dividends from the Local Subsidiary from Netherlands tax. The US may grant a foreign tax credit for the tax paid by the Local Subsidiary.

There is a need to review potential CFC issues for the use of intermediate holding companies, as there may be CFC taxation if the intermediate holding company, in this case the Netherlands Co, provides any related tax concessions. The benefits of the Netherlands tax concessions may be lost at the level of US CFC taxation on the USA Parent.

THE DOUBLE IRISH DUTCH SANDWICH

One structure which has reportedly been used by several US multinationals to potentially reduce their tax liabilities is known as the 'Double Irish Dutch Sandwich structure.' In general terms, income from royalties, the sale of products, or the sale of advertising, is derived by a first Irish company within a multinational group. This Irish company then pays a deductible royalty to a Netherlands company, with Irish tax at 12.5% tax applying to the margin. The Netherlands company then pays royalties to a second Irish Company and may be taxed in the Netherlands only on the margin. The majority of the income is derived by the second Irish company, which may potentially be exempt under Irish tax rules where it is treated as controlled by management located in another country. The management was generally claimed to be provided from a tax haven jurisdiction, for example in Bermuda.

It remains to be determined whether the Double Irish Dutch Sandwich arrangement would be effective against the respective transfer pricing and anti-tax avoidance provisions of the countries concerned, however it is understood that several of the taxpayers may have obtained related tax rulings from the US tax authorities. One issue is whether any transfer of intangible property from the US to the offshore companies was made at their fair market values and was subject to exit tax. There is also an issue whether the related valuation of that intellectual property was made based on current costs and circumstances at the time of the valuation, or if the valuation was based on the present value of the related future income streams. In general, a US taxpayer may be deemed to have sold intangible property at rates commensurate with the income attributable to that intangible property, regardless of the actual consideration received, and such deemed income may then be taxed in the US as ordinary income.

US CFC taxation under Subpart F may potentially apply to the related royalties derived in a foreign subsidiary in a low-taxing country. However, the transaction may potentially have been structured as a cost sharing arrangement by several companies in the multinational group to jointly develop the intangible property. The non-US rights in the intangible property developed under the cost sharing arrangement may be treated as created in the jurisdiction where the intellectual property is intended to be utilised by the foreign subsidiary, and therefore may potentially not be subject to US CFC taxation.

In general terms it may be argued that the US requires an effective general anti-abuse rule (GAAR) to address such planning structures. A GAAR rule was introduced in the UK in 2013.[19] The UK GAAR applies to 'tax arrangements' which are 'abusive'. In broad terms a tax arrangement is any arrangement which, viewed objectively, has the obtaining of a tax advantage as its main purpose or one of its main purposes. A transaction is then regarded as abusive when the course of action taken by the taxpayer aims to achieve a favourable tax result that Parliament did not anticipate when it introduced the tax rules in question and where that course of action cannot reasonably be regarded as reasonable.[20] The existence of an effective US GAAR provision would potentially have raised issues including whether the respective companies had sufficient commercial reasons to achieve the desired tax result.

19. *Finance Bill 2013*, section 208(2) (United Kingdom).
20. HMRC's GAAR Guidance (Approved by the Advisory Panel with effect from 15 April 2013) at www.hmrc.gov.uk/avoidance/gaar-part-abc.pdf on 25 July 2013.

CFC PROVISIONS AND THE GROUP FINANCE COMPANY

Figure 28.2 Group Finance Company

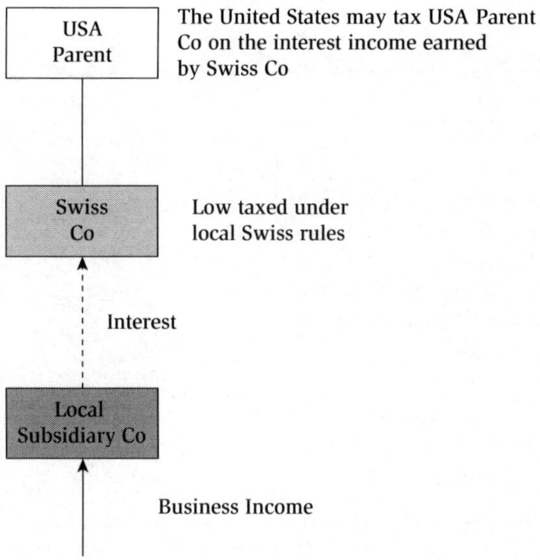

This issue relates to the funding of a multinational energy group through an intermediate group financing company, for example a group treasury or financing company located in Switzerland. The US may seek to impose CFC taxation under Subpart F,[21] on the USA Parent in respect of the interest income derived by the Swiss Co.

Switzerland is likely to apply a low effective tax rate in this structure. In this case there may be a Swiss Cantonal tax ruling substantially reducing the combined Swiss Federal and Cantonal tax.

The principal issue with the structure is that the parent country's CFC rules, in this case in the US, may apply to tax the USA Parent on the interest income derived by the Swiss Co. There may be less scope for tax planning arrangements to reduce CFC taxation on interest income in such group treasury structures, compared to the potential use of tax planning based on structures such as cost contribution arrangements potentially used in intangible property structures.

US CHECK-THE-BOX PROVISIONS

The US tax provisions include entity classification or check-the-box measures. These rules allow certain entities to elect to be taxed on a tax transparent, look through, or disregarded basis, or alternatively on a corporate basis, by making an election, known as checking the box, on the relevant form. The election is not available for trusts. The

21. *Internal Revenue Code*, 26 USC (1986) Part III, Subpart F, § 951–965 (United States).

elections can also potentially affect whether the results of foreign subsidiaries are brought into US taxation.

Foreign entities, where the liability of all members is limited, are by default treated as corporations for tax purposes. These entities can, however, elect to be treated as partnerships for transparent tax treatment so that it is the partners that are taxed. Foreign entities, with two or more members, where at least one member's liability is not limited, are by default treated as transparent for tax purposes. These entities can, however, elect to be treated as corporates for tax purposes so that it is the entity which is taxed.

US domestic entities cannot elect their own tax status if they are organised under a US statute that describes or refer to the entity as incorporated or as a corporation, a body corporate, a joint stock company or a joint stock association. US LLCs and partnerships can, however, elect their tax classification under these measures.

The election is not available to 'per se' listed corporations, Regulation 301.7701. The companies in this category which may not make the check-the-box election include, for example:

- Australia – Public Limited Company;
- Canada – Corporation and Company;
- France – Société Anonyme;
- Germany – Aktiengesellschaft;
- Netherlands – Naamloze Vennootschap; and
- Italy – Societe per Azioni.

THE OECD BEPS ACTION PLAN: CFC PROVISIONS

The OECD BEPS Action Plan has also focussed on CFC provisions and related anti-tax avoidance measures in Action 3 – Controlled Foreign Company regimes. The OECD released the related discussion draft in May 2015.[22] The related issues and recommendations are as follows:

Definition of a CFC

The OECD recommendation is to broadly define entities that are within the scope of the CFC rules, so that in addition to including corporate entities, the CFC rules would also apply to partnerships, trusts, and permanent establishments when those entities are either owned by CFCs or treated in the parent jurisdiction as taxable entities separate from their owners. A modified hybrid entity mismatch rule would prevent entities from circumventing the CFC rules by being treated differently in different jurisdictions.

22. OECD, Designing Effective Controlled Foreign Company Rules, BEPS Action 3, 2015 Final Report (OECD, 2015).

Threshold Requirements

The recommendation is to include a low-tax threshold where the tax rate calculation is based on the effective tax rate. The low-tax threshold should also use a tax rate that is meaningfully lower than the tax rate in the country applying the CFC rules.

Definition of Control

The definition of control requires two different determinations: (i) of the type of control that is required, and (ii) of the level of that control. The recommendation for control is that CFC rules should at least apply both a legal and an economic control test so that satisfaction of either test results in control. Countries may also include de facto tests where they achieve the same effect. A CFC should be treated as controlled where residents hold, at a minimum, more than 50% control, although countries that want to achieve broader policy goals or prevent circumvention of CFC rules may set their control threshold at a lower level. This level of control could be established through the aggregated interest of related parties or unrelated resident parties or from aggregating the interests of any taxpayers that are found to be acting in concert. CFC rules should also apply where there is direct or indirect control.

Definition of CFC Income

The OECD did not set out general recommendations for how to define CFC income, but it instead discusses several possible approaches that jurisdictions could adopt. Whichever approach is adopted, the CFC rules should accurately attribute income that raises base erosion and profit shifting concerns. The CFC rules should accurately define attributable income earned by CFCs that are holding companies, income earned by CFCs that provide financial and banking services, income earned by CFCs that engage in sales invoicing, income from IP assets, income from digital goods and services, and income from captive insurance and reinsurance. In practical terms, this means that CFC rules must be capable of dealing with at least the following types of income:

- Dividends;
- Interest and other financing income;
- Insurance income;
- Sales and services income; and
- Royalties and other IP income.

The OECD discussed two different approaches that jurisdictions could use to accurately attribute income earned by a CFC:

- The categorical approach is used under some existing CFC rules which have separate rules for different types of income, and this approach builds on these rules and has one rule for dividends, another rule for interest, and separate rules for other types of income. If jurisdictions adopt this approach, they could

have rules similar to those discussed above. The categorical approach allows jurisdictions to tailor their rules so that each type of income is treated accurately.
- The excess profits approach. This could involve a simpler and more mechanical approach than the categorical approach referred to above, and could also be used to deal with embedded IP. If such an approach were targeted at specific income, such as IP then jurisdictions could choose to implement an excess profits approach alongside other, more traditional CFC rules.

Rules for Computing Income

Computing the income of a CFC requires two different determinations: (i) which jurisdiction's rules should apply, and (ii) whether any specific rules for computing CFC income are necessary. The OECD recommended the use of the rules of the parent jurisdiction to calculate a CFC's income, and that jurisdictions should have a specific rule limiting the offset of CFC losses so that they can only be used against the profits of the same CFC or against the profits of other CFCs in the same jurisdiction.

Rules for Attributing Income

Income attribution can be broken into determining which taxpayers should have income attributed to them, determining how much income should be attributed, determining when the income should be included in the returns of the taxpayers, determining how the income should be treated, and determining what tax rate should apply to the income:

- The attribution threshold should be tied to the minimum control threshold when possible, although countries can choose to use different attribution and control thresholds depending on the policy considerations underlying CFC rules.
- The amount of income to be attributed to each shareholder or controlling person should be calculated by reference to both their proportion of ownership and their actual period of ownership or influence.
- Jurisdictions can determine when income should be included in taxpayers' returns and how it should be treated so that CFC rules operate in a way that is coherent with existing domestic law.
- Jurisdictions then apply the tax rate of the parent jurisdiction to the income.

Rules to Prevent or Eliminate Double Taxation

The OECD considered that jurisdictions are primarily concerned with double taxation where: (1) the attributed CFC income is also subject to foreign corporate taxes; (2) CFC rules in more than one jurisdiction apply to the same CFC income; and (3) where a CFC distributes dividends out of income that has already been attributed to resident shareholders under CFC rules, or a resident shareholder disposes of shares in the CFC.

The OECD recommended allowing a credit for foreign taxes actually paid, including CFC tax assessed on intermediate companies, and to exempt dividends and gains on disposition of CFC shares from taxation if the income of the CFC has previously been subject to CFC taxation, with the tax treatment of such dividends and gains left to individual jurisdictions.

EU ANTI-TAX AVOIDANCE DIRECTIVE

The Council of the EU adopted the Directive (EU) 2016/1164 (ATAD1) providing rules against tax avoidance practices that directly affect the functioning of the internal market on 20 June 2016.[23] The Directive required Member States to adopt minimum levels of protection against specific tax avoidance measures. In relation to CFC provisions, Articles 7 and 8 on the controlled foreign company rule is based on the following criteria:[24]

- the parent's interest in the entity is broadly more than 50% of the entity's voting power, capital or entitlement to profits;
- the entity is subject to a low tax rate, determined as 50% of the rate applicable in the parent state;[25]
- the entity is involved in non-genuine arrangements, and the parent state does not exclude it as being *de minimis*;[26] and
- the entity is not excluded as having specified passive income that is no more than one-third of its total income, or for a financial undertaking, no more than one-third of its specified passive income is from transactions with the parent or its 25% associated enterprises.

The amount attributed to the parent company is the non-distributed income:

- derived from a CFC's specified passive activities which, if the CFC is in the EU or EEA, doesn't carry on substantive economic activity there;[27] or
- arising from non-genuine arrangements involving the CFC which have been put in place for the essential purpose of obtaining a tax advantage.

23. Council Directive (EU) 2016/1164 of 12 July 2016 laying down rules against tax avoidance practices that directly affect the functioning of the internal market.
24. PWC, Tax Policy Bulletin, ECOFIN agrees EU-wide riles in Anti-Avoidance Directive, 29 June 2016. https://www.pwc.com/gx/en/tax/newsletters/tax-policy-bulletin/assets/pwc-ecofin-agrees-eu-wide-rules-in-anti-tax-avoidance-directive.pdf on 18 October 2017.
25. This is expressed as the actual rate being lower than the difference between the rate that would have been charged on it in the parent State and its actual rate.
26. This is based on accounting profits no more than EUR 750,000 and non-trading income no more than EUR 75,000, or accounting profits no more than 10% of its operating costs.
27. States can choose to apply a similar requirement for third countries.

CFC PLANNING

There are several potential CFC tax planning structures. These may include the following arrangements, however any planning arrangements will be subject to the specific CFC and anti-tax avoidance rules of the country concerned and consideration of OECD BEPS and EU measures which may potentially apply:

- The subsidiary company conducts an active business such as intellectual property contract management, and enters into agreements such as cost contribution arrangements with other group companies, rather than simply owning intellectual property and deriving the related royalty income. The subsidiary company may also derive income such as technical service fees for providing intellectual property support services.
- Income such as interest may be earned in an operating company in a low-taxing country which also has substantial other active business activities. Some CFC provisions may not apply if a sufficient portion of the subsidiary's income is active business income, rather than passive income such as interest, dividends, and royalties.
- Passive income may be derived by a 50% joint venture company, rather than a wholly owned company within the multinational group. Such a joint venture company may potentially not be controlled by any one parent company, and may therefore not be subject to CFC provisions.
- The company deriving the passive income may be a company in the multinational group which has carry-forward tax losses. CFC taxation measures should generally not apply where the tax losses are recognised under the parent country's tax rules.
- The parent company may not own the company deriving the passive income, but rather the parent company enters into a total return swap with a third-party bank. For example, the parent company may pay an upfront fee to the bank, and then receive a payment at the end of the swap transaction equivalent to the company's passive income, with the same general effect as if the parent company had held the shares in the company deriving the passive income. Taxation may, however, apply to this type of structure in the UK under the loan relationship rules,[28] and in Australia under the taxation of financial arrangements provisions (TOFA).[29]
- The CFC may also be located in a country with high headline tax rate, but with a low effective tax rate due to tax concessions. For example, the effective tax rate in Luxembourg may be reduced because Luxembourg allows tax deductions for payments made on preferred equity certificates.[30] The effective tax

28. *Corporate Tax Act 2009*, c. 4, part 6, Chapter 2A (United Kingdom).
29. *Income Tax Assessment Act 1997*, Act No. 38 of 1997, section 230-30(2) (Australia).
30. This is based on the substance over form approach of Luxembourg tax interpretation, and *Luxembourg Income Tax Law* Article 40 that the tax balance sheet is based on the commercial balance sheet.

rate in Malta may be reduced,[31] compared to the headline tax rate, because of the tax refunds which are paid to the parent company.[32]

- In the cashbox structure, the parent company may pay a fee to a bank for an option or forward contract to acquire a special purpose vehicle (SPV) in the future. The parent company exercises the option and acquires the SPV after several years. The parent company has made a gain through acquiring the SPV, however it may not be taxed as it has not derived income during the term of the transaction. Taxation may, however, apply to this type of structure in the UK under the loan relationship rules,[33] and in Australia under the TOFA provisions.[34]
- The parent company may make a capital gain on the sale of an asset or the sale of the subsidiary company. The related gain may potentially be protected from CFC taxation due to tax exemptions under tax treaty rules.
- The subsidiary company may derive leasing income from an active asset management business, or derive the subsidiary may derive insurance income, which may potentially not be treated as passive income subject to CFC taxation. In the US, however, taxation under CFC provisions can apply to leasing and insurance income because this income is still treated as passive income.
- An uncontrolled trust may hold the assets which generate passive income. The trustee generally acts under non-binding guidance from the parent company, such as guidance set out in a letter of wishes, rather than having the assets under the direct control of the parent company.

31. Jonathan Pisani, 'Malta Tax of Dividend Income', Chetcuti Cauchi, www.ccmalta.com/publications/malta_tax_dividend_income on 9 January 2014.
32. *Income Tax Management Act*, Ch. 372 of the Laws of Malta, section 48(4A) (Malta).
33. *Corporate Tax Act 2009*, c. 4, part 6, Chapter 2A (United Kingdom).
34. *Income Tax Assessment Act 1997*, Act No. 38 of 1997, section 230-30(2) (Australia).

CHAPTER 29

Introduction to Transfer Pricing

INTRODUCTION

Transfer pricing refers to the requirement under the tax laws of many countries that arm's length prices must be paid for goods and services purchased or sold between related parties to prevent the manipulation of tax liabilities. The arm's length price is essentially the market price which would apply if the parties to the transaction were completely independent. Related party transactions include the sale of goods and services, the interest rate and guarantee fees on loans, the sale prices of plant and machinery, the rate charged for technical services, the rate charged for administrative services such as accounting and finance, human resources, information technology and legal support, the amount of royalties charged for the use of intangible property, and the sale price on the transfer of a company or business. This chapter will introduce several of the most essential transfer pricing topics.

Some goods and services, such as commodity prices and interest rates, may have published market prices, for example benchmark prices may be quoted on a commodity trader's electronic Bloomberg or Thomson Reuters screen. The prices of manufactured goods and services are less likely to be quoted on the market.

Transfer pricing issues arise on intra group services such as allocation of head office expenses, provision of group purchasing of goods and services, group finance and guarantees, and payments for the use of intangible property such as royalties. One example of the broad scope of related party transactions is the United Kingdom (UK) *Waterloo* case,[1] which held that a UK company should be taxed as if it had charged a fee to related foreign companies for the providing share plan benefits to employees.

Transfer pricing tax assessments have been made in relation to mergers and acquisition transactions. In the *Shell India* case,[2] for example, shares which were

1. *Waterloo plc and Ors v. Inland Revenue Commissioners* [2002] STC (SCD) 95 (United Kingdom).
2. *Shell India Markets Private Limited v. The Union Of India, Through Ministry Of Finance And Ors,* High Court of Bombay, Case Number WP/10788/2012 (India).

issued by the Indian subsidiary to its overseas parent were considered to be underpriced compared to the value of the related assets in India.[3] The Indian tax authorities sought to impose annual additional tax, equivalent to GBP 64 million as a transfer pricing adjustment.[4]

The process of applying arm's length prices for transactions with related parties to prevent shifting of taxable profits includes:

- A functional analysis is undertaken to determine what products or services are provided and with which related and unrelated parties.
- There is a selection of the most appropriate transfer pricing method to determine arm's length pricing.
- There is an analysis of comparable transaction prices or comparable company profits.
- Necessary adjustments are made to those comparables for different circumstances.
- Documentation is prepared to prove that the entity has adopted arm's length prices.

OECD Approaches

The OECD issued Transfer Pricing Guidelines which have been generally adopted by many countries. The most recent release was the OECD 2017 Transfer Pricing Guidelines.[5] The contents of the Guidelines include:

- Chapter I: The Arm's Length Principle;
- Chapter II: Transfer Pricing Methods;
- Chapter III: Comparability Analysis;
- Chapter IV: Administrative Approaches to Avoiding and Resolving Transfer Pricing Disputes;
- Chapter V: Documentation;
- Chapter VI: Special Considerations for Intangible Property;
- Chapter VII: Special Considerations for Intra-Group Services;
- Chapter VIII: Cost Contribution Arrangements; and
- Chapter IX: Transfer Pricing Aspects of Business Restructuring.

The OECD is an organisation sponsored by more developed governments under the Convention on the OECD,[6] and so OECD positions on specific taxation and transfer pricing matters reflect the view of the related governments, and may therefore not fully reflect the optimal outcome for less developed countries, or from the viewpoint of

3. Mary Swire, *Shell India Denies Transfer Pricing Abuse*, Tax-News.com, 6 February 2013.
4. *Income Tax Act, 1961*, section 92B (India).
5. OECD Transfer Pricing Guidelines for Multinational Enterprises and Tax Administrations, 2017, para. 6.32 p. 257.
6. *Convention on the Organisation for Economic Co-operation and Development*, 14 December 1960 (entered into force 30 December 1961).

businesses and other market interests. The extent to which OECD guidelines may be applied is also subject to local tax laws and rules of interpretation in each country.

The United Nations Transfer Pricing Manual

The United Nations has also considered transfer pricing issues, and a United Nations Expert Committee published the United Nations Practical Manual on Transfer Pricing for Developing Countries.[7] The Manual essentially provides information for governments on how to draft transfer pricing legislation, set up special transfer pricing units, use transfer pricing databases, pursue simplified strategies for verifying the arm's length nature of transactions, and provide compliance strategies for companies. The Expert Committee endorsed the principles used in the OECD Guidelines, including the use of the arm's length principle.

ESSENTIAL TRANSFER PRICING METHODS

The OECD Transfer pricing guidelines set out the following methods for determining arm's length pricing for transactions between related parties:

- The comparable uncontrolled price (CUP) method is based on the comparison of prices charged in a controlled transaction to the price charged in an uncontrolled transaction in comparable circumstances for comparable products and services.
- The resale price method (RPM) is based on the resale price at which a product purchased from a related party would be sold to an independent enterprise. The transfer price of the intercompany transaction is calculated by deducting the resale price margin from the resale price in the uncontrolled transaction.
- The cost plus method (CPM) is based on the costs incurred by the supplier of property/services in a controlled transaction, with a markup added to the costs to determine the arm's length price in the controlled transaction taking into consideration the functions performed, risks assumed, and assets employed.
- The profit split method (PSM) is based on the identification and appropriate split of the combined profit realised by related entities from a controlled transaction.
- The transactional net margin method (TNMM) is based on determining the net profit margin from a controlled transaction relative to an appropriate base, for example cost, sales, or assets.

7. UN Practical Manual on Transfer Pricing for Developing Countries (2013), www.un.org/esa/ffd/documents/UN_Manual_TransferPricing.pdf on 15 July 2013.

Examples of Transfer Pricing Methods

The following are some simplified examples of the above principal transfer pricing methods. The United Nations Practical Manual on Transfer Pricing for Developing Countries also has a series of transfer pricing method examples.[8]

Comparable Uncontrolled Price

In the CUP method, the USA Co in United States (US) sells Product X, such as a drilling rig, to a Germany Corp, which is a subsidiary company in Germany. The USA Co also sells product X to a Third-Party Co for USD 100 million. If the products are identical, and the terms and conditions are identical, then the CUP is USD 100 million based on the price of the comparable sale to the Third-Party Co. In practice, however, the types of goods, contract terms, geographical markets, quantities, and business circumstances may differ, and so adjustments to the comparable transaction price are almost always required. If these adjustments are complex then another method may instead be required.

There is generally a distinction made between internal comparables, where the goods and services are purchased or sold by the company with third parties, and external comparables, where the goods and services are purchased or sold between third parties. In this example, the USA Co's sale of Product X to the Third-Party Seller would be an internal comparable transaction.

Resale Price Method

In the RPM example, the USA Co sells Product X to a related party Subsidiary and also to an unrelated party retail Austrian Co Buyer for USD 100 million. Distributors in the Product X business generally earn 20% of sales price as their margin. The RPM therefore gives a resale price of USD 100 million less 20% margin of USD 20 million, for a sale price of USD 80 million for the USA Co.

Cost Plus Method

In the CPM example, the USA Co manufactures Product X for USD 50 million for sale to the Subsidiary Co. The manufacturing margin in Product X industry is typically 30%. The cost plus sale price to the Subsidiary Co is therefore USD 50 million plus 30% of USD 50 million, for a price of USD 65 million for the USA Co.

8. *United Nations Practical Manual on Transfer Pricing for Developing Countries*, 187, www.un.org/esa/ffd/documents/UN_Manual_TransferPricing.pdf.

Profit Split Method

In the PSM example, the USA Co manufactures Product X, using their research and development in creating the product, and sells the product to the Subsidiary Co. The Subsidiary Co sells the product to retail buyers using their marketing intangibles from investing in related advertising. The total profits of the USA Co and the Subsidiary Co relating to Product X are USD 150 million. The USA Co considers that 25% of profits relate to marketing intangibles in the Subsidiary Co. The profit allocated to the Subsidiary Co is therefore 25% of total profit of USD 150 million, or USD 37.5 million profit for the Subsidiary Co. The USA Co considers that 75% of the total profits relate to the manufacturing and research and development of the product. Accordingly the profit allocated to the USA Co is 75% of the total profit of USD 150 million, for a USD 112.5 million profit for the USA Co.

Transactional Net Margin Method

In the TNMM example, the USA Co sells Product X to the Subsidiary Co. The Subsidiary Co's gross sales of Product X are USD 450 million. The total profits of the USA Co and the Subsidiary Co for Product X are USD 150 million. The ratio of net profits to gross revenue of distributors of comparable products in comparable markets to the Subsidiary Co is 1/10. On this basis, the profits of the Subsidiary Co would be 1/10 of USD 450 million gross sales, or USD 45 million. The profits of the USA Co would then be the total profits of the USA Co and the Subsidiary Co of USD 150 million, less the USD 45 million profit in the Subsidiary Co, for a USD 105 million profit for the USA Co.

The ratios typically used in the TNMM may include:

- The net profit to gross revenue;
- The net profit before tax to sales;
- The gross profit to operating expenses;
- The net profit before tax to shareholders' funds;
- Earnings before interest and tax to assets; and
- The net profit before tax to number of employees.

Methods relating to profits such as the transactional net margin can be supported by the use of transfer pricing software. For example, Bureau van Dijk 'TP Catalyst' programme allows the selection of comparable companies based on industry category, geographical region, and selected key words. The software then analyses company database information such as financial results, and produces reports with the related profit-based ratios for the selected comparable companies.[9]

9. Bureau van Dijk, TP Catalyst, www.bvdinfo.com/en-gb/products/bvd-s-vertical-solutions/vertical-solutions/tp-catalyst on 14 August 2013.

Summary of Method Examples

Table 29.1 Summary of Method Examples

	CUP	*RPM*	*CPM*	*PS*	*TNMM*
Costs	50	50	50		
3rd Party Sales	100	100			
Dist. Margin 20%		(20)			
Cost Plus Margin 30%			15		
Sale Price to S	100	80	65		
S Sales					450
Total Profit				150	150
Profit Allocation 25%				37.5	
Profit Ratio 1/10 Sales					45
USA Co Profit	50	30	15	112.5	105

The above examples of transfer pricing methodologies use simplified calculations to demonstrate the essential differences between the transfer pricing methods, and in practice applying the methodologies will be much more complex. For example, using the CPM requires determining costs which are directly related to the profits concerned for a direct allocation, and then determining the basis of indirect cost allocation for more general expenses such as accounting and finance, human resources, information technology, and legal services. The basis used for allocating indirect costs is commonly known as the allocation key. This would include allocating the total costs of payroll services provided by the parent company to related companies in the group using the number of staff in each subsidiary as the appropriate allocation key.

The main observation to be made from these examples is that there is generally a wide range of potential outcomes possible due to the different transfer pricing methods available, as can be seen from the range of resulting profits for USA Co. The issue of selecting the appropriate transfer pricing methodology may therefore lead to disputes with the respective tax authorities where those authorities consider that a different transfer pricing method should be used.

ISSUES IN THE TRANSFER PRICING PROCESS

Choice of the Tested Party

The OECD Transfer Guidelines comment that when applying a cost plus, resale price, or TNMMs, it is necessary to choose the party to the transaction for which a financial indicator such as markup on costs, gross margin, or net profit indicator is tested. The choice of the tested party should be consistent with the functional analysis of the transaction. As a general rule, the tested party is the one to which a transfer pricing method can be applied in the most reliable manner and for which the most reliable comparables can be found, i.e., it will most often be the one that has the less complex functional analysis.[10] Issues can arise with this approach, however, where the focus for the transfer pricing analysis is the profits derived by a procurement, marketing, financing, or intangible property (IP) hub within a multinational group. The hub may actually be the more complex party where it performs a variety of different functions. Some flexibility may therefore be required in the selection of the tested party, or analysis of such an entity may be performed as a backup transfer pricing analysis, to test the results under the primary transfer pricing review.

Functional Analysis

The functional analysis is made to determine what products or services are provided and with which related and unrelated parties. This provides a full understanding and documentation of all the related party transactions, and the context of these transactions in the course of the multinational's business activities. This includes identifying the related party transactions, and the detailed analysis of the functions performed, assets used, and risks assumed (FAR) of the two related entities in relation to those transactions.

Selection of the Transfer Pricing Method

The selection of the transfer pricing method is made to establish arm's length pricing for the related party transactions. The OECD had previously expressed the preference for traditional transactional methods, using the CUP, resale price or CPMs, compared to transactional profit methods, such as the profit split and TNMMs. The OECD preference was, however, eliminated in the OECD 2010 and 2017 transfer pricing guidelines.[11]

10. OECD Transfer Pricing Guidelines for Multinational Enterprises and Tax Administrations, 2017, para. 3.18 p. 153.
11. OECD *Transfer Pricing Guidelines*, 2010, para. 2.2, and OECD *Transfer Pricing Guidelines*, 2017, para. 2.2.

The OECD transfer pricing guidelines require the selection of the most appropriate method to the circumstances of the case.[12] This can be compared to the US Treasury regulations, which require selection of the best method to give the most reliable measure of an arm's length result.[13]

The CUP method may be the most appropriate method where there are good internal comparables. This would potentially apply where the company sells the same or similar products or services to unrelated parties, with similar quantities, terms, and markets. On this basis there would be similar functions and risks applying to the comparable sales. The use of comparables is less accurate to the extent of any differences in circumstances, and where greater and more complex adjustments to comparable prices would need to be made.

The RPM may be appropriate where the reseller adds relatively little value to the process, for example where the reseller is a trading company which is essentially only purchasing and reselling the goods. The method is much less effective, for example, where the reseller creates related intangible property, such as a marketing intangible derived from extensive local advertising.

The CPM may be appropriate where a manufacturer performs few other activities besides manufacturing, for example a contract manufacturer may not provide any related services such as research and development, testing, or marketing. The method is also generally used for administrative services provided within a multinational group, including head office functions such as human resources, information technology, legal, and accounting services.

The PSM may be appropriate where there are insufficient comparables. The method considers the overall profit of both related parties to a controlled transaction, and then determines the profit split between them. The PSM may be the best method to determine the arm's length price where there are contributions such as intangible property which relate to the profits of both companies. The 2017 OECD Transfer Pricing Guidelines state that the method is appropriate for highly integrated operations, or where both parties to a transaction make unique and valuable contributions. The OECD consider that a transactional PSM would ordinarily not be used in cases where one party to the transaction performs only simple functions and does not make any significant unique contribution.[14] There have been different views expressed on this issue, however, including comments potentially supporting the wider use of the PSM by the Canada Revenue Agency (CRA).[15]

The TNMM may potentially be the most appropriate method where there are insufficient comparables. This method may be preferred to the PSM because information is more likely to be available on equivalent profit margins or other business ratios

12. Thomas Borstell, Ernst & Young, *OECD releases new and revised Transfer Pricing Guidelines* October 2010.
13. *Treasury Regulations*, Subchapter A, § 1.482-1(c) (United States).
14. OECD Transfer Pricing Guidelines for Multinational Enterprises and Tax Administrations, 2017, para. 2.115 p. 133.
15. OECD, Working Party No. 6 on the Taxation of Multinational Enterprises, Revised Guidance on Profit Splits annotated with country comments, 7-11 March 2016, OECD Conference Centre, Paris, CTPA/CFA/WP6/NOE2(2016)2/REV1, p. 3.

of other companies with similar business activities, and this information can be accessed from related databases based on published accounts and other financial data. There is a similar method in the US transfer pricing rules under the comparable profit method (CPM).[16]

RELATED TRANSFER PRICING CASES

The following is a selection of transfer pricing cases to illustrate several of the related tax issues:

Dixon's Case

In many cases it is likely that the CUP method may result in agreement on the methodology providing that an accurate comparable can be found. In practice, however, identifying suitable comparable transactions can be difficult. An example of this issue relating to the selection of a transfer pricing methodology was the UK decision in the *Dixons* case.[17] The case concerned the level of sales and profit commissions paid to the DSG Retail company in the UK, where DSG Retail was selling extended warranties on electrical products. The commissions were paid by a related insurance company located in a low-taxing jurisdiction of the Isle of Man. The tax authorities considered that commissions paid by the related insurance company to DSG in the UK were too low, resulting in more profit retained by the captive insurance company in the Isle of Man.

DSG Retail had argued that a third-party comparable of the level of commissions paid by an independent insurer to its customers supported the amount of the commissions. The tax tribunal rejected this comparable on the basis that the independent insurer was a powerful brand, and would only pay a lower commission. The tribunal determined the 'super profits' relating to the transactions, and allocated these profits using the PSM. The related insurance company was entitled to a market return on capital, however the residual profit over this amount should be returned to DSG Retail as a taxable commission.[18]

The Roche Products Case

The *Roche Products* case concerned the Australian company which distributed the pharmaceutical products of its Swiss parent company and other group companies, and was decided by the Administrative Appeals Tribunal in 2008.[19] The Australian Taxation Office considered that the TNMM should apply. The tribunal concluded,

16. *Treasury Regulations*, Subchapter A, § 1.482-5 (United States).
17. *DSG Retail and others v. HMRC* (TC 00001) (2009) ('*Dixons* case') (United Kingdom).
18. Anuschka Bakker & Marc M Levey, *Transfer Pricing and Intra-group Financing: The Entangled Worlds of Financial Markets and Transfer Pricing* 6 (2012).
19. *Roche Products Pty Ltd v. FCT* [2008] AATA 261.

however, that an arm's length price for the products would have yielded the Australian subsidiary a gross margin of at least 40% throughout its product range, based on the finding that the prices for sales to third parties would yield the third party this same gross profit margin. On this basis it was held that the gross profit margin in third-party comparable sales should apply to the Australian company's other products.[20]

The SNF Case

The *SNF* case,[21] concerned an Australian company which purchased products from related companies. The company used the CUP based on transactions between the suppliers and their arm's length customers. The company incurred losses due to commercial issues such as competition in the Australian market, excessive stock levels, and poor management, and partly due to a pricing strategy to penetrate the market. The Australian Taxation Office considered that the TNMM should be used, based on a 'benchmark operating profit' determined by the operating profits of other comparable distributors. The Federal Court accepted the company's pricing, however, and held that it could not be concluded that the purchase prices had been artificially inflated.[22]

OECD BEPS Changes to the Selection of Transfer Pricing Method

Several of the most significant changes to transfer pricing are likely to result from the OECD BEPS initiative and in particular the approach to functional analysis. The new approach is contained in BEPS Action Plans 8 to 10. Multinationals undertaking functional analysis will be required to ensure that 'transfer pricing rules secure outcomes that see operational profits allocated to the economic activities which generate them'. This means that entities must therefore be able to control the risks that give rise to potential rewards, and the mere legal ownership of an intangible asset is not sufficient to generate a significant return. The BEPS reports also provide that 'capital-rich entities without any other relevant economic activities will not be entitled to any excess profits,' which includes interest. These changes have been included in the OECD's 2017 Transfer Pricing Guidelines.[23]

EXAMPLES OF COUNTRY TRANSFER PRICING PROVISIONS

The following brief summaries of transfer pricing provisions in certain countries based on sources including the PricewaterhouseCoopers International Transfer Pricing 2015/2016, and the Ernst & Young 2016–2017 Worldwide Transfer Pricing Reference Guide. The related provisions are subject to changes over time, and so these summaries

20. Michael A Heimert & Michelle Johnson, *Guide to International Transfer Pricing: Law, Tax Planning and Compliance Strategies* 50 (2010).
21. *SNF (Australia) Pty Ltd v. FCT* [2010] FCA 635.
22. Greg Thompson, BDO, 'Federal court decides in favour of taxpayer in transfer pricing case'.
23. OECD Transfer Pricing Guidelines for Multinational Enterprises and Tax Administrations, 2017, para. 6.32 p. 257.

are primarily intended to show the similarities in the provisions of Australia, the Netherlands, and the UK which are closely based on the OECD transfer pricing guidelines, and the somewhat different approaches used in the US. The recent changes in several of these provisions also show that specific rules are also changing quite rapidly over time.

Australia

Australia introduced revised transfer pricing laws applying from 1 July 2013. These laws primarily focus on arm's length profit and profit allocation, as opposed to the previous priority on the arm's length pricing of transactions.[24] These rules may also apply to cross-border dealings between third parties where those parties have not dealt with one another on an arm's length basis. The revised rules included the following measures:[25]

- Self-assessment – The new provisions are based on self-assessment by taxpayers, rather than applying through determinations by the Commissioner of Taxation. Taxpayers therefore need to address compliance with the provisions in their tax returns.
- Time limit for amendments – There was previously no limitation on the period for transfer pricing adjustments, however a seven-year limit now applies.
- Endorsement of OECD material – The new provisions endorse the OECD guidelines, and so must be applied 'so as best to achieve consistency with' the OECD's Transfer Pricing Guidelines and Model Tax Convention and its Commentaries. The provisions also include the most appropriate method rule for selecting the transfer pricing method, and the use of comparability factors for selecting and applying arm's length pricing methods.
- Reconstruction – The provisions include the relevance of economic substance in applying the arm's length principle based on a reconstruction rule. This requires that arm's length conditions be determined based on what independent parties might be expected to have done in comparable circumstances. The controlled transaction is required to have economic substance, makes commercial sense, and would be entered into by independent parties acting in a commercially rational manner. The rules also refer to the availability of comparables, and the need to consider the options realistically available to the parties, their relative bargaining power, and which party controls relevant risks.
- Documentation and penalties – The failure to prepare transfer pricing documentation when the relevant tax return is lodged means that a company

24. *Tax Laws Amendment (Countering Tax Avoidance and Multinational Profit Shifting) Act 2013*, No. 101, 2013, and *Income Tax Assessment Act 1997*, Subdivisions 815-B (separate entities), 815-C (branches) and 815-D (partnerships and trusts) (Australia).
25. Cameron Smith & Janelle Sadri, *New Transfer Pricing Legislation Introduced into Parliament* (Deloitte, 2013) and Deloitte, *The New Transfer Pricing Landscape in Australia* (Deloitte, 2013).

cannot have a reasonably arguable position (RAP) for penalty purposes which could otherwise reduce the penalty rate to 10%. The general penalty rate of 25% of the tax shortfall is therefore likely to apply.

There are several new provisions relating to the interaction of the thin capitalisation and transfer pricing rules. In particular, a company with international related party borrowings may be required to show that the amount of its debt is at arm's length for purposes.[26] This rule follows the approach taken by the Australian Taxation Office in Taxation Ruling TR 2010/7.

The Netherlands

The current transfer pricing provisions in the Netherlands have applied from 2002 under Article 8b of the Dutch Corporate Income Tax Act,[27] and these measures are generally based on Article 9 of the OECD's Model Tax Convention. Related measures include Transfer Pricing Decree IFZ 2013/184M issued in 2013.[28]

The provisions can apply where there is control between affiliated businesses, which is determined where there are businesses that are directly or indirectly participating in the capital, management, or supervision of another company, and where there is sufficient influence on the prices charged between these companies.

The Advance Pricing Agreement (APA) decree IFZ2004/124M was issued on 11 August 2004, 'Procedure for dealing with requests for upfront certainty on transfer prices to be used in cross-border transactions (advance pricing agreements).'[29] This provides guidance on how the OECD Guidelines on APAs are applied in the Netherlands.

The Decrees on financing companies, IFZ2004/126M,[30] and IFZ2004/127M,[31] provides a transfer pricing regime for Netherlands finance companies including back-to-back intercompany loans and intercompany licensing transactions. A Netherlands finance or licence company is required to incur economic risk, and have sufficient operational substance in the Netherlands. The compensation to be derived from back-to-back intercompany loans and intercompany licensing transactions needs to be established and documented on a case-by-case basis, and the compensation

26. *Income Tax Assessment Act 1997*, section 815-140 (Australia).
27. *Income Tax Act 2001*, Articles 3.8 and 3.25, and *Corporate Income Tax Act* 1969, Article 8 and 8b (Netherlands).
28. Decree of 14 November 2013, No IFZ 2013/184M, Directorate-General for Taxation, Department of International Tax Affairs, 'Transfer pricing, application of the arm's length principle and the Transfer Pricing Guidelines for Multinational Enterprises and Tax Administrations (OECD Guidelines)' (Netherlands).
29. *Decree IFZ2004/124M*, 'Procedure for dealing with requests for upfront certainty on transfer prices to be used in cross-border transactions (advance pricing agreements)' on 11 August 2004 (Netherlands).
30. *Decree IFZ2004/126M* on 11 August 2004 (Netherlands).
31. *Decree IFZ2004/127M* on 11 August 2004 (Netherlands).

typically needs to consist of a handling fee component and a risk premium.[32] The requirement for operational substance generally means:

- The company would have professionally skilled Netherlands resident directors for at least half the board, and have real decision-making power.
- The major decisions of the company must be made in the Netherlands.
- All the related administrative activities must be performed in the Netherlands.

The requirement for economic substance generally means:

- The company should have real business risks and have sufficient equity capital at stake to meet those risks.
- The risks for finance companies need to include both credit and market risk.
- The company should have equity at risk of at least 1% of the amount of the company's outstanding receivables, or EUR 2 million, whichever is the lower amount.

The Decree on attribution of profits to permanent establishments IFZ2010/457M in 2011,[33] concerned how the Netherlands tax authorities determine the attribution of profits to permanent establishments. The Decree generally follows OECD recommendations that the permanent establishment should be evaluated as if it was a legally distinct and separate enterprise. The assets and risks of the business are then attributed between the head office and the permanent establishment based on a functional analysis. The amount of any free capital and loans is then allocated to the permanent establishment, and interest is then determined for loans attributed to the permanent establishment.[34]

United Kingdom

The current transfer pricing provisions were released in 2010,[35] and can substitute an arm's length price for intercompany transactions with UK or foreign affiliates including UK to UK transactions.[36] The participation condition requires that one of the two affected persons was directly or indirectly participating in the management, control, or capital of the other, or a third person was participating in the management, control, or capital of both these persons.[37] The rules can also apply to persons that collectively

32. PricewaterhouseCoopers, *International Transfer Pricing 2013/14* (PricewaterhouseCoopers, 2014) 623.
33. *Decree IFZ2010/457M*, Decree on attribution of profits to permanent establishments, on 15 January 2011 (Netherlands).
34. PricewaterhouseCoopers, *International Transfer Pricing 2013/14* (PricewaterhouseCoopers, 2013) 624.
35. *Taxation (International and Other Provisions) Act 2010*, c. 8, Part 4 (United Kingdom).
36. PricewaterhouseCoopers, *International Transfer Pricing 2013/14* (PricewaterhouseCoopers, 2013) 798.
37. *Taxation (International and Other Provisions) Act 2010*, c. 8, section 148 (United Kingdom).

control a business and have acted together with respect to the financing arrangements for the business.[38]

The provisions can apply where there is a potential advantage in relation to UK taxation, such as where a person's taxable profits for a chargeable period are reduced, or tax losses for a period are created or increased, as an effect of the provision of goods and services not being made on an arm's length position.[39] There is an exemption for small and medium-sized enterprises (SME) unless the UK does not have a tax treaty with a non-discrimination article with the related country.[40] In relation to these rules, small enterprises generally have a maximum of fifty staff, annual turnover of EUR 10 million, and a balance sheet total of EUR 10 million. Medium enterprises generally have a maximum of 250 staff, annual turnover of EUR 50 million, and a balance sheet total of EUR 43 million.[41]

Taxpayers are required to prepare their tax returns using the arm's length principle on a self-assessment basis, and are required to retain adequate records or other documentation to support their compliance. The related legislation is to be interpreted in a manner that best secures consistency with the arm's length principle in Article 9 of the OECD Model Tax Treaty, and the OECD Transfer Pricing Guidelines.[42]

The UK has provided specific APAs since 1999, and the current provisions for APAs were introduced in 2010.[43] A UK business may request an APA, and APAs may also be requested by non-residents trading in the UK through a permanent establishment or branch, and by UK residents trading through branches or permanent establishments outside the UK.[44] APAs are intended to enable businesses to achieve greater certainty over their tax liabilities. This can be an advantage where there is considerable difficulty or doubt in determining the method by which the arm's length principle should be applied, and the transfer pricing issues can be more efficiently dealt with in real time as they arise. The APA process generally comprises an expression of interest, the formal submission of application, evaluation of the proposed methodology and critical assumptions, and drawing up the APA agreement.[45]

HMRC guidance generally recommends that APA applications are bilateral rather than unilateral, except where: (1) the extension to a bilateral APA would unnecessarily complicate and delay the process; (2) the other party to the transaction is resident in a jurisdiction with no related tax treaty or the treaty partner has no APA process; or (3) there is little extra to be gained by seeking a bilateral agreement, such as where the UK

38. Ernst & Young, *Worldwide Corporate Tax Guide 2014* 1441 (Ernst & Young, 2014).
39. *Taxation (International and Other Provisions) Act 2010*, c. 8, section 155 (United Kingdom).
40. *Taxation (International and Other Provisions) Act 2010*, c. 8, section 167(3) (United Kingdom).
41. HMRC International Manual, INTM412080 – Transfer pricing: legislation: rules: exemptions: SME definition, www.hmrc.gov.uk/MANUALS/intmanual/INTM412080.htm on 11 March 2014.
42. *Taxation (International and Other Provisions) Act 2010*, c. 8, section 164 (United Kingdom).
43. *Taxation (International and Other Provisions) Act 2010*, c. 8, Part 5 (United Kingdom).
44. *Taxation (International and Other Provisions) Act 2010*, c. 8, section 218(2) (United Kingdom).
45. HMRC, Statement of Practice SP2/10 – Advance Pricing Agreements, www.hmrc.gov.uk/agents/sop.pdf on 11 March 2014.

is at the hub of arrangements with associated enterprises and the trade flows involved with any one country are modest in scale.[46]

United States

In the US, the threshold test for the transfer pricing provisions is whether the parties are under common control based on the facts and circumstances rather than on specific ownership thresholds. Control is defined to include direct or indirect control, whether legally enforceable, and however exercisable or exercised. The reality of control is decisive, rather than a focus on record ownership.[47]

The provisions apply the best method rule to select the transfer pricing method, given the facts and circumstances of the transactions, to provide the most reliable measure of an arm's length result relative to other potentially applicable methods. The method that yields the most accurate result should therefore be selected.[48]

In general, no adjustment may be made to a taxpayer's transfer pricing results if those results are within an arm's-length range based on two or more comparable uncontrolled transactions with fairly high standard of comparability. If inexact comparables are used then the range is based on results between the 25th and 75th percentile from a range of comparable transaction prices.

The taxpayer is required to report an arm's-length result on its tax return even where this differs from prices originally set out on invoices and in the taxpayer's books and records.[49]

There are specific regulations for several transfer pricing issues.[50] In relation to the transfer of intangible property, such as where patents and trademarks are sold by a US company to a related foreign company, the regulations apply a commensurate with income standard, which can result in adjustments long after the transfer takes place. This can require periodic adjustment to transfer prices where the transfer prices relied on projected results such as projected profit or cost savings. Periodic adjustments are generally not required where the related cumulative benefits are within a range of plus or minus 20% of the forecast.[51]

46. *HMRC International Manual*, INTM422030 – Transfer pricing: methodologies: Advance Pricing Agreements: types of agreement, http://www.hmrc.gov.uk/manuals/intmanual/intm422030.htm on 11 March 2014.
47. Treas. Reg. § 1.482-1(a)(3), 1968-1 C.B. 218; Treas. Reg. § 1.482-1T(g)(4), 1993-1 C.B. 90; Treas. Reg. § 1.482-1(i)(4), 1994-2 C.B. 93. (United States).
48. PricewaterhouseCoopers, *International Transfer Pricing 2013/14* 818 (PricewaterhouseCoopers, 2013).
49. PricewaterhouseCoopers, *International Transfer Pricing 2013/14* 821 (PricewaterhouseCoopers, 2013).
50. *Internal Revenue Code*, 26 USC (1986) §§482, 6038A, 6038C and 6662, *Treasury Regulations* §§1.482, 1.6662, 1.6038A, 1.6038C, and *Revenue Procedures* 2006–54, 99–32, and 2006–9 (United States).
51. PricewaterhouseCoopers, *International Transfer Pricing 2013/14* 822 (PricewaterhouseCoopers, 2013).

The IRS and the Treasury issued final regulation for transfer pricing for services in 2006.[52] These regulations retained the services cost method (SCM) safe harbour for low-margin services which allow some services to be charged without markup where they meet all of the following criteria:[53]

- The service must be a covered service based on a white list of 101 covered services the related ruling,[54] which relates to back office activities, or a service where the median of the arm's length range of cost markups is less than or equal to 7%.
- The service must not be on the black list of nine excluded activities, which include R&D, manufacturing and financing.
- The taxpayer is required to maintain books and records which evidence the intention to apply the SCM and which allow the IRS to verify the related costs and the methods of allocation and apportionment.
- The taxpayer must reasonably determine that the service does not contribute significantly to the key competitive advantages, core capabilities or the fundamental risks of success or failure of the group.

There are also specific rules for cost sharing arrangements (CSA), where related parties together contribute to the development of a product or service. The platform contribution transaction (PCT) rules relate to methods for valuing buy-ins under CSAs, such as contributions by a foreign subsidiary to a US parent developing new intangible property. The related final regulations were issued in 2011, together with 2011 temporary regulations on the use of discount rates, and 2011 proposed regulations on the related income method. The allowed methods for PCTs include the comparable uncontrolled transaction method (CUT); income method; acquisition price method (APM); market capitalisation method (MCM), residual PSM; and other unspecified methods.

The US has a number of acceptable transfer pricing methods for different goods and services. These methods include:[55]

Tangible Goods

- CUP;
- Resale price;
- Cost plus;
- Profit split, including comparable and residual uses;
- Comparable profits method, equivalent to the OECD TNMM; and
- Other unspecified methods.

52. Department of the Treasury and Internal Revenue Service 26 CFR Parts 1 and 31 [TD 9278] RIN 1545-BB31, 1545-AY38, 1545-BC52 Treatment of Services Under section 482 Allocation of Income and Deductions from Intangibles Stewardship Expense (United States).
53. Eric D Ryan & Paul Flignor, DLA Piper, 11 August 2009 *United States Final US Regulations on Intercompany Services: The IRS Sticks to Its Guns* (DLA Piper, 2009).
54. Revenue Procedure 2007-13, 2007-1 C.B. 295 (United States).
55. Ernst & Young, *2012 Transfer Pricing Global Reference Guide* 181 (London: Ernst & Young, 2011).

Intangible Goods

- Comparable uncontrolled transaction (CUT), similar to the CUP;
- Profit split;
- Comparable profits method, equivalent to the TNMM;
- Other unspecified methods; and
- Methods for platform contribution transactions (PCTs) under cost sharing arrangements, as compensation for contributions to developing cost shared intangibles.

Services

- Services cost method (SCM), as a safe harbour regime;
- Comparable Uncontrolled Services Price Method (CUSPM), similar to the CUP;
- Gross Services Margin Method (GSMM), similar to the RPM;
- Cost of Services Plus Method (CSPM);
- PSM;
- Comparative Profits Method, equivalent to the TNMM; and
- Other unspecified methods.

Platform Contribution Transactions (PCTs) (Cost Sharing)

- Comparable uncontrolled transaction method (CUT);
- Income method;
- Acquisition price method (APM);
- Market capitalisation method (MCM);
- Residual PSM; and
- Other unspecified methods.

TRANSFER PRICING AND PERMANENT ESTABLISHMENTS

Introduction

This issue concerns determining the profits of a branch as a permanent establishment, including the attribution of business profits under Article 7 of the OECD Model Tax Treaty.[56] This issue has been relevant, for example, to the amount of interest expenses allowed as deductions for the permanent establishment. The OECD considered this issue in the 2008 Report on the Attribution of Profits to Permanent Establishments.[57]

56. OECD, *Model Tax Convention on Income and on Capital* (2017) (OECD, 2017).
57. OECD *2008 Report on the Attribution of Profits to Permanent Establishments.*

General Business Activities

The OECD analysis of the allocation of profits to permanent establishments and the authorised OECD approach (AOA) is based on the 'functionally separate entity approach', which applies where the profits of the permanent establishment would be the profits derived on an arm's length basis if the permanent establishment was a distinct and separate enterprise. This approach can however result in taxation even where the head office or the permanent establishment are not in profit.

The allocation is required to be a two-step process, based on: (1) hypothetical treatment of the permanent establishment as a distinct and separate entity 'engaged in the same or similar activities under the same or similar circumstances'; and (2) allocating profits to this hypothetical entity taking into account the functions performed, assets used and risks assumed through the permanent establishment and through other parts of the enterprise as discussed in the Model Tax Treaty commentary.[58] This allocation is generally based on the location of 'significant people functions', where assets and risks are to be allocated between the permanent establishment and the home office by reference to the place of performance of these functions.[59]

The OECD has rejected the 'force of attraction' principle, which provides that where once a company has a permanent establishment in a state, then all the income arising in that state may be subject tax whether or not that income involved the permanent establishment.

The OECD released the Discussion Draft on the Additional Guidance on Attribution of Profits to Permanent Establishments relating to BEPS Action 7 in 2017. The guidance relates to the BEPS measures to prevent the artificial avoidance of permanent establishment status through the use of commissionaire arrangements and the specific activity exemptions of Article 5(4) and 5(5) of the OECD Model Tax Treaty, and the basis of profit attribution where the new BEPS measures will result in a permanent establishment.[60]

The Financial Sector

The OECD Report provided that capital is to be allocated according to the assets and risks attributable to the permanent establishment. In relation to the financial sector, this allocation is based on the location of key entrepreneurial risk taking functions (KERT). This includes origins of assets and risks, and their ongoing management. This is based on the arm's length principle a permanent establishment should have sufficient capital to support the functions it undertakes, the assets it economically owns and the risks it assumes. The OECD promote a functional and factual analysis to

58. OECD *Model Tax Convention on Income and on Capital* (2014), C(7)-6 para. 15.
59. OECD *Model Tax Convention on Income and on Capital* (2014), C(7)-8 para. 21, and W Joseph Murphy & Geoffrey Armstrong, *Transfer Pricing in the Context of a PE: The OECD View* (PricewaterhouseCoopers, 2007) <http://www.pwc.com/en_US/us/transfer-pricing-strategies/assets/transfer_pricing_and_permanent_establishments_oecd_view.pdf>.
60. OECD, Public Discussion Draft, BEPS Action 7, Additional Guidance on Attribution of Profits to Permanent Establishments, 22 June–15 September 2017.

attribute free capital, being funding that does not give rise to a tax-deductible return in the nature of interest, to the permanent establishment.

The OECD Report on Attribution of Profits to Permanent Establishments in 2010 concerned the related assets and risks, and required a functional analysis identifying the following functions, the company performing the functions, and where the functions were performed:

- Functions involved in creating a new financial asset, for example a loan.
- Functions involved in managing an existing financial asset.
- The key entrepreneurial risk-taking functions involved in creating and subsequently managing that asset.
- Support, middle or back office functions.
- Assets used.
- Risks assumed.
- Capital and funding.
- Creditworthiness.
- Capital adequacy requirements.
- Other regulatory requirements.
- Significance of free capital.

The activities and conditions of a hypothetical independent entity are determined by the following means:

- Attributing functions, assets, and risks to the permanent establishment.
- Attributing creditworthiness to the permanent establishment.
- Attributing capital to the permanent establishment.

The profits of the hypothetical entity are then determined which can relate to the following:

- Sales and support.
- Treasury functions, movement of funds, and payment of interest.
- Internal guarantees.
- Sales/trading functions.
- Risk management functions and transfers of risk.
- Transfers of existing financial assets.
- Support, middle or back office.
- Agency or conduit functions.

The issue of capital allocation was considered in the *National Westminster Bank* cases in the US.[61] Treasury Regulation § 1.882-5 generally requires: (1) determining the average tax basis of assets used in the US trade or business; (2) apportioning liabilities to the US business assets, by the actual ratio of the company's worldwide liabilities to worldwide assets, or a fixed ratio of 95% for banks and 50% for other companies; and

61. *Nat West II Limits IRS Power to Determine Interest Expense of Foreign Company*, Intl. Tax Advisory, 15 January 2004 (Alston & Bird LLP, 2004).

(3) applying an interest rate to these liabilities based on the interest rate of the US business, or the rate on USD liabilities not connected to that business. The liabilities and interest expenses associated with intra-company loans are disregarded in these calculations:

- In the *NatWest I* case,[62] the Court held that under the prior 1975 US/UK tax treaty,[63] branch interest expense should be based on actual liabilities of the branch, and not based on a formula that treats the branch as a unit of a worldwide enterprise.
- In the *NatWest II* case,[64] the Court held that Article 7 of the 1975 US/UK tax treaty overrode the Treasury regulations that would have imputed additional capital to the US branch of a foreign bank, and would therefore reduce the branch's interest expense deductions.

It is interesting that the newer 2003 US/UK tax treaty,[65] potentially overrules the *NatWest I and II* cases, on the basis that the related diplomatic note states that the OECD Transfer Pricing Guidelines will apply for purposes of determining profits attributable to a permanent establishment and, in particular, that the permanent establishment should be treated as having the same amount of capital that it would need to support its activities if it were a distinct and separate enterprise.

TRANSFER PRICING DOCUMENTATION AND AUDITS

Documentation Requirements

Most transfer pricing provisions and related rulings set out the documentation that must be prepared and retained by taxpayers. Increasingly, this documentation must be prepared and updated in each tax year, and not in response to a transfer pricing audit. An example of the detailed documentation requirements is provided under the related US regulations,[66] which require the following:

- An overview of taxpayer's business, including an analysis of the economic factors that affect the pricing of its products and services.

62. *National Westminster Bank, PLC v. United States*, 44 Fed. Cl. 120 (1999) ('*NatWest I* case') (United States).
63. *The Convention between the Government of the United States of America and the Government of the United Kingdom of Great Britain and Northern Ireland for the Avoidance of Double Taxation and the Prevention of Fiscal Evasion with respect to Taxes on Income*, 31 December 1975, 31 UST 5668 (no longer in force).
64. *National Westminster Bank, PLC v. United States* (Ct. Cl. 14 November 2003) ('*NatWest II* case') (United States).
65. *Convention between the Government of the United States of America and the Government of the United Kingdom of Great Britain and Northern Ireland for the Avoidance of Double Taxation and the Prevention of Fiscal Evasion with Respect to Taxes on Income and on Capital Gains*, 24 July 2001, 2224 UNTS 247 (entered into force 31 March 2003).
66. *Income Tax Regulations* § 1.6662-1 26 CFR Ch. I (United States).

- The taxpayer's organisation structure covering all parties relevant to the related party transactions at issue.
- Documentation required by regulations.
- The transfer pricing method selected and explanation of why that method was selected.
- The alternate transfer pricing methods which were considered, and why they were not selected.
- A description of the controlled transactions evaluated and any internal data used to analyse those transactions.
- What comparables were utilised in the analysis, how their comparability was evaluated, and a detailed description of any adjustments to the comparable prices.
- An explanation of the economic analysis and projections which were relied on in the process of developing the transfer pricing methodology.
- Any relevant data which was obtained after the end of the taxable year and before filing the return.
- An index of the related documents and a description of the record keeping system.

Selection for Audit and Some Suggested Responses

A threshold issue is whether companies may be selected for transfer pricing audits. The tax authorities may accept that companies have satisfactory current documentation which supports the use of arm's length pricing and therefore not conduct a tax audit. This can take place where the tax authorities are updated by the taxpayer on methods used to improve their tax compliance including their commitment to arm's length transfer pricing. The indicators for possible transfer pricing audits which may be used by tax authorities may include abnormally low profits, transactions with low tax regimes, cross-border business restructures, and any significant legal or economic transfers of intangible property.

If an audit is commenced, it is advisable for the company concerned to assemble the available information, determine if satisfactory documentation exists, and determine which prices can be supported as made at arm's length. Management support is an essential requirement in this process to ensure a coordinated response, and this process also requires cooperation from other companies in the group. This process also requires contact procedures for liaising with the tax authorities to ensure that they are provided with correct information.

It may be an advisable practice to resolve other tax matters where possible, such as tax issues relating to prior year tax returns. In the event that additional tax is considered a likely outcome of the audit, consideration may potentially be given to agreeing to making related tax payments to reduce penalties and related interest charges. There may also be an opportunity to reach a settlement on a positive basis which establishes the approaches for future transfer pricing in the group.

Following the audit, the company concerned may need to determine whether future prices should be adjusted due to the tax audit result. This determination may partly depend on the likely response of the tax authorities in the other countries concerned, and in particular whether they will accept the revised prices.

Approaches to Dispute Resolution

The response to a transfer pricing audit can include challenging the related tax adjustment in court. Transfer pricing litigation is frequently complex, however, and the result is particularly uncertain as courts are not experts at economic analysis, and generally do not dispute the transfer pricing methods adopted by tax authorities.

There are also subjective issues relating to the use of comparables, such as which companies were undertaking similar business, and which adjustments should be made for the inevitable differences in the circumstances relating to the comparables. The best approach is generally to achieve a reasonable basis of transfer pricing prior to the litigation process commencing. An APA, as an agreement or ruling with the tax authorities concerning the basis transfer pricing, is likely to be the best approach to prevent related disputes.

Competent Authority Mutual Agreement Procedures (MAP) and Compensating Adjustments

Double taxation can potentially arise where a transfer pricing adjustment is made by one country, but the revised prices which were used in that adjustment are not accepted by the other country. Where the tax authorities of the two countries do not agree then the Competent Authority procedure may assist in resolving the issue under tax treaty procedures to resolving disputes and prevent double taxation. The related tax treaty generally designates a 'competent authority' for each country which is generally a member of the tax department or tax commissioner and their respective delegates.

A company may petition the competent authority in their country of residence where the actions of one or both of the treaty countries results in taxation not in accordance with the provisions of the agreement. The MAP in Article 25 of the 2017 OECD Model Tax Treaty requires cooperation between the tax authorities of the two countries, however the result may be agreement to prevent double taxation arising from any transfer pricing adjustments. The MAP provisions in tax treaties may be amended by the measures in the OECD BEPS Action 14 Report,[67] and Action 15 Report.[68]

67. Making Dispute Resolution Mechanisms More Effective, Action 14: 2015 Final Report (OECD, 2015).
68. Developing a Multilateral Instrument to Modify Bilateral Tax Treaties, Action 15: 2015 Final Report (OECD, 2015).

OECD BEPS Action Plan: Documentation and Country-by-Country Reporting

The OECD released the report and updated guidelines on transfer pricing documentation and country-by-country (CbC) reporting under BEPS Action Plan 13.[69] The transfer pricing proposals are particularly significant as they incorporate new measures against tax evasion relating to transfer pricing.

The proposals include transfer pricing documentation based on a master file and local country files. The OECD has released the new Chapter V of the OECD 2017 Transfer Pricing Guidelines. This sets out a new three-tier global standard for transfer pricing documentation requirements, including a common template for country-by-country reporting and blueprints for a global master file and local files for transfer pricing documentation. The new guidelines set out the content of the new requirements, and the OECD are continuing to work on important questions of implementation, including how the country-by-country report and master file should be filed, and how transition to the new model will occur.[70]

The information required for the master file comprises the following five categories:

(1) The multinational enterprise (MNE) group's organisational structure.
(2) A description of the MNE's businesses.
(3) The MNE's intangibles.
(4) The MNE's intercompany financial activities.
(5) The MNE's financial and tax positions.

The local file for each country is required to refer to material transactions of the local taxpayer and containing the required transfer pricing analysis to validate the arm's length nature of those transactions.[71]

The potentially more significant development relates to country-by-country reporting. The country-by-country report will require the ultimate parent entity of a multinational group to set out global data by country for its fiscal year in a prescribed template, together with a list of entities by country of residence and indication of their activities. The report will be for tax administrations only, and will not be made public. The country-by-country report will include information, aggregated by country, from all 'constituent entities' that make up the consolidated group for financial reporting purposes. In addition, any entity or business unit that is not consolidated solely on the

69. OECD, Transfer Pricing Guidelines for Multinational Enterprises and Tax Administrations, Chapter V, and Action 13: Guidance on the Implementation of Transfer Pricing Documentation and Country-by-Country Reporting, (OECD, 2015) <http://www.oecd.org/ctp/beps-action-13-guidance-implementation-tp-documentation-cbc-reporting.pdf>.

70. Deloitte, BEPS Action 13: Transfer Pricing Documentation and Country-by-Country Reporting, (Deloitte, 2015) <https://www2.deloitte.com/content/dam/Deloitte/global/Documents/Tax/dttl-tax-uk-beps-action-13.pdf>.

71. PricewaterhouseCoopers, *The Future Directions in Transfer Pricing Arising under the BEPS Recommendations* (PricewaterhouseCoopers, 2014).

grounds of materiality will need to be included.[72] The OECD report provides that the data points that will be required to be reported for each country:

- Revenues, from both related and unrelated party transactions.
- Profit before income tax.
- Income tax paid, on a cash basis.
- Current year income tax accrual.
- Stated capital.
- Accumulated earnings.
- Number of employees.
- Tangible assets, excluding cash, and equivalents.

It can be considered that the template is designed to highlight those low-tax jurisdictions where a significant amount of income is allocated without some 'proportionate' presence of employees. This may mean that there will be pressure to assure that profit allocations to a particular jurisdiction are supported by the location in that state of sufficient appropriately qualified employees who are able to make a 'substantial contribution' to the related business activities such as the creation and development of intangibles.[73] The country-by-country report may potentially highlight business restructures which have an economic transfer of profit potential, for example where activities have ceased in one country and have commenced in another country.

TRANSFER PRICING AND TAX TREATIES

Tax treaties generally contain some form of transfer pricing measures, and these are usually based on the OECD Model Tax Treaty as follows.[74]

General Provisions

The OECD Model Tax Treaty essentially provides that where conditions are made between related enterprises which differ from those between independent enterprises, then any profits which would have accrued to one of the enterprises may be included in their profit. Article 9(1) of the 2017 Model Tax Treaty states this rule as follows:

> Where
>
> a) an enterprise of a Contracting State participates directly or indirectly in the management, control or capital of an enterprise of the other Contracting State, or

72. Deloitte, BEPS Action 13: Transfer Pricing Documentation and Country-by-Country Reporting, (Deloitte, 2015) <https://www2.deloitte.com/content/dam/Deloitte/global/Documents/Tax/dttl-tax-uk-beps-action-13.pdf>.
73. BEPS Action Plan: *Action 13 – Transfer Pricing Documentation* (PricewaterhouseCoopers, 2015) <http://www.pwc.com/gx/en/tax/tax-policy-administration/beps/transfer-pricing-documentation.jhtml>.
74. OECD, *Model Tax Convention on Income and on Capital* (2017) (OECD, 2017).

b) the same persons participate directly or indirectly in the management, control or capital of an enterprise of a Contracting State and an enterprise of the other Contracting State,

and in either case conditions are made or imposed between the two enterprises in their commercial or financial relations which differ from those which would be made between independent enterprises, then any profits which would, but for those conditions, have accrued to one of the enterprises, but, by reason of those conditions, have not so accrued, may be included in the profits of that enterprise and taxed accordingly.

The 2017 Model Tax Treaty then provides for a corresponding adjustment to be made by the other country to prevent double taxation. For example, the tax authority in the selling country may raise the sales price for tax purposes in their country because they considered the original price was less than the arm's length price. The tax authority in the purchasing country should then use that same deemed price, with this increased purchase cost then reducing tax in the purchasing country. Article 9(2) of the 2017 Model Tax Treaty states the following rule:

2. Where a Contracting State includes in the profits of an enterprise of that State – and taxes accordingly – profits on which an enterprise of the other Contracting State has been charged to tax in that other State and the profits so included are profits which would have accrued to the enterprise of the first-mentioned State if the conditions made between the two enterprises had been those which would have been made between independent enterprises, then that other State shall make an appropriate adjustment to the amount of the tax charged therein on those profits. In determining such adjustment, due regard shall be had to the other provisions of this Convention and the competent authorities of the Contracting States shall if necessary consult each other.

Branches and Transfer Pricing

Transfer pricing rules relating to permanent establishments such as branches are also included in the OECD Model Tax Treaty. The business profits provision requires the determination of the profits of a permanent establishment as if it was a separate and independent enterprise. The 2017 OECD Model Tax Treaty Business Profits Article 7(1) and (2) provides as follows:[75]

1. Profits of an enterprise of a Contracting State shall be taxable only in that State unless the enterprise carries on business in the other Contracting State through a permanent establishment situated therein. If the enterprise carries on business as aforesaid, the profits that are attributable to the permanent establishment in accordance with the provisions of paragraph 2 may be taxed in that other State.
2. For the purposes of this Article and Article [23A] [23B], the profits that are attributable in each Contracting State to the permanent establishment referred to in paragraph 1 are the profits it might be expected to make, in particular in

75. OECD, *Model Tax Convention on Income and on Capital* (2017) (OECD, 2017).

> its dealings with other parts of the enterprise, if it were a separate and independent enterprise engaged in the same or similar activities under the same or similar conditions, taking into account the functions performed, assets used and risks assumed by the enterprise through the permanent establishment and through the other parts of the enterprise.

The 2017 Model Tax Treaty and the prior 2014 and 2010 Models include a significant development in the OECD approach, as this required analysis of the functions performed, assets used and risks assumed by the permanent establishment in determining its attributable profits.

Article 7(3) of 2017 Model Tax Treaty then requires a corresponding adjustment where transfer pricing adjustment has been made to the profits of the permanent establishment:

> 3. Where, in accordance with paragraph 2, a Contracting State adjusts the profits that are attributable to a permanent establishment of an enterprise of one of the Contracting States and taxes accordingly profits of the enterprise that have been charged to tax in the other State, the other State shall, to the extent necessary to eliminate double taxation on these profits, make an appropriate adjustment to the amount of the tax charged on those profits. In determining such adjustment, the competent authorities of the Contracting States shall if necessary consult each other.

Interest Expenses and Tax Treaties

The 2017 Model Tax Treaty includes transfer pricing provisions for specific types of income. For example, Article 11(6) can apply where related party interest expenses are too high, and can deny tax treaty protection for the excessive portion of interest as follows:[76]

> Where, by reason of a special relationship between the payer and the beneficial owner or between both of them and some other person, the amount of the interest, having regard to the debt-claim for which it is paid, exceeds the amount which would have been agreed upon by the payer and the beneficial owner in the absence of such relationship, the provisions of this Article shall apply only to the last-mentioned amount. In such case, the excess part of the payments shall remain taxable according to the laws of each Contracting State, due regard being had to the other provisions of this Convention.

The MAP

The MAP provision in Article 25(1) of the 2017 Model Tax Treaty can be used to try to resolve cases of double taxation through negotiation between the respective tax

76. OECD, *Model Tax Convention on Income and on Capital* (2017) (OECD, 2017).

authorities, for example where transfer pricing adjustments would otherwise cause unrelieved double tax:[77]

> Where a person considers that the actions of one or both of the Contracting States result or will result for him in taxation not in accordance with the provisions of this Convention, he may, irrespective of the remedies provided by the domestic law of those States, present his case to the competent authority of either Contracting State. The case must be presented within three years from the first notification of the action resulting in taxation not in accordance with the provisions of the Convention.

In practice, however, MAPs are not often effective, particularly where the respective tax authorities do not agree on essential matters such as the appropriate transfer pricing method.

THE GLAXOSMITHKLINE CASE

Figure 29.1 GlaxoSmithKline Case

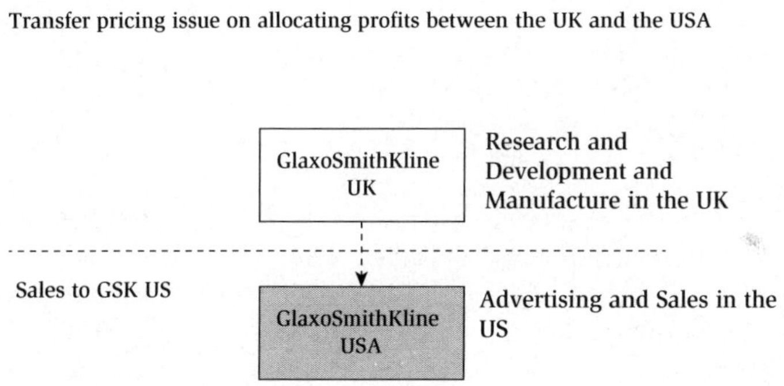

One of the most significant transfer pricing disputes was considered in the *GlaxoSmith-Kline* case,[78] which concerned the price at which the UK parent company GlaxoSmith-Kline PLC (GSK) sold pharmaceuticals to its US subsidiary. This issue included determining the value of the research and development and manufacturing of the product in the UK, compared to the advertising and sales marketing efforts made in the US.[79]

The US Internal Revenue Service (IRS) considered that 'embedded' marketing intangibles existed due to the advertising and marketing activities performed in the US, and that these marketing intangibles were economically owned by the US taxpayer. The IRS therefore adjusted the amount paid by the US taxpayer to the UK parent for the

77. *Ibid.*
78. *GlaxoSmithKline Holdings (Americas) Inc. v. Commissioner*, 117 T.C. No. 1 (2001).
79. Michael Kobetsky, *International Taxation of Permanent Establishments: Principles and Policy* (2011) 77.

pharmaceutical products to a much lower contract manufacturing basis, essentially based on a of markup on manufacturing costs.

In 2004, GlaxoSmithKline sued the IRS, claiming it should not have increased the US subsidiary's income by USD 7.8 billion (USD 4.5 billion for cost of goods sold, USD 1.9 billion for royalties, and USD 1.4 billion for interest) in relation to these intercompany transactions.

The IRS had asserted that the advertising and marketing activities were more valuable because the related product, called Zantac, was the second drug of its type to enter the market. The embedded marketing intangibles developed in the US should therefore substantially increase the profit allocation to the GSK subsidiary in the US. The taxpayer and the UK tax authorities (HMRC), however, considered that a much higher transfer price was reasonable, because the related research and development activities were was more valuable. In 2006, GSK and the IRS agreed to a USD 3.4 billion settlement, which was the largest tax settlement to that date for the IRS. The settlement was 60% of the total amount contested.

For planning purposes, there may have been scope to have the related research and development performed in a separate company with substantial commercial substance, and fees paid to this company for the use of the final product. This structural approach may, potentially, have reduced the amount of profit subject to the conflicting UK and US tax claims.

THE APA PROCESS

There are several steps to establishing an APA. The APA can include transfer pricing method, comparables, appropriate adjustments, and critical assumption as to future events. An APA may include agreement for specific transactions, groups of transactions, or on all transfer pricing issues, and may include agreement to resolve open issues of past years.

The use of an APA may not be an ideal situation where a company has reliable comparables which require only small adjustments. APAs are generally more appropriate for complex issues where significant adjustments are required to comparables, or where there are issues relating to intangible assets. APAs may also be used for cost sharing agreements, and allocating profits to permanent establishments such as branches.

Unilateral APAs are agreements between a taxpayer and one tax authority, whereas bilateral and multilateral APAs are agreements between the tax authorities in two or more countries respectively. There may be differences in country transfer pricing approaches which can prevent bilateral or multilateral APAs from being concluded. One country's tax authorities may, for example, attribute more value to product research and development, and another country's tax authorities may attribute more value to marketing activities.

APA Procedures in the US

In the US, Revenue Procedure 2006–9 generally provides that the following documentation is needed when a company requests an APA:[80]

- Taxpayer contact and identification details.
- The organisations, trades, businesses, and transactions that will be subject to the APA.
- A general description of the history of the business operations, worldwide organisational structure, ownership, capitalisation, financial arrangements, principal businesses, places of business, and major transaction flows for the parties.
- Representative financial and tax data of the parties for the last three years, including pertinent information and tax returns filed with the IRS, financial statements, annual reports, existing intercompany pricing agreements, marketing and financial studies, company accounting procedures, budget projections, business plans, and worldwide product line or business segment reports.
- The functional currency of each party and the currency in which payments between the parties are made for the transactions.
- A description of significant financial accounting methods and any significant differences between financial and tax accounting methods that have a direct bearing on the APA.
- Discussion of relevant statutory provisions, tax treaties, court decisions, regulations, revenue rulings, or procedures relating to the APA.
- An explanation of the taxpayer's and the IRS's respective positions on issues that are currently under audit, IRS appeals, litigation, or competent authority proceedings.

Documentation is then required to support the arm's length nature of the proposed transfer pricing method requested by the company in the APA application. This information includes:

- The measures of profitability and return on investment, such as gross profit margins, the ratio of gross income to operating expenses, net operating profit margins, or return on assets.
- A functional analysis describing the economic activities performed, assets employed, economic costs incurred, and risks assumed by the related parties.
- A list of competitors and discussion of any uncontrolled lines of business that may be comparable.
- A detailed presentation of criteria used to identify possible comparable transactions or similar businesses.
- A detailed explanation of any adjustment factors.

80. *Revenue Procedure 2006-9,* released 19 December 2005 (United States).

The guidelines for the APA process are principally set out in Revenue Procedure 2006–9 and the Proposed Revision of Procedures for Advance Pricing Agreements, Notice 2013-79.[81] The application process is generally as follows:

> The advance pricing and mutual agreement programme (APMA) of the IRS will meet with the taxpayer in a pre-filing conference prior to the filing of the APA request. APMA may require the taxpayer to submit a pre-filing memorandum. The meeting generally clarifies the data, documentation and analyses likely to be necessary, the suitability of the proposed transfer pricing method, and the procedure to be used for coordinating with IRS officials.
>
> The formal APA process is based on filing a written APA application, which will include financial information and related 'covered issue diagrams' including the group structure, explanation and functional analysis of the transactions under consideration, description of the proposed transfer pricing method, illustration of its application to prior years' financial and tax data, the economic analysis demonstrating why the proposed transfer pricing method is appropriate under the circumstances, copies of related intercompany agreements, and the proposed draft APA.
>
> The APA application is submitted to APMA, which then assigns a team leader to review the application and to negotiate with the taxpayer. The related procedures include APMA issuing case plans, conducting due diligence, and conveying APMA's views on the request to the taxpayer. Follow-up requests for information will generally be issued to the taxpayer, and meetings will be held to obtain information and negotiate the agreement. The APA team and the taxpayer should reach agreement on the transfer pricing method to be applied, and draft and execute the APA.

A bilateral APA can be available where a company is entitled to relief from double taxation under the MAP provisions of a tax treaty. The IRS may enter into an agreement with the foreign competent authority. Where the foreign entity is in a tax treaty jurisdiction, the IRS generally prefers negotiating a bilateral APA under Revenue Procedure 2004–40.[82] The related MAPs are set out in the Proposed Revision of Procedures for Requesting Competent Authority Assistance under Tax Treaties, Notice 2013-78.[83]

The APA request includes a list of critical assumptions, which are facts about the taxpayer, third parties or the industry that may significantly affect the terms of the APA. An APA may need to be renegotiated or terminated where a critical assumption contained in the APA is changed.

APMA may revoke the APA if it determines that there has been fraud, malfeasance or disregard by the taxpayer in connection with material facts in the APA request, in subsequent annual reports or in other taxpayer submissions, or where there has been a lack of good faith. The APA may be revised by agreement of the parties, which will include foreign competent authorities for bilateral and multilateral APAs. The

81. *Proposed Revision of Procedures for Advance Pricing Agreements*, Notice 2013-79, released on 22 November 2013 (United States).
82. *Revenue Procedure 2004–40*, released on 19 July 2004 (United States).
83. *Proposed Revision of Procedures for Requesting Competent Authority Assistance under Tax Treaties*, Notice 2013-78, released on 22 November 2013 (United States).

taxpayer may request the renewal of a current APA which can be based on an abbreviated request where the applicable law, facts and circumstances, economic conditions, and other factors are substantially unchanged.

The EU Common Approach

The EU Joint Forum on Transfer Pricing has developed a common approach for APA negotiations for EU Member States with an approximate time-table of eighteen months for APAs based on the following steps:

- Pre-filing and the formal application stage of three months.
- Evaluation and production of position papers of nine months.
- Competent authorities review each other's position papers in month thirteen.
- Negotiations finalised and the taxpayer consulted on the result in month seventeen.

The pre-filing stage is an informal discussion between the taxpayer and the tax authorities on the feasibility of the APA and the documentation required for the application. The information required includes the description of the activities and transactions covered, the transfer pricing methods to be applied, the countries involved, and the desired terms of the APA.

The application requires the documentation listed in the related country's APA regulations. The Best Practice document generally lists the related information and requires a functional analysis. The related documentation would include:

- The transactions covered.
- The group companies and permanent establishments concerned.
- The countries involved.
- The organisational structure.
- Financial information on the entities concerned.
- The related supply chain.
- A functional analysis.
- An industry analysis.
- The choice of the transfer pricing method.
- Analysis of selected comparables.
- The determination of the arm's length range.
- A comparison of transactions concerned with the selected comparables.
- The critical assumptions and effect of divergence.
- The related market conditions.
- The tax years to be covered.
- Demonstrations of compliance with applicable laws, treaty provisions and OECD Guidelines.

The tax authorities will then evaluate the proposal, request additional information, and conduct their own research on comparables. The authorities will then determine their view on applying the arm's length principle, and the required terms and conditions for the APA. Negotiations would then take place to agree on the APA terms and conditions.

The APA agreement may be unilateral, bilateral, or multilateral. The final APA agreements generally include critical assumptions, such as economic circumstances, the impact of potential changes in these assumptions, and the requirement to report changes in the assumptions. The APA will generally also include conditions to be met to enable the taxpayer to keep the APA valid, such as related record keeping and annual reporting requirements.

TRANSFER PRICING: MAP DEVELOPMENTS

The OECD BEPS measures included Action 14: Dispute Resolution include the following minimum standards relating to MAP:[84]

- Ensuring that treaty obligations related to the MAP are fully implemented in good faith and that MAP cases are resolved in a timely manner. This included the requirement that tax treaties contain a provision which requires competent authorities to endeavour to resolve by mutual agreement any difficulties or doubts arising as to the interpretation or application of their tax treaties.
- Ensuring the implementation of administrative processes that promote the prevention and timely resolution of treaty-related disputes. This included the requirement that tax treaties contain the related Article 25(1) of the OECD Model Tax Treaty. If the tax treaty does not permit a MAP request to be made to either Contracting Party and the competent authority who received the MAP request from the taxpayer does not consider the taxpayer's objection to be justified, the competent authority should implement a bilateral consultation or notification process which allows the other competent authority to provide its views on the case. The measures also include publication of clear rules, guidelines, and procedures on access to and use of the MAP.
- Ensuring that taxpayers can access the MAP when eligible. This included the requirement that tax treaties contain a provision which requires that the competent authority who receives a MAP request from the taxpayer shall endeavour, if the objection from the taxpayer appears to be justified and the competent authority is not itself able to arrive at a satisfactory solution, to resolve the MAP case by mutual agreement with the other competent authority, with a view to the avoidance of taxation which is not in accordance with the tax treaty.

The BEPS Action 14 measures include a peer review process for implementation of the dispute resolution measures, including identifying strengths and areas for improvement with information collected through questionnaire to assessed jurisdiction, peers, and taxpayers, and with the peer review report to be discussed and agreed

84. OECD, Action 14: Dispute Resolution, Making Dispute Resolution Mechanisms More Effective, (OECD 2015).

by the OECD Forum on Tax Administration (FTA) MAP Forum and adopted by the Inclusive Framework (IF) for publication.

The MAP measures were included in the BEPS Action 15 Report relating to the Multilateral Instrument,[85] and were then adopted in Articles 16 and 17 of the MLI.[86]

MAP AND COMPULSORY ARBITRATION PROCEDURES

MAP Arbitration Issues

The MAP in most tax treaties requires the competent authority of each state to negotiate in the event of double taxation. However the typical tax treaty, if viewed as a form of contract, generally lacks the essential terms for compulsory dispute resolution. This is a significant shortcoming, particularly with transfer pricing, where the respective states may not agree on the correct transfer pricing methodology, such as the in the *GlaxoSmithKline* case discussed above.[87]

The OECD have however included provisions for compulsory arbitration in Article 25(5) of the 2017 Model Tax Treaty as follows:

> 5. Where,
>
> a) under paragraph 1, a person has presented a case to the competent authority of a Contracting State on the basis that the actions of one or both of the Contracting States have resulted for that person in taxation not in accordance with the provisions of this Convention, and
>
> b) the competent authorities are unable to reach an agreement to resolve that case pursuant to paragraph 2 within two years from the date when all the information required by the competent authorities in order to address the case has been provided to both competent authorities,
>
> any unresolved issues arising from the case shall be submitted to arbitration if the person so requests in writing. These unresolved issues shall not, however, be submitted to arbitration if a decision on these issues has already been rendered by a court or administrative tribunal of either State. Unless a person directly affected by the case does not accept the mutual agreement that implements the arbitration decision, that decision shall be binding on both Contracting States and shall be implemented notwithstanding any time limits in the domestic laws of these States. The competent authorities of the Contracting States shall by mutual agreement settle the mode of application of this paragraph.

The principal issue is that these terms have not been adopted to date in most tax treaties, which are based on earlier versions of the Model Tax Treaty.

85. OECD, Developing a Multilateral Instrument to Modify Bilateral Tax Treaties, Action 15: 2015 Final Report (OECD, 2015).
86. Multilateral Convention to Implement Tax Treaty Related Measures to Prevent Base Erosion and Profit Shifting, opened for signature 7 June 2017.
87. *GlaxoSmithKline Holdings (Americas) Inc. v. Commissioner*, 117 T.C. No. 1 (2001).

EU Arbitration

A significant step forward in resolving transfer pricing disputes has been provided in the EU under the EU Arbitration Convention.[88] This provides a procedure which can resolve disputes and prevent double taxation. The procedure does not prevent transfer pricing adjustments by a EU country, however at least sixteen states have agreed to suspend tax collections during the dispute resolution procedure.

The provisions may not apply if there has been a final ruling, and 'serious penalties' have been imposed. Where the arbitration process applies, an advisory commission is established to resolve the case, and which can require the competent authorities to eliminate double taxation within six months of the commission's ruling.

The OECD BEPS Action Plan Arbitration Proposals

The OECD under the BEPS initiative released the Action 14 Final Report in 2015 Making Dispute Resolution Mechanisms More Effective. The intention is to address obstacles that prevent countries from solving treaty-related disputes under the MAP of Article 25 of the OECD Model Tax Treaty. Related comments by Deloitte noted that the key issue was mandatory binding arbitration to prevent double taxation, and that adoption of these measures has not been as broad as expected. Whilst extending the coverage of binding arbitration is generally the OECD's objective, one option is that countries with reservations on the use of binding arbitration may limit its scope, perhaps to certain articles of the treaty, or to exclude cases involving treaty or domestic anti-abuse rules. The two options for arbitration are: (a) the independent opinion approach based on the evidence presented and resulting in a written opinion from the arbitrator; and (b) the final offer approach where each competent authority presents their final offer for resolution, with reasons, and the arbitrator would select one outcome from the two offers presented.[89] Provisions for optional binding arbitration were included in the OECD BEPS Action 15 measures,[90] and in the MLI in Articles 18–26.[91]

88. *Convention on the Elimination of Double Taxation in Connection with the Adjustment of Profits of Associated Enterprises*, EU, 90/436/EEC.
89. Deloitte, United Kingdom, *BEPS Action 14: Make Dispute Resolution Mechanisms More Effective* (Deloitte Touche Tohmatsu Limited, 2014) <http://www2.deloitte.com/content/dam/Deloitte/ie/Documents/Tax> at June 2015.
90. OECD, Developing a Multilateral Instrument to Modify Bilateral Tax Treaties, Action 15: 2015 Final Report (OECD, 2015).
91. Multilateral Convention to Implement Tax Treaty Related Measures to Prevent Base Erosion and Profit Shifting, opened for signature 7 June 2017.

CHAPTER 30

Transfer Pricing Issues for Energy Production and Distribution

COMMODITY TRANSACTIONS

Transfer pricing provisions require that arm's length prices should be charged for commodity transactions such as oil, gas, coal and uranium sales between related parties. Generally, a reference for commodity pricing is established and available on computer trading systems. Oil and gas, for example, have published market prices as commodities, for example oil benchmark prices which include Brent Oil Crude, West Texas Intermediate (WTI), and Dubai Crude, and natural gas benchmark prices which include NYMEX Natural Gas and Henry Hub Natural Gas. These prices are quoted on the trader's electronic Bloomberg or Thomson Reuters screen.

Related transfer pricing issues include the following:

- Government licences including oil and gas production sharing contracts (PSCs) may specify an official sales price. This may be higher or lower than the market price, and the tax authorities in the other country may deem the market price to have been paid.
- The Norwegian Tax Administration calculates tax based on official oil sale prices. This causes significant issues for oil and gas companies which have used forward sales, and derived income less than the Norwegian official price used to calculate tax.

A group trading company should have purchases and sales with unrelated companies, in addition to the related party purchases and sales, together with local country directors, board meetings and trading staff, and sufficient capital to meet business risks. These measures should assist in establishing that the trading company carries on real trading activities and has commercial substance.

On this basis, there should also be transactions which are internal comparables to establish arm's length prices for purchases and sales to support the related party pricing used. The prices from third-party trading would establish comparable prices for the related party transactions.

Significant transfer pricing issues arise in practice, however, due to the different grades of oil and gas, and different delivery locations than the benchmark prices.

EXPLORATION SERVICES: SEISMIC SURVEYS AND GEOLOGICAL AND GEOPHYSICAL ANALYSIS

Exploration services are used to analyse potential commodity resources. Based on active seismic surveys to map underground structures, the surveys can include magnetic, gravity and passive seismic activities. The surveys are followed by geological and geophysical analysis (G&G) of the related data to determine potential resource structures and suggest locations for exploration and appraisal drilling.

Transfer pricing issues arise when companies seek to deduct these costs, or include the costs in cost oil under PSC regimes, when they are paid to related service companies in the group. Costs charged by a company's seismic and G&G team should be at arm's length, compared to services provided by independent contractors. However, the quality and type of these services can substantially differ.

Geological and geophysical experts may be located in the group parent country. The issue arises as to whether the exploration country tax authorities may consider that an excessive markup over costs was applied in the charges for these services. The group parent country may, however, consider that a higher markup over costs should have been used.

Transfer pricing defence files should demonstrate the markup is made at arm's length rates, or that the services are at similar prices to those used by independent contractors. For the larger oil, gas and mining companies, seismic and G&G services may be provided to or from third parties, and this may establish a strong comparable for the Comparable Uncontrolled Price (CUP) method. In other cases, the cost plus method may be more appropriate, especially where it is shown that any margin on the services is not excessive.

In upstream oil and gas, field operators may charge oil field partners and may establish comparable prices, especially where the other field partners have conducted related cost audits. Revenue authorities may use cost plus method based on an acceptable margin, or profit-based methods such as transaction net margin or profit split using comparison to similar companies' profit margins. The Norwegian Tax Administration may use a scale of hourly charges for experts, with limited variations for levels of knowledge and experience.

Exploration, appraisal and production drilling are significant costs for upstream operations. Exploration well costs may be particularly high, with the first Tupi offshore well in Brazil costing over USD 270 million. Transfer pricing issues arise when the local company is seeking to deduct these costs, or include the costs in cost oil under PSC regimes, when they are paid to related parties. The costs charged by the company's drilling team should be at arm's length, compared to services provided by independent contractors. There may be comparables as many drilling companies are independent. The oil and gas company may also use the services of independent companies, and may therefore establish comparable arm's length pricing. Drilling charges may vary however, depending on location, well depth, and geological formations.

FINANCIAL, COMPLETION AND ENVIRONMENTAL GUARANTEES

Financial guarantees may be given by a parent company to support its overseas subsidiary. This may, for example, be a guarantee by a parent company for a local bank loan, or a guarantee to a foreign government or national oil company for the financial obligations under an exploration or production licence. Arm's length price for financial guarantees can be established, and guarantees may be provided by several financial institutions for a fee, or may be indicated by the decrease in the interest rate on a loan.

It may be argued that the arm's length fee should be reduced for 'implicit support' of a parent company which would in many cases support its subsidiary without a guarantee, based on the *GE Capital Canada* case in 2011.[1] In this case, the court reduced a financial guarantee fee to 1%, on the basis that the parent company would provide 'implicit support' even without guarantee. The guarantee fee was therefore based on the interest rate difference between subsidiary credit ratings, less this implicit support.[2]

Completion guarantees relate to agreements to pay the whole or part of the debt of an energy construction or infrastructure project, such as a power station or electricity transmission network, until the project commences commercial operation.

Environmental guarantees may be given by a parent company to guarantee to pay costs in the event of a major environmental incident. The Greenland Government, for example, has required guarantees in excess of USD 1 billion for upstream oil and gas projects. The arm's length price of such guarantees may be difficult to determine as there are few commercial equivalents. Some companies may consider there is nominal value as the parent commercially must pay costs in a disaster, or lose its ability to obtain future licences in other countries.

TRANSFER PRICING AND PROCUREMENT

A group procurement company may purchase goods and services required by the multinational energy group, and then resell those goods and services to the various group companies. The group procurement company typically derives a profit margin which may be taxed in a low-taxing country. The related transfer pricing issue is what level of profit is appropriate for the procurement company. Tax authorities in the countries with group subsidiaries purchasing from the procurement company may

---

1. *The Queen v. General Electric Capital Canada Inc* 2010 FCA 344.
2. Anuschka Bakker & Marc M Levey, *Transfer Pricing and Intra-group Financing: The Entangled Worlds of Financial Markets and Transfer Pricing* (2012) p. 159.

adjust the related purchase prices downward, increasing local taxable profits, if the purchase prices are considered to exceed arm's length amounts.

The use of a group purchasing company was considered in *J S Ejendoms og Investeringsellskab*, TfS 1999, 950 in Denmark.[3] The purchasing function was transferred to the purchasing company, and 5% commission was received on these activities. The court held that there was no real business risk, and ignored the business transfer for transfer pricing purposes.[4]

The OECD considered group procurement companies in the OECD 2017 Transfer Pricing Guidelines.[5] The related example concerned a group procurement company which purchased in large volumes for the multinational group at substantial volume discounts. The OECD considered that the procurement company should receive a return based on its services of coordinating purchasing activity, rather than deriving the profit based on the amount of the discounts. The OECD commented:

> Company A, based solely on the negotiating leverage provided by the purchasing power of the entire group is able to negotiate with a supplier to reduce the price of widgets from USD 200 to USD 110. Under these circumstances, the arm's length price for the resale of widgets by Company A to other members of the group would not be at or near USD 200. Instead, the arm's length price would remunerate Company A for its services of coordinating purchasing activity. If the comparability and functional analysis suggests in this case that in comparable uncontrolled transactions involving a comparable volume of purchases, comparable coordination services resulted in a service fee based on Company A's costs incurred plus a mark-up equating to a total service fee of USD 6 per widget, then the intercompany price for the resale of the widgets by Company A would be approximately USD 116.

TRANSFER PRICING AND OIL, GAS, COAL, AND URANIUM TRADING

There may be scope to establish a group trading company in a low tax country such as Switzerland or Singapore. The trading company purchases commodities from related production companies, and then sells the commodities on the international market. The principal issue is whether significant profits can be booked in the trading company, where arm's length prices are charged for the commodity purchases from the related companies.

There was a review of issues relating to oil and gas trading in the United States (US) case of *Texaco, Inc and Subsidiaries v. Comr of Internal Revenue*,[6] involving Chevron, Exxon, Mobil, and Texaco. The case concerned sales by US oil companies to foreign subsidiaries at prices set by the Saudi Arabian government. The result was the sale of oil without markup from the companies' branches in Saudi Arabia, which was

3. J.S Ejendoms og Investeringsellskab, TfS 1999, 950.
4. Jens Wittendorff, *Transfer Pricing and the Arm's Length Principle in International Tax Law* (2010) p. 159.
5. OECD Transfer Pricing Guidelines for Multinational Enterprises and Tax Administrations, 2017, Chapter I, para. 1.168, p. 93.
6. *Texaco, Inc and Subsidiaries v. Comr of Internal Revenue* (No. 95-60696) (US Ct of Apps (5th cir), 17 October 1996).

subject to US tax, to foreign subsidiaries which were not subject to US tax. The IRS claimed over USD 6.5 billion in tax by adjusting the sale price to market prices. In 1993 the Tax Court decision was made in favour of the oil companies as the price was required under the oil companies' respective agreements with Saudi Arabia. The decision was affirmed by the Court of Appeal in 1996. The IRS petitioned the Supreme Court to hear a further appeal which the Supreme Court declined in 1997.[7]

The use of a group trading company was considered by the Swedish courts in the *Shell Sweden* case,[8] which concerned sales by a Shell United Kingdom trading company to a related group company in Sweden. The issue was whether a normal trading commission should be derived in the trading company, or only an administrative fee, for example of two cents per barrel. The Swedish Supreme Court of Administrative Appeal held that the United Kingdom (UK) trading company was entitled to a significant trading margin. The trading company purchased oil and gas from independent sources, such as state-owned oil producers, as well as from related parties, and the company carried real trading risk. The Court also considered that security and flexibility of supply also justified the higher price paid to the trading company.[9]

There may be scope for increasing the profits of a group trading company with the use of derivatives. Derivatives are generally instruments which are based on another asset. For example, an option to sell shares at a certain price, known as a put option, is a derivative based on the underlying shares. In oil and gas trading, derivatives used include forward contracts, which are frequently used to sell oil or gas at an agreed price at a future date. The use of forward contracts may be made on a speculative basis to attempt to increase profits, or as a hedging strategy to stabilise prices. The trading desk may increase profit margins in a tax effective location using derivatives such as the forward sale of oil and gas.

The Danish courts considered the group trading company in the *Texaco Denmark* case,[10] which concerned sales by a Texaco company to a related Texaco local country seller in Denmark. The issues included whether the long-term contracts used for the sales were a benefit to the overseas supplier, and so purchase costs for Danish subsidiary should be reduced below spot prices, increasing Danish taxable profit. The Court did not decide on this specific issue however the spot prices were accepted in the case.[11]

Danish courts also considered spot versus forward prices in the BP Denmark case (*BP Case*, TfS 1988, 292 (Denmark)).[12] The Danish Tax Office considered that spot prices should be used to give higher Danish taxable profits. The Court agreed with BP

7. Reuven S Avi-Yonah, *International Tax as International Law* (2007) p. 122.
8. *Shell Sweden case* (RÅ 1991 Ref 107).
9. Jens Wittendorff, *Transfer Pricing and the Arm's Length Principle in International Tax Law* (2010) p. 385.
10. *Texaco Case*, TfS 1987, 60.
11. Jens Wittendorff, *Transfer Pricing and the Arm's Length Principle in International Tax Law* (2010) p. 136.
12. *BP Case*, TfS 1988, 292.

that long-term contract prices should be different to spot prices due to the certainty of supply.[13]

ENERGY AND GLOBAL VALUE CHAINS

Global value chains are relevant in many respects for energy production and distribution. A common example is where an integrated oil and gas business conducts upstream oil and gas exploration and production (E&P) activities, midstream transportation activities, and downstream refining and distribution activities. The global value chain analysis seeks to allocate profits to the respective entities based on their respective function, assets, and risks (FAR) contributions.

Each of the transfer pricing methods may potentially be used in the transfer pricing analysis of global value chain. Where there is a closely integrated business there has been particular discussion on the use of the transactional profit split method.

The OECD BEPS Action Plan 10 provides for proposed changes to the transfer pricing rules in relation to global value chains used by multinational enterprises (MNE), based on the full range of firms' activities, from the conception of a product to its end use and beyond, including activities such as design, production, marketing, distribution, and support to the final consumer. The Action Plan was as follows:

> Action 10 – Assure that transfer pricing outcomes are in line with value creation/other high-risk transactions. This relates to addressing transactions that would generally not occur between third parties, including adopting related characterisation rules, applying transfer pricing methods in global value chains, and base eroding payments such as management fees and head office expenses.

The OECD Public Discussion Draft on global value chains was released in February 2015 in relation to the circumstances in which the application of a transactional profit split method is likely to be appropriate, and the ways in which the factors used to split the profits can align profits and value creation. The Discussion Draft examined the circumstances where the transactional profit split method may be more appropriate than other transfer pricing methods:[14]

> A global value chain is likely to involve extensive and varied functions involving many enterprises and multiple transactions; there seems to be very little experience of using a transactional profit split method in a way that could appropriately and comprehensively reflect the range of contributions to value in a diverse value chain. The fact that an MNE group disseminates its value chain amongst a number of enterprises in different jurisdictions does not imply that transactional profit split methods will be necessary or appropriate to benchmark arm's length returns for those enterprises. In many cases, the structure of the MNE group's value chain will allow the identification of relatively discrete, stand-alone elements which can be reliably priced using one-sided methods.

---

13. Jens Wittendorff, *Transfer Pricing and the Arm's Length Principle in International Tax Law* (2010) p. 333.
14. OECD, *Public Discussion Draft, BEPS Action 10: Discussion Draft on the Use of Profit Splits in the Context of Global Value Chains*, 16 December 2014–6 February 2015 <www.oecd.org/ctp/transfer-pricing/discussion-draft-action-10-profit-splits-global-value-chains.pdf>.

> However, there seems to be some experience of using transactional profit splits to address challenges posed by specific features of global value chains, in a way that one-sided transfer pricing methods may be less well equipped to do … . One-sided methods may not be able to account reliably for the interdependence of the key functions and risks, or for the synergies and benefits created by such integration. In such cases transactional profit split methods may be an appropriate means of determining an arm's length outcome, which takes into account the specific contributions of the parties to value creation.

The Discussion Draft suggested significant support for profit split methods for transfer pricing relating to global value chains used by many multinational groups engaged in manufacturing and distribution. The Discussion Draft was particularly significant in developing profit allocation keys such that transfer pricing outcomes are aligned with value creation. The concept of value creation is based on identifying the real economic contributions to total profits in the global value chain, and so allocating the greater tax revenue depending on the real contributions made by the respective companies in different countries.

The OECD released a Public Discussion Draft – Revised Guidance on Profit Splits in 2017.[15] This included draft guidance on how to accurately delineate the actual transaction between the associated enterprises, including an understanding of the broader context of the value chain to which they contribute, the requirement to select the most appropriate transfer pricing method to the circumstances of the case, and relevant guidance on identifying and evaluating intangibles. The OECD draft guidance included comments on the potential strengths and weaknesses transactional profit split method, including:

- The main strength of the transactional profit split method is that it can offer a solution for cases where both parties to a transaction make unique and valuable contributions (e.g., contribute unique and valuable intangibles) to the transaction. In such a case independent parties might effectively share the profits of the transaction in proportion to their respective contributions, making a two-sided method more appropriate.
- The transactional profit split method can also provide a solution for highly integrated operations in cases for which a one-sided method would not be appropriate.
- Another strength of the transactional profit split method is that it offers flexibility by taking into account specific, possibly unique, facts and circumstances of the associated enterprises that are not present in independent enterprises. Moreover, where there is a high degree of uncertainty for each of the parties in relation to a transaction, for example in transactions involving the shared assumption of economically significant risks by all parties, the flexibility of the transactional profit split method can allow for the determination of arm's length profits for each party that vary with the actual outcomes of the risks associated with the transaction.
- A further strength of the transactional profit split method is that both parties to the transaction are directly evaluated as part of the pricing of the transaction.
- A weakness of the transactional profit split method relates to difficulties in its application. On first review, the transactional profit split method may appear

15. BEPS Action 10, Revised Guidance on Profit Splits, 22 June–15 September 2017.

> readily accessible to both taxpayers and tax administrations because it tends to rely less on information about independent enterprises. However, associated enterprises and tax administrations alike may have difficulty accessing information from foreign affiliates. In addition, it may be difficult to measure the relevant revenue and costs for all the associated enterprises participating in the controlled transactions, which could require stating books and records on a common basis and making adjustments in accounting practices and currencies. Further, when the transactional profit split method is applied to operating profit, it may be difficult to identify the appropriate operating expenses associated with the transactions and to allocate costs between the transactions and the associated enterprises' other activities. Identifying the appropriate profit splitting factors can also be challenging.

One essential issue is whether different countries will agree to the processes used in global value chains, and therefore assign similar profits to the respective activities in each country, or may disagree on the processes involved or their value. One example of this issue is the *GlaxoSmithKline* case discussed above,[16] where there was disagreement of the value of the respective activities performed. The analysis of global value chains and the application of transactional profit split methods may require more effective arbitration procedures, as proposed by the OECD, to prevent double taxation.

On this basis the use of the transactional profit split method offers one approach to determining arm's length profits for enterprises in a global value chain, however this is generally perceived by the OECD as where both parties to a transaction make unique and valuable contributions such as intangibles, or for highly integrated operations.

16. *GlaxoSmithKline Holdings (Americas) Inc. v. Commissioner*, 117 TC No. 1 (2001).

CHAPTER 31

Intangibles and Transfer Pricing

THE OECD AND INTANGIBLES

This chapter considers the most significant transfer pricing issues relating to intangible property (IP). Intangible assets can be defined as assets that lack physical substance, such as patents, copyrights, franchises, goodwill, trademarks, and trade names. The OECD defined intangibles to be business rights associated with commercial activities which include:

- Marketing intangibles, such as trademarks and trade names connected with the exploitation of a product, customer lists, distribution channels, unique names, symbols, and pictures.
- Trade intangibles, such as patents, know how, designs, models, and computer software.

It is possible to transfer intangible property by making a contribution to a business, by sale of the intangible, or by licensing another to use the intangible. The owner of the intangible property can charge a royalty for use on an exclusive licence basis, allowing the licensee to have sole use in their country or region, or can charge a royalty for the non-exclusive use of the intangible property, which allows the owner to grant licences to other parties.

The transfer pricing issue is that the transfer or provision of intangible property to related parties should be made for arm's length consideration.

The OECD Guidelines

The OECD Transfer Pricing Guidelines 2017 comment that the arm's length principle requires that all members of the group receive appropriate compensation for any functions they perform, assets they use, and risks they assume in connection with the development, enhancement, maintenance, protection, and exploitation of intangibles.[1] This is done using a functional analysis establishing which members perform and exercise control over development, enhancement, maintenance, protection, and exploitation functions, which members provide funding and other assets, and which members assume the various risks associated with the intangible.

Considerations connected with the valuation of intangibles can include:

- The expected benefits from the use of the intangibles.
- Any limitation of the geographic area for use of the intangible under the related sale or licensing agreements.
- Any export restrictions on the use of the intangibles.
- Whether the related use is of an exclusive or non-exclusive character.
- Any capital investment made.
- The related start-up expenses and development work required.
- Whether the related agreements allow the possibility of sub-licensing.
- The licensee's distribution network.
- Whether there are any rights to participate in further development of the intangibles.

The OECD Transfer Pricing Guidelines considered that the principal factors affecting the valuation of intangibles would include the product nature, degree, and duration of protection, period of economic value, and the value the process contributes to the company's profits. For marketing intangibles such as trademarks in particular, the OECD considered that these factors also include consumer acceptability, geographical significance, market shares, and the sales volume related to the use of the intangibles.

In relation to transfer pricing methods, the comparable uncontrolled price method can potentially be used to determine the pricing for transfers or licensing of intangibles where same owner has transferred or licensed a comparable intangible under comparable circumstances to an independent party. The comparable uncontrolled price and resale price methods may potentially be used for arm's length pricing for the sale of goods which incorporating significant intangibles. The profit split method may be used where both parties to a transaction contribute valuable intangibles and where there are no effective comparable transactions.

United States Regulations for Intangibles

The United States (US) transfer pricing regulations require the selection of the best transfer pricing method.[2] Regulation 1.482-4 on intangibles includes the comparable uncontrolled transaction, comparable profit, and profit split methods. The comparable uncontrolled transaction method may be used where there is a high degree of comparability for related transactions. In cases where may be no exactly comparable

1. OECD Transfer Pricing Guidelines 2017, para. 6.48.
2. 26 CFR 1.482-1 – Allocation of income and deductions among taxpayers.

transactions, other comparables may be accepted to determine royalties in the 25%–75% inter-quartile range of results.

The comparable profit method can be used for intangibles where there is sufficient information on operating profits of similar businesses available. In general at least 50% of the income attributable to the related intangibles should be retained by licensee of the intangible.

The profit split method may be applied where both parties to a transaction have contributed intangibles which are in practice difficult to value, under regulation 1.482–6T. The regulations require that the profit relating to the routine contributions of the related parties is first calculated, which can be derived from similar contributions by unrelated parties. The remaining residual profit after deducting these routine contributions relates to the intangibles, and this residual profit is allocated as the profit split between the parties to the transaction.

Royalty Arrangements

In relation to royalty payments, the OECD Guidance on Transfer Pricing Aspects of Intangibles issued under Action Plan 8 of the Base Erosion and Profit Shifting (BEPS) Action Plan in 2014 identified the following factors relevant in determining the comparability of royalties arrangements:[3]

- Exclusivity.
- Extent and duration of legal protection.
- Geographic scope.
- Useful life.
- Stage of development.
- Rights to enhancements, revisions, and updates.
- Expectation of future benefit.
- Comparison of risk.

There are certain databases available which contain details of the royalty arrangements used by a large number of companies. RoyaltyStat is an example of such a database, and includes over 6,000 agreements filed with the US Securities Exchange Commission (SEC). The database software allows searches for royalties used in specific industries based on their related Standard Industrial Classification (SIC) codes. The database includes copies of the related agreements, together with information on intangible transfers and related pricing. The related website is www.royaltystat.com.

3. OECD *Guidance on Transfer Pricing Aspects of Intangibles*, (OECD, 2014) <www.oecd-ilibrary.org/docserver/download/2314291e.pdf>.

The Residual Profit Issue

Figure 31.1 Residual Profit and Deemed Royalties

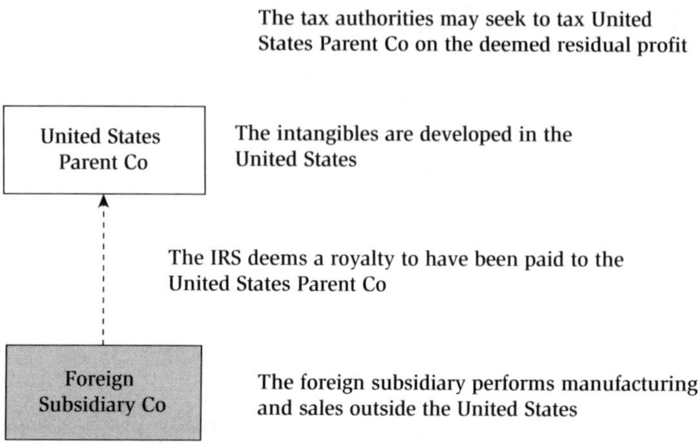

The above structure concerns the use of a residual profit approach which may be used by tax authorities. In this case, the Foreign Subsidiary Co's profits are adjusted downward to a deemed income based on its related costs plus a margin, for the manufacturing and sales activities performed in that country. The residual profit is deemed to relate to intangibles provided by the US Parent Co.

In this case the US Parent Co may be taxed in the US on an arm's length royalty notionally paid by the Foreign Subsidiary Co based on the deemed profit arising under the residual profit approach.

The principal issue is whether the deemed royalty is reasonable based on the nature of the intangible property transferred and the related terms and conditions. There may be a need to consider potential transfer pricing defences in relation to this type of audit outcome, which resulted in US deemed taxable royalty income, with no corresponding foreign tax deduction. Tax audits may deem a high level of royalty income to be derived in respect of intangibles, particularly where the value of other parts of the related party dealings, such as the manufacturing performed in this example by the Foreign Subsidiary Co, are calculated on a cost plus basis.

One approach to this issue is to establish the strongest transfer pricing basis for an arm's length royalty, rather than any approach based on the residual profits in the foreign country. This may, for example, include the use of the comparative profit method, on the basis that the profit margins of comparative entities provide the best method of determining an arm's length royalty rate.

INTELLECTUAL PROPERTY IN ENERGY PRODUCTION AND DISTRIBUTION

Energy Industries and Trademarks

Multinational energy groups frequently use technology which is subject to patents, ranging from technology used in upstream oil and gas and mining activities, to the technology used in power stations and electricity distribution networks. This process has been accelerating in recent times, including the current emphasis on new renewable energy technologies.

Energy companies may also have a high value on intangible property such as trademarks, on the basis that retail energy markets may have significantly higher prices for energy companies with well-known trademarks. The parent company's tax authorities may argue for taxation based on a related deemed royalty. A local country tax office would however generally limit deductions to any trademark royalties which were actually paid.

Energy group companies may have significant proprietary intangible property, and the tax authorities in the parent country may therefore seek to tax:

- Profits relating to manufacturing processes and patents.
- Profits relating to the use of valuable trademarks.
- Profits relating to customer intangibles such as the customer base and marketing relationships.

There may be scope to limit the potential tax exposures by using a group intangible property holding company, particularly for new intangible property, in country with limited tax on royalty income. Capital gains or exit taxes may mean that it may not be effective to move existing intangible property from a high taxing country.

Royalties paid for the use of various types of energy technology within a multinational group are often structured so that only one royalty is generally paid on all technology intangible property, and there are generally no separate royalty charges for each individual piece of intangible property.

THE TRANSFER OF IP AND OECD GUIDELINES

The OECD has been developing guidelines relating to the transfer of intangibles,[4] and issued a Revised Discussion Draft in July 2013.[5] The OECD considered several issues which may substantially affect tax on transfers.[6]

---

4. Discussion Draft of its revision of Chapter VI, Special Considerations for Intangible Property, of the OECD Transfer Pricing Guidelines, <http://www.oecd.org/ctp/transfer-pricing/50526258.pdf>.
5. OECD, *Revised Discussion Draft on Transfer Pricing Aspects of Intangibles*, <http://www.oecd.org/ctp/transfer-pricing/revised-discussion-draft-intangibles.pdf>.
6. PriceWaterhouseCoopers, *OECD Releases Highly Anticipated Draft of Intangibles Transfer Pricing Guidelines*, 22 June 2012, <http://www.pwc.com/en_US/us/washington-national-tax/newsletters/wnts/assets/pwc-oecd-draft-intangibles-transfer-pricing-guidelines.pdf>.

The OECD considered that goodwill and going concern value, which may not be transferable separately from other business assets, may have a significant impact on determining arm's length compensation, and should therefore be treated as intangibles for transfer pricing purposes. Intangible property ownership should be based on the performance and control of the important functions related to the development, enhancement, maintenance, and protection of the intangible, and bearing the necessary costs and risks. Accordingly where a party passively bears costs related to the intangible property, but does not control the risks or related critical functions, then the OECD considered that ownership should not be attributable to that party.

It is interesting that the OECD cautioned against the adoption of a transfer pricing methodology that 'too readily assumes that all residual profit from transactions after routine returns' should necessarily accrue to the owner of the intangibles or the party entitled to the returns on the intangibles. The OECD calls for a 'thorough understanding of the group's value chain, business process and its interaction with its IP'.

In the Guidelines, the OECD did not endorse or prefer any specific valuation or financial evaluation method. The OECD cautioned that valuations made for accounting purposes may not be relevant for transfer pricing purposes. The OECD reviewed the use of discounted cash flows for valuing intangible property, and highlighted several issues for consideration, including:[7]

- Financial projections should not be extended in time beyond the point where a business enterprise can reasonably forecast its results and can question the reliability of related assumptions of growth.
- The projections need to account for business cycles and other fluctuations relating to the experience of the company and the industry.
- The discount rates used need to reflect the risks which are associated with the related cash flows.

One potentially effective approach to group intangible property may be to use a cost contribution arrangement, where group companies contribute to the development of intangible property in return for the right to use this property in their respective countries, or a contract R&D arrangement, where a central intangible management company contracts with related companies in the group and with third parties to produce new intangible property. There may also be opportunities to transfer intangible property on a merger or acquisition, particularly where any potential tax on the transfer of the intangible property may be offset by the use of carry-forward tax losses in the transferring company.

7. Shanto Ghosh, John Wells & Todd Wolosoff, *Discussion Draft: OECD's Discussion Draft on Intangibles, A Positive Step Forward,* Intl. Tax Rev., Supplement, 17 December 2012, <http://www.internationaltaxreview.com/IssueArticle/3132168/Supplements/Discussion-draft-OECDs-discussion-draft-on-intangibles-A-positive-step-forward.html?supplementListId=87533>.

OECD TRANSFER PRICING GUIDELINES AND BUSINESS RESTRUCTURES

A very significant change in the OECD 2017 Transfer Pricing Guidelines was the inclusion of guidance on business restructures which have an economic transfer of profit potential.[8] The Guidelines now specifically apply transfer pricing to a broad definition of business restructuring, which include:

- cross-border transfers of something of value, e.g., of valuable intangibles; and
- termination or substantial renegotiation of existing arrangements, e.g., manufacturing arrangements, distribution arrangements, licences, and service agreements.

The Guidelines therefore apply transfer pricing to the cessation of activities in one country and their commencement in another country. This provides support for countries to apply exit taxes on business restructures which transferred the profit potential of activities such as R&D to another country, including where there has been no express transfer of the related activities.

THE OECD BEPS MEASURES AND INTANGIBLES: ACTIONS 8–10

The OECD BEPS Actions 8–10 measures included the following developments which can potentially apply to international IP planning structures:

- Returns not based on mere ownership of IP – This measure provides that merely having ownership of IP in a tax effective location will not mean that the related profits should be derived in that location. The OECD commented that other members of the legal owner's multinational enterprise (MNE) group may have performed functions, used assets, or assumed risks that are expected to contribute to the value of the intangible. The revised approach is that the ultimate allocation of the returns derived by the MNE group from the exploitation of intangibles, and the ultimate allocation of costs and other burdens related to intangibles among members of the MNE group, is to be accomplished by compensating members of the MNE group for functions performed, assets used, and risks assumed (FAR) in the development, enhancement, maintenance, protection, and exploitation of intangibles.[9]
- Charges based on costs of intangible development are discouraged – The OECD considered that there rarely is any correlation between the cost of developing intangibles and their value or transfer price once developed. The relevant considerations should include the functions performed, assets used, and risks assumed by the respective parties to the transaction, business reasons for engaging in the transaction, perspectives of and options realistically available to each of the parties to the transaction, competitive advantages

8. OECD 2017 Transfer Pricing Guidelines, Chapter IX, p. 369.
9. OECD BEPS Action 8-10 Final Report 2015, p. 73.

conferred by the intangibles including especially the relative profitability of products and services or potential products and services related to the intangibles, expected future economic benefits from the transaction, and other comparability factors such as features of local markets, location savings, assembled workforce, and MNE group synergies.[10]

OECD BEPS ACTION 13: CbC REPORTING

The BEPS Action 13 Country-by-Country (CbC) reporting measures may impact the use of group IP entities. As discussed, the CbC reports generally include these entities under the Main Business Activity heading in the Holding or Managing Intellectual Property category, with related information including related and unrelated party revenues, profits before tax, income tax paid, and number of employees. This may result in follow-up analysis based on additional information which can include whether profits allocated to such IP entities are commensurate with the functions performed, assets used, and risks undertaken by these entities. The CbC measures were adopted in the 2017 OECD Transfer Pricing Guidelines.[11]

HARD-TO-VALUE INTANGIBLES

The BEPS Action 8–10 measures provided for the development of transfer pricing rules for transfers of hard-to-value intangibles (HTVI) aimed at preventing BEPS by moving intangibles among group members.[12] The approach to pricing hard-to-value intangibles allows the taxpayer to demonstrate that its pricing is based on a thorough transfer pricing analysis and leads to an arm's length outcome, while the approach at the same time protects the tax administrations from the negative effects of information asymmetry. It does so by ensuring that tax administrations can consider after the fact, ex-post outcomes as presumptive evidence about the appropriateness of the before the event, ex-ante pricing arrangements, and the taxpayer cannot demonstrate that the uncertainty has been appropriately taken into account in the pricing methodology adopted.

The OECD released the related discussion draft in 2017 on hard to value intangibles, which is intended to assist tax jurisdictions that are implementing rules on hard-to-value-intangibles for transfer pricing purposes. The guidance should address the information imbalance between taxpayers and tax administrations. The proposed approach to pricing HTVI should follow these principles:[13]

10. OECD BEPS Action 8–10 Final Report 2015, p. 99.
11. OECD Transfer Pricing Guidelines for Multinational Enterprises and Tax Administrations, 2017, Chapter V, p. 233.
12. BEPS Action 8–10 on aligning transfer pricing outcomes with value creation, Final Report 2015, p. 109.
13. KPMG, OECD Discussion Draft on HTVI, 31 May 2017.

- Tax administrations can consider after-the-fact outcomes as presumptive evidence about the appropriateness of the original transfer pricing arrangements.
- The tax administration should not evaluate a taxpayer's actual income or cash flows without considering what the probability of achieving that income or cash flow was at time that the HTVI were transferred.
- If a revised valuation shows that the intangible was transferred at an undervalued or overvalued amount compared to the arm's length price, then the revised value of the transferred intangible may be assessed for tax, taking into account contingent payments and price adjustment clauses, irrespective of the payment profiles asserted by the taxpayer.
- Tax administrations should apply audit practices to ensure that presumptive evidence based on after-the-fact outcomes are identified and acted upon as early as possible.

The guidance therefore offers greater flexibility in related intangible valuations, particularly by looking at results after transfers of intangibles to review their correct valuation at the time of transfer because tax administrations can consider after-the-fact outcomes for the appropriateness of the before the event pricing arrangements. The after the event analysis for HTVI is included in the 2017 Transfer Pricing Guidelines.[14]

14. OECD Transfer Pricing Guidelines for Multinational Enterprises and Tax Administrations, 2017, Chapter V, p. 308.

CHAPTER 32

Intra-group Services, Cost Contribution Arrangements, and Transfer Pricing

INTRODUCTION

A significant issue for all multinational energy groups is how to charge subsidiary companies for many of the supporting services which are performed by the parent and other related companies. Transfer pricing rules require that an arm's length fee should be charged for all services provided between related parties. The services provided by a parent company, for example, are likely to include:

- Administration functions, such as accounting and budget services, payroll support, human resources services, and employee training.
- Commercial functions, such as product marketing.

Transfer pricing rules require companies to identify services with related parties, including services provided in multiple countries, and then determine and document the related arm's length fee for these services. The services which can be provided by the parent company to related companies may include:

- Management and control.
- Government, shareholder, and public relations.
- Project evaluation and approval.
- Accounting and finance.
- Performance evaluation.
- Technical and information technology services.
- Management of know-how, administration of patents, and licences.
- Procurement of commodities, goods and services.
- Leasing of assets for use in the business.
- Management and distribution of goods.
- Engineering support.

- Human resource services including recruitment and training.
- Financial services including group treasury functions.
- Fund raising with bond and capital issues.
- Legal and tax services including compliance and advice.
- Advertising of products.
- Research and development for new products.

There is an issue where certain services provided by a parent company relate to the parent company's role as a shareholder in subsidiary companies, and where the benefit of these services may actually be derived by the parent company itself. This issue typically relates to shareholder functions, which include directors and shareholder meetings, funding to invest in the subsidiary, performance and quality control, and group financial reporting. It is arguable that no charge should be made for services which are entirely for the parent company's benefit.

THE DOW SVERIGE CASE AND HEAD OFFICE CHARGES

Figure 32.1 Dow Sverige Case

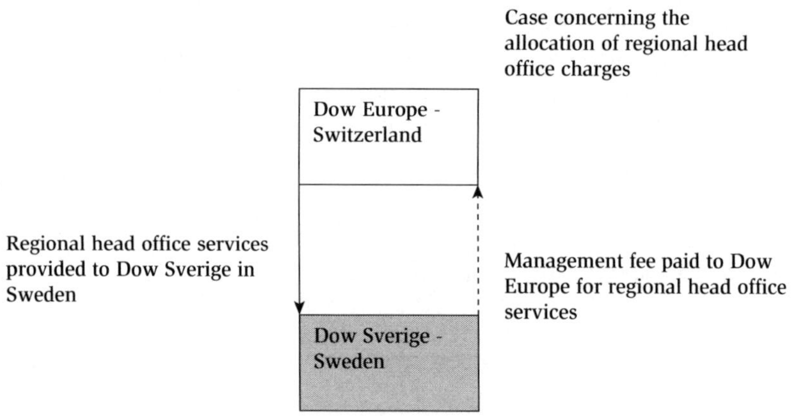

Overview

The basis of charging head office services was considered in the *Dow Sverige* case,[1] Management fees were paid by Dow Sverige A.B. in Sweden for marketing, production, administrative, human resources, and management services provided by Dow Europe, the regional head office company which was located in Switzerland.

The basis used by Dow Europe to determine the fee charged was an indirect allocation of related costs, based on net sales for marketing services, production results for production services, accounts receivable for administrative services, and the

1. *Dow Sverige AB*, Supreme Administrative Court, SAC ruling 7338-7339-01.

number of personnel for human resources services, which were then charged to Dow Sverige and other related companies with a cost plus 10% markup.

The Swedish Supreme Court held that the transfer pricing policy adopted by the group was reasonable, that allocated costs were proportionate for the businesses concerned, and that the 10% markup margin was acceptable.[2]

Cost-plus markups rarely exceed from about 10% to 12%, and a more common range is currently from about 5% to 8%, as the related benchmark examples generally do not support higher percentages. The rules can vary in different countries, for example Brazil allows, the charge for imported services should not be higher than the costs incurred plus a 20% markup.

INDIRECT CHARGES AND USE OF ALLOCATION KEYS

A summary of the related issues concerning the selection of allocation keys, together with several related examples, was made by the Canada Revenue Agency (CRA) in transfer pricing memorandum TPM-15:[3]

> 35. The CRA states, in paragraph 171 of IC87-2R, that 'When choosing an allocation key ... the taxpayer should consider the nature and use made of the service.'
> 36. Auditors should refrain from accepting the proportion of sales revenues as a single allocation basis for management fees. Sales can vary greatly from year to year, which can lead to wide fluctuations in the amount of group costs allocated when there has been little change in the benefits received. It may be preferable to implement a multiple allocation basis for intra-group services to better reflect the benefits received. It is not necessary to select a different allocation basis for each department, but a certain degree of aggregation of similar transactions may improve the reliability of the allocation. For example, time spent could be an appropriate allocation basis to allocate costs of the tax services, legal services, data processing, and the usage cost of a corporate jet, while the number of employees may be an appropriate basis on which to allocate the costs of the human resources department. In the same light, sales may be an appropriate allocation basis for advertising expenditures. The use of two or more allocation keys would reflect the diversity of the intra-group services allocated and allow for a more comprehensive matching of costs to the benefits received.

This transfer pricing memorandum is an interesting example of the current approach of one revenue authority, including the discussion of time spent, number of employees, and sales as allocation keys for specific expenses, and the acceptance of the use of two or more allocation keys to reflect the diversity of intra-group services.

---

2. Pim Fris & Sébastien Gonnet, NERA Economic Consulting, *The Emergence of a European Dimension for Transfer Pricing*, 25, <http://www.nera.com/extImage/PUB_European_Dimension_TP1373.pdf>.
3. Canada Revenue Agency, TPM-15, *Intra-group Services and Section 247 of the Income Tax Act*, 29 January 2015, <http://www.cra-arc.gc.ca/tx/nnrsdnts/cmmn/trns/tpm15-eng.html>.

OECD 2017 TRANSFER PRICING GUIDELINES AND ALLOCATION KEYS

The 2017 OECD Transfer Pricing Guidelines include the direct charging of costs, where a company charges for the specific services which have been provided to particular group companies. Direct charging was considered to be preferred compared with indirect charging, where a proportion of total expenses is allocated and charged to related companies based on factors such as operating profit of each company or the number of employees. Indirect charging is generally not permitted where the services concerned are a main business activity of the company and these services are provided to third parties.[4]

There may be internal comparable prices for use with the comparable uncontrolled price method, particularly where similar services are provided to unrelated parties. There may also be external comparable prices available for services which are available on the market, such as accounting, legal, and information technology support services.

The cost plus method may be the most appropriate method where there are no internal comparables, and this is the most common method in practice. It is generally necessary to establish an arm's length markup when charging for these services.

The Guidelines also provide for indirect charging for services which do not form a main business activity, and require that regard is given to the value of the services to recipient, and whether comparable services are provided between independent enterprises.

Indirect charging should generally be used where the value of the services to the related entities cannot be quantified except by using an estimation, and where separate reporting of services for each recipient would involve a disproportionate burden.

The Guidelines provide comments on the use of direct and indirect charging. In relation to direct charging the OECD commented:

> 7.21 In certain cases, the arrangements made for charging for intragroup services can be readily identified. These cases are where the MNE group uses a direct-charge method, i.e. where the associated enterprises are charged for specific services. In general, the direct-charge method is of great practical convenience to tax administrations because it allows the service performed and the basis for the payment to be clearly identified. Thus, the direct-charge method facilitates the determination of whether the charge is consistent with the arm's length principle.

In relation to indirect charging and the related use of allocation keys, the OECD commented:

> 7.24 In some cases, an indirect-charge method may be necessary due to the nature of the service being provided. One example is where the proportion of the value of the services rendered to the various relevant entities cannot be quantified except on an approximate or estimated basis. This problem may occur, for example, where sales promotion activities carried on centrally (e.g. at international fairs, in the international press, or through other centralised

4. OECD, *Transfer Pricing Guidelines 2017*, para. 7.21.

advertising campaigns) may affect the quantity of goods manufactured or sold by a number of affiliates. Another case is where a separate recording and analysis of the relevant services for each beneficiary would involve a burden of administrative work that would be disproportionately heavy in relation to the activities themselves. In such cases, the charge could be determined by reference to an allocation among all potential beneficiaries of the costs that cannot be allocated directly, i.e. costs that cannot be specifically assigned to the actual beneficiaries of the various services. To satisfy the arm's length principle, the allocation method chosen must lead to a result that is consistent with what comparable independent enterprises would have been prepared to accept.

7.25 The allocation should be based on an appropriate measure of the usage of the service that is also easy to verify, for example turnover, staff employed, or an activity based key such as orders processed. Whether the allocation method is appropriate may depend on the nature and usage of the service. For example, the usage or provision of payroll services may be more related to the number of staff than to turnover, while the allocation of the stand-by costs of priority computer back-up could be allocated in proportion to relative expenditure on computer equipment by the group members.

The United States (US) regulations on intra-group services do not express a preference for direct charging. Indirect charging can typically be made using a shared services arrangement (SSA) and applying the services cost method (SCM) safe harbour regime to determine the arm's length price.[5] The SCM does not require a markup on costs.

OECD BEPS ACTIONS 8–10: ALIGNING TRANSFER PRICING OUTCOMES WITH VALUE CREATION

BEPS Action 10 concerned the development of transfer pricing rules to provide protection against common types of base eroding payments, such as management fees and head office expenses. This included new guidance on low value-adding intra-group services to achieve balance between appropriately allocating to group members charges for intra-group services in accordance with the arm's length principle, and the need to protect the tax base of payor countries. The Report proposed an elective, simplified approach which:

- Specifies a wide category of common intra-group services which command a very limited profit markup on costs.
- Applies a consistent allocation key for all recipients for those intra-group services.
- Provides greater transparency through specific reporting requirements including documentation showing the determination of the specific cost pool.

This approach aimed to provide payor countries that the system through which the costs are allocated leads to an equal treatment for all associated enterprises that are

5. Treasury Reg. 1.482-9(b).

operating in similar circumstances. The approach also aimed to provide that no overpricing takes place due to general agreement on the categories of costs included in the cost base, and general agreement on the moderate markup of 5% that should be charged. The transparency of the approach is intended to make clear to payor countries whether intermediary companies have been interposed which may have no or low functionality and may inflate intra-group service charges. The 5% markup basis was included in the OECD 2017 Transfer Pricing Guidelines.[6]

OECD 2017 TRANSFER PRICING GUIDELINES AND LOW VALUE-ADDING SERVICES

The 2017 OECD Transfer Pricing Guidelines adopted the BEPS simplified approach for allocating certain costs within a multinational group.[7] The approach applies to 'low value-adding services' defined as follows:

> 7.45 Low value-adding intra-group services for the purposes of the simplified approach are services performed by one member or more than one member of an MNE group on behalf of one or more other group members which:
> - are of a supportive nature,
> - are not part of the core business of the MNE group (i.e. not creating the profit-earning activities or contributing to economically significant activities of the MNE group),
> - do not require the use of unique and valuable intangibles and do not lead to the creation of unique and valuable intangibles, and
> - do not involve the assumption or control of substantial or significant risk by the service provider and do not give rise to the creation of significant risk for the service provider.

The Guidelines list related services which may be low value-adding services, including:

- accounting and auditing;
- processing and management of accounts receivable and accounts payable;
- human resources activities;
- monitoring and compilation of data relating to health, safety, environmental, and other standards regulating the business;
- information technology services where they are not part of the principal activity of the group;
- internal and external communications and public relations support;
- legal services;
- activities with regard to tax obligations; and
- general services of an administrative or clerical nature.

6. Aligning Transfer Pricing Outcomes with Value Creation, Actions 8–10, 2015 Final Reports, 141, and 2017 OECD Transfer Pricing Guidelines for Multinational Enterprises and Tax Administrations, p. 341.
7. 2017 OECD Transfer Guidelines, Chapter VII, p. 319.

The related steps in applying the approach included: (1) determination of the related cost pools, (2) removing costs attributable by one member solely for another member, and (3) allocate among members of the group the costs in the cost pool that benefit multiple members of the group.

The Guidelines provide comment on charges for low value-adding services, including the use of allocation keys, and the use of the BEPS 5% cost plus markup for the provision of these services to related companies:

> 7.59 The third step in this simplified charge method for low value adding intra-group service costs is to allocate among members of the group the costs in the cost pool that benefit multiple members of the group. The taxpayer will select one or more allocation keys to apply for this purpose based on the following principles. The appropriate allocation key or keys will depend on the nature of the services. The same allocation key or keys must be used on a consistent basis for all allocations of costs relating to the same category of services. In accordance with the guidance in paragraph 7.24, the allocation key or keys selected with respect to costs for each relevant category of services should reasonably reflect the level of benefit expected to be received by each recipient of the particular service. As a general rule, the allocation key or keys should reflect the underlying need for the particular services. By way of examples, the allocation key for services related to people might employ each company's share of total group headcount, IT services might employ the share of total users, fleet management services might employ the share of total vehicles, accounting support services might employ the share of total relevant transactions or the share of total assets. In many cases, the share of total turnover may be a relevant key …
>
> 7.61 In determining the arm's length charge for low value-adding intragroup services, the MNE provider of services shall apply a profit mark-up to all costs in the pool with the exception of any pass-through costs as determined under paragraphs 2.99 and 7.34. The same mark-up shall be utilised for all low value-adding services irrespective of the categories of services. The mark-up shall be equal to 5% of the relevant cost as determined in Section D.2.2. The mark-up under the simplified approach does not need to be justified by a benchmarking study. The same mark-up may be applied to low value-adding intra-group services performed by one group member solely on behalf of one other group member, the costs of which are separately identified under the guidance in paragraph 7.57.

The Guidelines also provide guidance on related documentation and reporting requirements for these services.

OECD 2017 TRANSFER PRICING GUIDELINES AND COST CONTRIBUTION ARRANGEMENTS

The 2017 OECD Transfer Pricing Guidelines provide detailed commentary on the use of cost contribution arrangements (CCAs), also known as cost sharing agreements (CSAs).[8] The same transfer pricing analytical framework is used, including the delineation of the actual transaction undertaken, the contractual agreement provides

8. 2017 OECD Transfer Guidelines, Chapter VIII, p. 345.

the starting point for delineating the actual transaction, and the division of responsibilities, risks, and anticipated outcomes as determined by the functional analysis of the transaction.

In relation to the CCA, the OECD comment that a key feature is the sharing of contributions. In accordance with the arm's length principle, at the time of entering into a CCA, each participant's proportionate share of the overall contributions to a CCA must be consistent with its proportionate share of the overall expected benefits to be received under the arrangement.

In particular the OECD commented on whether independent parties would have accepted the terms of the CCA:

> 8.13 The expectation of mutual and proportionate benefit is fundamental to the acceptance by independent enterprises of an arrangement for sharing the consequences of risks materialising and pooling resources and skills. Independent enterprises would require that the value of each participant's proportionate share of the actual overall contributions to the arrangement is consistent with the participant's proportionate share of the overall expected benefits to be received under the arrangement. To apply the arm's length principle to a CCA, it is therefore a necessary precondition that all the parties to the arrangement have a reasonable expectation of benefit. The next step is to calculate the value of each participant's contribution to the joint activity, and finally to determine whether the allocation of CCA contributions (as adjusted for any balancing payments made among participants) accords with their respective share of expected benefits.

An important issue relates to entry, withdrawal or termination of the CCA. The Guidelines also include recommendations for structuring and documenting CCAs to meet the transfer pricing documentation requirements at commencement and over the term of the CCA. An entity that becomes a participant may obtain an interest in any results of prior CCA activity, such as completed or work-in-progress intangibles or tangible assets. The OECD commented that under the arm's length principle, any such transfer of intangibles or tangible assets must be compensated based on an arm's length value for the transferred interest based on a related 'buy-in' payment. A participant leaving a CCA should be compensated under a 'buy-out' payment.

The greatest potential impact of these measures is likely to be in relation to intangible property contributed under CCAs, where increased attention may be given to the valuation of the related intangibles, and whether the intangible provider has received an arm's length benefit under the CCA for transfer pricing purposes.

OECD BEPS ACTION 13: CBC REPORTING

The BEPS Action 13 Country-by-Country (CbC) reporting measures may impact the use of group service entities, where CbC reports generally include these entities under the Main Business Activity heading as Administration, Management, or Support Services category, with related information including related and unrelated party revenues, profits before tax, income tax paid, and number of employees. This may require analysis as to whether profits allocated to such service entities are commensurate with the functions performed, assets used, and risks undertaken by these entities. The CbC measures were adopted in the 2017 OECD Transfer Pricing Guidelines.[9]

9. 2017 OECD Transfer Pricing Guidelines for Multinational Enterprises and Tax Administrations, Chapter V, p. 233.

Chapter 33

Loan Financing, Interest Payments, and Transfer Pricing

INTRODUCTION

There are several transfer pricing issues relating to the funding provided by group parent companies, treasury companies, and in-house banking entities to related companies in other countries. The essential issue is that the interest rate charged on the related party loan must be made on an arm's length basis, given the amount, risk, and term of the loan. There are also related taxation issues such as thin capitalisation and interest barrier rules which can deny interest deductions.

The funding provided to an existing energy business with a good profit record is arguably made at a low level of risk. Funding new production and development activities may have inherently greater risk, and higher interest rates should generally apply. The parent company or group treasury company making such a loan is taking a calculated risk on the basis of potential future profits, and may extend funding where a third party would not lend to the subsidiary on a stand-alone basis.

There is a tax planning opportunity for energy subsidiaries to obtain interest deductions in a high taxation regime, such as upstream oil and gas taxes, and have the corresponding income taxed at lower tax rates where the group treasury company is located in a lower tax regime. Accordingly there is the potential for an effective tax result even with a modest interest rate on these loans.

There is an issue whether the amount of interest on such loans should be grossed up for local country withholding tax. A third-party foreign lender would generally require such grossing up, and so this should arguably be used for an arm's length loan. The local subsidiary may, however, be able to obtain a loan from a local bank without the need to gross up for tax. There is generally no common practice in relation to this issue, however a related point is that a foreign lending company may potentially be able to obtain a foreign tax credit for withholding tax.

ANALYSING GROUP LOANS

A parent company or a group treasury company may make a loan to another company in the group to fund a new business, finance business expansion, or to assist a group company which is in financial difficulties. Transfer pricing rules require that an arm's length interest rate should be paid on the outstanding loan balance. The rate of interest on the loan should therefore be the rate which would be charged between unrelated parties in similar facts and circumstances. The facts and circumstances of a loan between related companies may include:

- The repayment terms of the loan, for example whether the loan is at call, or has been made for a shorter or longer term.
- Whether there are any loan covenants, such as restrictions on the borrower preventing it from making other borrowings.
- Whether the loan is secured against assets and therefor carries less risk, for example there may be rights to take ownership of the borrower's plant and equipment in case of default on the loan.
- Whether financial guarantees are provided by any party which may reduce the risk on the loan.
- The facility may be in the form of a lines of credit, where the loan is made available when requested.
- The loan may relate to funding trading accounts, such as accounts payable or receivable, and so may carry less risk.
- The credit rating of the borrower's may indicate a higher risk on the loan.
- The business circumstances of the borrower may mean that the loan is more or less risky.
- The loan may relate to high risk activities such as research and development.
- The loan may be affected by foreign exchange rate risks, for example where the loan is in euros, while the borrower earns income in United States (US) dollars.
- There may be differences in the respective financial markets in the two countries, such as the level of financial liquidity and the level of market interest rates.

Group loans may carry more risk in the energy industry, for example where funds are used to finance new oil and gas exploration and production facilities, and where the local country subsidiary does not yet have substantial related income. The parent country tax authority may argue that a higher interest rate should apply. There is a corresponding risk that the higher interest rate applied in the lending country will not be accepted by the local country tax office in the borrowing country, which may seek to limit deductions to the interest rate paid on standard commercial loans.

One current issue is whether the arm's length interest rate should be reduced for 'implicit support' provided by the parent company. This issue is based on the view that the parent would in many cases financially support its subsidiary, on a similar basis to the discussion of a guarantee fee in the *GE Capital Canada* case in 2011,[1] and so a lower interest rate should be charged because the risk of the subsidiary company defaulting is actually very low.

The group's treasury department may evaluate several factors to establish an arm's length interest rate for the related party loan, including the level of debt compared to capital in a subsidiary, the risk of the loan, and the repayment terms. On this basis the lending company may undertake a similar analysis as if a bank or other financial institution was making the loan. There are several related software packages which can assist in establishing market interest rates, including the LoanConnector software provided by Thomson Reuters.[2] There is also an opportunity to potentially obtain evidence from an independent bank as to the interest rate which that bank would have charged the borrowing company on the loan. There has also been recent argument that a lower interest rate should be applied on an unsecured loan, on the basis that security would have been required on a loan between independent parties.

The transfer pricing of related party loans was considered by the Full Federal Court in Australia in the *Chevron* case.[3] The case concerned a five-year loan of AUD 2.5 billion, and the related interest payments were at the rate of 9%. The loan created a tax deduction in Australia against operating revenue from the North West Shelf gas project. The finding of the original judge was confirmed, in that 'the borrower would have given such security and operational and financial covenants and the interest rate, as a consequence, would have been lower.' The decision was summarised by Greenwoods & Herbert Smith Freehills as follows:[4]

- The Full Federal Court has now made it very clear that an Australian subsidiary of a multinational group is not to be treated as if it were an 'orphan' when undertaking transfer pricing arm's length calculations. In fact, some level of parental support may need to be assumed to exist depending on the facts/situation.
- If a borrower is part of a group that has a policy to borrow externally at the lowest cost and that has a policy that the parent will generally provide a third-party guarantee for a subsidiary that is borrowing externally, then in the case of related party debt, the interest rate payable by an Australian subsidiary should probably be set at a level that assumes a parent company guarantee has been given.
- As a result, the appropriate interest rate on internal debt will likely be closer to the parent's global cost of funds for the relevant currency.

The OECD adopted a similar approach in relation to related party interest rates the OECD 2017 Transfer Pricing Guidelines.[5] In the OECD example, a group parent

1. *The Queen v. General Electric Capital Canada Inc.* (2010 FCA 344) (Canada).
2. Thomson Reuters, *LoanConnector*, www.loanconnector.com at 11 December 2013.
3. *Chevron Australia Holdings Pty Ltd v. Commissioner of Taxation* [2017] FCAFC 62.
4. Greenwoods & Herbert Smith Freehills, Tax Brief, Lessons from Chevron, 27 April 2017.
5. OECD Transfer Pricing Guidelines for Multinational Enterprises and Tax Administrations, 2017, Chapter I, para. 1.164, p. 92.

company (P) has a credit rating of AAA, and the subsidiary (S) has a stand-alone credit rating of Baa. Because of the subsidiary's membership in the parent company group, large third-party independent lenders (T) are willing to lend to the subsidiary at interest rates that would be charged to independent borrowers with an A credit rating. The OECD commented that a related party loan should be based on the A credit rating, rather than Baa, because the A credit rating is used by the third party:

> Under these circumstances the interest rate charged on the loan by T to S is an arm's length interest rate because (i) it is the same rate charged to S by an independent lender in a comparable transaction; and (ii) no payment or comparability adjustment is required for the group synergy benefit that gives rise to the ability of S to borrow from independent enterprises at an interest rate lower than it could were it not a member of the group because the synergistic benefit of being able to borrow arises from S's group membership alone and not from any deliberate concerted action of members of the MNE group.

The OECD Transfer Pricing Guidelines 2017 also considered guarantee fees in a similar way.[6] In the OECD example, a group parent company (P) has a credit rating of AAA, and a subsidiary (S) has a stand-alone credit rating of Baa. As in the previous example, because of the subsidiary's membership in the parent company group, large independent lenders are willing to lend to it at interest rates that would be charged to independent borrowers with an A rating. Where the parent provides a guarantee to the subsidiary on a third-party loan, the parent should charge a lower guarantee fee, based on an effective credit upgrade from A to AAA, rather than a larger fee based on a credit upgrade of Baa to AAA. The OECD commented as follows:

> In calculating an arm's length guarantee fee, the fee should reflect the benefit of raising S's credit standing from A to AAA, not the benefit of raising S's credit standing from Baa to AAA. The enhancement of S's credit standing from Baa to A is attributable to the group synergy derived purely from passive association in the group which need not be compensated under the provisions of this section. The enhancement of S's credit standing from A to AAA is attributable to a deliberate concerted action, namely the provision of the guarantee by P, and should therefore give rise to compensation.

THE OECD BEPS MEASURES AND GROUP FINANCING

The OECD BEPS Action plan includes review of base erosion arrangements using excessive interest deductions and other financial payments in Action Plan 4 as follows:

> Action 4 – Limit base erosion via interest deductions and other financial payments. This includes the use of related-party and third-party debt to achieve excessive interest deductions or to finance the production of exempt or deferred income, and other financial payments that are economically equivalent to interest payments.

These proposals include thin capitalisation and interest barrier provisions.

6. OECD Transfer Pricing Guidelines for Multinational Enterprises and Tax Administrations, 2017, Chapter I, para. 1.167, p. 93.

The OECD BEPS Action plan also includes a specific review of transfer pricing relating to intra-group funding as part of Action 9:

> Action 9 – Assure that transfer pricing outcomes are in line with value creation/risks and capital. This issue relates to transferring risks or excessive capital to group members, including preventing inappropriate returns solely for the provision of capital or assumption of risks.

The related OECD Public Discussion Draft proposes attention to the provision of capital including the use of group treasury and financing companies:[7]

> Often a MNE group will centralise treasury functions with the result that the implementation of risk mitigation strategies relating to interest rate and currency risks are performed centrally in order to improve efficiency and effectiveness. It may be the case that the operating company reports in accordance with group policy a currency exposure, and the centralised treasury function organises a financial instrument that the operating company enters into. As a result, the centralised function can be seen as providing a service to the operating company, for which it should receive compensation on arm's length terms. More difficult transfer pricing issues may arise, however, if the financial instrument is entered into by the centralised function or another group company, with the result that the positions are not matched within the same company, although the group position is protected.

The OECD are therefore adopting a combined approach to base erosion and profit shifting for group treasury, and finance companies, based on thin capitalisation measures combined with transfer pricing measures. The centralised function of a group financing company is seen as providing a service to the operating company, for which it should receive compensation on arm's length terms. There is also a recognition that more complex transfer pricing issues arise where the group treasury company is managing group risk rather than the risks of a particular group company.

The OECD guidance provides that capital-rich entities without any other relevant economic activities ('cash boxes') will not be entitled to any excess profits. The OECD therefore consider that the profits the cash box is entitled to retain will be equivalent to no more than a risk-free return, such as would be received by a passive investor from an absolutely risk-free investment. On this basis there may be related analysis as to whether the functions performed, asset used, and risks assumed (FAR) by the group treasury company will be sufficient to prevent this potential cash box analysis.[8]

---

7. OECD, *Public Discussion Draft, BEPS Actions 8, 9 and 10: Discussion Draft on Revisions to Chapter I of the Transfer Pricing Guidelines* (Including Risk, Recharacterisation, and Special Measures) <http://www.oecd.org/ctp/transfer-pricing/discussion-draft-actions-8-9-10-chapter-1-TP-Guidelines-risk-recharacterisation-special-measures.pdf> 22.
8. OECD BEPS Actions 8–10 Final Reports 2015, 11.

OECD BEPS ACTION 13: CbC REPORTING

The BEPS Action 13 Country-by-Country (CbC) reporting measures will also impact the use of group treasury and financing entities.[9] The CbC reports will include these entities under the Main Business Activity heading as Internal Group Finance, with related information including related and unrelated party revenues, profits before tax, income tax paid, and number of employees. Accordingly the reports will identify group treasury companies with high related party earnings compared to the number of related employees.

Tax administrations may then review whether profits allocated to the group treasury companies are commensurate with the functions performed, assets used, and risks undertaken by these companies. This analysis is likely to include the extent to which financing risks are managed by the group treasury company, entitling it to more than a risk-free return. Issues may arise where activities are subcontracted by the group treasury company, and tax authorities may consider that a risk-free return may be appropriate where essential functions have been subcontracted by the group treasury company. The CbC measures were incorporated in the 2017 Transfer Pricing Guidelines.[10]

9. OECD Transfer Pricing Documentation and Country-by-Country Reporting, Action 13, 2015 Final Report.
10. OECD Transfer Pricing Guidelines for Multinational Enterprises and Tax Administrations, 2017, Chapter V, p. 229.

CHAPTER 34

OECD BEPS and the Changing Tax Environment

INTRODUCTION

The OECD BEPS measures potentially address a broad range of international tax planning, particularly in relation to a large number of tax treaties and amendments to be made under the Multilateral Instrument (MLI).[1] There have also been related developments in the OECD 2017 Transfer Pricing Guidelines. In the European Union (EU), the new anti-tax avoidance directives (ATAD 1 and ATAD 2) will also have important impacts on international taxation.[2] The following comments highlight several of these developments.

PERMANENT ESTABLISHMENTS

The OECD BEPS Action 7 measures include several developments to prevent the artificial avoidance of permanent establishments which can otherwise prevent local country taxation of business activities under tax treaties.[3] These measures were

1. Multilateral Convention to Implement Tax Treaty Related Measures to Prevent Base Erosion and Profit Shifting (MLI), opened for signature 7 June 2017, http://www.oecd.org/tax/treaties/multilateral-convention-to-implement-tax-treaty-related-measures-to-prevent-beps.htm on 1 December 2017.
2. Council Directive (EU) 2016/1164 of 12 July 2016 laying down rules against tax avoidance practices that directly affect the functioning of the internal market (ATAD 1), http://eur-lex.europa.eu/legal-content/EN/TXT/?uri=CELEX:32016L1164, and Council Directive amending Directive (EU) 2016/1164 as regards hybrid mismatches with third countries (ATAD 2), http://data.consilium.europa.eu/doc/document/ST-6661-2017-INIT/en/pdf, on 1 December 2017.
3. OECD, Preventing the Artificial Avoidance of Permanent Establishment Status, Action 7: 2015 Final Report.

included in the Action 15 for the MLI, and related MLI provisions.[4] This included restrictions on the preparatory and auxiliary activities treaty exemption, the use of contract splitting to use the time limits on construction activities, and the use of local agents to negotiate but not conclude contracts. The permanent establishment measures are less likely to be relevant to large upstream oil and gas companies and coal mining companies, however these measures are very relevant to service providers such as seismic, geological and geophysical (G&G) survey contractors, contract drilling, contract engineering, and technology consulting. The outcome is likely to be the increased use of local subsidiaries to provide these services, however transfer pricing issues may arise particularly where these subsidiaries are remunerated on a cost plus basis.

FINANCING AND HYBRID INSTRUMENTS

The principal development relating to financing structures is the tightening of thin capitalisation measures, including the BEPS Action 4 measures for the use of local country interest deduction limits based on earnings before interest, tax, depreciation and amortisation (EBITDA), rather than limits based on debt-to-equity ratios and other approaches.[5] The EU, for example, is requiring interest limitation measures in Member States to limit interest deductions in Member States in ATAD 1. In general, net borrowing costs are deductible in the tax period in which they are incurred only up to 30% of the taxpayer's EBITDA.

The use of hybrid entities and hybrid financial instruments is also being addressed. These structures are potentially very common, for example including the use of the United States (US) 'check the box' entity classification provisions,[6] and limited partnership structures including the use of the Netherlands commanditaire vennootschap (CV). BEPS Action 2 includes developing model treaty provisions and recommendations for the design of domestic rules to neutralise the effects of hybrid mismatches, including double non-taxation, double deduction, and long-term deferral.[7]

The recommendations include both primary and secondary measures, with secondary measures for example allowing one country to take measures against hybrids where measures are not taken by the other country. Treaty related measures against the use of hybrid mismatches are an optional provision in the MLI. An important aspect of these measures is that they may address imported mismatches, which can, for example, allow denying an interest deduction on a non-hybrid loan where a hybrid entity or financial instrument was used elsewhere in the multinational group as part of the transaction.

4. OECD, Developing a Multilateral Instrument to Modify Bilateral Tax Treaties, Action 15, 2015 Final Report, and Multilateral Convention to Implement Tax Treaty Related Measures to Prevent Base Erosion and Profit Shifting, opened for signature 7 June 2017).
5. OECD, Limiting Base Erosion Involving Interest Deductions and Other Financial Payments, Action 4 – 2016 Update.
6. Treasury Regulation 26 CFR 301.7701-3.
7. OECD BEPS, Neutralising the Effects of Branch Mismatch Arrangements, Action 2.

The EU introduced anti-hybrid measures in ATAD 1. To the extent a hybrid mismatch results in a double deduction, the deduction shall be given only in the Member State where such payment has its source. To the extent a hybrid mismatch results in a deduction without inclusion of the related income, the Member State of the payer is required to deny the related deduction. The measures have been extended to provide for minimum standards for hybrid mismatches involving third countries (non-EU countries) in ATAD 2.

It is also important to highlight the increased use of Production Sharing Contracts (PSC) in upstream oil and gas, which limit potential tax planning in several ways, and may therefore limit the need for the OECD BEPS anti-avoidance measures. The most significant of these is that financing costs including interest expenses are generally not recoverable costs under most PSCs, which immediately limits debt push down structures to maximise local debt deductions, and the need for thin capitalisation measures.

INTANGIBLE PROPERTY

The most interesting OECD development has been the rejection of mere ownership of intangibles as justifying the full income generated by those intangibles.[8] The OECD approach requires that all members of the group receive appropriate compensation for any functions they perform, assets they use, and risks they assume in connection with the development, enhancement, maintenance, protection, and exploitation of intangibles. This is based on a functional analysis establishing which members perform and exercise control over development, enhancement, maintenance, protection, and exploitation functions, which members provide funding and other assets, and which members assume the various risks associated with the intangible.

The OECD 2017 Transfer Pricing Guidelines provided new guidance on business restructures which have an economic transfer of profit potential.[9] The Guidelines specifically apply transfer pricing to a broad definition of business restructuring, which include cross-border transfers of something of value such as intangibles, and the termination or substantial renegotiation of existing arrangements such as manufacturing arrangements, distribution arrangements, licences, and service agreements.

The Transfer Pricing Guidelines also provide greater flexibility in valuating intangibles. This includes analysing results after the transfer of intangibles to review their correct valuation at the time of transfer. Tax administrations can consider after the fact, ex-post outcomes for the appropriateness of before the event, ex-ante pricing arrangements.[10]

8. OECD Transfer Pricing Guidelines 2017, para. 6.48.
9. OECD Transfer Pricing Guidelines 2017, para. 9.39 p. 380.
10. OECD Transfer Pricing Guidelines for Multinational Enterprises and Tax Administrations, 2017, Chapter V, p. 308.

DIVERTED PROFITS

There has also been increased focus on entities with little or no economic substance. The United Kingdom (UK) Diverted Profits Tax (DPT) provisions, for example, impose a charge of 25% of diverted profits, including where a person carries on activity in the UK in connection with the supply of services, goods, or any property by a foreign trading company, and it is reasonable to assume that the activities are designed to ensure that no permanent establishment is created in the UK.[11] Australia has also introduced DPT measures with significant similarities.[12]

The key to this type of provisions is whether there is an effective tax mismatch due to the use of a lower tax rate, and whether there is 'insufficient economic substance'. The related issues may include whether profits have actually been diverted, particularly where related functions, assets, and risks are subcontracted to related parties in other countries. The use of DPT type provisions may increase, including further guidance on the analysis of economic substance.

TREATY SHOPPING

The OECD BEPS Action 6 measures address preventing access to inappropriate treaty benefits including the use of treaty shopping.[13] The related OECD BEPS Action 15 Multilateral Instrument (MLI) minimum standards include inserting a new preamble into covered tax agreements which expressly states that the purpose of the treaty is to eliminate double taxation without creating opportunities for non-taxation or reduced taxation through tax evasion or avoidance. The MLI then includes a minimum standard to modify bilateral treaties to include:[14]

- Principal Purpose Test (PPT) – to deny treaty benefits where obtaining benefit was one of the principal purposes of the arrangement unless granting treaty benefits would be in accordance with the object and purpose of the treaty; and optionally.
- Supplementary (and optional) rule – Simplified Limitation on Benefits (S LOB) – to grant treaty benefits only to specified 'qualified persons' which include individuals, government entities, listed companies, non-profits, pension funds, together with potential active business or ownership requirements.

These measures are likely to impact the use of intermediate entities in countries with extensive tax treaty networks which do not have commercial substance in relation to their activities. This may particularly impact dividend, interest, and royalty flows

11. Pt.3 Finance Act 2015 and HMRC Diverted Profits Guidance, https://www.gov.uk/government/publications/diverted-profits-tax-guidance> on 12 May 2017.
12. Income Tax Assessment Act 1936, section 177J.
13. OECD, Preventing the Granting of Treaty Benefits in Inappropriate Circumstances, Action 6: 2015 Final Report.
14. Multilateral Convention to Implement Tax Treaty Related Measures to Prevent Base Erosion and Profit Shifting, opened for signature 7 June 2017, Articles 6 and 7.

where withholding tax reductions are claimed on the basis of treaty benefits for the intermediate treaty company.

The anti-treaty shopping measures are also important to mergers and acquisitions and private equity transactions. The related impacts are likely to include the use of treaty countries to sell local country investments, and claims for treaty protection from tax on the sale due to the absence of a permanent establishment.

TRANSPARENCY AND REPORTING

The OECD BEPS Action 13 Country-by-Country (CbC) Reporting measures require multinationals with annual consolidated group revenue equal to or exceeding EUR 750 million to file information on activities in countries where they have activities, which provides tax authorities with an understanding of global and local operations and the related global value chain. The measures also include development of formats for the electronic exchange of CbC information.[15] The adoption of the CbC reporting measures in the 2017 OECD Transfer Pricing Guidelines will facilitate the wider adoption of these measures.[16]

The related requirements include the master file, the local country file, and the CbC report. As discussed, the CbC report in particular is likely to increase transparency in understanding a multinational group, including disclosure on the amount of revenue (related and unrelated party), profits, income tax paid and taxes accrued, employees, stated capital and retained earnings, and tangible assets annually for each tax jurisdiction in which the multinational does business.

The larger potential impact of the CbC reporting measures for many energy multinational groups may concern the use of group marketing companies, where CbC reports will generally include these entities under the Main Business Activity heading as Sales, Marketing and Distribution category, and disclose related information on related and unrelated party revenues, profits before tax, income tax paid and number of employees. This will potentially result in review of these entities as to whether they have the appropriate commercial substance for the related trading profits or commissions, and transfer pricing analysis based on the functions performed, assets used, and risks undertaken (FAR) relating to these activities.

Recent disclosures of offshore tax structures including the Panama Papers,[17] and the Paradise papers,[18] have highlighted the use of non-disclose of offshore structures and bank accounts. Transparency and reporting developments include the Foreign Account Tax Compliance Act (FATCA) enacted by the US in 2010 imposes certain due diligence and reporting obligations on foreign financial Institutions, including the

15. OECD, Transfer Pricing Documentation and Country-by-Country Reporting, Action 13: 2015 Final Report.
16. OECD Transfer Pricing Guidelines for Multinational Enterprises and Tax Administrations, 2017, Chapter V.
17. The International Consortium of Investigative Journalists, ICIJ, The Panama Papers, https://panamapapers.icij.org/ on 1 December 2017.
18. The International Consortium of Investigative Journalists, ICIJ, Paradise Papers, https://www.icij.org/tags/paradise-papers/ on 1 December 2017.

obligation to report US citizen or US tax-resident account holders to the Internal Revenue Service (IRS).[19]

The OECD developed the Common Reporting Standard (CRS) as the single global standard for the collection, reporting, and exchange of financial account information on foreign tax residents.[20] These measures were approved by the OECD Council in 2014. CRS exchanges may be made under the Multilateral Competent Agreement (MCAA),[21] or made under bilateral agreements. Financial institutions such as banks and other deposit taking institutions, custodial institutions, investment entities, and specified insurance companies collect and report to their tax authorities financial account information on non-residents using the standard. Information includes details of the account holder, interest, dividends, account balance, or value and other income generated, or payments made, with respect to the account.

MUTUAL AGREEMENT PROCEDURES (MAP)

A development which should assist multinationals which are cooperating with tax authorities is the inclusion of MAP procedures under BEPS Action 14 on Dispute Resolution.[22] These measures were then included in the BEPS Action 15 MLI minimum standards.[23] This should provide a more effective tax treaty based dispute resolution procedure, and ensure effective and timely resolution of disputes regarding interpretation or application of treaties. The broader adoption of effective MAP procedures has the potential to reduce double taxation which may arise from transfer pricing adjustments. These developments will also include the adoption of binding arbitration between many significant trading partner countries.

GENERAL ANTI-ABUSE RULES (GAAR)

There has also been a general expansion of the use of GAAR provisions. The EU included a GAAR in the ATAD 1 in 2016.[24] The GAAR can apply to counteract aggressive tax planning when other rules do not apply. EU Member States are required to ignore arrangements which, having been put into place for the main purpose or one of the main purposes of obtaining a tax advantage that defeats the object or purpose of the applicable tax law, are not genuine having regard to all relevant facts and circumstances.

19. Foreign Account Tax Compliance Act, Public Law 111–147, Mar. 18, 2010 (FATCA), and 26 US Code § 1471–§ 1474.
20. OECD, Standard for Automatic Exchange of Financial Account Information in Tax Matters, OECD Publishing, http://dx.doi.org/10.1787/9789264216525-en on 6 December 2017.
21. Multilateral Competent Authority Agreement, signed 29 October 2014, (MCAA) http://www.oecd.org/tax/exchange-of-tax-information/multilateral-competent-authority-agreement.htm on 6 December 2017.
22. OECD, Making Dispute Resolution Mechanisms More Effective, Action 14 Final Report.
23. Multilateral Convention to Implement Tax Treaty Related Measures to Prevent Base Erosion and Profit Shifting (MLI), opened for signature 7 June 2017, Article 16.
24. EU, Directive (EU) 2016/1164 of 12 July 2016.

CHAPTER 35

Design of Energy Fiscal Systems

Fiscal systems for extractive industries such as oil and gas production and coal mining may include taxes under licence/concession regimes, production sharing contract (PSC) regimes, service contract, and royalties, and commonly include various combinations. In general terms, both licence/concession regimes and PSC regimes are in common use for upstream oil and gas, whereas the use of licence/concession regimes is much more prevalent in mining.[1] Renewable energy is characterised by tax regimes commonly combined with related tax and non-tax incentives.

The different fiscal systems have specific advantages and disadvantages for government and industry. It is likely that there is no one ideal fiscal system for all circumstances, however certain limitations in the regimes have arisen in several cases. The following is a discussion of the related issues to highlight several significant issues.

An initial comment is that the same fiscal outcome can potentially be replicated under the different regimes. The terms of an upstream oil and gas PSC, for example, can effectively be made very similar to a licence/concession regime by removing cost recovery limits and limiting the government profit oil share. Licence/concession regimes can also have an additional or supplementary tax in recognition of the use of the country's oil and gas resources. Similarly, royalty regimes can potentially be made similar to licence/concession regimes by increasing the royalty rates based on the return from an upstream oil and gas project.

1. Emil M Sunley & Thomas Baunsgaard, The Tax Treatment of the Mining Sector: An IMF Perspective, Background paper prepared for the World Bank workshop on the taxation of the mining.
   sector, 4–5 April 2001, p. 6.

INDUSTRY CHARACTERISTICS

The International Monetary Fund (IMF) discussed the particular characteristics of extractive industries, including mining and oil and gas, which relate to the design of related fiscal systems:[2]

- Potentially sizable rents arise. These are an especially attractive tax base on efficiency grounds – and on equity grounds too if, as is often the case, they would otherwise accrue to foreigners.
- Pervasive uncertainty, most obviously but not only on commodity prices, the most fundamental difficulty being less their wide variability than the difficulty of predicting them. Substantial uncertainty also arises in relation to geology, input costs, and political risk, ranging from expropriation to changes in future fiscal regimes, including those potentially arising from climate and environmental policies.
- Asymmetric information. Private investors undertaking exploration and development are likely to be better informed than host governments on technical and commercial aspects of a project. The host government will be better informed on its own future fiscal intentions.
- High sunk costs, creating time consistency problems. Projects commonly involve very substantial upfront outlays by investors that cannot be cashed in if the project is terminated. The balance of negotiating power thus shifts dramatically from investor to host government once these costs are sunk. Even the best-intentioned government has an incentive to offer attractive fiscal terms before a project is begun, but afterwards – as the tax base becomes much less elastic – reset the regime in its own favour; and investors' awareness of this can discourage investment (the 'hold-up' problem), to the detriment of both sides.
- Extensive involvement of multinational enterprises in many countries. This raises complex tax issues, with multinationals likely more expert than most developing country administrations, and sensitivities on sharing the benefits from national resources.
- Involvement of state-owned enterprises in others, potentially easing asymmetric information issues, however raising concerns on the efficiency of operations and allocation of taxing responsibilities.
- Producers may have substantial market power where they control a significant part of global resources.
- Exhaustibility. The importance of the finiteness of petroleum to long-term economic performance and commodity price developments is questionable. At project level exhaustibility can be a major concern.

2. International Monetary Fund, Fiscal Regimes for Extractive Industries: Design and Implementation, 15 August 2012, https://www.imf.org/external/np/pp/eng/2012/081512.pdf on 18 May 2017.

One industry characteristic is the timing of the related commercial risks and potential benefits. There is commonly a higher risk of the exploration and development stage of an upstream oil and gas project, for example due to the high cost of offshore exploratory and appraisal drilling, combined with a high profit potential in the event of a successful commercial discovery. In contrast, there may potentially be lower risks during the exploration and development stage of a mining project, combined with a higher risk profile during production, for example due to political circumstances.

In general, the combined government revenue rates on upstream oil and gas are higher in the majority of countries than for mining. The IMF Report commented that effective tax rates are commonly higher in upstream oil and gas (around 65%–85%) than in mining (45%–65%), and increase with earnings, most markedly for upstream oil and gas.[3] The principal fiscal objective is to incentivise exploration and development, while retaining the ability for governments to recover significant economic benefits from successful projects.

CORPORATE INCOME TAXES

The use of the corporate tax system is common in licence/concession regimes used by many countries for upstream oil and gas, and in nearly all countries for the mining industry including coal and uranium.[4] The income tax system may also be used to tax oil and gas companies on income from profit oil under PSC regimes. The corporate income tax regime in most cases is used together with a royalty system.

One dominant consideration in the use of the tax system is the issue of carry-forward tax losses. In general there are large carry-forward tax losses in the exploration and development stages of an upstream oil and gas or mining project, and taxable income is typically generated only once production has commenced. Tax is then deferred for a substantial period of time as the carry-forward tax losses are utilised. This issue is partly addressed by combining the tax regime with a royalty regime, where royalties are paid as soon as production commences. Other fiscal structures which can allow earlier access to corporate income tax include the approach used in Brazil, where carried forward tax losses may only be used to offset up to 30% of a company's taxable income in a given year.

There is also a significant consideration as to whether the tax losses from one project may be used to offset income from other projects in the same country. Approaches to this issue include ring fencing, where losses from one project can only be carried forward against profits of that same project. The use of ring fencing may, however, discourage investment in exploration and development as the related expenses may never be recoverable. Countries which have an additional tax rate on

3. *Ibid*, p. 35.
4. Countries using licence/concession regimes on current or prior fields include Algeria, Australia, Brazil, Cameroon, Columbia, Denmark, Ghana, Kazakhstan, Mozambique, Namibia, Netherlands, New Zealand, Peru, Romania, Russia, Trinidad and Tobago, United Kingdom, United States, and Uzbekistan, Columbia Centre on Sustainable Development, ccsi.columbia.edu on 6 September 2017.

upstream oil and gas activities may also have ring fencing between activities, generally to prevent losses from general business activities from reducing tax at the higher rate on upstream oil and gas activities.

There are potential advantages in providing incentives for exploration and development. This can include allowing exploration costs to be recovered in the year incurred, and allowing development costs to be recovered on an accelerated basis.[5]

There are some examples of a resource rent tax (RRT) in upstream oil and gas, where tax is generally imposed only if the accumulated cash flow from the project is positive. The calculations are usually based on an uplift of related expenses. The use of a RRT has theoretical advantages because it recognises the cost of capital and the time value of money. In practice this has not raised significant revenue, generally due to issues of complexity and the related cost of capital.[6]

Licence/concession regimes are subject to a greater potential for international tax planning, and the adoption of the BEPS measures in relation to issues such as treaty shopping and an effective transfer pricing system are essential for an effective fiscal regime. Transfer pricing is a particular concern where local country deductions may be inflated by paying excessive interest, royalties, and management fees to related parties which would not be paid between independent parties. The adoption of BEPS Action 13 for CbC reporting in particular is likely to lead to a greater understanding or multinational groups, with separate disclosures for procurement, marketing, finance, and IP entities within the multinational group. Future developments may potentially include greater conformity on determining reasonable allocations to respective functions within multinational energy groups, including development of benchmark or safe harbour returns for typical activities of respective entities within multinational groups based on functions performed, assets used, and risks assumed (FAR) analysis.

Corporate tax systems may create a bias towards debt financing as these costs are generally deductible. This issue is considered in OECD BEPS Action 4, Limiting Base Erosion Involving Interest Deductions and Other Financial Payments. The recommended approach under these measures is based on a fixed ratio rule which limits an entity's net deductions for interest and payments economically equivalent to interest to a percentage of its earnings before interest, taxes, depreciation and amortisation (EBITDA). This measure can be supplemented by a worldwide group ratio rule which allows an entity to exceed this limit in some circumstances. Licence/concession countries can partially address this issue by making financing costs not deductible under their regimes for additional tax on upstream activities.[7]

5. Emil M. Sunley, Thomas Baunsgaard & Dominique Simard, 'Revenue from the Oil and Gas Sector: Issues and Country Experience', World Bank, 2012, p. 3.
6. *Ibid*, p. 6. There are some limited aspects of RRT in the expenditure uplift provisions of other countries, such as the 100% first-year allowance for the corporation tax and supplementary charge in the United Kingdom, and the 22% additional allowances for the special tax in Norway.
7. This is the case with the United Kingdom's Supplementary Charge, and on the limits on interest deductions under Norway's Special Tax regime.

PRODUCTION SHARING CONTRACTS

An important consideration supporting the use of PSCs, particularly for upstream oil and gas, concerns resource sovereignty, where the countries concerned require ownership of natural resources.[8] In general there is a limitation on resource sovereignty under licence /concession regimes, as rights to the oil and gas reserves are directly granted to the oil and gas company. There is a closely-related issue of a country's requirement for control over its natural resources. This may take the form of a government or national oil company equity interest in an upstream project, or the option to acquire this interest.

The PSC can also offer practical advantages by consolidating conditions governing exploration and development in one agreement. The PSC also provides the opportunity to tailor terms and conditions to the characteristics of particular oil and gas fields.[9] A related practical concern is where the government oil ministry supervises the profit sharing, and then tax is imposed under somewhat different criteria by the government tax ministry. The more effective systems generally use the profit oil determined under the PSC to impose taxation without a separate calculation of tax liability.

The IMF commented that production sharing has been little used in the minerals industry, though it is very common in the petroleum sector. One reason might be that there may be less profit to share in the mining industry compared to oil and gas, and that there is no demand on the domestic market for some of the minerals. In mining, governments may therefore look either to get cash up front in royalties or capture some value added in downstream processing.[10]

There may potentially be a higher level of government revenue under a PSC system, typically where the government derives royalties, a share of profit oil, bonuses, and corporate tax on the oil and gas company. Certain PSC terms may discourage upstream oil and gas investment. Many PSCs apply ring fencing, for example, where carry-forward recoverable cost balances may only be utilised against income under the same PSC. Consideration may be given to allowing recoverable costs to be used against other PSCs. In this respect, upstream oil and gas PSCs generally protect against excessive recovery of costs by use of the annual cost oil limitation.

The use of PSCs can provide a sound basis for sharing project risks. This can apply, for example, where profit oil shares under the PSC are based on an R factor which takes into account the real project returns. This can provide an increased government profit oil share, for example, where the R factor used to determine the

8. Countries using PSCs for current terms or older fields include Angola, Brazil, China, Columbia, Ecuador, Gabon, Kazakhstan, Kenya, Libya, Malaysia, Mozambique, Nigeria, Pakistan, Peru, Senegal, Trinidad and Tobago, Uzbekistan, and Vietnam. Columbia Centre on Sustainable Development, ccsi.columbia.edu on 6 September 2017.
9. Emil M. Sunley, Thomas Baunsgaard & Dominique Simard, 'Revenue from the Oil and Gas Sector: Issues and Country Experience', World Bank, 2012, p. 9.
10. Emil M. Sunley & Thomas Baunsgaard, The Tax Treatment of the Mining Sector: An IMF Perspective, p. 9.

profit oil split is based the contractor's cumulative revenues compared to the contractor's cumulative costs.[11]

A significant issue for fiscal system design is that financing expenses including interest are specifically excluded from recoverable costs under most PSCs. The general exclusion of financing expenses such as interest from recoverable costs effectively addresses the common tax planning structure of debt push down, where a local entity borrows and creates substantial interest deductions. In practice this may discourage smaller oil and gas firms from investing as they may be more reliant on debt funding. The exclusion of interest expenses may tend to move the issue of related interest deductions to the parent investor country.

Cost control is a significant government concern with upstream fiscal regimes. In licence/concession regimes, amounts may be paid to related party entities for services such as seismic surveys, drilling, support services, and specialist rig employees and engineers, and there is a related transfer pricing issue whether these amounts are paid at cost or with a markup profit margin. Joint ventures and joint operating agreements can assist in controlling costs, because the other parties may be incentivised to review the related party costs claimed by the operator. Other approaches taken to this issue include the use of major accounting firms to review annual costs recovery claims.

The most interesting development concerning the treatment of costs under PSC regimes is the recent Indonesian gross split PSCs, where gross production is allocated between the state and the contractor based solely on production splits, without involving a cost recovery mechanism.[12] This is likely to bring forward state collection under PSCs, as there is no recoverable carry-forward of costs, while also removing incentives for 'gold plating' to inflate related costs.

SERVICE CONTRACTS

Service contracts are used in several countries where the oil and gas company essentially receives a fee for exploration, drilling, and production services, and does not have direct access to hydrocarbons.[13] In regular service contracts, the fee may be paid irrespective of the outcome of the oil and gas project, however risk service contracts can incentivise companies to reach production by a target date, and achieving set rates of production during the contract term.

The advantages for host countries include greater resource sovereignty, with ownership of oil and gas retained. There is also potentially less exposure to institutional deficiencies that may prevent effective collection under other fiscal regimes. Service

11. International Monetary Fund, Fiscal Regimes for Extractive Industries: Design and Implementation, 15 August 2012, 17, https://www.imf.org/external/np/pp/eng/2012/081512.pdf on 18 May 2017.
12. Ashurst, Indonesia abandons cost recovery mechanism for new production sharing contracts, Oil and gas update 20 January 2017, https://www.ashurst.com/en/news-and-insights/legal-updates/indonesia-abandons-cost-recovery-mechanism/ on 4 September 2017.
13. Countries using service contracts include Iran, Kuwait, Venezuela, Mexico, Bolivia, Ecuador, Iraq, and Turkmenistan, Abbas Ghandi and C Y Cynthia Lin, Oil and Gas Service Contracts around the World, A Review, p. 5.

contracts can be designed to provide for cost recovery plus interest together with a return on cumulative investment, such as the Iraq RSA. The disadvantages can include lack of profit maximisation, for example due to prioritising targets such as undiscounted revenue or cumulative production.[14] The contractors may also not have a significant incentive to controlling term costs, as the agreements are generally for a much shorter term than PSCs, and the field is likely to be under the control of the government.[15]

Service contracts may potentially provide the greatest government share of upstream oil and gas revenue, however this may therefore provide the least commercial incentive for upstream exploration and production. It is significant that Mexico has adopted PSC terms for oil and gas exploration and production rather than service contracts for the most recent licensing rounds.[16]

ROYALTIES

Royalties are a significant part of most upstream oil and gas and mining regimes, and in particular provide governments with revenue from the commencement of production, compared to the delay in revenue caused by carry-forward tax losses under corporate tax regimes, and recoverable cost balances under PSC regimes. The use of royalty regimes and other payment regimes such as bonus payments on certain project milestones are likely to minimise government risk. Consideration needs to be given to determining the basis for the royalty, for example with coal royalties where mine price is significantly lower than the export terminal price. The fixed percentage basis is simplest to calculate, however there may be advantages in using sliding scale royalties based on several factors, for example Alberta in Canada using royalties based on production and price.[17] This can potentially allow adjustments to revenue sharing or for a very successful project or high oil and gas, coal, or uranium prices.

STATE EQUITY PARTICIPATION

The government or national resources company may take an equity interest in a project, particularly in upstream oil and gas. This interest can take several forms, including free equity where the government receives a percentage of dividends without payment of any costs, carried equity where the government pays for its equity share out of production proceeds, and paid equity or full working interest where the state pays its share of costs when these are incurred. The IMF reported a mixture of paid equity and

14. Ghandi & Lin, Oil and Gas Service Contracts around the World: A Review, 2014, p. 5.
15. Carole Nakhle, Petroleum Taxation, Sharing the Oil Wealth: a study of petroleum taxation yesterday, today and tomorrow, Routledge 2008, p. 47.
16. Clare Ribando Seelke, Michael Ratner, M. Angeles Villarreal & Phillip Brown, Mexico's Oil and Gas Sector: Background, Reform Efforts, and Implications for the United States, 28 September 2015, Congressional Research Service, www.crs.gov.
17. Petroleum Royalty Regulation, 2017, under the Mines and Minerals Act, RSA 2000 c M-17 (Alberta).

carried equity in a series of oil and gas projects, and free equity and carried equity in mining projects.[18]

State equity participation is generally used to share in any upside resulting from a project, however non-economic reasons may include retaining a national interest in oil and gas resources, to facilitate transfer of technology and know-how, or to provide more direct control over project development. Full equity participation may be costly to government due to the related cash-calls to cover the state's portion of project costs. The government may potentially be in a better position taxing and regulating a project, rather than being directly involved in management.[19]

The option to participate on concessional terms may be a significant discouragement to investment, where the government or national resource company exercises an option to acquire equity in the project and the company does not fully recover its costs relating to that new interest. A better result may be achieved by the use of increased royalty and R factors in PSC regimes to increase the government share in a successful project.

POWER GENERATION, TRANSMISSION, AND DISTRIBUTION

Investment in power generation, transmission, and distribution infrastructure has been characterised by large scale privatisations, together with the building of new infrastructure where investment conditions are favourable. The related projects may have foreign and/or local country investment, and may also include public-private partnerships (PPP) between the private sector and government, including independent power producers with long-term contracts under which the government and/or a public sector utility guarantees to purchase output at a guaranteed price under power purchase agreements (PPAs).

In relation to power generation, characteristics outside the company income tax system, such as funding incentives, PPAs and feed-in tariffs, renewable energy quota obligations, carbon taxes and carbon trading, are likely to have the greatest impact on energy development. Feed-in tariffs and renewable energy quota obligations will significantly encourage supplies from renewable sources, and carbon taxes and trading can significantly discourage supplies from non-renewable sources.

The related fiscal terms are generally based on corporate income tax for power plants, transmission and distribution networks, with the trend toward renewable energy production being characterised by related investment subsidies and tax credits, tax holidays, and R&D concessions and incentives.[20] Tax provisions for interest

18. International Monetary Fund, Fiscal Regimes for Extractive Industries: Design and Implementation, 15 August 2012, 22, https://www.imf.org/external/np/pp/eng/2012/081512.pdf at 18 May 2017.
19. Emil M. Sunley, Thomas Baunsgaard & Dominique Simard, 'Revenue from the Oil and Gas Sector: Issues and Country Experience', World Bank, 2012, p. 10.
20. Nathalie McGregor & Sebastian James, Providing Incentives for Investments in Renewable Energy, Advice for policymakers, World Bank Group, Investment Climate in Practice, No. 19 November 2011.

deductions on borrowing costs are important, including large scale power privatisations and PPP investment structures. This includes the trend towards interest deduction limits based on EBITDA introduced by several European Union states, and also set out in BEPS Action Plan 4. One current issue is that renewable energy sources other than hydroelectricity may not provide base load power, so that energy shortages can arise when there are less favourable wind or solar conditions. There may be a trend towards targeted incentives for renewable energy storage, such as battery backup systems and pumped hydroelectric energy storage, and renewable energy projects which incorporate these systems.

FISCAL ADMINISTRATION

There are several opportunities to increase the effectiveness of fiscal administration and transparency. Several countries use different tax administrations for different taxes, which may result in potential conflicts such as where fiscal and commercial responsibilities are performed by oil and gas administrations or national oil companies. Several of these issues may be addressed by the adoption of self-assessment, together with targeted audit functions by the tax administration.[21] This structure is well adapted to licence/concession regimes, where the tax administration is primarily responsible for revenue collection. Effective administration may also combine PSC and tax supervision with the administration of royalties, with practical benefits such as the ability to reconcile royalty returns to other taxpayer information.

FISCAL STABILITY CLAUSES AND INVESTMENT TREATIES

In planning for fiscal regimes, where upstream oil and gas, mining, power plant and electrical transmission, and distribution investments are generally long-term and large-scale projects, a particular concern for investors is the risk of unexpected tax policy changes. Investors may generally seek to minimise this risk by the inclusion of a fiscal stability clause in related project agreements. This may take a form which essentially 'freezes' the tax system at the time of the project agreement, or may seek to guarantee the total investor take against material tax or royalty changes. The related issue is the impact on the government's flexibility to set tax policy in the future.[22]

The related issue is the availability and enforcement of bilateral investment treaties (BIT), which may provide protection or compensation for investors against privatisation or other significant changes in fiscal terms. BIT terms can apply to a large number of upstream oil and gas and mining investments made from related treaty countries.

21. International Monetary Fund, Fiscal Regimes for Extractive Industries: Design and Implementation, 15 August 2012, https://www.imf.org/external/np/pp/eng/2012/081512.pdf on 18 May 2017.
22. Emil M Sunley & Thomas Baunsgaard, The Tax Treatment of the Mining Sector: An IMF Perspective, p. 8.

The design of fiscal systems should take onto account the potential limitations on changing fiscal terms under PSC fiscal stability clauses or the country's BIT network by providing a reasonable allocation of the potential upside of the project in the original agreements.

CONCLUSIONS

There may be no specific preference between the alternative fiscal regimes. The key requirement is to balance incentivising exploration, development, and infrastructure investment with effective returns to government for a successful project. It is useful to emphasise that where returns to the investor are too restricted then investments will not take place, and that all projects face local conditions and local political and social pressures notwithstanding the fiscal regime used.[23]

There are significant differences in country circumstances, including potential exploration, development, and production costs for specific regions, the nature of specific oil, gas, coal, and uranium deposits based on the available data, the characteristics of particular electricity power and distribution markets, and investor evaluations of commercial and political country risks. It is also likely for a country with proven and successful resource projects to negotiate better fiscal terms, however the fiscal terms of contracts are also likely to be influenced by prevailing commodity prices. There is scope to adopt best practices to make the administration of the respective regimes more effective, with potential benefits for both governments and energy companies.

For upstream oil and gas, both licence/concession regimes and PSC regimes have been successfully used in many countries, with PSC regimes in many cases providing the greater government share. There are issues with service contracts which do not provide potential upside benefits to the contractor, and which may be more suited to low-risk, short-term projects. Combining licence/concession regimes or PSC regimes with royalties is very common, however care is required with the design of the royalty rates to provide an equitable sharing of the potential upside benefits from a successful project.

There is the potential to develop a best practice approach where countries consider emulating the most successful licence/concession regimes or PSC regimes, with modifications to adapt to local conditions such as differing geological, political, and expenditure risks, and providing a higher return to investors who undertake greater project risks. This approach may be developed on the basis of evaluations obtained from both the upstream oil and gas and mining industries combined with evaluations from respective governments.

23. Carole Nakhle, *Petroleum Taxation, Sharing the Oil Wealth: A Study of Petroleum Taxation Yesterday, Today and Tomorrow* (Routledge, 2008) p. 49.

CHAPTER 36

General Conclusions

This book has introduced and discussed significant topics concerning the international taxation of energy production and distribution. The most important observation is that taxation laws continue to change and evolve at a rapid pace.

There have been several significant developments relating to energy, particularly in relation to changes in Production Sharing Contract (PSC) regimes, tax incentives for renewable energy offered by many countries, and the concessional tax regimes for research and development (R&D).

The use of tax havens and low tax regimes to derive income such as dividends, interest, and royalties has been partially reduced by controlled foreign company measures. Countries are also increasing disclosure requirements for tax haven transactions, and examination of new measures against the use of tax havens is included in the BEPS measures, particularly in the County-by-Country (CbC) reporting requirements in BEPS Action 13,[1] and their incorporation in the OECD 2017 Transfer Pricing Guidelines.[2] There is a strong emphasis on increased international cooperation and reporting, using treaties with exchange of information (EOI) provisions entered into with low-taxing countries. The United Kingdom (UK), United States (US), Canadian, and Australian national tax authorities established the Joint International Tax Shelter Information Centre (JITSIC), and Japan, Korea, and China have also joined this organisation.

The most significant international tax development has been the extension of transfer pricing provisions and the related administrations to enforce those provisions. Transfer pricing continues to be an area of international taxation where many of the largest tax adjustments have been made by tax authorities. The need to address this issue of tax risk management has been recognised by multinational groups with

1. OECD Transfer Pricing Documentation and Country-by-Country Reporting, Action 13, 2015 Final Report.
2. OECD Transfer Pricing Guidelines for Multinational Enterprises and Tax Administrations, 2017, Chapter I, para. 1.164, p. 92.

increased use of APAs to obtain agreement on arm's length pricing. Current developments include the increased use of bilateral and multilateral APAs, where the tax authorities in two or more countries agree to the transfer pricing used by a multinational group.

On a broader perspective, there may be scope for legitimate tax planning, where income is derived from active businesses established for real commercial purposes, and which have significant local staff, local directors, and directors meetings, significant business capital to establish real business substance, and derive the related income based on the actual functions performed, assets used, and risks assumed (FAR) transfer pricing analysis. The related planning structures potentially include regional sales and procurement companies, group treasury centres, and the ownership and management of group intangible property (IP) and the related R&D.

The use of tax havens to reduce tax has also been affected by court decisions on issues such as beneficial ownership. Tax treaties increasingly contain anti-avoidance and disclosure provisions, such as the US limitation on benefits (LOB) clauses which can deny treaty benefits where there is no real presence in treaty countries. This trend will be extending under the principal purpose test (PPT) and simplified LOB tests in the BEPS Multilateral Instrument (MLI).

The increased use of general anti-avoidance rules (GAAR) is an important development, and this may also reduce the use of more aggressive tax structures. The introduction of the GAAR in the UK was significant, and structures such as the recent Double Irish Dutch Sandwich raise the issue of whether the US should potentially also introduce a GAAR. There is a related requirement for a dominant commercial purpose for many transactions under anti-avoidance rules and the analysis of tax courts. This issue may mean reviewing whether the proposed transaction meets the real business needs of the group.

The BEPS measures and related provisions in the 2017 OECD Transfer Pricing Guidelines have significantly altered the tax planning landscape, including measures such as Action 3 on CFC measures, Action 4 on interest deductions, Action 6 on treaty abuse, Action 7 on preventing the artificial avoidance of permanent establishment status, and Action 8–10 on transfer pricing including global value chains and IP. The Action 13 CbC reporting measures are particularly important as providing much greater transparency to tax authorities on multinational group structures. The use of specialised entities within multinational groups which may benefit from lower tax rates is likely to require real and effective local commercial substance. There have also been BEPS developments which potentially benefit multinational groups, such as resolving double taxation under the Mutual Agreement Procedure (MAP) in Action 12 and the related measures in the MLI under Action 15. The most significant related issue is whether the specific BEPS measures will be implemented in the respective countries' tax laws and treaties including adoption of the MLI.

There are a large number of mergers and acquisitions transactions in the upstream oil and gas, coal mining, power generation, and electricity transmission and distribution industries. These transactions can involve the tax regimes in a large number of countries, particularly where the target company itself holds a large number of subsidiaries. Multinational energy groups will continue to analyse international tax issues for their existing structures and for the new acquisitions.

Energy production and distribution continues to be one of the most exciting areas of international business activity. Issues such as the increased use of global supply chains, the importance of related intangible property, and the development of incentives for renewable energy, will be presenting many new international tax challenges.

Case Studies

The following section includes the case study questions and the suggested answers concerning energy production and distribution and the related international tax issues:

1. Renewable Energy – The Offshore Wind Farm Project, Income Flows, and Permanent Establishments (PE)
2. Upstream Oil and Gas – The New Production Sharing Contract (PSC)
3. Treasury and Finance – The Group Treasury Center, Loans, and Derivatives
4. Mergers and Acquisition – Private Equity Sale of an Electricity Transmission Network
5. Group Research and Development (R&D) – Cost Contribution Arrangements (CCA)
6. Group Technology – The New Battery Storage System and Tax Treaties
7. Group Technology – The Solar Power Station, Transfer Pricing, and Mutual Agreement Procedures (MAP)
8. Group Marketing – The Liquefied Natural Gas (LNG) Marketing Hub and the Transfer Pricing Dispute

The purpose of the case studies is to open up issues for general discussion, and to practice tax analysis and problem solving approaches. There may be several correct answers or alternative outcomes to the related questions. Accordingly, please answer the questions at a general level, and suggest alternative structures where you consider there may be a better tax result. You may also wish to add additional comments relating to the case studies if one or more of the companies concerned was to be located in your own country.

CASE STUDY 1

Renewable Energy: The Offshore Wind Farm Project, Income Flows, and Permanent Establishments (PE)

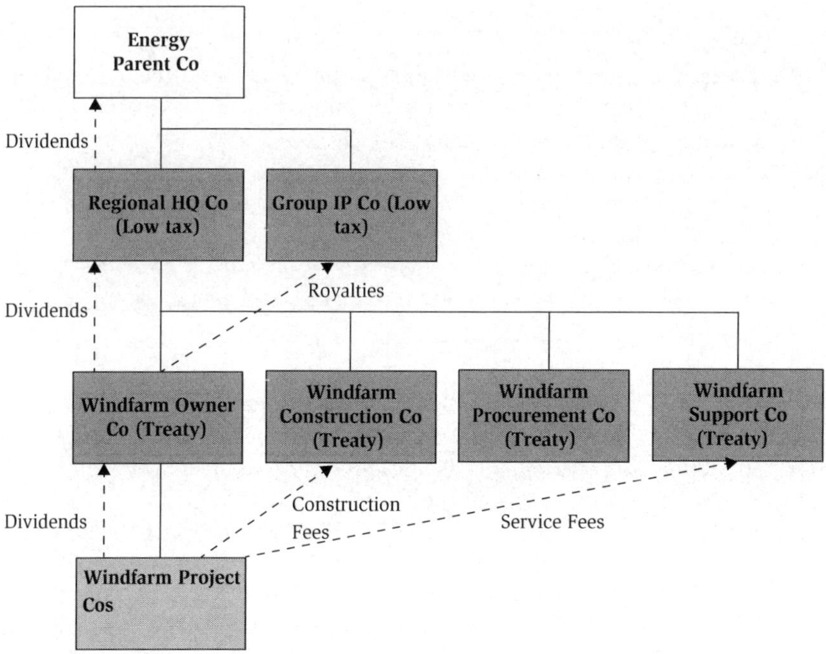

The Energy Parent Co is the parent company of a multinational renewable energy group. The Energy Parent Co holds the Regional HQ Co, which holds the Windfarm Owner Co, the Windfarm Construction Co, the Windfarm Procurement Co, and the

Windfarm Support Co. The Energy Parent Co also holds the Group IP Co which owns and manages the Group's intangible property including patents, trademarks, and computer software.

The Windfarm Owner Co holds several Windfarm Project Co companies in the local country. The Windfarm Construction Co constructs the windfarms in return for construction fees. The Windfarm Procurement Co purchases equipment required locally for the windfarm projects and also liaises with potential new projects. The Windfarm Support Co provides maintenance support for the windfarms in the local country in return for service fees including long-term support projects at particular windfarm sites.

All of the Group entities are located in different countries. The Regional HQ Co and the Group IP Co are located in low taxing countries. The Windfarm Owner Co, Windfarm Construction Co, Windfarm Procurement Co, and Windfarm Support Co are located in countries with tax treaties with the local country.

QUESTIONS

1. Discuss the dividend flow issues with this structure relating to the direct and indirect ownership of the Windfarm Project Cos, including the related tax planning, and the potential impact of the OECD BEPS anti-treaty abuse measures if the countries adopt the BEPS Action 15 Multilateral Instrument (MLI).
2. Discuss the permanent establishment issues with this structure, including the related tax planning and the potential impact of the OECD BEPS permanent establishment measures.
3. Discuss the controlled foreign corporation (CFC) issues with this structure, including the related tax planning, and the potential impact of the OECD BEPS CFC measures.
4. Discuss how OECD BEPS CbC Report may potentially assist in the local country tax authority analysis of this structure and the related tax planning.

ANSWERS

1. The dividend flows relating to the direct and indirect ownership of the Windfarm Project Cos include the dividends paid to the Windfarm Owner Co in a tax treaty country, the dividends then paid to the Regional HQ Co in a low tax country, and the dividends then paid to the Energy Parent Co.
   The dividends paid to the Windfarm Owner Co in a tax treaty country raise a treaty shopping issue, because the withholding tax on the dividends imposed by the local country may be reduced or eliminated under the tax treaty between the local country and the Windfarm Owner Co country, whereas the amounts received will then be paid on as dividends to the Regional HQ country which is located in a low tax country. It is arguable that

the tax treaty has been used to reduce tax where the income is then paid to a non-treaty country.

The BEPS Action 6 measures are intended to prevent inappropriate access to treaty benefits and include the following measures to be included in the OECD Model Tax Convention:

- A clear statement in treaties is proposed that the States that enter into a tax treaty intend to avoid creating opportunities for non-taxation or reduced taxation through tax evasion or avoidance, including through treaty shopping arrangements will be included in tax treaties.
- A specific anti-abuse rule is proposed for treaties, which may include the limitation-on-benefits (LOB) rule that limits the availability of treaty benefits to entities that meet certain conditions. These conditions, which are based on the legal nature, ownership in, and general activities of the entity, seek to ensure that there is a sufficient link between the entity and its state of residence.
- A more general anti-abuse rule may be used in treaties, based on the principal purposes of transactions or arrangements in the principal purposes test (PPT). If one of the principal purposes of transactions or arrangements is to obtain treaty benefits, the benefits are denied unless established that granting these benefits would be in accordance with the object and purpose of the treaty.

  The BEPS Action 15 MLI measures will implement treaty-related BEPS measures by modifying existing bilateral tax treaties where the respective countries both agree that their treaty should be included as a covered agreement. MLI Articles 6 and 7 implement the BEPS Action 6 – Minimum standard on preventing inappropriate access to treaty benefits.

  In relation to the Energy Parent Co multinational group structure, anti-treaty shopping measures may apply to the use of the Windfarm Owner Co.

- If the related countries adopt the PPT from the MLI for the tax treaty, then the commercial purposes of using the Windfarm Owner Co would be reviewed, and it may be necessary for that company to establish that the benefits of the tax treaty was not one of the principal purposes for the structure. This issue may potentially be addressed where the company carries out significant management activities relating to the subsidiaries using sufficiently senior staff in the treaty country.
- If the related countries adopt the S-LOB from the MLI for the tax treaty, then the rules will limit the availability of treaty benefits to entities that meet certain conditions, and the issue will be whether there is a sufficient link between the entity and its state of residence to be treated as qualified person. The related tests include whether the company is engaged in the active conduct of a business. Article 10(a)(i) of the MLI can potentially exclude operating as a holding company.

2. The permanent establishment issues relate to the construction services provided by the Windfarm Construction Services to the Windfarm Project Cos, the procurement and liaison services provided by the Windfarm Procurement Co, and the support services provided by the Windfarm Support Co to the Windfarm Project Cos.

   The BEPS Action 7 measures concern structures used to avoid having a taxable PE in a particular country. These measures were adopted in the BEPA Action 15 MLI Articles 12 to 14. The related measures to the case study include:

   - Commissionaire arrangements and similar strategies – These measures apply to commissionaire arrangements, where the agent does not own the products sold on behalf of the principal. The measures also concern arrangements where a dependent agent does not habitually concludes contracts but substantially negotiates those contracts. The BEPS Multilateral Instrument (MLI) provides the option that the PE extends to where the agent does not conclude contracts but habitually plays the role leading to the contracts in Article 12.
   - Fragmented Contracts using specific activity exceptions – This issue concerns contracts which are artificially divided or split up with the intention of allocating the resulting split contracts to a different related party in order to avoid the existence of a PE. The resulting several small operations under the separate contracts are then argued to be merely engaged in preparatory or auxiliary activities which do not constitute a PE. The MLI contains the related optional anti-fragmentation rule in Article 13.
   - Other strategies for avoidance of PE status and splitting up of contracts – These issues include the time exception for construction sites and the related practice of splitting-up contracts between closely related enterprises, so that each contract is below the time threshold to be treated as a PE. The MLI provides an option which can aggregate these contracts in Article 14.

     There is an issue concerning the liaison services by the Windfarm Procurement Co, which may not be a PE where these are merely representative office functions which are treated as preparatory or auxiliary activities which are exempt under Article 5(4)(e) of the Model Tax Treaty. These activities may however be a PE under the BEPS measures where the local office substantially negotiates the related windfarm contracts.

     The use of the Windfarm Procurement Co may also be an example of the fragmentation of contracts to avoid a PE. The procurement activities are an exception from PE status provided under Article 5(4)(d) of the OECD Model Tax Treaty. These are combined with liaison services which may be claimed to be preparatory or auxiliary activities which are exempt under Article 5(4)(e) of the Model Tax Treaty. However where these activities are combined with the other activities of the Energy Parent Group, the BEPS anti-fragmentation measures may hold there to be a PE in the local country.

There is also an issue with the Windfarm Support Co, which derives service fees from the Windfarm Project companies. These activities may constitute a PE where employees work in the local country at a fixed place of business. This will depend on the facts in the case, for example a team on a long-term assignment to a power station with a large number of turbines may result in a fixed place of business. The OECD Model Tax Treaty 2014 Commentary provides at C(5)-4 that a single place of business will generally be considered to exist where, in light of the nature of the business, a particular location within which the activities are moved may be identified as constituting a coherent whole commercially and geographically with respect to that business.

In relation to tax planning, however, the existence of a PE may not result in significant tax being derived by the local country. Related structures include maximising related expenses in the company with the PE, so that only a small margin is derived by that company. It is therefore necessary to examine the full global value chain, including the related party expenses of the multinational group companies.

3. The CFC issues relate to the income flows derived in low tax countries. This includes the dividends paid to the Regional HQ Co, and the royalties paid to the Group IP Co.

   The BEPS Action 3 measures are intended to respond to the risk that taxpayers with a controlling interest in a foreign subsidiary can reduce the tax base of their country of residence and, in some cases, other countries by shifting income into a CFC. The measures provide guidance on related issues, including:

   - Definition of a CFC – CFC rules generally apply to foreign companies that are controlled by shareholders in the parent jurisdiction. The report sets out recommendations on how to determine when shareholders have sufficient influence over a foreign company for that company to be a CFC.
   - CFC exemptions and threshold requirements – CFC rules should only apply to controlled foreign companies that are subject to effective tax rates that are meaningfully lower than those applied in the parent jurisdiction.
   - Definition of income – CFC rules should include a definition of CFC income, and the report sets out a non-exhaustive list of approaches or combination of approaches that CFC rules could use for such a definition.
   - Computation of income – CFC rules should use the rules of the parent jurisdiction to compute the CFC income to be attributed to shareholders.
   - Attribution of income – The attribution threshold should be tied to the control threshold and that the amount of income to be attributed

should be calculated by reference to the proportionate ownership or influence.

- Prevention and elimination of double taxation – The report emphasises the importance of both preventing and eliminating double taxation, and recommends that jurisdictions with CFC rules allow a credit for foreign taxes actually paid.

  In the case study example, the BEPS Action 3 measures concern whether the Energy Parent Co country has effective CFC measures so that the Energy Parent Co is taxed on dividends derived by the Regional HQ Co and royalties derived by the Group IP Co.

  In relation to the dividends, many countries provide a participation exemption from taxation of dividends where the dividends are derived from active business operations, and this exemption may apply notwithstanding CFC rules. It may however be appropriate to remove Regional HQ Co from the ownership structure to ensure the exemption applies. Other countries may tax foreign dividend income but allow a foreign tax credit. United States tax reforms applying from 2018 include a 100% deduction for foreign sourced dividends similar to the participation exemption in other countries.

  The royalty income derived by the Group IP Co is not likely to qualify for CFC exemptions. In relation to the BEPS CFC proposals, the Energy Parent Co would have control of the Group IP Co, the effective tax rate for the Group IP Co is likely to be significantly lower than in the Parent Co country, and the royalty income is likely to be passive income subject to CFC measures.

4. The OECD CbC Reporting measures include the Master File, the Local Country File, and the CbC Report.
   - The Master File provides tax administrations with high level information regarding a multinational enterprise's (MNE's) global business operations and transfer pricing policies.
   - The Local Country File provides a local tax administration with information regarding material related party transactions, the amounts involved, and the company's analysis of related transfer pricing determinations. The local county file may also be adapted to obtain additional information.
   - The CbC Report provides the amount of related and unrelated party revenue, profits, income tax paid and taxes accrued, employees, stated capital and retained earnings, and tangible assets annually for each tax jurisdiction.

     The CbC Report enables analysis of a multinational group's activities, including procurement hubs, IP and treasury centres. Ratios based on these reports such as related party revenues to total revenues, related party revenue to assets, and related party revenue to employees can also be analysed. In relation to the case study, the CbC

Report is likely to highlight the Regional HQ Co and the Group IP Co in particular.

The CbC Reports can include the holding company activities of the Regional HQ Co under the Main Business Activity heading Holding Shares or Other Equity Instruments, and the IP related activities of the Group IP Co under the Main Business Activity heading Research and Development, or Holding or Managing Intellectual Property categories.

The related information provided includes related and unrelated party revenues, profits before tax, income tax paid, and number of employees. The CbC report may assist in identifying group holding companies and IP centres with high related party earnings compared to the number of related employees.

The related analysis by tax authorities may include whether profits allocated to such holding or IP entities are appropriate to functions performed, assets used, and risks assumed (FAR) by these entities, or suggest that the use of the entity is potentially to reduce taxable profits in group companies with transactions with the entity.

The CbC measures were adopted in the 2017 OECD Transfer Pricing Guidelines for Multinational Enterprises and Tax Administrations, Chapter V, p.229.

CASE STUDY 2

Upstream Oil and Gas: The New Production Sharing Contract (PSC)

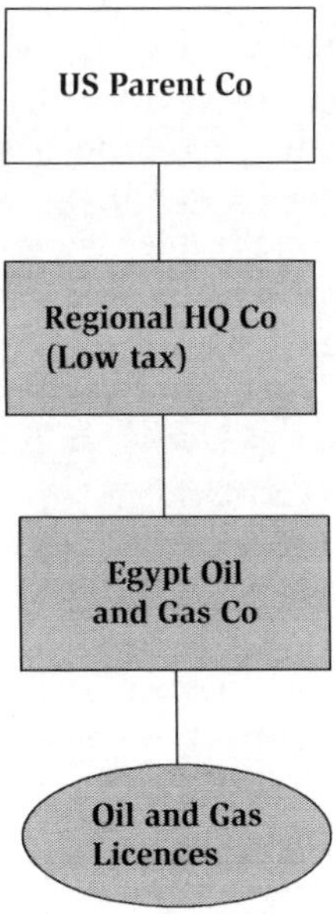

The US Parent Co is a United States based oil and gas company which is investing USD 800 million in a new oil field project in Egypt under the Egyptian Model PSC contract. Related extracts of the Egyptian Model PSC contract are set out in 'Egypt, Concession Agreement for Gas and Crude Oil Exploration and Exploitation (2012)' in the attached Annex.

QUESTIONS

1. What is the Egyptian government's principal revenue under this PSC?
2. How is Egyptian corporate tax paid under this PSC?
3. Discuss why this tax paying arrangement may be used with respect to a United States investor.
4. What is the importance of the general limitations on cost oil recovery?
5. What types of costs, which are not usually recoverable under most countries' PSCs, are potentially recoverable under this PSC?
6. What are the issues in relation to value added tax (VAT), customs tariffs and duties, and dividend withholding tax under these PSC terms?
7. What are the 'ring fencing' implications of the PSC, where the US Parent Co group has interests in other PSCs in Egypt?
8. Will the Egyptian Government benefit from the project at an earlier time before public sector partner EGAS derives its' share of profit oil?

ANSWERS

1. The Egyptian Government's principal revenue under the PSC is the production sharing under Article VII (b) of the PSC, generally known as a share of profit oil, to the Egyptian government public sector partner EGAS. This amount is determined after the oil and gas company is allowed cost recovery under Article VII (a), generally known as cost oil. It is significant that the production sharing under this PSC varies with the benchmark price of Brent oil, with the government obtaining a higher percentage with a higher Brent oil price. The Egyptian government or its public sector company will also obtain royalty income and specific bonuses under PSCs.
2. Corporate tax paid under this PSC is paid by EGAS as the public sector partner, which pays the tax in the name of, and on behalf of, the oil and gas company contractor. This amount is considered to be additional income for the contractor, so that the corporate tax paid by the public sector partner will be subject to corporate tax. The contractor is therefore required to add an amount to its taxable profit equal to the corporate tax amount paid by the public sector partner on its behalf.
3. The arrangement may potentially be used in respect of a United States investor to enable a credit for foreign taxes in the oil company's own country, for example where the parent company is located in the United States. This may include foreign taxes where the activities in Egypt as a branch under the Internal Revenue Code, 26 U.S. Code, § 901.

   The Internal Revenue Service (IRS) has issued the Internal Revenue Manual which generally provides that to be creditable, a foreign tax must be a compulsory payment to a foreign government, and an income tax, or a tax in lieu of an income tax. The tax on income is required to be a tax on net gain. A tax is likely to be a tax on a net gain if it meets three criteria:

- Realisation test, imposed generally when income would be realised under the Internal Revenue Code;
- Gross receipts test, based on the fair market value of amount realised; and
- Net income test, where gross income is reduced by allowable expenses.

  There is generally no United States foreign tax credit allowed for royalties, taxes based on sales, turnover, transaction, output, production, asset, property, or VAT.

  These structures are impacted by US tax law changes from 2018 in the Tax Cuts and Jobs Act (TCJA), which provides an exemption for foreign sourced dividends derived by US corporations in which the US corporation owns at least a 10% stake.

4. The general limitations on cost oil recovery provide limits on how much of the related costs of the project can be recovered in 'cost recovery petroleum' in each year. Article VII (a) of the Model PSC provides different percentages which may be recovered in each year for exploration, development, and operating expenses. The excess costs may be carried forward to be recovered in later years, however if the oil and gas project under the PSC is not successful then there is no recovery or refund of these costs.
5. This issue relates to financing costs, which are not usually recoverable under most countries' PSCs, and which may potentially be recoverable under this PSC. Leasing costs may also generally be recoverable. Limitations in other PSCs include the requirements for material amounts to be paid after competitive bids for the related contracts.
6. The issues in relation to other taxes including VAT, customs duty, and dividend withholding tax include:
   - The value added tax (VAT) on goods and services may be paid by Egypt Oil and Gas Co on its purchase of domestic and foreign goods and services used in the project. Where the oil and gas is exported then VAT free treatment may apply, so that the oil and gas exports are not subject to VAT but a credit or refund of VAT paid is then allowed. Certain PSCs may allow an exemption for VAT on the related purchases to remove the need to obtain a VAT refund or credit.
   - The customs tariffs and duties issue relates to taxes on imported plant and machinery for the project. Certain PSCs may allow an exemption for these taxes.
   - The dividend withholding tax issue relates to dividends paid by Egypt Oil and Gas Co to Regional HQ Co. It is necessary to review whether Egypt imposes withholding tax on dividends paid to non-residents such as Regional HQ Co, and whether the PSC provides any exemptions from withholding tax. If dividend withholding tax may be imposed it is necessary to review which company in the group should

make the investment, and which tax treaties and anti-treaty shopping provisions may potentially apply.

7. Ring fencing refers to the restrictions on the use of losses in one operation or entity to offset profits in another operation or entity. The use of PSC regimes is significant where the US Parent Co group has interests in other PSCs in Egypt because the initial losses on a new oil and gas project in the exploration stage under one PSC are generally not useable against the profits on an older profitable PSC in the production stage.
8. The Egyptian Government will benefit from the project as soon as the project enters into production, due to the 10% royalty to be paid by the oil and gas contractor under Article III(a). The royalty income will therefore be derived in the years prior to the government public sector partner EGAS deriving its share of profit oil.

CASE STUDY 3

Treasury and Finance: The Group Treasury Centre, Loans, and Derivatives

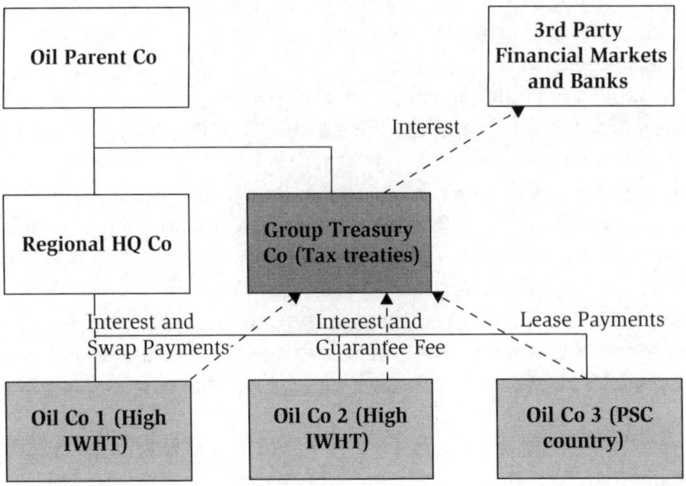

The Oil Parent Co is the parent company of the upstream oil and gas multinational group. The Oil Parent Co holds the Regional HQ Co and the Group Treasury Co, which are both located in countries with extensive tax treaty networks. The Regional HQ Co holds Oil Co 1 and Oil Co 2 companies, both located in countries with high interest withholding tax (IWHT), and the Oil Co 3 company located in a country with a PSC regime for upstream oil and gas. The Group Treasury Co borrows from 3rd party international financial markets and banks, and on-lends the funds to the Oil Co 1 and Oil Co 2 companies, and provides operating leases to the Oil Co 3 company.

QUESTIONS

1. What is the Oil Parent Co's principal tax issue with this financing structure?
2. What is the principal transfer pricing issue with the structure?
3. What is likely to be Oil Co 1 and Oil Co 2 companies' principal tax issue with this financing structure?
4. Why does the Group Treasury Co provide loans and currency swaps to the Oil Co 1 company? Discuss the related tax issues.
5. Why does the Group Treasury Co provide loans and loan guarantees to the Oil Co 2 company? Discuss the related tax issues.
6. Why does the Group Treasury Co provide operating leases to the Oil Co 3 company? Discuss the related tax issues.
7. What OECD BEPS transparency measures may impact transfer pricing analysis of the Group Treasury Co company?

ANSWERS

1. The Oil Parent Co's principal tax issue with this financing structure are controlled foreign corporation (CFC) provisions, which may apply to tax the Oil Parent Co on profits as they are derived in the Group Treasury Co. The CFC provisions in many countries apply to passive income such as interest, derived by controlled entities such as the Group Treasury Co, and which is subject to a low effective tax rate. There is a similar issue with countries with participation exemption for dividends, such as counties in the European Union, which can disallow the exemption if the dividends paid to the Oil Parent Co are paid from low taxed companies such as the Group Treasury Co which derive passive income such as interest.
2. The structure potentially provides a substantial profit to the Group Treasury Co because this company borrows from 3rd party international financial markets and banks at low interest rates, due to the volume of borrowing and the strength of the Parent Oil Co risk rating. The Group Treasury Co then typically on-lends the borrowed funds to group subsidiary companies at higher interest rates based on the subsidiaries' individual credit ratings. The principal transfer pricing issue is whether the Oil Co 1 and Oil Co 2 tax authorities would accept that the higher interest rate charged to their local subsidiaries in these circumstances. The OECD 2017 Transfer Pricing Guidelines, chapter I, para 1.164, p.92, for example, comment that because of the subsidiary's membership in the parent company group, large third party independent lenders are willing to lend to the subsidiary at interest rates that would be charged to independent borrowers with a higher credit rating.
3. The Oil Co 1 and Oil Co 2's principal tax issue with this financing structure is likely to be thin capitalisation provisions under their domestic tax rules. These provisions can potentially deny interest deductions where the level of

related party debt is considered to be excessive. The related provisions may be based in a debt to equity ratio, however the more recent measures are based on earnings before interest, taxes, depreciation and amortisation (EBITDA). The use of EBITDA for thin capitalisation generally reduces interest deductions compared to debt to equity ratios, as EBITDA depends on operating results in each year, and is also not subject to related measures such as asset revaluations. The OECD BEPS Action 4 measures recommended that countries use an EBITDA ratio between 10% and 30% of applicable EBITDA. This was designed to provide meaningful limits on net interest expense, while still allowing most multinationals to deduct all of their third party interest expenses.

4. The Group Treasury Co may provide loans together with currency swaps to Oil Co 1 to reduce the amount of interest, and therefore potentially reduce IWHT. This structure may be used where the local currency has a comparatively high interest rate. The loan is made in a lower interest currency such as USD, resulting in lower interest payments and lower IWHT. A swap is also made to provide the USD required to repay the loan, which results in net swap payments needing to be made by Oil Co 1. The potential result is a similar total financing expense for Oil Co 1, however local country IWHT only applies to the interest payment components of the arrangement. There are several related anti-avoidance issues, including determining what currency is actually required for Oil Co 1's commercial operations, and whether there is a dominant commercial purpose to the arrangement.
5. The Group Treasury Co may similarly provide loans together with loan guarantees to the Oil Co 2 to reduce the amount of interest and therefore reduce IWHT. The loan is made at a lower interest rate due to the guarantee, which potentially reduces local country IWHT. The guarantee fee is paid to increase the Oil Co 2's effective credit rating, and the guarantee payments are generally likely to be deductible. The potential result in a similar total financing expense for Oil Co 2, however IWHT potentially only applies to the interest payment components of the arrangement. The OECD 2017 Transfer Pricing Guidelines, Chapter I para 1.167 p.93, however comment that the guarantee fee should be based on the credit upgrade from a group company up to the parent risk rating, rather than the credit upgrade from the risk rating of an unsupported company. This is likely to substantially reduce the allowable deductions for transfer pricing purposes. There was a similar result concerning a guarantee fee in *The Queen v. General Electric Capital Canada Inc.* (2010 FCA 344).
6. The Group Treasury Co may provide operating leases to the Oil Co 3 as the related operating lease payments are less likely to be treated as financing costs for the Oil Co 3 under the related PSC terms. The terms of most PSCs do not allow financing costs including interest to be treated as recoverable costs. The lease payments are therefore more likely to be allowed as recoverable costs, allowing Oil Co 3 to recover them as cost oil.

7. The OECD BEPS transparency measure which may impact transfer pricing analysis of the Group Treasury Co is CbC Reporting. The CbC reports required from multinational groups, such as Parent Oil Co group, would include group treasury entities under the Main Business Activity heading as Internal Group Finance. The required related information includes related and unrelated party revenues, profits before tax, income tax paid, and number of employees. The CbC reports may therefore identify group treasury companies with high related party earnings compared to the number of related employees. The tax administrations concerned may then review whether profits allocated to the group treasury companies are commensurate with the functions performed, assets used, and risks assumed (FAR) by these companies.

Case Study 4

Mergers and Acquisition: Private Equity Sale of an Electricity Transmission Network

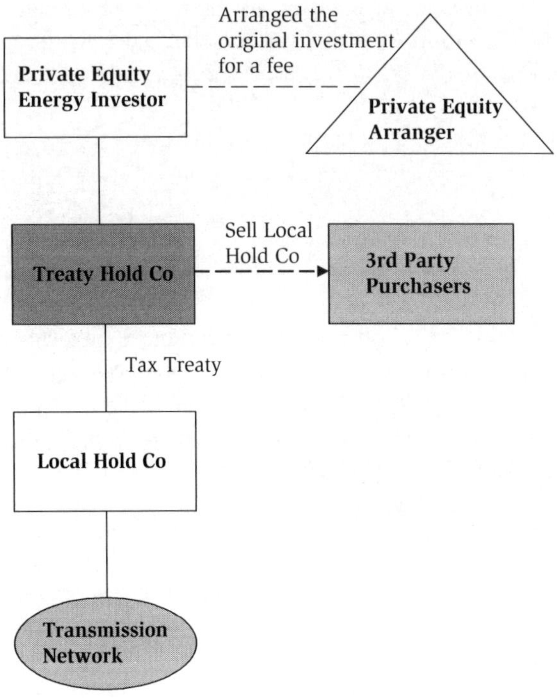

The Private Equity Energy Investor holds a subsidiary Treaty Hold Co located in a country with an extensive tax treaty network. The Treaty Hold Co holds the Local Hold Co, which holds a large scale local electricity transmission network. The Treaty Hold Co is selling all the shares in the Local Hold Co to the 3rd Party Purchasers. The original investment by the Private Equity Energy Investor was arranged by a 3rd party, the Private Equity Arranger, which is a tax transparent United States entity. All of these entities are located in different countries. There is a tax treaty between the Treaty Hold Co and the Local Hold Co countries which is based on the 2017 OECD Model Tax Treaty.

QUESTIONS

1. How could tax in the Local Country Co country apply to the sale?
2. What Local Country Co country tax exceptions or tax reductions may be relevant?
3. Discuss how tax treaty protection may apply to prevent the local country from taxing the Treaty Hold Co on the gain, including where the sale is treated as business profits, or where the sale is treated as a capital gain.
4. Discuss the characterisation issue for the electricity transmission network for tax treaty purposes.
5. Discuss the likely tax position of the Private Equity Energy Investor as it repatriates the profits from the Treaty Hold Co derived from the sale of the Local Hold Co.
6. Discuss the potential application of the OECD BEPS anti-treaty shopping measures.

ANSWERS

1. Tax may apply in the Local Country Co country on the basis that the gain is a revenue transaction, and has a sufficient link to the local country to allow tax to apply because the underlying assets are located in the local country. This issue generally depends on whether there are 'tracing upward' provisions which tax the sale of shares in a foreign holding company, such as the Treaty Hold Co in this example, where there are sufficient related assets located in the local country.
2. The Local Country Co country tax exceptions which may potentially be relevant include exemptions from tax on capital gains, the source of the profits being treated as outside the country, or that the profits do not relate to a local permanent establishment under domestic tax rules.
   - Local country taxation may potentially not apply to capital gains, or may apply tax at reduced tax rates. This issue may apply in countries with common law legal systems, and there may be relate case law on distinguishing transactions with a capital or revenue nature. The

related analysis may include the purpose of the original investment, whether it was intended to hold the investment for a long-term and derive income from the investment over several years, and whether the main intention of the investment was to hold the network for a limited period and to resell the network for a gain. A conclusion that the transaction was on revenue account is more likely where the Treaty Hold Co has a number of investments which are held for shorter periods of time.

- A non-resident entity such as the Treaty Hold Co may potentially only be taxed in the local country on local sourced profits. The source of the sale profits may potentially not be in the local country. This analysis would include the place of negotiation and conclusion of the related contracts, and may also include other activities undertaken by the investor or on their behalf, any improvements to the local investment, the nature of any agreements between the entities, and the extent and nature of any control or involvement in the management of the local investment.
- Many countries do not tax profits derived by non-residents which do not relate to a local permanent establishments unless the income is in certain categories which are subject to withholding tax, such as dividends, interest, or royalties. The local country may, however, seek to tax the profits because they relate to the Private Equity Arranger, which may have an office in the local country, and potentially may be treated as an agent for the non-resident Treaty Hold Co.

3. Tax treaty protection may apply to the sale under the tax treaty between the Treaty Hold Co and the Local Hold Co countries on the basis that the gain is in the nature of business profits, and these may only be taxed in local country if they relate to a permanent establishment in the local country under Article 7(1) of the Model Tax Treaty.

   If the gains are treated as capital gains, then treaty protection may apply under Article 13(5), which provides that gains from the alienation of any property, other than that referred to in paragraphs 1, 2, 3 and 4, shall be taxable only in the contracting state of which the alienator is a resident.

   The related issue is likely to be the application of Article 13(5), which provides that gains derived by a resident of a contracting state from the alienation of shares deriving more than 50% of their value directly or indirectly from immovable property situated in the other contracting state may be taxed in that other state. If this provision applies, then the Local Hold Co country may be prevented from taxing the Treaty Hold Co on the gain on the sale of shares in the Local Hold Co. The immovable property assets may, however, potentially comprise less than half the value of the Local Hold Co due to the related valuations. This issue can arise, for example, if there is a substantial value in Local Hold Co relating to other assets, such as government contracts, marketing intangibles and intellectual property such as patents, business methods, or computer software.

4. The characterisation of the electricity transmission network for tax treaty purposes is significant because these assets may not be treated as immovable property, so that the Local Hold Co country does not obtain the right to tax under Article 13(5). The term 'immovable property' is required under Article 6(2) to have the meaning which it has under the law of the contracting state in which the property in question is situated. In 2017, the IMF, OECD, UN and WBG discussed indirect transfers similar to this example in 'The Platform for Collaboration on Tax, Discussion Draft: The Taxation of Offshore Indirect Transfers – A Toolkit.' The report discussed the definition of immovable property and whether a definition with broader scope should be adopted.
   In several countries, immovable property includes land, buildings, and other benefits which arise out of land, and also gods and chattels which are affixed to land. In the *Australian Provincial Assurance Co Ltd v Coroneo* case, (1938) 38 SR (NSW) 700, for example, Jordan CJ commented that 'whether a chattel which has been to some extent fixed to land is a fixture is whether it has been fixed with the intention that it shall remain in position permanently or for an indefinite or substantial period … or whether it has been fixed with the intent that it shall remain in position only for some temporary purpose …'. Electricity transmission towers may therefore be treated as immovable property where they are fixed to land, and are likely to remain fixed to the land for substantial periods. This would allow the Local Hold Co country to tax the Treaty Hold Co where more than 50% of the value of the Treaty Hold Co was directly or indirectly derived from the immovable property.
5. The likely tax position of the Private Equity Energy Investor as it repatriates the profits on the sale would in many cases be reduced or nil local tax. Private equity investors generally include large institutional investors, pension funds, hedge funds, sovereign wealth funds, and high net worth individuals. The related entities may benefit from tax exemptions, such as pension funds, or be located in tax havens, with no local taxation. The related structures include pass through entities such as United States Limited Liability Company (LLC) entities, master limited partnerships (MLP), or collective investment vehicles (CIV), which are treated as tax transparent or disregarded entities for tax purposes. The related structures may also have investors located in high taxing countries, but with participation exemptions for the related dividends providing they meet certain conditions, such as minimum shareholding, underlying active or non-tax haven income, or relate to the purpose of the investment.
6. The OECD BEPS anti-treaty shopping measures may apply where the Local Hold Co country denies tax treaty protection to the Treaty Hold Co, and therefore not be prevented from taxing the Treaty Hold Co on the sale of the Local Hold Co. The OECD BEPS Action 15 Multilateral Instrument (MLI) will implement treaty-related BEPS measures by modifying existing bilateral tax treaties. These MLI Articles 6 and 7 relate to BEPS Action 6, minimum standard on treaty abuse, including treaty shopping structures which use tax

treaties to prevent the taxation of capital gains. The treaty shopping measures use principal purpose test (PPT) or limitation on benefits test (LOB) measures:

- Principal Purpose Test (PPT) – Denies treaty benefits where obtaining the benefit was one of the principal purposes of the arrangement, unless granting treaty benefits would be in accordance with the object and purpose of the treaty; and optionally,
- Supplementary and optional rule – Simplified Limitation on Benefits (S-LOB) test to grant treaty benefits only to specified 'qualified persons', including individuals, government entities, listed companies, non-profits, and pension funds, which meet active business or ownership requirements.

  This may potentially apply to investors, such as the Private Equity Investor, which invest through an intermediate holding company in a treaty country, such as the Treaty Hold Co, and claim that the gain on the sale is protected from local country tax as the Treaty Hold Co does not have a permanent establishment in the local country. The related treaty shopping issues will include the purpose of the investment, and the extent of related commercial substance in the treaty holding country.

CASE STUDY 5

Group Research and Development (R&D): Cost Contribution Arrangements (CCA)

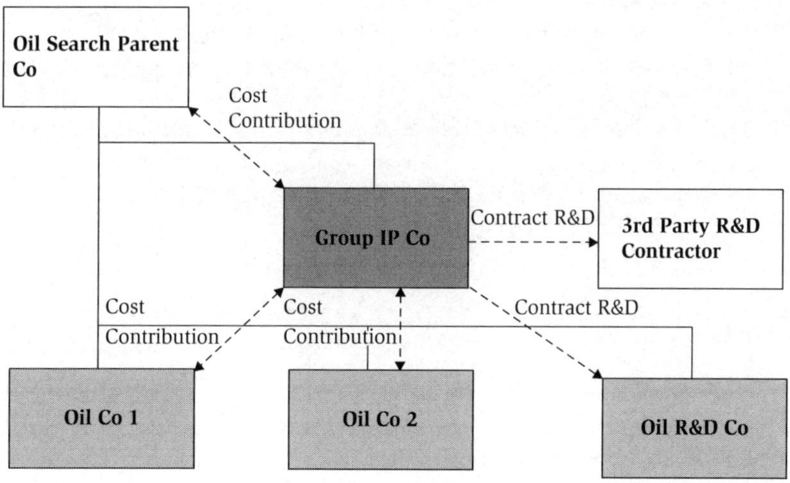

The Oil Search Parent Co is the parent company of a multinational group which conducts geological and geophysical (G&G) surveys to search for oil and gas. The surveys use advanced technology, including seismic reflection, seismic refraction, magnetic, gravity, gas sniffers, coring, and related computer software analysis to detect the presence of oil and gas in commercial quantities.

Each of these entities in this structure is located in a different country. The Group IP Co is located in a country with an extensive tax treaty network. The Oil Search Parent Co country does not have controlled foreign corporation (CFC) provisions.

The Group IP Co is the owner of the group's intangible property, including the technology used for the G&G process. The Oil Search Parent Co, the Oil Co 1, and the Oil Co 2 companies have entered into a cost contribution arrangement (CCA) with the Group IP Co. The CCA provides that these companies provide financial contributions, existing technology, or research and development (R&D) work, and share the related benefits of that technology.

The Group IP Co also engages the Oil R&D Co and 3rd Party R&D Contractor to provide R&D services. The Oil R&D Co is paid on a cost plus 10% margin basis for the R&D work. The 3rd Party R&D Contractor is paid on an hourly basis for specific projects based on the seniority of the related research staff.

QUESTIONS

1. What are the likely concerns of the Oil Search Parent Co country tax authorities with these arrangements?
2. What are the likely concerns of the Oil Co 1 country tax authorities with these arrangements?
3. Discuss the tax position of the Group IP Co if this company is located in the Netherlands.
4. Is there any tax or fiscal impact on this arrangement if the Oil Co 2 is in a country with a Production Sharing Contract (PSC) tax regime for upstream oil and gas?
5. What are the principal developments in the OECD 2017 Transfer Pricing Guidelines which may impact the use of these IP arrangements?
6. What are the principal OECD BEPS developments which may impact the use of these IP arrangements?

ANSWERS

1. The likely concerns of the Oil Search Parent Co country tax authorities with these arrangements include whether there are appropriate benefits to the Oil Search Parent Co in respect of the level of contributions made under the CCA.
   - The OECD 2017 Transfer Pricing Guidelines at Chapter VIII comment that a key feature of CCAs is the sharing of contributions. In accordance with the arm's length principle, at the time of entering into a CCA, each participant's proportionate share of the overall contributions to a CCA must be consistent with its proportionate share of the overall expected benefits to be received under the arrangement. In particular, the OECD commented on the essential issue of whether independent parties would have accepted the terms of the CCA.
   - The principal issue for the Oil Search Parent Co with the CCA is that it is likely to have provided substantial intangible property under the

CCA, and it is not clear that it will receive a significant benefit in return. This is particularly an issue where the Group IP Co becomes the owner of the related IP. The likely tax authority response is to identify what IP has been transferred, obtain an independent valuation of that IP, and then apply exit taxes to the extent that there is no commensurate benefit to arise to the Oil Search Parent Co.
  - The Oil Search Parent Co country may also have an issue in taxing the return of profits from the Group IP Co. Many countries provide a participation exemption which reduces or eliminates tax on dividends from foreign companies where sufficient control and other tests are met. The payment of any dividends from the Group IP Co to the Oil Search Parent Co may potentially not qualify for the participation exemption due to the low effective tax rate for the Group IP Co under the related IP tax concession regime.
2. The concerns of the Oil Co 1 country tax authorities with these arrangements are likely to include:
  - Whether the level of financial contributions to the Group IP Co are appropriate to support a full tax deduction, in view of the likely benefits to be derived from the use of the IP. It may be established, for example, that the Oil Co 1 could obtain the use of technology without a related fee or royalty, for example where the company is engaged in a Joint Operating Agreement (JOA), and the Operator under that JOA is providing the related intangibles under that agreement.
  - There is a withholding tax issue where the payments may be considered to be payments for the use of IP, so that royalty withholding tax should therefore be imposed. The Oil Co 1 may need to demonstrate that it has ownership or significant rights to the IP under the CCA, rather than making payments which are in substance for the use of IP owned by the Group IP Co.
3. The tax position of the Group IP Co if this company is located in the Netherlands is based on the Innovation Box regime:
  - The related intangible intellectual property must relate to patent rights, or have a related government issued R&D declaration. The tax base of the related income is reduced by 80%, and so the effective tax rate on related income is reduced to 5%. The regime is particularly significant in this case, as it can apply to self-developed and patented intangible intellectual property, and also to the contract R&D used in this structure.
  - There are significant conditions which apply to obtain benefits under the regime. This includes the requirement for sufficient commercial substance in the Netherlands entity, which must bear the risks and costs relating to the R&D, and have sufficiently skilled personnel who manage and control the research and development process, and manage and control the related risks.

- The most significant change following the OECD BEPS Action Plan 5 on Countering Harmful Tax Practices is the nexus approach applying in the Netherlands after 30 June 2016. This provides that only a portion of the benefits attributable to innovation are eligible for the reduced rate. The concession is based on calculations for qualifying expenditure, comprising in-house development activities which are not subcontracted within the group, and expenditure on development activities subcontracted to third parties.

4. The tax or fiscal impact on this arrangement where the Oil Co 2 is in a country with a Production Sharing Contract (PSC) tax regime will depend on the terms of each specific PSC.
   - The issue for upstream oil and gas companies relates to whether the payments under the CCA are recoverable costs under the PSC, allowing recovery of these amounts as cost oil. The majority of PSCs list the types of expenses which are allowed as cost recoverable, and payments relating to the production or use of technology may not be included. The PSC may also require that any material amounts must result from competitive bid contracts, and the CCA payments are unlikely to meet this condition.
   - In general, time based charges for the use of services are more likely to be allowed as recoverable costs, and consideration may need to be given to meeting these requirements where companies in the Oil Search Parent Co group are located in PSC countries.
5. The principal developments in the OECD 2017 Transfer Pricing Guidelines which may impact the use of these IP arrangements include:
   - In relation to the potential transfer of IP from the Oil Search Parent Co under the CCA, the 2017 OECD Transfer Pricing Guidelines in Chapter IX provided guidance on business restructures which have an economic transfer of profit potential. These measures may potentially support the Oil Search Parent Co tax authorities in applying exit taxes on business restructures which transferred the profit potential of activities such as R&D to another country, including where there has been no express transfer of the related activities.
   - In relation to the profits derived by the Group IP Co, the 2017 OECD Transfer Pricing Guidelines in Chapter VI commented that IP ownership should be based on the performance and control of the important functions related to the development, enhancement, maintenance, and protection of the intangible, and on bearing the necessary costs and risks. The OECD cautioned against the adoption of a transfer pricing methodology that 'too readily assumes that all residual profit from transactions after routine returns' should necessarily accrue to the owner of the intangibles. These measured follow the OECD BEPS Action 8–10 Report that returns should not be based on the mere ownership of IP. This issue potentially limits attributing significant profits to the Group IP Co unless it has significant related function

performed, assets used, and risks assumed (FAR), and exercises significant control over the intangibles.

6. The principal OECD BEPS developments which may impact the use of these IP arrangements include:
   - The OECD BEPS Action Plan 3 Strengthening CFC Rules focused on CFC provisions and related anti-avoidance measures. These measures are intended to respond to the risk that taxpayers with a controlling interest in a foreign subsidiary can reduce the tax base of their country of residence by shifting income into a CFC. The OECD guidance included the definition of a CFC, CFC exemptions and thresholds, and the definition, computation and attribution of the related income. The Oil Search Parent Co country may introduce CFC provisions which would potentially tax the Oil Search Parent Co on income derived by the Group IP Co which benefit from the low tax IP regime.
   - The BEPS Action 13 Country-by-Country (CbC) reporting measures include IP related entities under the Main Business Activity heading in the Research and Development or Holding or Managing Intellectual Property categories, with related information including related and unrelated party revenues, profits before tax, income tax paid, and number of employees. The CbC report may assist in identifying group IP centres such as the Group IP Co with high related party earnings, and the related transfer pricing analysis may include whether the level of related party profits is appropriate to functions performed, assets used, and risks assumed (FAR) by these entities. These measures were adopted in the 2017 OECD Transfer Pricing Guidelines in Chapter V.

Case Study 6

Group Technology: The New Battery Storage System and Tax Treaties

Power Storage Country Only Has a Tax Treaty with Regional HQ Country

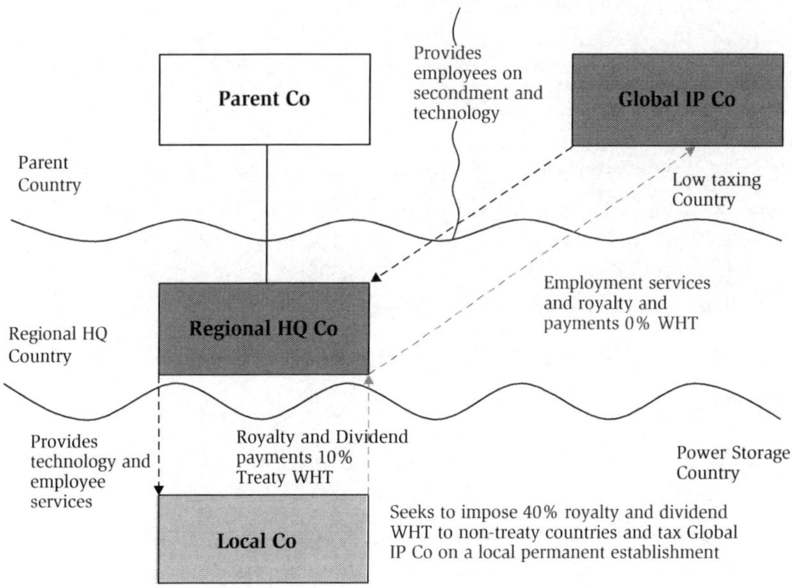

The Parent Battery Group provides large scale battery power storage to support gas, wind, and solar power stations to store electricity to meet peak load needs.

- The legal owner of the group's intangible property (IP) is the Global IP Co, which provides technology to the Regional HQ Co, which then provides technology to the Local Co.
- Global IP Co employees are seconded to the Regional HQ Co and then provide supporting services to Local Co on visits to that country.
- Dividends are paid by the Local Co to the Regional HQ Co, which in turn pays dividends to the Parent Co.

The local country considers that no tax treaties apply to the royalty and dividend payments and to the seconded employees.

EMPLOYEE SERVICES

The Global IP Co has seconded employees to the Regional HQ Co company under short-term employment contracts. These employees travel to the Local Country for short periods to assist the Local Co companies with specific projects. The related projects and employee duties are however substantially controlled by the Parent Co. The Regional HQ Co does not have a permanent establishment (PE) in the local country under the Regional HQ country/local country tax treaty. This is based on the OECD 2017 Model Tax Treaty, where there is no PE where the building site or construction or installation project lasts less than twelve months.

ROYALTIES

The Parent Co company developed the IP, and then transferred the foreign rights to the IP to the Global IP Co under a cost contribution/cost sharing agreement. The Global IP Co company licensed the IP to the Regional HQ Co, which then sublicensed the IP to the Local Co. The Global IP Co company has legal ownership of the IP, however the Parent Co company has substantial control over developing the related technology. The Global IP Co company contracts research and development (R&D) relating to further developments of the IP to other entities in the group including the Parent Co and the Local Co, which are paid a cost plus 10% fee for the R&D work.

DIVIDENDS

The ownership structure is that the Parent Co company holds 100% of the shares of both the Regional HQ Co and the Global IP Co companies. The Regional HQ Co holds 100% of the shares of the Local Co company. The Local Co company pays dividends out of local profits to the Regional HQ Co company, which in turn pays dividends using this income to the Parent Co. The Regional HQ Co has a small number of staff organising operations in the geographical region, however services such as information technology (IT), human resources (HR), finance, and legal functions are generally subcontracted to other companies in the group.

QUESTIONS

1. Common IP and Holding Structures
   This example is based on transferring the ownership of IP to a group subsidiary in low-taxing country, together with the use of regional holding companies to hold shares in local operating companies.
   Discuss the parts of this structure which may give rise to treaty abuse such as treaty shopping, and discuss what additional circumstances could potentially result in the case not being one of treaty abuse.
2. Permanent Establishment Adjustment
   The local country considers that the Global IP Co has a taxable local permanent establishment because it does not accept the employee secondments to the Regional HQ Co.
   Discuss why the local country considers that treaty abuse arises in this case.
3. Royalty WHT Adjustment
   The local country determines that royalties are in substance being paid to the Global IP Co. There is no tax treaty with the Global IP country. The local country considers that the tax haven royalty withholding tax (WHT) rate of 40% should apply.
   Discuss why the local country considers that treaty abuse arises in this case.
4. Dividend WHT Adjustment
   The local country determines that dividends are in substance paid to the Parent Co, and that the tax haven dividend WHT rate of 40% should apply.
   Discuss why the local country considers that treaty abuse arises in this case.
5. Entitlement to Treaty Benefits – The Principal Purpose Test
   The BEPS Action 15 Multilateral Instrument (MLI) Article 7(1) includes the anti-treaty abuse measures from BEPS Action 6. Countries may agree to adopt the Principal Purpose Test (PPT) under the MLI, which generally provides that a benefit under the treaty shall not be granted in respect of an item of income or capital if it is reasonable to conclude, having regard to all relevant facts and circumstances, that obtaining that benefit was one of the principal purposes of any arrangement or transaction.
   Discuss how this BEPS standard may apply.
6. Entitlement to Treaty Benefits – Simplified Limitation on Benefits Test
   The BEPS MLI Article 7(8) provides an alternative to the PPT where countries may agree to adopt the Simplified Limitation on Benefits test

(S-LOB). This provision would generally deny treaty benefits to a resident of a Contracting State who is not a 'qualified person'. This includes the definition of situations where a resident would be a qualified person, which would cover … e) a person other than an individual, provided that persons who are residents of that Contracting State and are qualified persons by reason of subparagraphs a) to d) own, directly or indirectly, more than 50% of the beneficial interests of the person.
Discuss how this BEPS standard may apply.

7. Entitlement to Treaty Benefits – Simplified Limitation on Benefits Test
The BEPS MLI Article 7(10)(a) for the S-LOB test includes a provision that would provide treaty benefits to certain income derived by a person that is not a qualified person if the person is engaged in the active conduct of a business in its State of residence and the income is derived in connection with, or is incidental to, that business.
Discuss how this BEPS standard may apply.
8. Entitlement to Treaty Benefits – Simplified Limitation on Benefits Test
The BEPS MLI Article 7(9)(e) for the S-LOB test includes a provision that would provide treaty benefits to a person that is not a qualified person if at least more than an agreed proportion of that entity is owned by certain persons entitled to equivalent benefits.
Discuss how this BEPS standard may apply.
9. Entitlement to Treaty Benefits – Simplified Limitation on Benefits Test – Conduit arrangements
The BEPS MLI Article 7(15)(a) for the S-LOB test relates to denying treaty benefits to arrangements where a resident of Contracting State that would otherwise qualify for treaty benefits is used as an intermediary by persons who are not entitled to these benefits.
Discuss how this BEPS standards may apply.
10. Remedies Available to Local Country
The local country may have several domestic and international anti-tax avoidance provisions available in this case. Domestic provisions may apply to the deduction and permanent establishment issues, and international provisions may apply including other BEPS Action items.
Discuss the potential domestic and international remedies including other BEPS Actions for the Local Co country.
11. Adopting the BEPS Action 15 Multilateral Instrument (MLI) allows the BEPS 6 Minimum Standards to be met by treaty countries.
    - Part III Article 7(1) contains the Principal Purpose Test.
    - Part III Article 7(8) contains the Simplified Limitation on Benefits (S-LOB) provisions;
    Would the Local Co country and the Regional HQ country be likely to adopt the MLI?

12. Which of the above two measures may be more effective for the Local Co country in this case?

ANSWERS

1. The principal issue is that dividend and royalty flows and employee services have apparently been channelled through the Regional HQ country because it has a tax treaty with the Local Co country. In general if there is related commercial substance in the Regional HQ Co, looking beyond the legal agreements, then this case may potentially not be treaty abuse.
2. The Global IP Co employees are seconded to the Regional HQ Co. For legal purposes they are likely to have short term employment contracts with the Regional HQ Co, and the Regional HQ Co may have a service agreement with the Local Co to provide the related services. The economic reality is that they are still Global IP Co employees operating in the Local Co country. This may constitute a taxable permanent establishment of the Global IP Co in the Local Co country. Protection from tax under the permanent establishment rules in the tax treaty with the Regional HQ country should therefore not apply.
3. The Local Co pays royalties to the Regional HQ Co based on related legal agreements, however the IP is actually owned by the Global IP Co. The Regional HQ Co performs no significant functions in relation to the IP and is therefore being used as a conduit to obtain the lower withholding tax rate under the tax treaty.
4. The Local Co pays dividends to the Regional HQ Co based on the ownership of Local Co shares. The Regional HQ Co performs no significant functions in relation to this ownership, and the ultimate economic owner is Parent Co. The Regional HQ Co is therefore being used as a conduit to obtain the lower withholding tax rate under the tax treaty.
5. There may be no significant economic or commercial benefits for the Regional HQ Co to be used in this structure. The employees are in substance employees of the Global IP Co, ownership of shares ultimately traces through to the Parent Co, and the IP is ultimately owned by the Global IP Co. The tax benefits of the tax treaty therefore appear to be one of the principal purposes of the arrangement. The PPT arguably provides less certainty to taxpayers as to whether treaty abuse measures apply, however it allows evaluation of the specific circumstances in each case.
6. The Local Co country would be able to deny treaty benefits in relation to this part of the definition of qualified person. This is because 100% of the ownership of the Regional HQ Co is outside the Regional HQ country. All the direct and indirect ownership of the Regional HQ Co is in the Parent Co country.

7. The Local Co country may potentially be required to provide treaty benefits in relation to this part of the definition of qualified person. This would apply if there was related active conduct of the business by the Regional HQ Co. A related issue is whether an active business includes subcontracting services to other group companies. This issue would however need to be determined on the facts, and may for example include examination of the functions performed, assets used and risks assumed (FAR) by the Regional HQ Co.
8. The Local Co country would potentially be able to deny treaty benefits in relation to this part of the definition of qualified person. This would apply because the ownership of the Regional HQ Co is held by the Parent Co, which is not in a tax treaty country, and is therefore not entitled to treaty benefits.
9. The conduit measures may be significant to deny treaty benefits, particularly if the Regional HQ Co potentially qualifies under the above S-LOB tests.
10. The Local Co country may seek to apply several measures besides BEPS Action 6 and the Action 15 MLI, including:
    - Domestic and treaty transfer pricing rules to reduce or deny the deduction for the royalty payments on the basis that the amount exceeds the arm's length consideration for use of IP.
    - Domestic anti avoidance provisions, such as general anti-avoidance rules (GAAR). The tax treaty may provide that it does not override GAAR rules.
    - Deny treaty benefits on the basis the ultimate 'beneficial owner' of royalty and dividend income is not the Regional HQ Co, for example under the OECD 2017 Model Tax Treaty, Article 10(2) for dividends, and Article 12(1) for royalties. The interpretation of this term, however, currently differs.
    - Measures under BEPS Action 7, Preventing the Artificial Avoidance of Permanent Establishment Status, in relation to the Global IP Co employees.
    - Apply Article 31 of the Vienna Convention on the Law of Treaties, which requires that treaties to be interpreted in good faith, on the basis that the treaty does not apply to tax abusive arrangements.
11. The Local Co country appears likely to adopt either or both measures where it is typically an inward investing country likely to pay interest, dividends, and royalties. This may potentially not be the case with the Regional HQ country, if it is typically an intermediate in international tax structures. This issue may however be addressed if the Regional HQ Co meets the related active business requirements.
12. This issue largely depends on the detailed facts and circumstances in each case. In general terms:
    - The Principal Purpose Test may be most effective unless the taxpayer has evidence of strong commercial benefits to the use of the Regional HQ Co.

- The Limitation on Benefits rules may potentially be satisfied by the active income rules, however the Action 6 Minimum Standard also requires anti-conduit measures which may apply.

CASE STUDY 7

Group Technology: The Solar Power Station, Transfer Pricing, and Mutual Agreement Procedures (MAP)

Power Station Country Issues Additional Tax Assessments. Power Station Country Only has a Tax Treaty with Regional HQ Co.

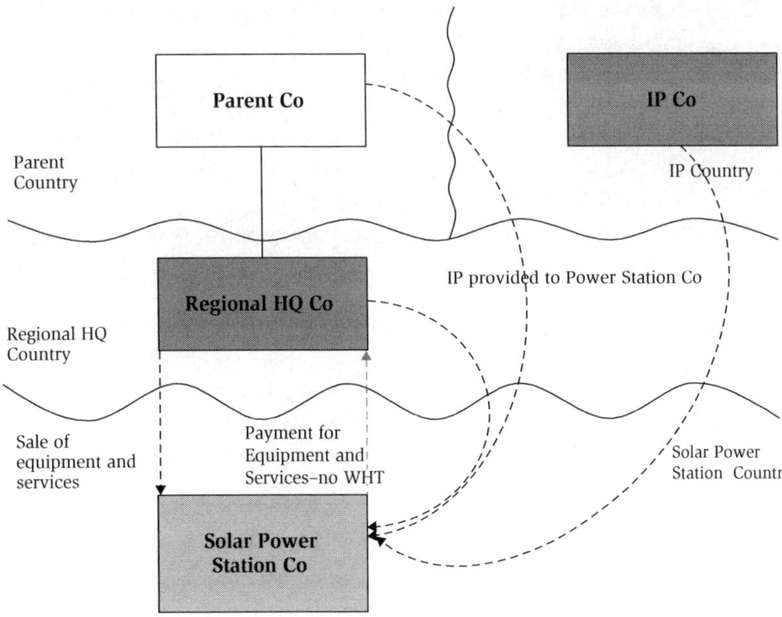

The Parent Co Group builds the Solar Power Station in the Solar Power Station country, providing equipment and services from the Regional HQ Co company, and intangibles including patents and designs from the IP Co company. Solar Power Station Co transfer pricing uses the Transactional New Margin Method (TNMM), with the Operating Margin as Profit Level Indicator (PLI).

The Solar Power Station country tax authorities, however, apply the Residual Profit Split method to increase tax paid by the Solar Power Station Co. The Solar Power Station country also determines that a royalty was in substance paid to the IP Co, the Regional HQ Co and the Parent Co companies, and imposes withholding tax on the deemed royalty payments.

QUESTIONS

1. Equipment and services have been provided to the Solar Power Station Co company by its related party Regional HQ Co. Intangible Property (IP) has been provided to the Solar Power Station Co from the Parent Co (power station plans), the IP Co (use of patents), and the Regional HQ Co (control software customisation). No royalties are paid by the Solar Power Station Co company.
   Discuss how double taxation arises in this case.
2. The BEPS Action 14 minimum standards for MAP are essentially:
   - Jurisdictions should ensure that treaty obligations related to MAP are fully implemented in good faith and that MAP cases are resolved in a timely manner;
   - Jurisdictions should ensure that administrative processes promote the prevention and timely resolution of treaty-related disputes; and
   - Jurisdictions should ensure that taxpayers that meet the requirements of paragraph 1 of Article 25 of the OECD Model Tax Convention can access the MAP.

   This case concerns a quite common combination of related party entities, including the Parent Co, the IP Co, the Regional HQ Co, and the Solar Power Station Co companies.
   Discuss why this gives rise to specific risks under BEPS Action 14.
3. Preventing Disputes – Elements of the Minimum Standard
   The tax treaty contains a provision which requires the competent authority (CA) of their jurisdiction to endeavour to resolve by mutual agreement. The Regional HQ Co country and the Power Station Co country are willing to consider a bilateral APA, however the Regional HQ country does not agree to roll-back the APA to prior years.
   Discuss how the BEPS Action 14 Minimum Standards may apply.
4. Availability and Access to MAP – Elements of the Minimum Standard
   The Regional HQ Co country is considering whether to advise that there are domestic tax law remedies available, and so MAP should not apply. The Regional HQ Co country is considering whether to advise that the taxpayer's

objections are not justified, and so MAP should not apply. The Solar Power Station country considers that a treaty anti-abuse provision should apply as there is not much commercial substance in the Regional HQ Co, and so MAP should not apply.
Discuss how the BEPS Action 14 Minimum Standards may apply.

5. Resolution of MAP Cases – Elements of the Minimum Standard
The Regional HQ country receives a MAP request from the Regional HQ Co but does not refer the case to the Solar Power Station country CA because it considers the case is likely to require a corresponding adjustment reducing local tax. The Regional HQ country CA advises that it cannot resolve the transfer pricing case without approval of its Anti-Tax Avoidance panel due to the treaty abuse issue. The Solar Power Station country will not accept binding arbitration of the case because this is not included in the tax treaty.
Discuss how the BEPS Action 14 Minimum Standards may apply.
6. Implementation of MAP Agreements – Elements of the Minimum Standard
The Solar Power Station Co country is willing to partly reduce the tax under a MAP, however they need six to twelve months to hire external consultants to review the refund amount. The Regional HQ country is prepared to make a corresponding adjustment to reduce Regional HQ Co tax, however it has just declared a new tax audit and made a substantial tax assessment.
Discuss how the BEPS Action 14 Minimum Standards may apply.
7. Adopting the BEPS Action 15 Multilateral Instrument should allow the BEPS 14 Minimum Standards to be met by treaty countries as follows:
   - Allows taxpayers option to present the case to the CA of either treaty jurisdiction,
   - Requires taxpayers to request MAP assistance within three years from first notification of action resulting in tax not in accordance with treaty,
   - Requires the CAs, if the objection appears to be justified and the CA is unable to arrive at a satisfactory solution, to endeavour to resolve case by mutual agreement and to implement resulting agreement, and
   - Requires the CAs to endeavour to resolve by mutual agreement difficulties arising on interpretation or application of the treaty, and allows the CAs to consult for elimination of double taxation in cases not provided in treaty.

     Would the Solar Power Station country and the Regional HQ country be likely to adopt the Multilateral Instrument?
8. The Multilateral Instrument Part VI is intended to apply binding arbitration only between jurisdictions that expressly choose to apply it with respect to their tax agreements. These rules cover:
   - Eligibility for arbitration, relevant timelines, and other operational rules,
   - The appointment of arbitrators,
   - The confidentiality of arbitration proceedings,
   - The resolution of cases prior to the conclusion of arbitration,

- Types of arbitration processes,
- Agreement (by the CAs) on a different resolution, and
- Costs of arbitration proceedings.

  Would the Solar Power Station country and the Regional HQ country be likely to adopt Part VI binding arbitration under the Multilateral Instrument?

ANSWERS

1. Equipment and services have been provided to the Solar Power Station Co company by its related party Regional HQ Co. The Solar Power Station Co company transfer pricing uses Transactional Net Margin Method (TNMM) with Operating Margin as the Profit Level Indicator (PLI). This compares the operating margins of comparable power station companies in the Solar Power Station country and other countries in the region, and determined that its profit margin was acceptable within the interquartile range (25%–75% of outcomes). The Solar Power Station country, however, applies a different transfer pricing method of Residual Profit Split, where the Solar Power Station Co and the Regional HQ Co are each allocated a routine return, and the residual profit is allocated using keys such as sales, research and development expenses, operating expenses, assets, or headcount. This increased taxable profit in the Solar Power Station Co because significant value was allocated to the local marketing intangibles. The Solar Power Station Co has not changed its payments to the Regional HQ Co. The Regional HQ Co country continues to tax based on the actual payments from the Solar Power Station Co.

   Intangible Property (IP) has been provided to the Solar Power Station Co from the Parent Co (power station plans), the IP Co (use of patents), and the Regional HQ Co (control software customisation). No royalties are however paid by the Solar Power Station Co company. The Solar Power Station Co country tax rules allow recognition of deemed royalties in these circumstances, with deemed royalties paid to the Regional HQ Co, the Parent Co, and the IP Co companies. Royalty withholding tax (WHT) was imposed on the deemed payments, reduced to 10% on payments to the Regional HQ Co under the tax treaty, and at a 30% rate on payments to the Parent Co and the IP Co as they are considered to be tax haven countries. The Parent Co, the Regional HQ Co and the IP Co countries do not consider there were royalties, and do not allow any related foreign tax credit.
2. Transfer pricing conflicts potentially arise concerning the allocation of profits between the Parent Co, the IP Co, the Regional HQ Co, and the Solar Power Station Co companies. The analysis should be based on analysis of the functions performed, assets used, and risks assumed (FAR) by the respective entities, however double taxation can arise where the companies and governments concerned do not agree on the transfer pricing method or the

comparable transactions or companies used in the related analysis. The MAP should address these issues, however in practice significant issues may arise.

3. In relation to the BEPS requirement for preventing disputes that jurisdictions should ensure that treaty obligations related to MAP are fully implemented in good faith and that MAP cases are resolved in a timely manner:
   - The tax treaty contains a provision which requires the CA of their jurisdiction to endeavour to resolve by mutual agreement. This complies with Minimum Standard 1.1.
   - The Regional HQ Co country and the Power Station Co country are willing to consider a bilateral APA, however with Regional HQ country does not agree to roll-back the APA to prior years. This does not comply with Minimum Standard 2.7.
4. In relation to the BEPS requirement for availability and access to MAP that jurisdictions should ensure that administrative processes promote the prevention and timely resolution of treaty-related disputes:
   - The Regional HQ country is considering whether to advise that there are domestic tax law remedies available, and so MAP should not apply. This does not comply with Minimum Standard 1.1 that applies notwithstanding domestic remedies.
   - The Regional HQ country is considering whether to advise that the taxpayer's objections are not justified, and so MAP should not apply. This does not comply with Minimum Standard 3.1, as both countries are concerned whether MAP requests are accepted or rejected.
   - The Solar Power Station country considers that a treaty anti-abuse provision should apply as there is not much commercial substance in the Regional HQ Co, and so MAP should not apply. This does not comply with Minimum Standard 1.1 that applies notwithstanding domestic anti-avoidance measures.
5. In relation to the BEPS requirement for resolution of MAP cases that jurisdictions should ensure that taxpayers that meet the requirements of paragraph 1 of Article 25 of the OECD Model Tax Convention can access the MAP:
   - The Regional HQ country receives a MAP request from the Regional HQ Co but initially does not refer the case to the Solar Power Station country CA because considers the case is likely to require a corresponding adjustment reducing local tax. This may not comply with Minimum Standard 1.1 that treaty obligations are implemented in good faith.
   - The Regional HQ country CA advises that it cannot resolve the transfer pricing case without approval of its Anti-Tax Avoidance panel due to the treaty abuse issue. This does not comply with Minimum Standard 1.2.
   - The Solar Power Station country will not accept binding arbitration of the case because this is not included in the tax treaty. This complies

with Minimum Standard 1.7, however countries may agree to binding arbitration under the Multilateral Instrument BEPS Action 15.

6. In relation to the BEPS requirements for the implementation of MAP agreements:
   - The Solar Power Station country is willing to partly reduce the tax under a MAP, however they need six to twelve months to hire external consultants to review the refund amount. This does not comply with Minimum Standard 2.3.
   - The Regional HQ country is prepared to make a corresponding adjustment to reduce Regional HQ tax, however it has just declared a new tax audit and made a substantial tax assessment. This may not comply with Minimum Standard 1.1 that treaty obligations are implemented in good faith.
7. Adopting the BEPS Action 15 Multilateral Instrument allows the BEPS 14 Minimum Standards to be met by treaty countries. The MLI measures:
   - Allow taxpayers the option to present the case to the CA of either treaty jurisdiction.
   - Require taxpayers to request MAP assistance within three years from first notification of action resulting in tax not in accordance with the treaty.
   - Require the CAs, if the objection appears to be justified and the CA is unable to arrive at a satisfactory solution, to endeavour to resolve case by mutual agreement and implement resulting agreement. There is an issue if majority of adjustments expected to reduce tax in the Regional HQ country.
   - Require the CAs to endeavour to resolve by mutual agreement difficulties arising on interpretation or application of treaty, allows the CAs to consult for elimination of double taxation in cases not provided in treaty. There is a significant issue with recharacterisation or reconstruction of payments as royalties.
8. The Multilateral Instrument Part VI is intended to apply binding arbitration only between jurisdictions that expressly choose to apply it with respect to their tax agreements. These rules cover:
   - Eligibility for arbitration, relevant timelines, and other operational rules,
   - The appointment of arbitrators,
   - The confidentiality of arbitration proceedings,
   - The resolution of cases prior to the conclusion of arbitration,
   - Types of arbitration processes,
   - Agreement (by the CAs) on a different resolution, and
   - Costs of arbitration proceedings.

   The most significant current issue is which countries choose to adopt binding arbitration under the Multilateral Instrument.

Case Study 8

Group Marketing: The Liquefied Natural Gas (LNG) Marketing

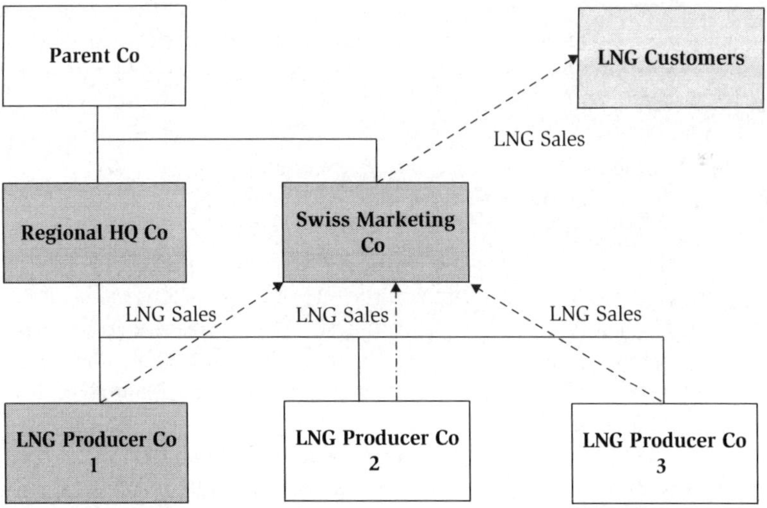

The Parent Co is the parent company of an upstream oil and gas multinational group. The Parent Co holds the Regional HQ Co, which holds liquefied natural gas (LNG) producing subsidiaries LNG Producer Co 1, LNG Producer Co 2, and LNG Producer Co 3 located in different countries. The Parent Co also holds the Swiss Marketing Co company. The LNG Producer Co 1, LNG Producer Co 2, and LNG Producer Co 3 companies sell the LNG to the Swiss Marketing Co, which then sells the LNG to the third party LNG Customers.

The Swiss Marketing Co company also performs other functions for the group, including oil and uranium sales, and also coordinates the development of Sales

Coordinator computer software, which coordinates sales, insurance, and deliveries between producers and purchasers. All the related party entities are located in different countries. The Swiss Marketing Co company has a low tax rate in Switzerland.

The LNG Producer Co 1, LNG Producer Co 2, and LNG Producer Co 3 companies each pay a 3% commission to the Swiss Marketing Co for selling the LNG, based on the sale price of the LNG to the third-party LNG Customers. For transfer pricing purposes, the 3% commission is determined using the Comparable Uncontrolled Price (CUP) method, where the 5% commission is the average rate of the LNG commissions charged by ten unrelated companies.

QUESTIONS

You represent the tax authorities in the LNG Producer Co 1's country. Discuss your issues with the transfer pricing for LNG sales by the LNG Producer Co 1.

ANSWERS

The principal transfer pricing issue with the commission is whether an independent party would pay 3% for the marketing services provided by the Swiss Marketing Co company, to establish that this was an arm's length commission rate, rather than the use of non-arm's length transfer pricing to derive profits within the multinational group in a low taxing jurisdiction.

The functions performed, assets used, and risks assumed (FAR) for the LNG Producer Co 1 and the Swiss Marketing Co companies should be examined. The principal issue is that although the Swiss Marketing Co is deriving very substantial profits from the LNG trading activities in a low taxing jurisdiction, for transfer pricing purposes, this does not mean that the rate of commission paid is necessarily above an arm's length rate. The FAR analysis may, however, suggest that the commission rate is too high because there is minimal commercial substance in the Swiss Marketing Co, and that significant marketing activities are actually carried out by the LNG producer Co 1.

The ten companies used in the transfer pricing benchmarking to support the 3% commission would be examined. The analysis would consider: (1) the geographical location and the related political risks in LNG production countries used as comparables, where lower commissions may apply for marketing production from lower risk locations, (2) the volumes of LNG sold, where lower commissions may apply for larger volumes, and (3) the nature of the related markets, where lower commissions may apply for sales to mature LNG markets with a well-established customer base.

It is also advisable to examine profits of comparable LNG producing companies using another transfer pricing method, for example using the transactional net margin (TNMM) method. This would provide a useful check of the transfer pricing basis and whether the commission paid by the LNG Producer Co 1 company was leaving too low a profit level compared to other LNG producing companies. The TNMM approach may be the preferred approach by the tax authorities particularly where other LNG producers not paying such a marketing commission are making substantially higher profits.

Certain tax authorities may adopt a transactional profit split method, where the total profits between the LNG Producer Co 1 and the Swiss Marketing Co companies are split, for example on the basis of the FAR analysis. The 2017 OECD Transfer Pricing Guidelines suggest, however, that the method is appropriate for highly integrated operations, or where both parties to a transaction make unique and valuable contributions. The OECD consider that a transactional profit split method would ordinarily not be used in cases where one party to the transaction performs only simple functions and does not make any significant unique contribution. There may however be scope for certain tax authorities to adopt this method in wider cases.

There may also be an opportunity where the Swiss Trading Co company is selected as the tested party for transfer pricing purposes, and then to review whether the profits derived were comparable to unrelated trading companies. This approach has a significant difficulty because the Swiss Trading Co company carries out other activities besides LNG trading, such as coordinating the development of the Sales Coordinator computer software. In relation to the identification of the tested party for the transfer pricing analysis, while there may be reliable and accurate data available for comparison, it may not be the least complex entity amongst the parties to the transaction, and the data available may require more than minimal adjustments.

A common threshold issue is obtaining financial information on the Swiss Marketing Co company, including the financial reports and management accounts. The management accounts in particular may be used to determine the basis for a reasonable apportionment of the profits in the Swiss Marketing Co company which relate to LNG Production Co 1. This issue can depend on taxpayer cooperation, or the Tax Treaty or Exchange of Information (EOI) agreements between the countries concerned.

The Country-by-Country (CbC) Reports for the Parent Co Group should be examined. The Parent Co Master File, LNG Producer Co 1 Local File, and the CbC report will assist the tax authorities to understand the Parent Group's global value chain, and in particular to determine the level of related party profits which are derived by the Swiss Marketing Co company. The CbC Report in particular will indicate group trading centres such as the Swiss Marketing Co, with high related party earnings compared to the number of related employees. The current CbC reports would not, however, indicate the related party expenses of the Swiss Marketing Co, and the extent it had subcontracted activities to other entities in the multinational group.

The follow up CbC analysis will include whether profits allocated to such trading entities are commensurate with the functions performed, assets used, and risks undertaken by these entities, and may therefore suggest that the use of the marketing entity is potentially to reduce taxable profits in the group companies making sales to the marketing entity.

There may also be scope for the potential application of other tax provisions, for example the use of a General Anti-Avoidance Rule (GAAR) or a Diverted Profits Tax (DPT). This can particularly apply where there is little commercial or economic substance in the Swiss Marketing Co, such as where the principal traders do not work in Switzerland, or where significant activities are subcontracted by the Swiss Marketing Co company to other entities in the multinational group.

ANNEX EGYPTIAN MODEL CONTRACT - EXTRACTS

CONCESSION AGREEMENT FOR GAS AND CRUDE OIL EXPLORATION AND EXPLOITATION BETWEEN THE ARAB REPUBLIC OF EGYPT AND THE EGYPTIAN NATURAL GAS HOLDING COMPANY AND [CONTRACTOR]

ARTICLE III GRANT OF RIGHTS AND TERM

The GOVERNMENT hereby grants EGAS and CONTRACTOR, subject to the terms, covenants and conditions set out in this Agreement, which insofar as they may be contrary to or inconsistent with any provisions of Law No. 66 of 1953, as amended, shall have the force of law, an exclusive concession in and to the Area described in Annexes "A" and "B".

a) The GOVERNMENT shall own and be entitled to, as hereinafter provided, a royalty in cash or in kind of ten percent (10%) of the total quantity of Petroleum produced and saved from the Area during the Development period including its extension, if any. Said royalty shall be borne and paid by EGAS and shall not be the obligation of CONTRACTOR. The payment of royalties by EGAS shall not be deemed to result in an income attributable to the CONTRACTOR.

   (...)

   (g)

   (1) Unless otherwise provided, CONTRACTOR shall be subject to Egyptian income tax laws in A.R.E. and shall comply with the requirements of such laws with respect to the filing of returns, the assessment of tax, and keeping and showing of books and records.

   (2) CONTRACTOR shall be liable to prepare the income tax return statement. CONTRACTOR shall submit the tax return statement to EGAS at least twenty five (25) days prior to the due date of submitting thereof to the tax authority. EGAS shall have the right to review the tax return statement in order to approve the tax calculation therein. EGAS shall provide comments on such tax return statement within fifteen (15) days of the date of receiving the tax return statement from CONTRACTOR. In any case CONTRACTOR

shall be responsible for submitting the tax return statement to the tax authority within the legal due date.

(3) CONTRACTOR's annual income for Egyptian income tax in A.R.E. purposes under this Agreement shall be an amount calculated as follows:

The total of the sums received by CONTRACTOR from the sale or other disposition of all Petroleum acquired by CONTRACTOR pursuant to Article VII(a) and (b);

Reduced by:

(i) The costs and expenses of CONTRACTOR; and
(ii) The value of EGAS' share of the Excess Cost Recovery Petroleum, if any, to be paid to EGAS in cash or in kind as determined according to Article VII.

plus:

An amount equal to CONTRACTOR's Egyptian income taxes in A.R.E. grossed-up in the manner shown in Article VI of Annex "E".

For purposes of abovementioned tax deductions in any Tax Year, Article VII(a) shall apply only in respect of classification of costs and expenses and rates of amortization, without regard to the percentage limitation referred to in the first paragraph of Article VII(a)(1). All costs and expenses of CONTRACTOR in conducting the operations under this Agreement which are not controlled by Article VII (a) as above qualified shall be deductible in accordance with the provisions of the Egyptian Income Tax Law.

(4) EGAS shall assume, pay and discharge, in the name and on behalf of CONTRACTOR, CONTRACTOR's Egyptian income tax in A.R.E. out of EGAS' share of the Petroleum produced and saved and not used in operations under Article VII. All taxes paid by EGAS in the name and on behalf of CONTRACTOR shall be considered as income to CONTRACTOR.

In case CONTRACTOR dispose all or part of its share of production sharing Gas and excess cost recovery Gas, if any, by itself to local market and after obtaining the competent authorities in A.R.E. approval, CONTRACTOR shall bear and pay to EGAS an amount equal to the CONTRACTOR's Egyptian income tax in respect of such Gas, the payment of such tax by CONTRACTOR shall not be considered as income to CONTRACTOR and be deemed to be non-recoverable cost.

ARTICLE VII RECOVERY OF COSTS AND EXPENSES AND PRODUCTION SHARING

(a) COST RECOVERY:
(1) Cost Recovery Petroleum:

Subject to the auditing provisions under this Agreement, CONTRACTOR shall recover quarterly all costs, expenses and expenditures in respect of all the Exploration, Development and related operations under this Agreement to the extent and out of ----------percent (%) of all Petroleum produced and saved from all Development Leases within the Area hereunder and not used in Petroleum operations. Such Petroleum is hereinafter referred to as "Cost Recovery Petroleum".

For the purpose of determining the classification of all costs, expenses and expenditures for their recovery, the following terms shall apply:

1. "Exploration Expenditures" means all costs and expenses for Exploration and the related portion of indirect expenses and overheads.
2. "Development Expenditures" means all costs and expenses for Development (with the exception of Operating Expenses) and the related portion of indirect expenses and overheads.
3. "Operating Expenses" means all costs, expenses and expenditures made after the Commercial Production Commencement, which costs, expenses and expenditures are not normally depreciable.
   (...)

Exploration Expenditures, Development Expenditures and Operating Expenses shall be recovered from Cost Recovery Petroleum in the following manner:-

(i) "Exploration Expenditures", including those accumulated prior to the Commercial Production Commencement, shall be recoverable at the rate of -------- percent (---%) per annum starting either in the Tax Year in which such expenditures are incurred and paid or the Tax Year in which the Commercial Production Commencement occurs, whichever is the later date.

(ii) "Development Expenditures", including those accumulated prior to the Commercial Production Commencement, shall be recoverable at the rate of -------- percent (---%) per annum starting either in the Tax Year in which such expenditures are incurred and paid or the Tax Year in which the Commercial Production Commencement occurs, whichever is the later date.

(iii) "Operating Expenses", incurred and paid after the Commercial Production Commencement, shall be recoverable either in the Tax Year in which such costs and expenses are incurred and paid or the Tax Year in which the Commercial Production Commencement occurs, whichever is the later date.

(iv) To the extent that, in a Tax Year, costs, expenses or expenditures recoverable per preceding paragraphs (i), (ii) and (iii), exceed the value of all Cost Recovery Petroleum for such Tax Year, the excess shall be carried forward for recovery in the next succeeding Tax Year(s) until fully recovered, but in no case after the termination of this Agreement, as to CONTRACTOR.

(...)

(b) PRODUCTION SHARING

(1) The remaining ---------- percent (----- %) of the Petroleum shall be divided quarterly between EGAS and the CONTRACTOR based on Brent value and according to the following shares.

i) Crude Oil and Condensate:

(...)

BRENT PRICE

US$/bbl Crude Oil produced and saved under this Agreement and not used in Petroleum operations. Barrel of Oil Per Day (BOPD) (quarterly average) EGAS'

SHARE CONTRACTOR'S SHARE %

More than 100 US$ and less than or equal to 120 US$ That portion or increment less than 5 000 BOPD

That portion or increment from 5 000 BOPD and less than 10 000 BOPD

That portion or increment from 10 000 BOPD and less than 20 000 BOPD

That portion or increment equal to or more than 20 000 BOPD

(...)

ANNEX "E" ACCOUNTING PROCEDURE

ARTICLE II COSTS, EXPENSES AND EXPENDITURES

Subject to the provisions of the Agreement, CONTRACTOR shall alone bear and, directly or through the Joint Venture Company, pay the following costs and expenses, which costs and expenses shall be classified and allocated to the activities according to sound and generally accepted accounting principles and treated and recovered in accordance with Article VII of this Agreement:

(...)

(l) Taxes:

All taxes, duties or levies paid in the A.R.E. by CONTRACTOR or the Joint Venture Company with respect to this Agreement other than those covered by Article III(g)(1) of the Agreement.

(...)

(n) Other Expenditures:

Any costs, expenses or expenditures, other than those which are covered and dealt with by the foregoing provisions of this Article II, incurred by CONTRACTOR or the Joint Venture Company under approved Work Programs and Budgets.

Appendices

APPENDIX I

OECD Model Tax Convention 2017: Condensed Version

© OECD (2017), Model Tax Convention on Income and on Capital: Condensed Version 2017, OECD Publishing, Paris.

http://dx.doi.org/10.1787/mtc_cond-2017-en

TITLE OF THE CONVENTION

Convention between (State A) and (State B)

for the elimination of double taxation with respect to taxes on income and on capital and the prevention of tax evasion and avoidance

PREAMBLE TO THE CONVENTION

(State A) and (State B),

Desiring to further develop their economic relationship and to enhance their cooperation in tax matters,

Intending to conclude a Convention for the elimination of double taxation with respect to taxes on income and on capital without creating opportunities for non-taxation or reduced taxation through tax evasion or avoidance (including through treaty-shopping arrangements aimed at obtaining reliefs provided in this Convention for the indirect benefit of residents of third States),

Have agreed as follows:

CHAPTER I SCOPE OF THE CONVENTION

Article 1 Persons Covered

1. This Convention shall apply to persons who are residents of one or both of the Contracting States.
2. For the purposes of this Convention, income derived by or through an entity or arrangement that is treated as wholly or partly fiscally transparent under the tax law of either Contracting State shall be considered to be income of a resident of a Contracting State but only to the extent that the income is treated, for purposes of taxation by that State, as the income of a resident of that State.
3. This Convention shall not affect the taxation, by a Contracting State, of its residents except with respect to the benefits granted under paragraph 3 of Article 7, paragraph 2 of Article 9 and Articles 19, 20, 23 [A] [B], 24, 25 and 28.

Article 2 Taxes Covered

1. This Convention shall apply to taxes on income and on capital imposed on behalf of a Contracting State or of its political subdivisions or local authorities, irrespective of the manner in which they are levied.
2. There shall be regarded as taxes on income and on capital all taxes imposed on total income, on total capital, or on elements of income or of capital, including taxes on gains from the alienation of movable or immovable property, taxes on the total amounts of wages or salaries paid by enterprises, as well as taxes on capital appreciation.
3. The existing taxes to which the Convention shall apply are in particular:
   a) (in State A): ....
   b) (in State B): ....
4. The Convention shall apply also to any identical or substantially similar taxes that are imposed after the date of signature of the Convention in addition to, or in place of, the existing taxes. The competent authorities of the Contracting States shall notify each other of any significant changes that have been made in their taxation laws.

CHAPTER II DEFINITIONS

Article 3 General Definitions

1. For the purposes of this Convention, unless the context otherwise requires:
   a) the term "person" includes an individual, a company and any other body of persons;
   b) the term "company" means any body corporate or any entity that is treated as a body corporate for tax purposes;

c) the term "enterprise" applies to the carrying on of any business;
d) the terms "enterprise of a Contracting State" and "enterprise of the other Contracting State" mean respectively an enterprise carried on by a resident of a Contracting State and an enterprise carried on by a resident of the other Contracting State;
e) the term "international traffic" means any transport by a ship or aircraft except when the ship or aircraft is operated solely between places in a Contracting State and the enterprise that operates the ship or aircraft is not an enterprise of that State;
f) the term "competent authority" means:
   (i) (in State A): ....
   (ii) (in State B): ....
g) the term "national", in relation to a Contracting State, means:
   (i) any individual possessing the nationality or citizenship of that Contracting State; and
   (ii) any legal person, partnership or association deriving its status as such from the laws in force in that Contracting State;
h) the term "business" includes the performance of professional services and of other activities of an independent character.
i) the term "recognised pension fund" of a State means an entity or arrangement established in that State that is treated as a separate person under the taxation laws of that State and:
   (i) that is established and operated exclusively or almost exclusively to administer or provide retirement benefits and ancillary or incidental benefits to individuals and that is regulated as such by that State or one of its political subdivisions or local authorities; or
   (ii) that is established and operated exclusively or almost exclusively to invest funds for the benefit of entities or arrangements referred to in subdivision (i).

2. As regards the application of the Convention at any time by a Contracting State, any term not defined therein shall, unless the context otherwise requires or the competent authorities agree to a different meaning pursuant to the provisions of Article 25, have the meaning that it has at that time under the law of that State for the purposes of the taxes to which the Convention applies, any meaning under the applicable tax laws of that State prevailing over a meaning given to the term under other laws of that State.

Article 4 Resident

1. For the purposes of this Convention, the term "resident of a Contracting State" means any person who, under the laws of that State, is liable to tax therein by reason of his domicile, residence, place of management or any other criterion of a similar nature, and also includes that State and any political subdivision or local authority thereof as well as a recognised pension

fund of that State. This term, however, does not include any person who is liable to tax in that State in respect only of income from sources in that State or capital situated therein.

2. Where by reason of the provisions of paragraph 1 an individual is a resident of both Contracting States, then his status shall be determined as follows:
   a) he shall be deemed to be a resident only of the State in which he has a permanent home available to him; if he has a permanent home available to him in both States, he shall be deemed to be a resident only of the State with which his personal and economic relations are closer (centre of vital interests);
   b) if the State in which he has his centre of vital interests cannot be determined, or if he has not a permanent home available to him in either State, he shall be deemed to be a resident only of the State in which he has an habitual abode;
   c) if he has an habitual abode in both States or in neither of them, he shall be deemed to be a resident only of the State of which he is a national;
   d) if he is a national of both States or of neither of them, the competent authorities of the Contracting States shall settle the question by mutual agreement.
3. Where by reason of the provisions of paragraph 1 a person other than an individual is a resident of both Contracting States, the competent authorities of the Contracting States shall endeavour to determine by mutual agreement the Contracting State of which such person shall be deemed to be a resident for the purposes of the Convention, having regard to its place of effective management, the place where it is incorporated or otherwise constituted and any other relevant factors. In the absence of such agreement, such person shall not be entitled to any relief or exemption from tax provided by this Convention except to the extent and in such manner as may be agreed upon by the competent authorities of the Contracting States.

Article 5 Permanent Establishment

1. For the purposes of this Convention, the term "permanent establishment" means a fixed place of business through which the business of an enterprise is wholly or partly carried on.
2. The term "permanent establishment" includes especially:
   a) a place of management;
   b) a branch;
   c) an office;
   d) a factory;
   e) a workshop, and
   f) a mine, an oil or gas well, a quarry or any other place of extraction of natural resources.
3. A building site or construction or installation project constitutes a permanent establishment only if it lasts more than twelve months.

4. Notwithstanding the preceding provisions of this Article, the term "permanent establishment" shall be deemed not to include:
   a) the use of facilities solely for the purpose of storage, display or delivery of goods or merchandise belonging to the enterprise;
   b) the maintenance of a stock of goods or merchandise belonging to the enterprise solely for the purpose of storage, display or delivery;
   c) the maintenance of a stock of goods or merchandise belonging to the enterprise solely for the purpose of processing by another enterprise;
   d) the maintenance of a fixed place of business solely for the purpose of purchasing goods or merchandise or of collecting information, for the enterprise;
   e) the maintenance of a fixed place of business solely for the purpose of carrying on, for the enterprise, any other activity;
   f) the maintenance of a fixed place of business solely for any combination of activities mentioned in subparagraphs a) to e),

   provided that such activity or, in the case of subparagraph f), the overall activity of the fixed place of business, is of a preparatory or auxiliary character.

4.1 Paragraph 4 shall not apply to a fixed place of business that is used or maintained by an enterprise if the same enterprise or a closely related enterprise carries on business activities at the same place or at another place in the same Contracting State
   and
   a) that place or other place constitutes a permanent establishment for the enterprise or the closely related enterprise under the provisions of this Article,
      or
   b) the overall activity resulting from the combination of the activities carried on by the two enterprises at the same place, or by the same enterprise or closely related enterprises at the two places, is not of a preparatory or auxiliary character,

   provided that the business activities carried on by the two enterprises at the same place, or by the same enterprise or closely related enterprises at the two places, constitute complementary functions that are part of a cohesive business operation.

5. Notwithstanding the provisions of paragraphs 1 and 2 but subject to the provisions of paragraph 6, where a person is acting in a Contracting State on behalf of an enterprise and, in doing so, habitually concludes contracts, or habitually plays the principal role leading to the conclusion of contracts that are routinely concluded without material modification by the enterprise, and these contracts are
   a) in the name of the enterprise, or
   b) for the transfer of the ownership of, or for the granting of the right to use, property owned by that enterprise or that the enterprise has the right to use, or

c) for the provision of services by that enterprise,

that enterprise shall be deemed to have a permanent establishment in that State in respect of any activities which that person undertakes for the enterprise, unless the activities of such person are limited to those mentioned in paragraph 4 which, if exercised through a fixed place of business (other than a fixed place of business to which paragraph 4.1 would apply), would not make this fixed place of business a permanent establishment under the provisions of that paragraph.

6. Paragraph 5 shall not apply where the person acting in a Contracting State on behalf of an enterprise of the other Contracting State carries on business in the firstmentioned State as an independent agent and acts for the enterprise in the ordinary course of that business. Where, however, a person acts exclusively or almost exclusively on behalf of one or more enterprises to which it is closely related, that person shall not be considered to be an independent agent within the meaning of this paragraph with respect to any such enterprise.
7. The fact that a company which is a resident of a Contracting State controls or is controlled by a company which is a resident of the other Contracting State, or which carries on business in that other State (whether through a permanent establishment or otherwise), shall not of itself constitute either company a permanent establishment of the other.
8. For the purposes of this Article, a person or enterprise is closely related to an enterprise if, based on all the relevant facts and circumstances, one has control of the other or both are under the control of the same persons or enterprises. In any case, a person or enterprise shall be considered to be closely related to an enterprise if one possesses directly or indirectly more than 50 per cent of the beneficial interest in the other (or, in the case of a company, more than 50 per cent of the aggregate vote and value of the company's shares or of the beneficial equity interest in the company) or if another person or enterprise possesses directly or indirectly more than 50 per cent of the beneficial interest (or, in the case of a company, more than 50 per cent of the aggregate vote and value of the company's shares or of the beneficial equity interest in the company) in the person and the enterprise or in the two enterprises.

CHAPTER III TAXATION OF INCOME

Article 6 Income from Immovable Property

1. Income derived by a resident of a Contracting State from immovable property (including income from agriculture or forestry) situated in the other Contracting State may be taxed in that other State.
2. The term "immovable property" shall have the meaning which it has under the law of the Contracting State in which the property in question is situated. The term shall in any case include property accessory to immovable

property, livestock and equipment used in agriculture and forestry, rights to which the provisions of general law respecting landed property apply, usufruct of immovable property and rights to variable or fixed payments as consideration for the working of, or the right to work, mineral deposits, sources and other natural resources; ships and aircraft shall not be regarded as immovable property.

3. The provisions of paragraph 1 shall apply to income derived from the direct use, letting, or use in any other form of immovable property.
4. The provisions of paragraphs 1 and 3 shall also apply to the income from immovable property of an enterprise.

Article 7 Business Profits

1. Profits of an enterprise of a Contracting State shall be taxable only in that State unless the enterprise carries on business in the other Contracting State through a permanent establishment situated therein. If the enterprise carries on business as aforesaid, the profits that are attributable to the permanent establishment in accordance with the provisions of paragraph 2 may be taxed in that other State.
2. For the purposes of this Article and Article [23 A] [23 B], the profits that are attributable in each Contracting State to the permanent establishment referred to in paragraph 1 are the profits it might be expected to make, in particular in its dealings with other parts of the enterprise, if it were a separate and independent enterprise engaged in the same or similar activities under the same or similar conditions, taking into account the functions performed, assets used and risks assumed by the enterprise through the permanent establishment and through the other parts of the enterprise.
3. Where, in accordance with paragraph 2, a Contracting State adjusts the profits that are attributable to a permanent establishment of an enterprise of one of the Contracting States and taxes accordingly profits of the enterprise that have been charged to tax in the other State, the other State shall, to the extent necessary to eliminate double taxation on these profits, make an appropriate adjustment to the amount of the tax charged on those profits. In determining such adjustment, the competent authorities of the Contracting States shall if necessary consult each other.
4. Where profits include items of income which are dealt with separately in other Articles of this Convention, then the provisions of those Articles shall not be affected by the provisions of this Article.

Article 8 International Shipping and Air Transport

1. Profits of an enterprise of a Contracting State from the operation of ships or aircraft in international traffic shall be taxable only in that State.
2. The provisions of paragraph 1 shall also apply to profits from the participation in a pool, a joint business or an international operating agency.

Article 9 Associated Enterprises

1. Where
   a) an enterprise of a Contracting State participates directly or indirectly in the management, control or capital of an enterprise of the other Contracting State,

   or

   b) the same persons participate directly or indirectly in the management, control or capital of an enterprise of a Contracting State and an enterprise of the other Contracting State,

   and in either case conditions are made or imposed between the two enterprises in their commercial or financial relations which differ from those which would be made between independent enterprises, then any profits which would, but for those conditions, have accrued to one of the enterprises, but, by reason of those conditions, have not so accrued, may be included in the profits of that enterprise and taxed accordingly.
2. Where a Contracting State includes in the profits of an enterprise of that State — and taxes accordingly — profits on which an enterprise of the other Contracting State has been charged to tax in that other State and the profits so included are profits which would have accrued to the enterprise of the first-mentioned State if the conditions made between the two enterprises had been those which would have been made between independent enterprises, then that other State shall make an appropriate adjustment to the amount of the tax charged therein on those profits. In determining such adjustment, due regard shall be had to the other provisions of this Convention and the competent authorities of the Contracting States shall if necessary consult each other.

Article 10 Dividends

1. Dividends paid by a company which is a resident of a Contracting State to a resident of the other Contracting State may be taxed in that other State.
2. However, dividends paid by a company which is a resident of a Contracting State may also be taxed in that State according to the laws of that State, but if the beneficial owner of the dividends is a resident of the other Contracting State, the tax so charged shall not exceed:
   a) 5 per cent of the gross amount of the dividends if the beneficial owner is a company which holds directly at least 25 per cent of the capital of the company paying the dividends throughout a 365 day period that includes the day of the payment of the dividend (for the purpose of computing that period, no account shall be taken of changes of ownership that would directly result from a corporate reorganisation, such as a merger or divisive reorganisation, of the company that holds the shares or that pays the dividend);

b) 15 per cent of the gross amount of the dividends in all other cases.

The competent authorities of the Contracting States shall by mutual agreement settle the mode of application of these limitations. This paragraph shall not affect the taxation of the company in respect of the profits out of which the dividends are paid.

3. The term "dividends" as used in this Article means income from shares, "jouissance" shares or "jouissance" rights, mining shares, founders' shares or other rights, not being debt-claims, participating in profits, as well as income from other corporate rights which is subjected to the same taxation treatment as income from shares by the laws of the State of which the company making the distribution is a resident.
4. The provisions of paragraphs 1 and 2 shall not apply if the beneficial owner of the dividends, being a resident of a Contracting State, carries on business in the other Contracting State of which the company paying the dividends is a resident through a permanent establishment situated therein and the holding in respect of which the dividends are paid is effectively connected with such permanent establishment. In such case the provisions of Article 7 shall apply.
5. Where a company which is a resident of a Contracting State derives profits or income from the other Contracting State, that other State may not impose any tax on the dividends paid by the company, except insofar as such dividends are paid to a resident of that other State or insofar as the holding in respect of which the dividends are paid is effectively connected with a permanent establishment situated in that other State, nor subject the company's undistributed profits to a tax on the company's undistributed profits, even if the dividends paid or the undistributed profits consist wholly or partly of profits or income arising in such other State.

Article 11 Interest

1. Interest arising in a Contracting State and paid to a resident of the other Contracting State may be taxed in that other State.
2. However, interest arising in a Contracting State may also be taxed in that State according to the laws of that State, but if the beneficial owner of the interest is a resident of the other Contracting State, the tax so charged shall not exceed 10 per cent of the gross amount of the interest. The competent authorities of the Contracting States shall by mutual agreement settle the mode of application of this limitation.
3. The term "interest" as used in this Article means income from debt-claims of every kind, whether or not secured by mortgage and whether or not carrying a right to participate in the debtor's profits, and in particular, income from government securities and income from bonds or debentures, including premiums and prizes attaching to such securities, bonds or debentures. Penalty charges for late payment shall not be regarded as interest for the purpose of this Article.

4. The provisions of paragraphs 1 and 2 shall not apply if the beneficial owner of the interest, being a resident of a Contracting State, carries on business in the other Contracting State in which the interest arises through a permanent establishment situated therein and the debt-claim in respect of which the interest is paid is effectively connected with such permanent establishment. In such case the provisions of Article 7 shall apply.
5. Interest shall be deemed to arise in a Contracting State when the payer is a resident of that State. Where, however, the person paying the interest, whether he is a resident of a Contracting State or not, has in a Contracting State a permanent establishment in connection with which the indebtedness on which the interest is paid was incurred, and such interest is borne by such permanent establishment, then such interest shall be deemed to arise in the State in which the permanent establishment is situated.
6. Where, by reason of a special relationship between the payer and the beneficial owner or between both of them and some other person, the amount of the interest, having regard to the debt-claim for which it is paid, exceeds the amount which would have been agreed upon by the payer and the beneficial owner in the absence of such relationship, the provisions of this Article shall apply only to the last-mentioned amount. In such case, the excess part of the payments shall remain taxable according to the laws of each Contracting State, due regard being had to the other provisions of this Convention.

Article 12 Royalties

1. Royalties arising in a Contracting State and beneficially owned by a resident of the other Contracting State shall be taxable only in that other State.
2. The term "royalties" as used in this Article means payments of any kind received as a consideration for the use of, or the right to use, any copyright of literary, artistic or scientific work including cinematograph films, any patent, trade mark, design or model, plan, secret formula or process, or for information concerning industrial, commercial or scientific experience.
3. The provisions of paragraph 1 shall not apply if the beneficial owner of the royalties, being a resident of a Contracting State, carries on business in the other Contracting State in which the royalties arise through a permanent establishment situated therein and the right or property in respect of which the royalties are paid is effectively connected with such permanent establishment. In such case the provisions of Article 7 shall apply.
4. Where, by reason of a special relationship between the payer and the beneficial owner or between both of them and some other person, the amount of the royalties, having regard to the use, right or information for which they are paid, exceeds the amount which would have been agreed upon by the payer and the beneficial owner in the absence of such relationship, the provisions of this Article shall apply only to the last-mentioned amount. In such case, the excess part of the payments shall remain taxable according to the

laws of each Contracting State, due regard being had to the other provisions of this Convention.

Article 13 Capital Gains

1. Gains derived by a resident of a Contracting State from the alienation of immovable property referred to in Article 6 and situated in the other Contracting State may be taxed in that other State.
2. Gains from the alienation of movable property forming part of the business property of a permanent establishment which an enterprise of a Contracting State has in the other Contracting State, including such gains from the alienation of such a permanent establishment (alone or with the whole enterprise), may be taxed in that other State.
3. Gains that an enterprise of a Contracting State that operates ships or aircraft in international traffic derives from the alienation of such ships or aircraft, or of movable property pertaining to the operation of such ships or aircraft, shall be taxable only in that State.
4. Gains derived by a resident of a Contracting State from the alienation of shares or comparable interests, such as interests in a partnership or trust, may be taxed in the other Contracting State if, at any time during the 365 days preceding the alienation, these shares or comparable interests derived more than 50 per cent of their value directly or indirectly from immovable property, as defined in Article 6, situated in that other State.
5. Gains from the alienation of any property, other than that referred to in paragraphs 1, 2, 3 and 4, shall be taxable only in the Contracting State of which the alienator is a resident.

[Article 14 Independent Personal Services]

[DELETED]

Article 15 Income from Employment

1. Subject to the provisions of Articles 16, 18 and 19, salaries, wages and other similar remuneration derived by a resident of a Contracting State in respect of an employment shall be taxable only in that State unless the employment is exercised in the other Contracting State. If the employment is so exercised, such remuneration as is derived therefrom may be taxed in that other State.
2. Notwithstanding the provisions of paragraph 1, remuneration derived by a resident of a Contracting State in respect of an employment exercised in the other Contracting State shall be taxable only in the first-mentioned State if:
   a) the recipient is present in the other State for a period or periods not exceeding in the aggregate 183 days in any twelve month period commencing or ending in the fiscal year concerned, and

b) the remuneration is paid by, or on behalf of, an employer who is not a resident of the other State, and
c) the remuneration is not borne by a permanent establishment which the employer has in the other State.

3. Notwithstanding the preceding provisions of this Article, remuneration derived by a resident of a Contracting State in respect of an employment, as a member of the regular complement of a ship or aircraft, that is exercised aboard a ship or aircraft operated in international traffic, other than aboard a ship or aircraft operated solely within the other Contracting State, shall be taxable only in the first-mentioned State.

Article 16 Directors' Fees

Directors' fees and other similar payments derived by a resident of a Contracting State in his capacity as a member of the board of directors of a company which is a resident of the other Contracting State may be taxed in that other State.

Article 17 Entertainers and Sportspersons

1. Notwithstanding the provisions of Article 15, income derived by a resident of a Contracting State as an entertainer, such as a theatre, motion picture, radio or television artiste, or a musician, or as a sportsperson, from that resident's personal activities as such exercised in the other Contracting State, may be taxed in that other State.
2. Where income in respect of personal activities exercised by an entertainer or a sportsperson acting as such accrues not to the entertainer or sportsperson but to another person, that income may, notwithstanding the provisions of Article 15, be taxed in the Contracting State in which the activities of the entertainer or sportsperson are exercised.

Article 18 Pensions

Subject to the provisions of paragraph 2 of Article 19, pensions and other similar remuneration paid to a resident of a Contracting State in consideration of past employment shall be taxable only in that State.

Article 19 Government Service

1. a) Salaries, wages and other similar remuneration paid by a Contracting State or a political subdivision or a local authority thereof to an individual in respect of services rendered to that State or subdivision or authority shall be taxable only in that State.
   b) However, such salaries, wages and other similar remuneration shall be taxable only in the other Contracting State if the services are rendered in that State and the individual is a resident of that State who:

(i) is a national of that State; or
(ii) did not become a resident of that State solely for the purpose of rendering the services.

2. a) Notwithstanding the provisions of paragraph 1, pensions and other similar remuneration paid by, or out of funds created by, a Contracting State or a political subdivision or a local authority thereof to an individual in respect of services rendered to that State or subdivision or authority shall be taxable only in that State.
   b) However, such pensions and other similar remuneration shall be taxable only in the other Contracting State if the individual is a resident of, and a national of, that State.
3. The provisions of Articles 15, 16, 17, and 18 shall apply to salaries, wages, pensions, and other similar remuneration in respect of services rendered in connection with a business carried on by a Contracting State or a political subdivision or a local authority thereof.

Article 20 Students

Payments which a student or business apprentice who is or was immediately before visiting a Contracting State a resident of the other Contracting State and who is present in the first-mentioned State solely for the purpose of his education or training receives for the purpose of his maintenance, education or training shall not be taxed in that State, provided that such payments arise from sources outside that State.

Article 21 Other Income

1. Items of income of a resident of a Contracting State, wherever arising, not dealt with in the foregoing Articles of this Convention shall be taxable only in that State.
2. The provisions of paragraph 1 shall not apply to income, other than income from immovable property as defined in paragraph 2 of Article 6, if the recipient of such income, being a resident of a Contracting State, carries on business in the other Contracting State through a permanent establishment situated therein and the right or property in respect of which the income is paid is effectively connected with such permanent establishment. In such case the provisions of Article 7 shall apply.

CHAPTER IV TAXATION OF CAPITAL

Article 22 Capital

1. Capital represented by immovable property referred to in Article 6, owned by a resident of a Contracting State and situated in the other Contracting State, may be taxed in that other State.

2. Capital represented by movable property forming part of the business property of a permanent establishment which an enterprise of a Contracting State has in the other Contracting State may be taxed in that other State.
3. Capital of an enterprise of a Contracting State that operates ships or aircraft in international traffic represented by such ships or aircraft, and by movable property pertaining to the operation of such ships or aircraft, shall be taxable only in that State.
4. All other elements of capital of a resident of a Contracting State shall be taxable only in that State.

CHAPTER V METHODS FOR ELIMINATION OF DOUBLE TAXATION

Article 23A Exemption Method

1. Where a resident of a Contracting State derives income or owns capital which may be taxed in the other Contracting State in accordance with the provisions of this Convention (except to the extent that these provisions allow taxation by that other State solely because the income is also income derived by a resident of that State or because the capital is also capital owned by a resident of that State), the firstmentioned State shall, subject to the provisions of paragraphs 2 and 3, exempt such income or capital from tax.
2. Where a resident of a Contracting State derives items of income which may be taxed in the other Contracting State in accordance with the provisions of Articles 10 and 11 (except to the extent that these provisions allow taxation by that other State solely because the income is also income derived by a resident of that State), the firstmentioned State shall allow as a deduction from the tax on the income of that resident an amount equal to the tax paid in that other State. Such deduction shall not, however, exceed that part of the tax, as computed before the deduction is given, which is attributable to such items of income derived from that other State.
3. Where in accordance with any provision of the Convention income derived or capital owned by a resident of a Contracting State is exempt from tax in that State, such State may nevertheless, in calculating the amount of tax on the remaining income or capital of such resident, take into account the exempted income or capital.
4. The provisions of paragraph 1 shall not apply to income derived or capital owned by a resident of a Contracting State where the other Contracting State applies the provisions of this Convention to exempt such income or capital from tax or applies the provisions of paragraph 2 of Article 10 or 11 to such income.

Article 23B Credit Method

1. Where a resident of a Contracting State derives income or owns capital which may be taxed in the other Contracting State in accordance with the provisions of this Convention (except to the extent that these provisions allow taxation by that other State solely because the income is also income derived by a resident of that State or because the capital is also capital owned by a resident of that State), the firstmentioned State shall allow:
   a) as a deduction from the tax on the income of that resident, an amount equal to the income tax paid in that other State;
   b) as a deduction from the tax on the capital of that resident, an amount equal to the capital tax paid in that other State.

   Such deduction in either case shall not, however, exceed that part of the income tax or capital tax, as computed before the deduction is given, which is attributable, as the case may be, to the income or the capital which may be taxed in that other State.
2. Where in accordance with any provision of the Convention income derived or capital owned by a resident of a Contracting State is exempt from tax in that State, such State may nevertheless, in calculating the amount of tax on the remaining income or capital of such resident, take into account the exempted income or capital.

CHAPTER VI SPECIAL PROVISIONS

Article 24 Non-Discrimination

1. Nationals of a Contracting State shall not be subjected in the other Contracting State to any taxation or any requirement connected therewith, which is other or more burdensome than the taxation and connected requirements to which nationals of that other State in the same circumstances, in particular with respect to residence, are or may be subjected. This provision shall, notwithstanding the provisions of Article 1, also apply to persons who are not residents of one or both of the Contracting States.
2. Stateless persons who are residents of a Contracting State shall not be subjected in either Contracting State to any taxation or any requirement connected therewith, which is other or more burdensome than the taxation and connected requirements to which nationals of the State concerned in the same circumstances, in particular with respect to residence, are or may be subjected.
3. The taxation on a permanent establishment which an enterprise of a Contracting State has in the other Contracting State shall not be less favourably levied in that other State than the taxation levied on enterprises of that other State carrying on the same activities. This provision shall not be construed as obliging a Contracting State to grant to residents of the other Contracting State any personal allowances, reliefs and reductions for taxation purposes

on account of civil status or family responsibilities which it grants to its own residents.

4. Except where the provisions of paragraph 1 of Article 9, paragraph 6 of Article 11, or paragraph 4 of Article 12, apply, interest, royalties and other disbursements paid by an enterprise of a Contracting State to a resident of the other Contracting State shall, for the purpose of determining the taxable profits of such enterprise, be deductible under the same conditions as if they had been paid to a resident of the first-mentioned State. Similarly, any debts of an enterprise of a Contracting State to a resident of the other Contracting State shall, for the purpose of determining the taxable capital of such enterprise, be deductible under the same conditions as if they had been contracted to a resident of the first-mentioned State.
5. Enterprises of a Contracting State, the capital of which is wholly or partly owned or controlled, directly or indirectly, by one or more residents of the other Contracting State, shall not be subjected in the first-mentioned State to any taxation or any requirement connected therewith which is other or more burdensome than the taxation and connected requirements to which other similar enterprises of the firstmentioned State are or may be subjected.
6. The provisions of this Article shall, notwithstanding the provisions of Article 2, apply to taxes of every kind and description.

Article 25 Mutual Agreement Procedure

1. Where a person considers that the actions of one or both of the Contracting States result or will result for him in taxation not in accordance with the provisions of this Convention, he may, irrespective of the remedies provided by the domestic law of those States, present his case to the competent authority of either Contracting State. The case must be presented within three years from the first notification of the action resulting in taxation not in accordance with the provisions of the Convention.
2. The competent authority shall endeavour, if the objection appears to it to be justified and if it is not itself able to arrive at a satisfactory solution, to resolve the case by mutual agreement with the competent authority of the other Contracting State, with a view to the avoidance of taxation which is not in accordance with the Convention. Any agreement reached shall be implemented notwithstanding any time limits in the domestic law of the Contracting States.
3. The competent authorities of the Contracting States shall endeavour to resolve by mutual agreement any difficulties or doubts arising as to the interpretation or application of the Convention. They may also consult together for the elimination of double taxation in cases not provided for in the Convention.
4. The competent authorities of the Contracting States may communicate with each other directly, including through a joint commission consisting of

themselves or their representatives, for the purpose of reaching an agreement in the sense of the preceding paragraphs.

5. Where,
   a) under paragraph 1, a person has presented a case to the competent authority of a Contracting State on the basis that the actions of one or both of the Contracting States have resulted for that person in taxation not in accordance with the provisions of this Convention, and
   b) the competent authorities are unable to reach an agreement to resolve that case pursuant to paragraph 2 within two years from the date when all the information required by the competent authorities in order to address the case has been provided to both competent authorities,

   any unresolved issues arising from the case shall be submitted to arbitration if the person so requests in writing. These unresolved issues shall not, however, be submitted to arbitration if a decision on these issues has already been rendered by a court or administrative tribunal of either State. Unless a person directly affected by the case does not accept the mutual agreement that implements the arbitration decision, that decision shall be binding on both Contracting States and shall be implemented notwithstanding any time limits in the domestic laws of these States. The competent authorities of the Contracting States shall by mutual agreement settle the mode of application of this paragraph.

Article 26 Exchange of Information

1. The competent authorities of the Contracting States shall exchange such information as is foreseeably relevant for carrying out the provisions of this Convention or to the administration or enforcement of the domestic laws concerning taxes of every kind and description imposed on behalf of the Contracting States, or of their political subdivisions or local authorities, insofar as the taxation thereunder is not contrary to the Convention. The exchange of information is not restricted by Articles 1 and 2.
2. Any information received under paragraph 1 by a Contracting State shall be treated as secret in the same manner as information obtained under the domestic laws of that State and shall be disclosed only to persons or authorities (including courts and administrative bodies) concerned with the assessment or collection of, the enforcement or prosecution in respect of, the determination of appeals in relation to the taxes referred to in paragraph 1, or the oversight of the above. Such persons or authorities shall use the information only for such purposes. They may disclose the information in public court proceedings or in judicial decisions. Notwithstanding the foregoing, information received by a Contracting State may be used for other purposes when such information may be used for such other purposes under the laws of both States and the competent authority of the supplying State authorises such use.

3. In no case shall the provisions of paragraphs 1 and 2 be construed so as to impose on a Contracting State the obligation:
   a) to carry out administrative measures at variance with the laws and administrative practice of that or of the other Contracting State;
   b) to supply information which is not obtainable under the laws or in the normal course of the administration of that or of the other Contracting State;
   c) to supply information which would disclose any trade, business, industrial, commercial or professional secret or trade process, or information the disclosure of which would be contrary to public policy (ordre public).
4. If information is requested by a Contracting State in accordance with this Article, the other Contracting State shall use its information gathering measures to obtain the requested information, even though that other State may not need such information for its own tax purposes. The obligation contained in the preceding sentence is subject to the limitations of paragraph 3 but in no case shall such limitations be construed to permit a Contracting State to decline to supply information solely because it has no domestic interest in such information.
5. In no case shall the provisions of paragraph 3 be construed to permit a Contracting State to decline to supply information solely because the information is held by a bank, other financial institution, nominee or person acting in an agency or a fiduciary capacity or because it relates to ownership interests in a person.

Article 27 Assistance In The Collection of Taxes[1]

1. The Contracting States shall lend assistance to each other in the collection of revenue claims. This assistance is not restricted by Articles 1 and 2. The competent authorities of the Contracting States may by mutual agreement settle the mode of application of this Article.
2. The term "revenue claim" as used in this Article means an amount owed in respect of taxes of every kind and description imposed on behalf of the Contracting States, or of their political subdivisions or local authorities, insofar as the taxation thereunder is not contrary to this Convention or any other instrument to which the Contracting States are parties, as well as interest, administrative penalties and costs of collection or conservancy related to such amount.

---

1. In some countries, national law, policy or administrative considerations may not allow or justify the type of assistance envisaged under this Article or may require that this type of assistance be restricted, e.g. to countries that have similar tax systems or tax administrations or as to the taxes covered. For that reason, the Article should only be included in the Convention where each State concludes that, based on the factors described in paragraph 1 of the Commentary on the Article, they can agree to provide assistance in the collection of taxes levied by the other State.

3. When a revenue claim of a Contracting State is enforceable under the laws of that State and is owed by a person who, at that time, cannot, under the laws of that State, prevent its collection, that revenue claim shall, at the request of the competent authority of that State, be accepted for purposes of collection by the competent authority of the other Contracting State. That revenue claim shall be collected by that other State in accordance with the provisions of its laws applicable to the enforcement and collection of its own taxes as if the revenue claim were a revenue claim of that other State.
4. When a revenue claim of a Contracting State is a claim in respect of which that State may, under its law, take measures of conservancy with a view to ensure its collection, that revenue claim shall, at the request of the competent authority of that State, be accepted for purposes of taking measures of conservancy by the competent authority of the other Contracting State. That other State shall take measures of conservancy in respect of that revenue claim in accordance with the provisions of its laws as if the revenue claim were a revenue claim of that other State even if, at the time when such measures are applied, the revenue claim is not enforceable in the firstmentioned State or is owed by a person who has a right to prevent its collection.
5. Notwithstanding the provisions of paragraphs 3 and 4, a revenue claim accepted by a Contracting State for purposes of paragraph 3 or 4 shall not, in that State, be subject to the time limits or accorded any priority applicable to a revenue claim under the laws of that State by reason of its nature as such. In addition, a revenue claim accepted by a Contracting State for the purposes of paragraph 3 or 4 shall not, in that State, have any priority applicable to that revenue claim under the laws of the other Contracting State.
6. Proceedings with respect to the existence, validity or the amount of a revenue claim of a Contracting State shall not be brought before the courts or administrative bodies of the other Contracting State.
7. Where, at any time after a request has been made by a Contracting State under paragraph 3 or 4 and before the other Contracting State has collected and remitted the relevant revenue claim to the first-mentioned State, the relevant revenue claim ceases to be
   a) in the case of a request under paragraph 3, a revenue claim of the first-mentioned State that is enforceable under the laws of that State and is owed by a person who, at that time, cannot, under the laws of that State, prevent its collection, or
   b) in the case of a request under paragraph 4, a revenue claim of the first-mentioned State in respect of which that State may, under its laws, take measures of conservancy with a view to ensure its collection

   the competent authority of the first-mentioned State shall promptly notify the competent authority of the other State of that fact and, at the option of the other State, the first-mentioned State shall either suspend or withdraw its request.
8. In no case shall the provisions of this Article be construed so as to impose on a Contracting State the obligation:

a) to carry out administrative measures at variance with the laws and administrative practice of that or of the other Contracting State;
b) to carry out measures which would be contrary to public policy (ordre public);
c) to provide assistance if the other Contracting State has not pursued all reasonable measures of collection or conservancy, as the case may be, available under its laws or administrative practice;
d) to provide assistance in those cases where the administrative burden for that State is clearly disproportionate to the benefit to be derived by the other Contracting State.

Article 28 Members of Diplomatic Missions and Consular Posts

Nothing in this Convention shall affect the fiscal privileges of members of diplomatic missions or consular posts under the general rules of international law or under the provisions of special agreements.

Article 29 Entitlement to Benefits[2]

1. [Provision that, subject to paragraphs 3 to 5, restricts treaty benefits to a resident of a Contracting State who is a "qualified person" as defined in paragraph 2].
2. [Definition of situations where a resident is a qualified person, which covers
   — an individual;
   — a Contracting State, its political subdivisions and their agencies and instrumentalities;
   — certain publicly-traded companies and entities;
   — certain affiliates of publicly-listed companies and entities;
   — certain non-profit organisations and recognised pension funds;
   — other entities that meet certain ownership and base erosion requirements;
   — certain collective investment vehicles.]
3. [Provision that provides treaty benefits to certain income derived by a person that is not a qualified person if the person is engaged in the active conduct of a business in its State of residence and the income emanates from, or is incidental to, that business].

2. The drafting of this Article will depend on how the Contracting States decide to implement their common intention, reflected in the preamble of the Convention and incorporated in the minimum standard agreed to as part of the OECD/G20 Base Erosion and Profit Shifting Project, to eliminate double taxation without creating opportunities for non-taxation or reduced taxation through tax evasion or avoidance, including through treaty-shopping arrangements. This may be done either through the adoption of paragraph 9 only, through the adoption of the detailed version of paragraphs 1 to 7 that is described in the Commentary on Article 29 together with the implementation of an anti-conduit mechanism as described in paragraph 187 of that Commentary, or through the adoption of paragraph 9 together with any variation of paragraphs 1 to 7 described in the Commentary on Article 29.

4. [Provision that provides treaty benefits to a person that is not a qualified person if at least more than an agreed proportion of that entity is owned by certain persons entitled to equivalent benefits].
5. [Provision that provides treaty benefits to a person that qualifies as a "headquarters company"].
6. [Provision that allows the competent authority of a Contracting State to grant certain treaty benefits to a person where benefits would otherwise be denied under paragraph 1].
7. [Definitions applicable for the purposes of paragraphs 1 to 7].
8. a) Where
   (i) an enterprise of a Contracting State derives income from the other Contracting State and the first-mentioned State treats such income as attributable to a permanent establishment of the enterprise situated in a third jurisdiction, and
   (ii) the profits attributable to that permanent establishment are exempt from tax in the first-mentioned State,

   the benefits of this Convention shall not apply to any item of income on which the tax in the third jurisdiction is less than the lower of [rate to be determined bilaterally] of the amount of that item of income and 60 per cent of the tax that would be imposed in the first-mentioned State on that item of income if that permanent establishment were situated in the first-mentioned State. In such a case any income to which the provisions of this paragraph apply shall remain taxable according to the domestic law of the other State, notwithstanding any other provisions of the Convention.

   b) The preceding provisions of this paragraph shall not apply if the income derived from the other State emanates from, or is incidental to, the active conduct of a business carried on through the permanent establishment (other than the business of making, managing or simply holding investments for the enterprise's own account, unless these activities are banking, insurance or securities activities carried on by a bank, insurance enterprise or registered securities dealer, respectively).

   c) If benefits under this Convention are denied pursuant to the preceding provisions of this paragraph with respect to an item of income derived by a resident of a Contracting State, the competent authority of the other Contracting State may, nevertheless, grant these benefits with respect to that item of income if, in response to a request by such resident, such competent authority determines that granting such benefits is justified in light of the reasons such resident did not satisfy the requirements of this paragraph (such as the existence of losses). The competent authority of the Contracting State to which a request has been made under the preceding sentence shall consult with the competent authority of the other Contracting State before either granting or denying the request

9. Notwithstanding the other provisions of this Convention, a benefit under this Convention shall not be granted in respect of an item of income or capital if it is reasonable to conclude, having regard to all relevant facts and circumstances, that obtaining that benefit was one of the principal purposes of any arrangement or transaction that resulted directly or indirectly in that benefit, unless it is established that granting that benefit in these circumstances would be in accordance with the object and purpose of the relevant provisions of this Convention.

Article 30 Territorial Extension[3]

1. This Convention may be extended, either in its entirety or with any necessary modifications [to any part of the territory of (State A) or of (State B) which is specifically excluded from the application of the Convention or], to any State or territory for whose international relations (State A) or (State B) is responsible, which imposes taxes substantially similar in character to those to which the Convention applies. Any such extension shall take effect from such date and subject to such modifications and conditions, including conditions as to termination, as may be specified and agreed between the Contracting States in notes to be exchanged through diplomatic channels or in any other manner in accordance with their constitutional procedures.
2. Unless otherwise agreed by both Contracting States, the termination of the Convention by one of them under Article 32 shall also terminate, in the manner provided for in that Article, the application of the Convention [to any part of the territory of (State A) or of (State B) or] to any State or territory to which it has been extended under this Article.

CHAPTER VII FINAL PROVISIONS

Article 31 Entry into Force

1. This Convention shall be ratified and the instruments of ratification shall be exchanged at .... as soon as possible.
2. The Convention shall enter into force upon the exchange of instruments of ratification and its provisions shall have effect:
   a) (in State A): ....
   b) (in State B): ....

3. The words between brackets are of relevance when, by special provision, a part of the territory of a Contracting State is excluded from the application of the Convention.

Article 32 Termination

This Convention shall remain in force until terminated by a Contracting State. Either Contracting State may terminate the Convention, through diplomatic channels, by giving notice of termination at least six months before the end of any calendar year after the year ...... In such event, the Convention shall cease to have effect:

a) (in State A): ....
b) (in State B): ....

TERMINAL CLAUSE[4]

4. The terminal clause concerning the signing shall be drafted in accordance with the constitutional procedure of both Contracting States

APPENDIX II

North America Free Trade Agreement (NAFTA): Extracts

The North America Free Trade Agreement is a very long document, and so the following extract includes several of the terms of Part 2, Trade in Goods, for further reference, comprising: Chapter Three, National Treatment and Market Access for Goods; Chapter Four, Rules of Origin; and Chapter Five, Customs Procedures,. The complete Agreement is located at: <https://www.nafta-sec-alena.org/Home/Legal-Texts/North-American-Free-Trade-Agreement>

Extract

PART TWO: TRADE IN GOODS

CHAPTER THREE: NATIONAL TREATMENT AND MARKET ACCESS FOR GOODS

Article 300: Scope and Coverage

This Chapter applies to trade in goods of a Party, including:

a) goods covered by Annex 300-A (Trade and Investment in the Automotive Sector),
b) goods covered by Annex 300-B (Textile and Apparel Goods), and
c) goods covered by another Chapter in this Part, except as provided in such Annex or Chapter.

Section A – National Treatment

Article 301: National Treatment

1. Each Party shall accord national treatment to the goods of another Party in accordance with Article III of the General Agreement on Tariffs and Trade (GATT), including its interpretative notes, and to this end Article III of the GATT and its interpretative notes, or any equivalent provision of a successor agreement to which all Parties are party, are incorporated into and made part of this Agreement.
2. The provisions of paragraph 1 regarding national treatment shall mean, with respect to a state or province, treatment no less favourable than the most favourable treatment accorded by such state or province to any like, directly competitive or substitutable goods, as the case may be, of the Party of which it forms a part.
3. Paragraphs 1 and 2 do not apply to the measures set out in Annex 301.3.

Section B – Tariffs

Article 302: Tariff Elimination

1. Except as otherwise provided in this Agreement, no Party may increase any existing customs duty, or adopt any customs duty, on an originating good.
2. Except as otherwise provided in this Agreement, each Party shall progressively eliminate its customs duties on originating goods in accordance with its Schedule to Annex 302.2.
3. On the request of any Party, the Parties shall consult to consider accelerating the elimination of customs duties set out in their Schedules. An agreement between two or more Parties to accelerate the elimination of a customs duty on a good shall supersede any duty rate or staging category determined pursuant to their Schedules for such good when approved by each such Party in accordance with its applicable legal procedures.
4. Each Party may adopt or maintain import measures to allocate in-quota imports made pursuant to a tariff rate quota set out in Annex 302.2, provided that such measures do not have trade restrictive effects on imports additional to those caused by the imposition of the tariff rate quota.
5. On written request of any Party, a Party applying or intending to apply measures pursuant to paragraph 4 shall consult to review the administration of those measures.

Article 303: Restriction on Drawback and Duty Deferral Programs

1. Except as otherwise provided in this Article, no Party may refund the amount of customs duties paid, or waive or reduce the amount of customs duties owed, on a good imported into its territory, on condition that the good is:
   a) subsequently exported to the territory of another Party,
   b) used as a material in the production of another good that is subsequently exported to the territory of another Party, or
   c) substituted by an identical or similar good used as a material in the production of another good that is subsequently exported to the territory of another Party, in an amount that exceeds the lesser of the total amount of customs duties paid or owed on the good on importation into its territory and the total amount of customs duties paid to another Party on the good that has been subsequently exported to the territory of that other Party.
2. No Party may, on condition of export, refund, waive or reduce:
   a) an antidumping or countervailing duty that is applied pursuant to a Party's domestic law and that is not applied inconsistently with Chapter Nineteen (Review and Dispute Settlement in Antidumping and Countervailing Duty Matters);
   b) a premium offered or collected on an imported good arising out of any tendering system in respect of the administration of quantitative import restrictions, tariff rate quotas or tariff preference levels;
   c) a fee applied pursuant to section 22 of the U.S. Agricultural Adjustment Act, subject to Chapter Seven (Agriculture and Sanitary and Phytosanitary Measures); or
   d) customs duties paid or owed on a good imported into its territory and substituted by an identical or similar good that is subsequently exported to the territory of another Party.
3. Where a good is imported into the territory of a Party pursuant to a duty deferral program and is subsequently exported to the territory of another Party, or is used as a material in the production of another good that is subsequently exported to the territory of another Party, or is substituted by an identical or similar good used as a material in the production of another good that is subsequently exported to the territory of another Party, the Party from whose territory the good is exported:
   a) shall assess the customs duties as if the exported good had been withdrawn for domestic consumption; and
   b) may waive or reduce such customs duties to the extent permitted under paragraph 1.
4. In determining the amount of customs duties that may be refunded, waived or reduced pursuant to paragraph 1 on a good imported into its territory, each Party shall require presentation of satisfactory evidence of the amount

of customs duties paid to another Party on the good that has been subsequently exported to the territory of that other Party.

5. Where satisfactory evidence of the customs duties paid to the Party to which a good is subsequently exported under a duty deferral program described in paragraph 3 is not presented within 60 days after the date of exportation, the Party from whose territory the good was exported:
   a) shall collect customs duties as if the exported good had been withdrawn for domestic consumption; and
   b) may refund such customs duties to the extent permitted under paragraph 1 on the timely presentation of such evidence under its laws and regulations.
6. This Article does not apply to:
   a) a good entered under bond for transportation and exportation to the territory of another Party;
   b) a good exported to the territory of another Party in the same condition as when imported into the territory of the Party from which the good was exported (processes such as testing, cleaning, repacking or inspecting the good, or preserving it in its same condition, shall not be considered to change a good's condition). Except as provided in Annex 703.2, Section A, paragraph 12, where such a good has been commingled with fungible goods and exported in the same condition, its origin for purposes of this subparagraph, may be determined on the basis of the inventory methods provided for in the Uniform Regulations established under Article 511 (Uniform Regulations);
   c) a good imported into the territory of a Party that is deemed to be exported from its territory, or used as a material in the production of another good that is deemed to be exported to the territory of another Party, or is substituted by an identical or similar good used as a material in the production of another good that is deemed to be exported to the territory of another Party, by reason of
      (i) delivery to a duty-free shop,
      (ii) delivery for ship's stores or supplies for ships or aircraft, or
      (iii) delivery for use in joint undertakings of two or more of the Parties and that will subsequently become the property of the Party into whose territory the good was deemed to be imported;
   d) a refund of customs duties by a Party on a particular good imported into its territory and subsequently exported to the territory of another Party, where that refund is granted by reason of the failure of such good to conform to sample or specification, or by reason of the shipment of such good without the consent of the consignee;
   e) an originating good that is imported into the territory of a Party and is subsequently exported to the territory of another Party, or used as a material in the production of another good that is subsequently

exported to the territory of another Party, or is substituted by an identical or similar good used as a material in the production of another good that is subsequently exported to the territory of another Party; or

f) a good set out in Annex 303.6.

7. Except for paragraph 2(d), this Article shall apply as of the date set out in each Party's Section of Annex 303.7.
8. Notwithstanding any other provision of this Article and except as specifically provided in Annex 303.8, no Party may refund the amount of customs duties paid, or waive or reduce the amount of customs duties owed, on a non-originating good provided for in item 8540.11.aa (colour cathode-ray television picture tubes, including video monitor tubes, with a diagonal exceeding 14 inches) or 8540.11.cc (colour cathode ray television picture tubes for high definition television, with a diagonal exceeding 14 inches) that is imported into the Party's territory and subsequently exported to the territory of another Party, or is used as a material in the production of another good that is subsequently exported to the territory of another Party, or is substituted by an identical or similar good used as a material in the production of another good that is subsequently exported to the territory of another Party.
9. For purposes of this Article:
   customs duties are the customs duties that would be applicable to a good entered for consumption in the customs territory of a Party if the good were not exported to the territory of another party;
   identical or similar goods means "identical or similar goods" as defined in Article 415 (Rules of Origin Definitions);
   material means "material" as defined in Article 415;
   used means "used" as defined in Article 415.
10. For purposes of the Article:
   Where a good referred to by a tariff item number in this Article is described in parentheses following the tariff item number, the description is provided for purposes of reference only.

Article 304: Waiver of Customs Duties

1. Except as set out in Annex 304.1, no Party may adopt any new waiver of customs duties, or expand with respect to existing recipients or extend to any new recipient the application of an existing waiver of customs duties, where the waiver is conditioned, explicitly or implicitly, on the fulfilment of a performance requirement.
2. Except as set out in Annex 304.2, no Party may, explicitly or implicitly, condition on the fulfilment of a performance requirement the continuation of any existing waiver of customs duties.
3. If a waiver or a combination of waivers of customs duties granted by a Party with respect to goods for commercial use by a designated person can be

shown by another Party to have an adverse impact on the commercial interests of a person of that Party, or of a person owned or controlled by a person of that Party that is located in the territory of the Party granting the waiver, or on the other Party's economy, the Party granting the waiver shall either cease to grant it or make it generally available to any importer.

4. This Article shall not apply to measures subject to Article 303.

Article 305: Temporary Admission of Goods

1. Each Party shall grant duty-free temporary admission for:
   a) professional equipment necessary for carrying out the business activity, trade or profession of a business person who qualifies for temporary entry pursuant to Chapter Sixteen (Temporary Entry for Business Persons),
   b) equipment for the press or for sound or television broadcasting and cinematographic equipment,
   c) goods imported for sports purposes and goods intended for display or demonstration, and
   d) commercial samples and advertising films, imported from the territory of another Party, regardless of their origin and regardless of whether like, directly competitive or substitutable goods are available in the territory of the Party.
2. Except as otherwise provided in this Agreement, no Party may condition the duty-free temporary admission of a good referred to in paragraph 1(a), (b) or (c), other than to require that such good:
   a) be imported by a national or resident of another Party who seeks temporary entry;
   b) be used solely by or under the personal supervision of such person in the exercise of the business activity, trade or profession of that person;
   c) not be sold or leased while in its territory;
   d) be accompanied by a bond in an amount no greater than 110 percent of the charges that would otherwise be owed on entry or final importation, or by another form of security, releasable on exportation of the good, except that a bond for customs duties shall not be required for an originating good;
   e) be capable of identification when exported;
   f) be exported on the departure of that person or within such other period of time as is reasonably related to the purpose of the temporary admission; and
   g) be imported in no greater quantity than is reasonable for its intended use.
3. Except as otherwise provided in this Agreement, no Party may condition the duty-free temporary admission of a good referred to in paragraph 1(d), other than to require that such good:

a) be imported solely for the solicitation of orders for goods, or services provided from the territory, of another Party or non-Party;
b) not be sold, leased or put to any use other than exhibition or demonstration while in its territory;
c) be capable of identification when exported;
d) be exported within such period as is reasonably related to the purpose of the temporary admission; and
e) be imported in no greater quantity than is reasonable for its intended use.

4. A Party may impose the customs duty and any other charge on a good temporarily admitted duty-free under paragraph 1 that would be owed on entry or final importation of such good if any condition that the Party imposes under paragraph 2 or 3 has not been fulfilled.
5. Subject to Chapters Eleven (Investment) and Twelve (Cross Border Trade in Services):
   a) each Party shall allow a vehicle or container used in international traffic that enters its territory from the territory of another Party to exit its territory on any route that is reasonably related to the economic and prompt departure of such vehicle or container;
   b) no Party may require any bond or impose any penalty or charge solely by reason of any difference between the port of entry and the port of departure of a vehicle or container;
   c) no Party may condition the release of any obligation, including any bond, that it imposes in respect of the entry of a vehicle or container into its territory on its exit through any particular port of departure; and
   d) no Party may require that the vehicle or carrier bringing a container from the territory of another Party into its territory be the same vehicle or carrier that takes such container to the territory of another Party.
6. For purposes of paragraph 5, "vehicle" means a truck, a truck tractor, tractor, trailer unit or trailer, a locomotive, or a railway car or other railroad equipment.

Article 306: Duty-Free Entry of Certain Commercial Samples and Printed Advertising Materials

Each Party shall grant duty-free entry to commercial samples of negligible value, and to printed advertising materials, imported from the territory of another Party, regardless of their origin, but may require that:

a) such samples be imported solely for the solicitation of orders for goods, or services provided from the territory, of another Party or non-Party; or

b) such advertising materials be imported in packets that each contain no more than one copy of each such material and that neither such materials nor packets form part of a larger consignment.

Article 307: Goods Re-Entered after Repair or Alteration

1. Except as set out in Annex 307.1, no Party may apply a customs duty to a good, regardless of its origin, that re-enters its territory after that good has been exported from its territory to the territory of another Party for repair or alteration, regardless of whether such repair or alteration could be performed in its territory.
2. Notwithstanding Article 303, no Party may apply a customs duty to a good, regardless of its origin, imported temporarily from the territory of another Party for repair or alteration.
3. Annex 307.3 applies to the Parties specified in that Annex respecting the repair and rebuilding of vessels.

Article 308: Most Favoured Nation Rates of Duty on Certain Goods

1. Annex 308.1 applies to certain automatic data processing goods and their parts.
2. Annex 308.2 applies to certain colour television tubes.
3. Each Party shall accord most favoured nation duty-free treatment to any local area network apparatus imported into its territory, and shall consult in accordance with Annex 308.3.

Section C – Non-Tariff Measures

Article 309: Import and Export Restrictions

1. Except as otherwise provided in this Agreement, no Party may adopt or maintain any prohibition or restriction on the importation of any good of another Party or on the exportation or sale for export of any good destined for the territory of another Party, except in accordance with Article XI of the GATT, including its interpretative notes, and to this end Article XI of the GATT and its interpretative notes, or any equivalent provision of a successor agreement to which all Parties are party, are incorporated into and made a part of this Agreement.
2. The Parties understand that the GATT rights and obligations incorporated by paragraph 1 prohibit, in any circumstances in which any other form of restriction is prohibited, export price requirements and, except as permitted in enforcement of countervailing and antidumping orders and undertakings, import price requirements.

3. In the event that a Party adopts or maintains a prohibition or restriction on the importation from or exportation to a non-Party of a good, nothing in this Agreement shall be construed to prevent the Party from:
   a) limiting or prohibiting the importation from the territory of another Party of such good of that non- Party; or
   b) requiring as a condition of export of such good of the Party to the territory of another Party, that the good not be re-exported to the non-Party, directly or indirectly, without being consumed in the territory of the other Party.
4. In the event that a Party adopts or maintains a prohibition or restriction on the importation of a good from a non-Party, the Parties, on request of any Party, shall consult with a view to avoiding undue interference with or distortion of pricing, marketing and distribution arrangements in another Party.
5. Paragraphs 1 through 4 shall not apply to the measures set out in Annex 301.3.

Article 310: Customs User Fees

1. No Party may adopt any customs user fee of the type referred to in Annex 310.1 for originating goods.
2. The Parties specified in Annex 310.1 may maintain existing such fees in accordance with that Annex.

Article 311: Country of Origin Marking

Annex 311 applies to measures relating to country of origin marking.

Article 312: Wine and Distilled Spirits

1. No Party may adopt or maintain any measure requiring that distilled spirits imported from the territory of another Party for bottling be blended with any distilled spirits of the Party.
2. Annex 312.2 applies to other measures relating to wine and distilled spirits.

Article 313: Distinctive Products

Annex 313 applies to standards and labelling of the distinctive products set out in that Annex.

Article 314: Export Taxes

Except as set out in Annex 314, no Party may adopt or maintain any duty, tax or other charge on the export of any good to the territory of another Party, unless such duty, tax or charge is adopted or maintained on:

a) exports of any such good to the territory of all other Parties; and
b) any such good when destined for domestic consumption.

Article 315: Other Export Measures

1. Except as set out in Annex 315, a Party may adopt or maintain a restriction otherwise justified under Articles XI:2(a) or XX(g), (i) or (j) of the GATT with respect to the export of a good of the Party to the territory of another Party, only if:
   a) the restriction does not reduce the proportion of the total export shipments of the specific good made available to that other Party relative to the total supply of that good of the Party maintaining the restriction as compared to the proportion prevailing in the most recent 36month period for which data are available prior to the imposition of the measure, or in such other representative period on which the Parties may agree;
   b) the Party does not impose a higher price for exports of a good to that other Party than the price charged for such good when consumed domestically, by means of any measure, such as licenses, fees, taxation and minimum price requirements. The foregoing provision does not apply to a higher price that may result from a measure taken pursuant to subparagraph (a) that only restricts the volume of exports; and
   c) the restriction does not require the disruption of normal channels of supply to that other Party or normal proportions among specific goods or categories of goods supplied to that other Party.
2. The Parties shall cooperate in the maintenance and development of effective controls on the export of each other's goods to a non-Party in implementing this Article.

Section D – Consultations

Article 316: Consultations and Committee on Trade in Goods

1. The Parties hereby establish a Committee on Trade in Goods, comprising representatives of each Party.

2. The Committee shall meet on the request of any Party or the Commission to consider any matter arising under this Chapter.
3. The Parties shall convene at least once each year a meeting of their officials responsible for customs, immigration, inspection of food and agricultural products, border inspection facilities, and regulation of transportation for the purpose of addressing issues related to movement of goods through the Parties' ports of entry.

Article 317: Third Country Dumping

1. The Parties affirm the importance of cooperation with respect to actions under Article 12 of the Agreement on Implementation of Article VI of the General Agreement on Tariffs and Trade.
2. Where a Party presents an application to another Party requesting antidumping action on its behalf, those Parties shall consult within 30 days respecting the factual basis of the request, and the requested Party shall give full consideration to the request.

APPENDIX III

European Union: Union Customs Code*

The new Union Customs Code is intended to generally apply in the European Union from 1 May 2016. The complete Code is a very long document available at: < http: //eur-lex.europa.eu/legal-content/EN/TXT/PDF/?uri = CELEX:32013R0952&rid = 1 > . The following preamble from that document sets out the major parts of the new Union Customs Code.

EXTRACT

REGULATION (EU) No 952/2013 OF THE EUROPEAN PARLIAMENT AND OF THE COUNCIL

of 9 October 2013 laying down the Union Customs Code (recast)

THE EUROPEAN PARLIAMENT AND THE COUNCIL OF THE EUROPEAN UNION,

Having regard to the Treaty on the Functioning of the European Union, and in particular Articles 33, 114 and 207 thereof,

Having regard to the proposal from the European Commission,

After transmission of the draft legislative act to the national parliaments,

Having regard to the opinion of the European Economic and Social Committee,

Acting in accordance with the ordinary legislative procedure,

Whereas:

(1) A number of amendments are to be made to Regulation (EC) No 450/2008 of the European Parliament and of the Council of 23 April 2008 laying down the

* http://eur-lex.europa.eu, © European Union, 1998-2015.

Community Customs Code (Modernised Customs Code). In the interests of clarity, that Regulation should be recast.

(2) It is appropriate to ensure that Regulation (EC) No 450/2008 is consistent with the Treaty on the Functioning of the European Union (TFEU), in particular Articles 290 and 291 thereof. It is also appropriate that the Regulation take account of the evolution of Union law and that some of its provisions are adapted in order to facilitate their application.

(3) In order to supplement or amend certain non-essential elements of this Regulation, the power to adopt delegated acts in accordance with Article 290 TFEU should be delegated to the Commission. It is of particular importance that the Commission carry out appropriate consultations during its preparatory work, including at expert level. The Commission, when preparing and drawing up delegated acts, should ensure a simultaneous, timely and appropriate transmission of relevant documents to the European Parliament and to the Council.

(4) In particular, when preparing and drawing up delegated acts, the Commission should ensure that Member States' experts and the business community are consulted in a transparent manner, and well in advance.

(5) In order to ensure uniform conditions for the implementation of this Regulation, implementing powers should be conferred on the Commission in order: to specify the format and code of the common data requirements for the purpose of the exchange of information between the customs authorities and between economic operators and customs authorities and the storage of such information and the procedural rules on the exchange and storage of information which can be made by means other than electronic data-processing techniques; to adopt decisions allowing one or several Member States to use means for the exchange and storage of information other than electronic data-processing techniques; to specify the customs authority which is responsible for the registration of economic operators and of other persons; to specify the technical arrangements for developing, maintaining and employing electronic systems; to specify the procedural rules on the conferral and proving of the entitlement for a customs representative to provide services in a Member State other than the one where he or she is established; the procedural rules on the submission and acceptance of an application for a decision relating to the application of the customs legislation, and on the taking and the monitoring of such a decision; the procedural rules on the annulment, procedural rules on the use of a decision relating to binding information after it ceases to be valid or is revoked; the procedural rules on the notification to the customs authorities that the taking of such decisions is suspended and on the withdrawal of such suspension; to adopt decisions requesting Member States to revoke decisions relating to binding information; to adopt the modalities for the application of the criteria for the granting of the status of authorised economic operator; to adopt measures to ensure uniform application of customs controls, including the exchange of risk information and analysis,

common risk criteria and standards, control measures and priority control areas; to determine the ports or airports where customs controls and formalities are to be carried out on cabin and hold baggage; to lay down the rules on currency conversion; to adopt measures on the uniform management of tariff quota and tariff ceilings and the management of the surveillance of the release for free circulation or export of goods; to adopt measures to determine the tariff classification of goods; to specify the procedural rules on the provision and the verification of the proof of non-preferential origin; the procedural rules on the facilitation of the establishment in the Union of the preferential origin of goods; to adopt measures to determine the origin of specific goods; the granting of a temporary derogation from the rules on preferential origin of goods benefiting from preferential measures adopted unilaterally by the Union; the determination of the origin of specific goods;
to specify the procedural rules on the determination of the customs value of goods; to specify the procedural rules on the provision of a guarantee, the determination of its amount, its monitoring and release and the revocation and cancellation of an undertaking given by a guarantor; to specify the procedural rules regarding temporary prohibitions of the use of comprehensive guarantees; to adopt measures to ensure mutual assistance between the customs authorities in the event of the incurrence of a customs debt; to specify the procedural rules on repayment and remission of an amount of import or export duty and the information to be provided to the Commission; to adopt decisions on repayment or remission of an amount of import or export duty; to specify the procedural rules on the lodging, amendment and invalidation of an entry summary declaration; to specify the time-limit within which a risk analysis is to be carried out on the basis of the entry summary declaration; to specify the procedural rules on the notification of arrival of sea- going vessels and aircraft and on the conveyance of goods to the appropriate place; to specify the procedural rules on the presentation of goods to customs; the procedural rules on the lodging, amendment and invalidation of the temporary storage declaration and on the movement of goods in temporary storage; the procedural rules for the provision and verification of the proof of the customs status of Union goods; the procedural rules on the determination of competent customs offices and on the lodging of the customs declaration where other means than electronic data processing techniques are used; the procedural rules on the lodging of a standard customs declaration and on the making available of supporting documents; the procedural rules on the lodging of a simplified declaration and a supplementary declaration; the procedural rules on the lodging of a customs declaration prior to the presentation of goods to customs, the acceptance of the customs declaration and the amendment of the customs declaration after the release of the goods; to adopt measures for the determination of the tariff subheading of the goods which are subject to the highest rate of import or export duty where a consignment is made of goods falling under different tariff subheadings; to specify the procedural rules on centralised clearance and on the waiver from

the obligation for goods to be presented in that context; the procedural rules on entry in the declarant's records; the procedural rules on the customs formalities and controls to be carried out by the holder of the authorisation in the context of self-assessment; to adopt measures on the verification of the customs declaration, the examination and sampling of goods and the results of the verification;

the procedural rules on the disposal of goods; the procedural rules on the provision of information establishing that the conditions for relief from import duty for returned goods are fulfilled and on the provision of evidence that the conditions for relief from import duty for products of sea-fishing and other products taken from the sea are fulfilled; the procedural rules on the examination of the economic conditions in the context of special procedures; the procedural rules on the discharge of a special procedure; the procedural rules on the transfer of rights and obligations and the movement of goods in the context of special procedures; the procedural rules on the use of equivalent goods in the context of special procedures; the procedural rules for the application of the provisions of international transit instruments in the customs territory of the Union; the procedural rules on the placing of goods under the Union transit procedure and on the end of that procedure, on the operation of the simplifications of that procedure and on the customs supervision of goods passing through the territory of a country or territory outside the customs territory of the Union under the external Union transit procedure; the procedural rules on the placing of goods under the customs warehousing or free zone procedure; to lay down the time-limit within which risk analysis is to be carried out on the basis of the pre-departure declaration; to specify the procedural rules on the exit of goods;

the procedural rules on the lodging, amendment and invalidation of the exit summary declaration; the procedural rules on the lodging, amendment and invalidation of the re-export notification; to adopt a work programme supporting the development of related electronic systems and governing the setting up of transitional periods; to adopt decisions authorising Member States to test simplifications in the application of the customs legislation, especially when those simplifications are information technology (IT) related. Those powers should be exercised in accordance with Regulation (EU) No 182/2011 of the European Parliament and of the Council of 16 February 2011 laying down the rules and general principles concerning mechanisms for control by Member States of the Commission's exercise of implementing powers.

(6) Considering the cooperation which is needed between the Member States and the Commission to develop, maintain and employ the electronic systems required for the implementation of the Union Customs Code (the Code), the Commission should not adopt the work programme supporting that development and governing the setting up of transitional periods where no opinion is delivered by the committee examining the draft implementing act.

(7) The advisory procedure should be used for the adoption of: decisions allowing one or several Member States to use means for the exchange and storage of information other than electronic data-processing techniques, given that those decisions do not affect all Member States; decisions requesting Member States to revoke decisions relating to binding information, given that those decisions affect only one Member State and aim at ensuring compliance with the customs legislation; decisions on repayment or remission of an amount of import or export duty given that those decisions directly affect the applicant for that repayment or remission.

(8) In duly justified cases, where imperative grounds of urgency so require, the Commission should adopt immediately applicable implementing acts relating to: measures to ensure uniform application of customs controls, including the exchange of risk information and analysis, common risk criteria and standards, control measures and priority control areas; the determination of the tariff classification of goods; the determination of the origin of specific goods; measures temporarily prohibiting the use of comprehensive guarantees.

(9) The Union is based upon a customs union. It is advisable, in the interests both of economic operators and of the customs authorities in the Union, to assemble current customs legislation in a code. Based on the concept of an internal market, that code should contain the general rules and procedures which ensure the implementation of the tariff and other common policy measures introduced at Union level in connection with trade in goods between the Union and countries or territories outside the customs territory of the Union, taking into account the requirements of those common policies. Customs legislation should be better aligned on the provisions relating to the collection of import charges without change to the scope of the tax provisions in force.

(10) In order to ensure effective administrative simplification, the views of economic operators should be taken into account when the customs legislation is further modernised.

(11) In accordance with the Commission Communication of 9 August 2004 entitled "Protecting the Communities' financial interests – Fight against fraud – Action Plan for 2004-2005", it is appropriate to adapt the legal framework for the protection of the financial interests of the Union.

(12) Council Regulation (EEC) No 2913/92 of 12 October 1992 establishing the Community Customs Code was based upon integration of the customs procedures applied separately in the respective Member States during the 1980s. That Regulation has been repeatedly and substantially amended since its introduction, in order to address specific problems such as the protection of good faith or the taking into account of security requirements. Further amendments to that Regulation were introduced by Regulation (EC) No 648/2005 of the European Parliament and of the Council of 13 April 2005 – and subsequently included in Regulation (EC) No 450/2008 – as a consequence of the important legal changes which have occurred in recent years, at both

Union and international level, such as the expiry of the Treaty establishing the European Coal and Steel Community and the entry into force of the 2003, 2005 and 2011 Acts of Accession, as well as the amendment to the International Convention on the simplification and harmonisation of customs procedures (the Revised Kyoto Convention), the Union's accession to which was approved by Council Decision 2003/231/EC of 17 March 2003.

(13) It is appropriate to introduce in the Code a legal framework for the application of certain provisions of the customs legislation to trade in Union goods between parts of the customs territory to which the provisions of Council Directive 2006/112/EC of 28 November 2006 on the common system of value added tax or Council Directive 2008/118/EC of 16 December 2008 concerning the general arrangements for excise duty apply and parts of that territory where those provisions do not apply, or to trade between parts where those provisions do not apply. Considering the fact that the goods concerned are Union goods and considering the fiscal nature of the measures at stake in that intra-Union trade, it is justified to introduce, appropriate simplifications to the customs formalities to be applied to those goods.

(14) In order to take into account the special fiscal regime of certain parts of the customs territory of the Union, the power to adopt delegated acts in accordance with Article 290 TFEU should be delegated to the Commission in respect of the customs formalities and controls to be applied to the trade in Union goods between those parts and the rest of the customs territory of the Union.

(15) The facilitation of legitimate trade and the fight against fraud require simple, rapid and standard customs procedures and processes. It is therefore appropriate, in line with the Commission Communication of 24 July 2003 entitled "A simple and paperless environment for customs and trade", to simplify customs legislation, to allow the use of modern tools and technology and to promote further the uniform application of customs legislation and modernised approaches to customs control, thus helping to ensure the basis for efficient and simple clearance procedures. Customs procedures should be merged or aligned and the number of procedures reduced to those that are economically justified, with a view to increasing the competitiveness of business.

(16) The completion of the internal market, the reduction of barriers to international trade and investment and the reinforced need to ensure security and safety at the external borders of the Union have transformed the role of customs authorities giving them a leading role within the supply chain and, in their monitoring and management of international trade, making them a catalyst to the competitiveness of countries and companies. The customs legislation should therefore reflect the new economic reality and the new role and mission of customs authorities.

(17) The use of information and communication technologies, as laid down in Decision No 70/2008/EC of the European Parliament and of the Council of 15 January 2008 on a paperless environment for customs and trade, is a key

element in ensuring trade facilitation and, at the same time, the effectiveness of customs controls, thus reducing costs for business and risk for society. It is therefore necessary to establish in the Code the legal framework within which that Decision can be implemented, in particular the legal principle that all customs and trade transactions are to be handled electronically and that information and communication systems for customs operations are to offer, in each Member State, the same facilities to economic operators.

(18) In order to ensure a paperless environment for customs and trade, the power to adopt delegated acts in accordance with Article 290 TFEU should be delegated to the Commission in respect of common data requirements for the purpose of the exchange and techniques, cases where other means may be used for such exchange and storage and registration of persons. Means other than electronic data processing techniques could be used in particular on a transitional basis, where the necessary electronic systems are not yet operational, but not beyond 31 December 2020. Insofar as centralised clearance is concerned, those transitional measures would consist, until the necessary electronic systems are operational, in maintaining the procedure currently known as the 'single authorisation for simplified procedures'.

(19) Use of information and communication technologies should be accompanied by harmonised and standardised application of customs controls by the Member States, to ensure an equivalent level of customs control throughout the Union so as not to give rise to anti-competitive behaviour at the various Union entry and exit points.

(20) In the interests of facilitating business, while at the same time providing for the proper levels of control of goods brought into or taken out of the customs territory of the Union, it is desirable that the information provided by economic operators be shared, taking account of the relevant data-protection provisions, between customs authorities and with other agencies involved in that control. Those controls should be harmonised, so that the economic operator need give the information only once and that goods are controlled by those authorities at the same time and at the same place.

(21) In the interests of facilitating business, all persons should continue to have the right to appoint a representative in their dealings with the customs authorities. However, it should no longer be possible for that right of representation to be reserved under a law laid down by one of the Member States. Furthermore, a customs representative who complies with the criteria for the granting of the status of authorised economic operator for customs simplifications should be entitled to provide his or her services in a Member State other than the Member State where he or she is established. As a general rule, a customs representative should be established in the customs territory of the Union. That obligation should be waived where the customs representative acts on behalf of persons who are not required to be established within the customs territory of the Union or in other justified cases.

(22) All decisions relating to the application of the customs legislation, including to binding information, should be covered by the same rules. Any such

decisions should be valid throughout the Union and should be capable of being annulled, amended except where otherwise stipulated, or revoked where they do not conform to the customs legislation or its interpretation.

(23) The streamlining of customs procedures within an electronic environment requires the sharing of responsibilities between the customs authorities of different Member States. It is necessary to ensure an appropriate level of effective, dissuasive and proportionate penalties throughout the internal market.

(24) Compliant and trustworthy economic operators should enjoy the status of 'authorised economic operator' subject to the granting of an authorisation for customs simplifications or an authorisation for security and safety, or both. Depending on the type of authorisation granted, authorised economic operators should be able to take maximum advantage of widespread use of customs simplifications or benefit from facilitations relating to security and safety. They should also be given more favourable treatment in respect of customs controls, such as fewer physical and document-based controls.

(25) Compliant and trustworthy economic operators should benefit from international mutual recognition of the status of 'authorised economic operator'.

(26) In order to secure a balance between, on the one hand, the need for customs authorities to ensure the correct application of the customs legislation and, on the other, the right of economic operators to be treated fairly, the customs authorities should be granted extensive powers of control and economic operators a right of appeal.

(27) In accordance with the Charter of Fundamental Rights of the European Union, it is necessary, in addition to the right of appeal against any decision taken by the customs authorities, to provide for the right of every person to be heard before any decision is taken which would adversely affect him or her. However, restrictions to that right may be justified in particular where the nature or the level of the threat to the security and safety of the Union and its residents, to human, animal or plant health, to the environment or to consumers so requires.

(28) In order to minimise the risk to the Union, its citizens and its trading partners, the harmonised application of customs controls by the Member States should be based upon a common risk management framework and an electronic system for its implementation. The establishment of a risk management framework common to all Member States should not prevent them from controlling goods by random checks.

(29) In order to ensure a consistent and equal treatment of persons concerned by customs formalities and controls, the power to adopt delegated acts in accordance with Article 290 TFEU should be delegated to the Commission in respect of determining other cases where the customs representative is not obliged to be established in the customs territory of the Union and rules relating to decisions taken by the customs authorities, including those relating to binding information, authorised economic operator and simplifications.

(30) It is necessary to establish the factors on the basis of which import or export duty and other measures in respect of trade in goods are applied. It is also appropriate to lay down more detailed provisions for issuing proofs of origin in the Union, where the exigencies of trade so require.

(31) In order to supplement the factors on the basis of which import or export duty and other measures are applied, the power to adopt delegated acts in accordance with Article 290 TFEU should be delegated to the Commission in respect of rules on origin of goods.

(32) It is desirable to group together all cases of incurrence of a customs debt on import, other than following the submission of a customs declaration for release for free circulation or temporary admission with partial relief, in order to avoid difficulties in determining the legal basis on which the customs debt was incurred. The same should apply in cases of incurrence of a customs debt on export.

(33) It is appropriate to establish the place where the customs debt is incurred and where the import or export duty should be recovered.

(34) The rules for special procedures should allow for the use of a single guarantee for all categories of special procedures and for that guarantee to be comprehensive, covering a number of transactions.

(35) A comprehensive guarantee with a reduced amount, including for customs debts and other charges which have been incurred, or a comprehensive guarantee with a guarantee waiver, should be authorised under certain conditions. A comprehensive guarantee with a reduced amount for customs debts and other charges which have been incurred should be equivalent to the provision of a guarantee for the whole amount of import or export duty payable, in particular for the purposes of the release of the goods concerned and of the entry in the accounts.

(36) In order to ensure better protection of the financial interests of the Union and of the Member States, a guarantee should cover non-declared or incorrectly declared goods included in a consignment or in a declaration for which it is provided. For the same reason, the undertaking of the guarantor should also cover amounts of import or export duty which fall to be paid following post-release controls.

(37) In order to safeguard the financial interests of the Union and of the Member States and to curb fraudulent practices, arrangements involving graduated measures for the application of a comprehensive guarantee are advisable. Where there is an increased risk of fraud it should be possible to prohibit temporarily the application of the comprehensive guarantee, taking account of the particular situation of the economic operators concerned.

(38) It is appropriate to take account of the good faith of the person concerned in cases where a customs debt is incurred through non-compliance with the customs legislation and to minimise the impact of negligence on the part of the debtor.

(39) In order to protect the financial interests of the Union and of the Member States and to supplement the rules concerning the customs debt and the

guarantees, the power to adopt delegated acts in accordance with Article 290 TFEU should be delegated to the Commission in respect of the place of incurrence of the customs debt, the calculation of the amount of import and export duty, the guarantee of that amount and the recovery, repayment, remission and extinguishment of the customs debt.

(40) It is necessary to lay down the principle of how to determine the customs status of Union goods and the circumstances pertaining to the loss of such status, and to provide a basis for determining when that status remains unaltered in cases where goods are temporarily taken out of the customs territory of the Union.

(41) In order to ensure free movement of Union goods in the customs territory of the Union and customs treatment of non-Union goods brought into that territory, the power to adopt delegated acts in accordance with Article 290 TFEU should be delegated to the Commission in respect of the determination of the customs status of goods, the loss of the customs status of Union goods, the preservation of that status for goods temporarily leaving the customs territory of the Union and the duty relief for returned goods.

(42) It is appropriate, where an economic operator has provided, in advance, the information necessary for risk-based controls on the admissibility of the goods, to ensure that quick release of goods is then the rule. Fiscal and trade policy controls should primarily be performed by the customs office competent in respect of the premises of the economic operator.

(43) The rules for customs declarations and for the placing of goods under a customs procedure should be modernised and streamlined, in particular by requiring that, as a rule, customs declarations be made electronically and by providing for only one type of simplified declaration and for the possibility to lodge a customs declaration in the form of an entry in the declarant's records.

(44) Since the Revised Kyoto Convention favours the lodging, registering and checking of the customs declaration prior to the arrival of the goods and, furthermore, the dissociation of the place where the declaration is lodged from the place where the goods are physically located, it is appropriate to provide for centralised clearance at the place where the economic operator is established.

(45) It is appropriate to lay down at Union level the rules governing the destruction or disposal otherwise of goods by the customs authorities, since these are matters which previously required national legislation.

(46) In order to supplement the rules regarding the placing of goods under a customs procedure and ensure equal treatment of the persons concerned, the power to adopt delegated acts in accordance with Article 290 TFEU should be delegated to the Commission in respect of the rules relating to the customs declaration and the release of goods.

(47) It is appropriate to lay down common and simple rules for the special procedures, supplemented by a small set of rules for each category of special

procedure, in order to make it simple for the operator to choose the right procedure, to avoid errors and to reduce the number of post-release recoveries and repayments.

(48) The granting of authorisations for several special procedures with a single guarantee and a single supervising customs office should be facilitated and there should be simple rules on the incurrence of a customs debt in these cases. The basic principle should be that goods placed under a special procedure, or the products made from them, are to be assessed at the time when the customs debt is incurred. However, it should also be possible, where economically justified, to assess the goods at the time when they were placed under a special procedure. The same principles should apply to usual forms of handling.

(49) In view of increased security-related measures, the placing of goods into free zones should become a customs procedure and the goods should be subject to customs controls at entry and with regard to records.

(50) Given that the intention of re-export is no longer necessary, the inward processing suspension procedure should be merged with processing under customs control and the inward processing drawback procedure abandoned. This single inward processing procedure should also cover destruction, except where destruction is carried out by, or under the supervision of, customs.

(51) In order to supplement the rules on special procedures and ensure equal treatment of the persons concerned, the power to adopt delegated acts in accordance with Article 290 TFEU should be delegated to the Commission in respect of the rules relating to cases where goods are placed under special procedures, movements, usual forms of handling and equivalence of those goods and discharge of those procedures.

(52) Security-related measures relating to Union goods taken out of the customs territory of the Union should apply equally to the re-export of non-Union goods. The same rules should apply to all types of goods, with the possibility of exceptions where necessary, such as for goods only transiting through the customs territory of the Union.

(53) In order to ensure the customs supervision of goods brought into and taken out of the customs territory of the Union and the application of security-related measures, the power to adopt delegated acts in accordance with Article 290 TFEU should be delegated to the Commission in respect of the rules relating to entry summary declaration and pre-departure declarations.

(54) In order to explore further customs and trade facilitation, in particular by making use of the most recent tools and technology, Member States should be authorised, under certain conditions and upon application, to test for a limited period of time simplifications in the application of the customs legislation. That possibility should not jeopardise the application of the customs legislation or create new obligations for economic operators, who may take part in these tests on a purely voluntary basis. In accordance with the principle of proportionality, as set out in Article 5 of the Treaty on European

Union (TEU), it is necessary and appropriate, for the achievement of the basic objectives of enabling the customs union to function effectively and implementing the common commercial policy, to lay down the general rules and procedures applicable to goods brought into or taken out of the customs territory of the Union. In accordance with the first subparagraph of Article 5(4) TEU, this Regulation does not go beyond what is necessary in order to achieve those objectives.

(56) In order to simplify and rationalise customs legislation, a number of provisions contained in autonomous Union acts have, for the sake of transparency, been incorporated into the Code. Council Regulation (EEC) No 3925/91 of 19 December 1991 concerning the elimination of controls and formalities applicable to the cabin and hold baggage of persons taking an intra-Community flight and the baggage of persons making an intra- Community sea crossing, Regulation (EEC) No 2913/92, Council Regulation (EC) No 1207/2001 of 11 June 2001 on procedures to facilitate the issue or the making out in the Community of proofs of origin and the issue of certain approved exporter authorisations under the provisions governing preferential trade between the European Community and certain countries, and Regulation (EC) No 450/2008 should therefore be repealed.

(57) The provisions of this Regulation setting out the delegation of power and the conferral of implementing powers and the provisions on charges and costs should apply from the date of entry into force of this Regulation. The other provisions should apply from 1 June 2016.

(58) This Regulation should be without prejudice to existing and future Union rules on access to documents adopted in accordance with Article 15(3) TFEU. It should also be without prejudice to national rules on access to documents.

(59) The Commission should make every effort to ensure that the delegated and implementing acts provided for in this Regulation enter into force sufficiently in advance of the application date of the Code to allow its timely implementation by Member States,

HAVE ADOPTED THIS REGULATION:

APPENDIX IV

European Union: Union Customs Code*

The following extract from the Union Customs Code concerns the determination of tariffs including tariff classification and origin of goods.

<http://eur-lex.europa.eu/legal-content/EN/TXT/PDF/?uri=CELEX:32013R0952&rid=1>. The following preamble from that document sets out the major parts of the new Union Customs Code.

Extract

TITLE II FACTORS ON THE BASIS OF WHICH IMPORT OR EXPORT DUTY AND OTHER MEASURES IN RESPECT OF TRADE IN GOODS ARE APPLIED

Chapter 1 Common Customs Tariff and tariff classification of goods

Article 56 Common Customs Tariff and surveillance

1. Import and export duty due shall be based on the Common Customs Tariff. Other measures prescribed by Union provisions governing specific fields relating to trade in goods shall, where appropriate, be applied in accordance with the tariff classification of those goods. 2. The Common Customs Tariff shall comprise all of the following:
   (a) the Combined Nomenclature of goods as laid down in Regulation (EEC) No 2658/87;
   (b) any other nomenclature which is wholly or partly based on the Combined Nomenclature or which provides for further subdivisions to it, and which is established by Union provisions governing specific fields with a view to the application of tariff measures relating to trade in goods;

* http://eur-lex.europa.eu, © European Union, 1998-2015.

(c) the conventional or normal autonomous customs duty applicable to goods covered by the Combined Nomenclature;
(d) the preferential tariff measures contained in agreements which the Union has concluded with certain countries or territories outside the customs territory of the Union or groups of such countries or territories;
(e) preferential tariff measures adopted unilaterally by the Union in respect of certain countries or territories outside the customs territory of the Union or groups of such countries or territories;
(f) autonomous measures providing for a reduction in, or exemption from, customs duty on certain goods;
(g) favourable tariff treatment specified for certain goods, by reason of their nature or end-use, in the framework of measures referred to under points (c) to (f) or (h);
(h) other tariff measures provided for by agricultural or commercial or other Union legislation.

3. Where the goods concerned fulfil the conditions included in the measures laid down in points (d) to (g) of paragraph 2, the measures referred to in those provisions shall apply, upon application by the declarant, instead of those provided for in point (c) of that paragraph. Such application may be made retrospectively, provided that the time-limits and conditions laid down in the relevant measure or in the Code are complied with.
4. Where application of the measures referred to in points (d) to (g) of paragraph 2, or the exemption from measures referred to in point (h) thereof, is restricted to a certain volume of imports or exports, such application or exemption shall, in the case of tariff quotas, cease as soon as the specified volume of imports or exports is reached.
   In the case of tariff ceilings such application shall cease by virtue of a legal act of the Union.
5. The release for free circulation or the export of goods, to which the measures referred to in paragraphs 1 and 2 apply, may be made subject to surveillance.

Article 57 Tariff classification of goods

1. For the application of the Common Customs Tariff, tariff classification of goods shall consist in the determination of one of the subheadings or further subdivisions of the Combined Nomenclature under which those goods are to be classified.
2. For the application of non-tariff measures, tariff classification of goods shall consist in the determination of one of the subheadings or further subdivisions of the Combined Nomenclature, or of any other nomenclature which is established by Union provisions and which is wholly or partly based on the Combined Nomenclature or which provides for further subdivisions to it, under which those goods are to be classified.

3. The subheading or further subdivision determined in accordance with paragraphs 1 and 2 shall be used for the purpose of applying the measures linked to that subheading.
4. The Commission may adopt measures to determine the tariff classification of goods in accordance with paragraphs 1 and 2.

Article 58 Conferral of implementing powers

1. The Commission shall adopt, by means of implementing acts, measures on the uniform management of the tariff quotas and the tariff ceilings referred to in Article 56(4) and on the management of the surveillance of the release for free circulation or export of goods, referred to in Article 56(5).
   Those implementing acts shall be adopted in accordance with the examination procedure referred to in Article 285(4).
2. The Commission shall adopt, by means of implementing acts, the measures referred to in Article 57(4).
   Those implementing acts shall be adopted in accordance with the examination procedure referred to in Article 285(4).
   On imperative grounds of urgency relating to such measures, duly justified by the need to rapidly ensure the correct and uniform application of the Combined Nomenclature, the Commission shall adopt immediately applicable implementing acts in accordance with the procedure referred to in Article 285(5).
   Where the opinion of the committee referred to in Article 285(1) is to be obtained by written procedure, Article 285(6) shall apply.

CHAPTER 2 Origin of goods

Section 1 Non-preferential origin

Article 59 Scope

Articles 60 and 61 shall lay down rules for the determination of the non-preferential origin of goods for the purposes of applying the following:

(a) the Common Customs Tariff, with the exception of the measures referred to in points (d) and (e) of Article 56(2);
(b) measures, other than tariff measures, established by Union provisions governing specific fields relating to trade in goods; and
(c) other Union measures relating to the origin of goods.

Article 60 Acquisition of origin

1. Goods wholly obtained in a single country or territory shall be regarded as having their origin in that country or territory.
2. Goods the production of which involves more than one country or territory shall be deemed to originate in the country or territory where they underwent their last, substantial, economically-justified processing or working, in an undertaking equipped for that purpose, resulting in the manufacture of a new product or representing an important stage of manufacture

Article 61 Proof of origin

1. Where an origin has been indicated in the customs declaration pursuant to the customs legislation, the customs authorities may require the declarant to prove the origin of the goods.
2. Where proof of origin of goods is provided pursuant to the customs legislation or other Union legislation governing specific fields, the customs authorities may, in the event of reasonable doubt, require any additional evidence needed in order to ensure that the indication of origin complies with the rules laid down by the relevant Union legislation.
3. Where the exigencies of trade so require, a document proving origin may be issued in the Union in accordance with the rules of origin in force in the country or territory of destination or any other method identifying the country where the goods were wholly obtained or underwent their last substantial transformation.

Article 62 Delegation of power

The Commission shall be empowered to adopt delegated acts in accordance with Article 284, laying down the rules under which goods, whose determination of non-preferential origin is required for the purposes of applying the Union measures referred to in Article 59, are considered as wholly obtained in a single country or territory or to have undergone their last, substantial, economically-justified processing or working, in an undertaking equipped for that purpose, resulting in the manufacture of a new product or representing an important stage of manufacture in a country or territory, in accordance with Article 60.

Article 63 Conferral of implementing powers

The Commission shall adopt, by means of implementing acts, the procedural rules for the provision and verification of the proof of origin referred to in Article 61. Those implementing acts shall be adopted in accordance with the examination procedure referred to in Article 285(4).

Section 2 Preferential origin

Article 64 Preferential origin of goods

1. In order to benefit from the measures referred to in points (d) or (e) of Article 56(2) or from non-tariff preferential measures, goods shall comply with the rules on preferential origin referred to in paragraphs 2 to 5 of this Article. contained in agreements which the Union has concluded with certain countries or territories outside the customs territory of the Union or with groups of such countries or territories, the rules on preferential origin shall be laid down in those agreements.
3. In the case of goods benefiting from preferential measures adopted unilaterally by the Union in respect of certain countries or territories outside the customs territory of the Union or groups of such countries or territories, other than those referred to in paragraph 5, the Commission shall adopt measures laying down the rules on preferential origin.
   Those rules shall be based either on the criterion that goods are wholly obtained or on the criterion that goods result from sufficient processing or working.
4. In the case of goods benefiting from preferential measures applicable in trade between the customs territory of the Union and Ceuta and Melilla, as contained in Protocol 2 to the 1985 Act of Accession, the rules on preferential origin shall be adopted in accordance with Article 9 of that Protocol.
5. In the case of goods benefiting from preferential measures contained in preferential arrangements in favour of the overseas countries and territories associated with the Union, the rules on preferential origin shall be adopted in accordance with Article 203 TFEU.
6. Upon its own initiative or at the request of a beneficiary country or territory, the Commission may, for certain goods, grant that country or territory a temporary derogation from the rules on preferential origin referred to in paragraph 3.
   The temporary derogation shall be justified by one of the following reasons:
   (a) internal or external factors temporarily deprive the beneficiary country or territory of the ability to comply with the rules on preferential origin;
   (b) the beneficiary country or territory requires time to prepare itself to comply with those rules.

   A request for derogation shall be made in writing to the Commission by the beneficiary country or territory concerned. The request shall state the reasons, as indicated in the second subparagraph, why derogation is required and shall contain appropriate supporting documents. The temporary derogation shall be limited to the duration of the effects of the internal or external factors giving rise to it or the length of time needed for the beneficiary country or territory to achieve compliance with the rules.

Where a derogation is granted, the beneficiary country or territory concerned shall comply with any requirements laid down as to information to be provided to the Commission concerning the use of the derogation and the management of the quantities for which the derogation is granted.

Article 65 Delegation of power

The Commission shall be empowered to adopt delegated acts in accordance with Article 284, laying down the rules on preferential origin referred to in Article 64(3).

Article 66 Conferral of implementing powers

The Commission shall adopt by means of implementing acts:

(a) the procedural rules, referred to in Article 64(1), to facilitate the establishment in the Union of the preferential origin of goods;
(b) a measure granting a beneficiary country or territory the temporary derogation referred to in Article 64(6).

Those implementing acts shall be adopted in accordance with the examination procedure referred to in Article 285(4).

Section 3 Determination of origin of specific goods

Article 67 Measures taken by the Commission

The Commission may adopt measures to determine the origin of specific goods in accordance with the rules of origin applicable to those goods.

Article 68 Conferral of implementing powers

The Commission shall adopt, by means of implementing acts, the measures referred to in Article 67. Those implementing acts shall be adopted in accordance with the examination procedure referred to in Article 285(4). On imperative grounds of urgency relating to such measures, duly justified by the need to rapidly ensure the correct and uniform application of rules of origin, the Commission shall adopt immediately applicable implementing acts in accordance with the procedure referred to in Article 285(5).
Where the opinion of the committee referred to in Article 285(1) is to be obtained by written procedure, Article 285(6) shall apply.

CHAPTER 3 Value of goods for customs purposes

Article 69 Scope

The customs value of goods, for the purposes of applying the Common Customs Tariff and non-tariff measures laid down by Union provisions governing specific fields relating to trade in goods, shall be determined in accordance with Articles 70 and 74.

Article 70 Method of customs valuation based on the transaction value

1. The primary basis for the customs value of goods shall be the transaction value, that is the price actually paid or payable for the goods when sold for export to the customs territory of the Union, adjusted, where necessary.
2. The price actually paid or payable shall be the total payment made or to be made by the buyer to the seller or by the buyer to a third party for the benefit of the seller for the imported goods and include all payments made or to be made as a condition of sale of the imported goods.
3. The transaction value shall apply provided that all of the following conditions are fulfilled:
   - (a) there are no restrictions as to the disposal or use of the goods by the buyer, other than any of the following:
     - (i) restrictions imposed or required by a law or by the public authorities in the Union;
     - (ii) limitations of the geographical area in which the goods may be resold;
     - (iii) restrictions which do not substantially affect the customs value of the goods; (b) the sale or price is not subject to some condition or consideration for which a value cannot be determined with respect to the goods being valued;
   - (c) no part of the proceeds of any subsequent resale, disposal or use of the goods by the buyer will accrue directly or indirectly to the seller, unless an appropriate adjustment can be made;
   - (d) the buyer and seller are not related or the relationship did not influence the price.

Article 71 Elements of the transaction value

1. In determining the customs value under Article 70, the price actually paid or payable for the imported goods shall be supplemented by:
   - (a) the following, to the extent that they are incurred by the buyer but are not included in the price actually paid or payable for the goods:
     - (i) commissions and brokerage, except buying commissions;

(ii) the cost of containers which are treated as being one, for customs purposes, with the goods in question; and

(iii) the cost of packing, whether for labour or materials;

(b) the value, apportioned as appropriate, of the following goods and services where supplied directly or indirectly by the buyer free of charge or at reduced cost for use in connection with the production and sale for export of the imported goods, to the extent that such value has not been included in the price actually paid or payable:

(i) materials, components, parts and similar items incorporated into the imported goods;

(ii) tools, dies, moulds and similar items used in the production of the imported goods;

(iii) materials consumed in the production of the imported goods; and (iv) engineering, development, artwork, design work, and plans and sketches undertaken elsewhere than in the Union and necessary for the production of the imported goods;

(c) royalties and licence fees related to the goods being valued that the buyer must pay, either directly or indirectly, as a condition of sale of the goods being valued, to the extent that such royalties and fees are not included in the price actually paid or payable;

(d) the value of any part of the proceeds of any subsequent resale, disposal or use of the imported goods that accrues directly or indirectly to the seller; and

(e) the following costs up to the place where goods are brought into the customs territory of the Union:

(i) the cost of transport and insurance of the imported goods; and

(ii) loading and handling charges associated with the transport of the imported goods.

2. Additions to the price actually paid or payable, pursuant to paragraph 1, shall be made only on the basis of objective and quantifiable data.
3. No additions shall be made to the price actually paid or payable in determining the customs value except as provided in this Article.

Article 72 Elements not to be included in the customs value

In determining the customs value under Article 70, none of the following shall be included:

(a) the cost of transport of the imported goods after their entry into the customs territory of the Union;

(b) charges for construction, erection, assembly, maintenance or technical assistance, undertaken after the entry into the customs territory of the Union of the imported goods such as industrial plants, machinery or equipment;

(c) charges for interest under a financing arrangement entered into by the buyer and relating to the purchase of the imported goods, irrespective of whether the finance is provided by the seller or another person, provided that the financing arrangement has been made in writing and, where required, the buyer can demonstrate that the following conditions are fulfilled:
    (i) such goods are actually sold at the price declared as the price actually paid or payable;
    (ii) the claimed rate of interest does not exceed the level for such transactions prevailing in the country where, and at the time when, the finance was provided;

(d) charges for the right to reproduce the imported goods in the Union;

(e) buying commissions;

(f) import duties or other charges payable in the Union by reason of the import or sale of the goods;

(g) notwithstanding point (c) of Article 71(1), payments made by the buyer for the right to distribute or resell the imported goods, if such payments are not a condition of the sale for export to the Union of the goods.

Article 73 Simplification

The customs authorities may, upon application, authorise that the following amounts be determined on the basis of specific criteria, where they are not quantifiable on the date on which the customs declaration is accepted:

(a) amounts which are to be included in the customs value in accordance with Article 70(2); and

(b) the amounts referred to in Articles 71 and 72.

Article 74 Secondary methods of customs valuation

1. Where the customs value of goods cannot be determined under Article 70, it shall be determined by proceeding sequentially from points (a) to (d) of paragraph 2, until the first point under which the customs value of goods can be determined. The order of application of points (c) and (d) of paragraph 2 shall be reversed if the declarant so requests.
2. The customs value, pursuant to paragraph 1, shall be:
    (a) the transaction value of identical goods sold for export to the customs territory of the Union and exported at or about the same time as the goods being valued;
    (b) the transaction value of similar goods sold for export to the customs territory of the Union and exported at or about the same time as the goods being valued;

(c) the value based on the unit price at which the imported goods, or identical or similar imported goods, are sold within the customs territory of the Union in the greatest aggregate quantity to persons not related to the sellers; or
(d) the computed value, consisting of the sum of:
  (i) the cost or value of materials and fabrication or other processing employed in producing the imported goods;
  (ii) an amount for profit and general expenses equal to that usually reflected in sales of goods of the same class or kind as the goods being valued which are made by producers in the country of export for export to the Union;
  (iii) the cost or value of the elements referred to in point (e) of Article 71(1).

3. Where the customs value cannot be determined under paragraph 1, it shall be determined on the basis of data available in the customs territory of the Union, using reasonable means consistent with the principles and general provisions of all of the following:
   (a) the agreement on implementation of Article VII of the General Agreement on Tariffs and Trade;
   (b) Article VII of the General Agreement on Tariffs and Trade;
   (c) this Chapter.

Article 75 Delegation of power

The Commission shall be empowered to adopt delegated acts, in accordance with Article 284, in order to determine the conditions for granting the authorisation referred to in Article 73.

Article 76 Conferral of implementing powers

The Commission shall specify, by means of implementing acts, the procedural rules for:

(a) determining the customs value in accordance with Articles 70(1) and (2) and Articles 71 and 72, including those for adjusting the price actually paid or payable;
(b) the application of the conditions referred to in Article 70(3);
(c) determining the customs value referred to in Article 74.

Those implementing acts shall be adopted in accordance with the examination procedure referred to in Article 285(4).

Table of Cases

Table of Statutes and Directives

National Tax Code, Law No. 5172 (1966) (Brazil), **42**
New International Tax Arrangements (Participation Exemption and Other Measures) Act 2004, Act No. 96 of 2004 (Australia), **181**
North American Free Trade Agreement, 17 December 1992, 32 ILM 289, art 302 (entered into force 1 January 1994), **75, 104, 165**
Offshore Petroleum and Greenhouse Gas Storage Act (2006), section 75 (Australia), **41**
Petroleum and Natural Gas Act (British Columbia), **45**
Petroleum Profits Tax Act 2004 (CAP P13 LFN 2004) (Nigeria), **55**
Petroleum Resource Rent Tax Assessment Act 1987 (Act No. 142 of 1987) (Australia), **41, 102**
Petroleum Royalty Regulation, 2017, under the Mines and Minerals Act, RSA 2000 c M-17 (Alberta), **45**
Proposed Revision of Procedures for Advance Pricing Agreements, Notice 2013-79, released on 22 November 2013, Internal Revenue Service (United States), **314**
Proposed Revision of Procedures for Requesting Competent Authority Assistance Under Tax Treaties, Notice 2013-78, released on 22 November 2013, Internal Revenue Service (United States), **314**
Provisional Regulations of the People's Republic of China on Business Tax Detailed Rules for its Implementation, 13 December 1993 (Business Tax) (China), **47**
Provisional Regulations of the People's Republic of China on Value Added Tax Detailed Rules for its Implementation, 13 December 1993 (VAT) (China), **47**
Provincial Sales Tax Act 2012, SBC 2012 Chapter 35 (British Columbia), **46**
Regulation (EU) No 952/2013 (European Union), **165, 463–474**
Regulation (EC) No. 713/2009 of the European Parliament and of the Council of 13 July 2009 establishing an Agency for the Cooperation of Energy Regulators. ENTSO, European Network of Transmission System Operators for Electricity, https://www.entsoe.eu/Pages/default.aspx on 25 August 2017 (European Union), **119**
Regulation on administrative cooperation and combating VAT fraud (Council Regulation 904/2010 (OJ L268 of 12/10/2010) (European Union), **162**
Renewable Energy Act 2017 (Germany), **132**
Revenue Procedure 2004–40, released on 19 July 2004, Internal Revenue Service (United States), **314**
Revenue Procedure 2006-9, released on 19 December 2005, Internal Revenue Service (United States), **313, 314**
Stamp Tax Act (Inshi zei ho), Act No. 23 of 1967 (Japan), **53**
State Tax Act Statute of 1922 on Income Taxation to the State (Statsskatteloven) (Denmark), **47**
Tariff Act, 19 USC 1401a (United States), **171**
Tax Cuts and Jobs Act (TCJA), Public law no. 115-97, 131 Stat. 2054 (United States), **60, 61, 184**
Tax Equity and Fiscal Responsibility Act of 1982, Public Law 97–248 (United States), **61**
Tax Laws Amendment (Countering Tax Avoidance and Multinational Profit Shifting) Act 2013, No. 101, 2013 (Australia), **295**
Tax on Credit, Exchange Operations, and Insurance, or on Securities, Law No. 5143 (1966) (Brazil), **43**

Table of Treaties and International Agreements

Index

SERIES ON INTERNATIONAL TAXATION

1. Alberto Xavier, *The Taxation of Foreign Investment in Brazil,* 1980 (ISBN 90-200-0582-0).
2. Hugh J. Ault & Albert J. Rädler, *The German Corporation Tax Law with 1980 Amendments,* 1981 (ISBN 90-200-0642-8).
3. Paul R. McDaniel & Hugh J. Ault, *Introduction to United States International Taxation,* 1981 (ISBN 90-6544-004-6).
4. Albert J. Rädler, *German Transfer Pricing/Prix de Transfer en Allemagne,* 1984 (ISBN 90-6544-143-3).
5. Paul R. McDaniel & Stanley S. Surrey, *International Aspects of Tax Expenditures: A Comparative Study,* 1985 (ISBN 90-654-4163-8).
6. Kees van Raad, *Nondiscrimination in International Tax Law,* 1986 (ISBN 90-6544-266-9).
7. Sijbren Cnossen (ed.), *Tax Coordination in the European Community,* 1987 (ISBN 90-6544-272-3).
8. Ben Terra, *Sales Taxation. The Case of Value Added Tax in the European Community,* 1989 (ISBN 90-6544-381-9).
9. Rutsel S.J. Martha, *The Jurisdiction to Tax in International Law: Theory and Practice of Legislative Fiscal Jurisdiction,* 1989 (ISBN 90-654-4416-5).
10. Paul R. McDaniel & Hugh J. Ault, *Introduction to United States International Taxation* (3rd revised edition), 1989 (ISBN 90-6544-423-8).
11. Manuel Pires, *International Juridicial Double Taxation of Income,* 1989 (ISBN 90-6544-426-2).
12. A.H.M. Daniels, *Issues in International Partnership Taxation,* 1991 (ISBN 90-654-4577-3).
13. Arvid A. Skaar, *Permanent Establishment: Erosion of a Tax Treaty Principle,* 1992 (ISBN 90-6544-594-3).
14. Cyrille David & Geerten M.M. Michielse (eds), *Tax Treatment of Financial Instruments,* 1996 (ISBN 90-654-4666-4).
15. Herbert H. Alpert & Kees van Raad (eds), *Essays on International Taxation,* 1993 (ISBN 90-654-4781-4).
16. Wolfgang Gassner, Michael Lang & Eduard Lechner (eds), *Tax Treaties and EC Law,* 1997 (ISBN 90-411-0680-4).
17. Glória Teixeira, *Taxing Corporate Profits in the EU,* 1997 (ISBN 90-411-0703-7).
18. Michael Lang et al. (eds), *Multilateral Tax Treaties,* 1998 (ISBN 90-411-0704-5).
19. Stef van Weeghel, *The Improper Use of Tax Treaties,* 1998 (ISBN 90-411-0737-1).
20. Klaus Vogel (ed.), *Interpretation of Tax Law and Treaties and Transfer Pricing in Japan and Germany,* 1998 (ISBN 90-411-9655-2).
21. Bertil Wiman (ed.), *International Studies in Taxation: Law and Economics; Liber Amicorum Leif Mutén,* 1999 (ISBN 90-411-9692-7).
22. Alfonso J. Martín Jiménez, *Towards Corporate Tax Harmonization in the European Community,* 1999 (ISBN 90-411-9690-0).

23. Ramon J. Jeffery, *The Impact of State Sovereignty on Global Trade and International Taxation,* 1999 (ISBN 90-411-9703-6).
24. A.J. Easson, *Taxation of Foreign Direct Investment,* 1999 (ISBN 90-411-9741-9).
25. Marjaana Helminen, *The Dividend Concept in International Tax Law: Dividend Payments Between Corporate Entities,* 1999 (ISBN 90-411-9765-6).
26. Paul Kirchhof, Moris Lehner, Kees van Raad, Arndt Raupach & Michael-Rodi (eds), *International and Comparative Taxation: Essays in Honour of Klaus Vogel,* 2002 (ISBN 90-411-9841-5).
27. Krister Andersson, Peter Melz & Christer Silfverberg (eds), *Liber Amicorum Sven-Olof Lodin,* 2001 (ISBN 90-411-9850-4).
28. Juan Martín Jovanovich, *Customs Valuation and Transfer Pricing: Is It Possible to Harmonize Customs and Tax Rules?,* Second Edition, 2018 (ISBN 978-90-411-6134-5).
29. Stefano Simontacchi, *Taxation of Capital Gains under the OECD Model Convention: With Special Regard to Immovable Property,* 2007 (ISBN 978-90-411-2549-1).
30. Michael Lang, Josef Schuch, & Claus Staringer (eds), *Tax Treaty Law and EC Law,* 2007 (ISBN 978-90-411-2629-0).
31. Duncan Bentley, *Taxpayers' Rights: Theory Origin and Implementation,* 2007 (ISBN 978-90-411-2650-4).
32. Sergio André Rocha, *Interpretation of Double Taxation Conventions: General Theory and Brazilian Perspective,* 2008 (ISBN 978-90-411-2822-5).
33. Robert F. van Brederode, *Systems of General Sales Taxation: Theory, Policy and Practice,* 2009 (ISBN 978-90-411-2832-4).
34. John G. Head & Richard Krever (eds), *Tax Reform in the 21st Century: A Volume in Memory of Richard Musgrave,* 2009 (ISBN 978-90-411-2829-4).
35. Jens Wittendorff, *Transfer Pricing and the Arm's Length Principle in International Tax Law,* 2010 (ISBN 978-90-411-3270-3).
36. Marjaana Helminen, *The International Tax Law Concept of Dividend,* Second Edition, 2017 (ISBN 978-90-411-8394-1).
37. Robert F. van Brederode (ed.), *Immovable Property under VAT: A Comparative Global Analysis,* 2011 (ISBN 978-90-411-3126-3).
38. Dennis Weber & Stef van Weeghel, *The 2010 OECD Updates: Model Tax Convention & Transfer Pricing Guidelines - A Critical Review,* 2011 (ISBN 978-90-411-3812-5).
39. Yariv Brauner & Martin James McMahon, Jr. (eds), *The Proper Tax Base: Structural Fairness from an International and Comparative Perspective—Essays in Honour of Paul McDaniel,* 2012 (ISBN 978-90-411-3286-4).
40. Robert F. van Brederode (ed.), *Science, Technology and Taxation,* 2012 (ISBN 978-90-411-3125-6).
41. Oskar Henkow, *The VAT/GST Treatment of Public Bodies,* 2013 (ISBN 978-90-411-4663-2).
42. Jean Schaffner, *How Fixed Is a Permanent Establishment?,* 2013 (ISBN 978-90-411-4662-5).

43. Miguel Correia, *Taxation of Corporate Groups*, 2013 (ISBN 978-90-411-4841-4).
44. Veronika Daurer, *Tax Treaties and Developing Countries*, 2014 (ISBN 978-90-411-4982-4).
45. Claire Micheau, *State Aid, Subsidy and Tax Incentives under EU and WTO Law*, 2014 (ISBN 978-90-411-4555-0).
46. Robert F. van Brederode & Richard Krever (eds), *Legal Interpretation of Tax Law*, 2014 (ISBN 978-90-411-4945-9).
47. Radhakishan Rawal, *Taxation of Cross-border Services*, 2014 (ISBN 978-90-411-4947-3).
48. João Dácio Rolim, *Proportionality and Fair Taxation*, 2014 (ISBN 978-90-411-5838-3).
49. Paulo Rosenblatt, *General Anti-avoidance Rules for Major Developing Countries*, 2015 (ISBN 978-90-411-5839-0).
50. Gaspar Lopes Dias V.S., *Tax Arbitrage through Cross-Border Financial Engineering*, 2015 (ISBN 978-90-411-5875-8).
51. Geerten M.M. Michielse & Victor Thuronyi (eds), *Tax Design Issues Worldwide*, 2015 (ISBN 978-90-411-5610-5).
52. Oktavia Weidmann, *Taxation of Derivatives*, 2015 (ISBN 978-90-411-5977-9).
53. Chris Evans, Richard Krever & Peter Mellor (eds), *Tax Simplification*, 2015 (ISBN 978-90-411-5976-2).
54. Reuven Avi-Yonah & Joel Slemrod (eds), *Taxation and Migration*, 2015 (ISBN 978-90-411-6136-9).
55. Alexander Bosman, *Other Income under Tax Treaties: An Analysis of Article 21 of the OECD Model Convention*, 2015 (ISBN 978-90-411-6610-4).
56. John Abrahamson, *International Taxation of Manufacturing and Distribution*, 2016 (ISBN 978-90-411-6664-7).
57. Frederik Boulogne, *Shortcomings in the EU Merger Directive*, 2016 (ISBN 978-90-411-6713-2).
58. Angelika Meindl-Ringler, *Beneficial Ownership in International Tax Law*, 2016 (ISBN 978-90-411-6833-7).
59. Andreas Waltrich, *Cross-Border Taxation of Permanent Establishments: An International Comparison*, 2016 (ISBN 978-90-411-6832-0).
60. Sergio André Rocha & Allison Christians (eds), *Tax Sovereignty in the BEPS Era*, 2017 (ISBN 978-90-411-6707-1).
61. Peter Antony Wilson, *BRICS and International Tax Law*, 2018 (ISBN 978-90-411-9435-0).
62. Louise Otis, Brigitte Alepin & Blanca Moreno-Dodson (eds), *Winning the Tax Wars: Tax Competition and Cooperation*, 2018 (ISBN 978-90-411-9460-2).
63. Marta Castelon, *International Taxation of Income from Services under Double Taxation Conventions: Development, Practice and Policy*, 2018 (ISBN 978-90-411-9594-4).
64. D.M. Broekhuijsen, *A Multilateral Tax Treaty: Designing an Instrument to Modernise International Tax Law*, 2018 (ISBN 978-90-411-9872-3).
65. John Abrahamson, *International Taxation of Energy Production and Distribution*, 2018 (ISBN 978-90-411-9101-4).